STUDIES IN EUROPEAN HISTORY

XX

THE ANABAPTISTS AND THE CZECH BRETHREN IN MORAVIA 1526-1628

A STUDY OF ORIGINS AND CONTACTS

by

JAROLD KNOX ZEMAN

Acadia University, Wolfville, Canada

1969

MOUTON

THE HAGUE · PARIS

LIBRARY OF CONGRESS CATALOG CARD NUMBER: 69-17824

Printed in The Netherlands by Mouton & Co., Printers, The Hague.

FOREWORD

1967 is the four-hundred-fiftieth anniversary of the posting of the ninety-five theses by Martin Luther and thus of the beginning of the Reformation. Yet this was, in a real sense, not the beginning of the Reformation, as 1967 also reminds us; for it is at the same time the five-hundredth anniversary of the formation of the *Unitas Fratrum Bohemicorum*.

The connection between Luther's Reformation and the *Unitas Fratrum* has been a matter of interest to students of Luther, both friendly and hostile, ever since the days of the Reformation itself, as I have sought to show in my book, *Obedient Rebels* (London and New York, 1964). Less widely discussed, but in many ways even more interesting, is the connection between the Hussite movement and the radical Reformation, especially the Anabaptists. It has long been known that Bohemia and Moravia were the locale for some of the most important Anabaptist groups, and monographs such as that of Lydia Müller, *Der Kommunismus der mährischen Wiedertäufer* (Leipzig, 1927), have drawn the attention of scholars to the distinctive development of Anabaptism in the land of Hus. Yet the geographical coincidence of the two movements has usually been an object of curiosity rather than of scholarly research, at least partly because so few church historians have had the requisite combination of historical interest and linguistic equipment to undertake a responsible examination of the intricate relations and protracted negotiations between the Anabaptists and the Czech Brethren.

That shortage of trained scholars did not, however, preclude the invention of hypotheses about the connections between the two groups. Ludwig Keller set forth the bold, if quite bizarre, suggestion that there was what might be styled an "apostolic succession in the underground", by means of which the radical movements of the Middle Ages perpetuated themselves until they emerged in the Anabaptists and other *Schwärmer* of the sixteenth century. Keller's thesis — which was considered important enough to be refuted (and thus also enshrined) in successive editions of that vade mecum for generations of students of church history, the *Lehrbuch der Kirchengeschichte für Studierende* of Johann Heinrich Kurtz — made up in imagination what it lacked in documentation. Perhaps the most unfortunate result of Keller's vagaries, however, was the consequent neglect by later historians of the sort of 'succession', or at least historical nexus, that could have been established from a study of the right sources, which meant, to be sure, sources in Czech as well as in Latin and German.

The present monograph by Dr. Zeman is a substantial contribution to the historical clarification of that nexus. Without pretensions to completeness or finality, Dr. Zeman has analyzed in detail the positive and the polemical aspects of the interchange between the *Unitas Fratrum* and the Anabaptists. A Czech Baptist is in a unique position to undertake such an investigation, for his cultural ties and his denominational loyalties may act as a counterbalance upon each other. Having sought to achieve a similar set of checks and balances in my own study of the relations between Luther and the *Unitas Fratrum*, I realize both how fruitful and how deceptive such an enterprise can be. In any case, however, this combination of backgrounds has prepared Dr. Zeman to raise questions both about the history of the Anabaptists and about the development of the Hussites that do not occur in the conventional accounts of either.

One of the most useful features of this monograph is what its author has called 'historical topography'. The teaching and study of church history is carried on all too often in isolation from maps and atlases. In an examination on the history of Christian theology during the first five centuries, for example, how many Ph.D.'s could identify the approximate location of Samosata (where the heretical bishop of Antioch, Paul, was born) or of Mopsuestia (where Theodore was bishop from 392 to 428)? Yet each time one begins to put pins on the map locating men and movements, fascinating coincidences and intriguing parallels assert themselves. The topographical, ethnic, and archaeological evidence assembled in Chapter VI of this book will make it useful even to readers who are not primarily concerned with ecclesiastical and theological history.

I hope, therefore, that Dr. Zeman's study will serve to advance research by others in both of the movements whose encounter he has described, and that in coming years he himself will take up some of the historical problems raised by his investigations.

Yale University   JAROSLAV PELIKÁN
New Haven, Connecticut
October 31, 1967

PREFACE

The present study has taken a number of years to complete. This was due in part to several interruptions of work and in part to the considerable difficulties in locating and obtaining source materials and other books on Czech history in libraries outside Czechoslovakia.

My interest in the Czech Reformation was awakened first by my father during my childhood in Bohemia. It was deepened by the inspiring lectures of Professors František M. Bartoš, František Bednář, Otakar Odložilík and Rudolf Říčan at the Comenius (then Hus) Faculty and at the Charles University in Prague during my undergraduate studies there.

In my graduate research I owe a debt of gratitude to the professors of the Theological Faculty at the University of Zürich, Switzerland, and in particular to Professors Fritz Blanke, Arthur Rich and Eduard Schweizer. Without the example of their scholarly work, without their guidance and continued personal encouragement, the study would not have been completed.

In my search for rare sixteenth-century books and manuscripts I received inestimable assistance from many librarians on the continents of Europe and North America. I wish to express special thanks to the staff of the following libraries: Zentralbibliothek in Zürich; Burgerbibliothek in Bern; Universitätsbibliothek in Mainz (Dr. Josef Benzing); Stadtbibliothek in Nürnberg; Universitätsbibliothek in Freiburg i.B. and in Tübingen; Württembergische Landesbibliothek in Stuttgart; Österreichische Nationalbibliothek in Wien; Národní a universitní knihovna, Státní ústřední archiv and the library of the Comenius Faculty, all of Prague; Mennonite Historical Library (Mr. Nelson Springer) in Goshen, Ind.; Malin Library in the Archives of the Moravian Church, Bethlehem, Pa.; the library at Colgate-

Rochester Divinity School in Rochester, N.Y., and Mills Memorial Library at McMaster University in Hamilton, Ont., Canada.

I wish to express also my heartfelt thanks to many friends in the Baptist Convention of Ontario and Quebec, and especially to the Villa Nova Baptist Church and to the Department of Canadian Missions (Dr. Dixon A. Burns). It was only through their understanding and support that I was able to spend two years in graduate studies in Switzerland. The immediate opportunity as such was provided generously by the Baptist Theological Seminary in Rüschlikon-Zürich. To its three successive presidents, Dr. Joseph Nordenhaug, Dr. John D. Hughey and Dr. John D. W. Watts, and to the gracious Seminary librarian, Dr. Vella Jane Burch, I am profoundly grateful.

The printing of the book was made possible by generous assistance from Mr. David C. Simmonds and Mr. A. Springle, both of Toronto.

The original manuscript was submitted as a doctoral thesis to the Theological Faculty at the University of Zürich in the late summer of 1965. Subsequently, only minor revisions of the text were undertaken, mainly to incorporate the latest bibliographical references. Helpful suggestions for changes were made by Professor R. Říčan of Prague and Professor R. Friedmann of Kalamazoo. Mrs. C. Richards of Toronto read the manuscript and kindly offered advice on the literary style.

No one has contributed more to the progress and completion of this book than my wife and children. For several years, they gave up periods of vacation. They were deprived of much needed companionship. In more than one way the finished book represents our work together.

Toronto, Canada   J. K. Z.
March 1968

TABLE OF CONTENTS

LIST OF ABBREVIATIONS

1. SOURCES AND COLLECTIONS OF SOURCES (PRINTED)

BDS	*Martin Bucers Deutsche Schriften:*
1 ff.	Vol. 1, Frühschriften 1520-1524 (1960).
	Vol. 2, Schriften 1524-1528 (1962).
	Vol. 7, Schriften 1538-1539 (1964).
CS	*Corpus Schwenckfeldianorum.*
CR	*Corpus Reformatorum.*
DS	see *TQ.*
HS	see *TQ.*
LCC	*Library of Christian Classics.*
LW	*Luther's Works* (ed. Jaroslav Pelikan and Helmut T. Lehmann) (St. Louis, Mo. and Philadelphia, Pa., 1958 ff.).
QFRG	*Quellen und Forschungen zur Reformationsgeschichte.*
FRA	*Fontes rerum austriacarum* (Wien).
FRB	*Fontes rerum bohemicarum* (Prague).
TQ	*Quellen zur Geschichte der Täufer (Wiedertäufer).*

    I: Herzogtum Württemberg (1930).
    II: Markgraftum Brandenburg (Bayern, I) (1934).
    III: Glaubenszeugnisse oberdeutscher Taugesinnter, I (1938).
    IV: Baden und Pfalz (1951).
    V: Bayern, II (1951).
    VI: Hans Denck, Schriften: Teil 1, 2, 3 (1955, 1956, 1960) quoted always as *DS,* 1, 2, 3.
    VII: Elsass, I (1959).
    VIII: Elsass, II (1960).
    IX: Balthasar Hubmaier, Schriften (1962). quoted always as *HS.*
    X: Bibliographie des Täufertums (1962).
    XI: Österreich, I (1964).
    XII: Glaubenszeugnisse oberdeutscher Taufgesinnter, II (1967).

TQ Hessen: Urkundliche Quellen zur hessischen Reformationsgeschichte, Vol. IV (1951).

TQ Schweiz, I: *Quellen zur Geschichte der Täufer in der Schweiz,* Vol. I (Zürich, 1952).

(For editors and publishers of all *TQ* volumes, see *TQ,* XI, p. xvi).

WA   *Luthers Werke*, Weimarer Ausgabe.
WA, Br   *Luthers Werke, Briefe*, Weimarer Ausgabe.
Z   *Huldreich Zwinglis Sämtliche Werke.*
ZGL   *Die älteste Chronik der Hutterischen Brüder* (ed. A. J. F. Zieglschmid) (Ithaca, N.Y., 1943).
ZGLK   *Das Klein-Geschichtsbuch der Hutterischen Brüder* ed. A. J. F. Zieglschmid) (Philadelphia, 1947).

2. CZECH PERIODICALS
(all except ČMM published in Prague)

ČČH   *Český časopis historický.*
ČČM   *Časopis českého musea* (later: *Časopis národního musea*).
ČMM   *Časopis matice moravské* (Brno).
ČSČH   *Československý časopis historický.*
CV   *Communio viatorum.*
KJ   *Kostnické jiskry.*
KR   *Křesťanská revue.*
LF   *Listy filologické.*
RS   *Reformační sborník.*
ThEv   *Theologia Evangelica* (vols. 1-4, 1948-1951).
TPKR   *Theologická příloha Křesťanské revue.*
VKČSN   *Věstník královské české společnosti nauk.*

3. OTHER PERIODICALS

ARG   *Archiv für Reformationsgeschichte.*
CH   *Church History.*
JGPÖ   *Jahrbuch für die Geschichte des Protestantismus in Österreich.*
MGB   *Mennonitische Geschichtsblätter.*
MQR   *Mennonite Quarterly Review.*
ORP   *Odrodzenie i reformacja w Polsce* (Warsaw).
RHPR   *Revue d'histoire et de philosophie religieuses* (Strasbourg).
TZ   *Theologische Zeitschrift* (Basel).
ZBG   *Zeitschrift für Brüdergeschichte* (Herrnhut).
ZBKG   *Zeitschrift für bayrische Kirchengeschichte.*
ZDVGMS *Zeitschrift des Deutschen Vereines für die Geschichte Mährens und Schlesiens* (Brünn).
ZHVSN   *Zeitschrift des historischen Vereins für Schwaben und Neuburg* (Augsburg).
ZKG   *Zeitschrift für Kirchengeschichte.*
ZSKG   *Zeitschrift für schweizerische Kirchengeschichte.*

4. DICTIONARIES AND ENCYCLOPEDIAS

ADB   *Allgemeine Deutsche Biographie.*
EK   *Evangelisches Kirchenlexikon* (Göttingen, 1956-1961).
LTK   *Lexikon für Theologie und Kirche* (2nd ed., Freiburg i.B., 1957 ff).
RE   *Realencyklopädie für protestantische Theologie und Kirche.*
RGG   *Religion in Geschichte und Gegenwart* (2nd and 3rd editions).
ME   *Mennonite Encyclopedia.*
ML   *Mennonitisches Lexikon.*

I

INTRODUCTION

At the beginning of our century, a British historian, one of the editors of the *Cambridge Modern History*, characterized the Bohemian Brethren as "a relic of sectarian life of earlier centuries revived in the early years of the sixteenth".[1] Fifty years later, a fellow countryman who had learnt the Czech language in order to examine thoroughly one aspect of the teachings of the early Unitas Fratrum concluded his Oxford doctoral dissertation with the following evaluation:

While, therefore, from one point of view the appearance of Chelčický and the early Brethren marked the culminating point in the development of the social radicalism of the medieval sects, at the same time it ushers in the new social radicalism of the left-wing of the Protestant Reformation. ... In the West, historians of political and social ideas, in tracing back the origins of modern democracy or of contemporary movements like socialism and anarchism, have usually ignored the great contribution, which during the fifteenth century the Czech people made to their development in the form of the political and social doctrines of Chelčický and the Unity of Brethren. Nevertheless, the importance of these doctrines ... reaches far beyond the borders of the Czech lands. They deserve, indeed, a fitting place in the history of European political thought.[2]

A similar revolution took place, simultaneously, in the interpretation and evaluation of the Anabaptist movement of the sixteenth century.[3]

---

[1] A. M. Ward in *Cambridge Modern History*, Vol. III, 147 (Cambridge, 1907).
[2] Brock, 1957, 275 f.
[3] See the review of "The Changing Reputation of the Anabaptists" by Littell, 1958, 138-161 and the art. "Anabaptist" in *ME*, I, 113 ff. Cf. also Klassen, 1964, 13-27.

1. REVIEW OF RESEARCH

It would be superfluous to cite the long list of authors whose names represent the advance of critical research in Anabaptism as a whole.[4] However, a brief review of studies on Anabaptism in Moravia is in order.

The early publication of excerpts from the Hutterite chronicles by Wolny in 1850 and Wolf in 1878, and the subsequent critical editions by Beck (1883), Wolkan (1923) and Zieglschmid (1943 and 1947)[5] provided readily accessible source materials. At the same time, however, they contributed to the creation of a Hutterite image of Moravian Anabaptism. The extensive studies by Loserth, Wolkan, Dedic, Wiswedel and Friedmann[6] — to mention the five main historians of Moravian Anabaptism — were focused chiefly on the history and ideology of the Hutterites. The unusual interest in their communal way of life and its underlying philosophy resulted in many additional studies of the Hutterite brotherhood, both in its original form in sixteenth-century Moravia and in its contemporary phenomena in Canada and the United States of America.[7] One should not be surprised, therefore, to see the post-Hubmaier Moravian Anabaptism equated with Hutteritism.[8]

Admittedly, the Hutterite Brethren accounted for the majority of Moravian Anabaptists. Their proportionate strength kept increasing

[4] The recent publication of an exhaustive classified bibliography of Anabaptism, *TQ*, X (1962), renders unnecessary the inclusion of a comprehensive bibliographical review. Cf. also the critical reviews by Loserth, 1928a; Friedman, 1929, 170-187 and 1931, 240 f.; Dedic, 1938; Köhler, 1940; 1941; 1943 and 1948; Teufel, 1941; 1942; 1943; 1948; 1952; Williams, 1958 and Friedmann, 1961a, 299-312 (the Hutterites). Every year, the April issue of *Mennonite Life* brings up-to-date reports on Anabaptist research in progress. See also Bauman, 1968, 1 ff.
[5] See the corresponding entries in our list of bibliography (Anabaptist sources). Cf. also our review of topographical research, Zeman, 1966, 8 ff.
[6] Cf. the many entries under their names in our list of bibliography and in *TQ*, X. The fruit of Friedmann's life-long research of the Hutterite heritage can be seen at its best in the two volumes, Friedmann, 1961a and 1965b, and in his many articles in the *ME*.
[7] A listing and evaluation of the works on Hutterite communism was provided by Friedmann, 1961a, 299-312 (originally published in 1950) and Klassen, 1964, 20 ff.
[8] To quote only a few examples: The regional list of bibliography on Moravian Anabaptism bears the title "Moravia (Hutterites)" (*TQ*, X, 11). The topographical lists of Anabaptist settlements in Moravia include only the Hutterite colonies (*ML*, III, 419 ff.; *ME*, II, 859). Friedmann regarded the Hutterites as the only "continuous" Anabaptist group in Moravia (*ME*, II, 855 and III, 749).

in the second half of the sixteenth century.[9] Nevertheless, the non-Hutterite groups played a very important role in Moravian Anabaptism, both through their contacts with Anabaptist centers in other countries and by their relationship to the population of Moravia. In contrast to the Hutterites whose communal way of life could not but lead to general isolation from the local population, the non-communitarian Anabaptists had greater opportunities for regular involvement in the life of the secular communities of their residence. For that reason alone our present investigation of contacts between Moravian Anabaptists and the Czech Brethren makes it imperative that we pay special attention to the non-communitarian groups.

With the exception of Hubmaier,[10] most of the other leaders and groups have not received satisfactory treatment in previous research. Loserth paid only marginal attention to Glaidt and Göschl[11] and to the non-Hutterite groups.[12] He was, however, interested in Marbeck, published his *Verantwortung* and wrote several articles about him.[13] Friedmann and Wiswedel contributed to our knowledge of the Philippite Brethren.[14] Wiswedel edited an important treatise written by Gabriel Ascherham.[15] In his essay on Glaidt, Wiswedel did not, unfortunately, pursue the research into the later, Sabbatarian stage of Glaidt's theological development.[16] There are no critical monographs on Martin Göschl nor Christian Entfelder.[17] In spite of the great interest of scholars, especially the Mennonite, in the theology of the Swiss Brethren and of the Marbeck fellowship no attempt has been made to study their historical and theological development in Moravia.[18] One of the most unusual groups of religious radicalism in Moravia were Italian refugees. Some were anti-Trinitarians, others joined the Hutterites, still others remained unattached. References

[9] Cf. our "Group Analysis" in Chapter VI.
[10] For bibliography on Hubmaier's life and theology, see Chapter III, footnote 2. The best summary of Hubmaier research is found in Bergsten, 1961, 31-54.
[11] Loserth, 1897.
[12] Loserth, 1894.
[13] Loserth, 1929a; 1925a; 1928b.
[14] Friedmann, 1958 (reprinted in Friedmann, 1961a, 242-253) and Wiswedel, III, 146 ff. Cf. also Chapter IV footnote 201.
[15] Wiswedel, 1937a. Cf. also Chapter IV footnote 200 for other literature on the Gabrielites.
[16] Wiswedel, 1937b.
[17] On Göschl, cf. Chapter IV footnote 18. On Entfelder, see Chapter IV footnote 238.
[18] Cf. the art. "Swiss Brethren" and "Marbeck" in *ME*.

to their Moravian sojourn are found in several works[19] but a comprehensive picture of the Italian community in Moravia has not been depicted as yet.

The research of Moravian Anabaptism has been carried on almost entirely by German-speaking scholars. This in turn meant that most of the published studies were based only on in-group German sources. Out-group sources, written mostly in the Czech language, were used, in part, by Kameníček[20] and Hrubý.[21] A number of Czech authors who were not interested in Anabaptism as such brought to light interesting data about Anabaptists from many local archives in Moravia and published them in the large collection of topographical studies, *Vlastivěda moravská*.[22]

With the exception of Kameníček, Hrubý and Hošek,[23] Czech historical research up to now has practically ignored Moravian Anabaptism. The few published articles either summarize the Hutterite story known from their chronicles[24] or report bibliographical data.[25] More original work was displayed by Černohorský and Landsfeld in their excavation and identification of Hutterite pottery and ceramics. Landsfeld's reports in particular have furnished important information for the topography of Moravian Anabaptism.[26]

[19]   De Wind, 1954; 1955a; 1955b; Friedmann, 1955a; Comba, 1897. Cf. also *TQ*, X, Nos. 1120 ff. On Bernardino Ochino, cf. Bartoš, 1946a, 111 ff.; Bainton, 1940; Cantimori, 1949, 496; Williams, 1962, 744.

[20]   Kameníček, III, 467-494 is the only attempt in the Czech language to summarize the history of Moravian Anabaptism. The author used a number of local sources (cf. his bibliography, *ibid*, 292 ff.), especially the records of the Moravian diet. The same source was used later by Hrubý. A few sources concerning the taxation of Anabaptists in 1605 are quoted by Kameníček, 1894 and 1895.

[21]   Hrubý, 1929a; 1935b and 1937 (in Czech) and 1935a (in German). It is to be regretted that Hrubý could not publish many additional source materials with which he was familiar. Among other things, he had collected correspondences and other documents illustrating the manifold contacts between the Czech lands and Switzerland, during the sixteenth and early seventeenth centuries. Not all of these were, of course, related directly to Anabaptism. Cf. Hrubý, 1931, 45, n.l.

[22]   Cf. Zeman, 1966, 10.

[23]   Hošek, 1867 wrote the first (completed) critical biography of Hubmaier. Even though he was not without prejudice, as a Roman Catholic priest, he was well acquainted with the sources and discerned the basic issues in Hubmaier's theology. Cf. Bergsten, 1961, 36.

[24]   Machát, 1897; Dušek, 1962 and 1963a-b.

[25]   Dudík, 1875, 111-114 and Tobolka, 1929 (on the printer Simprecht Sorg Froschauer); Menčík, 1896; Kameníček, 1899 and Kretz, 1922 (hymnbooks); Volf, 1934 (description of a MS. Codex in Prague; cf. Friedmann, 1965b, 60).

[26]   Černohorský, 1931. Landsfeld, 1964 gives a summary report (in English) on

Among the Czech authors, Čapek displayed a remarkable acquaintance with in-group sources. Regrettably, in his only published work he used the accumulated knowledge mainly for a popular apology of the persecuted Brethren and for propagation of Keller's thesis.[27] The sporadic appearance of isolated Anabaptist groups in Bohemia was described by Winter and Mareš, both of whom utilized several local out-group sources.[28] The Marxist historian Husa has attempted to reformulate an older hypothesis about the genetic influence of the *Unitas Fratrum* on Thomas Müntzer and the Zwickau prophets in their rejection of infant baptism.[29] In keeping with the Marxist interest in the peasant uprisings during the early Reformation era, Macek published an exhaustive study on the Tirolese peasant rebellion and on Michael Gaismaier.[30] Up to the present time, the Czech Protestant historians have not contributed a single study on the history or theology of Anabaptism.[31]

Research on Anabaptism in Slovakia by Slovak historians shows signs of promise for the future. Čulen published a well-rounded historical and interpretative study of the Hutterites (*Habaner*) in Slovakia from their earliest settlements in the sixteenth century up to the assimilation of their non-Anabaptist descendants in Slovakia in the twentieth century.[32] A recent monograph on Andreas Fischer by Ratkoš brought to light new evidence from local sources on the early spread of non-communitarian Anabaptism in Slovakia.[33] By contrast, the older book by Kraus made no contribution whatsoever

---

thirty years of excavations. For topographical study, Novotný, 1959 provides new information on Hutterite settlements from local sources.

[27] Čapek, 1903. On Keller's thesis, see our discussion later in this chapter.

[28] Winter, 1895, 304-312 and Mareš, 1907. Both of them did their research independently of Loserth who earlier had published an article on Anabaptists in Bohemia (Loserth, 1892).

[29] Husa, 1956a; 1957 and 1958. Cf. the criticism by Macek, 1958c. See also Chapter II footnotes 22 and 148, and Friesen, 1965, 319.

[30] Macek, 1960b. Cf. also his shorter essays, Macek, 1958a; 1959 and 1960a.

[31] The statement applies to Hrejsa, Bartoš, Říčan and Molnár. Their works contain brief references to Anabaptists in the Czech lands but none of them devoted a special study to Anabaptism. Bartoš has written a comprehensive study on the contacts of the Czech Brethren "with the Reformers" (Bartoš, 1956b), with Luther (Bartoš, 1929 and 1934) and Erasmus (Bartoš, 1956a and 1958a) and brief essays on several representative thinkers of the "left-wing Reformation" such as Franck and Acontius (Bartoš, 1946b) or Ochino (Bartoš, 1946a, 111 ff.).

[32] Čulen, 1945. The developments in Moravia are included.

[33] Ratkoš, 1958. Cf. also Ratkoš, 1963.

to research.[34] The interest of the contemporary Sudeten German scholars seems to have been focused on the ethnic and linguistic characteristics of the Anabaptists in Moravia and Slovakia, or on their contribution to folklore.[35]

A student of Moravian Anabaptism soon discovers that its historical and theological development is inextricably interwoven with the rest of the continental Anabaptist movement of the sixteenth century. The best evidence of this striking interrelatedness of all strata of Anabaptism are the published volumes of the *Quellen zur Geschichte der Täufer*. All of them contain references to Moravia. The leaders moved from one country to another, especially during the early phase of the movement. The missioners (*sendboten*) and special messengers maintained regular contacts. Individuals and groups of refugees travelled to Moravia and some of them later returned to their native regions, either disillusioned about Anabaptism, or more frequently, to recruit additional converts for the brotherhood in Moravia.[36]

One cannot, therefore, study Moravian Anabaptism as an isolated phenomenon. Every leader, every event and every tenet of faith must be understood within the wider context of European Anabaptism and indeed, within the framework of the whole Reformation movement. The fact that in our preceding review of Anabaptist research we have singled out the works which dealt specifically with Moravia (and Bohemia and Slovakia) must be regarded only as a methodological convenience.

Our summary of research into the history and theology of the Czech Brethren will require considerably less space. The history of the *Unitas Fratrum* has been presented in three definitive works which are based on a thorough acquaintance with the primary sources and which also make good use of monographs. In their interpretation of

---

[34] Kraus, 1937. It is a pity that this beautifully printed book contains little more than the parallel texts of excerpts from German sources (known from previous publications by other authors) and their translations into Slovak.
[35] Cf. Schwarz, 1939, 72 ff. (with additional bibliography); Kasparek, 1956 and 1957.
[36] Cf. the summary of these movements and migrations by Wiswedel, 1943 and 1948; Neumann, 1957; Wiswedel's art. "Sendboten" in *ML*, IV, 152 ff.; Friedmann's art. "Hutterite Missioners" in *ME*, II, 866 f.; and the comprehensive new study by Schäufele, 1966. Most of the contacts were with German-speaking countries. The contacts with Dutch Mennonitism were minimal.

the historical and ideological development of the Unity, the three authors express divergent but complementary views.

A good beginning of critical historiography was made in 1857-1858 by Anton Gindely, an enlightened Catholic, who treated the Czech Brethren with remarkable sympathy and empathy.[37] He also wrote the first summary of their doctrinal position.[38] In many details as well as in the general interpretation, his work was superseded by the three-volume history written by the official historian of the 'Renewed Unity' (*Brüdergemeine*, The Moravian Church), Josef Th. Müller 1922-1931.[39] Müller's history represents the fruit of a life-long concentrated study of the primary sources. Although himself of German origin, he mastered the Czech language of the sixteenth and seventeenth centuries. In addition to many excellent monographs,[40] he translated the main collection of sources, *Acta Unitatis Fratrum* (see further below) into German. The first volume of Müller's *Geschichte* appeared also in a Czech abbreviated translation by F. M. Bartoš.[41] It includes many important revisions and supplementary documentation by Bartoš, himself the best authority on the history and literature of Hussitism and of some aspects of Czech Brethrenism.[42]

The recent one-volume history by Rudolf Říčan, professor of church history at the Comenius Faculty in Prague,[43] does not bring any major revisions nor any substantial new historical information beyond the work of Müller. It does, however, pay special attention to the inner life of the Unity, to its uniquely disciplined congregational life and to the decrees by which the members were guided in their daily life in society. This particular emphasis makes the book indispensable for a comparison of the ordered community life among the Czech Brethren and among the Anabaptists.

[37] Gindely, I-II. His work stops with the year 1609.
[38] Gindely, 1854a.
[39] Müller, I-III.
[40] Cf. our list of bibliography.
[41] Müller-Bartoš (1923).
[42] Cf. the special issue of *Church History*, Vol. 28 (1959), 227 ff., published in his honour, and the tribute by Říčan in *CV*, 7 (1964), 155-160.
[43] Říčan, 1957a (Czech original) and 1961a (an abbreviated German translation). Another German book by the same author, Říčan, 1957b (the Czech original was never printed), provides a concise introduction to the study of the history of the Christian church in Bohemia and Moravia. It deals mainly with the Reformation in the fifteenth and sixteenth centuries and the subsequent developments.

Whereas Gindely's interpretation was conditioned by his Roman Catholic background and Müller's sympathy was with the Lutheran Reformation, Říčan, in spite of, or perhaps because of his personal leaning toward the Calvinistic wing of the Reformation, has succeeded, probably more than anyone else, in grasping the inner logic of the paradoxical ideological development of the Unity.

The three definitive histories of the Unity, therefore, complement each other and should be consulted together on any particular issue. In addition to them, the broadly based six-volume *History of Christianity in Czechoslovakia* by Ferdinand Hrejsa [44] provides a wealth of material arranged in a chronicle-like fashion. It is a basic manual for any student of religious life in sixteenth-century Bohemia and Moravia. Many of the scholarly monographs and articles by Amedeo Molnár [45] are also extremely relevant for the subject under investigation.

There is no need to include a selected bibliography beyond the basic works just reported. Three all-inclusive classified lists have been published by Říčan.[46] Two works, however, deserve special mention. By coincidence, they are both doctoral dissertations and both written in English.

In 1957, Peter Brock published his book on the political and social doctrines of the Czech Brethren.[47] His penetrating analysis of the "typically Anabaptist" ethical teachings of the Old Brethren (civil power, oath, non-resistance) should be read as an introduction to our present study of the contacts and relationships between the Czech Brethren and the Anabaptists.

In 1964, Miloš Štrupl, a minister of Czech origin now living in America, completed a doctoral thesis on "The Confessional Theology of the Unitas Fratrum".[48] His work must be regarded as the first

---

[44] Hrejsa, I-VI. The work includes also developments in Slovakia. It stops with the year 1576. The subsequent volumes were not published although they were prepared in manuscript. Hrejsa's history is based on his lectures at the Hus Faculty in Prague. For his earlier monographs, important for the study of religious radicalism in Moravia, see our list of bibliography.

[45] Cf. our list of bibliography.

[46] Říčan, 1957a, 444-483; 1957b, 222-242; 1961a, 323-363. The list on the theology of the *Unitas* was compiled by A. Molnár. The works published since 1961 can be identified readily in our list of bibliography which is arranged chronologically.

[47] Brock, 1957. Cf. the reviews by A. Molnár in *KR*, 24 (1957), 213 ff. and *CV*, I, (1958), 75 ff.; H. Kaminsky in *CH*, 27 (1958), 171 ff.; Paul Peachey in *MQR*, 33 (1959), 260 ff.

[48] Štrupl, 1964a. A brief résumé was published in an article, Štrupl, 1964b. It is

major attempt to review the entire span of the Unity's theological development — with several changes in basic orientation — as it is reflected in the official confessional statements.

In agreement with the periodization suggested by Hrejsa [49] and Molnár,[50] Štrupl has divided the two centuries of the "ancient" Unity (1467-1670) [51] into the following six periods:

(1) The 'Old Brethren' (up to 1495)
(2) The Era of Lukáš (1495-1528)
(3) Under the leadership of Jan Roh: Lutheran orientation (1529-1546)
(4) Under the guidance of Jan Blahoslav and Matěj Červenka (1547-1572)
(5) The Last Fifty Years in Bohemia and Moravia: The Bohemian Confession and the Calvinistic orientation (1573-1628)
(6) The Exile and John Amos Comenius (1629-1670)

Since Štrupl based his interpretation exclusively on the confessions and did not use other theological writings of the Brethren, his work cannot be acclaimed as the definitive work on the development of the Unity's theology as such. Nevertheless, it can serve — supplemented by the earlier sketches of the Brethren's theology by Gindely, Hrejsa, Hromádka, and Molnár [52] — as a reliable introduction to the changing theological thought of the *Unitas Fratrum*.

To the best of our knowledge, no one thus far has published a comprehensive study on the historical contacts and theological relationships between the Czech Brethren and the Anabaptists. In 1910, Müller printed an abbreviated German translation of the Czech sources (*Acta Unitatis Fartrum*) pertaining to the colloquies between

---

to be hoped that the complete text of the thesis will be published before long. Part one of the thesis presents a historical and literary survey of all known confessions. Part two brings a theological analysis of the teachings in each period and of the confessional development as a whole.
[49]   Hrejsa, 1939.
[50]Molnár, 1957c; later included in Molnár's longer essay on the theology of the Unity, Molnár, 1957d (in German, Molnár, 1961e).
[51]   The first group of the Brethren settled at Kunvald in 1457-1458. It was not until 1467 that they chose their own priests and separated from the Utraquist church. The year 1670 marks the death of Comenius, the last leader of the Unity.
[52]   Gindely, 1854a; Hrejsa, 1939; Hromádka, 1939 and 1954; Molnár, 1957d (in German, 1961e). For bibliography of works on the theology of the *Unitas*, see footnote 46 above. The following important contributions have been published since 1961: Fousek, 1961 and 1965; Molnár, 1963d and 1964a-b-c; Pelikan, 1964; Peschke, 1964.

the two groups in 1528 and in 1559.[53] In his introduction, he did not attempt a historical analysis of the records. Apart from several brief references to the same sources[54] and apart from Husa's work on Müntzer,[55] no one has made any direct contribution to the subject under our study.[56] Many helpful insights have been furnished by the older essays on the Habrovanite Brethren,[57] the dissertation by Brock mentioned earlier, several articles by Molnár and the exhaustive study by Urban on anti-Trinitarianism in Bohemia, Moravia and Slovakia.[58] The unpublished dissertation of Dedic on religious life in Moravia during the sixteenth century[59] and two manuscripts essays by Cerroni[60] are of little value for the study of our subject.

2. THE RELATIONSHIP BETWEEN THE ANABAPTISTS AND THE CZECH BRETHREN

A scholarly examination of the historical contacts and theological relationships between the Anabaptists and the Czech Brethren can be viewed both as a premature undertaking and as a long-overdue project of research.

From one point of view it comes too early in the present stage of Anabaptist research. No definitive history of Moravian Anabaptism as a whole has been written thus far.[61] The in-group sources, apart from the works of Hubmaier and the Hutterite chronicles, are scattered in archives in many countries of Western and Eastern Europe and in the libraries and Hutterite colonies across North America.[62] The recent discoveries of manuscript codices *Kunstbuch*, *Geiser* and others[63] have demonstrated to what extent the total picture of

[53]   Müller, 1910. His article includes also the later contacts of the Hutterites with the *Brüdergemeine* in Herrnhut during the eighteenth century.
[54]   E.g., Friedmann, 1949, 31 f.; Molnár, 1952a, 111 f. and 1962c; Malínský, 1956.
[55]   Cf. footnote 29 above.
[56]   According to Bergsten, 1961, 24, n. 66, Alexander Rempel is preparing a thesis (Göttingen) on the genetic influence of the Czech Brethren on the rise of Anabaptism. Cf. Blanke, 1955, 86 and 1961, 76.
[57]   Brandl, 1882; Odložilík, 1923 and 1925; Hanák, 1928 and 1929.
[58]   Molnár, 1952a; 1957a; 1957d; 1958b; 1958c; 1962c; 1964a; 1964b; Urban, 1966.
[59]   Dedic, 1922.
[60]   Cerroni, I and II.
[61]   The best works on the subject (as of today), Loserth, 1893 and 1894, can hardly be called definitive. The recent short essay by Kuhn, II, 309-333 is worth noting.
[62]   Cf. the large catalogue of Hutterite manuscripts, Friedmann, 1965b.
[63]   See Bender, 1956a and Fast, 1956b. Cf. our discussion of the Marbeck fellowship in Chapter V.

Moravian Anabaptism, particularly of its non-Hutterite strata, must be redrawn and reinterpreted both in its historical development and in its theological character when new sources are brought to light. One must register disappointment that the present publication plans for the series, *Quellen zur Geschichte der Täufer* do not include a volume of in-group and out-group sources from Moravia.[64] Most sources of the Unity have been known and described for some time and it is doubtful that any future discoveries would affect the present knowledge of the *Unitas Fratrum* to any significant extent. The main task is that of interpretation.

From another point of view, the study of the subject under discussion has long been overdue. All sorts of conflicting and contradictory hypotheses concerning the relationship between the Anabaptists and the Czech Brethren have been proposed, some by scholars of reputation, others by writers of doubtful erudition. The ultimate result has been a chaotic state of research and an area of confusion to be avoided by discriminating scholars as a *terra incognita*. To list all such opinions would hardly serve the purpose of advancing research. By way of illustration, let us mention a few. They can be divided into two main categories: hypotheses concerning (1) the historical question of the genetic influence of the *Unitas Fratrum* on the rise of Anabaptism and (2) the theological question of doctrinal similarities between the two groups.

Albrecht Ritschl[65] and Ludwig Keller[66] expressed, independently and yet almost simultaneously (1885-1886), the hypothesis that there was an ideological similarity and therefore also an historical connection between the Czech Brethren and the Anabaptists. The basis for their respective hypotheses was different in each case. Ritschl sought the common roots of Anabaptism and the old Unity in the ascetic ideal of holiness of the Franciscan tertiaries. He did not offer any

---

[64] The first volume of *Glaubenszeugnisse oberdeutscher Taufgesinnter* (= TQ, III, ed. by Lydia Müller) and the forthcoming second and third volumes (ed. by Friedmann) contain important doctrinal writings which are related, in part, to Moravia. Excerpts from out-group sources have been published by Hrubý, 1935a. However, the continued existence of Anabaptism in Moravia for an entire century makes it imperative that the TQ series include at least one volume of local Moravian sources, translated where necessary from Czech (as Hrubý did).

[65] Ritschl, III, 221-240 ("wirklich im Grunde nahe verwandt"; p. 230). Ritschl's knowledge of the Unity was based on three works: Gindely, I-II, Goll, I-II and Niemeyer, 1840.

[66] Keller, 1885, 282-295 ("Die 'Brüder' in Böhmen"). Keller repeated his hypothesis in other writings.

historical proofs of the Franciscan influence, either for the Anabaptists or for the Czech Brethren. Ritschl's thesis was generally rejected by subsequent scholarship.[67] However, the issue has been reopened by evidence of Franciscan influence which was pointed out for the Anabaptists by Friedmann [68] and for the Unity by Molnár.[69]

Keller's hypothesis was a part of his general thesis according to which there were ideological parallels and historical links between "the old evangelical brotherhoods" of the late Middle Ages and the Anabaptists of the sixteenth century. The Waldenses living in several European countries played a crucial role in the transmission of ideas. In Keller's view, the founding of the *Unitas Fratrum* represented "a new phase in the history of the Bohemian Waldenses" [70] and the rise of Anabaptism was nothing more than "a new phase of an old brotherhood". The history of Anabaptism is "the history of reestablishment of the old evangelical congregations".[71] Views similar to those held by Keller had been expressed a century earlier by Robert Robinson, an English Baptist.[72]

---

[67]   See the critical refutation of Ritschl's hypothesis by Bender in his art. "Ritschl", *ME*, IV, 342 f.

[68]   Friedmann, 1956 and 1962, 351. Cf. also *ZGL*, 39 and art. "Olivi Petrus", *ME*, IV, 1113.

[69]   Molnár, 1957e.

[70]   Keller, 1885, 286.

[71]   *Ibid.*, 297 and 372. The following example will illustrate Keller's uncritical method in proving connections between the different "phases of evangelical brotherhoods". A congregation of the Major Party of the *Unitas Fratrum* was established in the town of Slavkov (Austerlitz) under the protection of Lord Oldřich of Kounice around 1510. In the spring of 1528, the non-resistant opponents of Hubmaier, *Stäbler*, were granted permission to settle at Slavkov by Oldřich's sons. As we shall demonstrate later (Chapter IV at footnotes 193 ff.) there were great doctrinal differences between the communitarian Anabaptists and the Major Party of the Unity. The *Stäbler* could not have been involved in the merger negotiations with the Unity in 1528. But Keller asserts that the same Lord of Kounice who received the (Czech) Brethren in 1511 later opened his domain to the (Anabaptist) Brethren from Germany, presumably because he was able to discern that the two groups represented but two phases of the same brotherhood. The only source for Keller's argument was, in this case, a footnote in Beck, p. 74! Had he examined the historical realities he would have discovered that Oldřich of Kounice died in 1519 and that the communitarian Anabaptists whom his sons allowed to settle in Slavkov in 1528 had few, if any dealings with the Czech Brethren, let alone a consciousness of ideological affinity or historical dependence (cf. our analysis of the references to the Czech Brethren in the writings of Hubmaier and in the Hutterite chronicles). For another example of Keller's method, cf. Chapter III footnote 95 and Oyer, 1964, 113.

[72]   Robinson, 1792, tried to trace a continuous Baptistic witness through the centuries and is often regarded as a precursor of the later champions of the successionist concept of Baptist history, such as Orchard, 1855. Robinson was familiar

A number of scholars who in many other respects have disagreed in their interpretation of the origins and nature of Anabaptism, have rejected Keller's thesis.[73] Without subscribing to Keller's uncritical concept of continuity and dependence, others have cautiously suggested that sixteenth-century Anabaptism could hardly be regarded merely as a radicalization of the Zwinglian or Lutheran Reformation. The theology of several Anabaptist leaders shows acquaintance with late medieval mysticism and apocalypticism, with the *devotio moderna* and with the teachings of some pre-Reformation "sectarian" movements.[74]

The genetic influence of the *Unitas Fratrum* on Anabaptism has been both defended and rejected. Among the historians who were familiar, to a greater or lesser degree, with the primary sources for the early Anabaptism, Wiswedel and Husa considered such influence as most probable,[75] whereas Bender, Blanke, Friedmann and Brock ruled it out.[76] It should be noted, however, that Brock and Husa

---

with many sixteenth century sources. He included the *Unitas Fratrum* in the broad stream of Baptist history: ". . . the Baptists ought always to honour this Church; it was a cradle in which many of their denomination were cherished" (508). In his book, he made contradictory statements on the relationship between the Anabaptists and the *Unitas Fratrum*: "None of them [Czech Brethren] ever attempted to deny that they baptized adults on a profession of faith, before they received them into the church; on the contrary they apologize for it and they all allow that the Anabaptists of Moravia proceeded from a schism in this church" ((508). "Let us turn our attention to that of the Baptists of this country [i.e. Anabaptists in Bohemia and Moravia], for though they were increased and multiplied by parties who withdrew from the *Unitas Fratrum*, yet none of these parties were their founders" (508). We are indebted to Prof. W. Morgan Patterson of Louisville, Kentucky, for having brought Robinson's work to our attention.

[73] Troeltsch, Holl, Köhler, Bender, Westin, Blanke, Friedmann and others. Cf. the bibliographical references in Bergsten, 1961, 23, n. 59.

[74] Cf. the summary by Bergsten, 1961, 23 ff.; Schäufele, 1966, 314 f.; Friedmann, 1962 and art. "Waldenses' 'in *ME*, IV. For the influences of medieval chiliasm and of the *devotio moderna* on the Czech Reformation, cf. Bartoš, 1959c; Molnár, 1956d and 1963c. A contemporary Czech Baptist author Josef Hovorka (using the pseudonym Konstantin Dušek) speaks of continuity and evolution of ideas in four phases: the Waldensians in Bohemia → the Taborites → the early *Unitas Fratrum* → the Anabaptists. According to his interpretation, the original theology of the *Unitas Fratrum* (1467-1478) can be regarded as a development of the Waldensian-Taborite ideas and anticipation of sixteenth-century Anabaptism. (Personal correspondence.)

[75] Wiswedel, III, 189 claims that the Anabaptists [which ones?] "read the tracts and writings of the Czech Brethren". Husa, 1956a; 1957, 93 ff. and 1958 proposed his hypothesis exclusively for Müntzer and the Zwickau prophets.

[76] Bender's art. "Bohemian Brethren" in *ME*, I, 383; Blanke, 1955, 86 (with limitation to the Anabaptists in Zürich); Friedmann, 1940, 111 ff. (reprinted in Friedmann, 1949, 31 f.); 1961a, 11 (rejection of Keller's thesis); 1962, 352 and art.

were the only two who were able to study the original Czech sources of the Unity.

The striking similarity of theological and ethical views has been pointed out by Wolf, Kameníček, Dedic, Hrubý, Molnár and others.[77] On the other hand, Enequist, Müller and Říčan regarded the two groups as basically different.[78]

The two issues, the one of historical dependence and the other of ideological affinity, cannot be easily separated. Referring to the problem of relationship between two other movements, in a different place and at an earlier point in history, a biblical scholar suggested that "sometimes direct contact or influence is pressed too far and not enough allowance is made for the influence of notions 'in the air'".[79] Obviously the historical and theological relationship between the *Unitas Fratrum* and the Anabaptists cannot be studied apart from the general problem of Anabaptist origins and sources of Anabaptist theology.[80] Furthermore, the relationship will be grasped and explained only with reference to the typology of both Anabaptism and the *Unitas Fratrum*.

3. THE QUEST FOR THE ESSENCE OF ANABAPTISM

It would lead us too far afield if we were to summarize and evaluate the many interpretations of Anabaptism which have been proposed since the early days of the Reformation. Such critical reviews have been made recently by several competent scholars.[81] For our present

---

"Moravian Church", *ME*, III, 750; Brock, 1957, 251 ff. claims that the Anabaptists (in Moravia) and the leader of the Minor Party of the Unity, Jan Kalenec, "reached a similar position on such subjects as the state, war and oaths independently". Brock also suggests that Kalenec was dependent upon the Anabaptists in advocating adult baptism and community of goods. Cf., however, Chapter IV footnotes 156 and 157.

[77] Kameníček, III, 473: "The Anabaptists did not consider themselves to be Protestants. . . . Nearest to them were the Czech Brethren, both in their doctrine and even more in their emphasis on moral life. In that sense one may regard Anabaptism *cum grano salis* as the German version of Czech Brethrenism." Wolf, 1878, 77 f.; Dedic, 1922, 14; Hrubý, 1935b, 65; Molnár, 1952a, 126 and 1962c.

[78] Enequist, 1884, 8; Müller, 1910, 185 f. and Müller, I, 452; Říčan, 1957a, 131. Friedmann has pointed out both similarities (especially between the 'Old Brethren' and the Anabaptists) and differences (Friedmann, 1961a, 11 and 36).

[79] G. R. Driver in *Hibbert Journal*, 55 (1957), 188.

[80] See the bibliography on this aspect of Anabaptist research in *TQ*, X, Nos. 2391-2418.

[81] See especially Friedmann, 1961a, 1-40 (reprint of two older articles, "Concep-

purpose it will suffice simply to list some of the concepts by which
the modern analysts have tried to describe the very essence of Anabaptism: [82] *Nachfolge* or *imitatio Christi*, discipleship (originally suggested by Johannes Kühn in 1923 and then reinterpreted by Harold
Bender in 1943); [83] theology of martyrdom (Ethelbert Stauffer);
restitution of the true church (F. H. Littell); existential Christianity
(Robert Friedmann in 1950 and Maynard Kaufman); biblical theology
in paradox (D. E. Smucker); apolitism (Walther Köhler); the free
church (Littell and Blanke); religious awakening (Blanke [84]); consistent biblicism (Yoder); kingdom-theology based on a dualistic
concept of two worlds (Friedmann's latest attempt of reinterpretation [85]).

These are but a few samples of Anabaptist typology. Whereas
every one of them describes an aspect of the teachings represented
by one particular group within the broad stream of Anabaptism,
none of them by itself can be regarded as a satisfactory definition
of the complex body of views included under the common name of
Anabaptism. Undoubtedly, the process of proposing, defending and
rejecting such theses can serve the purpose of clarifying our understanding of Anabaptist theology. But these attempts to reduce to
one basic idea such divergent and often mutually exclusive opinions,
as characterized Anabaptism, can be regarded only as a misleading
oversimplification of historical facts.

Nothing could illustrate the futility of the quest for a master key
that would unlock all doors within the sixteenth-century labyrinth
of Anabaptism better than the juxtaposition of the following quotations. These are taken from the writings of three leading Mennonite
historians who have been closely associated, for a quarter of a century,
in an admirable scholastic effort to distinguish the peaceful evangelical

---

tion of the Anabaptists", 1940 and "Recent Interpretations of Anabaptism", 1955)
and Friedmann, 1964b; Hillerbrand, 1959a, 1960b and 1962b, 1-5; Kaufman,
1957 and 1958; Bergsten, 1961, 13-30 and Durnbaugh, 1968. Cf. *MQR*, Jan. 1950.
[82] The bibliographical references to the particular works in which the concepts
were originally expressed by the respective authors will be found in the reviews
mentioned in the preceding footnote. See also Bauman, 1968, 3, n. 2.
[83] Bender's interpretation actually included three concepts: (1) the concept of
the essence of Christianity as discipleship, (2) the concept of the church based on
true conversion and involving a commitment to holy living and discipleship, (3) the
ethic of love and nonresistance (Bender's art. "The Anabaptist Vision", reprinted
by Herschberger, 1957, 42, 47, 51).
[84] With reference to the Anabaptist congregation in Zollikon in 1525 (Blanke,
1955, 36 ff.).
[85] Friedmann, 1964b, and the revised English version, Friedmann, 1967.

Anabaptists from the "illegitimate" children of the left-wing Reformation.

In his last article, published posthumously, Harold S. Bender wrote:

The Anabaptists stood at the crossroads of the Reformation, heirs of Lutheranism, Zwinglianism, and Mysticism, and though they did not develop a completely new and independent system of theology (why should they?), a leader like Marpeck . . . dealt in an astonishingly and impressively creative way with central questions of the Reformation.[86]

In his review of George H. Williams' "massive and overwhelming" history of *The Radical Reformation*, Cornelius Krahn asked:

One could raise the question whether some of the Radical Reformers did not have more in common with some Magisterial Reformers, at least in certain areas, than they had among themselves, as for example, the Swiss Brethren and the followers of Zwingli. . . . On the other hand, the Zwinglians had much more in common with the Swiss Brethren than with the magisterial Church of England. This does not deny the fact that all 'radicals' had certain basic things in common. On the other hand one could go a step further and point out that Luther and Müntzer not only labored together for the same cause for some time, but also had in common the mysticism of the Middle Ages which had quickened their faith.[87]

In his analysis of the relationship between Anabaptism and Protestantism, Robert Friedmann stated:

Anabaptism must not be considered as a form of Protestantism, not even as its "Left Wing" (Bainton), though Anabaptism arose in Central Europe at exactly the same period as Protestantism at large. Anabaptism, I claim, is as little Protestantism as is Quakerism in the Anglo-Saxon countries.[88]

Much later, Friedmann still claimed that the Anabaptists had developed a definite theology of their own, *sui generis*.[89]

---

[86]　Bender, 1964, 261.
[87]　*MQR*, 37 (1963), 248.
[88]　Friedmann, 1950, 14. Five years later, his list of "New Descriptive Categories" for Anabaptism included: existential Christianity; kingdom-mindedness; discipleship; obedience; fellowship of the Lord's Table; theology of martyrdom; Christian primitivism; restitution of the church; sanctification of life (*CH*, 24 [1955], 151; reprinted in Friedmann, 1961a, 40).
[89]　". . . the Anabaptists had an unequivocal, peculiar theology" (Friedmann, 1967, 21). The inherent paradox of Friedmann's interpretation becomes apparent in comparison with the following statement in which he compared the Czech Brethren with the Anabaptists: "The Bohemians had sacraments, hierarchy, confessions and Lent, like the Waldenses or the Donatists, while the Anabaptists lived according to the more Protestant pattern" (Friedmann, 1961a, 11).

For different reasons, Hans Hillerbrand also pleaded for the recognition of Anabaptism as "a Christian tradition in its own right":

We conclude that by and large the Anabaptist position [on justification] is
closer to Catholicism than to the Reformation; and it comes as no surprise,
then, that the Tridentine Canon on Justification is strongly reminiscent of
Peter Riedemann's view expressed in his *Rechenschafft*. . . . The picture of
Anabaptism is thus an ambiguous one. A definite affinity with the Reformation on the one hand gives validity to the description of the movement
as Radical Reformation. This is coupled, however, with a unique proximity
to Catholic thought, making it impossible to see the movement exclusively
as a result of the Reformation. The postulate of Anabaptism as a Christian
tradition in its own right may be the answer to our problem.[90]

The repeated attempts to define the 'genius' of Anabaptism inevitably
raised the related but different question of how the broad stream of
Anabaptism should be classified. The introduction of the term "the
Left Wing of the Reformation" by Bainton in 1941[91] and the still
more ambiguous nomenclature, "the Radical Reformation", proposed
by Williams in 1957,[92] made the division into categories and sub-
categories absolutely necessary.

Williams distinguished the Radical Reformation both from the
"Magisterial" Reformation of Protestantism and the "papal" Counter-
Reformation. In contrast to the latter two which retained the ecclesio-
political concept of *corpus christianum* embodied in territorial state
churches, the champions of the Radical Reformation were united in
their plea for a free church. Otherwise, they were divided into many
camps. Williams proposed the following classification of the Radical
Reformation: [93]

(1) THE ANABAPTISTS:
  (a) *Evangelical* (mostly pacifistic), e.g. the Swiss Brethren, Men-
      nonites, Hutterites, Hubmaier;
  (b) *Revolutionary*, e.g. Münster;
  (c) *Contemplative*, e.g. Hans Denck, Ludwig Haetzer, Adam
      Pastor.

[90] Hillerbrand, 1960b, 418. Endorsed by Armour, 1966, 135 ff. and 186, n. 2-3.
Cf. the comment by Bergsten, 1961, 30 and our discussion of the 'catholicizing'
trend in the final stage of Hubmaier's theological development, Chapter IV at
footnotes 47 ff.
[91] Bainton, 1941.
[92] Williams, 1957, 19 ff. and his *magnum opus*, Williams, 1962.
[93] Williams, 1957, 22-35. Cf. his review of earlier classifications by other authors,
in Williams, 1958, 46 ff. See also Bauman, 1968, 31.

(2) THE SPIRITUALISTS:
  (a) *Evangelical*, e.g. Schwenckfeld and Gabriel Ascherham (final phase);
  (b) *Revolutionary*, e.g. the Zwickau prophets, Carlstadt, Müntzer;
  (c) *Rational or Speculative*, e.g. Sebastian Franck, Valentine Weigel, Paracelsus.

(3) THE EVANGELICAL RATIONALISTS:
  (a) *Catholic Evangelicals and Speculative Ethical Theists*, including the early anti-Trinitarians;
  (b) *The Polish Brethren or the Minor Church of the Socinians*;
  (c) *Lithouanian and Transylvanian Unitarianism*.[94]

Five years later, Heinold Fast suggested the following revised grouping within the Left Wing of the Reformation: [95]

(1) TÄUFER:
  without any sub-categories. The group includes the Swiss Brethren, Hutterites, Mennonites, Hubmaier, Hut, Marbeck etc.

(2) SPIRITUALISTEN:
  (a) *Evangelical* (Denck, Schwenckfeld);
  (b) *Rationalistic* (Franck, anti-Trinitarians);
  (c) *Mystical* (Paracelsus, Weigel, Böhme).

(3) SCHWÄRMER:
  The group is characterized by "direct revelations", dreams and visions. Examples: Carlstadt, Müntzer, Melchior Hoffmann, Obbe Philips, Bernhard Rothmann.

(4) ANTITRINITARIER:
  Advocates of anti-Trinitarian views appeared in all three preceding categories. Examples: Michael Servet, Sebastian Castellio, Lelio and Fausto Sozzini, Bernardino Ochino.

---

[94]   The sub-categories of "Evangelical Rationalism" are not defined by Williams, 1957 but rather by his subsequent bibliographical treatment, Williams, 1958. Cf. also his later analysis of the classification, Williams, 1962, 846-865.
[95]   Fast, 1962b, IX-XXXV. Fast expressed reservations about Williams' term "Radical Reformation".

Other classifications have been proposed by Horsch,[96] Blanke,[97] Littell[98] and still others. The accrued benefits of all these attempts do not consist so much in the labelling of particular leaders and groups as in the gradual clarification of the main theological issues involved.[99]

4. NORMATIVE ANABAPTISM

Sooner or later, every student of Anabaptism must answer the question: What constitutes Anabaptism and how can it be delineated from other radical groups of the sixteenth century? Quite appropriately one might speak of NORMATIVE ANABAPTISM.

The problem can best be explained by applying any defined criteria of Anabaptism to such well-known leaders as Thomas Müntzer, Balthasar Hubmaier and Christian Entfelder. Was Müntzer an Anabaptist simply because he rejected infant baptism but did not actually practise believer's baptism and rebaptism? And even if he had constituted "a gathered church" on the basis of personal decision and subsequent baptism, would he be regarded as an Anabaptist in view of some of his socio-ethical views?

Are ethical issues such as Hubmaier's endorsement of Christian magistracy, oathtaking and even of defensive armsbearing involved in the "norm" for Anabaptism, or is Anabaptism defined merely in terms of theological issues?[100] It should be noted that the historians

[96] Horsch distinguished between (1) Evangelical Anabaptists, (2) Fanatical or Revolutionary Anabaptists (e.g. the Münsterites) and (3) Other groups (e.g. followers of Hubmaier). *MQR*, 7 (1933), 50 ff.
[97] Blanke differentiates between (1) Anabaptists who are biblicists, and as such children of the Reformation; (2) Spiritualists, such as Carlstadt, Müntzer, Schwenckfeld and Franck, "who had their roots in late medieval Catholic mysticism, with which they mingled ideas borrowed from the Reformation"; (3) Anti-Trinitarians. See Blanke, 1957, 57 f. and 1960, 72.
[98] Littell suggests four groups: (1) Religious revolutionaries (Müntzer, Rothmann); (2) Anti-Trinitarians; (3) Spiritualizers "opposed to institutionalized religion" (Schwenckfeld, Franck, Bünderlin); (4) Biblical restitutionists (Swiss Brethren, South German Brethren, Hutterites, Mennonites). Littell, 1963, 261.
[99] Cf. the discussion of the issues by Hillerbrand, 1959a and Bergsten, 1961, 13-30.
[100] Sachsse, 1963, 314 f. has proposed that Anabaptists be divided into two basic categories according to their attitude to society. Men like Hubmaier and his followers who approved of Christian participation in magistracy and other societal responsibilities, were in basic agreement with the Reformers (Zwingli, Luther) and had their origin in the Protestant Reformation. The other type of Anabaptists who withdrew from society did not originate in the Protestant Reformation but rather in the medieval sects. Their main ideal was a "holiness community" (*Heiligkeitsgemeinde*).

who have laboured most arduously to prove the origin of Anabaptism in Zwingli's Reformation have been also the most insistent on the pacifistic and apolitical nature of Anabaptism proper (*das eigentliche Täufertum*).[101]

One might, therefore, ask with justification whether or not this implies a dual norm, the one theological and the other ethical. If it does, one might then conceive of normative Anabaptism as a dichotomy of theological and ethical Anabaptism.

Such differentiation should be understood merely as a methodological tool since the dogmatic and the ethical aspect of the Gospel, "the divine indicative" and "the divine imperative", are but two sides of the same coin. Perhaps a more appropriate metaphor would be that of the two foci of an ellipse.

The oft-repeated observation that on the whole the Anabaptists laid a greater emphasis on new life than on dogmas, points in the same direction. It need not be interpreted as a symptom of Anabaptist work-righteousness nor of a perfectionist striving after holiness. Rather it confirms our hypothesis that Anabaptist ideology was a 'bifocal theology' with a balanced emphasis on doctrine and morality, faith and obedience.

It must be recognized, however, that such dual definition of normative Anabaptism does not necessarily imply a contrast to the 'magisterial' Reformation. All Reformers were forced to deal with issues in the realm of individual and social ethics. It should be admitted though that in the case of Luther, and even more so with his followers, the triumphant emphasis on the rediscovered Gospel of *sola gratia* and *sola fide* led to a neglect of the ethical consequences of the Gospel, particularly in the sphere of social ethics. A similar criticism would be less justified in the case of Zwingli and even less with Bucer or Calvin who laid great emphasis on the lordship and reign of Christ.

The theological aspect of normative Anabaptism has been usually defined as the practice of believer's baptism and the institution of a congregation of baptized believers (gathered church, free church) with the administration of the Lord's Supper and church discipline.[102]

---

[101]   This is true particularly of the Mennonite scholarship (cf. Yoder, 1962, 160 ff. and 173). A similar view was expressed by others, e.g. Blanke, 1957, 66 ff.

[102]   Some historians accept adult baptism (rebaptism) as the only mark of Anabaptism: Hillerbrand, 1962b, 2; Bergsten, 1961, 25, n. 69. Others combine it with the concept of a gathered (voluntary) church: Fast, 1960, 227,, n. 10; Wiswedel, 1943, 184. Still others regard the concept of the church as primary and believer's bap-

Such definition is of course limited to a minimal ecclesiological formula with a focus on the outward observance of the two sacraments. It says nothing about the theological interpretation of believer's baptism and of communion, let alone about the understanding of soteriology, pneumatology, christology or theology proper. Presumably the basic theological framework could be Lutheran, Zwinglian, Bucerian, spiritualizing, or even anti-Trinitarian. Such was, in fact, the case in the complex Anabaptist movement and no definition of normative 'theological' Anabaptism can avoid this dilemma.

The definition of normative 'ethical' Anabaptism is even more perplexing. Within the camp of the evangelical Anabaptists — to use Williams' typology — there were varying degrees of withdrawal from society, or "political abstinence" (Blanke) but there were also advocates of Christian magistracy [103] and finally those for whom community of goods was as indispensable a mark of a Christian as conversion and believer's baptism (the Hutterites). Furthermore, for many early Anabaptists, their *via crucis* of non-resistant suffering could be metamorphosed into an ethic of aggressive revolution — or vice versa — by the dialectic of their fervent apocalyptic expectations.[104]

Which of the contradictory viewpoints is the legitimate expression of 'ethical Anabaptism'? The discussion of this aspect of normative Anabaptism has barely been opened. The real issue has been clouded by the debate on the 'Zürich or Zwickau' cradle of the Anabaptist

---

tism only as a derivative; Littell, 1958, XVII ("the Anabaptists proper were those in the radical Reformation who gathered and disciplined a 'true church' upon the apostolic pattern as they understood it"); Blanke, 1957, 60 ("They sought a free church in a double sense: a congregation free from the state and based upon voluntary membership. This was the first goal of Anabaptism. Their real interest was not in baptism, but in the church."); cf. also Yoder, 1962, 166-174 and his essay, "The Prophetic Dissent" (Yoder, 1957). One must ask, however, whether Blanke's and Yoder's interpretations which are based on the events in Zürich (1523-1525) are applicable to Anabaptism elsewhere and at other times.
[103] Hubmaier was not the only Anabaptist who advocated Christian participation in government. Cf. Bergsten, 1961, 482-502 and 1957, 87 ff. (Marbeck). Local sources in Austerlitz (Slavkov) confirm that the Pilgramites were involved in municipal government up to the early seventeenth century (cf. Zeman, 1966, 22).
[104] Cf. Molnár, 1959b, 273: The sense of responsibility which characterized the Czech Reformation and the whole 'first Reformation' could be expressed either through courage for suffering or, by a dialectical reversal, through courage for a revolution. Similar observations on the revolutionary and apolitical phases of Anabaptism, its class origins and similarities with the Czech Reformation, have been made in Czechoslovakia by the Marxist historians Macek, 1960b, 537 ff. and Ratkoš, 1954, 414. Cf. also Cantimori, 1949, 28 ff.

movement. The discussion was initiated by Troeltsch and Holl many years ago but the problem has not yet been resolved.[105] The role of Thomas Müntzer in the genesis of Anabaptism is another related and unsolved issue.[106]

If it is true that "the Anabaptists are the Bible Christians of Reformation history, distinguished from the Reformers through the extension of the biblical norm beyond the purely religious into economic and social life", as Walther Köhler has pointed out,[107] then a bifurcated definition of normative Anabaptism as theological and ethical, is in order. Up to the present, however, the inclusion of the socio-ethical aspects has been limited to the definition of Anabaptism as "the free church". The concept represents the socio-political correlate of the ecclesiological definition of "the gathered church", the voluntary fellowship of believers.[108]

5. THE QUEST FOR THE ESSENCE OF CZECH BRETHRENISM

The quest for the essence of Czech Brethrenism [109] has parallelled the search for the essence of Anabaptism in several respects.[110] The three most striking similarities between the typological hypotheses proposed for the two groups are: (1) The dialectic tension between theses which stress the peculiar characteristics *sui generis* and those which emphasize ideological affinities with other theological camps, (2) the problem of relationship between Anabaptism or Czech Brethrenism and the 'magisterial' Reformations of Germany and Switzerland, and (3) the dual emphasis on ethical and theological characteristics.

---

[105] Cf. Hillerbrand, 1959a, 62 ff. and Zschäbitz, 1958, 13 ff.
[106] Cf. *TQ*, X, Nos. 2011-2150. The bibliography on Müntzer is longer than on any other leader of the Radical Reformation!
[107] W. Köhler in his art. "Wiedertäufer", *RGG*, V (2nd ed., 1931), col. 1916, translated by Littell, 1957, IX. Cf. also Hillerbrand, 1959a, 59, n. 51.
[108] Cf. Blanke, 1957, 60 ff. and 66 ff. See the analysis of the free church tradition by Littell, 1957 and the historical review by Westin, 1958. Cf. also our discussion of normative Anabaptism in Chapter II at footnote 156.
[109] The term is analogical to other such designations as Anabaptism, Zwinglianism etc. It has been common in Czech literature (*českobratrství*) for a long time and there is no reason why it cannot be introduced into English.
[110] No review of the typological hypotheses concerning the *Unitas Fratrum* has been published by anyone thus far. Brož, 1958a, 104 (1958b, 124 in English) devoted one paragraph to the problem. Our brief summary should not be regarded as a comprehensive treatment of the subject.

Three stages can be distinguished in the modern attempts to define the essence of the *Unitas Fratrum*. With few exceptions, all these were formulated by Czech Protestant scholars.

The first period was marked by a strong accent on the uniqueness (*svéráz, Eigenart*) of the *Unitas Fratrum*. The Brethren were said to have represented a specifically Czech type of piety and doctrine. In his remarkable apotheosis of the Czech Reformation, the founder of modern Czech historiography, František Palacký, regarded the Unity as the climax of the ideological development of the nation. Palacký saw the genius of the *Unitas* in its "greater concern for Christian practice than for dogmatic principles" and in its emphasis on the new, perfected character of Christians.[111] Palacký's interpretation was conditioned both by his political views as a leader in the Czech national awakening and by his philosophical sympathies with the ideals of Enlightenment.

Tomáš Garrigue Masaryk popularized Palacký's thesis in his philosophy of Czech history.[112] He saw Czech Brethrenism as the final and highest expression of the Czech religio-national traditions. As president of the newly founded republic he repeatedly declared that the Czech question was a religious question. In the context of his philosophy, he regarded "the humanitarian ideals" of Hus, Chelčický, Blahoslav and Komenský as a fully modern program for his nation.

There can be little doubt that the typology advocated by Jan Herben, Ferdinand Hrejsa, František Bednář and to a lesser degree by Jan B. Čapek[113] was greatly influenced by Palacký and Masaryk. The dependence upon Masaryk's philosophy of Czech history was pointed out by Josef L. Hromádka in a critical examination of Hrejsa's thesis in 1937.[114] A new generation of Protestant theologians led by Hromádka and influenced not a little by Karl Barth, undertook the task of reinterpreting the theological development of the *Unitas* in the context of the Continental Reformation.

In a series of monographs, the affinity with and partial dependence upon the Calvinistic theology was documented for the Unity's concept of the Lord's Supper and for other points of doctrine during the

---

[111] Cf. the quotations in Bartoš, 1948, 7 f.
[112] Especially in his work, *Česká otázka*, 1894. Cf. also his other basic works, *Ideály humanitní* and *Světová revoluce*. See the discussion of the Czech religious traditions by Říčan, 1939.
[113] Herben, 1926a-b; Hrejsa, 1939; Bednář, 1939 and Čapek, 1951.
[114] Hromádka, 1937.

latter part of the sixteenth and the early seventeenth century.[115] The thesis was by no means new. Already in 1741, J. C. Koecher had called the Brethren *Calviniani ante Calvinum* and in 1906 J. Bidlo observed that the late *Unitas* turned to Calvinism because of inner necessity.[116] Far from a one-sided reaction to the older school of interpretation, the new typology did not overlook the strong roots of the Brethren's theology in the Hussite movement and in the theology of Petr Chelčický. Nevertheless, it was recognized that after the death of Bishop Lukáš the Unity went through a period of strong Lutheran influence (1529-1546). A period of transition was followed by half a century (1573-1628) of growing alignment with the Calvinistic Reformation.[117] The approximation of the Brethren to Luther's Reformation in the second quarter of the sixteenth century was underscored by a number of scholars, most recently by Pelikan and Fousek.[118]

However, these were not the only reinterpretations of the essence of Czech Brethrenism in relation to other 'types' of Christianity. In 1904, Ivan Palmov, a Russian historian, claimed that the Czech Reformation, and particularly the *Unitas Fratrum*, represented a type of theology and piety which had no parallel in the Western Reformation. This he thought was owing to the consciousness of a basic affinity with the Eastern Church which existed in Moravia and Bohemia from the days of the missionary work of Cyril and Methodius in the ninth century. The fact that both the Hussites and the Czech Brethren had journeyed to the East to search for the remnants of an uncorrupted apostolic church was for Palmov a confirmation of his thesis. In a refutation, Müller [119] pointed out that a programmatic return to the apostolic model of the primitive church was a common characteristic of the medieval sectarian movements such as the Waldenses.

[115]   Souček, 1933; Hájek, 1934; Dobiáš, 1940 and 1941; Hromádka, 1939 (reprinted in a revised form in 1954) and 1956; Dobiáš, 1957 and 1960a-b; Souček, 1956 (cf. also Molnár, 1962 f.); Jeschke, 1958, 1959 and 1960a-b.
[116]   Koecher, 1741; Bidlo, 1906.
[117]   A good review of the Unity's changing theological orientation was written by Říčan, 1943 and Molnár, 1957d; a definitive work was prepared by Štrupl, 1964a. Cf. our reference at footnote 48 above.
[118]   Pelikan, 1946 and 1964, 120-146; Fousek, 1965, 60 claims that in their soteriology the Brethren (Bishop Lukáš) made "a genuinely pre-Lutheran discovery of the Gospel. . . . Without realizing it, Luther was more a 'Bohemian Brother' in his theological breakthrough than a 'Hussite', as he liked to call himself".
[119]   Palmov, 1904, first part. Müller's review appeared in *ZBG*, 1 (1907), 102-105.

A different interpretation was proposed by František M. Bartoš. The strong ethical accents of the Brethren and their differentiation between the essential, the ministrative and the incidental things reminded him of the theology of Erasmus. Through Comenius, Bartoš tried to detect a line of thought leading to deism and finally to modern free (creedless) Protestantism.[120] The thesis as such can hardly be defended but the ideological connection between the Unity and Erasmus (and the Left Wing of the Reformation) is worth noting.

The third phase of typology was ushered in by Amedeo Molnár, professor of historical theology at the Comenius Faculty in Prague, by his thesis on two Reformations.[121]

Molnár proposed that the term "the first Reformation" be used as a common designation for all reform movements aiming at the renewal of the church during the long period from the twelfth to the end of the sixteenth century. Among others, the Waldenses, the Hussites and the Left Wing of the sixteenth-century Reformation, particularly the Anabaptists, were included in the large group.

The first Reformation, "formally still medieval", displayed the following general characteristics. It recognized the sole authority of the Scriptures but the actual norm of truth and life was narrowed down to the synoptic Gospels, especially the Sermon on the Mount.[122] The Gospel was interpreted chiefly as a rule of life which demands obedience. This in turn led to a critical evaluation of sacramental acts of the church, particularly when performed by "unworthy priests". The first Reformation was further marked by strong eschatological or apocalyptic notes (the coming reign of Christ), an emphasis on the direct, unmediated work of the Holy Spirit and on the ethical demands of the Gospel, both in the life of individuals and in the life of society.

[120] Bartoš, 1939 and 1948 (enlarged). Cf. the reply to his thesis by Říčan in *KR*, 15 (1948), 315 ff. See also the essay on Erasmus' contacts with the Unity, Bartoš, 1956a and 1958a, and the summary of all ecumenical contacts of the Unity, Bartoš, 1956b.

[121] The thesis was first introduced in a Czech article, Molnár, 1957c and then included in Molnár's Czech essay on the theology of the *Unitas Fratrum*, Molnár, 1957d, 410 f. (also in German, 1961e, 284 f.). A French summary was included in his essay, 1963d. Molnár also applied the thesis to a number of specific problems of research, e.g. 1962c, 1962d (also in French in *CV*, 4 [1961], 329), 1962e and 1964a-b. Brož, 1958a (and 1958b in English) gave a good summary and supporting evaluation of Molnár's thesis. Lochman, 1963, 28 also referred to the thesis approvingly. The only open criticism came from Jeschke, 1960b. Thus far no evaluation has been expressed by scholars outside Czechoslovakia.

[122] Cf. a similar observation made by Friedmann, 1961a, 20.

As a result, the first Reformation found response mainly among the lower social classes, and was accompanied, at times, by revolutionary attempts to initiate the rule of Christ (the Hussite wars and the Peasant Revolt).

By contrast, the second or "classic" Reformation underscored the authority of the Scriptures as a whole even though it drew its understanding of the Gospel as a gracious gift of forgiveness and Christian freedom, primarily from the letters of Paul. By and large, eschatology was reduced to a personal hope for life after death. The socio-ethical dimensions of the Gospel were minimized. In its early years, the second Reformation appealed to all strata of society and was regarded as a direct continuation of the first Reformation. However, when the explosive message of the Gospel produced unexpected responses of religious and social radicalism, the Reformers refused to endorse them. Gradually, the second Reformation lost the support of the peasants and the lower nobility and became almost exclusively a movement of the rising bourgeoisie and the powerful high nobility. According to Molnár,[123] such social stratification took place in Lutheran Germany and later, in Calvinistic France.

The contrast between the two Reformations was, therefore, theological as well as socio-ethical. In theology, both Reformations were focused on soteriology but their interpretations differed. The first Reformation saw soteriological issues within the wider context of "koinonic" epistemology, of an eschatological existence of the church in society and of a refusal to rely on the support of political authorities.[124] The soteriological understanding of the second Reformation was narrowed down to individual justification.

According to Molnár, the two Reformations met, "walked hand in hand" for a time and then, tragically enough, parted their ways. The many colloquies between the Anabaptists and the Reformers in Ger-

---

[123] The socio-ethical contrast between the two Reformations was not fully demonstrated by Molnár's original presentation of the thesis, Molnár, 1957c-d (and 1961e). It was stressed in his subsequent articles, especially 1962e.

[124] One of Molnár's several attempts to define the theological difference between the two Reformations states: "La notion d'une noéthique théologique communautaire, d'une Eglise remplissant une fonction eschatologique au sein de l'humanité par discipline volontaire et renonçant à tout appui de la part de l'Etat, on la trouve exprimée déjà par les Vaudois du bas moyen-âge et particulièrement par les théologiens de l'Unité des Frères Tchèques. En Menno Simons nous rencontrons en plein XVIe siècle, époque classique de la 'deuxième Réforme', un représentant remarquable d'une pensée théologique structurée entièrement sur des données typiques de la 'première Réforme'" (CV, 4 [1961], 329).

many and Switzerland in the sixteenth century represented one form of the dialogue between the two Reformations.[125] The crucial issue involved in most of these debates was the concept of *corpus Christianum* and the related question of a free church. When the dialogue ended in the middle of the sixteenth century, the Reformers retained the medieval concept of a Christian society. Their territorial churches were controlled, to a greater or lesser degree, by civic authorities. As a result, the protagonists of the first Reformation had no other choice left to them than to withdraw into sectarian isolation. This development could not but be deplored as a betrayal of the strong sense of responsibility for all spheres of life which had characterized the original first Reformation.[126]

The unique position of the *Unitas Fratrum* in the history of Christian theology [127] can be discerned in the fact that the Czech Brethren never ceased to "lead a dialogue" between the two Reformations. Undoubtedly, the roots of the original Unity were in the first Reformation. The later generations welcomed the second Reformation.[128] In contrast to the Anabaptists, the Czech Brethren maintained friendly contacts with the leading spokesmen of the second Reformation (Luther, Melanchthon, Bucer, Calvin and others) even after these had denied some of the foremost principles of the first Reformation (free church, sympathy with the socially disinherited). The Czech Brethren never walked the whole way with the second Reformation, whether in its Lutheran or Calvinistic form. They did not hesitate to express reservations and objections. Their contacts should not be interpreted, therefore, as a betrayal of the first Reformation.

---

[125] Molnár, 1962c.

[126] "Verschiedene Wiedertäufergruppen stellten in dem klassischen Reformations-Zeitalter (16. Jahrhundert) in verschiedenem Masse und verschiedener Reinheit die erste schon in früheren Jahrhunderten einsetzende Reformation dar. Es führt ja eine direkte Zeugenlinie von den Waldensern und den Taboriten zu den Links-strömungen des 16. Jahrhunderts" (Molnár, 1961e, 285).

[127] In one sense, Molnár also speaks about the unique doctrinal position (*sváráz*) of the Unity as the Czech typologists did during the first period (see our review above). In another sense, Molnár provides a most original synthesis between the typologies of the first and second period. His *dogmengeschichtlich* interpretation is, of course, different from both.

[128] Molnár never states explicitly when the dialogue between the two Reformations began in the Unity, presumably, not until after Luther's writings became known to the Brethren. However, such historical dating is contradicted by the theological interpretations according to which the second-generation soteriology of the *Unitas* could be classified as "a genuinely pre-Lutheran discovery of the Gospel, of the truly good and reliable news of the gift of salvation in Christ" (Fousek, 1965, 60). We are not certain whether Molnár shares Fousek's view.

By way of critical evaluation, one must admit that Molnár's thesis provides the most ingenious way to dispose of the typological dilemma associated with the *Unitas Fratrum*. Somehow, its theology, and even less its ethics, could never be fitted into any existing typological or morphological categories of the Reformation. The Brethren had been claimed, with varying degrees of justification, for the Lutheran camp and for the Reformed camp. Without doing any violence to historical facts, one might align the Unity equally well with the Left Wing of the Reformation, particularly if one subscribes to the broad typology advocated by Littell or Williams. According to Molnár, the *Unitas Fratrum* cannot be lined up unequivocally with any defined segment of the sixteenth-century Reformation, not even for a limited period of time such as "the Lutheran spell" or "the Calvinistic spell" in its theological development.[129] It cannot be done for the simple reason that the Brethren continued to "sit on two chairs"[130] of the first and second Reformation and refused to give up either of them.

One can detect certain minor similarities between Molnár's thesis and Keller's concept of evangelical brotherhoods or even Troeltsch's differentiation between church and sect.[131] More pronounced is the influence of the social stratification of the sixteenth-century Reformation by Marx and Engels and by the contemporary Marxist historians.

Our main criticism[132] concerns Molnár's typology of sixteenth-century Anabaptism. The documented partial dependence of many Anabaptist leaders on the theology of Zwingli and of other Reformers makes it impossible to classify the Anabaptists exclusively as representatives of the first Reformation.[133] Might it be that the theology of men like Hubmaier, Denck, Marbeck, Riedemann and others should also be characterized as a dialogue between the two Reformations?

A number of questions beg an answer. To the best of our knowl-

---

[129] Odložilík, 1964, 102 f. claims that by 1614 the Unity had no longer any reservations about being regarded as a branch of the Reformed (Calvinistic) churches. In that year, the seniors gave an official permission to have the latest Latin confession of the Unity printed among the Reformed confessions in the second edition of the *Harmonia confessionum* planned by the theologians in Geneva.

[130] Molnár does not employ this phrase.

[131] Brož, 1958b, 125 refers to "an echo of Troeltsch's antithesis of church and sect".

[132] Our brief comments should not be regarded as a full evaluation of Molnár's thesis.

[133] Cf. footnote 126 above.

edge, Molnár himself has never related his thesis to the historical problem of genetic influence and ideological dependence of the one Reformation upon the other. A sympathetic interpreter of his thesis has suggested that the two Reformations are "quite independent of one another" and are "not to be derived one from the other".[134] Such explanation is of course contradicted by Molnár's classification of Anabaptism which we have just mentioned.

Does not Molnár's lumping together of so many varied strata of both Reformations lead to typological generalizations and over-simplifications which are useless for historical research? Broad categories of comparative theology such as were introduced by Molnár may be welcomed by those who are satisfied with tracing ideological (geistesgeschichtlich) parallels, but will not help greatly those who are trying to solve problems of complex historical and ideological relationships between groups and individual leaders. One may also doubt the wisdom of calling the two Reformations 'first' and 'second'.[135]

One of the most expressive descriptions of the Czech Reformation came recently from the pen of Jan M. Lochman.[136] He summarized the main accents of the Unity — an heir to the Hussite Reformation — under the following five points:

(1) Faith implies obedience and discipleship (Nachfolge). The knowledge of truth must be attested by new life. The Lordship of Christ extends over all spheres of life, "religious" and "secular".[137] No political and economic order of society can be regarded as permanent

---

[134]   Brož, 1958b, 125.
[135]   Brož, ibid., stresses that the two Reformations must not be conceived of as two successive stages in the evolution of Reformation theology. Molnár's thesis "frees us from historical evolutionism and from the poorly founded distinctions between the Czech, German, Swiss, Italian or perhaps 'World' Reformations". Gelder, 1961 distinguished two Reformations in the sixteenth century: Protestant and humanistic. Brož, ibid., made a plea for a separate classification of a third (Erasmian) Reformation. By a "third" Reformation, Wenger, 1963 designated Anabaptism. Friedmann, 1961a, 8 proposed the term "fourth Reformation" as an alternative to Bainton's "Left Wing of the Reformation". In his itinerary, Fynes Moryson, an Englishman, described his visit at the Bethlehem Church in Prague (1591) in the following terms: "they show a pulpit in which John Hus used to preach at the first Reformation of Religion" (Moryson, 1617, 16). In June 1524, Ludwig Hetzer reportedly applied the expression "second Reformation" to the radical Reformation which must go beyond Luther's Reformation (Williams, 1962, 97).
[136]   Lochman, 1963, 26 ff.
[137]   Cf. Köhler's remark about the Anabaptist extension of the biblical norm into economic and social life, quoted at footnote 107 above.

for it stands under the judgment of the coming kingdom of Christ (strong eschatological undertones and a trend towards communitarian life among the Taborites and the early Brethren).

(2) Christian witness often includes martyrdom. The story of the Czech Reformation, as seen by Comenius, was an *historia persecutionum*.[138]

(3) Both the Hussite churches (the Calixtines and the Taborites) and the *Unitas Fratrum* came into being as reform movements of the people. They were not initiated by decisions of feudal lords or city councils. In that sense, they were — particularly the Unity — the first free churches.[139]

(4) From its beginnings in the days of Hus until the death of Comenius, the Czech Reformation was marked by strong ecumenical consciousness. In the ecclesiological terminology of the Brethren the word 'church' was reserved for the one universal Christian church. Its branches were designated merely as 'unities' (*jednoty*).[140]

(5) In spite of, or perhaps owing to the fact that the Czech Reformation was born in wars, it bore a meaningful witness to peace in later times. Consistent pacifism became the creed of only small minorities: the followers of Petr Chelčický, the first generation of the Unity and afterwards its Minor Party, and the Habrovanites. However, a sense of responsibility for the maintenance of peace in the world marked the Czech Reformation from Hus' *Sermo de pace* (1414)[141] to King George's plan for a Peace League of Christian Princes (1462)[142] and to Comenius' vision of universal peace in his *Angelus pacis* (1667).[143]

No one could fail to see the striking similarities between 'the essence' of Czech Brethrenism as defined by Lochman, and the basic characteristics of Anabaptism. The strong ethical accent is common to both movements. The 'bifocal' typology of Anabaptism as theo-

[138] That was the title of the second Latin ed. published in 1648. For the Czech version, see *Historie*, 1902.
[139] Cf. Říčan, 1964b and 1965a; Zeman, 1957 and 1962.
[140] On the ecumenical motifs in the Czech Reformation, cf. Dobiáš, 1957; 1960a-b; Molnár, 1964c; Říčan, 1964b.
[141] Hus, 1963. The text was prepared for delivery before the Council of Constance.
[142] Heymann, 1965, 293-315.
[143] Komenský, 1938. A comprehensive plan was developed by Comenius in his large work, *De rerum humanarum emendatione consultatio catholica*. The major part of the manuscript remained unpublished until the recent critical edition in Prague (1966).

logical and ethical which we have proposed earlier may be advocated with equal justification for the *Unitas Fratrum*. Not only the first generation of the 'Old Brethren' and the split-away Minor Party but also the main stream of the Unity was characterized by a concern for a *regnum Christi* in all spheres of life.[144]

It is obvious that the increasing knowledge of Anabaptist history and thought and the gradual discovery of the theological heritage of the *Unitas Fratrum* by scholars outside Czechoslovakia will bring about a reinterpretation of the relationship between the two movements. New typological categories are needed in order to preserve the characteristic concepts of Anabaptism and Czech Brethrenism and to describe adequately their historical and ideological relationship.

The road which leads from our present realization of the issues, and of possible solutions, to the final answers — if there are any final answers in historical research — is long and will require many years of tedious studies.

6. THE PROPOSED PLAN OF STUDIES

We can envisage the following four stages of research required to clarify and define the relationship between the *Unitas Fratrum* and Anabaptism (the Radical Reformation).

(1) HISTORICAL CONTACTS:
   (a) In Moravia, the land of refuge for Anabaptists from many countries, from 1526 till 1628.
   (b) In Bohemia, Slovakia, Poland, Prussia and perhaps in other countries with opportunities for contact.
   The study of historical contacts should include not only a careful examination of all preserved records of personal and literary contacts (colloquies, correspondences, literary polemics, catechisms, hymns etc.) but also the listing of opportunities for contact, particularly in terms of historical topography.

[144]   In his book (Brock, 1957) Brock exaggerated the "break with the past" which the Major Party under Brother Lukáš carried out in the 1490's. There was a continuity of development in the theological and ethical teachings of the Unity. Cf. other studies on social ethics of the Brethren, e.g. Dobiáš, 1961; Molnár, 1949b; 1957f-g; Smolík, 1948; 1956; Válka, 1959 (cf. critical review by Říčan in *TPKR*, 1961, 27 ff.). However, Brock's main thesis is most pertinent for our present discussion. See the quotation at footnote 2 above.

(2) THEOLOGICAL (IDEOLOGICAL) COMPARISON:
   (a) Theological concepts.
   (b) Ethical concepts, particularly in the field of social ethics, and
       including the relationship between church and state.

> Sweeping generalizations which attempt to compare Ana-
> baptist theology with the theology of the Czech Brethren are
> of little use. What is needed is a series of monographs on
> particular issues and on individual representative leaders in
> both camps. Comparative studies on persons whose biograph-
> ical data make mutual acquaintance and influence possible
> or probable, should then be undertaken. For example, the
> theology of Bishop Lukáš should be compared with the
> theology of Hubmaier, Ascherham, Plener, Denck, Entfelder,
> Glaidt and Andreas Fischer. Similarly, the theology of Jan
> Blahoslav may be set over against the views of the later
> leaders of Moravian Anabaptism, both among the Hutterites
> and among the non-communitarian groups (Marbeck). One
> must not fail to take into account the differences in doctrine
> which were typical of the particular groups within Ana-
> baptism and of the successive stages in the theological devel-
> opment of the Unity. A comprehensive theological confronta-
> tion of the two movements can be made only on the basis of
> many sectional studies.
>
> A theological comparison should also include the problem
> of sources from which the respective groups drew. It is quite
> possible that some parallel teachings can be traced to a com-
> mon source which each group utilized independently. Further-
> more, the image of the Anabaptists and of the Czech 'Picards'
> as it is preserved in the polemical writings of their common
> opponents, Catholic and Protestant, should also be compared.
> Some reformers had important dealings with both groups.
> How did Bucer, for instance, evaluate Anabaptist theology
> and how did he judge the position of the Unity?

(3) SOCIOLOGICAL COMPARISON:
   A number of monographs on 'non-theological factors' such as
   social background, educational system, marriage and family life,
   ethnic and linguistic characteristics, crafts and professions, and
   on other sociological aspects of Anabaptism have already been

published.[145] Similar studies are needed for the *Unitas Fratrum*. With such materials in hand, a comparative analysis should not involve a great deal of additional research.

(4) TYPOLOGICAL RELATIONSHIP BETWEEN ANABAPTISM AND 'UNITAS FRATRUM':

On the basis of the historical, theological and sociological research outlined under 1, 2 and 3, the following three basic questions should be answered:

(a) What were the respective relationships of Anabaptism and of the *Unitas Fratrum* (1) to medieval theology and piety, (2) to sixteenth-century Reformation?

(b) Was there (1) a genetic influence and (2) later influence of the *Unitas Fratrum* upon Anabaptism?

(c) What was the typological relationship of the *Unitas Fratrum* to sixteenth-century Anabaptism as seen within the context of the whole Reformation?

7. THE LIMITATIONS OF OUR PRESENT STUDY

Our present investigation shall deal mainly with the historical contacts between the Anabaptists and the *Unitas Fratrum* in Moravia (Section 1.a. of our "Proposed Plan of Studies"). The following comments will explain the self-imposed limitations.

a. *Geographical Limitation*

Moravia, as the classical land of religious toleration during the sixteenth and early seventeenth centuries, afforded the best and longest opportunity for contacts between the two groups. Anabaptists of all shades of persuasion found shelter there for an entire century and were able to develop their congregations or communal settlements as nowhere else in Europe at that time. In the second half of the century, Moravia became also the stronghold of *Unitas Fratrum* when its activities in Bohemia were curbed after the persecution in 1546-1547.

---

[145] E.g. Correll, 1925; Dedic, 1939a; Kreider, 1953; Sommer, 1953; Peachey, 1954a-b; Clasen, 1963a; Klassen, 1963 and 1964; Friedmann, 1961a, 103-150 and the older general works, Kautsky, I-II and Troeltsch, 1912. The sociological research of the *Unitas Fratrum* has been very limited.

There is an additional reason why the study should be limited to the margraviate. Moravian Anabaptism had contacts mainly with Austria, southwestern Germany and Switzerland (and to a lesser degree with Silesia) whereas the sporadically appearing isolated small groups of Anabaptists in Bohemia seem to have been oriented more towards Saxony. The different type of radicalism there (Thomas Müntzer and the Zwickau prophets) presents a distinct problem and should be the subject of a separate investigation. It also involves the issue of the genetic influence of the *Unitas Fratrum* on the rise of antipaedobaptism in Saxony.[146]

The contacts between Anabaptists and the Unity in Slovakia were excluded for the simple reason that the Czech Brethren did not begin to settle there until after their expulsion from Moravia in 1628.[147] There was, therefore, no opportunity for contacts between the two groups during the period under our investigation. Since the vast majority of Anabaptists came to Moravia as refugees from other lands, the geographical limitation cannot be adhered to strictly. In order to investigate the possible genetic literary influence of the Unity upon Hubmaier, considerable attention will be given to the beginnings of Anabaptism in Switzerland and South Germany (Chapter III).

b. *Chronological Limitation*

The chronological span of our research is dictated by the geographical limitation. Anabaptists did not appear in Moravia until 1526. Most of them were expelled in 1622. The main decree of expulsion for the Czech Brethren in Moravia was issued in 1628. The terminal points, 1526-1628, happen to coincide with two important political events in the history of the margraviate. The year 1526 marked the beginning of the Habsburg rule in the Czech lands. In 1628, a new constitution (*Obnovené zřízení zemské*) sealed the doom of all liberties in the little land, the name of which had been known as a symbol of survival by all persecuted heretics throughout Europe.

The one hundred years of Anabaptist sojourn in Moravia will not receive equal attention in our present study. The first three years (1526-1528) are treated in three long chapters whereas the subsequent one hundred years are reviewed briefly in one chapter. There are several reasons for this seeming lack of balance.

[146]   Cf. the studies by Husa, 1956a, 1957 and 1958.
[147]   Hrejsa, B, 78 and Ďurovič, 1956.

The initial years of contact were most crucial for the formulation of relationships between Anabaptists and *Unitas Fratrum*. During that early period, the Anabaptists represented a greater variety of views than in the later periods when Moravian Anabaptism was stabilized into two or three main patterns, the Hutterite brotherhood and the non-communitarian Pilgramites or Swiss Brethren. The Czech Brethren were also experiencing a confrontation with several theological trends (Lutheran, Zwinglian, spiritualist) and under the leadership of Lukáš had not yielded to such influences but retained their own theology. This in turn made possible an encounter of Anabaptism with "genuine Czech Brethrenism".

We shall attempt to answer the question of a genetic influence of the Unity on the rise of Anabaptism in Moravia and to deal with the related issue of Hubmaier's knowledge of the Czech Reformation. Furthermore, the only recorded negotiations for a merger between the Anabaptists and the *Unitas Fratrum* took place in 1528.

All these factors make it necessary that we concentrate our attention on the early period and that the subsequent recorded contacts be only summarized in a concise review.[148] The later stratification of Moravian Anabaptism and the opportunities for contact with the Czech Brethren are treated fully in our topographical analysis.[149]

c. Bibliographical Limitations

A historian who undertakes research into a phase of Moravian history and does not have access to the archives and libraries in Czechoslovakia works under a serious handicap. Fortunately, in our age, microfilms and photocopies of manuscripts and rare books can be procured in most cases.

A glance at our list of bibliography will show that our present investigation is based mainly on printed primary sources and on an extensive knowledge of literature. In particular, we shall endeavour to acquaint the Western reader with the remarkable fruit of recent Czech historical scholarship.[150]

At the same time, it must be stressed that over a period of ten

---

[148] The later period should receive balanced attention in a theological comparison of the two groups, as outlined in our Proposed Plan of Studies.
[149] See Chapter VI and Zeman, 1966.
[150] Many important essays published in Czech periodicals remain unnoticed by scholars outside Czechoslovakia. We are referring especially to the works of Bartoš, Hrejsa, Říčan and Molnár.

years, we have pursued every lead that might have resulted in the discovery of additional source materials illustrating the contacts between Anabaptists and the Unity. The printed catalogues for archives in Czechoslovakia, Switzerland and Germany were checked and direct enquiries were made. In this way, we were able to 'discover' a manuscript essay written against the Anabaptists by a member of the Unity in 1589.[151]

In our use of sources we have been guided by the following principle. For items which are related directly to the central issue of our investigation, i.e. the historical (personal and literary) contacts between the two groups in Moravia, we have used always the original primary sources.[152] For items which are treated only as part of the historical or theological framework we have used primary sources wherever possible but in some cases we have accepted the quotations or summaries by reputable scholars.[153]

Our two lists of printed sources (*Anabaptistica* and *Bohemica*) indicate what extensive use of sixteenth-century prints [154] we were able to make.

However, we have excluded the hymnbooks altogether. A comparative study of the Anabaptist hymnology and the German hymnbooks of the Unity will furnish additional evidence of contacts.[155] The subject has been regarded, usually, as a special field of study. The main reason for our omission was a practical consideration. We did not have access to the various editions of the hymnbooks of the Unity.

8. THE SOURCES

In addition to the preceding statement on the bibliographical limitaitons, the following notes should facilitate an orientation in the sources used for our present study.

[151] Cf. Chapter V.

[152] In most cases microfilms or photocopies. We have published the Czech text of the main manuscript source for the first time in a critical edition (Zeman, 1958).

[153] This applies particularly to the sources of the Habrovanite Brethren (Chapter II) which have been analyzed independently by Odložilík, 1923, Hanák, 1928-1929 and, to some extent, by Brock, 1957.

[154] Most of the prints which we have used are stored in the amazing collections of the Zentralbibliothek in Zürich.

[155] According to Hrejsa Bohuš, 1931, 20 the first printed German hymnal of the Unity, *Ein New Geseng buchlen* (prepared by Michael Weisse in 1531) contained four Anabaptist hymns. Cf. the list of bibliography for the hymnology of the *Unitas* in Říčan, 1961a, 339 f. and for the Anabaptist hymnology in *TQ*, X, Nos. 4139-4277c.

(a) In-group Sources of the *Unitas Fratrum*: The only record of the colloquies between the Anabaptists and the Czech Brethren has been preserved in the official collection of documents known as *Acta Unitas Fratrum (AUF)*.[156] The thirteen (fifteen) volumes cover all but the last four decades (up to 1589) of the Unity's history in Bohemia, Moravia (and Poland). They contain chronologically arranged documents such as theological treatrises, polemical writings, correspondence within the Unity and with Reformation leaders in other lands, records of meetings and brief historical narratives of events.

The long history of research which led to the identification of editors, scribes and dates of origin for each volume has been told elsewhere.[157] The pertinent information about the particular sections used in our study will be found at the appropriate places. The contents of all thirteen codices were described accurately by Müller.[158] Only two volumes have been printed thus far in a critical edition.[159] Other selected portions were edited by Gindely, Zelinka and others.[160]

In contrast to the large selection of Czech, Latin and German documents collected in the *Acta,* the second important source, *Historia Fratrum,* is a Czech chronicle which merely lists events and records titles of written works or published books of the Unity in chronological order. For more than a century, Czech and German scholars have struggled with the question of authorship and date of origin. The most recent hypothesis by Bartoš suggests Jan Kálef as the probable author.[161]

Three other important manuscripts sources must be mentioned: (1) *Dekrety*, an official collection of decrees issued by the synods of

---

[156]   The name of the collection has its own history. The nomenclature includes such terms as *Lissauer Folianten, Herrnhuter Folianten* ('H', used by Gindely), *Archiv bratrský* (A.B.) and *Akta Jednoty bratrské* (A.J.B.). We adhere to the name introduced by Müller conforming to the original name chosen by Blahoslav for volumes VII and VIII. Cf. Müller, 1913, 66-80.

[157]   Müller, 1913, 66-80; Müller, I, 578 ff.; Bidlo, 1923 and his introduction in *Akty,* I, 8 ff.; Krofta, 1946, 85 ff.; Štěříková, 1964. See Appendix 1 for a table showing the chronology and authorship of all volumes.

[158]   Müller, 1913 and 1915. He also prepared a chronological list of all materials in the *AUF* for the years 1461-1528 (Müller, I, 585-604). See also Hobza, 1967.

[159]   *Akty* I and II.

[160]   Gindely, 1859 and Zelinka, 1942.

[161]   Bartoš, 1954b. Kálef died in 1588. *Historia Fratrum (HF)* is a Ms. codex in two volumes which cover the period from 1458 till 1542. A detailed synopsis of contents was published by Šafařík, 1862. Cf. Müller, I, 604 ff. and Krofta, 1946, 90 ff. and 110. See also Kaňák, 1967, 138 ff.

the Unity,[162] (2) a Czech *Necrologue* [163] which contains brief characteristics of ministers of the Unity (from 1467 to 1606) and (3) *Meč Goliášův* [The Sword of Goliath] by Jan Jafet, a work complementary to the *Necrologue*, giving a succession of ministers and bishops from 1457 to 1606.[164] We have also utilized a Czech manuscript codex preserved in Stuttgart.[165] The examination of three other codices in Prague led to the discovery of Czech polemical literature against the Anabaptists.[166] The many printed primary sources require no special description in the present context.[167]

(b) Anabaptist In-group Sources: With the exception of *Codex Kunstbuch* [168] we have not used any Anabaptist manuscript sources for our present study. Of the printed sources, we have made abundant use of the published Hutterite chronicles [169] and of the collection of sources, *Quellen zur Geschichte der Täufer*.[170] Other primary sources, such as confessions, catechisms and the published works of Ascherham, Marbeck, Riedemann and others, will be found listed in our bibliography. Friedmann's reports on his life-long research of the manuscript sources for Moravian (chiefly Hutterite) Anabaptism make a further discussion here superfluous.[171] It is doubtful that the famous Beck Collection in Brno contains any material that would

---

[162]   Ms. Codex II F 10 (Museum Library, Prague). Two preserved volumes cover the period up to 1575. Two additional volumes (1576-1617) have not been found thus far (Krofta, 1946, 145 f.). The text was published by Gindely, 1865.

[163]   Written by Vavřinec Orlík up to the year 1586 and contributed by a second hand up to 1605 and by a third hand up to 1606. Full text published in *Todtenbuch* (1863).

[164]   A reliable digest was published by J. Jireček in 1861 (Jafet). On the other historical works of Jafet, see Krofta, 1946, 146-156.

[165]   Ms. Codex of Jan Kamenický (copied in 1572), described by Bartoš, 1932.

[166]   Psaní, 1589 in Codex Skalský and Codex Crupp (see Chapter V at footnote 93) and several paragraphs in Codex XVII G 26 (University Library in Prague) (see Chapter V footnote 142). We are indebted to Prof. R. Říčan for his kind assistance.

[167]   The best introduction to the historiography and sources of the Unity was written by Krofta, 1946. Cf. also Brock, 1957, 277-292. The only larger collection of printed sources for the Unity outside Czechoslovakia (not to mention Herrnhut) is the Malin Library in the Archives of the Moravian Church, Bethlehem, Pa. Cf. the catalogue, Malin, 1881.

[168]   See the description by Fast, 1956b and Bender, 1956a, 75 ff.

[169]   Published in several editions: Wolny, 1850, Beck (1883), Wolkan, 1923, and the excellent editions by Zieglschmid, *ZGL* and *ZGLK*. Cf. Friedmann, 1961a, 151-156.

[170]   *TQ*, I-XII, and one volume each on Hessen and Switzerland. The series includes the works of Hubmaier (*HS*) and Denck (*DS*). Cf. the report on future volumes in *MQR*, 38 (1964), 368 ff.

[171]   See his large catalogue, Friedmann, 1965b, and his earlier works on Anabap-

bring to light additional evidence of historical contacts between the Anabaptists and the Czech Brethren.[172]

(c) Out-group Sources: We have paid special attention to the polemical literature in which both Catholic and Protestant writers attacked the Czech Picards (Institoris, Augustinus Moravus, Ziegler, Dungersheim and others) or the Anabaptists in Moravia, and in particular to the writings of Johann Faber, the Bishop of Vienna, who dealt with both groups.

Local secular sources were utilized chiefly for topographical research.[173]

As a rule, German and Latin sources are quoted in the original language [174] whereas the Czech sources are reproduced in an English translation.

9. THE PROBLEM OF TERMINOLOGY

A comparative study of Anabaptism and the *Unitas Fratrum* involves a problem in terminology. Both groups were known as 'the Brethren'. In either case, the term had been chosen by the group itself whereas the opponents used other, mostly deprecatory names such as *Wieder-täufer*, *Täufer*,[175] *Schwärmer* in the one case, and *Picards* or *Waldensians* (*fratres Waldenses*) in the other.

When the Anabaptist movement divided into several streams, the individual factions were given qualifying designations such as the Swiss Brethren, Hutterite Brethren, Gabrielite Brethren, Philippite Brethren or Austerlitz (Slavkov) Brethren. Similarly, when the Czech

---

tist sources, especially Friedmann, 1929; 1931-1932; 1952; 1956; 1961a, 151-253 and 286-312.

[172] Cf. the descriptive list of Beck's collection in Friedmann, 1965b, 86 ff. and Bender, 1949. The materials, copied by Beck's hand, have been used quite thoroughly by Loserth, Dedic and Wiswedel, all of whom were interested in the relationship between the Anabaptists and the Moravian religious groups. None of them reported documents related to the *Unitas Fratrum*.

[173] Cf. Zeman, 1966, 10 ff.

[174] The texts in German and Latin are reproduced in the original spelling except for the archaic German diphthongs which have been replaced, for technical reasons, by the modern *Umlaut* (ä, ö, ü). For the same reason, double 'ss' appears in place of the German ß.

[175] In the present usage, most German scholars prefer the term *Täufer* to *Wieder-täufer*. In the English language it is impossible to replace the word Anabaptist with Baptist since the latter designates exclusively the later Baptist movement. Some English-speaking historians have applied the shorter designation to both movements.

Brethren gradually developed three geographical units of administration, a differentiation was made between the Bohemian and
Moravian Brethren, and the Brethren in Poland.[176] Other names, of
more local usage, were derived from the main centers of the Unity,
such as the Brethren of Boleslav (*Bratří Boleslavští*) or of Ivančice.

Modern scholars have not adhered to a consistent pattern of nomenclature. In German, *Böhmische Brüder*, and in Italian, *Fratelli
Boemi*, have been used without exception. But in French and English,
Frères Tchèques and *Czech Brethren* have replaced, although not
with all authors, the former designation of Bohemian Brethren.[177]

The problem does not exist in the Czech language where one word,
český, serves to designate (1) the ethnic character of the Slavic population in Bohemia and Moravia, (2) the language and (3) the geographical area of Bohemia (*Čechy*), or of both Bohemia and Moravia
since these constitute 'the Czech lands', the lands of the Czech crown.
The word 'Moravian' refers primarily to the geographical area of
Moravia although it has been employed, both in the sixteenth century
and in modern times, also as a designation for the Czech dialects
spoken in Moravia and for the Slavic inhabitants of Moravia.[178]

None of the possible solutions of this dilemma in English nomenclature is fully satisfactory. Strictly speaking, 'Bohemian Brethren'
should designate members of the Unity, whether of Czech or German
ethnic origin, who resided in Bohemia. Similarly, 'Moravian Brethren'
ought to refer to the Brethren, Czech and German, living in Moravia.
The *nomen corporale*, Czech Brethren, should include both the Bohemian and the Moravian Brethren, irrespective of their ethnic origin.
One must admit, however, that the term 'Czech' is open to misunderstanding as though it excluded the German-speaking branch of the
Unitas Fratrum. The designation of the old Unity as 'the Moravian
Church' [179] should be ruled out for the same reason as the replace-
ment of the term 'Anabaptist' by 'Baptist'. The Moravian Church is

[176]   The term 'Polish Brethren' (*bracia polscy*) refers to the Polish anti-Trinitarians
but not to members of the *Unitas Fratrum* who emigrated to Poland after 1547.
[177]   Cf. Tapié, 1934 and Brock, 1957. Both Brock and Štrupl, 1964, 17, n. 19 have
pleaded for a general acceptance of the term Czech Brethren. On the other hand,
Pelikan, 1964 and Fousek, 1965 continue to use "Bohemian Brethren".
[178]   A source in 1521 refers to hymn singing "in the Moravian tongue" (Kameníček,
III, 276, n. 4). In 1616, a Moravian baron distinguished between his "Moravian
and German subjects" (*ibid.*, 761). The title of Faber's sermons in Znojmo in
1528 reads *Sermones ... habiti apud Morauos* (Faber, 1528c).
[179]   Used by Molnár Enrico, 1953, "with apology". Cf. also the works of
Schweinitz.

the official name of the Renewed Unity (founded by Zinzendorf) in the English-speaking countries.

It should be noted that in the latter part of the fifteenth century and in the early part of the sixteenth century, the word *Bohemi, Böhmen* as used in religious tracts and historical writings, referred to the Hussite church, i.e. the Utraquists or Calixtines who were thus differentiated from the Picards or the Waldenses (*Unitas Fratrum*).[180]

The problem of the Unity's nomenclature, confusing as it is by itself, is further complicated by the application of the term 'Moravian Brethren' to the Moravian Anabaptists, particularly the Hutterites. It was used both in the in-group and in the out-group sources.[181] At the same time, members of the Unity in Moravia were also being described as *Moravi*.[182] Fortunately, the name 'German Brethren' seems to have been applied, at least during the Anabaptist era in Moravia, to Anabaptists only.[183]

To prevent confusion or ambiguity in terminology we shall, in our present study, refer to any Anabaptist group always as the Anabaptists,[184] or apply the term 'Brethren' to them only with a qualifying designation such as the Swiss Brethren or the Hutterite Brethren.

References to the *Unitas Fratrum* will include such terms as the Unity, the Czech Brethren (all-inclusive designation), or, exceptionally, the Brethren.

In our use of personal and local names we shall adhere, wherever possible, to the original form and spelling in accordance with the

[180] Cf. Chapter II footnote 117 and Chapter III, footnotes 161 and 165.

[181] E.g., "Rechenschaft von den Mährischen Brüdern" (Ehrenpdeis, 1652, 165 referring to 1556). In 1661, Comenius referred to the Hutterites as "the Moravian Brethren" (quoted by Friedmann, 1949, 33). Kot, 1957, 1 *et passim* used the same terminology. Cf. also Neubaur, 1912 (on the Hutterites).

[182] Letter of William Aragosius to Professor J. J. Grynaeus in Basel written from Moravia in 1589: "Anabaptistae, qui Moravorum numerum facile superant ..." (Hrubý, 1935a, 40). Already Ottius, 1672, 51 complained about the confusion which prevailed with respect to the two kinds of Moravian Brethren.

[183] Letter of Friedrich of Žerotín in 1581: "... die Teutschen Brieder ..." (Hrubý, 1935a, 38).

[184] This will correspond to the designation used by the Czech population of sixteenth-century Moravia most frequently, *toufar, tufař, taufiř* (a Czech mutilation of the German word *Täufer*). The popular designation of the Hutterites as *habáni* (*Habaner*) had its origin in Slovakia, probably not until during the seventeenth century. Several etymological explanations have been suggested. Čulen, 1945, n. 5, claims that the original form was not German but rather Slovak and simply echoed the frequent use of the auxiliary verb 'haben' in the language of the Hutterites whom their Slovak neighbours did not understand. Cf. art. "Habaner" in *ML*, II and *ME*, II.

ethnic origin of the persons concerned, or the language of the country in which a particular town or village is located. Exceptions will be made in the case of Latinized personal names (Comenius) and the names of a few large cities such as Vienna (Wien) where the English form has been generally accepted. The German equivalents of the Czech geographical names in Moravia and Bohemia will be added, as a rule, in brackets since most historians of Anabaptism are more familiar with the German forms appearing in the Anabaptist sources.[185]

---

[185] For similar reasons, the German names of localities in Silesia and in other parts of post-war Poland have been given preference over the Polish names, e.g. Liegnitz - Legnica, Brieg - Brzeg, Wohlau - Wołów, Breslau - Wrocław. Cf. also list of "Place Names in Different Languages" in Heymann, 1965, xii ff. For the Anabaptist settlements in Moravia, our German-Czech and Czech-German topographical lists in Chapter VI (List A and B) will be found useful.

II

THE INFLUENCE OF THE GERMAN AND SWISS
REFORMATION IN SOUTH MORAVIA PRIOR TO THE
ARRIVAL OF THE ANABAPTISTS (1526)

The Anabaptists appeared in Moravia during the second half of a decade which was characterized by a strong echo of the German and Swiss Reformation.[1] In contrast to the Czech Hussite movement of the fifteenth century which had left the German population of Bohemia and Moravia almost entirely in the Roman Catholic church, the sixteenth-century Reformation of the German-speaking lands was bound to exercise an equally disturbing influence on both the Czech and German residents.

The motives for the eager acceptance of the ideas of Luther, Zwingli and other Reformers were different in each case. The Czech heretics greeted the rise of the Wittenberg Reformer as a vindication of their century-old struggle with Rome and as a deliverance from their unhappy isolation. For the Germans, the consciousness of ethnic and linguistic affinity with the new Reformation helped to remove the obstacles which had prevented them from joining the Hussite camp.[2]

The population of South Moravia — approximately the area located to the south of an imaginary line which connects the cities of Jihlava (Iglau), Brno (Brünn) and Kroměříž (Kremsier) — belonged to two distinct ethnic groups.

---

[1] For a general picture of the Czech Reformation, see Thomson, 1953a, Chapter 5, and Říčan, 1957b, Chapters III-XI. For an introduction to the period under study, see Hrejsa, IV, 242-329 and V, 5-26; Müller, I, 389-455. For political developments in Moravia, see Dvořák, 1900 and 1901; Kameníček, III and Hrubý, 1938.
[2] Cf. Luther in his *Vom Anbeten des Sakraments* addressed to the Czech Brethren (1523): "Ich will ... dissen artickel dargeben, wie wyr deutschen glewben und wie auch tzu glewben ist nach dem Euangelio" (*WA*, 11, 431; *LW*, 36, 276). Similarly Hubmaier in the dedicatory preface to his first book printed in Moravia (July 21, 1526): "wir Teütschen" (*HS*, 227 and 241).

The majority of the native people spoke the Czech language and belonged to the Slavic family of nations. A German-speaking minority was resident in the four larger royal cities — Jihlava, Brno, Znojmo (Znaim) and Olomouc (Olmütz) — which were almost entirely German,[3] and in several smaller manorial towns, such as Mikulov (Nikolsburg). Not many Germans lived in rural areas.

The Moravian Germans were the descendants of German settlers who had penetrated into all border areas of Bohemia and Moravia and had also established isolated settlements among the Czech populace in the interior of the two lands during the late Middle Ages. The Hussite Wars (1420-1434) with their strong national and social undertones brought the large-scale German *Ostsiedlung* in Bohemia and Moravia to an abrupt end.[4]

In following years, the coincidence of ethnic and religious differences reduced communications between the two ethnic groups to a minimum. The royal cities followed a policy of not accepting into their guilds, and consequently not for citizenship as such, any persons who could not speak the German tongue. The policy served not only to safeguard the German character of the cities, but also to prevent the spread of 'Czech heresy' among the burghers.[5] For the growth of their population, the cities depended almost entirely on a continuous influx of German craftsmen from cities in South Germany, Austria and Silesia. This small but regular immigration served not only to offset the serious losses of population due to periodic outbreaks of epidemic diseases but also to keep up important business contacts with the commercial centers in the neighbouring countries. Long before the birth of the Reformation in Germany, the German Catholic cities in Moravia were known abroad as important points on the international commercial routes. After the Hussite Wars, the new routes bypassed heretic Bohemia. The paths connecting the German cities in Silesia and Poland with Nürnberg, Augsburg, Linz and Vienna, led through Moravia.[6]

[3]   In 1527, the population of Olomouc numbered 649 burghers resident within the city walls and 585 living outside the walls. Of the former, only 30 had Czech names, of the latter only 43. Taking into consideration frequent intermarriage, a Czech name in a German-speaking city was no reliable indication of Czech nationality (Hrubý, 1935c, 97, n. 2, with reference to sources). On royal cities in Moravia, see Heymann, 1965, 174 ff. and 449 ff., and especially Marek, 1965.
[4]   On German settlement in Moravia, see Kuhn, I, 84-96 and 125-135; II, 306-333; with bibliography.
[5]   Cf. illustrations from sources quoted by Hrubý, 1935c, 97 f.
[6]   Cf. Husa, 1957, 58 and Näf, 1944, 224.

An understanding of these secular links between the Moravian Germans and their compatriots in the neighbouring countries helps to explain why so many German-speaking refugees began to flock to Moravia in the third decade of the sixteenth century. The newcomers were 'evangelicals' of many shades of persuasion who were escaping persecution in Germany, Austria, Silesia and later also in Switzerland. From 1526 onward the little trickle grew into a stream. Moravia became the land of refuge for thousands of Anabaptists who spoke many dialects of the German language and represented the whole spectrum of views typical of the Left Wing of the Reformation.

In many respects, the basic outlook and mentality of the uprooted 'refugee Germans' — even prior to the arrival of the Anabaptists — stood in sharp contrast to the ideals of the socially stable 'native Germans'. The difference came into sharp focus in some of the early controversies in the Moravian Anabaptist camp, as we shall observe in subsequent chapters. But first, we shall outline briefly the respective responses to the German and Swiss Reformation by the Czech and German population in Moravia.

1. THE CZECH AND GERMAN ROMAN CATHOLICS

Since the Hussite revolution, the Roman Catholic church in Moravia had remained a small but influential minority. It was considerably stronger and better organized in Moravia than in Bohemia since the episcopal see in Olomouc had suffered no interruption in occupancy.[7] For almost half a century, Bishop Stanislav I Thurzo (1497-1540) attempted to exercise a firm control over both the Czech- and German-speaking parishes in Moravia. He could not, however, prevent the gradual transition of most German-speaking parishes to Lutheranism.[8] By way of contrast, the Czech-speaking Catholics, few as they were, showed little sympathy for the 'German innovations'. Bishop Thurzo, a highly educated man, the leading humanist in the land and a friend of Erasmus, did not hesitate to

---

[7] At the see of Prague, no archbishops were appointed by Rome during the whole period from 1421 to 1561. The Utraquist Archbishop Jan Rokycana (died 1471) was never confirmed by the Pope. Cf. Heymann, 1959, 1961 and 1965.

[8] By 1560, under the rule of Bishop Thurzo's weaker successors, the number of Roman Catholic parishes in Moravia, both Czech- and German-speaking, was reduced to fifty out of the total number of 600 parishes (Hrubý, 1935c, 91).

advocate strict measures to suppress the Lutheran heresy. In 1523, he instigated the arrest and trial of the Lutheran Reformer Paul Speratus in the city of Jihlava.[9] At the Bohemian diet held in Prague in the middle of July 1524, he pleaded that "Lutherans and others in error be hindered and not tolerated".[10]

During the first half of the sixteenth century, the Roman Catholic church in Moravia suffered from a chronic lack of priests. There was not a single training institution for the priesthood in the land. Monks were leaving monasteries, priests were marrying and then, sometimes for fear of punishment, joining the Czech Utraquist or German Lutheran churches. On most domains, secular lords controlled the appointment of priest to parishes. Disciplinary measures of the bishop were ignored. During the second quarter of the sixteenth century, the Roman Catholic church in South Moravia was in a state of disintegration.[11]

2. THE CZECH UTRAQUISTS

The Utraquist church was the national Hussite church of the Czech population in Bohemia and Moravia.[12] It traced its origin to the introduction of communion *sub utraque specie* by Jakoubek of Stříbro (Jacobellus de Misa) in Prague in October 1414 and to the *Compactata* of Basel (1433). Bishop Jan Rokycana[13] more than anyone else shaped the theological and liturgical character of the church. Through the first century of its existence, the church suffered from an ongoing struggle between the radical and the conservative wing. The conservative party longed for a complete reconciliation with Rome. The conflict within the church was intensified by the strong echoes of Luther's Reformation.[14]

Since 1519 Luther had been in personal contact with the radical leaders in Prague and in 1523, he dedicated his proposals for reconstitution of the Utraquist ministry, *De instituendis ministris*

[9]   See below at footnote 88.
[10]   Hrejsa, IV, 274.
[11]   For a detailed description of the situation see Kameníček, III, 307-403.
[12]   For recent characteristics of the Utraquist church, see Heymann, 1959 and 1961; Molnár, 1965c and Říčan, 1965a.
[13]   See note 7 above.
[14]   F. Hrejsa introduced the term "Neo-Utraquists" to designate the more radical (pro-Lutheran) wing of the church in contrast to the conservative "old Utraquists".

ecclesiae, to "the Senate and People of Prague".[15] The brief period of Neo-Utraquist supremacy in the consistory and city council of Prague ended with the violent suppression of the Lutheran sympathizers in the summer of 1524. One of the chief lay leaders in the radical Utraquist movement was the knight Burián Sobek of Kornice. After studies in Wittenberg where he became a personal friend of Luther he returned to Prague in 1521 as doctor of law. In 1523 he was appointed city chancellor only to be deposed and imprisoned by the restored reactionary party on August 9, 1524.[16] On October 27, 1524, Luther wrote him a comforting letter addressed to *Christi captivo et servo fideli, Domino Buriano de Skornicz, secretario Pragensi, meo in Domino carissimo.*[17]

Early in May 1525, Sobek was released from jail and banished from Prague. He went to Moravia where in 1527 Hubmaier dedicated to him his treatise on the liturgy of the Lord's Supper.[18] Nothing else is known about his early stay in Moravia.[19] He remained a member of the Utraquist church and later lived in Olomouc.[20] He maintained close relations with the Czech Brethren during the 'Lutheran era' of Bishop Jan Augusta and translated two of their confessions (*Rechenschafft* 1533 and *Apologia verae doctrinae* 1538, both printed in Wittenberg) into German and Latin respectively. He even accompanied Bishop Augusta on his visit to Luther in the spring of 1538.[21]

According to a hypothesis proposed recently by Husa, Sobek is supposed to have been the main initiator of Thomas Müntzer's visit

[15] Latin original in *WA*, 12, 169-195. English tr. in *LW*, 40, 7-59. A translation into German was made by Paul Speratus. A Czech translation was provided by Burián Sobek of Kornice who in 1521 had rendered four other writings of Luther into Czech (Müller-Bartoš, 274, note 198).

[16] Hrejsa, IV, 275. Cf. also Müller-Bartoš, 268-274.

[17] *WA*, *Br*, 3, No. 786.

[18] *HS*, 364. In contrast to his practice in the other dedicatory prefaces, Hubmaier made no reference to Sobek's domain or place of residence. Sobek's family was of Silesian origin. The Bohemian branch lived at Lipka near Chrudim. Of the Moravian branch, Hynek Bilík of Kornice at Veselí is known to have granted special privileges to the congregation of the *Unitas Fratrum* in Veselí on September 6, 1528. (Hrejsa, B, 94; Zeman, 1966, 84 f.).

[19] According to Ms. 642, fol. 66 in the Archives of the National Museum in Prague he submitted to the Chamber Court a petition for his rehabilitation in 1528 (Husa, 1957, 65, n. 208).

[20] Kameníček, III, 284 and 435. Bergsten's claim (Bergsten, 1961, 430 and *HS*, 353) that Sobek later joined the *Unitas Fratrum* is unfounded. Cf. the correction by Říčan in *TPKR*, 1962, 163. Nor did Sobek publish a "Chronik der böhmischen Brüder 1482-1532" (Bergsten in *HS*, 353) but instead translated into Czech in 1539 the chronicle of J. Carion (printed at Litomyšl in 1541). Cf. Kraus, I, 209 f.

[21] Hrejsa, V, 40, 44, 47.

to Prague (from the end of June till the end of November, 1521) and his host and protector for three months. The conjecture is based on one ambiguous source.[22]

Before we turn to the discussion of Czech Utraquist circles in Moravia, a mention must be made of three unusual religious leaders whose activities were also closely related to the revolutionary events in Prague in the early twenties. Like Burián Sobek of Kornice, they, too, found refuge in Moravia.

Jan Kalenec, a Prague cutler, had been brought up in the Utraquist church. For a short time, he was influenced by Luther's doctrines as they were proclaimed by his followers in Prague. However, he soon established contact with the congregations of the *Unitas Fratrum* in Bohemia and even met Bishop Lukáš in Boleslav. Finally, he joined a small group of the Minor Party[23] in Prague. By its aged leader Amos — after whom the sect was known also as the Amosites — he was 'ordained' a priest and chosen as successor to Amos in 1522. When persecution set in two years later, Kalenec was arrested,

---

[22]   Husa, 1957, 64-66 and 117 (German summary). The contemporary Czech source (Bartoš Písař, 103; reprinted by Husa, *ibid.*, 96) refers to an anonymous prominent citizen who, being "one eye of this city" and of radical views concerning sacraments, especially the sacrament of the altar, kept in his house for three months "a German Master Thomas, a priest, who had recently come from Saxony, from Luther", preached in German in Prague and then returned to Meissen where he aroused the serfs against their lords until Duke George of Meissen ordered his execution. The Czech chronicler might have referred to Thomas Müntzer. However, the identification of the anonymous citizen with Burián Sobek of Kornice is questionable. Husa himself admits that the conjecture rests on two assumptions: (1) that the phrase "eye of the city" (*oculus civitatis*) was a contemporary designation for a city secretary (*písař*, i.e. scribe); (2) that Sobek had been employed by the city of Prague as one of the secretaries during Müntzer's stay in Prague in 1521, an assumption for which there is no evidence. He did not become the chief secretary (chancellor) of the joint administration of the Old and New Town of Prague until 1523. Even though one might admit that the promotion to a high post would seldom come to a man not previously employed in a lower rank in the same office, one must not, at the same time, forget the historical circumstances under which Sobek received his appointment in 1523. It was related directly to the takeover of the Utraquist Consistory and the city administration by the radical pro-Lutheran circles. Sobek must have been associated with this group ever since his return from Wittenberg some time in 1521. It is hardly conceivable that with such views he would have found entrance into the city office while it was controlled by a conservative administration. According to Husa's undocumented assertion, Sobek was more radical in his theological position than most citizens in the Neo-Utraquist camp and his views "were close to the views of Müntzer" (Husa, 1957, 1965). Cf. also Molnár, 1958b-c, Macek, 1958c and Gritsch, 1967, 52 ff.
[23]   On the split within the Unity in the 1490's and the issues which led to the separation of the 'Minor Party', see Müller-Bartoš, 150-174; Brock, 1957, 103 ff.; Peschke, 1957 and Urban, 1966, 12 ff.

branded on the face and banished from Prague in December 1524. He was reported to have practised rebaptism and to hold anti-Trinitarian views.[24] During the years 1523-1524 he exchanged polemical writings with Brother Lukáš and Brother Krasonický. Little is known about Kalenec during the two following decades. In 1542 he resumed his literary activities from Letovice, a small town on the river Svitava, not far from Boskovice (north of Brno). Presumably, he went there soon after his expulsion from Prague [25] and gathered around himself the last remnants of the Minor Party.

Another 'selfgrown' prophet who found refuge in South Moravia was Matěj Poustevník (Matthias the Hermit). Originally a furrier from the region of Žatec (Saaz) in western Bohemia — an area well-known for its Waldensian heresies and links with the town of Zwickau — he made his appearance in Prague in the middle of November 1519 after a prolonged solitude "in the wilderness". He was accompanied by a small group of followers and began to preach, mostly in the open air since he had been refused permission to preach in churches. According to contemporary sources his forceful messages were characterized by apocalyptic urgency and a devastating critique of the rich and of the priests. Chiliastic visions motivated his call to repentance. An epidemic of pestilence in Prague during 1520 helped to increase the wide popular interest in his preaching.

While the apocalyptic framework of Matěj's theology will be re-created, with striking similarity, by the Anabaptist refugees led by Hans Hut and opposing Hubmaier at Mikulov (Nikolsburg) in 1527, the actual roots can be traced back to Chelčický's critique of society and to the Taborite concepts of the church, its ministry and sacraments. In a letter written by an Utraquist priest in Prague on November 1, 1526, Matěj was praised for "the spiritual riches apparent in him through his hard work, continuous prayers, reading and meditation in the law of the Lord (Scriptures) and his frequent communion of the body and blood of the Lord Jesus Christ". However, he was at the same time accused of "making light of the food and drink of the Lord in that he followed the teachings of the old Taborite writings and distinguished between three 'modes of presence' (*byty*) of Christ,

---

[24] Marta of Poříčí confessed in Prague in 1527 that she had been baptized for the second time by Kalenec because her first baptism had been administered by unworthy priests (Bartoš Písař, 219).

[25] Odložilík, 1923, 12-15 and 351; Brock, 1957, 244-250; Husa, 1957, 77; Urban, 1966, 15 ff. Sources in Bartoš Písař, 68 f., 92, 211, 219. Cf. also footnotes 152 f. below and Chapter IV footnotes 156 f.

namely the highest and natural mode which is the body of Christ in heaven, the second or 'middle' mode which is Christ's presence in believing men; and the third or lowest mode which is Christ's sacramental presence in the sacraments".[26]

In his reply, Matěj did not deny the Taborite teachings on the eucharist and stated: "According to the Scriptures, Christ left for us in this world the sacrament of his body and blood as a remembrance (*ku památce*) under the kind (*pod způsobou*, i.e. *sub specie*) of bread and wine, and does not indicate that he would return before the judgment day. . . . Soon, however, the Lord God will lead his people out of the Babylonian imprisonment, from the power of Rome, the cursed antichrist, your father. . . ." [27]

The letter quoted above also accused Matěj of having spread heretical writings which poisoned the minds of many people, including Lord Vilém Křinecký of Ronov "who was baptized for the second time and is a Picard".[28] It is not clear whether the writer inferred that Křinecký had received rebaptism from Matěj himself, or whether it was merely Matěj's influence which led Lord Křinecký into the Unity.

In any case, Matěj's radical views could not be tolerated by the conservative Utraquist party which returned to power in Prague in 1524. He was arrested in March 1525 and was not released till October 23, 1526, the day on which Ferdinand was elected king by the Bohemian diet in Prague. He was ordered to leave the city the same day. Most likely, he went directly to the Moravian village of Habrovany where with the knight Jan Dubčanský of Zdenín — whom he might have met in Prague — he became one of the co-founders of the new Unity of Habrovanite Brethren on February 23, 1528.[29]

Matěj's relationship to the *Unitas Fratrum* is not clear. Hrejsa regards him as "one close to the Brethren, perhaps a former member of the Unity". During his long imprisonment in Prague, he wrote a letter to Brother Vavřinec Krasonický "and to all other Brethren beloved in the Lord".[30]

---

[26]   Bartoš Písař, 200.
[27]   *Ibid.*, 204 f.
[28]   *Ibid.*, 200. Cf. Husa, 1957, 69, n. 215.
[29]   According to Hejnic, 1957, 66 and Urban, 1966, 26 Matěj later left the Habrovanites, lived in Boskovice in 1542 and died likely during his imprisonment in Prague in 1542, or soon afterwards.
[30]   Bartoš Písař, 150 f. (dated November 1, 1525). The main primary source on

Another person representative of the "theological fringe zone" which included many independent seekers oscillating between the radical views of pro-Lutheran Utraquism and the position of the *Unitas Fratrum*, was Václav of Lileč. He was an Utraquist priest and rector of the Hussite monastery at Vilémov (southeast from Kutná Hora in eastern Bohemia). From the middle of the fifteenth century the monastery had been an important center of religious life. The "Brethren of Vilémov" had contacts with the early *Unitas Fratrum*.[31] On October 31, 1521, the famous work of Peter Chelčický, *Síť víry* [The Net of Faith] appeared here in its first and only printed edition during the Reformation era.

Not many details are known about the origin and life of Václav of Vilémov.[32] Some time in 1526 or 1527 he joined Jan Dubčanský at Habrovany to form with him and with Matěj Poustevník the founding trio of the Unity of Habrovanite Brethren. He was a well educated man, equally at home in the medieval heritage of the church of Rome (in his writings he refers to Jerome, Albert the Great, Thomas Aquinas, the papal decrees) and in the Czech Reformation movement. He was also familiar with the writings of Luther and Erasmus. Later in Moravia he became acquainted with the writings of Zwingli, Oecolampad and Lambert. He is regarded as the author of several of the writings of the Habrovanite Brethren (from 1527 on). He might have also mediated the emphasis of Chelčický on Christian political abstinence (refusal of oaths, non-participation in government and war) for the syncretistic doctrines of the Habrovanites.[33]

We have sketched the portraits of Jan Kalenec, Matěj Poustevník and Václav of Lileč in some detail in order to show the type of persons who were congregating in South Moravia at the time when the German and Swiss Reformation spread its influence there. Each leader brought with him a circle of followers from Bohemia. Thus in the second half of the third decade of the sixteenth century South

Matěj is Bartoš Písař. See also Husa, 1957, 67 f.; Hrejsa, IV, 255, 279, 304; Müller, I, 397, 446 and Hejnic, 1957.

[31] Cf. Müller-Bartoš, 28; Urbánek, 1930, 645 f.; Brock, 1957, 41, 74.

[32] The most comprehensive treatment is Hrejsa, 1915 (a summary in Hrejsa, V, 11).

[33] This is the contention of Brock, 1957, 253-256. According to Odložilík,, 1923, 343-344, the Habrovanite sources show inconsistencies in their discussion of "worldly power". This is to be expected if the Habrovanite position on problems of social ethics represents an amalgamation of Zwinglianism and the "ethical proto-Anabaptism" of Chelčický.

Moravia became a place of refuge and a rallying point not only for German refugees but also for Czech-speaking refugees who were fleeing from religious persecution in Bohemia. Few of them were mere adventurers suffering from an unstable character.[34] Most of them were earnest seekers of truth. Their existential search for a better understanding of the Scriptures and for a personal assurance of salvation, their longing for the true apostolic church and for a faithful obedience and witness to Christ in society, were paralleled in the lives of countless pilgrims of faith all over Europe at that time.

What made the spiritual pilgrimage of the Czech seekers more difficult was the inevitable dichotomy between the challenging heritage of their own century-old reform movement, with the many choices it offered — from conservative Utraquism to radical Taboritism and even anti-Trinitarianism — and the new voices from Wittenberg, Strasbourg, Basel and Zürich. Luther, Melanchthon, Carlstadt, Corvin, Johannes Hess, Bucer, Erasmus, Zwingli, Bullinger, Sebastian Franck, Urbanus Rhegius: all of these are referred to by Kalenec in his preserved writings.[35]

Perhaps the most typical representative of a lay seeker and self-appointed Reformer in Moravia was the knight Jan Dubčanský of Zdenín (died 1543). His small domain embraced only three villages, Habrovany, Nemojany and Lulč, located to the north of Slavkov (Austerlitz). In spite of his limited material possessions he played an important role in the political and religious life of the margraviate.[36]

In the early part of 1519 he took part in a public debate between the Utraquists and the Czech Brethren which was held at the request of the local Utraquist priest Jan in the townhall of Třebíč, a town located halfway between Znojmo and Jihlava. The main issue

---

[34] In the official opinion of the Unity (1533) such was Matěj Poustevník. The Brethren described him as follows: "He never wanted to be subject to anyone. He could not agree with those with whom he had fellowship first. Instead he put forth his own doctrines, and then, leaving his friends, he boldly declared himself to be a messenger of God unto all. When others pointed it out to him he would not listen but instead would blow his own horn and even arrange conferences with many in Prague . . . Then leaving that again, he joined still others . . ." (quoted in Czech by Müller-Bartoš, 280, n. 228).

[35] Documented by Odložilík, 1923, 356.

[36] There are three comprehensive Czech essays on Dubčanský and his Habrovanite Unity: Odložilík, 1923 (a German summary, Odložilík, 1925); Hanák, 1928-1929 and Brandl, 1882.

seems to have been the adoration of the sacrament of the altar, the same question to which Luther was to address himself four years later in his epistle to the Czech Brethren, *Vom Anbeten des Sakraments*. Dubčanský was among the spokesmen for the Utraquist side while the chief defender of the Unity was Krasonický from Litomyšl.[37]

Dubčanský must have had a special liking for theological debates. In the spring of 1526, he was co-responsible for a debate at Slavkov (Austerlitz) between the Czech Utraquists and the German evangelical ministers (see below). Soon after the founding of his own Unity of the Habrovany Brethren (February 23, 1528) he arranged for a colloquy with Jan Kalenec, the leader of the small group of the 'Minor Party' centered in the nearby village of Letovice.[38] He also made repeated preludes to the *Unitas Fratrum*. A meeting between the two 'unities' was to take place in Prostějov on October 1, 1531. However, it was suppressed by King Ferdinand. Finally, a debate between the leaders of the two groups was held at Kyjov (Gaya) on February 28, 1535. The meeting was arranged by Lord Vilém Kuna of Kunštát who, although he was not a member of either unity, favoured their merger.[39] The meeting, like all previous ones, ended in failure. It was Dubčanský's last attempt at reconciling the splintered groups of Moravian Protestantism. He was imprisoned by King Ferdinand in May 1537.

The examples of five men — Burián Sobek of Kornice, Jan Kalenec, Matěj Poustevník, Václav of Lileč and Jan Dubčanský, all of whom had, by 1526, moved from original Utraquism to positions which went all the way from modified Lutheranism to extreme radicalism

---

[37] A detailed account of the strife between the two Czech Reformation parties in Třebíč is given by Krasonický himself in his "Hystoria . . ." preserved in Ms. Codex V F 41, fol. 219-348 (National Museum of Prague). The manuscript was not accessible to us. Cf. Odložilík, 1923, 16-17.

[38] The Habrovanite sources contain only two vague references to the colloquy which took place at Olešnice, most likely sometime in 1528. See Hrejsa, 1915, 170 and Odložilík, 1923, 45 f. and 305.

[39] Vilém Kuna leaned towards the Schwenckfeldian position and translated into Czech two of Schwenckfeld's writings. A detailed record of the unfinished colloquy is preserved in *AUF*, IV, fol. 199a-214a. Nine articles were to be considered: (1) the essence of salvation, (2) Lord's Supper, (3) baptism, (4) the powers of the ministerial office, (5) shedding of blood, (6) oathtaking, (7) church, (8) covenants (*závazkové*) and (9) Christian liberty. Only the first two were discussed and when no agreement could be reached, the meeting was concluded. Cf. a summary by Odložilík, 1923, 307 f.

— might lead to a misleading conclusion that during the same period of time, the entire Czech Utraquist church in South Moravia had undergone a similar development.

The situation, inasmuch as it can be reconstructed from the sparse sources, was anything but that. The response of the ordinary people as well as of the priests in the Czech Utraquist parishes to the ideas of Luther, Zwingli and others was slow. The views expressed by the Utraquist priests at the meeting in Slavkov, March 14-15, 1526 (see further below) indicate how little the Czech ministers, in their original position, had been influenced by Luther or Zwingli. There were remarkable exceptions such as Beneš Optát of Telč, the Utraquist priest in Velké Meziříčí (Gross-Messeritsch).[40] By and large, however, the common people were not affected by the "rediscoveries of the Gospel" made in Wittenberg and Zürich, until much later in the century.[41] Such lack of response calls for explanation.

Three factors stand out as the main reasons. In the first place, the Utraquist church in general and its parishes in Moravia in particular, were deprived, for decades, of good and well educated priests. The Moravian deaneries were related only loosely to the Utraquist consistory in Prague[42] which was unable to supply a sufficient number of priests. The local deans, and quite frequently the secular lords, were forced to recruit less desirable candidates who could perform only the minimal liturgical functions. As a result, education of the people and a finer theological discernment and interest were lacking.

In the second place, the language barriers were sufficient to delay the penetration of new ideas for a decade or even a generation. Several writings of Erasmus and Luther had, of course, been trans-

[40]   See the important essays by Hrejsa, 1915, 179-216 and Hrejsa, 1918. Optát was in close contact with Paul Speratus who found temporary refuge in Optát's parish at Velké Meziříčí in 1523. It is not certain whether later (1528) he served the Czech population in Jihlava for a short while. From 1530 on he lived at Náměšť as tutor (in Czech and German) of the children of Václav of Lomnice. On his part in the Czech translation of the New Testament in 1533, see footnote 200 in the next chapter.

[41]   See the well documented essays, Hrubý, 1935c and 1939. Hrubý contends that from about 1540 onwards the Czech Utraquist church in Moravia became virtually Lutheran and independent of the Utraquist administration in Prague. In his polemic with Hrubý, Hrejsa, 1938 defended his earlier position, viz. that in spite of strong Lutheran and Calvinistic influences the Neo-Utraquist church remained faithful to its Hussite roots.

[42]   Cf. our discussion of the "Twenty Articles" (1524) below at footnote 110.

lated into Czech at an early date [43] and printed on the presses of Utraquist owners or by the *Unitas Fratrum*. No Czech translations of the works of Zwingli are known to have been printed,[44] although the widespread knowledge of the Zwinglian concepts among the Czech radical groups in Moravia would suggest that some translations must have been circulated at least in manuscript.

The Czech humanist Jan Šlechta of Všehrdy could boast in his letter to Erasmus written on October 10, 1519: *"Omnes enim libros tuos, quoscunque scripsisti et Basileae Ioanni Frobenio, viro docto et in arte calcographica Daedaleo ingenio praedito, imprimendos dedisti, habeo, mirificeque lectione eorum delector...."* [45] Similarly, the leading Moravian nobleman, Arkleb of Boskovice — to whom Hubmaier later dedicated his last book printed in Moravia [46] — was able to report to Erasmus in a letter sent from Znojmo some time in October 1520: *"Libri et scripta Martini Luteri vulgo hic in manibus hominum habentur perlegunturque cum tuis".* [47]

But both of these were voices of highly educated men who did not have to depend on translations. The first book in the Czech language was printed in Moravia only in 1527.

A final aspect of the slow penetration of Lutheran and Zwinglian views among the Czech population was the fact that the transition from Roman Catholicism or Utraquism to Lutheranism seems to have been, in most instances, a case of magisterial Reformation *par excellence*. Hrubý [48] has brought to light sufficient evidence to indicate that, with some notable exceptions, the process of Lutheranization followed the pattern *cuius regio, eius religio*. Once the owner of a domain changed his confessional allegiance, the parish churches were expected to follow his example. Small dissenting groups such as the *Unitas Fratrum* or the Anabaptists were tolerated in most

---

[43] Erasmus' *Encomion Moriae* appeared already in 1513 in the Czech translation by Řehoř Hrubý of Jelení whose son Zikmund (Gelenius) joined Erasmus in Basel ten years later as an editor in the printing shop of Frobenius. In 1519 knight Oldřich Velenský translated and printed the *Enchiridion* on the press of the Unity in Bělá pod Bezdězem. Other writings were translated later. Similarly, Luther's writings appeared in Czech translations by Burián Sobek of Kornice (cf. note 15 above) already in 1521, and 1523. The Unity published a translation of *Vom Anbeten des Sacraments* at Litomyšl in 1523. Other translations followed. Cf. Chapter III note 196 and Říčan, 1967.

[44] Müller-Bartoš, 280.

[45] *E*, 4, No. 1021, line 48-51.

[46] *HS*, 434.

[47] *E*, 4, No. 1154, line 33-34.

[48] See footnote 41 above.

places. Such a practice — which stood in sharp contrast to the popular Hussite movement of the previous century — tended to minimize the personal religious involvement of the individual as well as his quest for truth.

3.   *UNITAS FRATRUM:* CZECH AND GERMAN

In spite of its early attempts to establish liaison with the Waldensians, and its many subsequent ecumenical encounters at home and abroad,[49] the *Unitas Fratrum* was and remained a legitimate child of the Czech Hussite Reformation. As such, it was predominantly Czech-speaking and of Czech ethnic origin.

However, in 1480, several hundred German-speaking Waldensian refugees from Mark Brandenburg were received into the Unity and established its German-speaking branch.[50] They were never absorbed by the Czech majority but rather continued their separate ethnic existence until the suppression of Protestantism in the Czech lands after 1620. In fact, secret adherents survived in northern Moravia until the early part of the eighteenth century when some of them made their way to Herrnhut and thus provided an historical link between the old *Unitas* and the *Brüderunität* of Count Zinzendorf.[51]

The original Waldensian refugees from the area of Königsberg and Angermünde (Mark Brandenburg) settled in two German-speaking areas: in and around Lanškroun (Landskron) on the Bohemian-Moravian border (east of Litomyšl) and around Fulnek on the domain of Jan of Žerotín in northeastern Moravia (between Olomouc and Moravská Ostrava). In contrast to the rapid growth of the Czech Unity, particularly during the first half of the sixteenth century, the German-speaking Unity does not seem to have made any inroads among the German population of Bohemia and Moravia, not even in its immediate German-speaking neighbourhood.[52]

---

[49]   Cf. Enequist, 1884; Říčan, 1943 and 1964b; Dobiáš, 1957 and 1960a-b; Bartoš, 1956b; Molnár, 1964c.
[50]   Müller-Bartoš, 114 ff.
[51]   Goll, 1916, 152.
[52]   Such is the view expressed by Müller, I, 180 f. and Müller-Bartoš, 114 f. The claim should be re-examined in the light of detailed genealogical studies of the two German congregations if sources for such studies are available. The fact that the German *Unitas* failed to make converts from among the native German population, even during the course of the sixteenth century, provides an interesting parallel to

They do not appear to have been affected by the expulsion orders of the Hungarian King Matthias (Corvinus) in 1481 which forced large numbers of the Moravian Brethren into their first temporary exile in Moldavia.[53] Nor were they involved in the prolonged controversies between the 'Major Party' and the 'Minor Party' from 1494 on. This is somewhat surprising in view of the fact that the 'Old Brethren' of the Minor Party held up the Waldensians as an example of true apostolic piety and obedience.[54] However, in the sixteenth century, individual members of the German branch served the Unity in good stead as interpreters, translators and messengers in the manifold contacts of the Brethren with the Reformation in the German-speaking lands.

The leaders of the Unity greeted Luther as a welcome ally in their lonely search for the true church. At the same time, many of them, especially the aging Bishop Lukáš himself,[55] reacted to Luther's theology and to the events in Wittenberg with the caution of a man who had defended his position in battles on many fronts and who — by the time Luther appeared on the scene — had finalized his views into a well-rounded system of theology. The initiative towards direct personal contacts with Luther as well as a literary exchange during the era of Lukáš came chiefly from two sources, both of them originally outside the Unity.

In the winter of 1517-1518,[56] three German monks from Breslau

the isolation of the German Anabaptist settlements in Moravia. There were no language barriers and no serious theological obstacles in the way, such as existed in the case of the Anabaptists (rebaptism, apolitism and later, communal life). Could it be that the laws of refugee block settlement applied as much in the case of the Waldensians and Anabaptists in sixteenth-century Moravia as they do in the case of Mennonite, Baptist, Lutheran, Greek Orthodox and other religio-ethnic pocket settlements in contemporary Canada and the U.S.A.?

[53] Müller, I, 182, n. 450. Müller-Bartoš, 115, n. 223. Hrejsa, B, 30, 48, 103 and C, 95 contradicts himself in his claims that the Waldensians were expelled to Moldavia. Cf. also Macek, 1958, 219. Moldavia is a province east of Transylvania (Siebenbürgen) in present day Roumania. Cf. also next chapter at footnotes 171-173.

[54] Říčan, 1957a, 80.

[55] Born ca. 1458, died 1528. On his life, see chapter IV beginning at footnote 101.

[56] HF, I, fol. 398 (Šafařík, 1862, 122) reports their arrival, obviously in retrospect, under the year 1525 which led Gindely, I, 192 to date their coming in the same year. The wording of the report ("at the time when Luther took his stand") and the evidence of other sources indicate that the three monks must have left Breslau some time during the winter 1517-1518. This date is accepted by Müller, I, 401, n. 301; Müller-Bartoš, 272, n. 172; Odložilík, 1923, 19; Hrejsa, IV, 287; Fornaçon, 1954, 36 and Říčan, 1957a, 122. The best evidence is the statement of HF which says that the three monks "came to Litomyšl to Brother Vavřinec (i.e. Krasonický) and Brother Roh". Jan Roh was in Litomyšl as assistant to Krasonický until his

(Wrocław) in Silesia arrived in Litomyšl, a center of the *Unitas*, second in importance only to Mladá Boleslav, the residence of Bishop Lukáš. They were 'John the Monk' (Jan Mnich in Czech sources), Michael Weisse and Johann Zeising, usually rendered Jan Čížek in Czech sources.[57]

In spite of the warnings of Bishop Lukáš, the local minister, Vavřinec (Lawrence) Krasonický received them into the membership of the Unity. Their presence strengthened the leanings of several ministers of the Unity towards the teachings of Luther. In particular, it influenced the young deacon Jan Roh,[58] assistant to Krasonický at Litomyšl till August 1518. As a native of a border town Domažlice, he spoke German.

We hear nothing more of the three former monks until 1522. During that year Brother Roh visited Luther in Wittenberg no less than three times, accompanied, most likely in each case, by Michael Weisse. Two more visits by the same ambassadors of the Unity followed in the fall of 1523 and in 1524. Whereas the first journey, in May 1522, was undertaken by Roh of his own initiative, without the prior knowledge of Bishop Lukáš, the subsequent visits were of an official nature and resulted in the literary exchange between Luther and Lukáš.[59] Direct communications with Luther were initiated only after the German Reformer Paul Speratus, then in

ordination at the Synod in Brandýs nad Orlicí, August 15, 1518. Soon afterwards, he moved to Bělá pod Bezdězem (Weisswasser) where he was in charge of the congregation till 1529. Müller, I, 401; Molnár, 1952a, 94. The reasons for the departure of the three monks from Breslau are not known. Several hypotheses were proposed by Fornaçon, 1954, 36 ff. and Matusik, 1960, 200 ff.

[57] Writing in 1636, Comenius regarded "Hanuš Čížek" as a German of Swiss origin obviously because he propagated the views of Zwingli (reprinted in Komenský, 1912, 308). Recently Williams, 1962, 229 even made him into "a Slav, possibly a convert from the Minor Unity". Both views are unfounded. Blahoslav mentions the polemical works of Lukáš against Čížek in his "Corollarium", 1567. (Molnár, 1956a, 151 f.) Cf. also footnote 188 in the next chapter.

[58] On Roh, who often used a German form of his name, Horn, or a latinized form, Cornu, see Müller, I, 400-403; Kaňák, 1957, 93-99, and Molnár, 1950. Cf. also Chapter IV at footnotes 123 ff. Roh had no relation to the Minor Party, nor was he an associate of Kalenec, as Williams, 1962, 217 claims (misreading the Czech text in Husa, 1957, 77).

[59] Luther's *Vom Anbeten des Sakraments des heiligen Leichnams*, printed in April 1523 (*WA*, 11, 431-456; English translation in *LW*, 36, 275-305). A Czech translation by Roh was printed in Litomyšl in the same year. A Czech reply of the Brethren was completed by Lukáš on June 23, 1523 and printed on September 16, 1523. A German translation of the reply in manuscript was sent to Luther with the messengers on their fourth visit, some time in the fall of 1523. Luther gave no written reply.

Jihlava, and the Czech Utraquist priest Beneš Optát of Telč had submitted to Luther their inquiries concerning the doctrinal position of the Czech Utraquists (*Bohemi*) and of the Czech Brethren (*Beghardi*) in the spring of 1522. The details of the correspondence and personal contacts have been recounted elsewhere and need not be reviewed here.[60]

With the fifth journey of Roh and Weisse to Wittenberg in 1524 the official contacts of the Unity with Luther ended. They were not resumed till 1533, five years after the death of Bishop Lukáš. The Brethren were disappointed by the apparent lack of new life and church discipline among the followers of Luther.[61] Nor could they agree with Luther on several theological issues. Besides, the attention and energy of Lukáš and of the Central Council of the Unity were to be totally absorbed by a vehement encounter with the Zwinglian influence in the Moravian branch of the Unity.

In the latter part of 1524, one of the newcomers from Silesia, Zeising, rendered an important service to the Unity. He translated from Czech into German two letters of apology which were submitted by the elders, the one to King Louis II, the other to the estates at the diet in Prague on January 25, 1525.[62] A few months later, towards the end of the first half of 1525, Zeising and his colleagues began to spread the Zwinglian concept of the eucharist in Moravia. According to Odložilík,[63] they circulated a copy of Zwingli's first treatise on the Lord's Supper, *Ad Matthaeum Alberum de coena dominica epistola*.[64]

Alarmed by the rapid dissemination of the new concepts, the elders of the Unity hastily drew up a brief refutation. It was finished in

---

[60] The most concise summary which compares the respective contacts of the Brethren with Erasmus and Luther is Bittner, 1954. Cf. also Thomson, 1953b; Peschke, 1935, 355-360 and 1940, 259-274 (German tr. of Speratus' "Conclusiones Beghardorum et Bohemorum"); Bartoš, 1929 and 1934; Čihula, 1897; Pelikan, 1946; 1948; 1949; 1964, 120-146; Molnár, 1959a; 1964a-b; Fousek, 1965, esp. pp. 60 ff. and Heymann, 1968.

[61] Cf. similar complaints expressed in Nürnberg during the same years by Hans Sachs in his booklet, *Ein Gespräch eines evangelischen Christen mit einem Lutherischen* (1524) and by Hans Greiffenberger, *Die Welt sagt, sie sehe keine Besserung von denen, die sich lutherisch nennen* (1523). Cf. Kiwiet, 1957b, 237.

[62] Cf. footnote 131 in the next chapter.

[63] In the following paragraphs, we follow Odložilík, 1923 (German summary, Odložilík, 1925). The Czech essay (a doctoral dissertation) includes long excerpts from the sources.

[64] Z, III, 322-354. Written originally on November 16, 1524, it was printed by Christopher Froschauer in March 1525. A German translation by Georg Binder appeared in Zürich in the same year.

writing on June 25, 1525 and printed at Boleslav on September 5.[65] Before the end of the year, the condemned 'innovators' prepared a Reply (*Odpis*) [66] which was a free paraphrase of Zwingli's Letter to Alber.

On February 2, 1526,[67] the Council of Elders met at Boleslav to hold a discussion about the doctrine of the Lord's Supper. Zeising and his friends were invited to defend their position. The elders, however, rejected their symbolic interpretation and agreed upon a statement [68] in which the old position of the Unity was maintained. In the Lord's Supper, Christ is present *sacramentaliter, spiritualiter, potentialiter et vere* (*posvátně, duchovně, mocně a pravě*). With the first two terms, the Brethren made a distinction between their position and the Roman Catholic or Lutheran concepts; with the other two expressions, they drew a line between their position and that of Zwingli or of the sacramentarians.

The statement was incorporated in an official reply to the *Odpis* which had been prepared in advance, likely by Lukáš himself, and approved at the same meeting of the elders. It was printed at Boleslav on April 25, 1526.[69] The personal confrontation at the February meeting did not terminate the strife.

Zeising and Weisse continued to spread their views. From the house of Brother Krasonický in Litomyšl each of them sent a Latin letter to Lukáš in which they showed no respect for the elderly leader of the Unity. Lukáš not only replied to both of them but also sent a warning letter to the Brethren in Moravia.[70] According to Lukáš,

[65]   *Spis dostičinící těm, jenž o svátosti těla a krve Páně méně, než pravda čtenie smysliti káže, smyslí pravíc ji znamením toliko a ne pravdou býti.* Only known copy in Brno, State Archives. Content in Odložilík, 1923, 19-21.

[66]   *Odpis*, not preserved but reconstructed by Odložilík on the basis of a new refutation by the Unity in 1526. Odložilík, 1923, 23-28, provides a detailed textual comparison of *Odpis* with Zwingli's Letter to Alber and proves that the author, most likely Zeising, borrowed his arguments and even his wording from Zwingli. Molnár, 1952a, 108, suggests that Zeising's *Odpis* appeared in print. Odložilík assumes only a manuscript copy. It is not clear whether the work was in German or in Czech.

[67]   Molnár, 1952a, 108, n. 139 corrects the dating by Odložilík (January 29, 1526) who in turn revised the dating of Müller, 1920, 518 and Müller, I, 443.

[68]   The Czech statement is printed in full by Odložilík, 1923, 28-30. Cf. Peschke, 1935, 281-289.

[69]   *Spis proti v nově povstalým odporem, že by svátost těla a krve Páně znamením toliko a ne pravdou byla.* Copy in Brno, State Archives. Content summarized by Odložilík, 1923, 30-33.

[70]   *Psaní Bratra Lukášovo z příčiny Michala Weysa, a Čížka,* AUF, V, fol. 349b-350b. A German translation, not always accurate, was printed by Müller, 1920,

Zeising and Weisse were trying to prove that there was no difference between the Zwinglian concept of *signum* (*est* equals *significat*) and the teaching of the Brethren about the sacramental presence of Christ in the eucharist (*sacramentaliter, significanter, posvátně neb znamenaně*).[71]

The letter of Bishop Lukáš makes it abundantly clear that the Zwinglian concepts were spreading in the Moravian branch of the Unity, even among some of the (Czech) leaders. He writes in part:

I certainly notice that some are leaning toward it [i.e. Zeising's position] and some have even said that his arguments are more persuasive etc. Therefore, youngsters [literally, children] begin a war and a division comes to the head [i.e. the leadership] and how it will end with others I do not know. That is why I bring it to your attention, Brethren, so that you may take care of it, leaving everything else aside. Watch these people who have arisen against the Unity with their fancy German ways. They have more confidence in Germans and the German views. They boast of their [knowledge of] languages and exegesis.[72] For they wish to build up the Germans and carry their fire [of controversies] into our midst. But know assuredly that this is as though Satan had conspired against the Unity through them.

Two additional documents from the same period (1525-1526) confirm how widespread the Zwinglian influence was in the Unity. The anonymous *Four Articles*,[73] written in Czech, must have had their origin in the Zeising circle. The first article "on the spiritual mode of Christ in the outward word and sacraments" says:

No one can prove that the Lord Christ in his spiritual mode is [present] in the word or sacraments, that is, in the outward signs (*znamení*) instituted

---

521-524. For brief excerpts of the Czech text in Molnár, 1952a, 108-109. This letter is the only preserved item of the correspondence. The letter is not dated but sufficient time must have elapsed after the publication of *Spis* (see footnote 69) on April 25, 1526, to allow Zeising and Weisse to write their critical letters from Litomyšl, and Lukáš to prepare his replies.

[71] *AUF*, V, fol. 350a.

[72] In spite of a more positive attitude toward higher education in the Unity after 1494 ('the Major Party'), Lukáš remained in opposition to the use of the original languages in the exposition of the Scriptures. This was one of Luther's criticisms of the Brethren in his writing, *Vom Anbeten des Sakraments* (1523): ". . . wolt ich bitten, das yhr die sprachen nicht also verachtet, sondern . . . ewre prediger unnd geschickte knaben altzu mal liesset gutt latinisch, kriechisch unnd Ebreisch lernen. Ich weyss auch furwar, das, wer die schrifft predigen soll und auslegen . . . und solls alleyne aus seyner mutter sprach thun, der wirt gar manchen schonen feylgriff thun" (*WA*, 11, 455; Eng. tr. *LW*, 36, 304).

[73] *Čtyři články*, preserved in *AUF*, XI, fol. 173-179, escaped the attention of Odložilík, Müller and Bartoš. In our dating, we follow Hrejsa, IV, 307. The reply, *Odpověď na spis, odpírající v služebnících Božích, ve křtu Kristově, v večeři jeho milostnému Kristovu bytí* is preserved in *AUF*, XI, fol. 181-193b.

by Christ. In his spiritual mode Christ can be [present] only in the souls of men. But the word and sacraments are not superfluous. Although they do not impart grace and truth, they nevertheless offer 'ministrative benefits' (*služebné užitky*). Sacraments are meant for profession (*vyznání*), remembrance (*připomínání*) and mediation (*zprostředkování*) of holy things in Christ.

The second article distinguishes between the outward, 'ministrative' word of God, which is mere letter, and the inward, 'essential' word of God, which is spirit and life. The third article concerning the bread and wine in the Lord's Supper declares that the body and blood of Christ are involved only as a remembrance and not as a present reality (*ne přítomně, ale pamětně*). The fourth article refers to the words of institution.

The anonymous reply, *Odpověď na spis* ..., likely prepared by Lukáš, repudiates the views contained in the *Four Articles*. However, the tone of the reply is quite different from the letter of Lukáš quoted above. The writer calls the author of the *Four Articles* "dear friend, dear comrade, dear brother". Both documents support the thesis that the controversy affected not only the small German minority within the Unity, but also its Czech majority.

For Lukáš, the intensive struggle against Zwinglianism involved more than the doctrine of the eucharist. Rightly he sensed that the basic premises in the theology of Zwingli (and Luther!) were different from those on which he had built the doctrines of the Unity. Earlier in his letter to the Brethren in Moravia he wrote: "The issue affects the entire Unity, the decisions of the councils, synods, faith itself, the essential truth and the ministrative truth. ..."

In addition, the elderly bishop could not overcome his aversion to foreign innovations, particularly if they were represented by men of such unpredictable behaviour as Zeising. Of the three Silesian ex-monks nothing more is known about John the Monk. The records simply report that he disappeared.[74] Michael Weisse must have

---

[74] "John the Monk with Zeising wanted to reform the Unity. The former disappeared somewhere." (*HF* under the year 1525; cf. Šafařík, 1862, 122.) The letter of Lukáš, however, refers to Michael 'the Monk' (i.e. Weisse) and John 'the German' (*Jan Němec*, i.e. Johann Zeising). No mention is made of John the Monk at all. (Cf. also Müller, I, 444, n. 395 and Matusik, 1960, 202 ff.) The statement in the closing paragraph of the letter, "I have never known the Monk until recently, nor spoken with him", can hardly apply to Michael Weisse who had accompanied Jan Roh to Wittenberg four of five times during 1522-1524. The document in the *AUF* is genuine. A note added at the end by the scribe, W[avřinec] O[rlík], states that he copied it from a letter written by the hand of Brother Lukáš. It is possible that in the opening paragraph of his letter, Lukáš confused 'John the Monk' with

parted ways with Zeising. In 1531, after the death of Bishop Lukáš, he received ordination as priest of the Unity and served as pastor of the German-speaking congregation in Lanškroun until his death in 1534.[75] Most likely, he had cared for the congregation ever since the passing of their previous minister, Thomas 'the German' (Tomáš Němec) in 1522. Lanškroun is about fifteen miles from Litomyšl. In 1532, Weisse was elected member of the Central Council of the Unity and this in spite of the fact that he never fully renounced his Zwinglian leanings.[76]

Zeising ignored the warnings by Lukáš as well as those written to him by his personal friends, Krasonický and Roh.[77] Instead, he propagated in Moravia at least two other writings of Zwingli, *Subsidium sive coronis de eucharistia*[78] and "On the Keys and the Confession".[79] Lukáš prepared Czech refutations of both in 1526 but

---

'Michael the Monk'. This would mean that Weisse — the only one among the three who stayed in the Unity till his death in 1534 — stood aside and did not take part in the strife which was perpetuated by John the Monk and Zeising. Both of these must have moved to Moravia during the summer of 1526. Lukáš enclosed his reply to them with his letter to the Brethren in Moravia (presumably Bishop Škoda in Přerov). This indicates that when he wrote his letters, the two Silesians must already have left Litomyšl for Moravia and were in contact with the leaders of the Unity there.

[75] *HF* (Šafařík, 1862, 122) has an obscure reference to his end: "Then he wavered (*se zvrtkal*) and after a dinner with Vojtěch of Pernstein, he expired." It is not clear whether he "wavered" in his faith (relapse into Zwinglianism?) or his moral behaviour. The Necrologue (Todtenbuch, 227) describes him as "a hard (stubborn) man who began again to take a stand against the Brethren and to make friendship with priests". Cf. Müller, II, 28, n. 74. On Weisse, see Lehmann, 1922, Fornaçon, 1954 and Matusik, 1959.

[76] His Zwinglian concept of the eucharist can be traced both in his German hymnbook of the Brethren (Gesengbuchlen, 1531; cf. Fornaçon, 1954, 42 and Matusik, 1960, 203, n. 68) and in his unauthorized German translation of the Confession, *Rechenschafft des Glaubens* (printed by Chr. Froschauer in Zürich, 1532). Cf. Molnár 1956a, 130.

[77] *HF* (Šafařík, 1862, 122) and Odložilík, 1923, 34. The text of these letters is not preserved.

[78] Z, IV, 440-504. Preface of the Latin original is dated August 17, 1525. Printed by Chr. Froschauer in Zürich the same month. A German tr. by Georg Binder was printed by Johann Hager in Zürich on November 30, 1525 and again by Chr. Froschauer in 1526. The title of the German tr. is *Naachhut von dem Nachtmal oder Dancksagung Christi*. HF calls it *O svátosti dobré milosti*. Cf. Müller, I, 442, n. 389; I, 444, n. 397; Müller, 1920, 517, n. 7, and 519, n. 15.

[79] A separate reprint of Zwingli's exposition of Articles 50-52 from his major work *Auslegen und Gründe der Schlussreden*, Preface dated July 14, 1523 (Z, II, 1-457). The short reprint of Art. 50-52 appeared under the title *Ein kurtz gut vnd gründtlich vnterricht was die schlüssel der kirchen sein vnd vermügen vnd von der Beicht. Von Huldrich Zwinglin in seiner aussleggūg der artickel geschriben.*

neither of them has been preserved.[80] Quite likely they were not printed but sent as letters to Zeising and his circle.

According to the *Historia Fratrum*,[81] the Brethren repeatedly admonished Zeising and finally threatened him with excommunication. Zeising recanted in tears and promised to abide by the decisions of the Unity. Three days later, however, he declared he could not act against his conscience. He asked the Brethren to proceed against him according to their rules of discipline. He also solemnly promised that he would not attack the Unity as long as he lived. Soon after his excommunication, however, he wrote another letter, "full of poison", against the Brethren, and in particular, against their bishop in Moravia, Brother Škoda. His letter was sent from Tovačov (south of Olomouc) where he was staying (or merely visiting?) on the domain of the powerful magnate, the governor of Moravia, Jan of Pernstein at Tovačov and Helfenstein.[82] Later in 1526, or in 1527, he spent some time at Habrovany in the company of Jan Dubčanský.[83] During the same period (fall 1526 — early 1527) he must have visited Mikulov. He is referred to by Hubmaier as *mein lieber brueder Jan Zeysinger* at the end of his communion liturgy, *Ein Form des Nachtmals Christi*,[84] which Zeising was to deliver to Burián Sobek of Kornice. The dates for Zeising's stays at Habrovany and Mikulov seem to overlap. Quite likely, he remained an itinerant propagator of his changing views and kept visiting several centers of the radical Reformation in Moravia until his martyr's death in Brno in April 1528.

The final pronouncement of the Unity in their prolonged struggle against the Zwinglian influence among the Brethren in Moravia and among other groups there, such as the emerging Unity of the Habrovanites, did not come till November 1527. This important

---

1524. The print has no date, no place nor any name of printer (possibly Jobst Gutknecht in Nürnberg).

[80]   *Odpis na spis Voldřicha Zwinglia O svátosti dobré milosti* (mentioned in *HF*, fol. 578) and *Psaní o rozdíle mezi kázáním Čtení sv. a klíči Kristovými* (mentioned in *HF*, fol. 580). Cf. Müller, I, 561 f., Nos. 93 and 95.

[81]   *HF*, fol. 401-402. Cf. Odložilík, 1923, 35.

[82]   Jan of Pernstein was a Neo-Utraquist with strong sympathies for the radical movements in Moravia. At the end of 1526 Hubmaier dedicated to him his short treatise on the necessity of rebaptism, *Grund vnd Vrsach* (printed in Nikolsburg early in 1527; *HS*, 328). Cf. note 184 in the next chapter.

[83]   Reference in one of the Habrovanite tracts, quoted by Odložilík, 1923, 41, n. 1.

[84]   *HS*, 365. Cf. also Bergsten, 1961, 427.

work, "Against the incomplete and partial faith of the present-day innovators"[85] provided a classical summary of the theology of Lukáš and of the doctrinal position of the Unity during his era. In his view, both Luther and Zwingli were guilty of selecting only some truths from the whole witness of the Scriptures and over-emphasizing them to the neglect of some other equally important aspects of the Christian gospel. In the discussion of the sacraments, especially the eucharist, Lukáš rejected both Luther's and Zwingli's interpretation.

The encounter of the Brethren with Zwinglian thought in Moravia in the years 1525-1527 which we have described in some detail has direct bearing on the subject of our study. The negative attitude which the leaders of the Unity expressed in their writings and personal confrontations predetermined, to a large extent, the eventual outcome of contacts and negotiations between them and the emerging Anabaptists.

The rejection of Zwinglian theology in general, and of its concept of the eucharist in particular, also meant the rejection of the basic theological framework of early Moravian Anabaptism, at least as it was represented by Hubmaier. A realistic hope for a theological *rapprochement* and a union of the two movements, the Czech Brethren and the Anabaptists, was thereby reduced to a minimum.

By the same token, had the Unity yielded, in the mid-twenties, to the Zwinglian influence — as it did to the Lutheran in the thirties, and to the Calvinistic still later on — a theological platform would have been erected in Moravia on which a flourishing Anabaptist 'Unity of Brethren', German-speaking and Czech-speaking, might have been built through the merger of the *Unitas Fratrum*, or at least its Moravian wing, and of Hubmaier's type of Anabaptist congregations. The three branches of the *Unitas*, Bohemian, Moravian and Polish (after 1547) are known to have taken their separate courses of action particularly in their ecumenical relations. One can only speculate about the different course Anabaptist history and theology might have taken, both in Moravia and elsewhere in

---

[85] *Spis tento ... v němžto nynějších novověrcuov neplná a necelá, anobrž kusá viera s mnohými a jistými duovody písem svatých z zákona božieho se ukáže.* Printed in Boleslav, November 2, 1527. Copies in National Museum, Prague and State archives, Brno. Summary by Odložilík, 1923, 42-44 and Molnár, 1952a, 110. The treatise was prepared especially against the Habrovanite group. It contains no direct references to the Anabaptists although by November 1527 they had been settled in South Moravia for more than a year.

Europe, as a result of such a merger with the Czech Brethren in Moravia.

The rejection of Zwinglian theology by Bishop Lukáš had, therefore, far-reaching implications not only for the future relationships of the Unity to Anabaptism but also for the subsequent developments in the Left Wing of the Reformation as such.

4. THE GERMAN EVANGELICALS

In an earlier part of the chapter, we have pointed out that the German-speaking population in Moravia had not been influenced greatly by the Hussite Reformation of the fifteenth century. The vast majority remained in the Roman Catholic church until the ideas of Erasmus, Luther, Zwingli and others began to evoke an echo in Moravia around 1520. As a result, small groups of interested evangelicals met to discuss the new teachings. Public disputations were held. The Czech nobility, mostly in the Utraquist camp, encouraged the transition from Catholicism to a 'reformed' position.

It would be anachronistic to refer to such parishes as Protestant. Nor can they be designated simply as Lutheran [86] at this early stage of the Reformation movement in Moravia. In their theological outlook, they represented different strands of the Reformation. In South Moravia, the German evangelical circles were exposed more to Zwinglian, Elsatian and South German ideas than to an unequivocal influence from Wittenberg.

During the period 1524-1526, their views were undergoing continuous revision as new books and new refugees with varied backgrounds were arriving in the towns and villages of South Moravia. Because of the fluid state of their theology we shall designate them simply as 'German Evangelicals'.[87] In later years, most of them cast firm anchorage in the Lutheran camp.

The border city of Jihlava (Iglau) became one of the first centers of the Lutheran movement. Paul von Spretten (Speratus) stopped here on his way from Vienna to Wittenberg in March 1522 and was persuaded to stay. He soon won a great following among the Ger-

[86] Cf. the reference by Williams, 1962, 218 to "a German-speaking Lutheran parish in Nikolsburg" (prior to Hubmaier's arrival).
[87] Cf. the striking differentiation between 'Lutheran' and 'Evangelical' Christians in Hans Sachs' booklet, *Ain Gesprech aines Euangelischen Christen, mit ainem Lutherischen*, 1524 (Weller, No. 3148; Schottenloher, 1921, No. 49).

man population of the royal city. He also established contacts with the Czech Utraquists (Beneš Optát of Telč) and the Czech Brethren. Through his correspondence with Luther (May-June 1522) he furnished an incentive for the visits of the Brethren's emissaries in Wittenberg.

The work of Speratus in Jihlava came to an early end when, after many threats by the Bishop of Olomouc, Stanislav Thurzo, the king had Speratus arrested in the spring of 1523. He was imprisoned in Olomouc (April 16) and condemned to death by fire. Only the intercessions of Jan of Pernstein, Arkleb of Boskovice, Georg the margrave of Brandenburg and others, brought a release on July 7. Speratus left Jihlava on September 7, 1523 and after brief stops in Litomyšl — where he visited the Brethren — and in Prague (September 29) he reached Wittenberg early in November.[88]

---

[88] Born in the same year as Luther (1484) in Rötlen (diocese of Augsburg), Speratus studied philosophy, theology and law in Paris, Italy and perhaps also in Vienna. He became doctor in all three fields. In February 1519, he was appointed preacher at the cathedral in Würzburg. On account of his pro-Reformation views (and marriage), he was forced to leave the city. After a short stay in Salzburg where he was again appointed "Domprediger", he came to Vienna. His sermon against the monastic vows which he preached in St. Stephen's cathedral on January 12, 1522 — and later wrote down during his imprisonment in Olomouc in 1523 and had printed in Königsberg (September 1524) under the title *Von dem hohen gelübd der Tauff* — was censured immediately by the theological faculty of the university. He was expelled from the city on January 20, 1522. For a description of his stay in Moravia, see Tschackert, 1891, 9-16; Hrejsa, 1915, 201 ff.; Dedic, 1931, 152 f.; Altrichter, 1910, 150; Schenner, 1911, 222 ff. Speratus' well-known hymn, "Es ist das Heil uns kommen her", published originally in Luther's first hymnbook in 1524, includes the following lines which are worth noting in view of the subsequent theological development in South Moravia (cf. footnotes 123 and 145 below):

> Wer glaubt in mich und wird getauft, [!]
> Dem selben ist der Himmel erkauft,
> Dass er nicht wird verloren.
> Er ist gerecht vor Gott allein,
> Der diesen Glauben fasset . . .
> (Tschackert, 1891, 15)

After a stop in Wittenberg, Speratus became a court preacher in Königsberg (end of July 1524). In 1527, Speratus was ready to return to Jihlava (see correspondence in Schenner, 1911, 247 ff.). Later in his life, as the Lutheran Bishop of Pomesania in ducal Prussia (1530 till his death in 1551), he had occasion to meet Anabaptist refugees from Moravia (including Hans Spittelmaier and Oswald Glaidt) at the colloquy in Kętrzyn (Rastenburg) at the end of December 1531 (Williams, 1962, 408 ff.) and to welcome the Czech Brethren when they sought refuge in Prussia in 1548, after their expulsion from Bohemia by King Ferdinand (Müller, III, 2 ff.; Tschackert, 1891, 81 ff.; Śliziński, 1958, 147-199).

In the following year, the focal point of the German Reformation shifted to Mikulov (Nikolsburg), a border town on the main road from Brno to Vienna. At that time, the town with its castle was the center of the domain owned by Leonhart I of Lichtenstein (1482-1534) and his nephew Hans VI (1500-1552).[89]

Our knowledge of the religious developments in Mikulov, and in all of South Moravia, during the three years just prior to the arrival of Anabaptist refugees in the early summer of 1526, is based mainly on two printed sources. The first of these is a, German apology of Johannes (Hans) Spittelmaier entitled *Entschuldigung Joannis Spitelmayer prediger zu Nicolspurg* and dated March 6, 1524.[90]

In the dedicatory preface addressed to the Lords Leonhart and Hans of Liechtenstein, Spittelmaier referred to himself as the local minister (*vnnderteniger Caplan*) who had preached the Gospel in Mikulov for some time. Apart from this single autobiographical reference and a few mentions of his name in the Anabaptist sources [91] nothing is known about either his origin or the course of his life prior to his stay in Mikulov. [92] Judging by his detailed description of monastic life he might have been a monk before he embraced evangelical doctrines. His apology was prepared as a reply to repeated attacks against him by the Franciscan monks in the nearby Austrian town Feldsberg.[93] He knew Latin and Greek [94] and the style of his apology with its clear and witty presentation of arguments is equal if not superior to that of Hubmaier.

---

[89]   Leonhart and Hans were mistaken for brothers by many authors, e.g. Brock, 1957, 251.
[90]   Spittelmaier, 1524. With the assistance of Dr. J. Benzing we were able to identify the printer as Joh. Singriener in Wien. Original print in Goshen, two handwritten copies in Brno, Beck Collection (cf. Bergsten, 1961, 399, n. 5). Although the booklet had been listed by Beck, 160 in 1883 and again by Wiswedel, 1937b, 550, n. 2, its contents were never reported until Bergsten provided a brief summary. Using the handwritten copies, Bergsten gives the date of the preface as March 16, 1524. It should be corrected to read March 6, 1524, on the basis of the printed copy. Friedmann in his art. on Spittelmaier in *ME*, IV, 599 makes no mention of *Entschuldigung*.
[91]   *ZGL*, 50, 52, 53, 86 and *TQ*, II, 40. All for the years 1526-1528.
[92]   Friedmann in *ME*, IV, 599 assumes Bavarian or Austrian origin and even suggests that Hans might have been related to Ambrosius Spittelmaier, a native of Linz, executed as Anabaptist on February 6, 1528. On the latter, see Klassen, H., 1958.
[93]   Feldsberg (Valtice), since 1918 on the territory of Czechoslovakia.
[94]   Spittelmaier, 1524, fol. b iij[r] and c iv[v]. In our summary of the apology we shall include folio references in the text above.

The work is divided into three parts: a brief dedicatory preface (fols. a^v - a ij^r), an apology addressed to "all who love the divine word on which rests the salvation of our soul" (fols. a ij^v - b iv^v) and seven articles in which the author states his position (fols. c^r - d iij^v).

From the beginning of the world — so begins Spittelmaier his apology — men have despised the voice of God and persecuted those who believed his word. Spittelmaier himself had tasted persecution for the sake of the Gospel when he was called a seducer of people and a heretic by "the bestial unlearned bunch Behemoth in Feldsberg" (fol. a iiij^r), i.e. the monks in the monastery there. They were the hypocrites (*geleichsner*) who put on a show of outward piety but inside were like the graves filled with dead bones (fol. b^v). By their continued attacks the monks had forced Spittelmaier to prepare a printed reply, first in German and then in Latin.[95]

Although he does not regard himself as a bishop he nevertheless follows the injunction of the apostle Paul that a bishop should exhort people in sound doctrine (*in huilsamer ler*) and discipline those who oppose it [Titus 1:9-11] (fol. b iij^r). Like the Israelites who rebuilt the walls around Jerusalem in the days of Nehemiah [Neh. 4:17] he, too, is ready to fight against the enemies with his left hand and to build the walls with his right hand.

"For the evangelical preacher will not be frightened by any persecution, not even by death itself. He will not allow himself to be pushed into a corner but instead will freely speak the truth among his own and will not keep silent out of fear" (fol. b iij^v). As pastor of the Christian congregation (*christenliche versamlung*) in Mikulov, Spittelmaier stood up against all sects and divisions (*allerlay segkten oder zertrennung*) and pointed the people to Christ who alone is the Saviour (*seligmacher*) and giver of all grace and mercy (fol. b iv^v).

In reply to the accusations made against him by the monks, Spittelmaier outlines his theology in the following seven articles.

(1) All men have sinned and become righteous through Christ alone. He is the only Saviour (*seligmacher, gerechtfertiger*) who took upon his shoulders all our sin and unrighteousness. He reconciled and united human nature with the divine.

(2) Man becomes righteous by faith alone. Faith is *die guette zuuorsicht, hofnung götlicher gnad vnd barmhertzigkait, in Christo verhaissen* (fol. c^v). "Faith is a gift of God, the rock on which Christ has built his church" (fol. c ij^r). Through faith man receives the Holy

---

[95] No copy of the Latin apology — if ever printed — is known.

Spirit who fills the heart with joy and good will so that it might do the whole will of God, not out of fear of hell, nor out of desire for reward (fol. c ij^r). Such will which stems from faith and the Spirit, works the genuine good works. The principal righteousness is therefore faith and the principal evil is unbelief.

(3) In prayer, man lifts up his mind and heart to God. One should call upon God at all times, yet not like the monks who do nothing else but sing and recite prayers all day long so that one cannot hear a single sermon unto salvation.

(4) God alone must be worshipped. Since Christ is the only advocate no man should pray to any human creature nor to angels.

(5) To praise God in his sanctuary [Ps. 150:1] or in holy places [Ps. 68:35] does not require holy vows as practised by the monks. God should be praised by his saints [96] to whom he has shown such grace and mercy.

(6) The monasteries, whether they be of Franciscan, Dominican or Augustinian order, are places of hypocrisy, idolatry and impurity. Instead of humility, members of one order take pride in their own particular rules and consider themselves to be better than members of another order. As for the vows of purity "a prostitute in a public house will be saved sooner than a monk or nun in a monastery" (fol. c iv^r).

(7) The call to repentance (*metanoite*) means 'better yourselves' (*bessert euch*). Through repentance, man lays aside the old Adam and puts on the second Adam, Christ. The original sin (*erbsündt*, fol. d i^r) of Adam affects all of us. Through repentance and faith we participate in the righteousness of Christ.

Spittelmaier distinguishes between four kinds of repentance. Repentance (*büsswertigkait*) is, first of all, an inner acknowledgment and confession of sin to God which then leads to hatred of sin and to love of righteousness. According to the Scriptures, confession of sin (*beicht oder bekentnüss*) is necessary and commanded by God. It was exemplified by David and other men in the Bible.

But there is another kind of repentance which Christ commanded in the Gospel of Matthew, Chapter 18.[97] Such repentance which is to

---

[96]   "Gott soll man loben in seinen heiligen".

[97]   The reference to Mt. 18:15 ff. (fol. d ij^r) as the basis for public repentance in a Christian congregation is most interesting. In the letter written by Conrad Grebel and his associates in Zürich to Thomas Müntzer later that year (September 5, 1524) Article 23 refers to "the rule of Christ (Mt. 18:15-18) without which the Lord's Supper should not be observed" (*TQ Schweiz*, I, 15; Eng. tr. Williams, 1957, 77).

be practised by a Christian congregation, refers not to secret sins but to known (*offenwerlich*) sins which become an offense to all men. The rule should apply also to prelates and priests whose public sins, especially their open keeping of women, have become such a stumbling block. "Therefore, Christ gave to his royal priesthood [I Peter 2:9], i.e. to all Christians, the power of the keys of the kingdom of heaven so that they would deal with public sins" [98] (fol. d ij^v).

The third kind of repentance is personal reconciliation with a person whom one has harmed [Mt. 5:23 f.; 6:12, 14 f.]. Without such repentance or reconciliation with fellow men one can receive no forgiveness of sins from God.

The fourth kind of repentance is auricular confession (*orenbeicht*). The Scriptures know nothing of it, nor did the early church practice it. There is no need for special deeds of satisfaction which the Roman church prescribes. "They are nothing else but tyranny and ridicule of the true satisfaction which is the death of Christ" (fol. d iij^v).

In the concluding paragraph of his *Entschuldigung*, Spittelmaier stated that he had preached the Evangel and the foregoing articles publicly at Mikulov and was prepared to give an account before all men. His final scriptural quotation about the plentiful harvest and few labourers [Mt. 9:37 f.] suggests the heavy burden of loneliness which he must have borne as a pioneer preacher of evangelical Christianity in Mikulov in the early spring of 1524.

At that time, the views of Spittelmaier displayed the characteristic emphases of the early Lutheran Reformation. The Scriptures by themselves are the sufficient source of truth (*solu Scriptura*).[99] Christ is the

---

Beginning with the Schleitheim Confession of Faith, the passage became the *locus classicus* for the Anabaptist practice of church discipline and especially, the practice of ban. Cf. Jenny, 1951, 11, lines 73-85; Eng. tr. in Lumpkin, 1959, 25.

[98] Spittelmaier does not spell out how a Christian congregation should practise public repentance, nor how the public sins of the priests should be censured. By implication his demand that all Christians should have the right to deal with offensive sins, whether these be committed by laity or by clergy, is reminiscent somewhat of the Hussite program, the *Four Articles of Prague* (1420). The last article stipulated that "all mortal and public sins be censured and hindered in every estate by those in authority". Cf. the full Latin text in Müller, I, 521 f. and the original Czech text in Říčan, 1951a, 50 f. A similar echo of the third article, viz. "that large material possessions controlled by priests and monks be taken away from them according to the commands of Christ" (Müller, *ibid.*, 520 f. and Říčan, *ibid.*, 47 f.) can be heard in Spittelmaier's statement, "der Euangelisch prediger sol nit die guetter diser welt begern" (fol. b iij^v). It is doubtful that he was familiar with the original Hussite program.

[99] "in der heiligen götlichen schrifft begründet ... ich als liebhaber des heiligen

only mediator of salvation.[100] The law and the gospel stand in sharp contrast. Man is justified only by faith in Christ (*sola fide*).[101]

This was the Evangel that Spittelmaier preached. The concept of the church [102] and of the ministry [103] appear only as marginal concerns. The priesthood of all believers is implied but not explained in practical terms.[104] Spittelmaier's personal experience of persecution seems to have occasioned his passionate plea for the freedom of preaching.[105]

In the broader context of our inquiry into the rise of the German Reformation movement in South Moravia, it is important to notice the absence of several doctrinal issues in the apology of Spittelmaier. Most striking is his silence about the sacraments, especially the sacrament of the altar. This had been the issue in the personal contacts and literary exchanges between Luther and his friends in Bohemia and Moravia during the two preceding years. In the fall of 1522 in

---

götlichen worts ... allen Christgelaubigen menschen, die alain das gotsswort fürpilden" (fol. a jv - a ijr).

[100] "Christus vnd kain ander ist der seligmacher" (fol. bv). "Ach wie mit ernstlichen wortten wirt ... angezaigt, das wir alle sünder sein vnd kain andern gerechtfertiger oder seligmacher haben dan Christum ..." (fol. cr). "In dem ain götlichen Euangelischen befelch gibt seinen nachuolgern, allain die zerstretten schefflen auff Christum vnd sein creütz zuweisen, vnd den allain anzaigen" (fol. b ivr).

[101] "Durch das gesatz erkennen wir die sünd. ... Darumb ist es von nötten das wir fliehen zu dem Euangelio, des ain wort ist aller genaden vnd barmhertzikait. ... Das haist das heilig Euangelium predigen. Zum ersten den glauben Christi, vnd darnach durch in verzeichung der sindt." (fol. b ijr).

[102] "sein christenliche kirchen ... die nichts anders ist dan alle die menschen von got ewigklich ausserwelt, glauben in seinem sun Jesum Christum, dürch in verzeihung vnd nachlassung der sündt" (fol. b ijr).

[103] The twofold office of the minister consists in leading man to an understanding of self as sinner and to a saving knowledge of God through Christ. "Aber warlich dise zway stuck seindt das ambt aines ydlichen predigers. ... Das erst ist den weg des hernn beraytten, das ist lernen wie nur der mensch ain hey sey [Is. 40:3-8]. Das ander, den hernn zaigen vnd das lamp gottes. Oder also auff kurtzen verstandt, den menschen im selbs, vnd got anzaigen, darmit der mensch sich selbs, vnd got erkhen." (fol. b iijv - b ivr).

[104] "dem künigtlichen briesterthumb, das ist allen Christen" (fol. d ijv). Cf. the quotation at footnote 98 above for the context.

[105] "Der Euangelisch prediger ... sol sich nit lassen erschreckhen durch kain veruolgung auch biss in den tödt, las sich in khainen winckhel truckhen, vnd bey den seinigen, die warhait frey redt, vnd nit aus forcht verschweig." (fol. b iijv). Spittelmaier's statement antedates Hubmaier's famous plea for religous toleration of heretics (*Von Ketzern und ihren Verbrennern*, HS, 95-100) which was written in the fall of the same year. Not unlike Spittelmaier's apology, Hubmaier's treatise was directed against a monastic order, in this case against the Dominicans who were in charge of inquisition. None of Hubmaier's thirty-six articles parallels the statement of Spittelmaier.

Moravia, Speratus published his correspondence with Luther [106] concerning the theology of the eucharist, both among the Czech Utraquists (Beneš Optát of Telč) and in the *Unitas Fratrum*. The same issue was the main subject of Luther's *Vom Anbeten des Sakraments des heiligen Leichnams* printed in April 1523.[107] Writing his apology at the beginning of March 1524, Spittelmaier seems to have been totally unaware of both the issues and the solutions proposed by the different parties. The fact that his brief writing was directed against abuses and attacks of the monks in Feldsberg cannot be regarded as a sufficient explanation of his strange silence.

Spittelmaier might have been familiar with Luther's *De instituendis ministris ecclesiae*.[108] There are several parallels of thought [109] between the two treatises even though the main subject of Luther's writing to the Bohemian Utraquists, the concept of ministry and ordination, is avoided by Spittelmaier.

His apology is saturated with quotations from the Scriptures, above all from the epistles of Paul (*der hochberümbt apostel*, fol. d i^r). The only non-scriptural authorities referred to by name are Jerome (fol. b iij^r) and Gerson (fol. c j^v).

From January 29 to February 2, 1524, a large synod of the Utraquist estates and priests from Bohemia and Moravia met in Prague. *Twenty Articles* which had been prepared by Master Havel Cahera, the administrator of the Utraquist consistory and a personal friend of Luther,[110] were approved first by the priests and then by the estates. The first six articles are concerned with examinations and appoint-

---

[106]   Hrejsa, IV, 293 dates the print "some time in July 1522". Müller, I, 405 refers to the fall. For content of the correspondence, see Peschke, 1935, 356-360; Müller, I, 401 ff. and Hrejsa, IV, 289-294. Cf. also footnote 60 above.

[107]   Cf. footnote 59.

[108]   Cf. footnote 15. Speratus arrived in Wittenberg in November 1523 and immediately translated the Latin treatise into German. It was printed in Wittenberg early in 1524 (WA, 12, 164).

[109]   Here are only a few examples: (1) Reference to "Behemoth" (WA, 12, 195; Spittelmaier, fol. a iiij^r). (2) The vain repetitions of prayers by priests and monks (WA, 12, 186 f.; Spittelmaier, fol. c ij^v). (3) The power of the keys which belongs to all Christians; reference to Matthew 18:15-18 (WA, 183 f.; Spittelmaier, fol. d ij^v).

[110]   On Havel (Gallus) Cahera, see Müller, I, 419 ff. The Czech text of the articles is printed in Bartoš Písař, 21-25 and summarized by Hrejsa, IV, 270 f. The Latin version (original?) was reprinted by Chaloupecký, 1925, 157-166. It follows a different order: "I. In nomine sanctae et individuae Trinitatis [historical introduction], II. De praedicatione et enarratione verbi dei, III. De sacramentis et ceremoniis sue ritibus ecclesiae, IV. De magistratu ecclesiastico, V. de festivitatibus."

ments of Utraquist priests by the consistory in Prague. Articles 7-12 define the authority of the word of God. The writings of church fathers and later theologians, including the works of the Czech Reformers Hus, Rokycana and others, are recognized alongside the Bible as long as they are in agreement with its teachings. The last eight articles treat of the sacraments. Following Luther — and against the Unity during the era of Lukáš — the Utraquists reduced the number of sacraments from seven to two. Baptized infants may, at the request of their parents, also receive communion.[111] The mass is replaced by a simpler Supper of the Lord with the omission of many liturgical practices which appear to be contrary to the Scriptures. The elevation of the host for adoration is allowed where people or priests request it. Nevertheless, the priests are admonished to instruct their people so that gradually such unscriptural practices would be abandoned.

The Twenty Articles which represented a compromise between the Neo-Utraquist (pro-Lutheran) and the conservative wing within the Utraquist Church did not remain in force too long. They were revoked in the early summer of 1524 when the pro-Catholic party regained control of the Prague consistory. Nonetheless, the doctrinal position expressed in them gained acclaim in wide circles of the church.

It is difficult to assess the significance of the *Articles* for the developments in South Moravia. Most likely some of the Czech Utraquist noblemen and priests from the area were present at the

---

[111] Infant communion was introduced by Jakoubek of Stříbro (Jacobelllus de Misa) in the early years of the Hussite movement, before 1420. Accepting, in agreement with Hus, the doctrine of transubstantiation, Jakoubek regarded both infant baptism and infant communion as necessary unto salvation. Cf. Peschke, 1935, 67 and Říčan, 1957b, 37. Even the radical Taborites practised infant communion as early as 1420 (Müller, I, 30 f.). The Latin article III, 1 of the Prague synod (January 29, 1524) stipulates: "Peracto baptismo, si infans aptus est et parentes aut compatres petierint et desideraverint, ut ei sacramentum corporis et sanguinis domini communicetur, re salubriter deliberata, poterit diaconus id praestare, etc." On the interpretation of the eucharist, Art. III, 5 states: "Censemus ad pietatem pertinere, ut omnes concomitantiarum praescriptiones circa sacramentum corporis et sanguinis domini nostri Iesu Christi, prout superflue igenia humana id faciunt, prorsus omittantur. Simpliciter enim, quemadmodum ipse dominus instituit et testatus est, credendum et asseverandum est de eo. Sumendum est autem integre, neque aliquid vel addendum, vel adimendum. Christus enim panem testatur esse suum corpus et vinum affirmat esse suum sanguinem, ac utrumque reliquit, ut minister ecclesiae una cum populo sub utraque specie digne his utrisque seorsim utatur ad recolendam memoriam [*nota bene!*] mortis et beneficiorum eius. Itaque hoc modo credendum et divina mensa eius finis causa, quem Christus intendebat, utendum est." (Chaloupecký, 1925, 161 and 163).

January synod in Prague.[112] It is doubtful that any German Evangelicals attended the Czech gathering. Most certainly, when Spittelmaier wrote his *Entschuldigung* one month later, he displayed no knowledge of the issues which had been discussed there.

If one may judge a complex historical situation on the basis of a single preserved source, one is inclined to believe that the German-speaking evangelical congregation (*christenliche versamlung*) at Mikulov came into existence under Spittelmaier's leadership. He appears to have acted independently of the preceding Reformation in Jihlava (Speratus) and in temporary isolation from the concurrent developments among the Czech Utraquists and in the *Unitas Fratrum*. Apart from the study of Scriptures, the sources of Spittelmaier's own transition from Catholicism to the evangelical position remain obscure.

Two years later, on March 14, 1526, a large gathering of priests and laymen, both German- and Czech-speaking, was convened in the town of Slavkov (Austerlitz) located a short distance east from Brno and about thirty miles north of Mikulov. A detailed account of the meeting was prepared by Oswald Glaidt and appeared in print shortly afterwards.[113] The short booklet constitutes the second main source for our knowledge of the religious developments among the German evangelicals prior to the arrival of the Anabaptists. We shall first summarize the contents of the printed report.[114]

It is presented in three parts: (a) An historical introduction in which Glaidt, a participant on the German side, describes the proceedings of the two day debate. His introduction is dated in Nikolsburg, March

[112] Drawing from a source in 1562, Komenský and Hartman in the seventeenth century reported, under the wrong date of January 1523, that the Moravian representatives included Paul Speratus, Benedikt Optát, Václav Litomyšlský and Jan Charpa (*Historie*, 1902, 79). The attendance by Speratus is doubtful since he was in Wittenberg at that time. Cf. also Hrejsa, 1915, 203, n. 3 and 4.

[113] *Handlung yetz den xiiij. tag Marcy dis. xxvi. iars. So zu Osterlytz inn Merhernn durch erforderte versammlung viler Pfarrer vnd priesterschafften auch etlicher des Adels vnd anderer in Christlicher lieb vnd ainikayt beschehen ...* (Glaidt, 1526). For a comparison of three printed editions of the report, see Appendix 2.

[114] Glaidt's report received unusual attention in the literature, perhaps due to the fact that an abbreviated version, without Glaidt's commentary, was included in Kessler's *Sabbata* (Kessler, 220-222). Summary of the content is given by Loserth, 1897, 68 f.; Odložilík, 1923, 35-38; Wiswedel, 1937b, 552-555; Bergsten, 1961, 401 ff. and Hrejsa, IV, 312 f. In our summary, we refer simply to fols. i to viii of the Zürich edition. Its folios are marked only a i - a v. There are no folios marked 'b'. The last page has no text.

29, 1526. (b) The text of seven articles of agreement. (c) Glaidt's own commentary which is inserted after the text of each article.

A meeting of priests [115] (*ein versamlung der briesterschafft*) took place at *Schlackaw* or *Vsserlitz*. The German ministers, at least those from the area of Mikulov, had been urged to attend by the 'Christian Bishop', i.e. Martin Göschl.[116] At the opening of the disputation, at 10 o'clock in the morning on March 14, 1526, there were 105 Czech Utraquist priests [117] present. Many more (*vil me*) of them came later. The number of German ministers was even higher (*noch vil me*). Seated at a middle table, to act as judges (*commissarii*), were members of the lower nobility, Jan Dubčanský,[118] Jan Lhotský, Jan Kytlice and N. Hřivín.[119] The debate was conducted in the Latin language. A copy of the Scriptures was placed on each table since all points were to be judged "only by the pure word of God".

According to Glaidt (fol. a ij^r) the purpose of the meeting was to compare the conflicting doctrines of the evangelical preachers (*Euangelisch prediger*). The common people did not know whom to follow and to whom to listen. It was highly desirable, therefore, that an agreement (*ein verglich*) be reached.

The three main topics of discussion during the two days' colloquy

[115]   The title of the report (*ouch etlicher des Adels vnd anderer*) suggests that there might have been some laymen present in addition to the ministers and members of nobility.

[116]   "Daruff hatt der Christenlich Bischoff Bropst zu Keynitz, vnser Nicolspurger dz wir personlicher erschinen gebetten." The biographies of Göschl and Glaidt will be reviewed in Chapter IV.

[117]   The Czech Brethren were not represented as Friedmann (*ME*, II, 522) assumes on the basis of his mistaken identification of the Utraquists with the Bohemian Brethren. Williams, 1962, 205 reports the meeting as an effort of Dubčanský to unite the Utraquists, the two parties of the Unity (Major and Minor Party) and the Lutherans. The German ministers could hardly be classified as Lutherans. Glaidt's report is quite explicit: "Beheimischer priester, die von bedin gestalten, wie man sy nennet", i.e. the Utraquists. The reported unanimous defense of infant communion by the Czech ministers furnishes an additional proof that they were all Utraquists.

[118]   Since Dubčanský's name is mentioned first and because of his repeated efforts in subsequent years to unite the different religious parties in Moravia, we may assume that he was, together with Göschl, the main initiator of the meeting.

[119]   Jan Lhotský of Ptení (Odložilík, 1923, 36) was Dubčanský's brother-in-law (Loserth, 1893, 125). According to Loserth, Kytlice and Hřivín were knights, i.e. members of the lower nobility. It is not known whether there were other noblemen in attendance. The absence of the Lords of Liechtenstein is striking, especially since the German ministers from Mikulov played an important role at the meeting. The absence of the Lords of Kounice on whose domain the town Slavkov was located, is also worth noting. They were members or adherents of the *Unitas Fratrum* which had a congregation in the town.

were: the ground of salvation, marriage of priests and the Lord's Supper.

The first question concerning the basis of salvation was raised by the Utraquists. The German ministers replied: "Faith in God, through Jesus Christ, which is exercised daily in the praise of God, the love of the neighbour and the mortification of the flesh". The Utraquists were in agreement except that they could see little love, the fruit of such faith, among the Germans. Instead, there was quarrel, hatred and disunity, far worse than among the Czechs. "The world", replied the evangelicals, "is full of weeds. Certainly, where there was no love towards fellow men, there could be no saving faith, which is a gift of God." They expressed their willingness to be taught better.

Then, the Utraquists opened debate on the issue of marriage of priests. Several German priests had married. This was "a work of the flesh and against the Scriptures" (fol. a ij^v). A disputation "with Scripture against Scripture" continued till five o'clock. During the debate, a hundred Utraquist priests stood up and went over to the German side admitting that it was permissible for a bishop or preacher (*Bischof oder prediger*) to marry. Finally, all Czechs gave in and agreement was reached on this point also.

The Utraquists suggested that articles be drawn up and pledged to accept them as long as they were based on the Scriptures. It was done accordingly and everybody went to rest "in joy and Christian love".

The meeting was resumed at six o'clock next morning. The prepared articles were read. The article on the sacrament of the altar was debated till three o'clock. But then agreement was reached and *seven articles* were signed by all present. Glaidt records each article and adds his own commentary.[120]

(1) "One must preach nothing but the word of God, namely the law to show sin and condemnation, and then the Gospel to proclaim grace and salvation. For according to the testimony of Christ [Mt. 13:52] a teacher in the kingdom of God is one who out of his treasure brings forth things new and old" (fol. a iij^r).

(2) "The last will or testament of Christ, bequeathed in the last supper, is nothing but a remembrance (*Widergedechtnuss*) of

---

[120] To separate the official articles of agreement from Glaidt's personal comments, we shall first enumerate all articles and then gather the comments. In his booklet, Glaidt inserts the commentary after each article. Sentences in quotation marks are literal translations of the German original.

Christ... ." Therefore, all human additions, such as elevation, adoration, processions etc., which are contrary to the Scriptures, should be abolished, but only after due instruction of the people so that no reason for offence and uprising be given.

(3) "Every believer should know and distinguish between two kinds of communion, an inward, spiritual communion (*Gemeinschaft*) and an outward communion of remembrance. The former, which is experienced through faith, is necessary for the forgiveness of sins and eternal life, and is sufficient unto salvation. The latter should not be despised but observed according to the testament of Christ" (fol. a iiij^v).

(4) "One must not dispense (*reichen*) the communion of the Lord's table to any one except to such as have been first born again by the word of God and nourished with the 'reasonable milk', that is, those who by [personal] faith know how to proclaim the death of the Lord and to discern his body." [121]

(5) "The blessing of water, candles, oil and other similar things — which leads to nothing else but to dangerous superstition and is contrary to the Scriptures — shall be abolished by all of us."

(6) "The evangelical freedom which does not forbid anything that God has not forbidden, allows marriage unto all men without exception. Therefore, ministers of the word who cannot restrain themselves should in no way be hindered from marriage so that they fall not into adultery — as unfortunately it often happens — and then under the judgment of God. Nevertheless, those who have received from God the gift of self-control, can rejoice in the Lord without wives."

(7) "It is obvious that neither the feast days of the saints, nor the prohibition of certain meals can be substantiated from the Scriptures. Every priest (*pfarrherr*) or minister of the word (*diener des worts*) should, therefore, instruct his people in the true faith, as best as he can, yet without giving occasion to uprising."

Glaidt's commentary on each article consists, to a large extent, of scriptural quotations, mostly from the New Testament.

He observes that the first article, *sola Scriptura*, is basic to all other articles. Man is justified by faith alone, without the works of the law. No amount of religious observances and good works, such as the burning of candles, pilgrimages, singing of masses and saying of

---

[121]   Article 4 was directed against the Utraquist practice of infant communion. Cf. also Glaidt's commentary on this article.

prayers, the founding of monasteries etc., can make one righteous in the eyes of God.

Commentary on Article 2: At the original last supper, Christ used no special garments, nor altar, candles or bells. Rather, he gave bread to his disciples, without walking around with it, and without adoration (*anbeten*). Adoration belongs to God alone. Nobody has ever seen God who himself said, "No man can see me and live". Christ said, "You will always have the poor with you but you will not have me . . . ." These words refer to his physical presence, for spiritually, God is always with us until the end of the world. The disciples believed that the body of Christ had been given for them and for the sin of the whole world as the one sufficient sacrifice. Afterwards they observed the supper in remembrance of him. Similarly, as we drink from the cup, we remember him and proclaim his death until he comes.[122]

Commentary on Article 3: Through a number of quotations from Scriptures Glaidt draws a distinction between the outward and inward (spiritual) circumcision and then continues: "So it is also in our sacraments (*sacramenten*) or symbols (*gnadenzeichen*). What will baptism and Christ's Supper help (*hulff*) me if I do not first, in faith, receive the inward (*inwendig*) baptism and supper? Does not Christ say: 'He who believes and is baptized is saved,' and concerning the supper, 'This do in remembrance of me'? Thus there must be first faith and remembrance of the death of Christ, through which we are set free. Otherwise, as Paul says, we shall not discern the body of the Lord and eat and drink damnation unto ourserves" (fol. a v^r). The rest of the long commentary on this article deals with the 'tyrannic' practices of the Roman Catholic church which makes people partake of the sacraments without faith.

Commentary on Article 4: Glaidt explains that this article was prepared chiefly against the Utraquist practice of infant communion. When the "Bohemians" were asked to prove their practice with the Scriptures, they were unable to do so. They only said: "If one allows baptism for small children, why should one not permit also this sign of grace (*gnadenrych zeychen*)?" The Germans replied: "Baptism is given as a sign of the beginning of the Christian life when a man,

---

[122] Glaidt's reference to the cup, and the absence of any arguments about the cup of the laity seem to indicate that communion in both kinds must have been practiced among the German Evangelicals for some time. See also our analysis of the report further below.

through faith, pledges himself to Christ, that is, to fight the old Adam and to become a new creature in Christ.[123] 'Do you not know', says Paul, 'that all of us who have been baptized into Christ, have been baptized into his death ... and have put on Christ?' But this sacrament of the cup which is the thanksgiving (*danksagung*), the supper, the remembrance (*widergedechtnuss*) of Christ, is administered (*gereicht*) in order to proclaim the Lord's death. However, small children, fools and the like can never do that" (fol. a vj^r).

According to Glaidt, the Utraquists finally stated they could not enter into any agreement without the consent of their parishioners (*on willen irer pfarrlüt*). The Germans replied: "Do the horses pull the wagon, or does the wagon pull them? Does the minister teach the people, or do the people teach him?" Thereupon, the Czechs requested that they be allowed a period of time during which they would instruct their people with sermons and Scriptures, and lead them from the old custom to the right order. Their request was granted.

The commentaries on Articles 5, 6 and 7 contain no addditional insights, nor details about the proceedings of the meeting.

In his comment on the agreement reached at Slavkov, Kessler explains why he copied the text of the *Handlung*. He wished to give an example of "how the one God of peace, through the prince of peace Christ Jesus, likes to unite his elect and to deliver them from sects and divisions".[124] He could not have known that the meeting was of little consequence for the subsequent development of religious life in Moravia. Far from being a 'union synod' between two official ecclesiastical parties, the disputation was but an episode soon to be forgotten and ignored by both parties. Nevertheless, Glaidt's record of the meeting makes it possible for us to assess the theological and ecclesiastical situation among the German Evangelicals in South Moravia, two years after Spittelmaier's *Entschuldigung* and only a few weeks before Hubmaier's arrival in Mikulov.

The fact that Glaidt's booklet is the only known record of the disputation [125] makes it necessary that we raise a few questions pertaining to the credibility of his account.

---

[123] "Antwurten wir darauff, der tauff wer ggeben zu eim anfang zeychen Christenlichs lebens, da der Mensch durch den glouben sich Christo zusagt, den alten adam zu kempffen, vnd in christo ein nüwe Creatur werden" (fol. a v^v).
[124] Kessler, 222.
[125] It is somewhat surprising that a meeting of such size should have remained unnoticed in the plentiful Czech polemic religious literature of the late twenties.

The number of participants, especially on the German side, is startling. The title of the report (*versammlung viler pfarrer vnd priesterschafften, ouch etlicher des Adels vnd anderer*) as well as the terminology used consistently by Glaidt (*pfarrer* or *priester* for the Utraquist priests, *Evangelisch prediger, diener des worts* for the German ministers) seems to imply that the meeting was a disputation of the clergy, with only a few laymen present. The number of those in attendance must have been around three hundred, with a German majority. If the total number of parishes in Moravia (the diocese of Olomouc) was over 600,[126] including both the Utraquist and the Roman Catholic parishes, Czech- and German-speaking, one might regard the attendance of 120 to 140 Czech Utraquist priests as possible. Even so they had to come from a fairly large area. Glaidt makes no hint whatsoever about the geographical area involved.

The number of German ministers (more than 150) can be accepted as realistic only if the majority of them belonged to the category of refugee preachers and run-away monks. Unless there were many German ministers from northern Moravia involved — which is quite unlikely — the few German parishes in South Moravia never could have supplied so many delegates. The terminology employed by Glaidt with reference to the German ministers makes it quite obvious that most of them were not in charge of a parish (*pfarrer*) but were rather itinerant preachers (*prediger, diener des worts*). There could have been several of these in one locality at any given time. The preponderance of refugee preachers on the German side

---

On the Czech side, Dubčanský, one of the main initiators of the Slavkov disputation, and his co-workers at Habrovany, wrote and published numerous works which contain frequent references to contemporary events and issues beyond the scope of their own circle. In 1527, Dubčanský published, in Prostějov, his correspondence with the Unity (Bishop Lukáš) in which he had made repeated proposals for "union meetings". The Slavkov meeting could have been mentioned as an example. Yet Odložilík, 1923 (39, n. 2), who studied all extant Habrovanite sources, found no reference to the meeting. On the German side, there seems to be at least one allusion to the disputation. In the preface to his first book printed in Moravia (July 21, 1526) Hubmaier rehearses the argument put forth by the Utraquists in defence of infant communion. Compare the wording of Glaidt's commentary on Article 4 (above) with Hubmaier's wording: HS, 227. One should remember that H. was writing the preface in Glaidt's room at Mikulov! Cf. also Bergsten, 1961, 424 ff.

[126] The total number of parishes (636) in the diocese of Olomouc (which included the northern regions of Opava and Krnov) was established by Hrubý, 1935c, 91 on the basis of several sources. Cf. footnote 8.

can be documented further by the theological views which dominated the disputation.

The seven articles agreed upon at Slavkov reflect a rapidly changing theological outlook among the German Evangelicals in South Moravia following Spittelmaier's *Enschuldigung* of March 1524. At that time, there was only one battlefront in the German community at Mikulov: an early Lutheran attack against the unscriptural doctrines and practices of the Roman Catholic church.

Two years later, the issues were far more complex. The encounter was taking place simultaneously on three fronts. The old battle against the Roman church conducted under the banners of the common Reformation principles, *sola Scriptura, sola fide* and *lex versus evangelium,* continued (compare Articles 1, 5, 6 and 7 as reported by Glaidt). However, the massive argumentation was now concentrated in another area, namely, the doctrine of the sacraments in general, and of the eucharist in particular (compare Art. 2-4).

For both of these battle lines, the refugee ministers brought experience and weapons from their former skirmishes in other lands. However, in Moravia, they soon became involved in yet another *Auseinandersetzung,* namely, the confrontation between the sixteenth-century Reformation and the older Czech Reformation. The Czech tradition could be represented by any number of mutually conflicting views, ranging from conservative old Utraquism to radical Neo-Utraquism, or from the self-assured Major Party of the *Unitas Fratrum* to the provocative extremism of more radical groups. At the meeting in Slavkov, the confrontation with the Czech Reformation was comparatively simple. The Neo-Utraquists were surprisingly radical in endorsing a symbolic interpretation of the eucharist as a mere *wider gedechtnuss* (Article 2). They subscribed to a highly spiritualized concept of communion. The eucharist was no longer regarded as necessary unto salvation and was neglected altogether by some, as the warning, included in Article 3, implied.

The only issues which necessitated heated argumentation were the marriage of the priests (Article 6) and *communio parvulorum* (Article 4). The Utraquists yielded in both cases.[127]

---

[127] Subsequent developments among the Moravian Utraquists show what little effect the Slavkov "agreement" had. As late as 1558, a regional agreement (*srovnání*) of Utraquist priests made in Prostějov, stipulated that communion should not be administered to infants but only to older children after they had been duly instructed in catechism (Hrejsa, 1938, 313).

It is somewhat surprising that in a confrontation of the German Evangelicals with the Czech Utraquists two other questions should have been bypassed altogether. The printed record makes no reference, *verbis expressis*, either to the problem of the ordination and appointment of ministers, or to the practice of communion *sub utraque specie* which had been the *raison d'être* of the Utraquist church ever since the Compacts of Basel (1433).

In the first instance, the silence about ordinations and appointments to parishes would suggest that the Utraquist church in South Moravia was developing rather independently from the Utraquist consistory in Prague. There, the issue was and remained in the center of interest, especially after 1523.[128]

In the second case, communion in both kinds must have been introduced in the German evangelical congregations some time before the disputation in Slavkov. If it had not been an accepted practice by then, the Utraquists would have raised their objections most certainly.[129]

---

[128] Cf. footnotes 15, 108 and 110 above.

[129] Whereas the Czech Reformation restored communion in both kinds at an early stage (October 1414), the sixteenth-century Reformation was slow in reinstating the cup of the laity. In Wittenberg, communion under both species was administered, for the first time, by Carlstadt — during Luther's stay at Wartburg — on Christmas Day 1521 (Barge, I, 358-362; Williams, 1962, 41 ff.). Clothed in plain clothes, he read the mass, with important omissions, in Latin. The observance was repeated three more times (up to January 6, 1522) but then suppressed. Carlstadt had demanded communion in both kinds in his tract *Von beiden Gestalten der heiligen Messe* (November 30, 1521; cf. Barge, I, 332 f.). Upon Luther's return from Wartburg, early in March 1522, Latin mass with communion in one kind, yet with the elimination of phrases referring to the sacrifice, was restored until December 1523 (Luther's *Formula missae et communionis*; WA, 12, 205-220). The main reason for the perpetuation of the mass was Luther's regard for the weak brethren. In his essay *Von beider gestalt des Sakraments zu nehmen* (printed in mid-April 1522 and reprinted in Zürich in June 1523, WA, 10, II, 11-41; LW, 36, 231-267), Luther was willing to tolerate both practices side by side. In Zürich, Zwingli (Z, II, 765 — with an appeal to Hus — and 792), supported by Hubmaier (Z, II, 787), pleaded for communion in both kinds at the second disputation, October 26-28, 1523. However, when the City Council ruled against any immediate reform of the mass, Zwingli and his associates followed the orders. Thus, the mass in Latin (with the omission of the sacrifice part) was perpetuated, side by side with evangelical preaching, in the churches of Zürich until Easter 1525. Zwingli's liturgy for the Lord's Supper, *Action oder Bruch des Nachtmals, Gedechtnus, oder Dancksagung Christi*, was printed on April 6, 1525 (Z, IV, 13-24). The preservation of the mass after the October disputation, 1523, was one of several factors which led to the gradual estrangement between Zwingli and the circle around Conrad Grebel. The emerging Anabaptists criticized severely the inconsistency of the practice and eventually observed the first communion in both kinds, in their own circle, the first Anabaptist congregation, at Zollikon, on

For our analysis of the theological developments among the German Evangelicals, Glaidt's report on the concepts of eucharist and baptism is of primary importance. It should be clearly understood that the text of the agreed articles contains no reference to baptism at all. However, in his commentary (on Art. 3 and 4) Glaidt discusses baptism together with the Lord's Supper. He also mentions that infant baptism was used as an argument by the Utraquists in their defense of infant communion.

5. THE ORIGINS OF ANABAPTISM IN MORAVIA

Referring to the German congregation in Mikulov — which Glaidt represented — Říčan describes its theological outlook as "Zwinglian with trend towards Anabaptism".[130] The concept of eucharist betrays the influence of Zwingli's teachings which must have been known there from his printed works.[131] The brevity of Glaidt's comments makes it difficult, if not impossible, to find verbatim quotations, or parallels in thought, as Odložilík was able to do for the more extensive writings of Zeising and his associates.[132] The terminology employed by Glaidt shows definite similarities to the vocabulary of Zwingli [133] but at the same time includes variations and differences which merit further investigation.

January 22 or 23, 1525. Cf. the detailed account in Blanke, 1955, 6-10, 24 f., and note on p. 85.

[130]   Říčan, 1957b, 90.

[131]   The list of Zwingli's main works on the subject of eucharist up to March 1526 would include: Art. 18 in *Die 67 Artikel* (1523); *Auslegen und Gründe der Schlussreden* (1523); *Ad Matthaeum Alberum de coena dominica epistola* (1524); *De vera et falsa religione commentarius* (1525), section "De eucharistia" (Z, III, 773-820) which appeared in German translation during 1525 in three separate editions, *Von dem Nachtmal Christi, widergedechtnus oder Dancksagung* (cf. Z, III, 625 f. Modern German tr. by F. Blanke in Zwingli *Hauptschriften*, Vol. 10, 58-136); *Subsidium sive coronis de eucharistia* (1525, also two editions of a German translation, *Nachhut von dem Nachtmal oder Dancksagung Christi*, 1525 and 1526); *Eine klare Unterrichtung vom Nachtmal Christi* (The first of the four editions published in 1526 is dated Zürich, February 23rd. Cf. Z, IV, 782 f.).

[132]   See footnotes 63 ff. above.

[133]   The expressions "widergedechtnus", "danksagung", "gnadenzeichen" are Zwinglian. However, we were unable to find, in Zwingli's writings up to 1526, a verbatim parallel to the distinction between the "inwendige, geistliche Gemeinschaft" and "auswendige Gemeinschaft" of Glaidt's Art. 3, nor a parallel to the differentiation between inward ("inwendig") and outward baptism. In his book, *Von der Taufe, von der Wiedertaufe und von der Kindertaufe* (May 27, 1525) Zwingli distinguishes between several types of baptism. He uses the dichotomy of

In view of Hubmaier's later stay in Mikulov and his close association with Glaidt, one might ask whether or not some of his earlier writings had reached Moravia prior to March 1526 and influenced Glaidt's thinking. With reference to eucharist and baptism, only three tracts could have been used by Glaidt. They are *Etliche Schlussreden vom Unterricht der Messe* (printed probably in Ulm before Easter 1525),[134] *Eine Summe eines ganzen christlichen Lebens* (printed in Augsburg, 1525)[135] and *Von der christlichen Taufe der Gläubigen* (printed in Strasbourg during the summer 1525).[136]

In these writings, Hubmaier repeatedly uses the terminology 'inward — outward',[137] yet he never applies it to 'communion' as Glaidt's third article does. His teaching on the Lord's Supper carries a strong emphasis on the fellowship of believers who eat and drink together and are bound together in love and discipline.[138] This 'horizontal' dimension of the communion, so typically Anabaptist,[139] is totally absent in Glaidt's report. Following Zwingli, Hubmaier conceives of the eucharist not only as an act of remembrance (*Gedächtniss*) but also of proclamation (*Verkündigung*) and commitment (*Verpflich-*

"der usser wassertouff" and "der inner touff oder gloub" (Z, IV, 223) and then again a distinction between two kinds of baptism of the Holy Ghost, viz. "der innerlich touff des heiligen geystes", without which no one can be saved, and "der usserlich touff des h.geystes" which is speaking with tongues (*ibid.*, 225 f.). Claidt uses consistently the terms "inwendig - auswendig" instead of Zwingli's "innerlich - ausserlich". He makes no use of Zwingli's translation of "sacrament" - "pflichtszeichen" (*ibid.*, 218). For a summary of Zwingli's teaching on the sacraments, and especially on the eucharist, up to 1526, see Baur, I, 420-438 and 482 ff. and Köhler, 1924, 61-117 and 301 ff.

134   *HS*, 101-104.
135   *HS*, 108-115.
136   *HS*, 116-163.
137   "ewsserlich Denckzaichen oder kreyd" (*HS*, 102); "vsswendig wortzaichen ains inwendigen Christenlichen wesens" (104); "nach dem vnd nun sich der mensch inwendig vnd im glauben in ain new leben ergeben hat, bezeügt er auch das ausswendig offenlich vor der Christenlichen kirchen, in dero gmainschafft er sich lasset verzaychnen vnnd einschreyben. ... vnd lasset sich tauffen mit dem ausswendigen wasser, in welchem er offenlich bezeüget seinen glauben vnd fürnemen" (111 f.); "der ausswendig tauff Christi ist nichs anders, dann ain offenliche zeugknuss der inwendigen pflichten, mit der sicht der mensch bezeugt ... das er sey ain sünder" (112 and 122).
138   "mit ainander gemainschafft haben, eben also soll vnser leyb vnd plut vnder ainander gemain sein ... Inn dem christmal soll man den thod Christi verkündigen vnd ... sich mit leyb vnd plût in brüederlicher dienstbarkeit zusamen verpflichten vnnd verbinden ..." (*HS*, 103).
139   Cf. Art. 3 of Schleitheim Confession (1527), Jenny, 1951, 11 f. On Hubmaier's dependence upon the Swiss Anabaptists, see Bergsten, 1961, 313 ff.

tung). In his comment on Art. 5, Glaidt develops his own scheme: thanksgiving, meal, remembrance, proclamation.

It is possible that in their definition of baptism the German Evangelicals at the disputation in Slavkov might have echoed Zwingli's argument about baptism as a sign of initiation.[140] Hubmaier, in his treatise on baptism (1525), quotes and ridicules Zwingli's thesis. If baptism is a sign of initiation or beginning (*ein anheblich zeichen*) what does really begin with infant baptism? Is it faith, or new life, or the spirit of God, Hubmaier asks,[141] and gives a negative answer in each case.

We may conclude that none of Hubmaier's books mentioned above was in circulation among the German Evangelicals in the spring of 1526. They did not find it inconsistent to postulate faith as a prerequisite of baptism, on the one hand, and to defend infant baptism, on the other hand.

The preface written by Hubmaier for his first book printed in Moravia, dated on July 21, 1526, "in the room" of Oswald Glaidt, furnishes an important additional source for our understanding of the religious climate in Mikulov at the time of the emerging Anabaptism.[142]

According to Hubmaier, the defenders of infant baptism fell into three categories. Among the Czechs, the Utraquists continued to defend infant communion chiefly because the Germans practised infant baptism.[143] Besides, the Czechs had a system of training and testing their children with which they also justified infant baptism.[144]

---

[140]   Cf. footnote 123 above with the following quotations from Zwingli's *Von der Taufe* ... (printed in Zürich, May 27, 1525): "Ietz kumpt das sterckest ort, das uns lert den wassertouff ein anheblich zeichen sin, damit wir uns in ein nüw leben got pflichtend . . .", (Romans 6:3-5) (Z, IV, 342). Cf. also *ibid.*, 231, 237, 241, 245. Zwingli refers to baptism as "signum ceremoniae initialis" in other writings, e.g. Z, III, 763 f.

[141]   *HS*, 137.

[142]   *HS*, 227-229 and 241-243. Strangely enough, no historian has exploited this source for an analysis of the situation in Mikulov.

[143]   It is difficult to decide whether Hubmaier was simply citing the argument from the Slavkov disputation, or whether at the time of his arrival, one could still hear the same debate going on. In view of the total picture presented by Hubmaier, we are inclined to regard the reference as a description of the contemporary scene rather than a mere quotation from Glaidt's report. This would imply also that on July 21, 1526, the Germans at Mikulov, natives and refugees, practised infant baptism. Cf. "das wir Teütschen vnsere khinder auch tauffen" (*HS*, 227). Cf. also footnotes 125 and 127 above.

[144]   Hubmaier's reference to "ein eingossne probation vnd bewerung für jre kindlen" (*HS*, 228) is rather obscure. There can be no doubt that he meant the

Among the Germans, some postulated faith in infants (*eingossner glaub*) while others became uncertain about *fides infantium* and baptized children on the faith of others, whether parents, godparents, or the church (*frembder glaub*).

Hubmaier's description of the theological attitudes towards baptism in South Moravia at the end of July 1526 supplements the picture presented by Glaidt at the end of March. Both sources provide trustworthy evidence that ANABAPTISM DID NOT ORIGINATE among the native population, whether German or Czech, IN MORAVIA. Nor does it seem to have emerged among the German evangelical refugees who began to settle in Moravia from the early twenties. Most certainly, there was no opposition to infant baptism recorded at the disputation in Slavkov, even though some of Glaidt's own comments on faith which must precede baptism prepared the way for an Anabaptist interpretation.[145] There are no other known sources which would shed additional light on the theological developments in South Moravia during the period from March 29 to July 21, 1526.

One might suspect that some among the German evangelical refugees began to question the validity of infant baptism prior to Hubmaier's arrival. One might also surmise that other Anabaptist refugees preceded Hubmaier to Mikulov. However, Hubmaier makes no allusion to such developments antedating his arrival. His reference to *herr Oswald* (Glaidt) — which stands in marked contrast to his later reference to *mein lieber brüeder Jan Zeysinger*[146] — implies that Glaidt did not embrace Anabaptism until later, under the direct personal influence of Hubmaier. The Hutterite chronicle, although not always reliable in its dating and of much later origin, connects the rise of Anabaptism in Moravia with the arrival of Hubmaier.[147]

Any genetic influence of the *Unitas Fratrum* on the rise of Ana-

---

Czechs. He distinguished clearly between "sie, die anndern" (i.e. the Czechs) and "wir Teütschen, die unseren". He might have been referring to the Utraquist practice of the sacrament of confirmation.

[145] "What will baptism and Christ's Supper help me if I do not first, in faith, receive the inward baptism and supper? Does not Christ say: He who believes and is baptized is saved ...? Thus there must be first faith ...". Cf. footnotes 123 and 185.

[146] *HS*, 229 and 365. Similar evidence is furnished by Hubmaier's references to Göschl as "gnädiger Herr" (*HS*, 229; July 21, 1526) and as "gnädiger Herr und Bruder" (*HS*, 307; December 10, 1526).

[147] *ZGL*, 49 and Beck, 48. "Im Jare 1526 kam Balthasar Huebmär gen Nikolspurg in Mähren, fing an zu leeren vnd predigen den waren tauff Christij. Das volck aber nam seine leer an vnd ward vil volck getaufft" (quoted from Beck).

baptism in Moravia is also highly improbable. On account of the common interest in Zwinglian theology, Zeising might have been in personal contact with the German Evangelicals in South Moravia prior to his move from Litomyšl to Moravia in the spring or summer of 1526. He might have mediated a knowledge of the Brethren's teachings on baptism and rebaptism. However, there is no proof of such contacts and even if they did exist, obviously they did not provide an impetus for the emergence of Anabaptism in South Moravia. The question of the Unity's influence on the rise of Anabaptism elsewhere is, of course, a different question and is not the subject of our present research.[148]

Finally, we must also rule out any influence of Jan Kalenec, the leader of the Minor Party of the Unity.[149] His presence in Moravia during the years 1525 and 1526, after his expulsion from Prague in December 1524, is not attested by any known sources but simply assumed on the basis of his later stay at Letovice. The issue that occupied Kalenec as the new leader of the diminishing Minor Party, especially during the years 1523-1527, was the old strife between the Major and Minor Party, namely, the question of the Christian participation in government and war. Polemical writings were exchanged between Kalenec on the one side and Lukáš and Krasonický on the other.[150] No doubt the attention of Kalenec was directed entirely towards this issue which, one must remember, was not introduced at Mikulov until 1527, during the confrontation between Hubmaier

[148]   The most recent attempt to trace Czech influences, esp. that of the Unity's practice of rebaptism, on the rise of anti-paedobaptism in Zwickau, Saxony, was made by Husa, 1956 and 1957, esp. 32 ff., 76 f., 92-95. The first reference in sources to criticism of infant baptism in Zwickau is dated December 17, 1521 ("certi scismatici in fide christiana credentes baptismum pueris nihil prodesse") and, therefore, follows the visit of Müntzer and Mark Thomae Stübner to Bohemia earlier in 1521. Furthermore, the chronist, Peter Schumann, accused the "arch heretic" Nicolaus Storch of having imported his views from Bohemia ("qui hoc scisma ex Boemia advexerat", Wappler, 1908b, 23, n. 230). Husa cautiously proposes that Müntzer might have become acquainted with the views of the Czech Brethren on baptism during his stay in Prague. He suggests the priest Jan Roh as well as Jan Kalenec, Matěj Poustevník and the book on the repetition of baptism, Lukáš, 1521a, as possible contacts. Husa's hypothesis is based entirely on the one source quoted by Wappler and he himself warns (Husa, 1957, 94) against overestimating the Bohemian influence on Müntzer and the Zwickau prophets. Husa makes no attempt to compare the widely divergent concepts of baptism in the Unity and in the Zwickau circles. Cf. the critical reviews by Macek, 1958c and Molnár, 1958b-c, and the reply by Husa, 1958. See also Gritsch, 1967, 62 ff.
[149]   On Kalenec, see above at footnote 23.
[150]   Cf. the account of the controversy in Müller-Bartoš, 275 ff. and Brock, 1957, 242-249.

and Hut. The problem of Christian magistracy, oathtaking and other ethical issues lay outside the orbit of interest at the disputation in Slavkov and — insofar as one can use the *argumentum ex silentio* — among the pre-Anabaptist Evangelicals in South Moravia in general. Kalenec rejected infant baptism altogether [151] but his contacts with the non-resistant and communitarian Anabaptists in Moravia did not develop until during a later period.[152]

In view of all these facts, we may conclude with Brock that "both sides — the Moravian Anabaptists and Kalenec — reached a similar position on such subjects as the state, war and oaths independently. In regard to adult baptism, however, and even more as regards community of goods, it was Kalenec who was probably indebted to the Anabaptists for his acceptance of these tenets".[153]

Our foregoing analysis of the Moravian Anabaptism *in statu nascendi,* during the spring and summer of 1526, demands a further clarification of the term 'Anabaptism'. What constitutes normative Anabaptism? Can the mere theological questioning of the validity of infant baptism — which was very widespread in the third decade of the sixteenth century — be classified as 'Anabaptism' alongside the more advanced manifestations of the same opposition which led to the practical institution of believer's baptism and rebaptism, as well as to the establishment of Anabaptist congregations? What about the issues in the realm of social ethics, such as Christian participation in government, taking of oaths, non-resistance and community of goods? Widely different opinions on these matters were held by those who were otherwise united in their rejection of infant baptism and agreed on the restitution of a church of baptized believers. There

---

[151]   Müller, I, 450 and II, 101.

[152]   Brock, 1957, 252 and Williams, 1962, 218 give the impression that Kalenec established contact with the communal Anabaptists soon after settling in Moravia at the end of 1524. However, Kalenec's favourable comment about the Anabaptists — which Brock translates from Odložilík, 1923, 357 without any date — comes from the "Book of Jan Kalenec", dated May 1, 1542 and preserved in *AUF*, IV, fols. 215-228. Cf. Müller, II, 100 f.; Gindely, I, 508, n. 40, and Urban, 1966, 21 ff.

[153]   Brock, 1957, 252. His view is endorsed by Paul Peachey in *MQR*, 33 (1959), 260. Peachey applies Brock's conclusion to the whole *Unitas Fratrum*. Brock's thesis about Kalenec's dependence upon the Anabaptists in the matter of believer's baptism must be questioned since already at the end of January 1524, Kalenec probably presented a statement on infant baptism to the synod of Utraquist estates and priests in Prague. Hrejsa, IV, 270 and Odložilík, 1923, 15, n. 1. Hrejsa's and Odložilík's assertion is based on an obscure reference to such statement in a letter of Kalenec to Augusta in 1543. The rejection of infant baptism by the Minor Party is of course documented as early as 1501. Cf. footnotes 24, 25 above and Chapter IV footnotes 156 f.

were even greater contrasts in the basic theological framework (theology proper, christology, pneumatology, anthropology, soteriology and eschatology) of such representative leaders within the early 'Anabaptist' movement as Müntzer, Hubmaier, Grebel, Hut or Denck. Several proposals for exact classification and typology of the Anabaptist movement have been made recently.[154]

It is obvious that the term 'Anabaptism', both in its etymological derivation and in its historical application during the Reformation era, refers primarily to the act of water baptism. To avoid confusion due to a loose usage of the term, we would suggest the following six stages of emerging Anabaptism. All of them can be illustrated by representative thinkers and groups from medieval and Reformation history. They serve as preparatory steps for the final, seventh stage which alone should be regarded as normative for genuine Anabaptism.[155]

(1) Theoretical questioning of the validity of infant baptism.[156]
(2) Theoretical rejection of infant baptism (anti-paedobaptism).[157]
(3) Theoretical advocacy of believer's baptism.[158]
(4) Theoretical justification of rebaptism.[159]
(5) Practical refusal to have one's child baptized.[160]
(6) Practical institution of believer's baptism through rebaptism.[161]

---

[154]   Cf. Chapter I at footnote 93.
[155]   Cf. Chapter I at footnote 99.
[156]   Several medieval sects, as well as the Reformers in their early development (Zwingli, Luther, Oecolampad, Bucer etc.), expressed doubts about infant baptism. Cf. Z, IV, 228 and 606.
[157]   In some of his writings, Schwenckfeld rejected infant baptism but did not advocate rebaptism and finally, on the basis of his spiritualism, regarded any water baptism as unimportant. Cf. Maier, 1959, 23-25. A similar attitude was expressed by Müntzer. See Armour, 1966, 61.
[158]   A stage in the development of all Anabaptists. E.g., Felix Mantz' *Protestation und Schutzschrift* written in December 1524, prior to Mantz' baptism on January 21, 1525. Text in *TQ Schweiz*, I, 23-28.
[159]   There is a difference between postulating believer's baptism and justifying rebaptism. The latter implies complete annulment of infant baptism. According to Williams, 1962, 50 Müntzer encouraged the postponement of baptism until children could understand the act but he never proposed rebaptism of adults. Cf. Husa, 1958, 503, n. 3 and Armour, 1966, 61, n. 38.
[160]   Both Grebel and Hut (Neuser, 1923, 12) refused to have their newborn children baptized in 1524. In both cases, this step — which aroused great attention in the community — preceded the step of their own rebaptism. Müntzer stopped baptizing infants at Allstedt as Carlstadt did at Orlamünde. It is highly significant that neither of them moved beyond this stage. Cf. Hillerbrand, 1962, 176.
[161]   Cf. the description of the first rebaptisms in Zürich on January 21, 1525, by

(7) Practical institution of a local congregation as an expression of the church of baptized believers, with the administration of the Lord's Supper and church discipline.[162]

Only the last phase can be classified as normative Anabaptism. It involved not only a new concept of the sacraments, especially baptism, but also a new concept of the church, "a free church, a Christian fellowship based on voluntary membership and independence of the state".[163]

6. SUMMARY OF THE SITUATION

In the mid-twenties of the sixteenth century, the impact of the German and Swiss Reformation upon the native population in Moravia was not widespread. The German-speaking people appear to have been affected more than the Czechs. The limited sources, which afford only a fragmentary knowledge of the situation, seem to indicate that there were three main centers of influence.

The focal point where Lutheran and Zwinglian ideas were introduced into the *Unitas Fratrum* was the city of Litomyšl in the north, on the border between Bohemia and Moravia. Three fugitive monks from Breslau, Michael Weisse, Johann Zeising and John 'the Monk', were welcomed there by Brother Vavřinec Krasonický and Brother Jan Roh, two influential ministers of the Unity. Gradually, Zwingli's writings and concepts were disseminated by the 'Silesian triumvirate' in some Moravian congregations of the Unity, both German-speaking (Lanškroun and Fulnek) and Czech-speaking.

In the southeastern part of Moravia, in and around Mikulov, there developed the main 'reception area' for German evangelical refugees from Austria, South Germany and later also from Switzerland and Silesia. The refugees as well as the native Germans were under the leadership of another 'triumvirate' made up of two Bavarian-Aus-

---

Blanke, 1955, 21 f. and in Waldshut, end of January and Easter 1525, by Bergsten, 1961, 304 f.

[162] The first Anabaptist confession, the *Schleitheim Articles* (1527), includes the following marks of "the brotherly union": baptism, ban (discipline), breaking of bread, separation from the world, election of pastors by the congregation, rejection of Christian participation in magistracy and rejection of oath. Cf. the text and commentary by Jenny, 1951 and the earlier analysis by Blanke, 1940b.

[163] Blanke, 1961, 15. Cf. also Fast, 1960, 224, paragraph 3. In genuine Anabaptism, the rejection of infant baptism went hand in hand with the repudiation of the concept of *corpus Christianum*. Likewise, the initiation of the practice of believer's baptism was accompanied by the restitution of a believer's church.

trian refugees, Johann Spittelmaier and Oswald Glaidt, and the native of Jihlava, Coadjutor Bishop Martin Göschl.

Central Moravia became the focal area of Czech Utraquist radicalism represented by the lay seeker Jan Dubčanský and the two refugees from Bohemia, Matěj Poustevník and Václav of Lileč who, with Dubčanský, were to form a third triumvirate at the time of birth of the Unity of Habrovanite Brethren in 1528. Furthermore, in the same area and in contact with them, there lived Jan Kalenec, the last apologist of the Minor Party.

One might regard the disputation in Slavkov in March 1526 as an important step towards interchange of ideas between the three 'triumvirates'. It is doubtful that Zeising was present at Slavkov. However, he was to establish contact with the central and southern area soon afterwards.

By the time Hubmaier arrived on the scene, the personal links and ideological cross-currents among the three camps were fully realized. Coming as he did with a basically Zwinglian theology, he found eager listeners among those whose concept of the Reformation had been moulded principally by the ideas of Zwingli.

However, before we begin to examine the records of the historical beginnings of Anabaptism in Moravia, we must raise one other question: From where did the Zwinglian and related ideas reach Moravia?

7. THE SOURCES OF 'ZWINGLIANISM' IN MORAVIA

In our summary of the Zwinglian controversy within the *Unitas Fratrum*, we have pointed out that Zeising and his colleagues used a number of Zwingli's own writings. These must have been brought to Moravia mainly from Zürich just as the writings of Erasmus were imported from Basel.

An important commercial route connecting the cities in South Germany and Austria with the German cities in Silesia and Poland led through Moravia. An interesting confirmation of regular 'mail' and book traffic between Augsburg and the city of Liegnitz (Legnica) in Silesia is preserved in the letter of Simprecht Sorg, the printer of Hubmaier's works in Moravia, to Zwingli written from Frankfurt am Main on September 17, 1528.[164] He was urging Zwingli

---

[164] Z, IX, 554 f. Christopher Froschauer had a branch office in Frankfurt (Z, IX, 50, n. 8).

to send a letter to Schwenckfeld and his colleagues and to let the Zürich printer Christopher Froschauer bring the letter to Augsburg. From there Sorg's brother-in-law could forward correspondence to Liegnitz every two weeks. He also mentioned that Bucer in Strasbourg was using the same route via Augsburg.[165]

Earlier, at the beginning of April 1526 — practically during the same week when Hubmaier made his public recantations in Zürich — Oecolampad in Basel, and Zwingli in Zürich received a messenger from Schwenckfeld and Crautwald and then sent a letter by him to Silesia.[166] Regular contacts between Zürich and Silesia must have existed already before 1526. The printer Caspar Lybisch in Breslau reprinted, during 1523-1524, at least six partial editions of Zwingli's *Auslegen und Gründe der Schlussreden*.[167] Judging by the subject matter of the Silesian editions, they might have been among the works of Zwingli which were circulated both by Zeising and by the Evangelicals in South Moravia.

It is worth mentioning that while Zwingli's works were being reprinted in Breslau, two of Schwenckfeld's writings appeared in Zürich. The first one was printed by Simprecht Sorg in 1524 and the second by Christopher Froschauer, with a preface by Zwingli, in 1528.[168] During Hubmaier's stay at Mikulov, Zwingli's new works published in Zürich arrived in Moravia promptly.[169]

Perhaps the most astonishing aspect of the spread of Zwingli's views and works in Moravia is the fact that Zwingli himself does not appear to have been aware of it. He exchanged letters with Silesia, he made a few references to Bohemia,[170] but his published

[165] Another confirmation of the traffic through Moravia is found in the letter of Paul Speratus to the City Council of Jihlava, written in Königsberg (Prussia) on February 9, 1527. He sent it with a visitor from Posen (Poznań) to Breslau where the carrier expected to meet several persons from Jihlava (Schenner, 1911, 248).
[166] Z, VIII, 559 f. (Oecolampad's letter to Zwingli, April 9) and *ibid.*, 567-570 (Zwingli's letter to Krautwald, Schwenckfeld etc., dated April 17). The messenger's name was Matheus Winclerus, or Matthias Wicklerus (Z, IX, 100). Cf. also Appendix 2, note 2. On Hubmaier's recantations, see the Chapter III at footnote 17.
[167] Cf. the list in Z, II, 5 f. The reprints included expositions of Art. 33, 33-43 with part of Art. 64, 47-49, 52-54, 57-59 and 61-63.
[168] Schwenckfeld, 1524 and 1528. Zwingli's preface is dated August 24, 1528 (reprinted in CS, III, 4 and Z, VI, Part 2, 258 f.).
[169] Examples given by Bergsten, 1961, 417.
[170] E.g., Z, IX, 282 (1527); X, 307 (1529). Cf. also references to Bohemia in letters written to Zwingli: Z, VIII, 56 (1523, reading "Boemiam" instead of "Bremiam"; see Oecolampad, 1927, 205 f., n. 11); X, 30 f. (1529); X, 424 (1530); X, 629 (1530); XI, 41 (1530).

correspondence does not include a single letter to or from Moravia. Nor is the land, to our knowledge, mentioned by name in any of Zwingli's works.

We may conclude that his writings were reaching Moravia both from Switzerland — via Augsburg and other South German cities — and from Silesia. However, there are additional reasons why Silesia must be regarded as one of the chief sources of the pre-Anabaptist evangelical views spreading in Moravia.

Duke Friedrich II of Liegnitz, Brieg and Wohlau (1480-1547) was regarded, together with his brother-in-law, Georg the Margrave of Brandenburg, as one of the best friends and protectors of the *Unitas Fratrum*. After the death of King Louis II of the Jagiellon dynasty in the summer of 1526, the leading barons of the Unity proposed Duke Friedrich as a candidate for the Czech crown, against Ferdinand.[171] A personal friendship existed between Friedrich and the Lords Kostka of Postupice, members and powerful protectors of the Unity who resided in the city of Litomyšl. There, the three former monks from Breslau were received into the Unity. It is reasonable to suspect that the Silesian exiles resumed contact with their homeland after the Duke and their home city of Breslau joined the Reformation.

At his court, Friedrich employed, from 1518 till 1523, a Silesian nobleman, a knight of the Teutonic order, Caspar Schwenckfeld of Ossig (1489-1561).[172] Schwenckfeld was among the first followers of Luther in Silesia and through his influence, Friedrich introduced the Reformation in 1522. On account of impaired hearing, Schwenckfeld left the ducal services at Liegnitz in 1523 but remained in close contact with the court until his departure from Silesia in April 1529.

During the summer and fall of 1525 — the same period in which the exiled Silesian monks began to spread Zwinglian views on the

---

[171]   Bidlo, 1900, 5; Hrejsa, V, 126; Müller, I, 433, n. 365; Matusik, 1960, 207. Friedrich's mother, Ludmila, was the daughter of the "Hussite king", George of Poděbrady. Friedrich spoke the Czech language. On the later personal contacts between him and Bishop Jan Augusta, see Müller, II, 233 ff. Friedrich was the brother-in-law of Albrecht, Duke of Prussia. Cf. also our footnotes 88 above and 190 ff. in the next chapter.

[172]   On Schwenckfeld's life, see Schultz, 1946. Wolfgang Knörrlich, *Kaspar Schwenckfeld und die Reformation in Schlesien* (diss., Bonn, 1957) was not available to us. For a concise summary of Schwenckfeld's life and early theological development see Williams, 1962, 106-117 and Maleczyńska, 1960, 232 ff.

eucharist within the Unity — Schwenckfeld's deviation from Luther's doctrine, especially his view on the real presence, became known. In July, he wrote *Duodecim Questiones oder Argumenta contra impanationem* [173] and in November he journeyd to Wittenberg. In the early days of December he discussed his new concept personally with Luther and with others.[174] Luther rejected it, as a species of Zwinglian symbolism.[175] Zwingli acknowledged the affinity of Schwenckfeld's view with his own and published, as late as August 1528, one of Schwenckfeld's treatises with a commendatory preface.[176]

Schwenckfeld himself, however, soon drew a clear line of demarkation between Zwingli's interpretation of *est* as *significat* in the sense of a mere remembrance, and his own emphasis on the inner, spiritual *participatio* and *manducatio* of Christ. In keeping with the basic dualism of his emerging theological system, he began to distinguish between an external celebration of the Lord's Supper, a *commemoratio*, and an internal, spiritual communion with Christ. The relationship between the two communions was not defined unequivocally in Schwenckfeld's subsequent writings. According to some of his statements, the inner communion must precede the outward communion. Elsewhere, they occur simultaneously. More and more, however, Schwenckfeld emphasized the inward communion as a spiritual experience which takes place apart from the external communion.

In a circular letter, signed by himself, Crautwald and the pastors at Liegnitz on April 21, 1526 — only a month after the disputation in Slavkov, Moravia — Schwenckfeld announced his *Stillstand*, a suspension of the outward observance of the sacrament until a radical reform of doctrine and life should transform the church. What was first intended as a temporary measure became a perma-

---

[173] CS, II, 132-140.
[174] During his visit, Schwenckfeld talked also with Dr. Johannes Bugenhagen (Pomeranus) about the Czech Picards and passed on to him a copy of their confession: "... ich habe ihm gegeben der Pickarden Büchlin, darinnen sie ihre entschuldigung thůn, für dem König vnd den Herren zů Böhem" (Schwenckfeld's Diary from Wittenberg visit, December 1-4, 1525; CS, II, 272; cf. Schultz, 1946, 91). Undoubtedly, Bugenhagen received two brief German apologies of the Unity which had been translated by Zeising and presented to King Louis II and to the estates of the Bohemian diet in January 1525. See Müller-Bartoš, 343, Nos. 90-91.
[175] A summary of Schwenckfeld's doctrine of the eucharist and baptism is found in Maier, 1959, 18-25. For a thorough analysis, see Loetscher, 1906, 352-386 and 454-500. Cf. also Schultz, 1946, 60 ff.
[176] See note 168 above and Maier, 1959, 19, n. 4.

nent characteristic of Schwenckfeld's spiritualistic Reformation of tht 'Middle Way'.[177]

Article 3 of the agreement reached at Slavkov [178] — in which a sharp distinction between "an inner, spiritual communion" and "an outward communion of remembrance" is made — is strongly reminiscent of the Silesian spiritualism. The warning clause that "the outward communion should not be despised but observed according to the testament of Christ" points in the same direction. Similarly, Glaidt's own differentiation between an inward and outward baptism, and his retention of infant baptism, represents a concept parallel to Schwenckfeld's teaching on baptism. Schwenckfeld did not begin to question paedobaptism until 1527.[179] In his later writings he condemned the misuses of external baptism by the church but because of his preoccupation with the inner baptism of the Holy Spirit, he relegated water baptism, whether infant or adult, to the periphery of Christian experience. He never rejected infant baptism nor consistently approved of rebaptism.[180]

Since our knowledge of the views among the pre-Anabaptist German Evangelicals in South Moravia is limited to one main source, the report and commentary of Glaidt from March 1526, it is difficult to determine the extent of the influence of Silesian spiritualism. The later connections between South Moravia and Silesia [181], as well as the routes of travel mentioned above, should make the hypothesis of Silesian origin rather plausible.

[177]   The text of the letter is reproduced in CS, II, 329-333. Eng. tr. in Schultz, 1946, 106 ff. For other quotations from Schwenckfeld's writings, see Maier, 1959, 20 ff. and Williams, 1962, 113 ff.
[178]   See above at footnote 120.
[179]   The letter of Schwenckfeld and Crautwald to Jacob von Salza, Bishop of Breslau, October 1527 (CS, II, 657). Maier, 1959, 23, n. 2 suggests that the first Silesian attack on the efficacy of external baptism as a means of grace in the Lutheran sense came from the pen of Crautwald, possibly already in 1526.
[180]   In one of his later writings, Schwenckfeld declared that for a thousand years the church had not administered the sacrament of baptism correctly (CS, VII, 252). Cf. Urner, 1948 and Ecke, 1952. On the relationship of the Spirit to baptism, see Seeberg, 1929.
[181]   Both Simprecht Sorg, the printer, and Oswald Glaidt found refuge in Liegnitz in 1528 when persecution broke out in Moravia (Z, IX, 554 f.; HS, 398 and Bahlow, 1928, 7 ff.). Hubmaier dedicated his second treatise on the freedom of the will to Duke Friedrich on May 20, 1527 (HS, 400). One should be careful to distinguish between the contacts during the pre-Anabaptist period and those during the Anabaptist era at Mikulov. The latter contacts might not have been initiated until after the arrival of Gabriel Ascherham and his group from Silesia. See Chapter IV at footnotes 200 ff.

In the absence of conclusive evidence, we must explore additional avenues of influence. The majority of the evangelical refugees came to Moravia along the established travel routes. One is justified, therefore, to look to their cities and towns of origin in South Germany and in the different provinces of Austria for possible sources.

The Tirolese town of Hall, near the city of Innsbruck, was the field where Jakob Strauss began his public ministry as an evangelical preacher.[182] A native of Basel and a graduate of the University in Freiburg i.B., Strauss came to Hall as a doctor of theology in June 1521. When his evangelical preaching — in agreement with Luther — evoked great response among the people, the ecclesiastical authorities forced his expulsion from Hall on May 10, 1522, in spite of repeated protests and petitions by the town council and the burghers. As a preacher in Eisenach (Saxony) from January 1523, he maintained contact with the Evangelicals around Innsbruck. His books were circulated and read in Tirol.[183] Unrest related to the Peasant War in Thuringia forced Strauss to leave Eisenach in the early fall of 1525. After a brief stay in Nürnberg he was appointed preacher in Baden-Baden by Margrave Philip I. Nothing more is known about him after October 1527.

His eighteen writings, mostly sermons, appeared in forty-three separate editions, of which eight were printed in Strasbourg, two in Nürnberg and twelve in Augsburg. The majority came off the presses in Erfurt. In 1523, Strauss published two sermons on baptism which he had preached at Eisenach.[184] The main argument deals with the Roman Catholic ceremonial practices which accompanied the administration of infant baptism. Strauss defends the abolition of these

---

[182]   On the life and teachings of Strauss, see Barge, 1937; Rogge, 1957 and Macek, 1960b, 93 ff. and 106. Cf. also an annotated list of Strauss' 18 writings printed from 1522 till 1527, in Barge, 1935 and Rogge, 1957, 152 f. Neither the date of birth nor the date of death is certain. Barge sets the dates as 1480-1483 and prior to 1532.

[183]   In 1523 and 1524, his and other evangelical books were sold publicly on the market in Hall (Barge, 1937, 27).

[184]   *Von dem ynnerlichen vnnd ausserlichen Tauff eyn Christlych begründt leer, geprediget durch D. Ja. Straus zu Eyssnnach* (printed by Ludwig Trutebul in Erfurt, 1523) and *Wider den symoneischen tauff vnd erkauftn, ertichten krysem vnd oel, auch warin die recht cristlich tauff (allain võ Christo auffgesetzt) begriffen sey* ... (Printed in three editions: by Ludwig Trutebul in Erfurt 1523, by Melchior Ramminger in Augsburg 1523 and in Strasbourg 1524. We quote the title of the Augsburg edition.) Cf. Barge, 1935, 118 f., No. 7 and 8. The prints were not accessible to us. We follow the summary provided by Barge, 1937, 50-52 and Rogge, 1957, 54-60.

and points out that for the average person the outward ritual is the center of interest, whereas the real meaning of baptism, the cleansing of sins, is being overlooked. Baptism is "an outward sign of the inward work of God in the soul". Its effect involves "the whole process and content of our redemption", namely, the washing away of sin. A newly born child cannot tell the difference between good and bad and does not bring, therefore, consciously and willingly any sin into the world. The children participate in Christ through a sacrament when their parents and godparents show a genuine faith. Only in this sense Strauss postulates faith as a prerequisite of baptism. When a child grows up, the outward baptism by itself is no longer sufficient unto salvation. The effect of the sacrament must be renewed daily through personal faith. Strauss' baptismal theology was and remained, in its basic concepts, Luther's theology of infant baptism.[185]

In his subsequent attacks on Zwingli and Oecolampad, Strauss defended the real presence in the sacrament of the eucharist, against the Swiss who gave the people "only dry bread and sour wine".[186] He distinguished clearly between inward and outward communion. The "inner, spiritual eating of the body of Christ" is identical with faith, requires no outward sign and takes place, through faith, all the time. The sixth chapter in the Gospel of John speaks only about such

[185]   There can be no doubt that this is the only possible interpretation of a similar statement made by Glaidt in his commentary on Article 3: "What will baptism and Christ's Supper help me if I do not first, in faith, receive the inward baptism and supper?" Hubmaier's reference to "frembder glaub" as an argument used by the Moravian Evangelicals in their defense of infant baptism confirms such interpretation. Cf. footnotes 123 and 145 above. In their theology of baptism both Strauss and Glaidt are in basic agreement with Luther's understanding of baptism as outlined in his *Eyn Sermon von dem heyligen hochwirdigen Sacrament der Tauffe*, first printed in Wittenberg on November 9, 1519 and then reprinted in not less than 15 different editions (up to 1523) in several cities, including Nürnberg (WA, 2, 727-737; LW, 35, 29-43). For a comparison of Luther's baptismal theology with that of Strauss, see Rogge, 1957, 58 ff. and Oyer, 1964, 112, n. 4 and 5.
[186]   Quoted by Barge, 1937, 124 and 141. The two polemical writings are the last known printed works of Strauss: *Wider den vnmilten Irrthum Maister Vlrichs zwinglins, So er verneünet, die warhafftig gegenwirtigkait dess allerhailligsten leybs vnd blůts Christi im Sacrament* (printed in Augsburg, June 1526) and *Das der war leyb Christi vnd seyn heiliges blůt, im Sakrament gegenwertig sey ...* (completed in January 1527 and printed in Augsburg in October 1527). Cf. Barge, 1935, 251 f., Nos. 17 and 18. E. Staehelin in Oecolampad, 1934, p. 13, n. 1, surmised that Strauss had difficulty finding a printer and finally had the last named treatise printed by Simprecht Sorg in Nikolsburg. The evidence which Barge cites in favour of Augsburg is conclusive and was accepted by Staehelin, 1939, 326, n. 1. Zwingli's reply to Strauss, *Antwort über Straussens Büchlein ...* was printed in Zürich early in January 1527 (Z, V, 453-547).

eating. The outward communion is based entirely on Christ's words of institution (Matthew 26, Mark 16, Luke 22 and I Cor. 11). In the eucharist, "Christ gives his body and blood in outward, visible signs which can be attested by human senses (*empfindliche Zeichen*) and are consumed bodily". But even in outward communion, "his most holy body and his precious blood remain invisible and incomprehensible to all senses and human reason. Nonetheless, they are truly present by the effective power of his eternal word".[187]

Strauss' polemic against Zwingli's interpretation of the eucharist was not printed until June 1526, three months after the disputation in Slavkov, and thus could not have prejudiced Glaidt — who expressed a symbolic and spiritualizing concept of the sacrament — against following some of Strauss' views on baptism outlined in his earlier sermons. The knowledge of Strauss' tracts in Moravia can be postulated as probable although it has not been attested by any known sources.[188] It is also worth noting that in the fall of 1524, the Anabaptist Brethren in Zürich regarded Strauss, alongside with Müntzer, Carlstadt and Michael Stiefel, as a champion of their cause.[189]

Recently, Hillerbrand has suggested that a common ideological influence of Erasmus, Carlstadt and Müntzer must be recognized as one of the decisive factors which led to the emergence of Anabaptism in Germany and especially in Zürich.[190] The two motifs which Hillerbrand defined as the common characteristics of the three leaders — so different in other respects! — were: "a revision, if not outright

[187] Quotations from Barge, 1937, 140 f. Cf. also Z, V, 454. For a discussion of the eucharistic controversy between Strauss and Zwingli (and Oecolampad) see Köhler, 1924, 400 ff. and Rogge, 1957, 131 ff.

[188] Odložilík, 1923, 346 and 356, enumerates the names of German and Swiss Reformers who were known to the Habrovanites and to Kalenec. Strauss is not included. Cf. footnote 35 above. Strauss' sermon on confession, *Ain New wunderbarlich Beychtbüchlein*, printed in seven editions in 1523-1524, might have been known to Hans Spittelmaier when he wrote his *Entschuldigung* in 1524. Cf. his Art. 7 at footnote 97 above and Barge, 1935, 112 ff.

[189] "Wir versehend unss fil gůtz zů Jacobo Struss und anderen etlichen. . . . Wann so du und Caralostadius, Jacobus Struss und Michel Stifel nit gar rein zeflissen sin woltind (alss ich aber und mine brüder hoffend, ir werdins tůn), were ess wol ein ellend evangelium in die welt kummen" (*TQ Schweiz*, I, 16 and 20: the letter of Grebel and the Brethren to Müntzer, September 5, 1524). The inclusion of Strauss seems to have been occasioned by Grebel's acquaintance with Strauss' booklet against usury which was printed in four editions in 1523 (Barge, 1935, 248 f., No. 13). Cf. Grebel's letter to Vadian, July 15, 1523 (*TQ Schweiz*, I, 2).

[190] Hillerbrand, 1962a, 152 ff. Cf. also his earlier article, Hillerbrand, 1960b. It is not necessary to refer, in this connection, to the extensive bibliography dealing with the relationship of Anabaptism to Erasmus, Carlstadt and Müntzer.

repudiation of Luther's basic distinction between Law and Gospel" and "the spiritualization of the Christian religion".[191] It is the latter trend, with its particular bearing on the concept of sacraments, which must be examined as another possible source of the views which characterized the pre-Anabaptist Evangelicals in Moravia.

The circulation of the works of Erasmus, both in their original editions and in Czech translations, is well attested in the sources from 1513 onward.[192] A distinction between the external and the internal, the physical and the spiritual, was basic for Erasmus' piety. The disparagement of the external in favour of the internal had significant implications for the concept of baptism and communion.[193] The statements of Glaidt concerning the sacraments could be interpreted as echoes of Erasmian thought.

Similarly, in the case of Andreas Bodenstein of Carlstadt we are interested, in the present context, only in his concept of eucharist and baptism.[194] His seven tracts on communion were brought to Zürich by his friend, Gerhard Westerburg, early in October 1524, and their printing in Basel was arranged by Felix Mantz. The printing of the eighth tract, *Von dem Touff der Kinder*, was prevented by Oecolampad, presumably because it rejected infant baptism. The manuscript has not been discovered thus far but Carlstadt's views on baptism are most likely reflected in Mantz' *Protestatio* which Mantz submitted to the City Council of Zürich.[195] Carlstadt estab-

---

[191]   Hillerbrand, 1962a, 178 f. Concerning the 'spiritualization', Hillerbrand explains further: "In this they betray the influence of Luther whose stress on the centrality of faith had established a precarious balance between the 'objective' and the 'subjective'. This balance is repudiated in favour of the latter and made identical with the 'spiritual'. This had implications particularly in regard to the sacraments, which could no longer be 'objective' vehicles of divine grace but had to be of 'subjective' or 'spiritual' significance" (*ibid.*, 179).

[192]   See footnotes 43-47 above. One should note especially the Czech translation of the *Enchiridion* in 1519.

[193]   Hillerbrand, 1962a, 160. Cf. also Köhler, 1924, 49 ff.; Auer, 1954; Bartoš, 1958a and Bergsten, 1961, 441 ff. Gottfried G. Krodel, *Die Abendmahlslehre des Erasmus von Rotterdam und seine Stellung am Anfang des Abendmahlsstreites der Reformatoren* (Unpubl. theol. dissertation, Erlangen, 1955) was not accessible to us.

[194]   The main work on Carlstadt is Barge, I and II. A new evaluation of Carlstadt was attempted by Rupp, 1959 and Hillerbrand, 1966. Cf. also Fuchs, 1954; Vasella, 1956; Hillerbrand, 1962, 161-168 and Bergsten, 1961, 258-261. A reprint of eight writings from 1523-1525 in Carlstadt, I and II (bibliography in vol. I, VIII f.).

[195]   The full text is reprinted in *TQ Schweiz*, I, 23-28. The hypothesis was proposed by Rupp, 1959, 321 f., n. 3. Krajewski, 1954, 1957 and 1962 ignored the influence of Carlstadt. Fast, 1962a, 470 ff. suggested that Mantz used a collection of prooftexts prepared by Conrad Grebel late in 1524. According to Fast, the same

lished personal contact with the Grebel circle in Zürich late in October 1524 but did not meet Zwingli.

Carlstadt's dichotomy between the physical (outward) and spiritual (inward) things can be traced to some of his earliest writings. Already in 1520, in his treatise" On Holy Water and Salt",[196] Carlstadt maintained that water and salt were mere signs pointing to spiritual realities. Water remains water and "even if one poured the whole river Tiber and Elbe, Rhine and Danube over a sinner, his sins would not be washed away". In his three early writings on the eucharist,[197] in 1521, he underlined the spiritual understanding of the sacrifice of Christ by the believer as the real communion, in contrast to the less important observance of the outward signs. Bread and wine possess no magic power but are signs and seals of God's manifold promises. The seven communion tracts published in Basel during the late fall of 1524 represent the final clarification of Carlstadt's symbolic and spiritualizing interpretation of the eucharist.[198]

In his concept of baptism, he began to differentiate, already in 1523, between the outward sign of water and the inward spiritual renewal of the person.[199] The ultimate consequence had to be a consistent rejection of infant baptism.[200]

---

collection was used by Hans Krüsi in the writing of his booklet, *Von dem Glaubenn ... Von dem Tauff Christi,* printed 1525, probably in Augsburg (*ibid.,* 473 f.).

[196] *Von geweihtem Wasser und Salz* (August 15, 1520), summary in Barge, I, 209-211.

[197] *Von den Emphahern Zeichen und Zusag des heiligen Sacraments, Fleisch und Blut Christi* (June 24, 1521); *Von Anbetung und Ehrerbietung der Zeichen des Neuen Testamentes* (dedicated to the artist Albrecht Dürer in Nürnberg, November 1, 1521) and *Von beiden Gestalten der heiligen Messe* (November 11/30, 1521); summary and quotations in Barge, I, 281-285, 328-338.

[198] Cf. Köhler, 1924, 67 ff. and Hillerbrand, 1966, 390 ff.

[199] "Das bedeutet auch die Taufe, damit die Apostel besprengt haben und wir jetzt eintauchen, dass die Hitze und Begierden und Lüste sollen ausgetilgt sein, wie man Feuer mit Wasser dämpfet oder auslöscht, und ist das Begräbnis in und mit Christo. Denn wie Christus im verneuten Leben ist aufgestanden und das sterbliche Leben in ein unsterblich verwandelt hat, also soll der alte Adam in uns mit allen seinen Begierden und Eigenwillen und Ungehorsam sterben und im Grabe liegen und unser leben neu sein in Gehorsam und Gottes willen." — "Wiewohl die Beschneidung und Taufe und andere äusserliche Zeichen weder fromm, weder böse machen, vereinen auch Gott nicht — da der ewige Gottes Wille, mit Herzen angenommen, den Menschen Gott vereint und anleimt — : dennoch mussten die Gläubigen solche äusserliche Ding in ihrer Weise annehmen und als Zeichen der innerlichen Gerechtigkeit und Einigkeit gebrauchen." Quoted by Barge, II, 84, from *Von Mannigfältigkeit des einfältigen einigen Willen Gottes* (March 1523). Cf. Carlstadt's statement with Glaidt's commentary on Art. 3 and 4 (at footnote 122 above).

[200] See quotations gathered by Hillerbrand, 1962, 166, n. 71.

Carlstadt's writings were known in Moravia,[201] at least among the Czech radicals. It is very likely that they had influenced also the thinking of the German Evangelicals, including Glaidt.

By contrast, any direct influence of the printed works of Müntzer is doubtful. His vocabulary, so strikingly different from the Moravian sources under discussion; his theological argumentation; his open attacks on infant baptism: [202] these and other considerations make it obvious that, in spite of his earlier sojourn in Bohemia (1521), his writings and ideas seem to have remained outside the Moravian orbit of interest as it is documented by the German and Czech sources up to the spring of 1526.[203]

An investigation of sources for the Moravian religious development should also include an examination of the theological views prevalent in the important Reformation centers in South Germany during the same years. Cities like Nürnberg,[204] Augsburg,[205] Regensburg,[206]

---

[201] Müller-Bartoš, 283, n. 234. Note also the reprints of Carlstadt's writings by Philipp Ulhart in Augsburg, 1524-1525 (Schottenloher, 1921, Nos. 80, 81, 104, 105, 106).

[202] *Protestation oder Entbietung* (1524): "Ich bitte alle Buchstabengelehrten, dass sie mir anzeigen, wo es in dem heiligen Buchstaben steht, dass ein einziges unmündiges Kindlein getauft sei von Christo und seinen Boten oder verordnet sei, unsre Kinder also wie jetzund zu taufen" (Brandt, 1933, 134). "Die rechte Taufe ist nicht verstanden. Darum ist der Eingang zur Christenheit zum viehischen Affenspiel worden. Aus einem sandigen Grunde haben die Schriftgelehrten die elende, traurige Mutter, die liebe Christenheit, über die Massen hoch betrogen" (135). "Da man unmündige Kinder zu Christen machte and liess die Catechumenos abgehen, wurden die Christen auch Kinder, wie ihnen doch Paulus verboten hatte, denn da verschwand aller Verstand aus der Kirche. Da ward die rechte Taufe verblümet mit der leidigen heuchlerischen Gevatterschaft, da man viel gelobt mit grossem Gepränge und hälts wie der Hund mit der Wurst" (136). "In dieser Entbietung ... habe ich gesagt von dem Schaden der Kirche, welcher durch die unverstandene Taufe und gedichteten Glauben uns überfallen hat" (143). Cf. also the quotations and analysis of Müntzer's thought by Hillerbrand, 1962a, 168-177 and Armour, 1966, 59 ff.

[203] The statement applies only to this period. The later echoes of Müntzerite theology in the controversy between Hans Hut and Hubmaier at Mikulov in 1527 are a different matter.

[204] The conditions in Nürnberg are of particular relevance. The city of Albrecht Dürer and Hans Sachs became a center of radicalism in 1524-1525. Müntzer visited N. and had his last attack on Luther, *Hoch verursachte Schutzrede*, printed by four employees in the printing shop of Hans Hergott in October 1524 (cf. Hillerbrand, 1964a). Hans Denck was schoolmaster at St. Sebald school and was involved in the procedings against the "godless painters" (Hans Greiffenberger, Sebald and Barthel Behaim, Georg Penz and Hans Platner) who denied the real presence in the eucharist and some of whom rejected infant baptism. The preserved protocol of the hearings (January 1525) shows the influence of Carlstadt and

Ulm [207] and Strasbourg [208] played a decisive role during the formative stage of the Reformation in general, and of the Radical Reformation in particular.

The enthusiasm for Luther's message was beginning to give way to an uncertainty about its specific implications to which a theological free-for-all promptly addressed itself. Pamphlets of all levels of theological sophistication appeared in great numbers. The result was frequently an open or latent deviation from the position of the Wittenberg reformer.[209]

Views not only deviating but deliberately mediating between the positions of the great Reformers were expressed. It was precisely these 'hotbeds' of evangelical radicalism which from 1526 onward became the focal points of the South German Anabaptist movement.

There were live connections between these cities and the evangelical refugee circles in South Moravia. An attempt, however, to review the situation in each of the cities mentioned above would lead far beyond the scope and purpose of our present investigation.

Finally, the theological heritage of the Czech Reformation must not be overlooked as an important source for the rise of religious radicalism in Moravia.

Hrejsa has pointed out [210] that the concept of the eucharist expressed in 1522 by Beneš Optát in his questions addressed to

---

Müntzer. Both Denck and the 'painters' distinguished between outward (*eusserlich*) and inward (*innerlich, inwendig*) bread in communion and between outward and inward baptism. Cf. Kolde, 1888 and 1902; Roth, 1885, esp. Chapter 6, "Der Abendmahlstreit und die Wiedertäufer"; Evans, 1924; Krodell, 1956; Baring, 1959; Philoon, 1962; Clasen, 1965 and Strauss, 1966.

[205] For the evangelical movement and early Anabaptism in Augsburg, see Meyer, 1874; Roth, 1901b; Schottenloher, 1921 and Schwab, 1962.

[206] Cf. *TQ*, X, Bibliography, Nos. 448 f.

[207] Cf. *TQ*, X, Bibliography, Nos. 496 ff.

[208] Cf. *TQ*, X, Bibliography, Nos. 476-492. The writings of the lay preacher Clemens Ziegler deserve special attention, esp. *Von der waren nyessung beid leibs und bluts Christi . . . und von dem Tauff* (Strasbourg, 1524). Excerpts reprinted in *TQ Elsass*, I, 11-17. According to Molnár, 1957a, 24 ff., Ziegler's concept of the eucharist and baptism corresponds to the teaching of the *Unitas Fratrum*. The editors of *TQ Elsass*, I (p. 18) suggest the influence of Jacob Strauss' second baptismal tract which we have discussed above at footnote 184. See also Peter, 1954. In one of his other books, *Ein fast schon büchlin* (Strasbourg, 1525) Ziegler condemned the Bohemians (Utraquists) for giving communion to small children who cannot confess faith (*TQ Elsass*, I, 32).

[209] Hillerbrand, 1962a, 153.

[210] Hrejsa, IV, 287-299. Cf. Peschke, 1935, 358.

Speratus — and then forwarded to Luther — differed both from Luther's and Zwingli's (later) interpretation and could, therefore, have its origin only in the older traditions of the Czech Reformation, especially those of the Taborites and the Unity. As could be expected, the Czech radical groups in Moravia, such as the followers of Dubčanský or Kalenec, drew more on the domestic than on foreign sources.[211]

However, the ideas of the Czech Reformation penetrated also into the German evangelical circles. Odložilík established evidence of Taborite teaching on the eucharist [212] in the writings of Zeising, who knew Czech.[213] Meetings such as the disputation in Slavkov, and other contacts with the Czech population must have spread some knowledge of the theological heritage of the Czech Reformation among the German Evangelicals in Moravia.

*

In this chapter we have attempted to draw a comprehensive picture of the religious scene in Moravia prior to the appearance of the Anabaptist refugees in 1526. We have also tried to demonstrate how complex were the influences which shaped the theological outlook of the Czech and German evangelical groups, and how widespread were their contacts, both in terms of geography and ideology.

The significance of all these factors for Moravian Anabaptism and for its encounter with other groups, in particular with the *Unitas Fratrum*, is obvious. One need no longer wonder why, from the very beginning, the Anabaptist refugees entered Moravia in such large numbers: They followed the routes already known to the evangelical refugees.

Nor can one be surprised at the heterogeneity of the Anabaptist movement in Moravia. This variety, too, was a continuation of the pattern established during the pre-Anabaptist phase and was due

[211] Cf. our analysis at footnotes 33 and 35 above.
[212] A figurative interpretation of 'est' in the words of institution. Odložilík, 1923, 23, n. 1; 25, n. 4; 26, n. 1, refers to a Taborite eucharistic tract by Jan Němec of Žatec. For the Taborite teachings, see Peschke, 1935, 83-95.
[213] Zeising translated two brief apologies of the Unity in 1525. Cf. Müller, I, 561, Nos. 90 and 91: "Verdolmetzt vom Behemischen yns Deutzsche. Durch Johannem Zeysinck."

to the complex sources of ideological influences and to varied strata
of ethnic background.

Moravia, the sixteenth-century haven for "hunted heretics", beck-
oned to all. Here they could find a refuge and feel at home.[214]

---

[214] Cf. Hubmaier's statement in the preface to his eucharistic tract, *Ein ainfeltige
vnderricht*, addressed to Leonhart of Liechtenstein in the fall of 1526. He compares Nikolsburg to Nicopolis, the new name for the biblical "Emmaus". He recalls how the two disciples walked to Emmaus and persuaded Jesus to break bread
with them in the evening. "Also sey eben Christus nach der freydenreychen
vrsteend seins lebendigen worts newlicher Jaren vnder dem aller Christenlichsten
Fürsten vnd Herren, Herrn Friderichen Hertzogen in Sachsen etc., durch D. Mar-
tinum Luther anfencklich beschehen, vnd darnach gen Emaus, das ist Nicolspurg,
gewalfartet, durch seine diener da zůbleiben erbetten, wann es fahe an nacht
werden vnd kummen die letsten tag, vnd ist also in der brechung des brots gnedigk-
lich von jnen erkennt worden . . . . Was Jch als ein vnwirdiger Pilgran Christi,
der . . . als ein verfierer, auffrürer vnnd ertzketzer verschreyt, was ich ja darzů
helffen mag, damit nun die Eer Gottes vnnd seyn heylig wort bezeügt werde, bin
ich vrbittig, willig vnnd berayt solchs zůthon . . ." (*HS*, 289).

III

HUBMAIER AND THE CZECH REFORMATION
(WHY HUBMAIER WENT TO MORAVIA)

In the preceding chapter, we have come to the conclusion that the
rise of Anabaptism in Moravia can be dated with the arrival of Balthasar Hubmaier at Mikulov in the summer of 1526. The character of
the earliest Moravian Anabaptism appears to have been moulded
chiefly by Hubmaier, either by his direct personal and literary influence, or by opposition to it. His books printed in Moravia from
July 1526 to June 1527 constitute the main source materials for our
knowledge of that period.[1] We shall, therefore, scrutinize his writings
for evidences of knowledge of the Czech Reformation groups as well
as of the (pre-Anabaptist) German Evangelicals in Moravia. Such
analysis should provide at least a partial answer to the question: Why
did Hubmaier go to Moravia?

The reasons which motivated Hubmaier to seek refuge in Mikulov
cannot be determined too readily nor finally. Among the many students of Hubmaier's life and theology, only Bergsten[2] offers a few
marginal suggestions in order to explain why the famous Anabaptist

---

[1]   Other in-group primary sources for this period consist of (1) a few court statements by Anabaptists who had been in Moravia during this period; (2) the Hutterite
chronicles which were written at a much later date.

[2]   Bergsten, 1961, prepared simultaneously with the critical edition of Hubmaier's writings (HS), represents the most dependable historical study of Hubmaier. Cf. the reviews by Říčan in TPKR, 1962, 150-154 and by Friedmann in
MQR, 36 (1962), 356-362. Other important studies on Hubmaier: Bergsten, 1959,
Hošek, 1867 (Eng. tr. 1891-1892), Loserth, 1891 and 1893, Macoskey, 1956, Mau,
1912, Newman, 1926, Sachsse, 1914, Schulze, 1957, Seewald, 1953, Teufel, 1941,
113-127, Theobald, 1941, Vedder, 1905, Wiswedel, 1939 and 1940a, Yoder, 1959,
Klaassen, 1966a and Armour, 1966 (Chapter I). Cf. also TQ, X, Bibliography,
Nos. 1602-1640a. For a complete list of all known sources for Hubmaier's life and
thought, incl. his correspondence and statements in court hearings, see Bergsten,
1961, 55-69.

leader decided to migrate from Zürich to "distant" Moravia. The subject of our research into the relationship between the Anabaptists and the Czech Brethren in Moravia calls for a more thorough investigation of Hubmaier's possible contacts with the Czech Reformation prior to his arrival at Mikulov. What — if anything — did he know about the situation in Moravia?

1. HUBMAIER'S LIFE AND RELIGIOUS DEVELOPMENT

Balthasar Hubmaier[3] was born in the small town of Friedberg near Augsburg in the early 1480's. After Latin schooling in Augsburg, he was matriculated as a student at the University of Freiburg i.B. on May 1, 1503. With the exception of a few months in 1507 which he spent earning a much needed income as teacher in Schaffhausen, Hubmaier stayed in Freiburg for almost nine years. He became *baccalaureus artium* in 1504, *magister artium* in 1505 or 1506, *baccalaureus biblicus* on August 1, 1511 and *sententiarius* on March 27, 1512. He was greatly influenced by his teacher and close personal friend, Dr. Johannes Eck (1486-1543), the famous opponent of Luther in later years. Another teacher in Freiburg was Wolfgang Capito, the future Reformer in Strasbourg. Hubmaier also made personal acquaintance with Urbanus Rhegius, subsequently the Reformer in Augsburg, and developed a life-long friendship with Dr. Johannes Faber (Heigerlin, 1478-1541), a student in Freiburg since 1509. In 1518, Faber became vicar general to the Bishop of Constance; in September 1523 he entered the services of Archduke Ferdinand (King of Bohemia and Moravia, 1526-1564) and moved to Vienna, where eventually he became the Bishop of Vienna in 1530.[4]

Most likely, Hubmaier was ordained into the priesthood in the city of Constance. In 1512 he followed his beloved teacher, Eck, to the University of Ingolstadt and was matriculated there on February 13. As a protégé of Eck, Hubmaier advanced quickly in his academic career. He was granted the degrees of a licentiate and of a doctor of

---

[3] In addition to the detailed biographies of Hubmaier listed in the preceding footnote, two concise summaries have been published recently: in German, Bergsten's historical introduction in *HS*, 9-43; in English, Chapter 4 of Estep, 1963. Cf. also Williams, 1962, 64 ff., 134 ff., 156 ff., 218 ff. In our biographical sketch, we follow mainly Bergsten.

[4] On Faber, see Staub, 1911, Helbling, 1933 and 1941, Rezek, 1882.

theology (August 31 and September 2, 1512). He became professor of theology, and, in 1515, vice-rector of the university. At the same time he served as a parish minister.

The spreading fame of his pulpit eloquence — and the probable assistance of Eck — led to his call to Regensburg where he became the chief preacher (*Domprediger*) at the cathedral in January 1516. For five years he stood in the center of the religious and civic life of the imperial city. He became one of the chief spokesmen in a turbulent crusade against the Jews, who were accused of charging exorbitant interest and were finally expelled from the city in February 1519.[5] On the site of the destroyed synagogue a chapel was erected and dedicated "to the Beauteous Mary" (*zur schönen Maria*). It became a center for pilgrimages. Hubmaier preached to large crowds of pilgrims who streamed to Regensburg from all over Germany and from the neighbouring countries.[6] He kept a daily record of miracles which reportedly took place. At that time, Hubmaier was one of the best-known popular Catholic preachers in South Germany. He appears to have been so preoccupied with his daily ceremonial and administrative duties that he paid little or no attention to the Leipzig disputation between his esteemed teacher Eck and Martin Luther, nor to the continuing debate.

His rather sudden departure from Regensburg for the small town of Waldshut on the border of Switzerland at the end of the year 1520, or early in 1521, can be understood in the light of Hubmaier's own reference to an outbreak of pestilence in Regensburg.[7] However, it also meant a return to a region with which he was familiar from his student days in Freiburg. Waldshut was subject to the episcopal see at Constance where Johannes Faber was vicar general, and was under the direct political rule of the Habsburgs. Important routes of travel and communication met and crossed in Waldshut: from

---

[5] Hubmaier's reputation as a crusader against the Jews was recorded in several contemporary chronicles, including the Czech *Kronika česká* (1541) by the Catholic priest Václav Hájek of Libočany (Wenceslaus Hagecius, d. 1553). It is one of the few references to Hubmaier in the Czech sources (German ed., Hagecius, 1697, 856).

[6] In the year 1520, nearly 120,000 special medallions made of lead or silver were sold to pilgrims (Bergsten, 1961, 87). A detailed account of the pilgrimages is given in Theobald, 1936, 49-98.

[7] Hubmaier's letter to Johannes Sapidus in Schlettstadt, dated in Waldshut, October 26, 1521, reprinted in *TQ Elsass*, I, 40-42. Reference to pestilence on p. 41, line 27. Cf. also *HS*, 279.

Strasbourg and Freiburg to Zürich and, along the river Rhine, to Basel.

Hubmaier took full advantage of the proximity of the two emerging centers of the Swiss Reformation. The preserved correspondence with his humanist friends during 1521 and 1522 [8] reveals that he used the relative quietness of the small town for a systematic study of the Pauline epistles. According to his letter to Sapidus, he was acquainted with Erasmus' *Paraphrases in epistolas Pauli ad Rhomanos, Corinthios et Galatas* (printed in Basel 1520) and *Ratio seu compendium verae theologiae* (Basel 1519). In the same year (1521) he sent a copy of the first edition of Oecolampad's *Judicium de doctore Martino Luthero* (1520-1521) to Beatus Rhenanus. On June 23, 1522, he reported his study of Luther's tracts on communion *sub utraque specie*.[9] Shortly before that he had visited Freiburg i.B. and Basel where, among other contacts, he discussed with Erasmus the question of purgatory and the exegesis of John 1:13.[10]

For a brief period (November 11, 1522-March 1, 1523) Hubmaier accepted the invitation of the city council of Regensburg and returned to the pilgrimage chapel *zur schönen Maria*, without resigning

[8]   Letters to Beatus Rhenanus (1521) and to Johannes Sapidus (October 26, 1521) in Schlettstadt (Alsatia), to Johannes Adelphius, physician in Schaffhausen (June 23, 1522) and to Wolfgang Rychard, city physician in Ulm (January 17, 1523). Cf. Bergsten, 1961, 57, Nos. 5-8 (with references to modern reprints of the correspondence) and his analysis, *ibid.*, 97-106.

[9]   "Libellos Lutheri sub utraque specie et de Coena habeo. Judicium Tuum de libello sub utraque specie exopto te." Letter to Joh. Adelphius printed by Veesenmeyer, 1826, 234. For identification of Luther's writings, see Sachsse, 1914, 132 and Bergsten, 1961, 101, n. 38. To the three suggestions made, another one might be added, viz., *Eyn Sermon von dem Hochwirdigen Sacrament des Heyligen Waren Leychnams Christi Und von den Bruderschafften* (first ed. before December 24, 1519; *WA*, 2, 742-758; *LW*, 35, 49-73). It contains a reference to the decree of the Council of Basel (1433) which allowed the Hussites to receive communion under both kinds (*WA*, 2, 742; *LW*, 35, 50).

[10] "Descendi Basileam, ubi Buschium accessi, hominem vere doctum, et Glareanum, item Erasmum salutavi; multa cum illo de Purgatorio contuli, ac super iis duobus passibus Jo. I: Neque ex voluntate carnis, neque ex voluntate viri. Erasmus aliquandiu de Purgatorio continuit se, sed tandem umbratilem adducens responsionem ad multa alia et varia quidem properavit. Libere loquitur Erasmus, sed anguste scribit. Sed de iis tecum. Veni et in Friburgum, quod longe aliter, quam nomen sonat, offendi. Plane liberum non est, sed captivum, discordiis et factionibus cum profanis et sacrilegis onustum. Dein rursus in Basileam migrans optimos comites meos Basileenses et ego recomitatus sum. Tractavimus multa in itinere et docta et profunda. Cum Pelicano non multa nugatus sum, qui tarde rediit ex capitulo suo." Letter to Adelphius, June 23, 1522 (Veesenmeyer, 1826, 233 f.). Discussion of the letter in Bergsten, 1961, 100 f.

from his post in Waldshut. A preserved letter written from Regensburg on January 17, 1523, indicates that the man who was asked to revive the declining pilgrimages was no longer interested in recording Marian miracles. Instead he began to expound the Gospel of Luke in a systematic fashion and rejoiced in the spread of evangelical doctrines in Bavaria.[11] Without any open hostility, he left the city and resumed his work in Waldshut.

The sustained study of the Scriptures, enforced by the influence of Luther and Erasmus, produced a gradual shift from Roman Catholicism to an evangelical position. The return to Regensburg in the winter of 1522-1523 no doubt accelerated the inner conflict and led to a break with the old church.[12]

From the spring of 1523 until his forced departure from Switzerland in April or May 1526, Hubmaier became oriented increasingly towards the Reformation in Zürich, with additional contacts in Basel, Schaffhausen, St. Gallen and Appenzell.[13]

On May 1, 1523, he conversed with Zwingli, *auff dem Zürchgraben*, about the scriptural basis for infant baptism. According to Hubmaier's own later testimony, Zwingli agreed with him that "children should not be baptized before they can be instructed in faith".[14] Elsewhere in retrospect, Hubmaier might have implied his doubts about infant baptism as early as 1520.[15]

In theological agreement with Zwingli, Hubmaier took part in the

---

[11] "Nobiscum per Bavariam multi sunt qui satis callent et evangelizant Evangelicam institutionem." Referring to Nürnberg, Hubmaier wrote: "Christus a tribus concionatoribus . . . syncerissime praedicatur." Letter to Wolfgang Rychard in Ulm quoted by Sachsse, 1914, 133.

[12] For the dating of Hubmaier's "inner change" we accept the conclusive evidence provided by Bergsten's meticulous research. See esp. Bergsten, 1961, 106, n. 56. Cf. also the reference "jnnerhalb fier jaren" (*HS*, 272) which points back to the fall of 1522.

[13] Since our main interest is in Hubmaier's relationship to the Czech Reformation, we shall not review in detail his contacts with Zwingli nor with the Swiss Brethren (Anabaptists). See Bergsten, 1961, 108-395 and his summary in *HS*, 16-33; Yoder, 1959 and 1962, 58 ff., 79 ff., 173. On Hubmaier's relationship to the rise of Anabaptism in St. Gallen, see also Fast, 1960, 226 f., n. 10.

[14] "Da Hastu mir recht geben, das man die Kinder nit Tauffen solle, ee sy im glauben vnderricht seyent." *HS*, 186. Cf. *TQ Schweiz*, I, 195.

[15] In his booklets against Zwingli's and Oecolampad's defense of infant baptism: *HS*, 173 (preface written in 1526) and 260 (completed in the fall of 1526, or possibly early 1527). The two references, identically phrased and somewhat indefinite in their meaning, can hardly be regarded as convincing evidence about such early questioning of infant baptism. See also Armour, 1966, 59 ff., for a discussion of influences on Hubmaier.

Second Disputation in Zürich, October 23-26, 1523. Gradually, he introduced Reformation practices in Waldshut. The repeated Austrian demands for his arrest and the increasing military threat to Waldshut forced him into temporary exile in Schaffhausen (August 29 to October 27, 1524). Upon his return he began to preach publicly against infant baptism. Wilhelm Reublin, a former priest, expelled from Zürich after the first rebaptism took place there on January 21, 1525, visited Waldshut a few days afterwards and baptized several local citizens. At that time, Hubmaier hesitated to put his preaching into practice. However, when Reublin returned at Easter time, Hubmaier and some sixty other persons submitted to rebaptism on April 15, 1525. Subsequently, Hubmaier baptized three hundred persons including the majority of the members of the town council. A parish church was transformed into an Anabaptist congregation.[16]

The bold introduction of Anabaptism could not mean anything less than the loss of friendship with the Reformers (Zwingli, Oecolampad, Hofmeister and Capito) for Hubmaier, and complete political isolation for the burghers of Waldshut in their struggle against the Habsburgs. The defeat of the peasants in the battle at Griessen (east of Waldshut) on November 4, 1525, eliminated the last ally. A few hours before Waldshut surrendered, without battle, Hubmaier escaped to Zürich on December 5, 1525.

He was received by his Anabaptist friends but arrested a few days later by order of the City Council. After a non-public disputation with Zwingli and his associates on December 19, Hubmaier prepared a recantation and agreed to read it at a service in the *Fraumünster* church on December 29. However, when he mounted the pulpit after Zwingli's sermon, he proceeded to defend believer's baptism. After prolonged imprisonment he read his recantation three or four times [17]

---

[16]   *TQ Schweiz*, I, 391 f.

[17]   The conflicting reports in the sources may be interpreted as complementary. The official record of the Zürich City Council (*TQ Schweiz*, I, 196 f.) sets the first recantation for Friday April 13 in the Fraumünster, the second for Sunday morning April 15 in the Grossmünster and then ("darnach") a third one in the St. Peter's Church in Zürich (no date given). Bullinger, 1838, 304 f., does not specify the number of recantations in Zürich but simply says that H. "that ein rächten widerrüff, zum ersten in der Statt Zürych, demnach zü Gossow in der herrschafft Grüningen". This could mean four recantations altogether. Loserth, 1893, 122, n. 1, misquoted Bullinger and confused his date for Hubmaier's release from the jail (April 6) with the date of recantation. Bullinger mentions places but gives no dates. The report of the Zürich Councillor Fridli Bluntschli (reprinted by Fast, 1959, 170) lists three recantations: in Fraumünster (no date), a second one on Sun

in the middle of April 1526. He was banished from the Zürich area, but in order to minimize the danger of his capture by Austrian authorities — who had repeatedly demanded his extradition — the Council allowed him to stay for a few more weeks, hidden in the house of an unnamed citizen.[18] The order of the Council to clear up his financial affairs and to reimburse the city for the expenses incurred by his case,[19] as well as the poor state of his health, were no doubt contributing factors.

In all likelihood, Hubmaier was not escorted to the Swiss border until the early or middle part of May.[20] He made a brief stop in Con-

---

day April 15 (no place given) and a third one, "demnach einer zů Grüningen" (no date). Yoder, 1962, 81, n. 9, misunderstood Bluntschli's dating. Stumpf, 1952, 291 records three recantations, without dates: two in Zürich and one in Gossau. For analysis of the mutual dependance of these sources, see Fast, 1959, 116. The wavering attitude of Hubmaier and the complex motives for his recantation are scrutinized by Bergsten, 1961, 383-394 and by Yoder, 1962, 79-89.

[18] Stumpf, 1952, 291: ". . . ward er eynem burger heimlich bevolhen, der in ein zyt lang in synem huss enthielt und in demnach mit sonderer practic uss dem land fertiget." Referring to the same provision, Bullinger, 1838, 305 says, "über ettlich wuchen". Zwingli claimed that the Council granted the extension of stay because of his and his colleagues' intercession: Reply to J. Fabri, April 30, 1526 (Z, V, 87) and letter to Gynoraeus, August 31, 1526 (Z, VIII, 705): "Audivit senatus preces nostras ac post revocationem, quam ex animo facere simulabat, quum nihil minus esset, spacium latendi immerenti dedit, donec occasione inventa tutus abire posset. Qua data per senatorem quendam, virum in euangelio Christi fidelissimum, ablegatus est clam, ut eius abitionem ne cives quidem senserint." Cf. footnote 20. It might be noted also that the Tirolese revolutionary peasant leader, Michael Gaismair, a personal friend of Zwingli, sought refuge in Zürich at the end of November 1525 and left early in January 1526 for fear of assassination by Austrian agents (Macek, 1960a, 115 ff. and 1960b, 416 ff.). There is no record of his contact with Hubmaier who was in Zürich at the same time. Had Hubmaier been a supporter of peasant revolts — as has been claimed by various authors, cf. Bergsten, 1961, 51 f. and 281 ff. — the two men would have sought friendship and alliance. At the time when Hubmaier made his journey to Moravia, Gaismair was organizing a peasant army in Graubünden, Appenzell and Tirol (see Macek, 1960b, 467 ff.). On Gaismair's later sympathies with Anabaptism, see Macek, 1960b, 542 f.

[19] TQ Schweiz, I, 197.

[20] The dating of Hubmaier's departure from Zürich depends on the interpretation of Bullinger's phrase "über ettlich wochen" and Stumpf's "ein zyt lang" (cf. footnote 18 above). In his reply to Fabri, Zwingli wrote: "Wir habend all dry [Zwingli, Leo Jud and Heinrich Engelhard] noch vergangner wochen in doctor Balthazars sach einen ersamen radt gebätten" (Z, V, 87). Zwingli's reply was completed on April 30 and printed immediately so that a friend of his, Gregor Mangolt, was able to take a number of copies to Constance before May 5. (Cf. his letter to Zwingli sent from Constance on May 5; Z, VIII, 581.) The meaning of the expression "vergangner wochen" is ambiguous. It can mean either "during the past weeks" or "during the (immediately) preceding week" (Z, V, 87, n. 12). Since there is no reference to Zwingli's intervention, nor to the extension of H.'s stay in

stance where, according to Zwingli's report,[21] he defended believer's baptism and boasted of a victory over the paedobaptists in Zürich. The presence of Anabaptist refugees from Waldshut in Constance no doubt encouraged Hubmaier to resume his witness. They had written him a letter during his imprisonment in Zürich.[22]

From Constance Hubmaier and his wife [23] made their way to Augsburg, near his native town of Friedberg. Neither the motives for his sojourn there nor the length of his stay can be determined with certainty. He might have been returning to his home region and seeking protection in the free imperial city with which he had maintained contact. The first book in which he had expressed his Anabaptist persuasion was printed in Augsburg in 1525.[24]

While in the city, he met with the evangelical ministers,[25] likely

---

Zürich in the official record of the Council session on April 11 (*TQ Schweiz*, I, 193-197), it must have taken place later, after H.'s public recantations, i.e. some time between April 15 (or later, depending on the unknown date of the recantation in Gossau) and April 30. Obviously, the permission to stay for several more weeks was granted only after Zwingli's intercession. For these reasons, we date Hubmaier's departure from Zürich later than Bergsten does (end of April, Bergsten, 1961, 393 and *HS*, 33).

[21] Zwingli's letter to Gynoraeus, August 31, 1526: "Nam ut primum Constantiam venit, apud ministros verbi sic nos calumniatus est victoriamque suam de catabaptismo iactavit, ut nesciam, an nullos in odium nostri traxerit" (Z, VIII, 705 f.).

[22] According to Hubmaier's own testimony before the Zürich Council in January 1526, he received a letter from Constance at the end of December 1525 in which the refugees from Waldshut encouraged him, "er sölte nun gedultig und frölich sin, dann gott wurd im zů siner zit wol helffenn" (*TQ Schweiz*, I, 392). Hubmaier's decision to make his first stop in Constance might have been connected also with the visit of Gregor Mangolt of Constance in Zürich (approx. April 29 - May 3; Z, V, 35 and VIII, 581). As we have mentioned in footnote 20 above, Mangolt mediated, at the time, Zwingli's contact with Constance. His three letters written to Zwingli from Constance on May 5 and 11 and on June 1, 1526 (Z, VIII, 581 ff., 587 ff. and 617 ff.) do not, however, contain any reference to Hubmaier. Cf. also the mention of a bag with Hubmaier's books which was kept in Constance by a certian Guldinast (record of trial before the Council of Zürich, April 11, 1526; *TQ Schweiz*, I, 197).

[23] Hubmaier married Elsbeth Hügline of Reichenau in January 1525. Cf. *HS*, 26 and Bergsten, 1962, 275, n. 110.

[24] *HS*, 109. The same printer, Melchior Ramminger, printed one of the four editions of Hubmaier's first printed work, *Achtzehn Schlussreden*, in 1524. *HS*, 71.

[25] Letter of Peter Gynoraeus (Frabenberger) to Zwingli, written in Augsburg on August 22, 1526 (Z, VIII, 688-690). Gynoraeus was a pupil of the humanists Sapidus and Rhenanus, studied in Basel from 1522 and served there as "people's priest" at St. Alban's Church until his expulsion from the city in November 1525 (Z, VIII, 688, n. 1). His letter is the only source for our knowledge of Hubmaier's stay in Augsburg.

including the Reformer Urbanus Rhegius, Hubmaier's colleague from student days in Freiburg and Ingolstadt. He complained to them about the "tyrannic" treatment he had suffered from Zwingli. He soon entered into a more intimate fellowship with a group of radicals who had been influenced by Ludwig Haetzer [26] until the latter's expulsion in the fall of 1525. At that time, Hans Denck [27] settled in Augsburg as a teacher of languages and became the leader of the pre-Anabaptist circle.

Through Hubmaier's influence many where baptized, including Denck.[28] Hubmaier can, therefore, be regarded as the founder of the Anabaptist congregation in Augsburg which was to play a crucial role in South German Anabaptism. On the other hand, Bergsten's hypothesis that Hubmaier might also have met Hans Hut — of whom we shall hear more in Nikolsburg — is hardly tenable.[29] Hut was baptized by Denck at Pentecost, May 26, 1526,[30] at which time he spent only three or four days in Augsburg [31] and stayed with Denck.[32] At an interrogation Hut stated plainly that he did not meet Hubmaier until in Nikolsburg.[33]

The absence of Hubmaier at Hut's baptism may provide a clue to the unsolved question concerning the length of Hubmaier's stay in Augsburg. Schulze assumes that Hut was baptized after Hubmaier's

---

[26]   On Haetzer's stay in Augsburg, see Goeters, 1957, Chs. 5 (42 ff.) and 7 (54 ff.).
[27]   On Denck's activities in Augsburg, see Walter Fellmann in DS, 2, 12 f. and Kiwiet, 1957b, 243 ff.
[28]   Letter of Gynoraeus to Zwingli: "Sed quidquid sit, plerosque suae farinae apud nos fere permovit, ut crederent." Referring to Denck, Gynoraeus wrote: ". . . e rebaptisatis praecipuus est" (Z, VIII, 689). This is the only source on the basis of which one assumes that Hubmaier himself rebaptized persons in Augsburg. Nowhere in his preserved writings does Denck mention Hubmaier in connection with his baptism. The fact that, during the same month, Denck baptized Hut, provides supporting evidence to Gynoraeus' report concerning the rebaptism of Denck. See footnote 29 below. Cf. Bergsten, 1961, 396 f.
[29]   Bergsten, 1961, 396 f. On Hut's stay in Augsburg, see Herbert Klassen, 1959, 179 and Neuser, 1913, 25.
[30]   TQ, II, 42, lines 24 ff. Meyer, 1874, 223, Art. 5; 224, Art. 8; 245, Art. 5; Neuser, 1913, 25 gives a wrong date (May 20).
[31]   Meyer, 1874, 224, Art. 9.
[32]   Meyer, 1874, 224, Art. 10.
[33]   The wording of Hut's statement (made on October 5, 1527) allows for no other interpretation. It was overlooked by Bergsten. "Er sei bei dem Denken hie [Augsburg] and zu Nurmberg, beim Hetzer hie und bei doctor Balthasarn Friedberger zu Niclaspurg bei denen von Lichtenstain, so landherren in Merern sein gewesen . . ." (TQ, II, 41, lines 23-26; printed also, with slight variations, by Meyer, 1874, 229, Art. 4).

departure from Augsburg.[34] This would mean that Hubmaier's stop in Augsburg was considerably shorter than has been suggested in recent research. The later dating for his departure from Zürich which we have proposed earlier [35] would further reduce the length of his stay. Such revision in chronology would also make possible an advanced dating of Hubmaier's arrival in Moravia, which was advocated by some of his earlier biographers.[36] On the other hand, it is conceivable that Hut, during his very short stay in Augsburg, failed to meet Hubmaier simply because the latter might have been ill, or temporarily away from the city, perhaps on a visit to his native town. In the absence of other sources, it is impossible to draw a final conclusion.

Hubmaier's itinerary from Augsburg to Mikulov in Moravia remains a matter of conjecture except for an obscure reference to his stop in the Austrian city of Steyr, southeast of Linz.[37] His route

---

[34] Schulze, 1957, 238. He dates Hut's baptism rightly on May 26 (250, n. 94), refers to Hubmaier's arrival in the city "in May", yet assumes a stay of two months ("at the most"). Such chronology is impossible. Bergsten, 1961, 395 f. (and *HS*, 34) dates Hubmaier's arrival "at the beginning of May" and refers to a stay of "about two months".

[35] Footnote 20.

[36] Hošek, 1867, 83; Dudík, 1875, 111; Wolf, 1878, 71 and Kameníček, III, 467 refer to "the month of June". Both admit, however, that the only *terminus ante quem* is the dating of Hubmaier's preface to *Der Lehrer Urteil*, July 21, 1526 (*HS*, 229).

[37] Oecolampad in his letter to Zwingli written in Basel on December 1, 1526, reported a rumour: "Baldassarem Waldshutanum ferunt rebaptizasse nobilem quendam in Stiria et adhuc dogma suum stabilire" (*Z*, VIII, 789). Schulze, 1957, 238 applied it to Leonhard of Liechtenstein who, according to his interpretation, was baptized by Hubmaier in Steyr and then took him to his Moravian domain at Mikulov. Others (Loserth, 1893, 125; Nicoladani, 1893, 25; Mecenseffy, 1956a, 36 and in *ME*, IV, 631; Bergsten, 1961, 406 f. and in *HS*, 34 and 284) have interpreted Oecolampad's report as a reference to the baptism of Leonhard of Liechtenstein which, however, took place at Mikulov (as is well attested in Anabaptist sources, e.g. *TQ*, II, 153, 187; *ZGL*, 50; Beck, 1883, 48, 52). It is rather surprising that the same report should be interpreted by these historians as a reference to the fact of Liechtenstein's baptism with a mistaken designation of its place, and yet, at the same time, accepted as a proof of Hubmaier's stop in the city of Steyr, "the wrong place". The extensive records of hearings which were conducted in Steyr and in other Anabaptist centers in Upper Austria by Ferdinand's procurator, Wolfgang Kunigl, in the fall of 1527 (printed in *TQ*, XI, 33 ff. and formerly in Nicoladani, 1893, 160 ff.) are completely silent about Hubmaier's supposed visit, or any other contact with the Anabaptists, in Steyr. Nevertheless, an *argumentum ex silentio* proves little. We may propose yet another hypothesis: Might not the rumour recorded by Oecolampad refer to Hubmaier's contact with Jakob Portner, an evangelical chaplain of baron Wilhelm of Rogendorf, at the castle in Steyr? In 1527, Portner became a co-worker of Hut, was sent out as a missioner and imprisoned in Augsburg. Cf. *TQ*, XI, 34, line 12 f.; Mecenseffy, 1956a, 36; *ME*, IV, 205 and 631.

probably followed the river Danube [38] through Ingolstadt, Regensburg, Passau and Linz. The fact that he left the imperial city and moved into the Austrian territory with an ever-increasing risk to his life, suggests that from Augsburg, he must have decided to go to Moravia, which at that time lay outside the Habsburg rule and was known for its wide religious toleration. He could not have foreseen that within a few weeks after his settlement at Mikulov, the young Jagiellon King Louis II would die in a battle against the Turks at Mohacs on August 29, 1526, and that Ferdinand would succeed him to the throne.[39]

2. OPPORTUNITIES FOR LITERARY CONTACT

In order to facilitate a quick chronological and theological orientation, we have reviewed Hubmaier's life and religious development. We have paid special attention to certain events which are of particular relevance for our inquiry into Hubmaier's possible knowledge of the Czech Reformation and into his contacts with the German Evangelicals in Moravia, prior to his arrival at Mikulov. Before examining the internal evidence of such relationship in Hubmaier's preserved writings, we shall enumerate briefly some of the opportunities for literary contact which are known to have existed.[40]

The Roman Catholic inquisitors and apologists displayed an un-

---

[38]   Hošek, 1867, 83 claims that Hubmaier sailed on a boat which was put at his disposal by "a certain Vilém Vyeland". He does not indicate the source of his information. Obviously, he applied, erroneously, Hubmaier's mention of Wieland's boat (*HS*, 279) to the journey to Moravia. Hubmaier referred, however, to his trip from Regensburg to Ulm (the opposite direction!) on his way to Waldshut, either in 1523, or, more probably, at the end of 1520. Cf. Bergsten, 1961, 91. The reference of Schulze, 1957, 238 to Hubmaier's itinerary through Uttenreuth near Erlangen is based on a wrong identification of a certain "Balthasar" with Hubmaier. Cf. *TQ*, II, 79, 81, 94, and note especially the dating of Balthasar's stop in Uttenreuth, "etwo vor 5 wochen", in 1528!

[39]   Ferdinand was elected king by the Bohemian diet (acting without any agreement with the Moravian estates) in Prague on October 23, 1526. The Moravian estates received him, without election, as king and margrave on the basis of the hereditary rights of his wife Ann (sister of the deceased King Louis) at a diet in Olomouc, November 11-18, 1526, on condition that he would confirm their freedoms and rights, including the broad religious freedom. Dvořák, 1901, 377 f.; Kameníček, 1900, 98.

[40]   No one, thus far, has paid attention to this aspect of Hubmaier's life and theological development. Amedeo Molnár has called for such a study in his review of *HS* (*CV*, VI, 1963, 98). Cf. also Molnár, 1965c, 6 ff.

usual interest in the Czech Picards or Waldensians during the first quarter of the sixteenth century. During the first half of the first decade, two Dominican theologians, Heinrich Krämer Institoris and Jacobus Lilienstein, as well as a Moravian humanist, Augustin Käsenbrod, launched their attacks against the *Unitas Fratrum*. Several years later, 1512-1514, Jakob Ziegler and Hieronymus Dungersheim wrote their scholarly refutations. Finally, Johannes Faber paid superficial attention to the Picards in several of his writings, from 1526 onward. We may speak of three successive stages of Catholic investigation into the theology and life of the Czech Brethren. Each phase was marked by a number of Latin works printed in Germany. Some of them contained verbatim reprints of the confessional statements of the *Unitas* and thus spread abroad some knowledge of the Brethren during the early years of the Reformation in Germany and Switzerland.

The first phase was initiated by the official Dominican inquisitor Heinrich Krämer, better known as Institoris. At the turn of the century, he was sent by Pope Alexander VI to Bohemia and Moravia to convert the heretics and to burn their books. His mission could hardly be called successful but his two books against the Waldensians, printed in Olomouc in 1501,[41] served the purpose of introducing the little-known Unity to a wider public outside the Czech circles. Institoris recorded the first known estimate of the number of Brethren in Bohemia and Moravia — a startling and likely exaggerated figure of 100,000 [42] — and no doubt helped to persuade the leaders of the Unity about the necessity of preparing confessional statements in the Latin language.

Simultaneously, the Brethren were attacked by the leading Moravian humanist, Augustin Käsenbrod (1467-1513),[43] a close friend of

[41] *Clippeum Adversus waldensium seu Pickardorum heresim* (Olomouc, Conrad Baumgarten, April 20, 1501; second ed. by the same printer on March 20, 1502) and *Opus perutile Sermonum in defensione s.rom. ecclesiae adversus Waldenses haereticos* (Olomouc, C. Baumgarten, 1501). Cf. Dudík, 1875, 109. On the mission of Institoris, the author of the ill-famed *Malleus maleficarum*, see Müller, I, 311 ff. and Hrejsa, IV, 110 f. and 158 ff.

[42] Institoris, 1501a, fol. 14b: "... quod in regno Bohemie noui insurgunt continue errores et precipue illorum, qui pickarti seu waldenses nuncupantur, quorum eciam numerus ad centum milia a quibusdam estimatur ...".

[43] Käsenbrod was known also under the name Augustinus Moravus or Olomucensis. On his life and strife with the Unity, see Müller, I, 307 ff.; Hrejsa, IV, 158; Truhlář, 1894, 64 ff., 112 ff. and 151 ff. and Wotke, 1898, 59 ff. Cf. also footnote 115 below. Although Käsenbrod visited Olomouc frequently, he did not reside

the Bishop of Olomouc, Stanislav Thurzo. After studies in Cracow and Padua, where he became doctor of laws in 1494, he entered the service of King Vladislav as secretary (1496-1511) in the royal Bohemian chancellary at Buda (Ofen in Hungary). He worked with another Czech Catholic humanist, Jan Šlechta of Všehrdy, of whom we shall hear more in connection with Erasmus. As provost of the cathedral in Olomouc since 1498, Augustin exchanged letters during the years 1500-1503, with Jan Černý (Niger), a brother of Bishop Lukáš and well-known physician.[44] The first letter appeared in Olomouc[45] even before it reached Černý. Augustin's four letters, in which he grossly distorts the views of the Brethren, were published in Ziegler's great polemical work of 1512,[46] whereas Černý's replies were never printed.

Through his correspondence, Käsenbrod pursued the goal of bringing about a persecution and eventual extermination of the heretical Picards. To that end he wrote two letters to the king[47], and finally succeeded in his efforts when the "St. James mandate" against the Unity was passed by the Bohemian diet in Prague in July 1508, and was endorsed, with some important modifications, by the Moravian diet meeting in Olomouc at the end of August 1508.[48]

Somewhat more sympathetic in his judgment about the Brethren was the Dominican theologian Jacobus Lilienstein who wrote his polemical treatise in 1505.[49] He censured their teachings but praised their morals.

All these literary attacks and the increasing threat of persecution forced the Brethren to prepare their Latin apologetic writings of

---

there permanently until after his resignation from the royal service in 1511. He died on November 3, 1513.

[44] See his biography by J. Doubková in Kaňák, 1957, 78-93, with a detailed summary of the correspondence. The physician Černý-Niger, who was an outstanding lay theologian, must not be confused with a later priest and historian of the Unity, bearing the same name, Jan Černý-Nigranus (ca. 1510-1565), a coworker of Blahoslav. Cf. his biography by the same author, *ibid.*, 119-143. Cf. also Chapter IV, footnote 121.

[45] *Ad eruditum virum Mag. Johannem Nigrum phisicum, Tractatus de secta Waldensium* (Olomouc, C. Baumgarten, October 29, 1500; copies in Olomouc and Brno).

[46] Ziegler, 1512, fols. B iij b - D i a.

[47] The first one dated on November 14, 1506, the second undated (some time in 1507), both printed in Ziegler, 1512, fols. D i b - D ij a.

[48] On the mandate, see Müller, I, 346 ff. and Hrejsa, IV, 174 f., 211 ff.

[49] *Tractatus contra Waldenses fratres erroneos* (1505). A brief summary in Allen,

1503,[50] 1507,[51] 1508 [52] and finally, the opus magnum, *Apologia verae scripturae*, printed by Hieronymus Höltzel in Nürnberg on December 16, 1511.[53] It was especially the daring step of having their large apology printed by a well-known printer in Germany that led immediately to scholarly refutations by two renowned theologians.

The first of these was the work of the Bavarian-born humanist and theologian, Jakob Ziegler (ca. 1470-1549). Educated at the universities in Ingolstadt and Vienna, he became a friend of Bishop Thurzo in Olomouc and from 1508 till 1511 lived in Moravia as tutor of Jindřich Kuna of Kunštát. The polemical treatise which he undertook to write, on their instigation, on November 9, 1510, was printed, at the expense of the Lord of Kunštát, by Melchior Lother in Leipzig, on October 31, 1512,[54] five years before the nailing of Luther's theses in Wittenberg. Ziegler based his work on the three earlier Latin confessions of the Unity, the full text of which he included, together with other

---

1914, 290-292, and Hrejsa, IV, 206. Cf. also a quotation in *E*, 5, 22 (notes) and Bartoš, 1934, 104, n. 2.

[50] *Oratio excusatoria atque satisfactiva fratrum regi Vladislao ad Ungariam missa,* 1503. Reprinted in Ziegler, 1512, fols. A iij a - A vj b; Dungersheim, 1514b (in paragraphs, *passim*); Aeneas Sylvius, 1523, 125-133; later reprinted also by Gratius, 1535, Freherus, 1602, Lydius, 1616 and Brown, 1690.

[51] *Confessio fratrum regi Vladislao ad Ungariam missa,* 1507. Printed in Ziegler, 1512, B i a - B iij b; Aeneas Sylvius, 1523, 133-138; not in Dungersheim (cf. Peschke, 1964, 66); later reprints by the same authors as listed in footnote 50.

[52] *Excusatio fratrum Waldensium contre binas litteras doctoris Augustini datas ad regem,* 1508. Printed in Ziegler, 1512, D ij b - F ij a; Aeneas Sylvius, 1523, 138-160; not in Dungersheim; later reprints by the same authors as listed in footnote 50.

[53] Only 100 copies were printed and transported immediately to Mladá Boleslav (Bohemia). The work became known chiefly through Dungersheim's *Confutatio* (Dungersheim, 1514a). As copies of the original print were unavailable, handwritten copies were procured by Emperor Maximilian as well as by the Augustinian monastery in Erfurt whence Luther left for Wittenberg (Bartoš in *ARG*, 31 [1934], 105). Müller, I, 531 knew of no extant copy. Since then, copies have been located in the British Museum, London; Prague, Leipzig and Breslau. A critical edition of the four Latin confessions (1503, 1504, 1507 and 1511) has been prepared by E. Peschke and A. Molnár and awaits publication (Peschke, 1964, 15, n. 1.). For a comprehensive study of these and other confessions of the Unity during the era of Lukáš, see Gindely, 1854c, Müller, I, 523 ff., Janoušek, 1923 and Štrupl, 1964a, 31-54.

[54] *Jacobi Ziegleri ex Landau Bavariae Contra Haeresim Valdensium Libri Quinque* (Ziegler, 1512), dedicated to Bishop Thurzo. Copies in Zürich, Leipzig, London and Prague. On Ziegler, see Schottenloher, 1910, esp. 23-35. A critical study of Ziegler's argumentation was provided by Peschke, 1964, 28-64. Cf. also Ziegler's later regrets in his letter to Erasmus written in Rome, Feb. 16, 1522 (*E*, 5, 21 f., lines 130-142).

sources, in his book.[55] He did not use the Apology of 1511, but learned about its publication shortly before the completion of his manuscript.[56]

A year and a half later, on March 23, 1514, a large refutation of the Brethren's Apology was printed in Leipzig, under the title *Confutatio apologetici cuiusdam sacrae scripturae falso inscripti*.[57] It came from the pen of the thomistic theologian at the University of Leipzig, Hieronymus Dungersheim of Ochsenfurt (1465-1540). He had been commissioned for the work by Duke George of Saxony, a grandson of the Hussite King, George of Poděbrady. Later in 1514, Dungersheim published, in Leipzig, a shorter *Reprobatio* of the 1503 Latin confession of the Brethren.[58]

The polemical writings of Ziegler and Dungersheim were known to Luther and formed, together with the *Apologia* of 1511, his initial knowledge of the Czech Picards.[59] Would it be unrealistic to suggest that the same works might have been read by Hubmaier? Their dates of publication (October 31, 1512 and March 23, 1514) coincide with Hubmaier's stay in Ingolstadt (February 1512-December 1515). There, the newly-made doctor of theology began to deliver his first lectures as professor of theology, under the aegis of Johannes Eck, the future chief apologist of the church against the 'Hussite' heresies of Luther. In the same month (October) Ziegler, *magister artium ac theologiae baccalaureus biblicus ingolstadiensis*, published his work against the

---

[55]   The first part of Ziegler, 1512 (fols. A iij a - F ij a) includes the full text of the Confessions of 1503, 1507 and 1508 (see footnotes 50, 51, and 52 above) as well as the polemical writings of Augustin Käsenbrod (listed in footnotes 46 and 47 above).

[56]   Ziegler, 1512, fol. Ee IV b.

[57]   Dungersheim, 1514a. A copy of the print was not accessible to us. Peschke, 1964, 65-108, made available a critical analysis of the text in comparison with Dungersheim's other work (Dungersheim, 1514b) and with the text of the Brethren's Apology of 1511.

[58]   *Reprobatio orationis excusatoriae picardorum regiae maiestati in Ungariam missae.* Lipsiae, Vulfgangus Monacensis 1514 (Dungersheim, 1514b). Copies in Leipzig and Prague. For analysis of content, see Peschke, 1964 (in previous footnote). The book contains the complete text of the 1503 Confession (cf. footnote 50 above). According to Peschke, 1964, 66, Dungersheim did not know the 1507 and 1508 Confessions even though these had been printed in Ziegler's book (published in Leipzig two years earlier).

[59]   The thesis was proposed first by Köhler, 1900, 175 ff., and then expounded by Bartoš, 1929 (in Czech) and 1934 (in German). Cf. also the subsequent discussion: Peschke, 1935, 333 ff.; Thomson, 1953, 164 ff.; Bittner, 1954, 121 f.; Molnár, 1959a, 184; Molnár, 1964a, 184 f.; Peschke, 1964, Chapter 4, "Luthers Stellung zu den Böhmischen Brüdern" (109 ff.) and Fousek, 1965, 41 ff.

Waldensian heretics in Bohemia and Moravia. Dungersheim's *Confutatio* created an even greater sensation in the German theological circles. Could Hubmaier have remained ignorant of both books?

Unfortunately, nothing at all is reported in the preserved sources about his teaching activities at the university.[60] We do not know what the subjects were on which he lectured, nor what 'theological line' he took. Most likely, he was an epigon of his teacher, Eck.[61] Even more relevant is the fact that after two years he made a clear choice between the academic career and the task of a popular preacher and religious leader. He decided in favour of the latter and left for the post of cathedral preacher in Regensburg. While in Ingolstadt, he was probably more involved in his priestly offices and his administrative duties as vice-rector of the university than in actual academic pursuits. He might have known of the books of Ziegler and Dungersheim, but there is no evidence that he ever studied them.[62]

Another opportunity for a direct knowledge of the confessional theology of the *Unitas* presented itself to Hubmaier several years later when he lived in Waldshut and established contact with several humanist friends. In the spring of 1523, a friend of Erasmus, Jacobus Sobius, a humanist scholar, orator and teacher at the University of Cologne (Köln), published anonymously a hitherto unknown Commentary on the Council of Basel by Aeneas Sylvius Piccolomini to which he appended, among other documents related to the Hussite and Wycliffite controversy, the full text of the three Latin confessions of the Unity.[63] The book was printed by Cratander in Basel shortly

---

[60] Sachsse, 1914, 123. In 1526, Hubmaier confessed to his ignorance of the Bible at the time when he became a doctor of theology (1512). He also enumerated the theologians whose books he had studied (*HS*, 309).

[61] On the theology of young Eck, cf. Joseph Greving, *Johann Eck als junger Gelehrter. Eine literar- und dogmengeschichtliche Untersuchung über seinen Chrysopassus praedestinationis aus dem J. 1514.* Cf. also Hubmaier's eulogy of Eck, Sachsse, 1914, 80 and 124; Loserth, 1893, 17, n. 1.

[62] Cf. our discussion of internal evidences further below. The book of Ziegler was recalled as late as 1604 by the statesman and leader of the Unity, Václav Budovec of Budov, in his *Poznamenání*. See Sliziński, 1958, 214; Bartoš, 1951a, 91, n. 7; Bartoš, 1959b, 238, n. 9.

[63] Aeneas Sylvius, 1523. The three confessions are reprinted — most likely from Ziegler, 1512 — on pp. 125-160. In the text, the full title of each of the three confessions (cf. footnotes 50-52) appears. The headings which appear at the top of each page read "Professio fidei fratrvm Vald. ad Vladislavm Vngariae Regem missa" for the first two confessions and "Responsio" for the third one. Sobius prepared his edition of sources as a corrective response to the *Catalogus haereticorum* (1st ed., Köln, 1522) of the Dominican Bernard of Luxembourg who, in his

after Hubmaier had returned to Waldshut from his short second stay in Regensburg, and after his professed change to an evangelical position.

The man who might have originated the plan to publish an impartial collection of sources on the Czech Reformation was none other than Erasmus.[64] His books were read and published in Czech translations in Bohemia and Moravia from 1513 onward.[65] More than a year before Luther did it at the disputation in Leipzig (July 1519), Erasmus defended Hus with his famous phrase: "Even though he was burnt, he was not defeated".[66]

From September 1518 to January 1521, Erasmus exchanged letters with two leading representatives of the Czech nobility, Jan Šlechta of Všehrdy, then living at Kostelec in central Bohemia, and Artleb of Boskovice, who wrote from Znojmo in South Moravia. When the

---

treatment of the Bohemian heretics, drew chiefly from the well-known work of Piccolomini, *Historia bohemica* (1475). With the subtle irony of a humanist, Sobius wrote in his (anonymous) preface: "Huic cohaerebat Professio fidei fratrum Valdensium ad regem Ungariae: quae non multum alicubi dissentit ab iis quae nunc vulgo traduntur a quibusdam, ut ab illis accepisse videri possint. Atque hinc melius cognosci possunt quales sint quam ex catalogo haereticorum, quem reverendus pater F. Bernhardus de Lutzemburgo, ordinis Praedicatorum, aedidit. Eiusmodi legere fortasse prodest, ut caveamus." On Sobius and his editorship of the book, see Clement, 1759, 241 f. (footnotes); Ritter, 1927, 43; Bartoš, 1948a, 131-135; Bartoš, 1956a, 39 f.; Bartoš, 1958a, 252 f.; *E*, 6, 447 f.; *ADB*, 34 (1892), 529 f.; Krafft, 1870, 36-48. The print bears no date nor place. Bartoš suggested Köln or Strasbourg, 1522. Molnár, 1957a, 27, pointed out evidence that it was printed by Cratanter in Basel, shortly before April 20, 1523. Cf. the letter of Andreas Cratander to Bonifacius Amerbach in Avignon (Basel, April 20, 1523) in which C. reported the printing of the book shortly before that (Amerbach, 1943, No. 914, 420 f.). A letter of Amerbach to Andreas Alciatus, written in Avignon, July 9, 1523, described the contents of the volume, incl. the "Waldensian" confession (Amerbach, 1943, No. 925, 434 f.). At the time when Aeneas Sylvius, 1523 was printed by Cratander, Oecolampad worked in the shop on the edition of his Latin transl. of *Psegmata Ioannis Chrysostomi* (Oecolampad, 1927, 207 and 217, n. 5; Staehelin, 1939, 173 ff.). It should be noted also that Cratander printed one of Hubmaier's tracts in 1524 (*HS*, 75).

64   Such is the hypothesis of Bartoš, 1956a, 39 (repeated in Bartoš, 1958a, 252). Erasmus met Sobius in the house of provost Hermann of Neuenahr during his visit in Köln in November 1520. A few months earlier, Erasmus had received a copy of the *Apologia* (1511) from two emissaries of the Unity who visited him in Antwerp in June 1520 (*E*, 4, 291 f.; Bittner, 1954, 115 f.; Bartoš, 1958a, 246; Molnár, 1952a, 90 f.). Sobius did not, however, publish the text of the Apology, but rather the three shorter confessions.

65   Bartoš, 1958a, 118. Cf. footnote 43 in the previous chapter.

66   "Cum alter [Hus] exustus fuerit, non reuictus, alterius [Wiclefi] libri non nisi post mortem damnati." (*E*, 3, 320, letter to Martin Lypsius, May 7, 1518, reprinted in many editions of Erasmus' correspondence, incl. 1518, 1519 and 1521.)

correspondence was printed in Basel late in 1521,[67] Šlechta's detailed
description of the three religious parties in Bohemia and Moravia —
the Roman Catholics, the Utraquists and the 'Picards' — as well as
Erasmus' rather mild judgment of the Czech heretics and his positive
evaluation of some of the teachings of the Unity,[68] certainly made it
possible for anyone interested to obtain a general picture of the
religious scene in the two lands.

In November 1521, Erasmus moved from Louvain to Basel where
Hubmaier visited him the following spring. They talked mainly about
two subjects: purgatory and the meaning of regeneration which, according to John 1:13, comes "neither by the will of the flesh nor by
the will of man".[69] Both subjects had been treated in the confessional
writings of the Unity.[70] During the early spring, Erasmus had been

---

[67]   A good summary of the correspondence was provided recently by Bartoš,
1956a, 10-12, 36-37; Bartoš, 1958a, 119-122, 248-249; and Bittner, 1954, 108-120.
The following table shows the chronological sequence of the letters and their first
reprints important for our study of Hubmaier:

Letter and Date	Original Reprint	Critical Edition
(1) Šlechta to Erasmus (Fall 1518)	(not preserved)	— —
(2) Erasmus to Šlechta (April 23, 1519, received on Sept. 11)	Erasmus 1519, 160 and 1521, 304	No. 950 (E, 3, 551-553)
(3) Šlechta to Erasmus (October 10, 1519)	Erasmus 1521, 547-551	No. 1021 (E, 4, 79-85)
(4) Erasmus to Šlechta (November 1, 1519) (Visit of two envoys of the Unity in Antwerp, June 1520)	Erasmus 1521, 551-556	No. 1039 (E, 4, 113-119)
(5) Artleb to Erasmus (October [?] 1520)	— —	No. 1154 (E, 4, 368-370)
(6) Erasmus to Artleb (January 28, 1521)	Erasmus 1521, 540-542	No. 1183 (E, 4, 438-442)

The epistolary collection Erasmus, 1521 bears the date of August 31, 1521 but
could not have been published until after November 22, 1521, since it contains
Erasmus' letter to Thurzo (Nov. 22) as the last item in point of time. Cf. footnote
71 below.

[68]   Šlechta's report on the Unity, including their practice of rebaptism and their
concept of the eucharist, is found in E, 4, 84 f. Erasmus' opinion about the Unity
is recorded in E, 4, 116 ff.

[69]   Cf. Hubmaier's recollection of the discussion quoted in footnote 10 above.

[70]   On purgatory, see the summary of arguments in Peschke, 1964, 53 f. and 100 ff.
Regeneration was treated in articles on baptism and confirmation. Cf. Palmov,
1904, 331 ff. and 340 ff.

reminded no less than three times of the Czech Brethren.[71] One may suspect that in the course of his conversation with Hubmaier he could have mentioned their teachings and even boasted about his correspondence with "distant" Bohemia and Moravia.[72]

[71] (1) The letter from Jakob Ziegler (Rome, Feb. 16, 1522) with his confession of remorse about the polemical work against the Picards (*E*, 5, 21 f., lines 130-142). (2) Erasmus' correspondence with Bishop Thurzo in Olomouc: (a) T.'s first letter to Erasmus, July 1521 (lost). (b) Erasmus' reply from Basel, ca. Nov. 21, 1521 (*E*, 4, 598 ff.) which is the first known letter of E. written upon his arrival in Basel on November 15. (c) Another letter of Erasmus to T., Basel, Nov. 22, 1521 (*E*, 4, 602). Both letters (b and c) were printed in Erasmus, 1521, 634 ff. and 639. (d) E. to T., March 21, 1522 (*E*, 5, 31 f.). (e) T. to E., April 10, 1522 (*E*, 5, 41 f.). All letters are humanist in content although Erasmus in his letter on March 21 refers to Luther and mentions his *Paraphrases* on Matthew and on the epistles of Paul. On Thurzo's extensive contacts with the leading humanists in Europe, see *E*, 4, 599 f.; Wotke, 1899 and Kopřiva, 1959. In the same year in which Hubmaier wrote his letter to Beatus Rhenanus (cf. footnote 8 above) R. dedicated his editio princeps of Tertullian to Bishop Thurzo (printed by Froben in Basel, July 1521; 2nd ed. in 1528). He also dedicated to Thurzo both editions of his collection *Autores historiae ecclesiasticae* (Basel, Froben, August 1523 and 1539). Erasmus dedicated to Thurzo his ed. of Pliny's *Historia naturalis* (March 1525) and *Enarratio* of Ps. 38 (March 1532). Cf. also Nyikos, 1937, 358 ff. (3) Another reminder of the Czech Brethren might have been Erasmus' *Paraphrases* on Matthew which came off the press on March 21, 1522 (*E*, 5, 4), just a few weeks before Hubmaier's visit in Basel. According to Bartoš, 1958a, 256, n. 4, Erasmus' use of the term 'resipiscere' as a translation of 'metanoein' (instead of his former use of 'renasci') shows a possible influence of the Unity's *Apologia*, 1511, a copy of which E. had received in 1520. Cf. also the analysis of the term 'Christianismus renascens' in the theology of young Zwingli by Rich, 1949, 9 ff.
[72] It should be noted, however, that the correspondence with Šlechta and Artleb of Boskovice as reprinted in Erasmus, 1521, contains no reference to the two subjects discussed by Erasmus and Hubmaier. In this connection, the question of a possible influence of the theology of the Unity — as expressed in the two books printed in Basel, Erasmus, 1521 and Aeneas Sylvius, 1523 — on other (future) Anabaptist leaders must be raised. Conrad Grebel lived in the house of Cratander from August 21 till October, 1521. Even if the collection of letters which was to appear in Erasmus, 1521 had been in Froben's printing shop during Grebel's stay with Cratander, it would take a great deal of imagination to suggest that the young humanist, who had just joined his fiancée in Basel, spent his time reading letters about the Bohemian heretics! Cf. Bender, 1950, 59 ff. Wilhelm Reublin — who introduced Anabaptism to Waldshut, baptized Hubmaier and in later years visited Moravia — was people's priest at St. Alban's Church in Basel from the spring of 1521 until his expulsion on June 27, 1522. The publication of Erasmus, 1521 coincides with his stay there. Later, as priest in Witikon, he was the first minister in the canton of Zürich who preached publicly against infant baptism (early in 1524), with the result that by Easter time 1524 parents in his parish were refusing to have their children baptized (*TQ Schweiz*, I, 10 f.; *ME*, IV, 304 f.). Had he been influenced by the baptismal theology of the Czech Picards as reported in Erasmus, 1521, and in the confessions of the Unity, printed in Aeneas Sylvius, 1523? We do not know. The same conclusion applies to Hans Denck, who worked as editor (corrector) in the shops of Cratander and Curio, from January or February until

In contrast to Erasmus, who was a great admirer of Jan Hus, Hubmaier never mentioned the name of the Czech Reformer in any of his writings. His silence stands also in sharp contrast to the bold public acknowledgments of Hus and the Hussites made repeatedly by Luther,[73] and the frequent references to Hus in the polemical writings of Catholic theologians such as Eck or Faber.[74] In Hubmaier's presence and with his support, Zwingli pleaded, at the Second Disputation in Zürich in October 1523, for communion under both kinds which had been defended before the Council of Constance by "Hans Hus, a pitiable martyr before God who had been killed without guilt".[75] Hubmaier's complete avoidance of the memory of Hus is even more puzzling when one recalls that he had personal ties with Constance,

---

September 1523 (DS 2, 9 and Kiwiet, 1957b, 233 f.). His knowledge about Aeneas Sylvius, 1523 which appeared in Cratander's shop in March or April 1523 can be assumed with a greater degree of probability than in the case of any other Anabaptist leader. Burckhardt, 1898, 10 f. rejected Keller's assertion (Keller, 1885, 327 ff. and 373 ff.) that as an international center of bookprint the city of Basel was also a center of evangelical brotherhoods under Waldensian and Bohemian influences and, therefore, became the cradle of Swiss Anabaptism. Because of Denck's birthplace in Upper Bavaria near the Bohemian border Keller (ibid., 329) surmised an early influence of "Brüdergemeinden" on Denck. Without any evidence, Burckhardt (ibid., 7) even suggested that Denck's family had ties with the Bohemian Brethren. For a discussion of the Erasmian influence on Anabaptism and some of its representative leaders, see Kreider, 1952; Fast, 1956a, 109 ff.; Hall, 1961; Hillerbrand, 1962, 157 ff.

[73] Luther to Spalatin (Feb. 1520): "... sumus omnes Hussitae ignorantes. Denique Paulus et Augustinus ad verbum sunt Hussitae" (WA Br, 2, 42). On Luther's statements about Hus and the Hussites, see Kraus, I, 150 ff. and Thomson, 1953, 163 ff. with a list of older bibliography (160). Cf. also the recent treatment by Pelikan, 1964, 106 ff.

[74] Faber's treatment of Hus is of particular interest since he was the vicar general in Constance (1518-1523) and a personal friend of Hubmaier. The biographers of Faber (listed in footnote 4 above) have made no study of his relationship to Hus nor to the various groups within the Czech Reformation. A research into Faber's manifold involvements in the Bohemian and Moravian religious and political life, from 1523 till his death in 1541, is long overdue. Faber paid attention to Hus in his two early works, Faber, 1526b (polemic against Zwingli), fols. Z iij - a i, and 1528f (reprinted in Latin version in 1537a): "Triginta articuli, in quibus Joannes Hus Martino Luthero tolerabilior minusque impius esse deprehenditur." He claims to have used Hus' De Ecclesia (Hus, 1520b) as the source for his treatise, but the expressed purpose was a polemic against Zwingli in the 1526 booklet, and against Luther in the enlarged version of 1528. "Vnd möge ein yeder Christen mensch wol spüren vnd mercken dz gegen dem zwingli der ketzer Johannes Huss ein frommer man vnd Christenlicher leerer gewesen ist, vnd so er bey vns hie zů gegen were, das er auch vnd wider den zwingli einen beystand thon wurde." (Faber, 1526a, fol. a i.)

[75] Z, II, 765. Cf. also footnote 129 in the previous chapter.

the city of Hus' martyrdom; [76] that his pamphlet "On the Heretics and Those Who Burn Them" was addressed to Anton Pirata, provincial vicar of the Dominican order in Constance; [77] and that the majority of his books were printed in Moravia, where the reverent remembrance and cult of Hus constituted the common heritage of all groups within the Czech Reformation.

During his short exile in Schaffhausen (September-October 1524), Hubmaier wrote his protest against the burning of heretics. Shortly afterwards, he defended himself and the citizens of Waldshut against accusations that he had misled them into "the cursed Hussite, heretical faith".[78] It is hardly necessary to add that in the Roman Catholic

[76]   The city of Constance is mentioned no fewer than seven times in the printed works of Hubmaier (*HS*, 500; Ortsregister). H. was probably ordained there into the priesthood and maintained frequent contacts with the bishop's office and especially with his friend Faber. He made his first stop there after release from Zürich in the spring of 1526. Yet he seems never to have associated the city with the memory of Hus. How different was the reaction of Erasmus during his visit in Constance in September 1522. Accompanied by Beatus Rhenanus and treated magnificently by his host, Johannes of Botzheim, the celebrated humanist recalled the fiery death of Hus and a few months later described his impressions thus: "Quae civitas nulla re magnopere celebris est quam ecclesia perquam vetusta nec ineleganti; tum synodo illic olim habita, praesidente Caesare; sed praecipue Ioanne Hus illic exusto". Letter to Marcus Laurinus, Feb. 1, 1523; *E*, 5, 214. For reprints from 1523 onward, see *E*, 5, 203.

[77]   *HS*, 95-100. It is difficult to imagine how a man with Hubmaier's education and contacts could have written — five years after Luther's acclaim of Hus at the disputation in Leipzig — thirty-six articles against the burning of heretics, addressed them to an inquisitor in Constance and not have mentioned Hus. One is inclined to suspect some definite reason behind such silence. Was Hubmaier, in his concept of church history, still a pupil of Eck — and this in spite of the fact that during his stay in Schaffhausen he wrote his *Axiomata* against Eck? On Hubmaier's relationship to Eck in the fall of 1524, see *HS*, 85 ff. and Bergsten, 1961, 176 ff. Neither Sachsse, 1914 nor Bergsten, 1961 studied Hubmaier's concept of history in general and church history in particular.

[78]   The accusation was made in a letter sent by the city of Freiburg i.B. to Waldshut on October 3, 1524: "... dass üch Euwer Pfaff wyt abgefürt und understanden hat, onerlaupt aller Oberkeyt in den verdampten hussischen, ketzerischen Glauben gantz zu pringen, und in alle Ungehorsam zu füren, dem hapt Ihr gefolgt ..." (Schreiber, 1863, 100). The reply, "Ein warhafftig enntschuldigung unnd clag gemeiner statt Waltzhůt", which was written entirely, or in part, by Hubmaier, towards the end of 1524, rejects the accusation: "... man muss gedencken ir wissen nit in allem üwerm glouben, was ketzer, ketzerisch, Huss oder hussisch sye, oder wie sich christen luten mit irrenden menschen halten sollen, ee und sy die fur ketzer ussrieefen ... irren macht nit ein ketzer, es were sunst Petrus ... und all apostel ketzer gewesen, dan Christus hat inen allen iren unglauben verwisen Mar. am XVI. ca., sonder im irsal und unglauben endtlich verharren und sich nit wellen wysen, das macht ein ketzer." "... dass ir uns ermanet, darmit wir uns luterischenn und hussischenn pfaffen abthient ... aber unser

usage of that day, the term 'Hussite' was void of any specific meaning related to the original teachings of Hus and was employed as a synonym for almost any heretical deviation from, or criticism of, the position of the church.

Yet during the early years of the Reformation, the writings of Hus were reprinted and circulated in large numbers. In March 1520, Hus' *De ecclesia* was printed, through the initiative of Luther, in Hagenau (Alsatia), in 2,000 copies.[79] Zwingli read it in May [80] and in July sent it to Oswald Myconius in Lucerne.[81] In August 1520, a second edition was printed in Mainz.[82] In 1524-1525, Otto Brunfels edited three volumes of what he claimed to be the writings of Hus.[83] Parts of them were translated into German by Wenzeslaus Linck of Aldenburg and printed in 1525.[84] Besides, countless popular pamphlets [85] were

---

pfaffen sindt nit lutherisch; sy sind zu Konstanz pfaffen worden, so hat man inen nitt lutherische oder hussische lere befolchen, sunder das evangelium zů predigen, pur, clar, luter on alle vermischung . . ." (Loserth, 1891, 109 f.). For Hubmaier's authorship, dating of the document and its relationship to the peasant war, see Sachsse, 1914, 96 ff.; Bergsten, 1961, 198 ff. Keller's interpretation of the accusation (Keller, 1885, 305 f.) as a reference to the teachings of the Czech Brethren cannot be accepted.

[79]   *De Causa Bohemica. Paulus Constantius* (Hus, 1520a). On Paulus Constantius Phrygio (Seidensticker), see *E*, 5, 65, n. 15.

[80]   Valentin Curio to Zwingli, May 16, 1520 (Z, VII, 313) and Zwingli to Vadian, June 19, 1520 (Z, VII, 328 f.).

[81]   Zwingli to Myconius, July 6, 1520 (Z, VII, 330). Myconius returned it to Zwingli on January 8, 1521 (Z, VII, 424). Cf. also Koehler, 1921, No. 253.

[82]   *Liber Egregius de unitate ecclesiae* (Hus, 1520b). Hrejsa, IV, 259 reversed the order of the two editions. A modern critical ed. of the Latin text was provided by S. H. Thomson, *Magistri Johannis Hus Tractatus de ecclesia* (Univ. of Colorado Press and W. Heffer, Cambridge, 1956, also a reprint in Prague, 1958). A modern Czech tr., based on additional Latin manuscripts, was published in Prague in 1965 (Hus, 1965). Eng. tr. by David S. Schaff was printed in New York, 1915. Cf. also Molnár, 1957b.

[83]   Vol. I, *De Anatomia Antichristi* contained writings of Matěj of Janov and others. Cf. Kraus, I, 169 ff. and Hrejsa, IV, 278. On Brunfels, cf. *TQ Elsass*, I, 24, n. 1.

[84]   *Von schedligkeit der menschen satzungen oder Tradition* (Weller, No. 3439); *Dass die Secten . . . sollen ausgetilgt werden* (Weller, No. 3438); and also a German tr. of Brunfels' Latin martyrology, *Processus Johannis Hus: Geistlicher Bluthandel Johannis Hussz* (Weller, No. 3437). Cf. Kraus, I, 170.

[85]   To mention but a few: *Beclagung eines Leyens genant Hanns Schwalb uber viel misbrauchs christenlichs lebens und darin begriffen kurtzlich von Johannes Hussen* (1521; cf. Kraus, I, 167 f.); *Anzeigung . . . wie die gefallene Christenheit widerbracht müg werden . . . das concilium zu Basel und die Böhem betreffende* by Martin Reinhart (1524; cf. Kraus, I, 173); *Wie Hieronimus von Prag ain anhänger Johannis Huss . . . verprent worden ist* by Poggio Bracciolini (1521; Weller, Nos. 1969, 1970 and Suppl. 23). For others, see Kraus, I, 157 ff. On the

being published throughout Germany and in Switzerland.[86] Their reading contributed, no doubt, to a gradual transformation of the former censorious attitude toward the Bohemian heretics into an expression of admiration for Hus and his followers, including the Picards or Waldensians.

---

influence of Hussite ideas in Germany, see also Macek, 1958, 223 ff., Seibt, 1962 and Molnár, 1965c, 6 ff.

[86]   Two pamphlets would merit further investigation with respect to their characteristics of "Bohemian Christians": (1) *Von drien Christen. Dem Römischen Christen. Dem Böhemischen Christen. Dem Thürckischen Christen. N.d., n.p.* Printed and probably written by Pamphilus Gengenbach in Basel, 1523 (Gengenbach, 1523). Reprint in Goedeke, 1856, 214-230. Cf. Weller, Nos. 2434-2435, and Benzing, 1963, 31 f. The Bohemian Christian is a merchant (*kouffman*) from the city of "Bilsen" (Plzeň). He speaks German well because he does business also in Prussia and Austria. His description of conditions in Bohemia is printed on the last three pages of the tract. He mentions the bringing of Wycliff's books to Bohemia in 1410 [sic!] and enumerates eleven articles of Hus. He stresses communion in both kinds, abolition of monasteries and separation from the Roman church. "Wir haltens nit gar mit der Rŏmschen kirchen, so halten wirs auch nit nach der Ewangelischen leer" (fol. C iv a). "Ir halten vnns in unserem land für kătzer, vnd sind wir besser Christen dann ir, dann wir halten das ewangelisch gesatz, so halten ir das păbstlich gesatz" (fol. C iij a). The short pamphlet (21 pp. of text with marginal illustrations, fols. a i - c iv) makes mention of the first disputation in Zürich (January 29, 1523) and was probably printed later in 1523. The date of Gengenbach's death can be set only between October 15, 1523 and May 26, 1525 (Benzing, 1963, 31 f.). Lendi, 1926, 69 questioned the authorship by Gengenbach whereas Raillard, 1936, 63 ff. — following Humbel, 1912, 156 f. and Wackernagel, 1924, 394 — defended it. None of these authors raised the question about Gengenbach's source for his portrait of the Bohemian Christian. His views reflect the position of an evangelical Utraquist (Neo-Utraquist), as Hrejsa, IV, 269 pointed out. The author expresses his preference for the faith of the Turkish Christian which is summarized as "love of God and love of fellow men" (fol. C iv a). His inclusion of the Bohemian Christian and the enumeration of the articles of Hus might have been occasioned by the publication of Aeneas Sylvius, 1523 in Basel in April 1523, or possibly by personal contact with the young Czech humanist Sigismund Gelenius (Zikmund Hrubý z Jelení, 1497-1554) who came to Basel, at the age of 26, some time in 1523 to become one of Erasmus' closest associates as editor of Greek and Latin works in the shop of Froben. On Gelenius, see Bartoš, 1954a (later reprinted in Bartoš, 1959a, 75-79); Bartoš, 1958a, 257, n. 53; Allen, 1934, 107 and an unpublished Prague dissertation by Jiří Lejdar (not accessible to us). Erasmus referred to him as "vir utriusque linguae non vulgariter doctus probaeque fidei" (April 30, 1526; E, 6, 330). During his student days in Wittenberg, Gelenius found a friend in Melanchthon, who sent him repeated greetings in his letters to Oecolampad (June 24, 1524; end of September, 1524; January 12, 1525: Oecolampad, 1927, 283, 318, 339). In 1533, Gelenius was matriculated at the university of Basel together with the first Czech student from Bohemia, Václav Mitmánek, who was sent there by the *Unitas Fratrum*. There were no Czech students in Basel prior to 1533 (Sita, 1954, 16). (2) The other booklet bears the title *Ain Cristenlich gesprech Bŭchlin vonn zwayen Weybern, Mit namen Margretha Bŏhemin vnnd Anna Kollerin ... von Petter Reychart. 1523.* N.p. With the kind assistance of Dr. J. Benzing,

Yet another example of the widespread awareness of the ideological affinity between the Hussite Reformation of the fifteenth century and the young Reformation of the sixteenth century was the controversy between Conrad Treger, a Swiss Augustinian from Freiburg (Fribourg) and head of the Rhine-Swabian province of the Eremite Augustinian order, and the Reformers of Strasbourg, Bucer and Capito, during the year 1524. The title of Treger's second book, *Vermanung*, contained a warning "against the Bohemian heresy".[87] Capito's reply, *Antwurt*, was dedicated to the mayor and council of the city of Mühlhausen in Alsace, where Nikolaus Prügner was the leading evangelical minister.[88] Earlier that year, in Strasbourg, Hubmaier had published one edition of his *Achtzehn Schlussreden* in one volume with Prügner's Twenty Propositions.[89] Bucer was informed about the situation in Waldshut and in his letter to Zwingli, written on October 31, 1524 — four days after Hubmaier's return to Waldshut

---

we were able to identify the printer, Heinrich Steiner in Augsburg. In the dialogue, the Bohemian Margaret teaches another woman. As Hrejsa, IV, 269 pointed out, some of her admonitions might be interpreted as faint echoes of the teachings of the Czech Brethren (e.g. the triad of faith, love and hope, fol. a iv) but the main deductions seem to reflect Lutheran and mystic piety. The author emphasizes faith over against good works, distinguishes between "innerlich mensch" and "eusserliche werke", and refers to an inward knowledge which is thought of in terms of steps on Jacob's ladder. He mentions a sermon of St. Bernhard (de Clairvaux? fol. B i) and underlines readiness for the second coming of Christ.
[87] The controversy has been summarized by Johannes Müller in *BDS*, 2, 17-36. Cf. also Baum, 1860, 271 ff. Treger published his *Paradoxa centum fratris Conradi Tregarij* in Strasbourg on March 12, 1524. Capito replied, early in April, with his *Verwarnung der diener des worts vnd der Brüder zu Strassburg*, addressed to the brethren "von Landen vnd Stetten gemeyne Eidgenossenschafft". Treger retorted with *Vermanung bruder Conradts Treger . . . an ein lobliche gemeyne Eydgenossenschafft vor der Böhemschen ketzerey*. It was written at the beginning of May, but due to difficulties in finding a printer, not published till August 20 in Strasbourg. After a violent reaction in the city and Treger's temporary incarceration (Sept. 5-Oct. 12), Bucer published, on October 20, his *Ein kurtzer wahrhafftiger bericht von Disputationen und gantzem handel . . .* (now available in critical ed., *BDS*, 2, 37-173); Capito wrote his *Antwurt D. Wolffgang Fab. Capitons auff Brüder Conradts . . .* on October 24, 1524, and Caspar Hedio wrote his *Ablenung . . .* (cf. *BDS*, 2, 32, n. 70). Bucer and particularly Capito defended Hus and his followers (cf. *BDS*, 2, 134 and 138). Capito included a detailed account of the events at the Councils of Constance and Basel. An attempt to analyze the sources of Capito's and Bucer's knowledge of the Czech Reformation would lead us far beyond the scope of our present study.
[88] His name is mentioned in Capito, 1524, fol. A ij b. On Prügner, cf. Z, VIII, 526.
[89] Under the title, *Acht vnd dreyssig schlussrede . . .* (Strasbourg, Joh. Schwan, June 11, 1524). Cf. *HS*, 69 ff. and Bergsten, 1961, 131.

from his brief exile in Schaffhausen — he praised the citizens of Waldshut and held them up as an example.[90] Hubmaier read Bucer's *Grund und Ursache* and quoted from it in his book *Der Lehrer Urteil*.[91] His large book on baptism was printed in Strasbourg in July or August 1525.[92]

One can assume with a high degree of probability that Hubmaier was acquainted with at least Capito's *Antwurt*, if not with the other printed works which issued from the controversy between Treger and the Strasbourg Reformers in 1524.[93] Capito's references to the "purer and more scriptural" religion in the margraviate of Moravia[94] are of particular interest in view of Hubmaier's decision to go to Moravia.

In the early twenties, no other work of the Czech Brethren received wider acclaim beyond the borders of Bohemia and Moravia than the German version of their catechism, known commonly under the name *Kinderfragen*. The original Czech version, which was based on the Hussite catechisms of the fifteenth century, had appeared in its first printed edition already in 1501 or 1502, and then again, as the first part of a larger tripartite catechism, in November 1523. The German version (prepared perhaps by Jan Roh) was published in not less than eight, and possibly more, editions within three years, 1522-1524. In

---

[90] Z, VIII, 242.

[91] First ed. of *Grund und Ursache* at the end of December 1524, second ed. in 1525. Crit. ed. in *BDS*, 1, 185-278. The treatise was written by Bucer but released in the name of nine ministers in Strasbourg whose names appear at the end of the book. The quotations by Hubmaier in *HS*, 236 and 251.

[92] *HS*, 116 f. On Hubmaier's close relations with the Strasbourg reformers in the fall of 1524, and on the changed attitude after his public endorsement of believer's baptism, see Bergsten, 1961, 163, 265 ff. and 340 ff. The issue of baptism stood in the foreground of theological debate in Strasbourg in the fall of 1524 (cf. *TQ Elsass*, I, 11-29). At the same time, Hubmaier was developing his concept of believer's baptism.

[93] Both the controversy and Hubmaier's political exile in Schaffhausen were related to the contemporary religio-political situation in Switzerland. Cf. the analysis by Bergsten, 1961, 186 ff. The accusation of "the cursed hussite heretical faith" which was contained in the letter sent by the city of Freiburg i.B. to Waldshut on October 3, 1524 (cf. footnote 78 above), might have echoed the vocabulary of Treger's attacks (cf. footnote 87).

[94] Referring to many sects in Bohemia and Moravia, Capito claimed: "Doch seind die in der marggraffschaft Morauien etwas reyner vnd näher bey der geschrifft bliben" (Capito, 1524, fol. E I a). "Uss der eschen [i.e. Hus' and Jeronym's ashes] sind newe christen erwachsen ... Nach irem seligen todt ist die gantz Marggraffschafft Morauia, mit vil mechtigen stetten, dem wort, das durch sie gepredigt, angehangen" (fol. H I a). Keller, 1885, 306 interpreted Capito's words as a reference to the ideas of the Bohemian Brethren ("der böhmischen Brüdergemeinden").

addition, several adaptations of the text were made for use by the Lutheran churches and also by the Reformers in St. Gallen, Switzerland. The widely-scattered places of printing can serve as an indication of the scope of influence which this first catechism in the German language must have exercised on the emerging concepts of catechetical work in the German and Swiss Reformation. It must be stressed that none of the editions prior to 1530 bears any identification of the Czech Brethren. Instead, several of them refer to Martin Luther on their title page. Nevertheless, the short catechism — which was hardly suitable, from the pedagogical point of view, for instruction of small children — disseminated an elementary knowledge of the basic theological emphases of the Unity. It is known to have contributed to Luther's interest in the teachings of the Brethren. We shall consider the contents of the booklet later in connection with Hubmaier's catechism of 1526.[95]

At the time when Hubmaier lived in Schaffhausen, Heinrich Bullinger met with Zwingli in Zürich on September 12, 1524. Zwingli confided to the twenty-year-old headmaster of the cloister school at Kappel on Albis his concept of the eucharist. In turn, Bullinger shared with Zwingli his doubts about the doctrine of transubstantiation and explained his new interpretation which he had derived from "a

---

[95] A critical ed. of the Czech text, *Otázky dětinské*, by Molnár, 1948, 120-133. Crit. ed. of the German text by Zezschwitz, 1863, 39-58; Müller, 1887, 9-28 and Kåstner, 1902. An English tr. by Schweinitz, 1869 (based on the text ed. by Zezschwitz). Cf. also the Czech prefaces to the larger catechism of 1523 which were reprinted by Molnár, 1956a, 66-69. On the origin and theology of the catechism, Müller, 1887 remains the best study. On the authorship (Lukáš probably edited an older version which had been in use among the Brethren in the 15th century), on the Hussite sources and the relationship of the German text to the Waldensian *Enterrogaciones menors*, see Havelka, 1938, 27.176; Havelka, 1955 and Molnár's reply, Molnár, 1955a; Molnár, 1948, 115 ff. The study of Bednář, 1939 deals only with the Czech catechisms of the early 17th century. Heubach, 1952, 16 ff. used Müller, 1887 as the only source for his brief treatment of the *Kinderfragen*. For the list of editions of the German catechism, 1522-1530, see Appendix 4. In his attempts to prove connections between "the older evangelical brotherhoods", Keller, 1885 failed to differentiate between the Waldensian catechism and the catechisms (Czech and German) of the Czech Brethren. Although he was aware of the three different versions (296 f.), he proceeded to outline the contents of the Waldensian (Provençal) version (307 ff.), and then referred to the different printed editions of the German catechism of the Unity (338) as though these contained the same text. He based his brief comments on the older study of Zezschwitz (1863), according to which the *Kinderfragen* of the Unity were dependent upon the Waldensian catechism. Zezschwitz himself later reversed his conclusions about the literary dependence of the two (in *RE*, 2nd ed., II, 658). Cf. Molnár, 1948, 118 f. and F. Cohrs in *RE*, 3rd ed., 10, 138 f.

certain writing of the Waldensian brethren and from the books of Augustine".[96]

The biographers of Bullinger have been puzzled by this reference to "an unknown writing of the medieval Waldensians"[97] who are known to have retained the doctrine of transubstantiation until their contacts with the Czech and Swiss Reformation.[98] A similar uncertainty has prevailed in the interpretation of Zwingli's appeal to Wycliff and the Waldensians as advocates of a symbolic interpretation of the eucharist. He included the argument in his book, *De vera et falsa religione commentarius,* which was written soon after Bullinger's visit and printed at the end of March 1525.[99] Köhler surmised that Zwingli might have been referring to the Czech Brethren and basing his hearsay knowledge on Luther's book, *Vom Anbeten des Sacraments* (April 1523), which Capito had mentioned in his letter to Zwingli on February 6, 1525.[100] Since Luther's book contains no direct reference to Wycliff, Staedtke suggested that Zwingli was actually recalling his conversation (*audio*) with Bullinger on September 12, 1524.[101]

---

[96]   The only source is Bullinger's own recollection recorded in his *Diarium* (Bullinger, 1904, 9), which was not written till after 1540: "12. Septembris [1524] primo aperuit mihi mentem suam Zuinglius, quid sentiret de sacramento corporis et sanguinis Domini. Nam bona fide illi exponebam sententiam meam, quam hauseram ex scripto quodam fratrum Vualdens. et Augustini libris. Interim prohibebat, ne cui id mysterii explicarem; nondum enim satis tempestivum esse, ut proferatur; velle se iusto tempore proferre. Coeperam autem hoc anno varia authorum evolvere scripta, ut ex his quid omnium sentiendum esset intelligerem."

[97]   Blanke, 1942, 77 and 171; before him Simler, 1575, 11; Pestalozzi, 1858, 26; Egli, 1904, 440; Bouvier, 1940, 16, n. 2.

[98]   Cf. Staedtke, 1960, 21 ff.; Molnár, 1952b; Molnár, 1958a; Gonnet, 1952.

[99]   "Audio, ut hoc primo loco dicam, Viclevum olim et Valdenses etiam hodie in hac esse sententia, ut 'est' hic sit positum pro 'significat', quorum tamen ipse fundamenta scripturae non vidi." (Z, III, 795; cf. Blanke's tr. in *Zwingli Hauptschriften,* 10, 96.)

[100]   "Wiclefi autem et tua frigidissime solvit [Luther] in libello, quem at Waldenses scripsit" (Capito to Zwingli, Feb. 6, 1525, Z, VIII, 304). On Luther's book, see footnote 59 in previous chapter. According to Köhler, 1921, 25 (No. 204), Luther's book was in the Stiftsbibliothek in Zürich.

[101]   Staedtke, 1960, 20 ff. However, his criticism of Köhler's hypothesis applies also to his own suggestion. The name of Wycliff was not mentioned in Luther's book, nor in Bullinger's entry in the *Diarium.* Bullinger refers to the Waldensians and to Augustine. On the other hand, Capito's letter mentions both Wycliff and the Waldensians. Zwingli might have been recalling simply Capito's reference without consulting Luther's book itself. Cf. also another explanation proposed by Köhler, 1924, 91 f. Zwingli could have combined the names of Wycliff and Waldensians as an echo of accusations raised against him ("Viclevianus est, Valdensis est, haereticus est", Z, III, 796).

Staedtke's identification of the Waldensians with the Czech Brethren is obviously correct, for the simple reason that Bullinger referred to *Fratres Valdenses*. This was a standard name for the Czech Brethren and, to the best of our knowledge, had not been used by the medieval Waldensians.[102] Staedtke then attempted to find the source for Bullinger's knowledge of the 'Waldensian' concept of the eucharist and suggested Ziegler's polemical work against the Unity (1512).[103] However, it is far more reasonable to suspect that Bullinger gained his information from the collection of sources which had been published in Basel in April 1523.[104] Several factors make this hypothesis highly probable.

The edition was prepared by Jakob Sobius, whose lectures Bullinger heard during his studies in Köln (fall 1519-spring 1522).[105] Sobius released his volume as a reply to the *Catalogus haereticorum* which was issued, in 1522, by the Dominican monastery in Köln at the time when Bullinger used its library.[106] Even though Bullinger left Köln a full year before Sobius' volume was printed in Basel, he might have known about the planned edition. Furthermore, the book contains a large section on the teachings of Wycliff.[107] Bullinger

---

[102]   This important differentiation in nomenclature has been overlooked by all students of Bullinger.

[103]   Staedtke, 1960, 24 f. On Ziegler, 1512, see above at footnote 54.

[104]   Aeneas Sylvius, 1523. Cf. footnote 63 above. Molnár, 1957a, 27 expressed the same hypothesis. The theology of the eucharist is presented in all three confessions reprinted in Aeneas Sylvius, 1523. See esp. 128 f.; 135 f., 140-142 and 150-157. Cf. also quotations in Staedtke, 1960, 24 f., footnotes 29-34. Bullinger might have read also some of the older editions of the confessions (Apologia, 1511, Ziegler, 1512, Dungersheim, 1514a-b) since his rejection of the doctrine of transsubstantiation can be dated already in 1521 (Staedtke, 1960, 19, n. 5). Bullinger used a large library in the Dominican monastery in Köln (Blanke, 1942, 50; Bullinger, 1904, 5) which likely had on its shelves the polemical volumes of Ziegler and Dungersheim. It is unlikely that Bullinger would have referred to the German catechism of the Unity. Its early editions (1522-1524) bore no identification of the Unity. They did, however, contain two long questions on the eucharist (Müller, 1887, 4 and 21 ff.).

[105]   Bullinger was enrolled at the Bursa montis and Sobius was associated with the Bursa Corneliana. However, Bullinger heard the lectures of Sobius "extra scholam in liberis, ut vocant, aut extraordinariis lectionibus" (Bullinger's letter, March 12, 1545, printed by Krafft, 1870, 13). On Sobius' career in Köln, see Krafft, 1870, 36-48. On Bullinger's studies in Köln, see Blanke, 1942, 35-53.

[106]   Krafft, 1870, 38. The *Catalogus* referred to is Bernardus, 1522. Later it became the main source for Franck's list of heretics in his *Chronica*, 1531. Cf. footnote 63 above and footnote 122 in Chapter V.

[107]   More than a third of the volume deals with Wycliff: "Articuli Io. Viclefi impugnati a Wilhelmo Widefordo" (161-260); "Articuli Io. Viclefi damnati per concilium Constantiense" (261-278); "Rationes et motiva, ac reprobationes articu-

could, therefore, have discussed with Zwingli, in September 1524, the eucharistic theology of both Wycliff and the Waldensians. This in turn would explain Zwingli's reference to both in his *Commentarius*.[108]

Some time prior to 1528, Bullinger must have studied the teachings of Hus, for he wrote a German exposition of twenty-four articles of Hus. Unfortunately, nothing more than the title of the lost work has been preserved.[109]

---

lorum Viclefi et sequacis sui Io. Huss in concilio Const. damnatorum" (279-297); "Sententia damnationis doctrinae Io. Wiclefi" (345 f.).

[108] Cf. note 99 above. Bullinger included Peter Valdes among the forerunners of a symbolic interpretation of the eucharist (Fast, 1959, 92, 435 and Staedtke, 1960, 22, n. 21). Further study is needed to determine Bullinger's understanding of the relationship between Valdes, medieval Waldensians and the Czech "fratres Valdenses". According to Staedtke, 1960, 21, n. 13, Bullinger refers to the Waldensian doctrine of the eucharist in two of his writings (Nos. 73 and 79 of Bullinger's Bibliography up to 1528; Staedtke, 1962, 287 and 289). Several other writings should be examined, in particular Nos. 38 and 48 (Staedtke, 1962, 276 and 280). Cf. also quotations in Staedtke, 1962, 244, n. 33; 245, n. 34; 254, n. 72. The definition of the Czech Brethren's doctrine of the eucharist in Šlechta's letter to Erasmus (October 10, 1519) is worth noting: "In sacramento Eucharistiae nihil esse diuinitatis credunt, sed solum panem et vinum consecratum, signis quibusdam occultis mortem Christi repraesentantem affirmantes; et propterea in idolatriam cadere omnes quotquot coram illo genua flectunt, et incuruant, vel illud adorant: cum in alium finem a Christo sacramentum illud institutum non sit, nisi ad memoriam passionis ipsius recolendam, et non vt hinc [1521 ed.: hic] et inde circumferatur, aut eleuatum a sacerdote videndum ostendatur; quoniam Christus ipse qui adorandus et cultu latriae honorandus est, sedet ad dexteram Dei patris, sicut in symbolo fidei Christiana confitetur Ecclesia." (*E*, 4, 84. Printed originally in Erasmus, 1521, 551. Cf. Staedtke, 1960, 24 f.) It is difficult to judge whether Bullinger might have seen the volume of Erasmus' correspondence which was printed by Frobenius at the end of 1521, a few months before Bullinger's return from Köln (April 1522). Erasmus' visit in Köln in October 1520 had left behind a lasting impression (Blanke, 1942, 46 f.). Bullinger repeatedly expressed his indebtedness to Erasmus for his biblical works and patristic editions (Staedtke, 1962, 33 f.). Note also Bullinger's praise for the printer Frobenius (*ibid.*, footnote 20).

[109] "Declaratio 24 articulorum Ioannis Huss, ad Annam Kolinam". The title was listed by Bullinger in his *Diarium* (Bullinger, 1904, 16) among the German works written during the six-year period 1523-1528. The treatise has been lost and even the identification of "Anna Kolin", for whom Bullinger wrote it, has not been unequivocal. (Cf. Braendly, 1950, 150 f.; Staedtke, 1954, 44, n. 72; Staedtke, 1962, 270 and 272.) Molnár, 1957a, 27 suggested that Bullinger might have used Aeneas Sylvius, 1523 as the source for the articles of Hus. This is somewhat questionable since the volume contains extensive materials on Wycliff, but no articles of Hus except the 44 articles listed under the joint authorship of "Wycliff and his follower Hus" on pp. 279-297 (cf. footnote 107). The extant writings of Bullinger from this period (Staedtke, 1962, 263-292 lists a total of 86, including correspondence) merit detailed study in view of Staedtke's claim that Bullinger paid considerable attention to Hus and Jerome of Prague, around 1525 (Staedtke, 1960, 32). Cf. also the

In this connection, we must point out additional evidence about the knowledge of the Czech Reformation among the leading men of the Swiss Reformation during its formative years. In 1530, Oecolampad stated in his reply to the emissaries of the Romance Waldensians that "for a long time he had known their teachings from the confession sent to King Vladislav many years ago".[110] We may conclude with certainty that he read the confession in the collection of documents which had been printed by Cratander in March or April

---

statement in Stumpf, 1952, 149 (referring to Luther's and Zwingli's theological development in 1519): "Doch warent anfengklich gemeynlich alle artickel des Wykleffen, Joannis Husssen unnd Hieromini von Prag uff der pan etc.".

[110] "Sane dogmata vestrae fraternitatis olim cognovimus ex his, quae ante multos annos Vladislao, Ungariae regi, responsa; quae in his, quae at Christum attinent, plane catholica et a nobis quoque recepta" (From Oecolampad's reply, October 13, 1530, reprinted in Oecolampad, 1934, 511). The questions of the Waldensian emissaries, George Morel and Pierre Masson, are printed *ibid.*, 503-510. On the contacts of the Waldensians with the Reformers in Neuchâtel, Bern, Basel and Strasbourg (in 1530), see a summary in Williams, 1962, 522-528; also Gonnet, 1952; Staehelin, 1939, 625-629; Molnár, 1952b and 1954a. In 1533, two other Waldensian messengers spent nearly half a year with the Brethren in Mladá Boleslav and returned with an official letter from the leaders of the Unity (dated June 25, 1533 and published by Molnár, 1952b, 85 f.). Since Oecolampad was dealing with the Waldensians from the Romance language area one must raise the question concerning the identity of the confessional statement designated by him as "Vladislao, Ungariae regi, responsa". Among the several items of Waldensian literature which were written in "la langue vaudoise" (the Waldensian dialect of the Provençal, Goll, 1916, 266) and represented free renditions of the writings of the Czech Brethren, there was preserved, in a manuscript at the library of Trinity College, Dublin, a letter bearing the title "[La epistola] Al serenissima princi Rey Lancelau, al duc barons a li plus velh del regne, lo petit tropel de li Xristians appella per fals nom falsament P.[icards] o.V.[audes]". The first part is a free translation of the Czech version of the 1507 letter to King Vladislav (published by Molnár, 1947, 12-21). The Latin counterpart — not a literal translation — is the *Confessio fratrum regi Vladislao ad Ungariam missa* (cf. footnote 51 above). According to Molnár's extensive research into the complex relationships between the Waldensian literature and the Czech and Latin writings of the Unity, the books were not brought from Bohemia to Italy by Lukáš during his visit to Italy in 1498, nor by the Waldensian emissaries to Bohemia in 1533, but rather through some other channels during the first quarter of the sixteenth century. (See Molnár, 1947, 10 ff.; 1949a; 1952b; 1954a; 1958a; 1962a). According to one source (letter of Jan Černý to Flacius Illyricus, May 10, 1556, reprinted by Gindely, 1859, 278), the Brethren sent emissaries to the Waldensians in Italy some time before 1516 ("ante annos plus quam XL"), perhaps with a copy of the large *Apologia* 1511 (Molnár, 1952a, 77). In a letter written from Bologne in 1510 Václav Písecký reported that the *Oratio excusatoria atque satisfactiva* (1503 — cf. footnote 50) was known there. A medical student, Peter of Třebsko — a pupil of Jan Černý "the Physician" who had defended the Unity in the literary polemic against Augustin Käsenbrod (cf. footnotes 43-47 and 52) — studied in Italy for several years and returned to Litomyšl in 1523 (Molnár, 1949a, 56 and 1962a, 31 with references to sources).

1523 while Oecolampad worked in the same shop on his edition of Chrysostom.[111]

Another man who must have been acquainted with 'the heretics' in Moravia is the mayor and Reformer of St. Gallen, Vadian (Joachim of Watt, 1485-1551). Between 1501 and 1518, he had spent a total of fourteen years in Vienna, first as a student, then as a teacher (from 1508 onward) and for one semester (1516-1517) rector of the university.[112] The great humanist scholar, orator, poet and patron of Swiss students at the university,[113] maintained regular personal and correspondence contacts with the humanists in Moravia, such as Bishop Thurzo,[114] Augustinus Moravus (Käsenbrod),[115] Marcus Rustimini-

---

[111]   Oecolampad, 1927, 207 and 217, n. 5. Cf. also footnote 63 above. Oecolampad had easy access to the three Latin confessions reprinted in Basel. The Provençal version of the 1507 confession was never printed. Nor does it discuss the question of baptism which Oecolampad mentioned in his reply to the Waldensian emissaries: "A papistis baptisatos non rebaptisamus, ut catabaptistae, absit; sed synaxim illorum refugimus" (Oecolampad, 1934, 512). Of the three confessions reprinted in Basel, only the first (1503) contains a statement on baptism: "'Fides a deo data, talia de baptismate primo sacramento cogit sentire: Quicunque matura iam aetate auditu uerbi dei fidem adeptus qua in anima renatus, illuminatusque uim nactus fuerit, talis exteriori lauacro in argumentum interioris mundiciae per fidem acquisitae baptisari tenetur in nomine patris, & filij, & spiritus sancti, in unitatem ecclesiae sanctae. Professio ista nostra etiam in pueros extenditur, qui Decreto apostolorum (prout Dionysius scribit) baptisari debent: post ductu compatrum in Christi lege eruditorum uitam fidei inuitandos esse, assuescendosque" (Aeneas Sylvius, 1523, 128). The subsequent article on the confirmation further substantiates the Unity's practice of infant baptism. None of the three printed confessions mentions rebaptism which was practised by the Unity until 1534. Did Oecolampad know also the Apology (1511) where rebaptism was discussed (Peschke, 1964, 80)? Or was he reacting merely to information obtained through conversations with the Waldensian emissaries? He might have read a reference to rebaptism in Šlechta's letter to Erasmus: "Qui ad haeresim eorum accedunt, coguntur singuli rebaptizari in aqua simplici" (E, 4, 84, line 211 f.; printed originally in Erasmus, 1521, 551). Oecolampad came to Basel in November 1522 and lived first in the house of Cratander.

[112]   On Vadian's stay in Vienna, see Näf, 1944, 117 ff.; Bonorand, 1965 and Bender, 1950, 17-26.

[113]   On the Swiss students in Vienna during Vadian's professorship, cf. Bender, 1950, 17 f. Among them were Conrad Grebel (September 1515 to June 1518) and Jacob Zwingli, brother of the Zürich Reformer.

[114]   Näf, 1944, 190, 228; Bonorand, 1965, 41 ff.

[115]   Cf. Augustin's dedicatory epistle to Vadian, Feb. 13, 1512 (Näf, 1944, 141, n. 1). In a letter to his brother Melchior, dated in Vienna, December 13, 1513, Vadian bewailed the death of Käsenbrod (on November 3, 1513; Vadian, I, 237). On December 11, 1516, Stephanus Taurinus Olomucensis requested Vadian to forward to him letters received from the late Käsenbrod so that they could be included in a printed collection (Vadian, I, 174). See also Näf, 1944, 221 ff.; Bonorand, 1965, 41 ff. and our mention of Käsenbrod above at footnotes 43-48.

cus [116] and Wolfgang Heligmaier 'Bohemus'.[117] Vadian visited Olomouc and Brno on his extensive journey from St. Gallen through Germany, via Breslau and Cracow to Vienna and back to Switzerland, in the spring of 1519.[118] He might have been to Moravia before. In Vienna, he also met Jakob Ziegler shortly after the latter had attended to the printing of his polemical work against the Unity in Leipzig in 1512.[119] He met him again in 1518 [120] and exchanged letters with him in later years.[121]

Even if one does not overlook the secular character of the Viennese humanism and the general orientation of Vadian to non-religious spheres of life during his stay in Vienna,[122] one may assume that at least through his contacts with Käsenbrod and Ziegler, the two chief literary opponents of the Unity who wrote their polemics in Moravia, Vadian must have acquired more than hearsay knowledge about the Hussites and the Czech Brethren. In one of his earliest religious

[116] Rustiminicus taught in Olomouc. Cf. his letters written from there to Vadian in Vienna on the following dates: May 24, 1512 (Vadian, I, 96, No. 14); Oct. 28, 1512 (ibid., 102, No. 18); June 16, 1514 (ibid., 121 f., No. 37); October 31, 1514 (ibid., 130 f., No. 44) and some time in 1517 (ibid., 207, No. 111). See also Näf, 1944, 223 and Bonorand, 1965, 38.

[117] Heligmaier came from Bohemia and studied with Vadian in Vienna. In 1516, he wrote four letters to Vadian from Brno: April 23 (Vadian, I, 151 f., No. 65); June 12 (ibid., 157, No. 69); Aug. 4 (ibid., 162, No. 73); Sept. 2 (ibid., 162 f., No. 74). When Vadian — accompanied by Conrad Grebel — left Vienna in June 1518, Heligmaier wrote to him from Vienna, Sept. 24, 1518, wishing for his return (Vadian, II, 201 f., No. 134). In 1519, he wrote to Vadian two letters from Olomouc: April 18 (ibid., 226 f., No. 148) and Sept. 16 (ibid., 247, No. 168). The only letter preserved from later years was written by H. in Gamnitz on June 17, 1539 (Vadian, V. 1, 563, No. 1063). Heligmaier was also a close friend of Conrad Grebel who called him "my patron" and sent greetings to him with Vadian when the latter returned to Vienna for a short visit in November 1518: "Mag. Volfgangum Bohemum, patronum meum, suosque tuosque, qui Viennae sunt, cum eo veneris, nomine meo multa salute" (Vadian, II, 203, No. 135, written in Zürich, Sept. 26, 1518). A similar expression of admiration for Heligmaier is found in Grebel's letter to Vadian sent from Paris, Jan. 29, 1519 (ibid., 215; cf. Bender, 1950, 22 and 232, n. 65). On Heligmaier, see also Bonorand, 1965, 47 ff.

[118] Näf, 1944, 221 f.

[119] Schottenloher, 1910, 35. Cf. footnote 54 above.

[120] They met in Buda (Ofen) (Schottenloher, 1910, 36).

[121] Ziegler's letter to Vadian from Ferrara, Aug. 1, 1526 (Vadian, IV, No. 466) and three letters from Strasbourg, April 18 and May 20, 1532 and March 23, 1533 (Vadian, V. 1, Nos. 679, 688 and 731). C. Näf, 1957, 372.

[122] Cf. Bender's characteristic, Bender, 1950, 20-26, and Näf's detailed description, Näf, 1944, 117-360. Recently, Bonorand has pointed out the unsolved question of the influence of the Viennese university upon the rise of the Reformation in the Austrian-Hungarian sphere, and in particular among the Slavic people (Bonorand, 1963, 596 ff.). Cf. also Bonorand, 1965, 44.

writings, dating from the end of 1521 or the beginning of 1522, Vadian argued against the primacy of the pope and the Roman church. He included a discussion of the arguments used by Jean Gerson against Hus at the Council of Constance.[123] Staedtke's suggestion that Vadian might have passed on information about the eucharistic doctrines of the Czech Brethren to Bullinger when he visited him at Kappel on July 12, 1524 [124] — only two months before Bullinger's visit with Zwingli in Zürich — remains an interesting but unconfirmed hypothesis.

On the preceding pages we have demonstrated the interest of some of the leading humanists and Reformers of the Swiss and South German area in the heritage of the Czech Reformation, either in its early phase of Hussitism, or in the *Unitas Fratrum*. Our findings seem to confirm the observation made by Staedtke that "the Bohemian traditions might have been more at work in Switzerland than one is perhaps inclined today to admit, particularly with reference to the observation of the Lord's Supper in both kinds".[125]

Hubmaier had personal or epistolary contacts with most of the leaders mentioned. He met Erasmus in Basel in the spring of 1522, Vadian in St. Gallen in April 1523 and again at the Second Disputation in Zürich at the end of October 1523 where Vadian was co-chairman along with Sebastian Hofmeister of Schaffhausen and Christoph Schappeler of St. Gallen. On June 8, 1524, Vadian wrote Hubmaier an encouraging letter.[126] A month later, Vadian visited Bullinger who does not appear to have made a personal acquaintance of Hubmaier.[127] The personal contacts between Hubmaier and Zwingli (May

---

[123] "Vadiani fasciculus argumentorum contra primatum pape et ecclesiae romanae, pro Luthero, contra Eccium et Gersonem ... quorum sophismata refutantur idque maxime ex Cypriano". (Ms. in St. Gallen Stadtbibliothek, Vadiana No. 58; cf. summary in Näf, 1957, 142 ff.)
[124] Bullinger, 1904, 9. Staedtke, 1960, 26. According to Staedtke, Vadian would have obtained his knowledge of the Unity's concept of the eucharist from the polemical work of Ziegler.
[125] Staedtke, 1960, 32. Cf. also Schweizer, 71.
[126] Vadian, III, 240. Reprinted also in Loserth, 1893, 195 f., with the wrong date 1523.
[127] Cf. footnote 124. In all likelihood, Bullinger was present, as a recorder, at all three disputations with the Anabaptists which were held in Zürich in January, March and November 1525 (cf. Fast, 1959, 17, n. 25 and 111 ff.). Hubmaier was not invited for the first two (Bergsten, 1961, 253). He was on his way to attend the November disputation but was forced to return to Waldshut on account of the military operations against the peasants in the Klettgau area (Fast, 1959, 169; Bergsten, 1961, 344 f.; Yoder, 1962, 74).

1523, October 1523 and fall 1524) during the 'pre-Anabaptist' phase of Hubmaier's theological development have been mentioned earlier. A brief note written to Zwingli in November 1524,[128] a letter to Oecolampad dated on January 16, 1525,[129] as well as the latter's reply on January 18,[130] fall already into the priod of Hubmaier's transition into Anabaptism and estrangement from the Swiss Reformers.

During the four years 1521-1524, so decisive for the genesis of his theology, Hubmaier lived and worked within the framework of the Swiss and South German Reformation and had access to the same printed sources which account for the limited knowledge of the Czech Reformation in that area. Before we attempt to trace any evidence of such influence in Hubmaier's preserved writings, we must point out three additional sources from a slightly later period (1525-1526).

In January 1525 — the same month in which the first rebaptisms took place in Zürich and in Waldshut — three short German apologies of the Czech Brethren were printed in Zwickau.[131] The first two were prepared expressly for the diet which convened in Prague on January 25, 1525. The third was a translation of a letter written and sent by Brother Lukáš to King Louis II in 1524. The common purpose of the three documents was to avert more severe persecution of the Unity. The petitions are not doctrinal in content. Instead, the Brethren attempt to clarify the historical origins of their Unity. They picture the beginnings from within the Hussite movement in the days of Rokycana and Chelčický and reject the accusations of their enemies who associated them with the Picards or the Waldensians. They also enunciate the principle of separation between secular and spiritual authority and deny any right to the secular power to rule in spiritual matters.

---

[128] Z, VIII, 254 f.
[129] Oecolampad, 1927, 341 ff.
[130] Oecolampad, 1927, 344 ff. See also the different interpretations by Bergsten, 1961, 261 ff. and Yoder, 1962, 58 ff.
[131] (1) *Eyn kurtz vnterricht von dem vrsprunck der Bruder yn Behmen, vnd desselben vrsach, Daryn sie auch beweysen das sie nicht aus der waldenser oder Pickarten rotten kommen* . . . . (2) *Eyn recht Christlich. Sende Brieff vn erbittung, der Bruder aus Behem Ann alle stende des Reychs* . . . . (3) *Eyn sende brieff der bruder aus Behem . . . an den grossmechtigen Herrn Luwig* [!] . . . . All three were printed by Jorg Gastel who worked in the Zwickau printing shop owned by Johann Schönsberger Jr. (Benzing, 1963, 498). Cf. also Keller, 1885, 338. The last two were translated by Johann Zeysinck — Čížek. No translator is indicated in the first booklet. The second is reprinted in Palmov, 1904, 365-381. For full titles and summary of content, see Müller, I, 425-429 and Molnár, 1952a, 105 f.

It is doubtful that the booklets printed in distant Saxony would have reached immediately Hubmaier in Waldshut. However, since two of them, if not all three, were translated into German by Jan Čížek-Zeising, one might suspect that he could have informed Hubmaier about their contents when the two men became friends in Mikulov late in 1526.[132]

Some time in 1526, one edition of Glaidt's *Handlung* was printed by Johannes Hager in Zürich.[133] Hubmaier displayed a knowledge of Glaidt's report when he wrote the preface to his first book published in Moravia, at Mikulov on July 21, 1526.[134] It would be tempting to suggest that Glaidt's manuscript was brought to Zürich and the report printed while Hubmaier was still in the city after his public recantations in mid-April. A knowledge about the religious situation in Moravia as reported by Glaidt could have been, no doubt, the decisive factor in Hubmaier's decision to go there. But even if one could postulate the printing during April,[135] one would still have to weigh the significance of two known facts. After his release from the jail, Hubmaier spent his last days in Zürich in strict confinement and could, therefore, have had few if any contacts with the people in the city. Then, he took a rather long time to reach Moravia, with several stops on the way. His extended stay in Augsburg seems to suggest that he and his wife had no definite destination in mind when they were leaving Zürich. This does not preclude some knowledge of the Moravian scene. However, in all probability, they did not decide finally for Mikulov until in Augsburg, the city which enjoyed regular traffic with Moravia and Silesia.[136]

A few weeks after Hubmaier's arrival at Mikulov, Johannes Faber published one of his polemical works against Zwingli.[137] In the fall of 1526 Hubmaier worked on the final textual revisions of his reply to Zwingli's *Taufbüchlein*. One might suspect that he was interested in Faber's book not only because of the common subject but also because of lifelong ties with Faber who was then engaged in Ferdi-

---

[132]   Cf. footnotes 175 and 210 below.
[133]   Glaidt, 1526. See Appendix 2.
[134]   Cf. our summary at footnotes 142-144 in the preceding chapter.
[135]   Bergsten, 1961, 403 and *HS*, 59. Our textual analysis of the three editions of Glaidt, 1526 rules out the hypothesis. Cf. Appendix 2, at footnotes 2 and 3.
[136]   Cf. Simprecht Sorg's letter to Zwingli (Sept. 17, 1528) cited at footnote 164 in the preceding chapter.
[137]   *Christenliche beweisung* (Faber, 1526b). The manuscript was completed at the disputation in Baden on May 21, 1526 but not printed till September 4, 1526 in Tübingen. For contents and analysis, see Helbling, 1933, 36-41.

nand's services in Vienna.[138] The name of Faber is mentioned no less than eleven times in Hubmaier's booklet.[139]

The third part of Faber's book contains a survey of heretical movements of the past. Among others, he enumerates thirty articles of Hus,[140] twenty-eight articles of the "Picards or Waldenses, a new sect which arose in Bohemia"[141] and thirty articles of Johannes Wessel.[142] Two years later, after Hubmaier's death, the "ninety articles" of Hus, the Picards and Wessel were published in Leipzig in an expanded form as a separate booklet, this time directed against Luther.[143] A Latin edition of the same work was included in Faber's *Opuscula* of 1537.[144]

According to Faber's own statement the articles of the Bohemian Picards were drawn from their two confessions which "had been submitted to King Vladislav and printed in 1508".[145] A textual comparison shows that for his Latin version Faber used verbatim quotations from the two Latin confessions of the Unity submitted to King Vladislav in 1503 and 1507.[146] Most likely, he copied them from the reprint in Ziegler's polemical work of 1512.[147] The quotations in the

---

[138] Cf. our references to Faber at footnotes 4 and 74 above.

[139] *HS*, 175-210 (*passim*).

[140] Faber, 1526b, fols. Z iij - a i. Cf. footnote 74 above.

[141] Fols. a i - a iij^v. Reference to the origin of the Picards in 1304 during the reign of King Wenceslas is found on fol. Z i. Faber might have used Bernardus, 1522 as his source. Elsewhere (fol. a j) Faber dates the origin of the Picards and other sects ("Hussiter, Rogkenzaner, Taboriter, Pickharder vnd ander vil mer secten) zů der zeit des künig Lassla aufferstanden". He refers likely to King Ladislav Posthumus (1453-1457) rather than to King Vladislav (1471-1516).

[142] Fols. a iij^v - b ij^v.

[143] Faber, 1528f. A copy of this edition was not accessible to us.

[144] Faber, 1537a: "XC Articuli in quibus Io. Hus et Pighardi Waldenses, ac Ioannes de Wesalia, tolerabiliores Martino Luthero inueniuntur", fols. f v - i iv. The articles of the Picards are found on fols. g vi^v - i j^v.

[145] "Haec ex Pighardorum scriptis duabus ad Regem Vladislaum Confessionibus, quas anno domini MDVIII exhibuerunt, dicta sint" (Faber, 1537a, fol. i j^v). A similar reference is found in the German version of 1526. For the complete list of the Picard articles see Appendix 3.

[146] Cf. footnotes 50 and 51 above.

[147] Cf. footnotes 54 and 55 above. In Ziegler, 1512, the confessions of 1503 and 1507 are printed together and separated from the 1508 confession by the letters of Augustin Käsenbrod (see footnotes 46-47 and 50-52 above). In Aeneas Sylvius, 1523, all three confessions appear together. The fact that Faber quotes only the first two, points to Ziegler's volume. Besides, Faber and Ziegler were personal friends and spent some time together in Rome 1521-1522 (Helbling, 1944, 20 ff.; Schottenloher, 1908, 31 ff.). Faber might have used the original prints of 1503 and 1507 of which no extant copies are known (Müller, I, 524 and 530; Štrupl, 1964a, 34 and 44).

German version of 1526 represent a rather free and abbreviated translation of the Latin text of the confessions. It must be remembered that in these early works Faber was not directly attacking the Czech heretics — this he did in some of his later works [148] — but rather exploiting some of their more orthodox views for polemical purposes against Zwingli [149] (in 1526) and against Luther [150] (in 1528). The sixth article on baptism may serve as an illustration of his method of work. He completely ignored the first part of the article which defines believer's baptism [151] and quoted only the last sentence which allows also infant baptism [152] on the authority of Dionysius Areopagita. Faber then used the bracketed reference to Dionysius as the basis for a separate (eighth) article.

Faber's book against Zwingli provided yet another opportunity for Hubmaier to learn something about the Czech Picards, fragmentary and distorted as Faber's information was. It is difficult to prove or disprove that Hubmaier read the book. We were unable to find any reference to it in Hubmaier's works published in the fall of 1526 or during 1527. On the other hand, Hubmaier read in Mikulov Zwingli's *De peccato originali declaratio ad Urbanum Rhegium* which was printed in Zürich practically at the same time that Faber's book was being published in Tübingen.[153] One should also remember that a year later, the imprisoned Anabaptist leader requested a visit by

---

[148]   E.g., Faber, 1528d, 1529a, 1537b and 1537c.

[149]   Cf. Faber's concluding statement at the end of the Picard articles: "Ich hoff es sey gnůg bewisen, wie gross ketzer die Pickharder seyend, dz doch dennest so zwingli zů jnen keme vnd wőlt sie den glauben lern, den er souil jar zů Zürich gelert vnd gepredigt hat, sy wurdent sturm über jn leüten vnd jn verbannen, auch jre kirchen vnd heüser vor jm beschliessen" (Faber, 1526b, fol. a iijᵛ). The irony of Faber's statement is its historical truthfulness. With the exception of some of its circles in Moravia, the Unity under the leadership of Lukáš closed its door to Zwinglian theology (see our exposition in the preceding chapter, at footnote 85).

[150]   Cf. Faber's statement: "Certe non ideo haec scripserim, ut ullum ex erroribus eorum aut defendere, aut iustificare (quod absit) uelim, sed utcunque ex istis collationibus intelligant Germani, quanto grauior intolerabiliorque sit doctrina haeresisque Lutheri ... quam sint haereses Pighardorum ...". (Faber, 1537a, fol. i jᵛ.)

[151]   The complete text of the article from the 1503 confession is quoted in footnote 111 above. English tr. in Robinson, 1792, 503.

[152]   Faber, 1526b, fol. a jᵛ: "Bekennend die Pickhardi, das der kindertauff von den zwőlff botten [Aposteln] auffgesetzt vnd erkant worden sey. Das aber zwinglius nit halt."

[153]   Z, V, 359-396. Hubmaier's references in HS, 264. Cf. also Bergsten, 1961, 416 f. and Z, V, 367. Zwingli's book was printed in August, Faber's book on September 4, 1526.

Faber.[154] The bonds of friendship nearly twenty years old were tested severely during the latter years of Hubmaier's life, renewed for a few weeks before his death and then bewailed for another decade in Faber's polemical works against the silenced enemy and friend.[155]

With the reference to Faber's books we have concluded our enumeration of the manifold opportunities for a knowledge about the Czech Reformation and the religious situation in Moravia which presented themselves to Hubmaier from his days in Ingolstadt until the initial period of his stay in Moravia. We now turn to an analysis of such knowledge as is evidenced in his preserved writings.

3. EVIDENCES OF CONTACT IN HUBMAIER'S WRITINGS

A literary analysis of Hubmaier's works has been completed satisfactorily by Sachsse and Bergsten.[156] Unless additional manuscripts are discovered — an event which seems to be quite improbable — the list prepared by Bergsten and his dating of Hubmaier's individual writings will require scarcely any major revisions.

The preserved writings ascribed to Hubmaier fall into three literary categories. (a) Twenty-four printed booklets which all appeared within three years (May 1524 - June 1527); (b) Personal letters, appeals to authorities, and statements in court hearings, all of which fall into the pre-Moravian period of Hubmaier's life, with the exception of two documents from his final imprisonment in 1528.[157] No correspondence nor documents of any other kind, apart from the printed books, have been preserved from Hubmaier's one-year stay in Moravia (June-July 1526 to July 1527). (c) Other correspondence or statements written mostly on behalf of the town of Waldshut (all from the pre-Moravian period). Apart from one insignificant reference to the Hussite heresies which we have discussed earlier,[158] the

---

[154] *HS*, 460. Bergsten, 1961, 478 ff.
[155] Faber, 1528a, 1528e and reprint in 1537a.
[156] Sachsse, 1914, 4-116; Bergsten, 1961, 55-58; *HS*, 58 ff. Bergsten's introductions to individual works reprinted in *HS*, revise, in several cases, Sachsse's dating of Hubmaier's writings, especially from the Moravian period.
[157] *Rechenschaft des Glaubens*, January 3, 1528, now reprinted in *HS*, 458-491; and *Urgicht*, March 1528, reprinted in Loserth, 1893, 215 f. and Boehmer, 1933, 13 f.
[158] Cf. footnote 78 above.

letters and other documents do not contain a single allusion to the Czech Reformation or to religious life in Bohemia or Moravia.

For the purposes of our present inquiry into Hubmaier's contacts with Moravia, the printed works can be divided, chronologically, into four groups.

(1) Works written and printed before Hubmaier's arrival in Moravia: *HS*, Nos. 1-8 (69-163). These contain no references whatsoever.

(2) Works which were written, fully or in part, prior to Hubmaier's arrival in Moravia but published there, with revisions and/or additions:

HS, Nos. 9-13 (164-269) and part of No. 17 (329-334) which was a reprint of an older tract, No. 8 (140-145). This group contains only one direct reference, viz., to the practice of infant communion by the Bohemians.[159]

On the basis of this one allusion Bergsten concludes that already in Waldshut, Hubmaier was acquainted with the Utraquist practice of infant communion.[160] Elsewhere, he mistakenly applies the same reference to the Czech Brethren and even suggests that Hubmaier "probably" knew about their practice of rebaptism.[161] The latter assertion can in no wise be substantiated from the sources. For our part, we are inclined to be sceptical even about Hubmaier's knowledge, in 1525, of Utraquist infant communion. When considered within the context of Hubmaier's total silence about Hus, the Hussites and the Bohemians, the one isolated sentence reads very much like a postscript added by Hubmaier later when he was finalizing the manuscript for printing in Moravia in the late fall of 1526 and after he had been involved personally in the Moravian discussions concerning infant baptism and infant communion.[162]

---

[159] "Jtem, so ist es nyendert von Christo verbotten, das die Behem jre Kindlen nit zů dem Nachtmal setzen sollen" (*HS*, 199). The reference appears at the end of the third part of Hubmaier's *Gespräch auf Zwinglis Taufbüchlein*, the manuscript of which was completed — according to Hubmaier's own statement in the dedicatory preface (*HS*, 171) — in Waldshut around November 30, 1525, a few days before its surrender to the Austrians and Hubmaier's escape to Zürich. Hubmaier might have been familiar with Clement Ziegler's book, *Ein fast schon büchlin . . .* (printed in Strasbourg in 1525) in which Ziegler condemned the Bohemians for giving communion to small children who cannot confess faith (*TQ Elsass*, I, 32).

[160] Bergsten, 1961, 424.

[161] *HS*, 34 (Historical Introduction). Footnote 3 in Bergsten, 1961, 424 probably explains his reference to the Brethren. However, in the literature of the early sixteenth century, the term 'Bohemi' was used consistently as a designation for the Utraquists. The Czech Brethren were known as 'Picardi' or '(fratres) Waldenses'.

[162] In the dialogue between Balthasar and Zwingli, Balthasar's concluding argu-

The literary evidence of Hubmaier's acquaintance with the Czech Reformation and with the situation among the German Evangelicals in Moravia, prior to his arrival there, can, therefore, be regarded as highly doubtful, if not fully negative. The question as to whether or not he knew anything about the Czech Brethren or the Utraquists before he left Waldshut in December 1525, or even Zürich in May 1526, remains a matter of speculation. Hubmaier himself left no unequivocal indication of such knowledge.

(3) Works written and published in Moravia:

HS, Nos. 14-24 (270-457) with the exception of the dedicatory prefaces listed below under (4). This large body of Hubmaier's writings which, when judged by the number of pages, accounts for nearly one half of his printed works, contains no more than four direct references to the Czech Reformation. All of them date from the fall of 1526.

In one place, Hubmaier ridicules the practice of infant communion (Khindlen pappen, porridge that is fed to small children) [163] without mentioning the Utraquist church. Elsewhere, he condemns the mere reinstatement of communion in both kinds without the prerequisite of (believer's) baptism.[164] The reference is directed against the Utraquist church and the baptismal tract itself is dedicated to Jan Dubčanský whom Hubmaier hoped to win for Anabaptism. The problem of infant communion is not involved in the latter reference.

---

ment in the last paragraph of the third part of the tract (HS, 199) is complete without the reference to the Bohemians. He appeals to biblical evidence in the Book of Acts, Chapter 2. The subsequent mention of the Bohemian practice is framed by a logical argument, "what is not expressly forbidden by Christ, is allowed", which is strongly reminiscent of Hubmaier's reasoning in the preface to his first book printed in Moravia (dated July 21, 1526). See especially HS, 229. For Hubmaier's involvement in the Moravian discussions, see our summary at footnote 142 in the preceding chapter.

[163]   HS, 346.

[164]   "Der ander Jrsal. Das man schier allenthalb das Nachtmal Christi auffgericht vnd die menschen vnder bayderlay gstalt (wie sy es haissen) communiciert, vnd ist doch nye kain tauff vorgangen wider die haittern schrifft . . ." (HS, 351). The argument could apply equally well to the followers of Luther and Zwingli, especially in view of the subsequent argument concerning the sparing of the weak ("schonen der schwachen") which was used repeatedly by the two Reformers and for which they were criticized by their Anabaptist or spiritualist opponents. However, Hubmaier's phrase, "wie sy es haissen", constitutes a parallel to his juxtaposition of "wir" — the German Evangelicals in Moravia — and "sy" — the Czech Utraquists. See HS, 227 f. and our interpretation in footnote 144 of the preceding chapter. Bergsten, 1961, 425 also applies the reference to the Czech Utraquists.

The other two references constitute the only two places in all of Hubmaier's preserved writings where he mentions by name the 'Picards', i.e. the Czech Brethren.[165] In contrast to his critical utterances about the Utraquists, Hubmaier expresses himself in an appreciative way about "the brethren which are called the Picards".[166] He regards their practice of rebaptizing converts from Catholicism as a continuation of the ancient custom decreed by the Council of Carthage (256) in the days of Cyprian, according to which those who had been baptized by the heretics (*Ketzer*) were rebaptized upon joining the Catholic church. By a casuistic argument, Hubmaier equates the contemporary 'papists' with the ancient heretics.

In his other reference, Hubmaier counts the Picards, together with "the Russians, Moscowites and Walachians", among those who have not trespassed against the truth concerning baptism, i.e. have rejected infant baptism.[167] Hubmaier's own admission that he is merely quoting a rumour (*als ich hör*)[168] is well justified. It shows that at that time, at least, he was not too familiar with the baptismal concept of the Brethren who had, on the whole, retained infant baptism for

---

[165]   The term 'Picard' had been applied to the early Czech Brethren by their Czech opponents from 1461 onward (Hrejsa, III, 221). Eventually, it became the common designation for the Brethren — along with '(fratres) Waldenses' — in the polemical literature, whether Czech, German or Latin. The origin of its meaning in Bohemia can be traced to the arrival in Bohemia, in 1418, of a small group of refugees from Picardy, an area of present northern France and southern Belgium. For the spiritualist views of the original Picards, see Bartoš, 1931, 176-208. For the spread of their views among the early Hussites and Taborites and the persecution of the Czech Picards by Žižka, see Vavřinec, 59, 94 f. and 107 and Bartoš, 1965a, 122 ff. Cf. also Gastius, 1544, 222 f. One of the crucial points in the Picard heresy was the denial of the real presence in the eucharist. Some groups in Bohemia were characterized by strong chiliastic and pantheistic notes. Infant baptism does not seem to have been questioned. Cf. "Articuli Picardorum" (1420), Hrejsa, II, 131 ff. A sub-group of the early Picards were the Adamites whom Žižka exterminated in the fall of 1421 (Bartoš, 1965a, 159 f.). Brock, 1957, 57, n. 104, suspects pacifist tendencies among the Picards and the Adamites. For the application of the term 'Pickardisch' to Luther, Zwingli and others in the polemical literature of the sixteenth century, see Lepp, 1908, 52 f.

[166]   *HS*, 334.

[167]   "Der erst Jrsal . . . ist, das wir all bissher in der gantzen Europa, nyemant denn Picarden, Reissenn, Moscouiten vnd Vualachen (als ich hör) aussgenommen, des wegs der warhait so groblich verfelet haben, jn dem das wir die kindlen getaufft . . ." (*HS*, 350). The reference appears in the short tract on baptism, *Ein Form ze Tauffen*, written in the late fall of 1526 and dedicated to Jan Dubčanský.

[168]   The expression provides an interesting parallel to Zwingli's appeal to a rumour ("audio") concerning the symbolical interpretation of the eucharist by Wycliff and the (Czech) Waldenses. Z, III, 795. Cf. footnote 99 above.

children of their own members but administered believer's baptism (rebaptism) to adults of Catholic or Utraquist background when these joined the Unity.[169]

The reference is noteworthy for an additional reason. How did the Russians, the Moscowites and the Walachians come to be joined into one camp with the Czech Picards? From whom did Hubmaier hear the rumour? [170] The informant might have been some one related to the Unity. In 1481, large numbers of the Brethren in Moravia had been forced, by a decree of King Matthias (Corvinus), to migrate to Moldavia.[171] They travelled through Hungary, Transylvania and Walachia which had been under Turkish rule since 1460. According to a preserved letter, the elders intended to establish a permanent settlement in Moldavia, which lay in the sphere of the Eastern church where the Brethren would be safe from persecution by the Roman church. They even regarded the Moldavian exile as a God-sent opportunity for missionary work.[172] It is not certain when the majority of exiles returned to Moravia. They came back in small groups in the 1490's and some of them, no doubt, stayed. An unconfirmed hypothesis suggests that they moved as far as the Caucasian region.[173]

From March 1491 to November 1492, Lukáš of Prague and three other members of the Unity traversed the eastern countries of Europe and parts of the Near East, on an official search for the remnants of an uncorrupted apostolic church. They travelled through Walachia and Moldavia — where they likely visited the remaining exiles — to

---

[169] On Lukáš' theology of baptism, see Müller, I, 466 ff. Cf. also the comment of Yoder, 1962, 161 on Hubmaier's ignorance about the Picards.

[170] Both the editors of HS and Bergsten, 1961, 429 left the obscure reference without comment. The attempt of Schulze, 1957, 256 f. to identify the four groups with "the descendants of the Waldensians, the Lollards (followers of Wycliff) and the Hussites, of whom some escaped persecutions by emigrating to the Balkans or to Russia", is hardly satisfactory. The source on which he based his assertion (Boehmer in RE³, Vol. 20, 824) contains no mention of Russia or the Balkans.

[171] Müller, I, 182; Müller-Bartoš, 115; Goll, 1916, 152 ff. and Hrejsa, B, 30, 48 and C, 95. Cf. also our reference at footnote 53 in the preceding chapter.

[172] A letter of the elders preserved in AUF, V, fol. 365, quoted by Müller, I, 182 f., Müller-Bartoš, 115 and Goll, 1916, 157. Its date 1494 has been corrected by Goll to 1491 and by Müller to 1484.

[173] Říčan, 1957a, 57 and 1961a, 37 rejects the hypothesis. Walachia (south of the Transylvanian Alps and north of the Danube river, with the city of Bucharest) and Moldavia (east from Transylvania, between the rivers Seret and Prut) were autonomous principalities until they united to form Roumania in 1861. Bessarabia, east of the river Prut, formerly also part of Roumania, was ceded to the Soviet Union in 1940. Transylvania, in the northwestern part of Roumania, formerly belonged to Hungary. Cf. map in Macek, 1958b, 221.

Constantinople. From there they pursued separate courses: Knight Mareš Kokovec visited Russia, Lukáš crossed the Balkan countries and Greece, a certain Kaspar from the German Waldensians (who had joined the Unity in 1480) remained in Constantinople, and Martin Kabátník, a burgher of Litomyšl — from where the journey was started and financed — covered the long trip through Asia Minor, Jerusalem and Egypt. They did not find a living church; but the adventures of the eastern journey lived on in memories and, in the absence of a printed report, were retold in many versions.[174] One of these might have been brought to Hubmaier's attention, perhaps by Čížek (Zeising) who must have learned about it in Litomyšl and afterwards could have shared it with Hubmaier during his visit in Mikulov in the fall of 1526.[175] This might explain not only Hubmaier's mysterious reference to the Russians, Moscowites and Walachians but also the linking together of such reference with a mention of the Czech Picards.[176] The claim that all of these rejected, or at least questioned, infant baptism, was most likely Čížek's own interpretation.[177]

[174] Kabátník's report, the only source for our knowledge of the journey, was not printed in Litomyšl till 1539. Cf. Müller, I, 249 f. and Müller-Bartoš, 161 f. Lukáš made a mention of the dangerous travel to Walachia and Turkey in his book *Obnovení církve* [Renewal of the Church], 1510. Cf. quotation in Goll, 1916, 157. Müller, I, 249 confused two Czech words, Vlachy (Italy) and Valachy (Walachia), and applied the reference wrongly to Lukáš' eastern journey in 1491/92 and to his later visit in Italy. There is no mention of Italy in the Czech text. Cf. also Müller-Bartoš, 162.

[175] On Čížek's stay in Litomyšl, see previous chapter at footnotes 56 ff. His visit with Hubmaier in Mikulov is attested only in *HS*, 365.

[176] By coincidence, Faber's book on the religion of the Moscowites (Faber, 1526a) appeared in print only a few months earlier. Ambassadors of Basil of Russia had visited Emperor Charles the Fifth in Spain and on their return journey met with Archduke Ferdinand and Faber in Tübingen in the fall of 1525. Subsequently, Faber wrote an enthusiastic report on their way of life and religion in Russia. It is doubtful that Hubmaier knew Faber's book which was printed in Tübingen in January 1526, during Hubmaier's imprisonment in Zürich. In any case, the book stressed the orthodoxy of the Eastern church, the cult of Mary and the saints, the use of images, infant baptism etc. (Cf. a summary in Helbling, 1941, 66-88.) It was hardly a suitable source for Hubmaier's inclusion of the Moscowites among the precursors of Anabaptism. Most likely, the 'Russians' were Orthodox Byelo-Russians and Ukrainians living in the Grand Duchy of Lithouania (cf. Williams, 1962, 642) whereas the 'Moscowites' were Russians under the Czar.

[177] One can only surmise that the orally transmitted story was based on an idealized picture of the Eastern church for which there was an old tradition in the Hussite movement dating back to the days of Jerome of Prague (cf. Hrejsa, II, 38 and Goll, 1916, 153). To an Anabaptist, such remnants of the pure apostolic church would be characterized by believer's baptism.

(4) Dedicatory prefaces written and printed in Moravia:
     (arranged in chronological order by date of preface composition)

Date of Preface	To Whom Dedicated Title of Tract	Date of Printing HS, pp.
(1) July 21, 1526	Martin Göschl *Der Lehrer Urteil*	1st ed. July/Aug. 1526 227-229 2nd ed. later in 1526 241-243
(2) (Fall) 1526	Leonhart and Hans of Liechtenstein *Gespräch auf Zwinglis Taufbüchlein*	late in 1526 167-173
(3) N.d. (Nov. 1526)	Leonhart of Lichtenstein *Einfältiger Unterricht*	late in 1526 286-289
(4) Dec. 10, 1526	Martin Göschl *Christliche Lehrtafel*	Dec. 1526-Jan. 1527 307-310
(5) N.d. (end 1526)	Jan of Pernstein *Grund und Ursache*	early 1527 328-329
(6) N.d. (late 1526)	Jan Dubčanský *Form zu Taufen*	early 1527 348-349
(7) N.d. (end 1526)	Burián Sobek *Form des Nachtmahls*	early 1527 364-365
(8) April 1, 1527	Georg of Brandenburg *Willensfreiheit* I	April 1527 380-382
(9) May 20, 1527	Friedrich of Liegnitz *Willensfreiheit* II	May-June 1527 400-402
(10) June 24, 1527	Arkleb of Boskovice *Von dem Schwert*	June-July 1527 434-435

The ten listed prefaces written in Moravia, two of which were addressed to Protestant lords in Silesia, contain several direct allusions to the religious situation in Moravia during the second half of the year 1526. The first preface to Göschl (*HS*, 227 ff.) has preserved a record of the theological argumentation concerning baptism as it developed in the German evangelical and Czech radical Utraquist circles following the meeting at Slavkov in March 1526. We have discussed its meaning in the previous chapter.[178] Two brief references in the short prefaces to the Lord of Pernstein (*HS*, 328) and to knight Sobek (*HS*, 364), both dating from the end of 1526, indicate that the Czech Utraquists who were in contact with the German Evangelicals

---

[178]   See at footnotes 142-147 in the previous chapter.

in the area of Mikulov and Slavkov, still hesitated to reject infant baptism outright.[179]

On the other hand, the prefaces furnish a proof that the zealous preaching and literary activities of Hubmaier bore early fruit among the German Evangelicals and that by November or December 1526, at the latest, both Leonhart of Liechtenstein and the three leading ministers in Mikulov, Spittelmaier, Glaidt and Göschl, had submitted to rebaptism.[180] Whether the two leaders in the nearby town of Ivančice, the Slovak-Czech preacher and poet Ján Sylván and the German spiritualist Christian Entfelder, whose names are mentioned in the preface to Dubčanský,[181] were also in Hubmaier's Anabaptist fold at that time remains uncertain. If we add the names of "brüeder Jan Zeysinger" (Čížek) who was to deliver Hubmaier's booklet to Burián Sobek (HS, 365), of the wife of Leonhart of Liechtenstein (Kateřina of Boskovice and Černá Hora; HS, 289) and of Göschl's wife (HS, 310), we have completed the list of all persons on the contemporary Moravian scene whom Hubmaier mentions in his printed works. The name of Hans Hut appears only in the Rechenschaft.[182]

A careful comparison of the ten dedicatory prefaces as to their form and contents will show that they fall into three distinct groups. The first four (of our numbering) which were addressed, two to each, to Göschl and to the Lord(s) of Liechtenstein during the earliest period of Hubmaier's stay in Moravia, reflect the intimate relationships which developed rather easily and quickly, between the Anabaptist leader and the German Evangelicals in the Mikulov area. The four

---

[179] "Jch waiss vil frommer leüt, die offentlich bekennen, das der kindertauff gar kainen grund in der schrifft hab. Ob aber die, so in irer kindischen vnwissenhait bissher getaufft, sich auff ein neues (als sy reden) zetauffen lassen schuldig seyent oder nit, an dem aichbom hangen noch vil leüt wie Absolon zwischen himel vnd erden, wissen nit wo auss. Da sehen sy das ernstlich tauffbot Christi, dort fürchten sy den schatten des Widertauffs, da doch kainer ist auss irer aignen bekantnuss." (Preface to Pernstein, HS, 328.)

[180] Cf. the striking contrast between Hubmaier's reference to "Herr" Martin Göschl in the preface on July 21 (written "in herren Oswalden zymmer", HS, 227-229) and his address "Gnediger Herr vnd brüder" on December 10 (HS, 307). Cf. also Hubmaier's praise of Spittelmaier and Glaidt in the preface to Liechtenstein in November (HS, 288) and his appreciative words about the Lords of Liechtenstein, "sonderliche liebhaber des heiligen Euangelions" (HS, 310). At their request, he wrote his brief apology (HS, No. 14; 272-283).

[181] HS, 348. Their relationship to Moravian Anabaptism will be discussed in the next chapter.

[182] HS, 475, 486 f. and 489 f. It was completed on January 3, 1528 during Hubmaier's imprisonment in the Kreuzenstein castle and remained in manuscript until it was published by Sachsse, 1914, 231-271 and in HS, 458-491.

long prefaces constitute the main source for our knowledge of the transition from a modified Zwinglianism [183] to Anabaptism of Hubmaier's type.

The following three prefaces (nos. 5 to 7 of our numbering) indicate a different relationship altogether. They are much shorter (one half of a printed page each) and quite formal in their tone for they were addressed to strangers whom Hubmaier likely never had met in person. Significantly enough, all three were directed to Czech noblemen, religious seekers on the 'left wing' of the Utraquist church: the powerful Lord Jan of Pernstein,[184] knight Jan Dubčanský [185] and knight Burián Sobek.[186] The prefaces date from the same period (end of 1526). There can be no doubt that the dedicatory prefaces were occasioned by the visit, or repeated visits, of Čížek in Mikulov at that time. We have pointed out elsewhere [187] that after his excommunication from the Unity, Čížek stayed first at Tovačov, the domain of the Lord of Pernstein, and then at Habrovany with Dubčanský. He must have been also in contact with Burián Sobek to whom he was to deliver Hubmaier's tract. It is worth noting how scrupulously Hubmaier distinguished in his writings between persons of Czech origin and those of German origin in his use of their Christian names. He consistently used the form 'Jan' for the Czechs [188] but 'Hanns' or 'Joannes' for the Germans.[189]

The last three prefaces (Nos. 8 to 10 of our numbering) constitute yet another distinct group. They were written during the spring of

[183]   Cf. our analysis in the preceding chapter beginning at footnote 164.
[184]   On Pernstein, see Chapter II, footnote 82 and Chapter IV footnote 194. He occupied the highest political offices in Moravia until his death in 1548. As governor, he led a delegation to Vienna in November 1526 and delivered a Czech speech to Archduke Ferdinand on behalf of the Moravian estates who had received him as their king and margrave on the basis of the hereditary rights of his wife Ann (Šembera, 1870, 102). He protected the Czech Brethren on his domains but never joined the Unity.
[185]   On Dubčanský, see previous chapter at footnotes 36 ff.
[186]   On Sobek, see previous chapter at footnotes 15 ff.
[187]   See previous chapter at footnotes 82 ff.
[188]   In Hubmaier's spelling: Jan von Bernstain, Jan Dubschanskij (in the preface and in a question of the baptismal liturgy; HS, 348 f.) and even Jan Zeysinger (in the main text; HS, 365; the marginal note reads, however, Joannes Zeysinger). Did Hubmaier think that Čížek-Zeising was of Czech, or perhaps Slavic background? Cf. footnote 57 in the previous chapter.
[189]   Hanns von Liechtenstein (in the prefaces and in the dialogue of the catechism; HS, 311 ff.) and Joannes Spitalmayer (HS, 288). The reference to "Herren Joan. Syluano, Christanno [sic] Endfelder . . ." (HS, 348) is probably a latinized form rather than an exception to the rule.

1527, the last period of Hubmaier's witness in Moravia. In size and content, they fit somewhere between the first two groups. They are basically theological (freedom of the will and the problem of 'the sword') and reflect, especially the last one, the controversies with Hans Hut and his followers. At the same time, they lack the note of personal friendship which characterized the first group. All three recipients played an important role in the political and religious life of Moravia. Margrave Georg of Brandenburg-Ansbach (1484-1543) was an unwavering champion of the Lutheran Reformation in Upper Silesia and a leader of the German evangelical party at the royal court of Louis II until the latter's death at Mohacs in August 1526.[190]

Duke Friedrich II of Liegnitz, Brieg and Wohlau (1480-1547), a grandson of the Czech Hussite King Jiří (George) of Poděbrady, had even closer ties with Bohemia and Moravia. As an early follower of Luther, and subsequently a supporter of Schwenckfeld, he — and the ministers at Liegnitz — established contacts with Strasbourg and Zürich. In 1526 he conceived a plan for establishing a university in Liegnitz with some twenty professors whom he hoped to obtain from the Reformation centers in Germany and Switzerland. Among the few who actually reached Liegnitz was the young biblical scholar from Zürich, later successor to Zwingli as professor of the Septuagint, Theodor Bibliander (Buchmann, died in 1564). He came in August or September 1527 but stayed only two years.[191]

Hubmaier's dedicatory preface to Friedrich (May 20, 1527) falls precisely into that early period of high hopes according to which Liegnitz was to become the focal point of the Reformation in Silesia. Hubmaier did not live to see the early dissolution of the school due to lack of qualified teachers and finances. However, the lively contacts between Moravia and Silesia which antedated Hubmaier's arrival at Mikulov must have become even more regular from 1526 onward. After Hubmaier's death, if not earlier, Simprecht Sorg established himself as "the printer of Liegnitz". Oswald Glaidt, too, went to Liegnitz. The Duke, who had learnt to speak Czech from his mother, had friendly contacts with the Czech Brethren.[192]

---

[190]   Margrave Georg was cousin of King Louis, brother-in-law of Duke Friedrich of Liegnitz and brother of Duke Albrecht of Prussia, the former grandmaster of the Teutonic Knights. See the biography by Müller, 1955. Cf. also *HS*, 379 f. and Chapter IV footnote 191. On January 6, 1528, Georg issued a mandate against Anabaptists (*ME*, III, 447).

[191]   Egli, 1901, 9 ff.

[192]   See our summary of the contacts with Silesia in the previous chapter beginning

The Lord Arkleb (also Artleb) of Boskovice to whom Hubmaier dedicated his last printed work, was, with the exception of Jan of Pernstein, the most influential member of the Moravian oligarchy of noble families. In 1525, he exchanged his domain of Vranov against Lord Pernstein's holdings at Třebíč in southwestern Moravia.[193] In October 1520, he had written a letter from Znojmo to Erasmus in which he asked for a theological assessment of the doctrines of the Czech Brethren. He was alarmed by their steady growth and disagreed with many of their teachings. He found himself more in accord with the views of Luther and Erasmus. The evasive answer which Erasmus wrote on January 28, 1521 [194] probably contributed to Arkleb's closer alignment with Lutheranism in subsequent years. At his request, the young Czech humanist and printer, Oldřich Velenský of Mnichov,[195] prepared an abbreviated translation of Luther's *Exposition of the Vision of Daniel concerning the Antichrist.*[196] It was printed in Prague in March 1522 with a dedication to Arkleb.[197] Later that year, and again the following year, Arkleb pleaded before the king on behalf of the Lutheran preacher Paul Speratus.[198]

---

at footnote 164. Cf. also *HS*, 398. More details on Sorg and Glaidt in the next chapter. On Friedrich, see Maleczyńska, 1960 and Matusik, 1960, 207 ff. and 216 ff.

[193] Šembera, 1870, 102. Cf. Hubmaier's dedicatory address, "auff Trebiz", *HS*, 434. There had been a growing congregation of the Unity in Třebíč, at least since 1491. In 1520, Jan of Pernstein donated a lot on which the Brethren erected a new church building (Hrejsa, B, 88).

[194] On Arkleb's correspondence with Erasmus, see footnote 67 above and Chapter II footnote 47.

[195] Velenský (Ulricus Velenus Mnichoviensis) studied at the universities of Prague, Wittenberg and perhaps also Paris. He learnt the printing trade in Nürnberg. From 1519 to 1521 he operated a printing shop in Bělá pod Bezdězem (Bohemia). Among the many humanistic and religious works, he printed a Czech translation of Erasmus' *Enchiridion* and Lukáš' book on the repetition of baptism. His Latin booklet, *In hoc libello ... probatur Apostolum Petrum Rhomam non venisse neque illic passum* (printed first by Cratander in Basel and then by Sylvan in Augsburg, both ed. in 1520) created a sensation. The name of the totally unknown author (his last name was misprinted "Minhoniensis") was regarded by many as a pseudonym for Erasmus. Among others, Seb. Franck reprinted a summary of the booklet in his *Chronica* (Franck, 1531, fols. 257-263). On Velenský and his works, see Bartoš, 1925 and 1946a, 83-85; Husa, 1957, 70; Hrejsa, IV, 258 f. and Bohatcová, 1962.

[196] *Ad librum M. Ambrosii Catharini Responsio. Cum exposita visione Danielis VIII de Antichristo* (1521, WA, 9, 689 ff.). According to Bartoš, 1925, 19, n. 68, Velenský translated mainly the second part.

[197] The full title of the Czech tr., *Výklad slavného Doktora Martina Lutera o Antikristu ...* and the dedication were reprinted by Šembera, 1870, 103.

[198] Šembera, 1870, 103 cites *Chronik der kön. Stadt Iglau* by Martin Leupold

It must also be mentioned that Arkleb's unmarried aunt, Marta of Boskovice, was one of the first members of nobility who became a member of the Unity. She lived in Litomyšl under the pastoral care of Vavřinec Krasonický and in 1507 sent a famous letter of protest against the persecution of the Brethren to King Vladislav.[199] Arkleb's two sisters, Johanka and Apolonie (both died in 1540) were abbesses, the former of the Queen's nunnery in Old Brno (1508-May 1532), the latter of the Cistercian cloister in Tišňov (1516-1540). Johanka must have shared the evangelical views of her brother, since the first edition of the Czech New Testament ever printed in Moravia was dedicated to her and in part financed by her. The translation was made from Erasmus' Latin text by none other than the radical Utraquist priest, friend of Speratus, Beneš Optát of Telč, and Petr Gzel of Prague. Its appearance in November 1533, and the preceding negotiations were probably related to Johanka's resignation from her abbess post on May 9, 1532.[200]

A contributing cause of her resignation might have been her involvement with the Anabaptists. As abbess she granted, in 1529, permission to the Anabaptists to settle in Hustopeče (Auspitz), which at that time was among the holdings of the nunnery.[201] Some of the later, less amicable dealings beween the Anabaptists in Hustopeče and the abbess of the Queen's nunnery in Old Brno fall into the period after her resignation.[202]

Arkleb himself had occupied the highest office of the governor of

---

(d. 1624) as published by Chr. d'Elvert, Brünn, 1861, 50. Cf. also footnote 88 in previous chapter.

[199] On Marta of Boskovice, see Císařová, 1942, 265 ff. and Šembera, 1870, 122 ff. Her letter to the king (reprinted by Šembera, 1870, 188 f. and Císařová, 1942, 405 f.) was accompanied by a copy of the Czech confession (List králi, Molnár, 1947, 9 ff.) and of the Latin Confessio (cf. footnote 51 above).

[200] On Johanka, see Šembera, 1870, 124-126; Císařová, 1942, 219 f.; Hrejsa, 1915, 209, n. 1 and Hrejsa, V, 43 f. The New Testament was printed at Náměšť on November 29, 1533 and the dedicatory preface (reprinted by Šembera) dated there on November 19. It refers to Johanka as "formerly abbess of the Queen's cloister in Old Brno". Cf. also Urban, 1966, 20, 23.

[201] Cf. ZGL, 97 and 105, n. 2. The note reprinted there from Beck, 103 f., n. 1, identifies the cloister wrongly as "Königskloster" (Maria-Saal). Hrubý, 1935a, 9 and 12, corrected it to "Königinkloster" (klášter Králové). According to Šembera, 1870, 125, the nunnery faced serious financial difficulties already in 1520 when Johanka pawned golden and silver chalices and other precious objects at the collegiate chapter of St. Peter in Brno. When the chapter later refused to return the objects, the new abbess, Barbara of Sovinec (Eulenburg) filed a legal suit against Johanka in 1536.

[202] See ZGL, 105, 143 and 145 f.

Moravia from 1519 to 1523 and served as the supreme chamberlain in 1526 and 1527. He died in the same city and on the same day as Hubmaier (March 10, 1528). He was buried in the chapel of an Augustinian monastery in Vienna.[203]

By way of summary, we must reiterate that Hubmaier's contacts in Moravia — insofar as they are demonstrated by his dedicatory prefaces and by other direct allusions to persons on the contemporary scene — remained limited to two circles: (1) the inner circle of German Evangelicals, natives and refugees, in and around Mikulov, many of whom Hubmaier was able to win for Anabaptism before the end of 1526 (the Lords of Liechtenstein, Göschl, Glaidt, Spittelmaier and perhaps Entfelder); (2) the outer circle of Czech radical Utraquists (the Lords Arkleb of Boskovice and Jan of Pernstein, knights Dubčanský and Sobek) who had been vitally interested in Luther's or Zwingli's Reformation for some time and who were, therefore, predisposed to pay some attention to the theological arguments of the learned Anabaptist preacher in Mikulov. These he failed to persuade.

The period during which Hubmaier attempted to bear witness also to the Czechs seems to have been the fall and winter of 1526. With the coming of Hut in the spring of 1527 and the resulting inner conflict in the Anabaptist congregation at Mikulov, his attention had to turn in that direction. His last book written and dedicated to the Lord of Boskovice at the end of June 1527 did not represent a return of missionary endeavour directed toward the Czech population but rather an attempt to dissociate himself and his followers from what appeared to be anarchic teachings of Hut and his group, as well as to seek the protection of a powerful political leader. The preface addressed to Arkleb confirms our observation: Its content is not missionary but apologetic.

The four members of the Czech nobility to whom Hubmaier appealed belonged to the Utraquist church. They are known to have protected the Czech Brethren. However, none of them joined the Unity.[204] The

[203] Šembera, 1870, 103.
[204] Only a few members of the nobility, mostly knights, were admitted into the membership of the Unity during the era of Bishop Lukáš. In spite of a changed attitude to secular power and Christian participation in government (after the division into Major and Minor Party in 1495), the Major Party retained a highly critical and suspicious attitude towards persons in authority. A change took place after the death of Lukáš. Cf. Říčan, 1957a, 94 ff. and 140 f.; Brock, 1957, 206 ff. Bergsten's claim that Sobek became a member of the Unity was based on older literature. Cf. footnote 20 in previous chapter.

only known personal link between Hubmaier and the Czech Brethren was Čížek. The information that he might have supplied could hardly be classified as unbiased: He had been excommunicated from the Unity a few months earlier.

4. CONCLUSIONS

In this chapter, we have examined in detail the known literary opportunities for Hubmaier's knowledge about (a) the Czech Reformation in general, (b) the Czech Brethren in particular, and also (c) the German Evangelicals in South Moravia. We have also scrutinized evidences of such knowledge in Hubmaier's preserved writings. The express purpose of our study has been not only to define Hubmaier's relationship to the non-Catholic [205] religious parties in Moravia, prior to and during his one-year stay at Mikulov, but also to attempt to find an answer to the unsolved question of why he decided to go to Moravia.

The examples of Hubmaier's friends in Switzerland and South Germany prove that for more than a decade he had ample opportunities to learn about the theology of Hus and the Hussites, and to read several Latin and German confessional writings of the Czech Brethren.[206] For some unknown reason, perhaps owing to his preoccupation with practical church affairs, Hubmaier missed or ignored all these opportunities.

Unbelievable as it is, his preserved writings do not contain a single mention of the name of Hus. The passionate fighter for religious freedom [207] never cited the example of the Czech hero burnt in Constance. It was left to the Catholic theologian and politician Faber to bring together the memory of Hus and Hubmaier after the latter's fiery death.[208]

---

[205] On Hubmaier's relationship to the Catholic Church in Moravia, see Bergsten, 1961, 431-434.

[206] To summarize our detailed analysis of printed sources available to Hubmaier: (1) Four Latin confessional statements (1503, 1507, 1508, 1511) which were printed and reprinted in five separate volumes: Apologia, 1511, Ziegler, 1512, Dungersheim, 1514a and 1514b, Aeneas Sylvius, 1523; (2) The German Catechism which was published in no less than eight, and likely more, editions in the years 1522-1524; (3) Three German apologies printed in January 1525. In addition, the views of the Brethren were propagated in other books, e.g. the correspondence of Erasmus (1521).

[207] Cf. the chapter on Hubmaier in Austen Kennedy de Blois, *Fighters for Freedom* (Philadelphia, 1929), 55-75.

[208] Faber, 1528a, reprinted in Loserth, 1893, 216: "... er [Hubmaier] sey wie Johannes Huss vnschüldenclich verbrennt ...".

Hubmaier's superficial knowledge of the Utraquist church can be traced to Glaidt's printed report on the meeting at Slavkov and to limited oral information which Hubmaier obtained after his settlement in Mikulov. He knew how to exploit their practice of infant communion for his own criticism of infant baptism. But so far as we know, he failed to persuade the Czech Utraquists in South Moravia, even those who subscribed to a basically Zwinglian theology, about the scriptural basis of believer's baptism. The most likely 'prospect' of all, Jan Dubčanský, ceased his efforts to unite the Utraquists with the German Evangelicals after some of the latter had turned to Anabaptism. After vain preludes made to the Czech Brethren in February 1527, Dubčanský proceeded with the establishment of his own Unity of Habrovanite Brethren on February 23, 1528, still during Hubmaier's lifetime.[209]

Hubmaier's relationship to the Czech Brethren is even less documented. Apart from two appreciative but marginal references to the Picards which were based obviously on hear-say knowledge (probably traceable to Čížek) he ignored the Unity. This is the more astonishing and tragic, when one considers the many doctrinal parallels between the teachings of Hubmaier and those of the Czech Brethren in the era of Brother Lukáš. The fact that Hubmaier refers only to the Picards rather than to the 'Waldensians' [210] demonstrates that he never read any of their Latin confessional writings. Had he known at least their Confession of 1503 he could have included their statement on believer's baptism in his collection of quotations from the teachers of the church, ancient and contemporary. He revised the text for a second edition in Moravia.[211] Similarly, he could have cited, in sup-

---

[209] Dubčanský's proposals to the Unity and the organization of his own group will be discussed in the next chapter. There can be no doubt that Dubčanský read some of Hubmaier's books. At least two ideological parallels seem to confirm it: (1) the image of a wreath which designates an inn (HS, 198 and in earlier writings not printed in Moravia; quotation from Dubčanský in Odložilík, 1923, 328 and Müller, I, 449; cf. Bergsten, 1961, 428) and (2) the proposal to meet for a colloquy in a place which is equally distant from the residence of both parties: Hubmaier made the proposal to Zwingli in his printed book at the end of 1526 (HS, 214); Dubčanský made an identical proposal in his letter to Brother Lukáš in Mladá Boleslav, Feb, 9, 1527 (AUF, IV, fol. 191). Was it a mere coincidence?

[210] If Čížek had brought to Mikulov copies of the German booklets he had translated (footnote 131 above) Hubmaier would have shown a better knowledge about the origin of the Czech Picards.

[211] Der Lehrer Urteil, HS, 224-255 (the full text of both ed.). For the article on baptism (Confession 1503), cf. footnote 111 above. The last sentence of the article refers, of course, to infant baptism.

port of his own teachings, the Brethren's concept of church and church discipline, or their catechetical practices,[212] or, finally, the division within the Unity with relation to oaths and Christian participation in government. The striking similarities between the conflict of Hubmaier's congregation at Mikulov with Hut's followers and the conflict of the Major Party of the Unity with the Minor Party, must be obvious to anyone who studies the history of the two movements in Moravia.

There was no congregation of the Unity in Mikulov nor in any village or town in the immediate area, south of the river Dyje (Thaya). Hubmaier's work seems to have been concentrated entirely in Mikulov which remained the main rallying point for local and incoming Anabaptists up to the time of his imprisonment. In all probability, he did not visit other towns. Thus, Čížek, an ex-member of the Unity, provided the only personal link with the Unity. It should be noted also that — apart from the record of negotiations for a merger in 1528 — the synchronous sources of the Czech Brethren make no mention of the Anabaptists.

In view of the foregoing conclusions it is impossible to agree with Bergsten's statement that Hubmaier sought contact with all religious parties in Moravia and that "he regarded himself as called to develop

---

[212]   Hubmaier wrote his catechism, *Leertafel* (*HS*, 305-326) in Moravia in the fall of 1526, at the request of Martin Göschl (cf. the preface: *HS*, 307 ff.). Since Hubmaier's references to the idea of a catechism are found exclusively in his writings from the Moravian period (*HS*, 246, 247 and 248: in the second ed. of *Der Lehrer Urteil* which was prepared in Moravia; there are no references to catechism in the first ed. of the same booklet) one may assume that the plan for a catechism was not conceived until after his arrival at Mikulov. The increasing influx of refugees and the need of pre-baptismal instruction (cf. the reports on the large number of baptisms, summarized by Bergsten, 1961, 409) must have occasioned the need for a catechism. It is difficult to decide whether the highly developed catechetical system of the Czech Brethren was a contributing factor. Their German catechism had been reprinted several times in different places in Germany during the years 1522-1524 (see Appendix 4). Göschl must have had some knowledge about the Brethren since he was a native of Jihlava and had been influenced by Speratus who, among others, had initiated the contact of the Brethren with Luther. As well, Čížek visited Mikulov in the fall of 1526. Our detailed comparison of the two catechisms (see Appendix 5) has not produced sufficient evidence of a literary dependence of Hubmaier on the German catechism of the Unity. It is interesting to note also that all of Hubmaier's references to the idea of a catechesis are made in the context of the ancient or medieval church (*HS*, 246, 247, 248). On the other hand, there were no printed Roman Catholic catechisms — prior to Luther's (1529) — which could have served as a model for Göschl, the former Coadjutor Bishop of Olomouc. (On R.C. catechisms, cf. the art. "Katechismus" by J. Hofinger in *LTK*, 6, col. 45 ff.)

further the Reformation which had begun in the Czech lands with the introduction of the cup for the laity".[213] On the contrary, Hubmaier's writings from the Moravian period prove that basically he remained oriented toward the Swiss and German Reformation. In his longer writings, he continued the theological debate with Zwingli, Oecolampad, Luther and Erasmus.[214] From Moravia he even proposed to Zwingli that they meet for a public debate in Regensburg, half way between Mikulov and Zürich.[215] His shorter writings were prepared as practical aids for the congregational life of the young Anabaptist church in Mikulov.[216] The dedicatory prefaces addressed to Czech noblemen could easily create the impression that Hubmaier sought to enter into a genuine theological dialogue with the Czech Reformation parties. A careful reading of the works themselves, however, will confirm our conclusion that, by and large, Hubmaier was ignorant about the current issues among the old Hussites and the Neo-Utraquists, the Czech Brethren of the Major and Minor Parties and the still smaller and more radical groups.

Such an attitude on the part of Hubmaier is understandable for several reasons. He arrived in Moravia with little or no previous knowledge about the situation. His stay was short and filled with exhausting organizational and literary activities. The language barriers did not make the contacts any easier.[217]

Why then did Hubmaier decide to go to Moravia? It was not because he admired the followers of Hus and was familiar with their teachings. Most probably, he did not know too much about the German Evangelicals either. Through contacts which can no longer be identified but which were likely related to the printer Simprecht Sorg and his friends in Zürich, Augsburg and elsewhere, he must have heard about the place of refuge for persecuted Evangelicals.

---

[213] Bergsten, 1961, 425. Cf. also the opening statement on p. 423. At the end of the chapter (p. 435) he admits the danger of overestimating Hubmaier's influence on the total religious life in Moravia.
[214] *HS*, No. 9 (against Zwingli); No. 13 (against Oecolampad); Nos. 22 and 23 (Luther and Erasmus on free will). In No. 15, a collection of statements in support of believer's baptism, Hubmaier retained the same selection of contemporary authors (Erasmus, Luther, Oecolampad, Zwingli etc.) in both editions and ignored the witness of the Czech Brethren. Cf. footnote 211.
[215] *HS*, 214.
[216] *HS*, Nos. 15-21.
[217] Hubmaier seems to have retained, in Moravia, a very definite sense of mission to "the German nation". Cf. his phrase "wir Teütschen" over against "sy", i.e. the Czech Utraquists (*HS*, 227 f.); "... das das pur, lauter vnd rain Gotswort ... in vnsere teütsche Nation ankummen" (*HS*, 309); and elsewhere.

Many reached Moravia before Hubmaier, many more followed him. The determinative motives for his decision were, therefore, personal and political, not theological or ecclesiastical: he was running away from the power of the 'tyrants' and seeking a sheltered place for himself and his wife.[218]

This interpretation is confirmed amply by several autobiographical passages in Hubmaier's writings. Perhaps the clearest confession of his intentions is recorded in his brief *Short Apology* written at the request of his protectors at Mikulov in the late fall 1526: "Where there exists brutal violence and tyranny, there I will not wait for the attack of the forty men but avail myself of the basket of Paul [Acts 9:25], escape and run, as Christ has told us [Matthew 10:23], so long as God wills . . . ."[219]

At Mikulov (Nikolsburg — 'Nicopolis'), the new Emmaus,[220] Hubmaier and his wife found a refuge before the dark night of persecution. It was their last escape. But the newly-found freedom was not to be enjoyed for long.

---

[218] A similar conclusion was reached by Bergsten: "Wichtiger als der religiöse war aber der politische Anlass" (*HS*, 34). Cf. Bergsten, 1961, 397.

[219] *HS*, 280. The first part of the *Kurze Entschuldigung* is autobiographical. The second part (280-283) contains a threefold appeal to the secular auhorities. The emotional tone and the vocabulary of the latter suggests that it must have been composed under the shocking impact of the news that Hubmaier's archenemy, Ferdinand, had been elected king of Bohemia (October 13) and received as margrave of Moravia in mid-November 1526.

[220] *HS*, 289. Hubmaier combined the title of Göschl, "Bishop of Nicopolis", with the new name for Palestinian Emmaus. Cf. the footnotes, *ibid.*, and our quotation of the whole passage in footnote 214 of the previous chapter.

NEGOTIATIONS FOR A MERGER (1528)

Apart from a few interruptions, the Anabaptist refugees found a relatively safe shelter in Moravia for nearly one hundred years. Yet only once during that long period of time are they known to have made a serious attempt of rapprochement to any indigenous ecclesiastical group. The effort came early in their Moravian sojourn and concerned the *Unitas Fratrum*. In contrast to the later contacts which took the form of colloquies between interested individuals or local groups, without any aim at a church union, the negotiations in 1528 were of an official nature and probably involved the top leaders on both sides. In order to demonstrate the significance of these early contacts, we shall first review some important events which set the stage for the merger talks.

1. THE EARLY DEVELOPMENTS AMONG THE ANABAPTISTS IN MORAVIA (1526-1528)

The two and a half years of the initial Anabaptist history in Moravia fall into three distinct periods. The first year (June/July 1526-July 1527) was marked by the dynamic personal leadership of Hubmaier. From his arrest in July 1527 until his death in March 1528, there occurred a period of transition during which the first open division happened. The execution of Hubmaier signalled a time of persecution which, however, could not take its envisaged course on account of the Turkish threat. The negotiations for a merger took place in the third period.

The story of Hubmaier's leadership in Mikulov, his arrest and martyrdom, as well as the genesis of the first Anabaptist congregations in Moravia has been narrated and reviewed several times.[1] There is no need to write yet another summary of the familiar events. The sources for this period are few and we have been unable to discover any additional ones which would shed more light on several unsettled issues.[2] Instead, we shall underscore those aspects of the situation which concern the relationship of the incoming Anabaptists to the native population of Moravia, both German and Czech, and especially the documented or hypothetical contacts with the Czech Brethren.

In the previous chapter, we have indicated [3] the response which

[1]   The most recent critical treatment, based on a good knowledge of sources, is Bergsten, 1961, 398-481 (summary in *HS*, 34-43). Earlier presentations include: Cornelius, 1860, 40 ff. *et passim*; Loserth, 1893, 124-192; Vedder, 1905, 146 ff. and 219 ff.; Mau, 1912, 111-181; Seewald, 1953 and Schulze, 1957, 239 ff. Cf. also footnote 2 in the preceding chapter.

[2]   The main unsolved problem remains the reconstruction of the disputations between Hubmaier and Hut (and their followers) which took place at Mikulov in May 1527, and the issues which are related to them, in particular the origin and authorship of the so-called "Nikolsburg Articles". The best study on the subject is Seewald, 1953 which would still merit publication. (Seewald's "Nachtrag zu den Nikolsburger Artikeln", cited by Bergsten, 1961, 461, n. 103, was not available to us.) Bergsten, 1961, 451 ff. utilized Seewald's research in repudiating the hypothesis which had been proposed first by Erich Meissner in a 1921 dissertation (unpublished) and later made known by Wiswedel, 1938 (and his art. in *ML* and *ME*, III, 886 ff.), namely, that the "Nikolsburg Articles" were a forgery, likely done by the Augsburg minister Urbanus Rhegius and used as a basis for interrogations at Anabaptist trials. Bergsten, 1961, 460-464 then developed his own thesis according to which Hubmaier wilfully distorted the views of his opponent, Hut, and himself composed the articles. Friedmann in his review of Bergsten's book (*MQR*, 36 [1962], 356 ff.) questioned the hypothesis and pointed out sources which antedate the actual disputation at Mikulov — if the dating, in the middle of May (established by Neuser, 1913, 35, n. 32 and independently by Seewald, 1953, 19), is correct — by about two months and contain nearly identical articles. Cf. *TQ Elsass*, I, 138 ff. and *TQ*, V, 8. In a recent article based on a 1964 doctoral dissertation, Stayer, 1965, 188 f. suggests that the real issue at the Mikulov disputation was Hut's chiliasm and not "the sword". From a careful examination of the sources, Stayer concludes that in his confessions during the trial in Augsburg in the fall of 1527 Hut never claimed to teach non-resistance; nor did Hubmaier accuse him of it. Cf. Stayer's interpretation of two paragraphs in Hubmaier's "Rechenschaft", *HS*, 489 f., as applicable to two different groups of opponents. The "non-resistant Hut" is a product of the Hutterite chronicles (*ZGL*, I, 50) written in retrospect almost half a century later. In spite of several studies (Neuser, 1913, Klassen, H., 1959, Bergsten, 1961, Stayer, 1965) the relationship between Hut and Hubmaier, both as an historical encounter in Mikulov and as a theological conflict, requires further research. The issue concerns primarily Anabaptist in-group development in 1527 and as such is of little consequence for our inquiry into the contacts between the Anabaptists and the Czech Brethren which took place after the death of Hubmaier and Hut. Cf. Friedmann, 1966c and 1967b, and Bauman, 1968, 59 ff.

[3]   Cf. our analysis of Hubmaier's dedicatory prefaces in Chapter III.

Hubmaier's work evoked in Mikulov and in South Moravia generally. The spread of Zwinglian doctrines prior to the arrival of the Anabaptists had provided a platform which the native German Evangelicals and the pre-Anabaptist refugees could regard as common ground with Hubmaier's version of Anabaptist theology. Before the end of 1526, the two ministers of the German evangelical congregation in Mikulov, Hans Spittelmaier and Oswald Glaidt, both former refugees, had embraced Anabaptism. So did two prominent Moravian Germans, Martin Göschl, the former Coadjutor Bishop of Olomouc, and Leonhart of Lichtenstein.

With the paucity of sources at hand, it is difficult to estimate what proportion of the converts to Anabaptism was recruited from the local German population. The Anabaptist sources, both Hutterite and non-Hutterite, seem to imply that the majority of the new members were refugees, some of whom came merely with Anabaptist leanings and were not rebaptized until at Mikulov.[4] An eye witness, Hans Nadler, reported that baptisms were performed openly in the church building and that as many as seventy-two were baptized in one day.[5] Contemporary estimates of the total number of baptized vary from 2,000 to 6,000, and even higher.[6]

At his trial in Augsburg in the fall of 1527, Hut counted ten Anabaptist ministers in Moravia.[7] No doubt he was referring to the time of his visit there in May 1527. In the same connection, the Hutterite chronicles enumerate eight ministers by name and mention "others besides" who were ordained to preach the word of God.[8] Hut himself

---

[4] Cf. the following examples of testimonies about the earliest Moravian Anabaptism (years in brackets refer to the dates of the documents): Hans Hut, *TQ*, II, 41 (1527) and Meyer, 1874, 229-237 (1527); Leonhard Schiemer, *TQ*, III, 80 (early 1528); Hans Weischenfelder, Wappler, 1913, 279 (early 1528); Hans Schlaffer, *TQ*, III, 123 (1528); Hans Nadler, *TQ*, II, 132 and 153 (early 1529); Georg Nespitzer, *TQ*, II, 187 (1530). Cf. also Beck, 47 ff. and 59, and *ZGL*, 49 ff. (late chronicles).

[5] *TQ*, II, 132.

[6] Referring to Hubmaier's days in Moravia, Kessler, 164 reports 6,000 rebaptized. He began to collect materials for his "Sabbata" in 1524 and to write the final manuscript in 1533 (*ibid.*, VI). Referring to his visit in Moravia late in 1530, Julius Lober of Zürich reported 2,000 (*TQ*, II, 238).

[7] *TQ*, II, 42.

[8] "In dem kam Johannes Hut auch gen Nikolspurg, vnd wurden andere Diener mer bestellt, as nämlich: Oswalt Glait, Hans Spitlmair, Christian [vnd] Rotmäntl, Klein Utz vnd Gross Utz, Hans Werner vnd der Strützl, deren Etliche vorhin Predicanten gewesen vnd andere mer . . ." (Beck, 49). *ZGL*, I, 50, and *ZGL*, II, 7 regard Christian Rotmäntl as one person and add the name of Annderle Mosel. We were unable to find biographical information on any of them except the first

mentioned the names of Oswald (Glaidt), Spittelmaier, Göschl (*weich-bischof*), Bastian (*des weichbischofs zu Niclaspurg prediger*) and Augustin, a preacher in an unnamed village on the Liechtenstein domain.[9] In addition, a number of Anabaptist leaders from other countries visited Moravia for brief periods of time.[10] To complete the list of preachers identified by name, one must recall Christian Ent-felder and Jan Sylván, to whom Hubmaier referred as ministers (*Ecclesiasten*) at Ivančice in the late fall of 1526,[11] then the itinerant Johann Zeising,[12] and finally, a certain Wetel who lived at Ivančice in 1528.[13] The arrival of Jakob Widemann and Philipp Jäger [14] who played a decisive role in the secession of the communitarian, non-resistant Anabaptists from Mikulov in 1528, and of Gabriel Ascherham and Philip Plener (Weber, "Blauärmel"),[15] the respective founders of the Gabrielites and the Philippites, should likely be dated in the period after Hubmaier's arrest.[16]

This compilation of names drawn from several sources represents a total of more than twenty Anabaptist leaders who were resident in Moravia for part or all of the period 1526-1528. As far as we are able to judge, only three of them were natives of Moravia or Slovakia: Jan Sylván, Martin Göschl and probably also "his preacher" Bastian about whom nothing more is known. The observation made by Ben-der about the Anabaptist movement and leadership in Strasbourg applies equally well to that in Moravia: "It was brought in by outside missioners, throughout its early history its leaders were all from the outside, and it was repeatedly strengthened by the coming of large

---

two. Wiswedel's art. on "Werner, Hans" in *ME*, IV, 917 obviously refers to Hans Weber. Cf. *TQ*, II, 113 f. and 116 f.

[9]   Mayer, 1874, 231 ff. Loserth, 1893, 127 mentioned Göschl's "Caplan Niklas" but later corrected it to Bastian (Loserth, 1897, 68 and *ML*, II, 138).

[10]   Cf. footnote 4. The list is not complete.

[11]   *HS*, 348.

[12]   *HS*, 365. Zeising, Entfelder and Silván are not mentioned in the Hutterite Chronicles.

[13]   "Wetel von Eywaczitz, der von garlitz [Görlitz] bürtig ist", an author of a short epistle dealing with the Lord's supper and baptism. Reprinted in Wappler, 1908a, 183-186. Cf. at footnotes 251 ff. below.

[14]   On Widemann, see *ME*, IV, 941; on Philipp Jäger (Weber), *ME*, IV, 906. Cf. also Beck, 50, n. 2; *ZGL*, 52.

[15]   On Ascherham, see *ME*, I, 174 f.; on Plener, *ME*, IV, 192 f. and 906.

[16]   On the conflicting dating of Widemann's and Jäger's arrival in the Hutterite chronicles, see Bergsten's summary of research, Bergsten, 1961, 453, n. 70. In connection with the secession from Mikulov, four additional leaders are introduced by name: Jakob Mändel (formerly Liechtenstein's "Rentmeister"), Franz Itzinger, Thoman Arbeiter and Urban Bader (Beck, 75; *ZGL*, I, 87).

numbers of refugees . . .".[17] Rightly or wrongly, one might suspect that the few native leaders who accepted the message of the refugees would have served as natural links with the indigenous religious parties. However, both Göschl and Sylván were peculiar personalities with uncommon careers.

In terms of social prestige, Martin Göschl [18] was the most prominent leader of the early Moravian Anabaptism. The rest of the preachers at Mikulov were strangers and newcomers. But Göschl, the Coadjutor Bishop of Olomouc, was a well-known man in the ecclesiastical and political circles of the margraviate. As one of the high hierarchy, he was a member of the *landfried* and attended the diets of the Moravian estates. There must have been widespread surprise and consternation throughout Moravia when the Bishop's name appeared in the dedicatory preface of Hubmaier's first book printed in Moravia, at the end of July 1526, and again, in the preface to Hubmaier's catechism dated on December 10, 1526.[19] What motivated Göschl to an espousal of Anabaptism?

Born of a well-known family in the city of Jihlava (Iglau), Martin entered, in 1500, the Premonstratensian cloister at Želiv (Selau) in Bohemia. Neither the date of his birth nor details about his education are known.[20] In 1507 he returned to his native city to become administrator, and then parish priest of the St. James church which was under the patronage of the Želiv monastery. In 1509 he was consecrated Coadjutor Bishop (*Weihbischof*) of Olomouc, with the title, "Bishop of Nicopolis". For more than a decade he must have made regular visits to the episcopal office in Olomouc and have learnt to know personally not only Bishop Stanislav Thurzo but also Dr. Augustin Käsenbrod who resided there during the last two years

---

[17]   Bender, 1964, 243.

[18]   On Göschl, see Beck, 53 ff.; Loserth, 1893, 125 ff. and 1897, 65-70, and summary in articles in *ML*, II, 138 f. and *ME*, II, 546; Hrejsa, IV, 312 and V, 21 f.; Bergsten, 1961, 404 ff.; *HS*, 36. The Catholic bias prevented Beck and Loserth from a more objective evaluation of Göschl's career. The Coadjutor Bishop of Olomouc deserves a better biography based on a new examination and interpretation of all preserved sources.

[19]   Cf. the different wording in the two prefaces: "Dem . . . Herrn Martino, etwan Bischoff zů Nicopol, yetz aber Christenlichen Bropst zů Khůnitz, seinem gnedigen herren" (*HS*, 227 and 241, two editions) and "Dem . . . herren Martin etwan Bischoff zů Nicopol, yetz aber in Christenlicher gemain zů Nicolspurg Eelichem mitwoner, seinem gnedigen herren" (*HS*, 307). Cf. also footnote 180 in previous chapter.

[20]   Loserth (*ML*, II, 138) calls him "Dr. M.G." without saying a word about his education in any of his biographies of Göschl.

of his life (1511-1513). Likely he also met Jakob Ziegler who dwelt in Moravia from 1508 to 1511. Both were close friends of Bishop Thurzo and adamant enemies of the Czech Brethren.

In 1517, Göschl was elected provost of the nunnery *Himmelsrose* at Dolní Kounice (Kanitz).[21] By 1522-1523 he must have been influenced towards Reformation teachings by the brief sojourn of Paul Speratus in Jihlava.[22] It is not clear when he declared himself publicly as an evangelical. In 1525 he married one of the nuns at Kounice but remained in charge of the cloister[23] and attempted to secularize its property. Early in 1526, he effected a legal transfer of the nunnery holdings to the Moravian governor, Jan of Pernstein, and to the chamberlain, Arkleb of Boskovice: these were the same leading men of the Moravian aristocracy to whom a year later, Hubmaier, no doubt on Göschl's advice, dedicated two of his writings. At the same time, Göschl secured for himself a substantial annual income.[24] The legal and theological implications of his transfer are worth noting. Acting likely in agreement with the aforementioned barons, both of whom were sympathizers with the Lutheran Reformation, Göschl advocated a different type of secularization of ecclesiastical property than that which applied in the subsequent Lutheranization of many areas in Moravia. The ecclesiastical holdings were to become the property or trust of the estates, that is, of the margraviate as a whole, rather than to pass into private ownership.

However, Bishop Thurzo intervened. With the support of King Louis, he paid two personal visits to Kounice in the spring of 1526. He declared Göschl deposed from his offices as provost and Coadjutor Bishop, released the nuns from obedience to him and, acting on behalf of the king's chamber, he took charge of the cloister properties until a new provost was elected. Göschl appealed for help to the

[21]   Bergsten, 1961, 404 gives the correct date of 1517 while all other authors (mentioned in footnote 18) date the election in 1521. Cf. Zeman, 1966, 41.
[22]   Cf. Chapter II at footnote 88. In his later letters written "to the beloved brethren" in Jihlava from Königsberg on February 15, 1527 and August 8, 1530, Speratus warned against strangers with new doctrines, against "Schwarmgeister, Sakramentirer, Wiedertäufer" (full German text in Schenner, 1911, 249 f. and 253).
[23]   In 1527, the city council of Jihlava filed a law suit against Göschl in which he was accused of having misappropriated for the nunnery Kounice a sum of money donated by a citizen's wife for the St. James parish church in 1520. Sources in Loserth, 1897, 66 and Schenner, 1912, 374 f.
[24]   The income consisted of the dues from one (unnamed) village and of one thousand "gulden" payable to Göschl annually by the Moravian estates (Loserth, 1893, 126).

Moravian estates in an open letter dated April 24, 1526.[25] He accused the Bishop of taking steps without orders from the King, sought the protection of the estates as a co-signer of the *landfried* and a member of the estates, and warned them that they would all suffer similar injustices if they did not defend his cause.

On May 5, Bishop Thurzo wrote a letter from Kroměříž (Kremsier) to the mayor and council of the royal city of Znojmo (Znaim).[26] He defended the actions he had taken against Göschl at the royal command and defined Göschl's guilt according to the ecclesiastical law. He accused him of having defied the authority of the King and promised to see to it that he be punished. He expressed the hope that the Znojmo council would be able "to discern between the just cause of the King, their lord, and the misdemeanors of the unfrocked priest".

The fact that the Bishop wrote his letter expressly to the council of Znojmo, requires interpretation. In all likelihood, Göschl was in contact with the council, or with individual citizens, and might have been negotiating for a parish in this city which was known for its Lutheran sympathies and which shortly afterwards tolerated Anabaptist refugees within its walls.[27]

Meanwhile, he maintained connections with the evangelical ministers in Mikulov where the St. Wenceslas parish church was controlled by the patronage rights of the nunnery at Kounice. In his dual capacity as provost of the nunnery and Coadjutor Bishop, Göschl encouraged the ministers of Mikulov to attend the large meeting between German Evangelicals and Czech Utraquists in Slavkov on March 14, 1526.[28] In the late spring, probably some time in May,[29]

---

[25] Summary of Göschl's letter in Loserth, 1897, 67 without reference to source. The content of the letter can also be reconstructed from the Bishop's reply. See the following footnote.

[26] The full text of the Czech original reprinted in Kameníček, III, 572 ff.; a German summary in Loserth, 1897, 67 f. Loserth overlooked the point that the letter was addressed expressly to Znojmo and was not an open letter to all estates.

[27] Cf. art. "Znaim", *ME*, IV, 1034 and Zeman, 1966, 88.

[28] In his printed report, Glaidt refers to Göschl as "der Christenlich Bischoff, Bropst zů Keynitz, vnser Nicolspurger" (cf. footnote 116 in Ch. II). The last designation is likely to be understood only in the context of the patronage rights.

[29] Loserth, 1893, 127 dated Hubmaier's arrival "in the summer of 1526". Later, 1897, 68 and in his art. "Göschl" in *ML* and *ME*, he revised the date to "spring", i.e. before the Slavkov meeting, without indicating any reasons (Glaidt's report?). Beck, 54 implied that G. left Kounice after his open letter to the Moravian estates (April 24). Müller, 1920, 516, n. 4 advocated a date after the Slavkov meeting. He was followed by Odložilík, 1923, 35, n. 4 and Bergsten, 1961, 405. We were un-

Göschl moved with his wife to Mikulov where he was regarded as the *Antistes Ecclesiae Reformatae*.[30]

The fragmentary story of Göschl's life and career up to his settlement at Mikulov — which we have been able to piece together[31] — is in itself a sufficient explanation of the motives which must have led him to join hands with Hubmaier.

Here were two men with comparable gifts, goals and experiences. Göschl's ecclesiastical career, his legal involvements and active participation in the political life of the margraviate can be regarded as parallel to Hubmaier's rise to ecclesiastical prominence in Ingolstadt and Regensburg, or to his civic entanglements in the crusade against the Jews in Regensburg and in the strategy of defense against the Habsburgs in Waldshut. Both men tasted of ecclesiastical power: first as influential churchmen within the structure of Rome, then as victims of the same power; and both displayed a sense of political realism as well as a responsibility for the whole life of society.

Prepared by Luther's and Zwingli's emphasis on the authority of the Scriptures, Hubmaier and Göschl yielded to the persuasive logic of the New Testament passages dealing with the subject of baptism. By theological arguments they were drawn into the wide Anabaptist tide but they never moved into its main stream. They did not witness the uncontrollable outbursts of religious enthusiasm and revivalism which characterized the birth and growth of the movement in so many places.[32] Nor did they see apocalyptic visions about the im-

---

able to discover where Göschl's open letter was written (cf. footnote 25 above). He might have appealed to the estates after he had been evicted from Kounice by the Bishop, some time in the spring. Thus the evidence for the later arrival at Mikulov cannot be regarded as fully conclusive. As late as July 21, 1526, Hubmaier referred to Göschl as "now the Christian provost at Kounice" (*HS*, 227; cf. footnote 19 above). In his letter to Znojmo, May 5, Bishop Thurzo regarded the cloister as no longer existent. The royal chamber took possession of all properties in April 1527. In 1528 they were in pawn to Jiří Žabka of Limburg, and in October 1537 were sold to him (Loserth, 1897, 70). Thurzo's promise in his letter to Znojmo, to renew the cloister and to return the properties to the new provost, was not fulfilled. Cf. *Vlastivěda moravská, Ivančický okres*, 145, with reference to sources.

[30]   We were unable to identify the source for this title as applied to Göschl. It is mentioned by Beck, 54; Müller, 1920, 517 and Hrejsa, IV, 312.

[31]   The only other source material which Loserth, 1897 utilized were the entries in the Moravian *Kniha Půhonů* [Book of Charges]. Göschl's name appears eleven times as the accused and five times as the accuser (1518-1527). All cases specified by Loserth concerned ecclesiastical income or properties.

[32]   As an example, see Blanke's vivid account of the conviction of sin and repentance manifested at the first baptisms in the Swiss village of Zollikon near Zürich

minent end of the world, in spite of the fact that they were closer to the Turks than most Anabaptist leaders. In keeping with their pre-Anabaptist experience, they preferred to support the government of the land in its defensive measures against the invaders, and to safeguard maximum continuity with the pre-Anabaptist parish life.

There can be no doubt that the presence of such a prominent Moravian churchman as Göschl, and Hubmaier's immediate alignment with him, exerted a considerable influence on Hubmaier during the final phase of his theological development, and on the pattern of Anabaptist church life in Mikulov. Although we do not know whether Göschl's rebaptism preceded Leonhart's, one may guess that Göschl's espousal of Anabaptism furnished a more persuasive argument for the Liechtensteins than all of Hubmaier's preaching and teaching. Hubmaier's own admiration for the Bishop can be judged not only by the affectionate words in his dedicatory prefaces but also by the fact that in his baptismal agenda he assigned the administration of baptism to a bishop.[33]

Hubmaier's and Göschl's positive orientation towards civil power and their readiness to endorse the *status quo*, stood in sharp contrast to the chiliastic dreams of the Anabaptist refugees who were arriving in Moravia. Their numbers were increasing in proportion to the intensified persecutions in other countries. The clash between a 'this-worldly' and an 'other-worldly' religion, between a high church and low church type of Anabaptism, was inevitable.

The bold criticisms by Hans Hut in May 1527[34] did not introduce the controversy. They merely voiced tensions which must have been latent at Mikulov since the earliest days of Anabaptism. Only now,

---

(January 1525) and his characterization of the movement as an awakening ("Erweckungsbewegung"). Blanke, 1953, 22 ff. and 1955, 36.

[33] As examples of praise for Göschl, see *HS*, 229 and 307. References to a bishop in the baptismal agenda are found *ibid.*, 349 f. It could be argued, of course, that in his nomenclature, Hubmaier equated 'bishop' with 'pastor' (Hirt) of a local church (*HS*, 315).

[34] As we have pointed out in footnote 2 above, it is difficult to define the exact nature of Hut's encounter with Hubmaier. It could not have been the issue of the sword since Hut did not teach non-resistance in principle (he approved of taking oaths, and even bearing arms: Meyer, 1874, 227 f. art. 60-63; cf. the interpretations by H. Klassen, 1959, 202 f. and Stayer, 1965, 188 ff.). Rather, the focal point seems to have been chiliasm (imminent end of the world) and the resulting difference of emphasis in their respective concepts of baptism and church discipline. Bergsten, 1961, 464 ff. defines attitude to authorities, echatology and baptism as the three issues of the controversy. See also Bauman, 1968, 59 ff.

as a result of the open disputations, held first in the church and then in the castle of the Liechtenstein — the combination and sequence of the two places is meaningful, too — were the lines drawn. Göschl and Spittelmaier took Hubmaier's (and Liechtenstein's) side. Glaidt, Bastian ("Göschl's preacher"), Augustin and others were on Hut's side.[35] Göschl likely presided at the disputation in the castle and eventually threatened the unyielding Hut with deliverance to the king.[36] Hut was retained in the castle but managed to escape and left Moravia, never to return.

By a tragic irony Hubmaier was in the hands of the authorities several weeks prior to Hut's incarceration. There are conflicting reports about Hubmaier's arrest.[37] Before July 22, 1527, he was immured. On that day, Ferdinand sent letters to Freiburg i.B. and to Innsbruck requesting incriminating documents about Hubmaier's seditious activities in Waldshut.[38]

Shortly before his death at the stake in Vienna on March 10, 1528, he is said to have written a letter to Göschl in Mikulov in which he expressed remorse about his dealings with Hut and supposedly retracted his position on "the use of the sword".[39] In view of Hubmaier's statements on the subject in his preserved *Rechenschaft* [40] it is very doubtful that he would have changed his mind on a subject on which his teaching had been so consistent. The content of the letter is likely one of the apocryphal stories included in the early part of the Hutterite chronicles. There is no need, however, to question the existence of a letter to Göschl as such.[41] Göschl became Hubmaier's closest associate in Mikulov. It would be surprising if he had not tried to send him a message from prison.

The two congenial leaders walked on a similar path towards a martyr's death. Both of them had to face their former lord bishops. Hubmaier sent for his (Faber).[42] Göschl, after arrest in April 1528

---

[35]   According to Hut's testimony in Augsburg; Mayer, 1874, 231 f.
[36]   The information is based only on Hut's own testimony; Mayer, 1874, 233.
[37]   Cf. Bergsten, 1961, 477. Hut was arrested in Augsburg on September 15, 1527 (H. Klassen, 1959, 185).
[38]   Partial text reprinted in Loserth, 1893, 173 f.
[39]   ZGL, 51 and Beck, 52. Cf. the comment by Stayer, 1965, 191.
[40]   HS, 489 ff.
[41]   Both Bergsten, 1961, 485 and Friedmann (*MQR*, 39 [1965], 191, n. 44) expressed doubts about the existence of the letter with the content as reported by the Hutterite chronicle.
[42]   Subsequently, Faber published a lengthy report on his conversations with Hubmaier in the prison at the Kreuzenstein castle (Faber, 1528e, later reprinted

and subsequent torture and trial in Prague, was delivered to Bishop Thurzo and left at his mercy. According to a Hutterite source, he died of starvation in the jail at Kroměříž.[43] Actually, he had been condemned by King Ferdinand to the same death as Hubmaier. But because of his recantation and the intercession by the Moravian lords, he was not punished by the civil power.

We have included a detailed account of Göschl's career for two reasons. In the first place, he was the only native Moravian churchman of importance whom Hubmaier succeeded in winning for Anabaptism. The former Coadjutor Bishop of Olomouc provided the main link between Hubmaier and the Moravian society outside the refugee community at Mikulov. Göschl must have had some knowledge about the Unity not only from his association with Augustin Käsenbrod and Jakob Ziegler,[44] authors of polemical writings against the Czech Brethren, but also through the influence of Paul Speratus and his interest in their doctrines. Besides, Göschl had personal dealings with a number of Moravian barons and knights who were among the adherents and protectors of the Unity.[45] When, in the fall of 1526, Göschl requested Hubmaier to write a catechism his idea might have been inspired, or at least influenced by the catechetical practices of the Czech Brethren and possibly even by their printed German catechisms.[46]

In the second place, Göschl likely exerted a theological influence on Hubmaier's thoughts and actions at Mikulov. There are no extant

in Faber, 1537a, fols. M ij^v - b vj^v). This long report must not be confused with his previous short statement on the reasons why Hubmaier had been burnt (Faber, 1528a, reprinted by Loserth, 1893, 210-216). Both of them bore dedications to Georg, Duke of Saxony, and were dated respectively in Vienna on March 11, 1528 and in Prague on July 1, 1528. The short booklet must have been printed in Vienna in the second half of March, for copies of it reached Innsbruck before April 4 (Loserth, 1893, 188). On June 29, Crautwald in Liegnitz mentioned it in his letter to Capito (TQ Elsass, I, 170, with a wrong identification of the booklet in footnote 12).

[43] ZGL, 52 and Beck, 53 f. Hrejsa, V, 22 refers to the jail in Olomouc. The date of his death is not known.

[44] We assume these contacts on the basis of Göschl's biographical data outlined earlier. We were unable to discover any confirmation in the sources. The same observation applies to Göschl's contact with Paul Speratus.

[45] So far as we know there was never a congregation of the Unity in Jihlava where Göschl spent most of his life. There were only a few brethren there who attended services in the town of Třebíč (Hrejsa, B, 49).

[46] Cf. our discussion of the dependance of Hubmaier's Leertafel on the catechism of the Brethren: footnote 212 in the previous chapter and Appendix 5.

theological statements which would allow us to estimate the depth of Göschl's inward separation from the position of the Roman church. But the nature of his quarrels with the Bishop of Olomouc, the definition of his guilt in the final process against him [47] and the fact of his recantation, all seem to indicate a rather superficial break with the old church. One may conclude, therefore, that Göschl's close associations with Hubmaier introduced a restraining element and retarded if not prevented the latter's rapprochement with the more radical refugees in the congregation at Mikulov.

By way of illustration, one may point to the following issues. Hubmaier's teachings on eschatology show a distinct shift of emphasis from a strongly personal, subjective consciousness of the near return of Christ to a mainly objective affirmation of the article of the creed concerning the second coming of Christ, the last judgment and eternal life. The change is noticeable in Hubmaier's writings from the Moravian period.[48] Psychologically, one might explain the shift by the more stable social environment in which Hubmaier found himself at Mikulov, or by a reaction to the eccentric chiliasm among some refugees. However, one should not dismiss a 'catholicizing' influence of Göschl. Some other features of church life at Mikulov under Hubmaier's leadership are symptomatic of the same influence.

Hubmaier restored, at Mikulov, the Catholic practice of church bell ringing three times a day as call to prayer, in spite of the fact that it had been abolished earlier by the pre-Anabaptist ministers under Spittelmaier's leadership.[49] The close cooperation between the Mikulov church and the local authorities, after Hubmaier's bitter disillusionments about such relationships in Waldshut and Zürich (arrest and torture), might have been conditioned also, to some extent, by Göschl's political orientation as a former member of the Moravian diet.

---

[47] "Quod episcopatu relicto ac sacerdotio, virgine vestali sibi in matrimonium copulata aliud vitae genus elegit, aliis et causis accedentibus . . ." (Loserth, 1897, 69 f.; Beck, 54, note). The indictment does not mention heretical teachings as such.
[48] Compare Hubmaier's frequent references to "these last days" in his earlier writings (e.g., HS, 72, 172, 218: "O mein herr Jesu Christe, verkürtze die täg, vnd kümm bald herab zů vns" — written in the Zürich jail) and even soon after his arrival in Moravia (e.g., 289; see the full quotation in footnote 214 of Ch. II), with his later impersonal treatment of the last day and judgment (e.g., 325, 364, 371 and in his *Rechenschaft*, 474 f.). See also the references listed under "Eschatologie", HS, 503. Sachsse, 1914 ignored Hubmaier's eschatology. The only brief treatment of the important subject is in Bergsten, 1961, 467-471.
[49] HS, 476 f. Cf. Bergsten, 1961, 410 f.

One should not, therefore, be unduly surprised by Hubmaier's endorsement of several Roman Catholic doctrines which he professed in his *Rechenschaft*[50] submitted to King Ferdinand in January 1528, after three days of talks with Faber. The Bishop expressed astonishment that Hubmaier should have separated himself from the Roman church when he differed so little with its teachings.[51] To explain Hubmaier's final theological stand exclusively as an attempt to save his life is hardly satisfactory. The views expressed in the *Rechenschaft* represent the last stage of a trend which can be detected throughout Hubmaier's Moravian period, brief as it was, and might well be traced to his association with Göschl.

The other two members of the Mikulov 'triumvirate' who had welcomed Hubmaier in June-July 1526 and soon followed his leadership, were Oswald Glaidt and Hans Spittelmaier. Earlier, we have reviewed their pre-Anabaptist views, expressed in Spittelmaier's *Entschuldigung* (1524)[52] and Glaidt's *Handlung* (1526).[53] In Glaidt's room Hubmaier wrote the preface to his first book printed in Moravia.[54] Late in the fall (1526) he had nothing but highest praise for both men.[55] A few weeks later, Glaidt stated his Anabaptist position in his second booklet, *Entschuldigung*, printed at Mikulov on January 26, 1527.[56] The

[50] E.g., art. 16, on the power of the keys in the absolution of sins; 17, on the obedience to the church as mother; 18, on celibacy and 20, on the intercession of saints. *HS*, 477 ff.

[51] Faber, 1528e, as reprinted in Faber, 1537a, fol. b ij^r. Faber reports on his discussions with Hubmaier, during which both had only a copy of the Bible for reference except for one of Faber's books against Zwingli which Faber handed to Hubmaier to read (*ibid.*, fol. V iv). Faber's account presents complementary material to Hubmaier's *Rechenschaft*. Both documents cover the same range of topics (see Appendix 3). The main reason, however, why Faber published his lengthy manuscript was not to provide an historical record of his talks with the Anabaptist leader (dead by then) but to polemize against Luther and Zwingli.

[52] See Chapter II, beginning at footnote 90. On Spittelmaier's life, cf. Friedmann's art. in *ME*, IV, 599 and *ML*, IV, 226 (more complete) and Bergsten, 1961, 399 f. *et passim*.

[53] See Chapter II, beginning at footnote 113. For Glaidt's biography, cf. Beck, 160 f. (note); Loserth, 1897, 70-73; Wiswedel, 1937b and Loserth's art. in *ML*, II, 117 ff. and *ME*, II, 522 f.

[54] On July 21, 1526 (*HS*, 229).

[55] *HS*, 288.

[56] *Enntschuldigung Osbaldi Glaidt von Chamb. Etwan zŭ Leybm in Osterreich, yetz predicant zŭ Nicolspurg in Merhern. Etlicher Artickel verklerung ... Gedruckt zu Nikolspurg durch Simprecht Sorg, gen. Froschauer 1527.* 4°, 14 fols. Copy in Brno, in the collection of Hubmaier's works which used to belong to Glaidt's son Tobias. The booklet was not accessible to us. A detailed summary in Wiswedel, 1937b, 556-561; the title in Dudík, 1875, 113 f. Not unlike Spittelmaier in his *Entschuldigung* (1524), Glaidt defends his position against the attacks of the

concept of baptism betrays Hubmaier's influence.[57] The silence about the problem of Christian participation in government and war may be interpreted as an indication that the issue was not in the open at Mikulov at that time. The range of the topics and the purpose of the booklet are similar to those of Spittelmaier's *Entschuldigung* of 1524. Glaidt might have written his anti-Catholic polemic earlier but did not publish it, with Anabaptist revisions, until January 1527.

The controversy between Hubmaier and Hut in May led to an estrangement between Glaidt and Hubmaier. Whatever the specific issues might have been, Glaidt sided with Hut[58] and soon afterwards left Mikulov for Vienna where he baptized Leonhard Schiemer some time before Pentecost.[59] Under the increasing peril of persecution he moved from place to place. In the fall[60] he was with Hans Schlaffer in Regensburg and eventually he appeared at Liegnitz in Silesia.

With Glaidt away and Hubmaier in prison (after June), Hans Spittelmaier seems to have assumed the main leadership. He had been the first evangelical minister in town and enjoyed the full confidence of the Liechtensteins.[61] The only event recorded in the Hutterite chronicles for the period from Hubmaier's arrest to his death, is Spittelmaier's strife with the non-resistant communitarian Anabaptists who were led by the one-eyed Jakob Widemann and Philip Jäger.[62] The omission of Göschl's name in the Hutterite record of the controversy is somewhat surprising in view of the fact that he had played a

---

Franciscan friars in nearby Feldsberg (Valtice) in the following 13 articles: (1) The twofold faith (historical and genuine). (2) The saints and their intercession. (3) Prayer. (4) Fasting. (5) Almsgiving. (6) Differences in food and (7) days, incl. a discussion of the true Sabbath. (8) Marriage of priests. (9) Images. (10) Altars. (11) Giving offense, uprooting of Catholic customs, e.g. fasting on Friday, infant baptism. (12) Burial (in blessed ground). (13) Sacraments: baptism (a pledge of faith) and Lord's Supper (a pledge of brotherly love). Loserth's list of articles (*ML*, II, 118 and *ME*, II, 523) differs somewhat from ours which is based on Wiswedel's summary of the booklet. Loserth adds art. 14 on freedom of the will. Cf. Bergsten, 1961, 437, n. 6.

[57]   Cf. Bergsten, 1961, 406, n. 30.

[58]   According to the testimony of Hut in Augsburg, October 5, 1527 (Meyer, 1874, 231 f.). Williams, 1962, 225 aligned Glaidt (wrongly) with Hubmaier.

[59]   *ZGL*, 59 and *TQ*, III, 80 (Schiemer's own testimony, January 14, 1528). The day of Pentecost fell on June 9, 1527.

[60]   He met Schlaffer after the "Martyrs' Synod" (Augsburg, August 20), not before it, as Wiswedel, 1937a, 562 assumed. Cf. Friedmann, 1961a, 260.

[61]   Cf. the title "vnndterteniger Caplan" in his *Entschuldigung* (1524) dedicated to the Lords of Liechtenstein (Chapter II at footnote 90). In October 1527, Hut referred to him as "pfarrer zu Niclausburg" (*TQ*, II, 40).

[62]   Beck, 70-76; *ZGL*, 52 ff. and 86 ff.

crucial part at the Mikulov disputation between Hubmaier and Hut in May. For lack of other information, one may only surmise that after the unpleasant experience in May, Göschl, a native Moravian, left the dealings with the feuding factions among the Anabaptist refugees to Spittelmaier, himself a newcomer.[63]

The development and dating of the first Anabaptist split and secession in Moravia is recorded in the Hutterite sources with minute detail and only minor ambiguities.[64] As new refugees kept arriving, the dissatisfaction with the leaders of the Mikulov Anabaptist church became more vocal. The points of tension lay not only in the theological and ethical spheres but also in the sociological contrasts. Even the Hutterite interpretation — written half a century later — allows us to discern that the most pressing problem had been the physical care of newcomers. Liechtenstein, Spittelmaier and those associated with them were accused of not providing shelter and not properly receiving "the guests and strangers from other lands".[65]

Persecuted refugees who were used to meeting secretly in houses or hideout places did not feel at home in the 'churchy' atmosphere which must have characterized the services in the parish church at Mikulov. A large congregation numbering several hundreds, if not thousands, could never implement the same type of church discipline and 'brotherly watchcare' to which the refugees had been accustomed from their small conventicles in other lands. They began to hold meetings on their own in homes, both at Mikulov and in the nearby villages on the Liechtenstein domains where they had settled. Quite

[63] It should be noted that Göschl's name occurs in the chronicles for the same period of time. ZGL, 51 f.

[64] In the text edited by Zieglschmid, the arrival of Wiedemann and Jäger is dated clearly after Hubmaier's arrest and separated from the controversy between Hubmaier and Hut (cf. the phrase, "wie auch vorhin zu des Balthasar Huebmörs Zeit", ZGL, I, 53). In his own piecing together of short excerpts from several manuscript chronicles, Beck, 50 f. inserted part of the story in an earlier context. It should have been printed in the section appearing on pp. 70-76. His arrangement gave rise to the thesis of two disputations at Pergen, one in Hubmaier's days (preceding the Nikolsburg disputation) and another under Spittelmaier. The mistake which is being perpetuated in the art. "Nikolsburg" and "Pergen" (by P. Dedic) in ML and ME, has been corrected by Seewald, 1953, 13. Cf. Bergsten, 1961, 452 f. (esp. notes 69-70). There was only one disputation at Pergen in 1527.

[65] ZGL, 53 and Beck, 73. The case provides an interesting parallel to the problems of modern refugee communities. Similar accusations can be heard and divisions have taken place in Protestant congregations and in Catholic or Orthodox parishes in Canada and the U.S.A. when the needs and outlooks of successive waves of immigrants or refugees clashed. The problem is as old as the Christian church. See Acts 6:1 ff.

naturally, in their crowded quarters and desperate poverty, they began to share food and other necessities of life.

Hubmaier had encouraged such tangible expressions of brotherly love but became critical of the separatist meetings of Hut's followers.[66] Spittelmaier later nicknamed them *Kleinhäufler*. The situation was explosive enough without the additional issue of Christian involvement in government and war. Yet the problem of "the sword" loomed large at the debate in Pergen, some time in the fall of 1527.[67] The threat of the Turkish invasion made urgent the problems of war taxes and active participation in defense.

The articles discussed at Pergen (Perná) included problems of brotherly discipline, bearing of arms, war taxes and "other things". The brief record is not specific enough about the persons involved in the debate. There were 'elders' of the congregation in Pergen, but perhaps also from the church at Mikulov. One chronicle mentions "the brethren and the elders".[68] There is no mention of Spittelmaier's name. Whoever was present, the group did not reach agreement.

Subsequently, Spittelmaier defended publicly the use of the sword and payment of war taxes. The controversy continued through the winter. A few days after Hubmaier's execution in Vienna, "in mid-lent" (March 19), a group of two hundred *Stäbler* (men of the staff) [69]

---

[66]   Cf. Hubmaier's statement on "ein christenliche gmeinschaft der gütter" in his recantation at Zürich (*TQ Schweiz*, I, 148). See also *HS*, 178 and a condemnation of Hut's followers in *HS*, 489 f. Cf. Stayer, 1965, 189.

[67]   Bergsten, 1961, 483 follows Müller, 1927, 84 in dating the debate at Pergen "at the beginning of 1528". Neither of them explains the reasons. *ZGL*, 52 and Beck, 51 state that (the brethren and) the elders met for a disputation, "after the spread of the alarming news that the Turks were about to march on Vienna", with the date 1527 (in Beck only). The siege of Vienna did not take place till fall 1529 but many false alarms must have preceded it. The chronicle offers a further clue. Some time after the debate at Pergen, Leonhard of Liechtenstein summoned the leaders of the "communitarians" (an expression coined by Williams, 1962, 229), Wiedemann and Jäger, and told them that unless they conformed to the teachings of "his preachers", they would have to vacate his domains. However, the two leaders replied that such an attitude was not worthy of one who boasted of being also a brother. Thereupon, Leonhard allowed them to stay. "And it remained like that for the winter until the next Lent" (*ZGL*, 53). The interview must have taken place some time in the late fall 1527. Cf. also Bauman, 1968, 59 ff.

[68]   Beck, 51. Cf. *ZGL*, 52.

[69]   According to *ZGL*, 96 (Beck, 73) it was Spittelmaier who called the non-resistant Anabaptists "Stäbler". Brock, 1957, 252 f. suggested that in adopting the stave (in place of a sword) as a symbol of their non-violent creed the Anabaptists might have been following the example of the Minor Party of the Unity. Lukáš referred to the custom of "wandering around with staffs" in his printed book

or *Gemeinschaftler* (communitarians) as the *Kleinhäufler* came to be called, parted company with the *Schwertler* (men of the sword) and left for an uncertain destination. Even though the number did not include the children, it represented but a small minority, drawn not only from Mikulov but also from the surrounding villages. The fact that they tried to sell their possessions would indicate that not all of them were destitute refugees of recent arrival.

After several weeks of wanderings they were permitted to settle at Slavkov (Austerlitz) under the protection of the Lords of Kounice.[70] The tiny secessionist group of communitarian Anabaptists became the prototype of the main stream of Moravian Anabaptism in the years to come.

The situation at Mikulov following the exodus of the *Stäbler* in mid-March 1528 is difficult to reconstruct. The Hutterite chroniclers ignored Mikulov, having turned their attention to other places such as Slavkov and Hustopeče, where communitarian Anabaptism was born and nourished during its years of infancy. It is doubtful that the two hundred adult persons who left represented the total force of non-resistant Anabaptism on the Liechtenstein domains. Many more must have stayed under the pastoral care of Hubmaier's successors. They were being strengthened by the continuous flow of refugees.

The leaders became the first target of Ferdinand's determined efforts to prevent Moravia from becoming an island of refuge and safety for heretics. Göschl was arrested some time in April and transported to Prague where Ferdinand, accompanied by his chief adviser on ecclesiastical policies, Johann Faber, made his residence from April 6 till the second half of September 1528.[71] Hans Spittelmaier and other refugee ministers were affected by the decree of the Moravian diet. It is not known when he left nor where he turned.[72]

---

against Kalenec in 1523. We do not know whether the followers of Wiedemann actually carried staffs as a symbolic gesture. Spittelmaier might have been acquainted with the practice of the Minor Party and applied the symbol to his opponents (Williams, 1962, 229). In any case, the word "Stäbler" was of new coinage. There was no Czech equivalent for it and the Minor Party was not known under that name.

[70]   Cf. the details of the "exodus" in ZGL, 87 ff. and a good summary in Williams, 1962, 229 ff.

[71]   Hrejsa, V, 14 f. They were attending the lengthy session of the Bohemian diet. Cf. footnote 77 below.

[72]   According to Williams, 1959, 224 and 1962, 408 f. (cf. also CS, IV, 450) Spittelmaier took part, together with Oswald Glaidt and Johann Bünderlin, in a colloquy at Kętrzyn (Rastenburg) in ducal Prussia, on December 29-30, 1531 (cf.

Spring and summer of the year 1528 brought the first wave of persecution of Anabaptists in Moravia. We shall now relate the course of events since they set the stage for the negotiations between Anabaptists and the Czech Brethren that year.

Already on August 20, 1527, Ferdinand had launched persecution in his lands in the general mandate against all non-Catholics.[73] In the subsequent months specific mandates against Anabaptists were issued separately for each province (land) under Ferdinand's rule.[74] The new year was ushered in with the ominous Imperial Edict of Speyer (January 4, 1528).[75]

Ferdinand and his advisers were persuaded that in the spring of 1528 the Anabaptists were contemplating a violent uprising comparable to the Peasants' Revolt of 1525. The chiliastic expectations of the end of the world at Pentecost 1528 which came to light at Anabaptist trials [76] likely served as the basis for the dating of the feared riots. In the instructions to his emissaries who were to attend the congress of the Bohemian estates in Prague on February 4, Ferdinand wrote: "Make them aware of the new Anabaptist heresy which has arisen in the Empire, in Moravia and Silesia, as well as in our hereditary lands and in the surrounding countries, and which has not a few adherents, as we are given to understand. From confessions extracted at trials from those who have been arrested, at our command, for their second baptism, it is most certainly known that they [the Anabaptists] have conspired to rise against the authorities (*vrchnost*) in

---

Tschackert, 1894, 46 and Maleczyńska, 1960, 235 ff.). The colloquy was convened by Duke Albrecht in order to deal with the sacramentarian views of the eucharist which were being spread by Schwenckfeldians and Anabaptists. Among the Lutheran spokesmen was Paul Speratus, then Bishop of Pomesania. After the colloquy, the Duke expelled the three "spiritualizing" Anabaptists (August 16, 1532) although he retained in his services other spiritualists, such as Christian Entfelder. Cf. footnote 242 below.

[73]   The text of the long document was written by Faber (Helbling, 1933, 63 and 168, No. 164). It is reprinted in *TQ*, XI, 3-12. The date of issue coincided with the opening day of the "Martyrs' Synod" in Augsburg (*ME*, III, 529).

[74]   Cf. the comprehensive list in *ME*, III, 447 f. The text of several mandates is reprinted in *TQ*, XI, e.g., 26 f., 55 f.

[75]   Reprinted in *TQ*, I, °1 f. and *TQ*, XI, 61, n. 1.

[76]   Cf. the source references in Bergsten, 1961, 467 f. In his first sermon against the Anabaptists preached at the diet of Znojmo, Faber said: "Quod Catabaptistae suis asseclis persuadent breui, ut ad proximum Penthecosten, aut ab hinc uno anno, extrema iudicij horrendi tempora adfulsura, qui error duos ante annos in Apocel [Appenzell], Catabaptistarum magnum numerum, in aeditum montem conscendere compulit . . ." (Faber, 1537a, fol. k iijʳ). The original German version of the sermons was not accessible to us.

the spring [1528] and have covenanted themselves in solemn oath".[77] The Bohemian estates were requested to suggest the best way to prevent the plot.

As the day of Pentecost (May 31) drew nearer, Ferdinand became more apprehensive. On May 1, 1528, he wrote a letter from Prague to the government of Lower Austria in which he referred to a group of four hundred "peasants or common people of the riotous evil sect" who had gathered in a place called "im Walld" in Moravia. Another group of the same size was supposed to have been at another place in Moravia.[78] The rumour which reached Ferdinand in Prague referred perhaps to groups of Anabaptists hiding in the mountains and woods on the Liechtenstein domains for fear that the striking commando (*streifende Rotte*) of Dietrich of Hartisch might cross the unprotected Moravian border.[79] There were also the *Stäbler* who had left Mikulov in mid-March and had been camping for several weeks in the open.[80] In a letter to the King on March 4 the government in Vienna had recommended that a small equestrian unit be sent also to Moravia, and especially to the area around Mikulov, the main hotbed of the heresy.[81]

The crucial moment in Ferdinand's strategy against Anabaptism in Moravia came at the diet in Znojmo which was convened during

---

[77] The Czech original is reprinted in Sněmy, I, 270. A congress ("Sjezd") of the estates used to be held a short time before the actual diet in order to prepare the business and take a stand on the proposals of the king. The Bohemian diet in 1528 opened on April 16 and lasted till September 28 (Sněmy, I, 288).

[78] The text of the letter was reprinted by Loserth, 1919a. Cf. also Loserth, 1899, 433.

[79] In his attempts to annihilate the Anabaptists, Ferdinand created a small equestrian force, "streifende Rotte", under the command of the commissioner (Provos) of Lower Austria, Dietrich of Hartisch. The hiding Anabaptists were literally hunted and when caught, executed on the spot. Many fled from Austria to the region around Mikulov. However, they feared that Dietrich might cross the unprotected border, and were hiding in the woods and mountains. According to the Hutterite chronicles, the Lords of Liechtenstein issued a warning to the Provos not to cross the Moravian border (ZGL, 54 and Beck, 57 f.) and later recalled the Anabaptists from their hiding places (ZGL, 85 and Beck, 58). The chronicles date the beginning of the wild persecution from the first week of Lent (February 9-15, 1528; ZGL, 53 and Beck, 57). Ferdinand's accrediting letter for Dietrich is not dated till March 20 (*TQ*, XI, 91 ff). Cf. also *ME*, II, 667 f. and footnote 81.

[80] ZGL, 87 f. and Beck, 74 ff. One of their criticisms of the Liechtensteins was that they were prepared to use force in protecting the Anabaptists against Dietrich of Hartisch.

[81] *TQ*, XI, 83. The lengthy report to the King contains also an explanation of the delays in the process against Hubmaier (80). Cf. Bergsten, 1961, 479.

the last days of March and the early days of April 1528.[82] Ferdinand, accompanied by Johann Faber, attended the sessions. But in spite of his personal pleas and regardless of the denunciatory sermons preached by Faber,[83] the Moravian estates consented to only two measures against the Anabaptists: (1) their preachers and leaders who were not native Moravians were ordered to leave the margraviate within one month and (2) their public meetings and services were prohibited in order to minimize the danger of a feared uprising.[84]

The decisions of the diet fell far short of the demands of Ferdinand who pressed for a general expulsion of all Anabaptists and for merciless executions of the leaders. But then, the King was obliged to give in on some issue if he was to receive the financial and military support of the estates for his crusade against enemy number one, the Turks. In fact the Turks, unknowingly, became the greatest allies of the Moravian Anabaptists through the entire time of Ferdinand's reign (1526-1564). Whenever their armies pressed the King's forces, Ferdinand relented in his efforts to induce the Moravian estates towards strict measures against the Anabaptists. When the Turks re-

[82]   The dates and decisions of the diet at Znojmo must be reconstructed from other sources since the official records are not preserved (Hrubý, 1935a, 8, n. 2). Ferdinand was still in Vienna on March 22 (TQ, XI, 94 ff.) and possibly March 24, (TQ, XI, 100). Faber was in Vienna on March 26 (Helbling, 1933, 169, letter No. 174). On the other hand, on April 4 and 5, the King was already at Německý Brod (Deutschbrod) in Bohemia, on his way to Prague. (Cf. his letters to Innsbruck, Loserth, 1893, 190 and to Georg, Duke of Saxony, regarding the plans and distinguishing marks of the Anabaptists, Wappler, 1913, 281 f.) Faber's sermons were preached "in the month of April" (cf. the title of Faber, 1528b-c). Dvořák, 1901, 388 mentions April 1 as the day on which Ferdinand pleaded in Znojmo for help against the Turks.

[83]   The sermons were preached in German which was not understood by many members of the Moravian nobility. Both the original version (Faber, 1528b) and a Latin translation (Faber, 1528c) were printed. The Latin version, with a dedicatory preface to the Bishop of Olomouc, dated in Prague on April 24, appeared in three editions (Vienna, Leipzig and Venice, all in 1528). Cf. our Appendix 3.

[84]   The assumption of Loserth, 1893, 189 and 1899, 431 (repeated still in TQ, XI, 113, n. 2 and elsewhere) that the diet decreed a general expulsion of all Anabaptists has been corrected by Hrubý, 1935a, 8 and Hrejsa, V, 14. The decision is reported clearly in the letter of Johann of Zwola to Dr. Johann Hess, the Reformer in Breslau. He wrote it from Tovačov where he was a guest of Jan of Pernstein. As an eyewitness of the diet, he reported on April 15: "... assensum tantum modo in hoc regi ut qui e Germania in Moravuiam confluxere Baptistarum concionatores infra mensem prouincia excederent, conuentus hiis inhiberentur ..." (Loserth, 1893, 217). The report is confirmed by Ferdinand's letters to Brno and Jihlava (dated Prague, April 13) in which he was reminding them of the dealings and decisions at Znojmo. (Full Czech text in Kameníček, III, 468, note. Cf. Schenner, 1912, 89.)

treated, or an armistice was agreed upon, the Anabaptists could expect renewed persecution.[85]

What the King could not accomplish without the consent of the nobility throughout South Moravia, he was determined to carry out at least in the four royal cities which stood under his direct control: Brno, Olomouc, Jihlava and Znojmo. He and his escorts arrived in Prague on the Monday before Easter (April 6). On Easter Monday (April 13), he wrote letters to the city councils at Brno and Jihlava [86] reminding them not only of the decision of the diet but also of his personal orders which he had issued to their delegates in Znojmo. The letters do not specify what these orders were. However, from Ferdinand's letters to Lower Austria (April 12 and 18) [87] one may conclude that he expected the councils of the Moravian royal cities to effect immediate arrests and punishment of all known Anabaptists. He also envisaged that escapees would enter Austria and were to be apprehended there.

Two days before or after Easter 1528,[88] three Anabaptists, including

---

[85] Dvořák, 1901, 386 ff. has shown that the three main persecutions of Anabaptists in Moravia during the sixteenth century (spring and summer 1528, 1534-1536 and 1547-1550) coincided with the three "periods of rest" from the Turkish danger and from the related political problems. (1) After Jan Zapolya was expelled from Hungary in the fall of 1527 and Ferdinand was received as King by the Hungarian diet on October 7, his hands were free to turn against the Anabaptists in the spring and summer of 1528. In the fall of 1528, Zapolya invaded Hungary in the hope of an early arrival of the Turks, his allies. The siege of Vienna did not materialize till the following fall (Sept. 21-Oct. 15, 1529). (2) In 1533, the first peace of Constantinople ended the wars till 1537. (3) The second peace of Constantinople (August 1547) initiated a five years' armistice. One must not forget, though, that the second persecution was related also to the 'Anabaptist' kingdom at Münster (1534-1535) and the third wave to the Smalcadian war (1546-1547). Hrubý, 1935a, 7 ff. furnished further evidence for the interrelatedness of the Turkish wars and the persecutions of Anabaptists in Moravia. An important factor was the strong stand on the principle of religious toleration by the Moravian estates. Cf. Zeman, 1962, 6 ff.

[86] Czech original of the two letters to Brno in Kameníček, III, 468, note. Cf. footnote 84 above.

[87] TQ, XI, 113 and 115 f. Cf. Loserth, 1893, 190.

[88] There are conflicting dates in the sources. The Hutterite chronicles (Beck, 65 and Wolny, 1850, 75 f.; no date in the text of ZGL, 63) date the execution on Good Friday (April 10). A contemporary source, the letter of Johann of Zwola (cf. footnote 83 above) written on April 15, contains a postscript which reads: "Apud Brunam Baptiste tres pridie incendio consumpti, in quibus Czizek et Thomas quidam" (Loserth, 1893, 217). Müller, 1920, 520, n. 18; Odložilík, 1923, 41; Hrejsa, V, 21 and Molnár, 1952a, 109 have accepted the date of Tuesday, April 14. One might ask whether the term "pridie" in sixteenth-century Latin meant exclusively "the day before".

Zeising (Čížek), were burnt in Brno.[89] The news about their martyrdom
— like the report about Hubmaier's death a month earlier — travelled
fast. On April 28, Crautwald in Liegnitz mentioned it in his letter to
Bucer and included a brief description of other atrocities in Moravia.[90]
He must have been referring to the persecution in the royal cities.

The city of Znojmo witnessed the burning of three Anabaptist men
and two women, probably also in April 1528.[91] Three or four were
burnt in Olomouc.[92] No executions are recorded in the sources for
Jihlava although Ferdinand sent similar orders there on April 13.[93]

The violent persecution seems to have affected mainly the Anabaptists residing in the royal cities. Those who had settled on the
domains of Moravian barons experienced protection rather than
persecution. This must have applied as much on the Mikulov domain
of the Liechtensteins [94] as in the other places where Anabaptist settle-

---

[89]   The identification of the three martyrs presents problems. The best source,
Johann of Zwola, refers to Zeising (Čížek) and a certain Thomas. Čížek used to
stay at Tovačov (cf. footnote 82 in Ch. II) and was known personally to Jan of
Pernstein, the host of J. of Zwola. Thomas is probably identical with Thoman
Waldhauser, a former Catholic priest in Grein, Austria (called also Thomas of
Grein). He attended the Martyrs' Synod in Augsburg (August 1527; *ME*, III, 529)
and was probably the main leader of the Anabaptist congregation in Brno to whom
he wrote an epistle from the jail in Brno on April 4 (title in Beck, 66, note and
Friedmann, 1965b, 70). See also *ME*, IV, 876. The Hutterite chronicles show
variant readings (Beck, 65 and *ZGL*, 63) but do not include Zeising unless he is
referred to under the name "Dominicus". Thoman and Balthauser may be two
persons (*ZGL*, 63, n. 1) or one, viz., Thoman Waldhauser (Beck, 65). Fischer,
1607a, fol. A ij[v] mentions "Thoma Balthasar". An anonymous contributor in *ME*,
IV, 714 identifies Thomas with Thomas Pelsser, a Hutterite (in 1528?) preacher.
[90]   "Atque paulo antequam haec scriberem, nunciabatur, mandante rege Ferdi-
nando, tres anabaptistarum magistros Brunnae in Moravuia igni accenso confla-
grasse, innumeram autem fere multitudinem vulgi aqua tinctam in carceribus esse
et indies crescere, conductis publicis exploratoribus et carnificibus, qui quoscumque
invenerint, aut si qui juditio proditi fuerint, partim in vincula conijciunt, partim
variis cruciatbus enecant . . ." (*TQ Elsass*, I, 158 f.).
[91]   *ZGL*, 71 f. and Beck, 66 f. The sources include a detailed account of a fanatical
judge, Lewisch (Lebisch, Lebusch). Johann of Zwola reported in his lettter to
Dr. Johann Hess, written at Tovačov on April 15: "Znoymensis concionator Euan-
gelii pulsus aut ad carcerem quesitus est, sed is inter Baptistas tum computabatur"
(Loserth, 1893, 217).
[92]   Beck, 66. A table of martyrs in *ZGL*, 232 lists the following executions: 4 in
Brno, 7 in Znojmo and 4 in Olomouc (plus 11 in Prague). A list which was con-
fiscated from Julius Lober of Zürich on April 10, 1531 included the following
martyrs: 3 burnt in Olomouc, 2 beheaded in Brno and 4 beheaded at Prague (*TQ*,
V, 278 f.).
[93]   Cf. footnote 86 above.
[94]   Cf. footnote 79 above.

ments are known to have existed in the spring of 1528: Ivančice (Eibenschitz), Rosice (Rossitz), Slavkov (Austerlitz) and perhaps also in Dačice (Datschitz) and "Neuwitzsch".[95]

Meanwhile, Ferdinand continued his efforts to uproot Anabaptism in spite of the fact that the feared rebellion did not take place at Pentecost 1528. While still in Prague, the King received reports, on June 23, from Český Krumlov (Böhmisch Krumau) about an Anabaptist group there. His strict orders were finally obeyed by the local baron, Jan of Rosenberg. An exodus of nearly one hundred Anabaptists from there to Slavkov (Austerlitz) took place late in 1528, or more likely in 1529.[96]

On July 24, 1528, Ferdinand issued a mandate ordering that "printers and booksellers of heretical books, as the chief seducers and 'poisoners' of all lands, be executed by drowning, without mercy and without delay".[97] The mandate probably caused the removal of the printing shop of Simprecht Sorg Froschauer from Mikulov to Liegnitz in Silesia, early in the month of August.[98] By September 17 he had already set up his shop in Liegnitz and travelled to the autumn book

[95] Cf. the topographical data for these Anabaptist settlements in Zeman, 1966 and also our discussion of the merger negotiations further below.

[96] The correspondence concerning the Anabaptists in Český Krumlov (report to Ferdinand on June 23; Ferdinand's reply on July 2 which includes reference to "Pelhřim Marchpeckh" who, with his wife, was reported in the same area, and 15 questions for interrogation of three imprisoned Anabaptists, Virgilius Plattner, Jan Rablender and Jiří Moser; Ferdinand's second letter on July 27) is reprinted in part by Mareš, 1907, 26 ff. The exodus to Austerlitz is reported in Beck, 86 f. and ZGL, 91. Cf. also Loserth, 1892.

[97] Translated from the Czech text quoted by Dudík, 1875, 111 f. Neither Dudík nor Mecenseffy, 1956a, 24 refers to the source where the text is found. It is not mentioned in TQ, XI. Cf. also Bahlow, 1928, 7.

[98] Simprecht was the son of Hans (Johann) Froschauer, a printer in Augsburg, 1594-1522. He might also have been related to another printer family in Augsburg, Anton Sorg, father and son. After the death of his father, early in 1523, Simprecht came to Zürich and worked in the shop of Christoph Froschauer with whom he also was related (refers to him as his "Vetter" in the letter to Zwingli; see the following footnote). In the fall of 1524, he printed Schwenckfeld, 1524 in Zürich. During his one-year stay in Moravia he printed 16 works of Hubmaier, Glaidt, 1526 and 1527 and perhaps also Jörg Haug's Ain Christlich Ordenung (cf. Schottenloher, 1921, 65 and 131, No. 155; TQ, X, No. 2693; not listed by Friedmann, 1965b, 134). In Liegnitz, he printed three works of Schwenckfeld (1529: CS, III, 391 ff.; 1530: CS, III, 493 ff.; 1532: CS, IV, 210) and Gmeine Practica (1530). For further details, see Dudík, 1875, 111-114; Bahlow, 1928, 7-14; Tobolka, 1929; Benzing, 1963, 378 and 327; HS, 37, n. 113 and 60, n. 13 and 398; Leeman, 1940, 14 ff. Maleczyńska, 1960, 241 claims that Sorg also printed in Liegnitz in 1528 Ludwig Hätzer's Büchlein von Christo. Cf. Goeters, 1957, 142.

fair in Frankfurt a.M. from which place he wrote a letter to Zwingli.[99]

On August 28, an Anabaptist bottler (*flašnéř*), Jiří, and a Lutheran, Václav, were burnt in Prague.[100] They were the last victims of Ferdinand's rage in 1528. Less than a month later, the King and his court returned from Prague to Vienna where he became preoccupied again with the Hungarian affairs and the Turks. The Anabaptists in Moravia were allowed to resume more normal life.

2. THE *UNITAS FRATRUM* DURING THE FINAL YEARS OF BISHOP LUKÁŠ

The earliest contacts between the Moravian Anabaptists and the *Unitas Fratrum* took place at the very end of the "era of Brother Lukáš, the second founder of the Unity".[101]

By choice or coincidence, the anonymous Anabaptist emissaries who entered into merger negotiations with the Unity in 1528 met the three foremost leaders of the Unity at that time: Bishop Lukáš, Vavřinec Krasonický and Jan Roh. Our subsequent analysis of the records of negotiations makes it necessary that we become acquainted with these three men.

The outward events of the long life of Lukáš (ca. 1458-1528) lack the variety and drama which was characteristic of so many religious

---

[99]   Z, IX, 554 f.
[100]   The source, Bartoš Písař, 241 f. reports both as Germans. Cf. Hrejsa, V, 15 and Winter, 1895, 87 and 307.
[101]   Both terms were coined by the great historian of the Unity, Josef Th. Müller and fully endorsed by the subsequent studies of Molnár, Říčan and others. No comprehensive monograph on the life and thought of Lukáš has been published in book form as yet. On his life and theological development, a series of French articles by Molnár covers the period from birth until 1515: Molnár 1960a (also in Czech, 1948b), 1961a-b-c, 1962a-b, 1963a-b. His period of leadership as minister and later bishop at Mladá Boleslav (from 1494 till his death in 1528) is covered in Molnár, 1952a. An excellent summary of his theological system is available in Molnár, 1948a. Further studies deal with aspects of the relationship between Lukáš and Luther (Molnár, 1959a [in German: 1964b] and between Lukáš and the Waldensians in Italy (Molnár 1949a). Molnár's unpublished dissertation, "Luc de Prague" (Strasbourg, 1948) was not accessible to us. In addition to Molnár's interpretation the following works should be consulted: for biographical sketches, Kaňák, 1957, 63 ff.; Peschke, 1958c; Říčan, 1956, 25 ff. and 1957b, 77 ff.; for aspects of his theology, Peschke, 1935, 221 ff.; 1956 and 1957; Dobiáš, 1940, 1952a-b, 1953a-b; Bednář, 1952; Fousek, 1965; Štrupl, 1964, 31 ff. and 196 ff. and Trtík, 1967. See also the treatment of Lukáš and his era in Müller, I, Müller-Bartoš, Říčan, 1957a (German: 1961a) and Brock, 1957, 206 ff.

leaders in Europe in his day. With the exception of two extended journeys to foreign lands, he appears to have spent most of the seventy years of his life in three Bohemian cities.

He was born in an Utraquist home in Prague (therefore called Lukáš of Prague) probably in 1458.[102] With his older brother Jan, called Černý (Niger), he spent his youth in the capital city and received his training at the university which in those days had been reduced to the faculty of arts and was under Utraquist control. On October 2, 1481, he received his baccalaureate.

Probably of greater consequence and of more lasting influence than the lectures at the decaying university was his personal study of the works of Cyprian, Jerome, Augustine, several scholastic theologians, and especially the works of the Hussite Reformation, in particular the books of Petr Chelčický. The reading of Chelčický's works, combined with the radical preaching of a Neo-Utraquist priest Michal 'Polák' (of Polish origin), imprisoned by King Vladislav and tortured to death in the fall of 1480, led to a spiritual unrest and to a search for assurance of salvation. On the advice of a student friend, Lukáš decided to seek out a local fellowship of the despised 'Picards', the Czech Brethren.

As there were only a few secret believers and no regular congregation in Prague, Lukáš journeyed to the foremost center of the Unity at that time in the city of Litomyšl in north-east Bohemia near the Moravian border. The first visit took place likely after he concluded his studies at the university. Soon afterwards, he sold all that he had in Prague and settled permanently among the Brethren in Litomyšl, at the end of 1481 or in 1482.[103]

Like so many other Utraquist seekers before him, he found "a sure faith" and experienced transformation of life. He was joined in Litomyšl by his intimate friend from student days in Prague, Vavřinec Krasonický (see below), and his older brother Jan who established himself in the city as a physician. All three joined the Unity. Lukáš and Vavřinec — who came as an Utraquist priest — were received into the priesthood of the Unity.

By 1494, Lukáš had become a member of the central council (úzká rada) of the Unity and in the ensuing division between the Minor Party and the Major Party, he soon assumed the leading position among the spokesmen of the Major Party. With others, he realized

---

[102] For the different datings, see Molnár, 1948b, 21, n. 2.
[103] We follow the dating suggested by Molnár, 1948b, 31 f.

that the original strict rules of separation from society which could be practised by small groups of Brethren in a rural withdrawal would have to be modified to meet the different situation in which many new members of the Unity found themselves as burghers in towns and cities, or as members of the nobility. Contrary to the accusations made against him, he and his associates believed that this revision of ETHICAL standards — concerning such matters as taking of oaths, participation in civic government and bearing of arms — could be carried out without opening the door wide to the world. The many detailed instructions to Brethren in different walks of life and the vocational guides which were issued in subsequent years prove that the Major Party represented by no means a complete break with the "ethical Czech Brethrenism" [104] of the first generation but rather a stage of growth which was marked by continuity.[105]

A more radical revision of the views held by 'the Old Brethren' took place in the THEOLOGICAL system of the Unity which Lukáš developed in more than a hundred of his smaller and larger treatises.[106] He was the only leader of the Unity (with the exception of Comenius, most of whose life and work falls outside the period under our study) who created an original, well-balanced system of theology. Without exaggeration he may be called "the greatest theologian of the Czech Reformation".[107]

His two journeys to foreign lands have been mentioned already in another context. From March 1491 to November 1492, Lukáš and three other members of the Unity visited the eastern countries of Europe and the Near East, on a vain search for the remnants of an uncorrupted apostolic church.[108] In 1498, he sought contacts with the Waldensians in Italy. He met them near Florence and probably in their northern centers in the Alps as well. But he also visited Rome and, like Luther a few years later, observed the appalling conditions in the center of Christianity. He spent five weeks in Florence seeking

---

[104] For a discusison of this term, see Chapter I at footnote 144.

[105] This view is confirmed by the meticulous research of Říčan into the ethical and vocational rules issued by the Unity during and after the era of Lukáš. Cf. the many examples quoted by Říčan, 1957a, 87 ff. (German: 1961a, 59 ff.). In his excellent study, Brock, 1957, 206 ff. seems to have overstressed the contrast between the first and second generation of the Unity.

[106] Cf. the list of 140 works and important letters in Müller, I, 535-177 and Müller-Bartoš, 334 ff. (with some revisions).

[107] Dobiáš, 1940, 4. A presentation of the theology of Lukáš cannot be included in our present historical study. For bibliography, cf. footnote 100 above.

[108] Cf. Chapter III at footnote 174.

medical help. He likely witnessed the burning of Savonarola and brought several of his writings to Bohemia.[109]

From 1494 until his death on December 11, 1528, Lukáš lived in the city of Mladá Boleslav (Jungbunzlau). As one of the two bishops for the Unity in Bohemia (1500-1520) and as the only Bohemian bishop from 1520 till 1528, he directed the course of the first free church — declared illegal by the St. James mandate of King Vladislav in 1508 [110] — through many successive persecutions and in numerous theological encounters with enemies and friends in the Czech and foreign lands.[111]

The most intimate friend of Lukáš was Vavřinec Krasonický [112] (ca. 1456-1532). Born as a son of an Utraquist knight residing at Krasonice near Jemnice (Jamnitz, a center of Anabaptism in the sixteenth century) in southwest Moravia, he spent his childhood and received his early education in the Moravian town of Třebíč. In 1519 one of his sisters lived there while two others resided in nearby Moravské Budějovice (Budwitz).[113] His continuing personal contacts with South Moravia may explain why he was involved in the merger negotiations with the Anabaptists in 1528.

In the late 1470's Krasonický studied in Prague and received his baccalaureate in 1479, the same year in which the older brother of Lukáš, Jan Černý, graduated. The three Utraquist students, Krasonický, Lukáš and Jan Černý, entered into a lifelong triumvirate of friendship which was sealed by their identical decision to become members of the Unity and to settle in Litomyšl. Krasonický himself had received ordination as an Utraquist priest before he joined the Unity. With Lukáš, he was elected to the central council in 1494 but never became bishop. From 1495 until his death on January 25, 1532, he was pastor of the congregation in Litomyšl which was second in importance only to that in Mladá Boleslav.

[109] For the Italian journey, see Müller, I, 273 ff.; Molnár, 1952a, 45 and 1949a. Cf. also Chapter III, footnote 110.
[110] Cf. Müller, I, 346 ff.
[111] As examples of such encounters, cf. our discussion of the apologies against the attacks of Roman Catholic writers (Chapter III, beginning at footnote 41); or the literary exchanges with Luther (Chapter II at footnotes 59 ff.) and the encounter with Zwinglianism (Chapter II, beginning at footnote 63).
[112] A monograph on Krasonický is long overdue. The only articles, apart from scattered references in the general histories of the Unity, are: Bartoš, 1946a, 86-88, Krofta, 1946, 26-31, and Kaňák, 1957, 73-78. Cf. also Malínský, 1948a, 7 ff.; Molnár, 1956a, 55 ff., 76 ff., 149 ff. (sources); Brock, 1957, 107 et passim; Müller, 1887, 31 f., n. 4; Molnár, 1961d, 48 ff.
[113] Molnár, 1956a, 58 (correction of Bartoš, 1946a, 86).

Krasonický seems to have excelled in the art of polemic and public debate. Again and again he was chosen by the Unity to represent it at colloquies with those who attacked the Brethren. In 1497 he successfully defended the Unity in a debate with the Roman Catholic Bishop Gabriel who accompanied King Vladislav on his return to Prague.[114] At that time he defended the thesis that the primacy of the Roman bishop could not be derived from the apostle Peter since the Scriptures did not contain any record of his stay in Rome.[115] In 1500 he took part in a Latin disputation with the inquisitor Heinrich Krämer Institoris in Olomouc.[116] In subsequent years he defended the Unity at several encounters with the Utraquists, including a public debate in the townhall of Třebíč where Jan Dubčanský was among his Utraquist opponents.[117]

Among his literary polemics are found several treatises against the Minor Party and their successive leaders Amos and Jan Kalenec,[118] including a treatise on the problem of oathtaking.

As we have noted earlier, Krasonický was directly involved, in the 1520's, in the Zwinglian controversy with the three Silesian fugitive monks, Michael Weisse, Johann Zeising and John 'the Monk' whom he had earlier received into the membership of the congregation at Litomyšl.[119] His final apology of the policies instituted by the Major Party was written in 1530, after the death of Lukáš. It is the important work *O učených* [On the Learned Men] which was both a plea for a more positive recognition of higher education among the Brethren and a first attempt at an historical review of the origins and development of the Unity. This written testament of Krasonický which, like all his other works, was not printed[120] provided a link between his

[114] Cf. Molnár, 1956a, 55 ff.

[115] The thesis was later defended in a Latin treatise by Oldřich Velenský, 1520. Cf. Chapter III footnote 195.

[116] Hrejsa, IV, 158 f. On Institoris, cf. Chapter III at footnote 41 f.

[117] Cf. Chapter II at footnote 37. See also Hanák, 1928, 60 ff.

[118] Several were used by Brock in his interpretation of the strife between the Major and Minor Party. Cf. his bibliography, Brock, 1957, 293 and references to Krasonický in the index.

[119] Cf. Chapter II at footnotes 56 ff.

[120] In contrast to the many works of Lukáš which were printed at the presses of the Unity during his lifetime, all of the works of Krasonický remained in manuscript. Some were perhaps destroyed in the fire of Litomyšl in 1546. Ms. Codex V F 41 in the National Museum in Prague contains a number of Krasonický's letters and writings, among them the main work, *O učených* published in full, for the first time, by Molnár, 1956a, 76-99 (quotations in Brock, 1957 and Urbánek, 1923). Excerpts of "Writing against Cahera" were published by Goll in *ČČM*, 1878, 390-404. Cf. Goll, I, 138 ff.

generation and the coming generations of Jan Blahoslav and Jan Amos Comenius both of whom, in their synthesis of higher learning and personal piety, were able to bring to fruition the unfulfilled aspirations of Lukáš, Krasonický and their fellow labourers.

A brief mention must be included here of the older brother of Bishop Lukáš, Jan Černý (Niger).[121] He was a famous physician, who practised medicine first in Litomyšl (from ca. 1485 until ca. 1500), then in the Moravian city of Prostějov (ca. 1500-1513, or 1517), again in Litomyšl for a few years and later again in Prostějov, from about 1520 until his death which occurred sometime between 1521 and 1530. He retained such an eager interest in theology that some of his opponents regarded him (mistakenly) as a priest of the Unity. He defended the Brethren against the printed attacks of Augustin Käsenbrod (1500-1503). In the early 1490's, he had written several treatises, among them one against oathtaking and another against the practice of rebaptism in the Unity.[122] The viewpoints expressed would indicate that at that time at least he sided with the conservative Minor Party against Lukáš and Krasonický.

The third leader of the Unity whom the Anabaptist emissaries most likely met during their merger negotiations in 1528 was Jan Roh (Horn, Cornu).[123] By the chronology of his life (ca. 1490-1547) he belonged to the next generation. However, he was already playing an important role in the ecumenical relations of the Unity during the final years of the era of Lukáš. Born in a Brethren family in the city of Domažlice (Taus) on the southwestern border of Bohemia, he spoke German well. As a youth, he was sent to Litomyšl where, under the influence of Krasonický, he prepared himself for the ministry. Before he left Litomyšl as an ordained priest to assume charge of the congregation of Bělá pod Bezdězem (Weisswasser) near Mladá Boleslav in 1518, he must have met the three refugee monks from Silesia whom we have mentioned earlier. One of them, Michael Weisse, probably accompanied Roh on his visits to Wittenberg in

---

[121] Biography by J. Doubková in Kaňák, 1957, 78-93. Cf. our earlier references to Černý's literary controversy with Dr. Augustin Käsenbrod in Chapter III at footnotes 44 ff. Molnár, 1961d, 48 refers to Lukáš, Krasonický and Jan Černý as "the big three" of the Unity.

[122] Kaňák, 1957, 83 f. Only the titles of these and other theological tracts are preserved.

[123] See the brief biography by Kaňák, 1957, 93-99; Molnár 1950 and Müller, I, 400 ff. et passim.

1522-1524.[124] During the same period, Roh was perhaps the author of the German translation of the Brethren's Catechism, *Kinderfragen*.[125]

After the death of Lukáš Roh became, together with Jan Augusta, the main spokesman for the new pro-Lutheran orientation in the Unity. As one of the newly elected bishops in 1529 he also succeeded Lukáš as the main pastor of the congregation in Mladá Boleslav.[126] From 1532 until his death in 1547 he occupied the office of the judge of the Unity (the main bishop). At the end of his life, after a quarter of a century of persistent efforts to align the Unity with the Lutheran camp, he publicly repented of his "blindness toward the great heritage of the Unity" and pleaded for a return to the theology of Lukáš.[127]

Recently, Husa has suggested that Roh could have been one of the personal contacts which Thomas Müntzer might have had with the Unity during his six months' visit in Prague in 1521.[128] According to Husa, Müntzer's subsequent questioning and rejection of infant baptism might have been induced, or at least influenced by the teaching of the Unity concerning rebaptism. In February 1521, the first edition of the treatise by Lukáš *On the Repetition of Baptism*[129] was printed by Oldřich Velenský in Bělá pod Bezdězem where Roh was pastor at that time. This coincidence no doubt led to the inclusion of Roh in Husa's hypothesis. There are no known sources to support the assertion. The town where Roh lived was farther away from Prague than Mladá Boleslav. The printer Velenský had of course regular contacts with the capital city.

It is somewhat surprising that the negotiations between the Anabaptists and the Unity in 1528 should have taken place in Litomyšl and Mladá Boleslav and thus bypassed the Moravian leaders of the

---

[124]   Cf. our summary of Roh's contacts with Luther, in Chapter II at footnotes 58 ff.

[125]   Cf. Chapter III footnote 95.

[126]   The era of Roh in Mladá Boleslav is portrayed by Molnár, 1952a, Chapter III.

[127]   He is reported to have said in tears: "I did not understand and could not appreciate the greatness and purity of our Unity. I have allowed German books to stand in my way . . .". At his request, the synod in 1546 read and endorsed the book of Lukáš, *Zprávy kněžské* [Directives to Priests, 1527; cf. Fousek, 1957]. Roh's "repentance" is retold from sources by Molnár, 1952a, 158 f.

[128]   Husa, 1957, 77. Cf. also Molnár, 1958b-c, Bergsten, 1961, 24 and our earlier discussion of another hypothesis of Husa in Chapter II footnote 22. Roh had no relations to the Minor Party, nor was he an associate of Kalenec, as Williams, 1962, 217 assumes (misreading the Czech text in Husa, 1957, 77).

[129]   Lukáš, 1521a. A second, revised ed. (Lukáš, 1521b) was printed in Litomyšl in the same year.

Unity.[130] The probable reasons will be mentioned further below. In our present biographical survey of the leaders with whom the Anabaptists could have come in contact we shall merely mention Brother Martin Škoda who was co-bishop from 1516 and then (after 1518) the only Moravian bishop of the Unity until his death in 1532. Not much is known about him. He resided first at Prostějov, then in Přerov. He gave his full support to the policies of Lukáš who in his last will requested that Škoda succeed him as the main bishop (judge) of the Unity.[131] His request was fulfilled but the actual leadership passed into the hands of the younger generation represented by Jan Roh. During the Zwinglian controversy in 1526, Škoda had received a letter, "full of poison", from the excommunicated Zeising.[132] It was to be expected that the aging bishop would show little interest in dealings with the Anabaptists two years later.

The timing of the negotiations was most unfortunate. The Anabaptist representatives met with two seventy-year old patriarchs, Lukáš and Krasonický, whose doctrinal system had been tested in many previous encounters and found fully reliable.[133] To open negotiations did not mean union talks of two equal partners but rather an unconditional surrender of the one party to the other.

To make things worse, the talks came immediately after three bitter controversies in which the leaders of the Unity had been personally involved from the early twenties.

There was, first, a lively exchange of polemical writings between the revived Minor Party under Jan Kalenec and the leaders of the Major Party, Lukáš and Krasonický.[134] Then followed the Zwinglian controversy with Zeising and his followers. We have recounted its course earlier and pointed out the implications which the outright rejection of Zwingli's theology by Lukáš had for the ensuing contacts with the Anabaptists.[135]

The third phase concerned Jan Dubčanský.[136] After his unsuccess-

---

[130] Only a year earlier, Lukáš and the elders of the Unity had rebuked Jan Dubčanský for having bypassed the leaders of the Unity in Moravia and approached Brother Lukáš directly with his request for a debate (AUF, IV, fol. 191b).

[131] The last will of Lukáš is reprinted by Müller-Bartoš, 285 f.

[132] Cf. Chapter II at footnotes 81 ff.

[133] Cf. Reply to Dubčanský quoted at footnotes 141 ff. below.

[134] See Chapter II at footnotes 23 f. The writings against Kalenec are listed by Müller, I, 263 f. and discussed by Molnár, 1952a, 102 ff. and Brock, 1957, 245 ff.

[135] See Chapter II beginning at footnote 63.

[136] Cf. our earlier mention of Dubčanský, with bibliographical references, in Chapter II footnote 36.

ful attempt at a union meeting between the Czech Utraquists and the German Evangelicals at Slavkov (Austerlitz) in March 1526 [137] and following the preludes of Hubmaier who hoped to win him for Anabaptism,[138] Dubčanský wrote a letter to Lukáš and the elders of the Unity on February 9, 1527 [139] in which he proposed that "a brotherly meeting" between representatives of the Unity and "his brethren" be convened at a suitable place, halfway between Mladá Boleslav and Habrovany, Dubčanský's residence. The purpose of the meeting was to discuss differences in doctrine between the two groups, to correct errors on either side and to seek unity. In an arrogant tone, Dubčanský reminded Lukáš and his associates that they were obligated to give an account of their faith to anyone. He went on to warn the Brethren that in case of their refusal he would feel bound to publicize "the doublefacedness" of the Unity to all people, and even to other nations.[140]

The reply written by Lukáš in the name of the elders from Bohemia and Moravia on February 20, 1527 [141] is worth noting, for in some respects it parallels the report issued by the Unity on its negotiations with the Anabaptists a year and a half later.

Lukáš expresses surprise that Dubčanský proposes a meeting with the Brethren from Bohemia instead of with the Moravian Brethren who are much closer and better acquainted with the local scene. Since Dubčanský does not name or identify "his brethren", the Unity cannot meet with a group about which nothing is known.

The main reason, however, for the rejection of Dubčanský's proposal is stated in the subsequent paragraphs of the letter. "For we are sure", the elders declare, "that in the hope of God, our Unity is truly of the universal Christian faith in accordance with the Scriptures ... and with the true meaning of faith in the ordered [way of] salvation".[142] Then the letter recounts the many meetings and debates

[137]   See our summary and analysis in Ch. II, beginning at footnote 113.
[138]   *HS*, 348 f.
[139]   *AUF*, IV, fol. 191a. Cf. Hanák, 1928, 65.
[140]   It is not clear whether he meant nations outside the borders of Moravia (cf. the report on the Slavkov meeting which was printed in Zürich and Worms) or whether he was referring to Germans in Moravia, perhaps especially the incoming Anabaptists.
[141]   *AUF*, IV, fol. 191b-193a. Brief summary in Müller, I, 447 f.; Müller-Bartoš, 281 f.; Hanák, 1928, 65 f. and Molnár, 1952a, 109 f.
[142]   "smyslu pravého víry zřízeného spasení". Cf. the discussion by Fousek, 1965, 51 f. of the difficulties in translating into English the theological terminology of Lukáš, especially the concept of "the ordered salvation". Fousek renders it "ordained salvation".

which the Brethren have held willingly from the beginning with the Roman and the Utraquist churches in order to give an account of their faith and to explain the reasons of their separation from both of these communions. Furthermore, they have published in three languages (Czech, Latin and German) a number of confessional statements, as well as replies to the attacks by their enemies, "spiritual and secular, noble and common".

This does not mean, however, that the Unity is prepared to hold meetings with any sect (*rota*) [143] which distorts the truth and is not willing to learn God's appointed way of salvation. In their bitter recent experiences with the Minor Party and with the followers of Čížek (Zeising) they have learnt "not to throw the pearls before the swine". Čížek especially has been guilty of "betraying the better knowledge of the Law (Word) of God, becoming stubborn and contaminating others", whereupon he has been duly excommunicated. The elders express their surprise that Dubčanský should be ignorant of these happenings. If he read the statements of the Unity against the errors of Čížek he "would know assuredly that the truth is with the Unity and not with all these factions (*roty*)". The elders have no desire to hold a debate with such "unlearned innovators (*novověrci*) who show no steadiness and are not accustomed to the Law of God".

What these new Reformers are only beginning to discover, the [Czech] Brethren have known for almost a hundred years and taught to their children as elementary truth. All that the innovators want is to talk instead of coming to a personal knowledge (experience) of genuine faith and salvation as it is appointed of God and truly administered in the Unity. Whoever sincerely desires salvation can come and talk freely with the Brethren. But there is no need for a colloquy.

This frank reply by the elders of the Unity shows that they were well informed about the circle of Dubčanský's adherents and that they rightly suspected his associations with Zeising. Dubčanský arrested and imprisoned for one day the messenger who delivered the letter.[144] Such treatment could hardly have served the purpose of improving the relations.

During 1527 Dubčanský exchanged further letters with Lukáš and

---

[143]   The Czech word "rota" which the letter uses in reference to the followers of Kalenec and Zeising implies both a meaning similar to the German "Schwärmer" in its original connotation, i.e. a swarm (of bees), and the idea of a wilful separation from the main body of the church. It can be rendered as "clique, faction, sect".
[144]   Hanák, 1928, 66 and Molnár, 1952a, 110.

then had three of his letters, together with the replies, printed at Prostějov (1527), "at the request of Jan of Lipé at Krumlov, Dobeš of Boskovice at Rosice, and Krištof of Boskovice at Třebová.[145] It was the first Czech book ever printed in Moravia.

When Dubčanský's attempts to influence the Unity failed, he proceeded with the founding of his own small religious society known as the Unity of the Habrovanite Brethren. The event took place on February 23, 1528 in the small village of Routka near the town of Letovice (not far from Boskovice, north of Brno) where the leader of the Minor Party, Jan Kalenec, likely resided at that time.

It would go beyond the purpose of our present study to recount the doctrinal position of the Habrovanite Brethren.[146] We shall only mention in passing that the tiny group, which does not appear to have spread in an organized way beyond the three villages on the small estate of knight Dubčanský,[147] combined in its teachings the Zwinglian concept of the sacraments, modified by strong spiritualistic undertones, with some of the principles of 'ethical Anabaptism' which had been expressed earlier in the first generation of the *Unitas Fratrum*, and then in the 1520's defended by Kalenec of the Minor Party. Since baptism and eucharist carried only a symbolic meaning and the main benefit was derived from spiritual baptism and communion, the insistence on infant or adult baptism was pointless. For their part, the Habrovanites retained infant baptism, thus drawing a line between their group and the Anabaptists as well as the Minor Party, which under Kalenec rejected infant baptism altogether. In agreement with Anabaptism and the Minor Party, and against the main body of the Unity in the days of Lukáš, the Habrovanites refused oathtaking, bearing of arms and participation in government. Of all the radical groups in Moravia, they were the most consistent in the

---

[145]   The names are included in the title, *Jana Dubčanského neb Habrovanského listové bratřím Boleslavským poslaní, i také jich odpovědi zase psané, tuto spolu jsou vytištěni k žádosti* . . . (with the names of the three barons). The book was printed by Kašpar Neděle Prostějovský, called Aorg. Only the title of the book is preserved. The text of the first letter and reply is known from the manuscript copy (summarized above). Cf. Dudík, 1875, 115; Šembera, 1870, 53; Hanák, 1928, 66 and Müller-Bartoš, 282.

[146]   See the comprehensive Czech treatment by Odložilík, 1923, 318-346 and German summary, Odložilík, 1925; Hanák, 1928, 277-348 and Brock, 1957, 253 ff. The Habrovanite teachings, especially their view of the eucharist, became the subject of a new controversy in the *Unitas Fratrum* in the 1590's when Turnovský defended the eucharistic theology of Bishop Lukáš against the Calvinistic interpretation (Bidlo, 1918, 179 ff.).

[147]   Habrovany, Lulč and Nemojany.

practical implementation of the general priesthood of all believers. They rejected all ministerial offices and had no ordained clergy.

One can observe that their doctrinal system — which they publisized widely in several Czech books and hymnbooks printed on their own press "in monte Liliorum" at Luleč from 1530-1536[148] — represented a syncretistic position in which several domestic and foreign strata of influence were amalgamated in an original way.

The contacts between Dubčanský and the Unity continued beyond the year 1527. Sometime in 1528, the Habrovanites published in Prostějov a polemic against the final work of Brother Lukáš in which he had condemned "the incomplete and partial faith of the present day innovators".[149] After the death of Lukáš (December 1528) Dubčanský visited Bishop Škoda in Přerov several times and arranged for a colloquy which was to have taken place at Prostějov in October 1531. It was prevented, however, by King Ferdinand, and eventually took place, without success, at Kyjov on February 28, 1535.[150]

The arrest of Dubčanský in 1537 signalled a quick dissipation of his small group. After his release from prison in Prague he does not appear to have resumed his former position of leadership. He died in 1543 and with the removal of his personality the main impetus for the Habrovanite movement was lost as well. According to Kameníček, the remnants of the Habrovanites joined the Anabaptists.[151]

An interesting report on the divisions within the *Unitas Fratrum* is preserved in Franck's *Chronica* which was printed at Strasbourg in September 1531. Whereas most of his entries concerning the Czech Reformation are nothing more than free translations of the same items in the *Catalogus haereticorum*[152] his sympathetic treatment of the Czech Picards is based on oral information supplied by travelling merchants.[153]

[148] Cf. analyses of all their writings by Odložilík, 1923, 44-70 and 301-318; and Hanák, 1928, 96-124. See also Vonka, 1936, 38 ff.

[149] For the book of Lukáš, see Chapter II footnote 85. The reply of the Habrovanites, *Spis proti Bratřím Valdenským aneb Boleslavským* ... (1528) is reported in *HF*, Vol. I, fol. 650 (cf. Odložilík, 1923, 52).

[150] A record of the unfinished colloquy is preserved in *AUF*, IV, fol. 199a-214a. Cf. Chapter II, footnote 39; Odložilík, 1923, 307 f. and Hanák, 1928, 78 ff.

[151] Kameníček, III, 472. He also suggests that the Habrovanites who became Anabaptists represented likely the only Czech element in Moravian Anabaptism. He does not refer to any sources. Odložilík, 1923, 348 ff. discusses the decay and dissipation of the Habrovanites but makes no mention of Kameníček's assertion.

[152] Bernardus, 1522 and 1529. Cf. our analysis of Franck's dependence upon Bernardus in Chapter V at footnotes 121 ff.

[153] "wie ich von Kauffleuten hab hören sagen" (Franck, 1531, fol. 434b).

In one of his two brief descriptions of the Czech Brethren, he reports: "Some say that they are now divided into a large group (*hauffen*) and a small one. The large one believes as before, the small one agrees with the Anabaptists".[154] In his other reference to the Czech Picards, Franck reports a division into three groups: "They are divided into two, or as some claim (*als etlich wöllen*), into three groups (*hauffen*), a large one, a small one and a very small one (*gar kleynen*). These [the last named] agree altogether with the Anabaptists, have all things in common, baptize no children and do not believe in the body of the Lord in the sacrament. But the large group believes the sacrament. They persecute each other, whereby they betray their spirit, however nice they may appear to be.... There are at least 80,000 of them".[155]

Franck's report mentions only Bohemia. It is probable that his informants were referring to the Major and Minor Parties of the Unity. The third party, "very small", was likely the little circle around Kalenec at Letovice in Moravia where the Minor Party found its last refuge and underwent further radicalization of its views. From a much later source (1542)[156] it is known that Kalenec not only defended the ethical principles of the 'Old Brethren' (rejection of oath-taking, bearing of arms and participation in government) but also renounced infant baptism, approved of community of goods and held anti-Trinitarian views. Franck's report — when interpreted as a reference to Kalenec and his group — makes it possible to date the further radicalization of the Minor Party (towards Anabaptism) into a much earlier period, namely the late 1520's.[157] It should be noted, however,

---

[154]   Franck, 1531, fol. 434b. Quoted in Czech translation by Bartoš, 1946b, 97.
[155]   Franck, 1531, fol. 483a. This second reference to the Picards was overlooked by Bartoš, 1946b.
[156]   *Knížka Jana Kalence* (*AUF*, IV, fol. 215a-228a) and *Psaní Kalencovo proti Janu Augustovi* (*AUF*, IV, fol. 231a-240a). A summary of both in Odložilík, 1923, 351 ff. and Urban, 1966, 21 ff. The first writing is signed at the end by "Jan Kalenec and Pavel of Hořice, Brethren of the Minor Party at Letovice, May 1, 1542". The letter to Augusta (without date, probably the same year, or 1543) is signed by "Jan Kalenec, Elder of the few Brethren of the Minor Party". Cf. also Chapter I footnote 76; Chapter II footnotes 24, 25 and 152-153.
[157]   One of the earliest records of the rejection of infant baptism by the Minor Party is the letter of Jakub Hladík of Kutná Hora to Martin Chlupáč in Třebíč, dated April 24, 1501. He enumerates four errors of the Minor Party: (1) They do not hold the correct belief concerning the body and blood of the Lord in the eucharist; (2) "They do not believe that baptism should be administered to children but only to adults, contrary to the teaching of Christ, saying: Suffer the little ones to come unto me and hinder them not, for of such is the kingdom of God, and

that Franck's record does not mention anti-Trinitarianism, which must have developed at a later stage.

An alternative interpretation would identify Franck's third party of the Unity with the Habrovanite Brethren who had appeared as a constituted group shortly before Franck's *Chronica* was prepared for print. The Habrovanites were regarded by their misinformed opponents as another faction of the Picards (Unity).[158] However, the fact that Franck's 'third party' rejected infant baptism and defended community of goods speaks against such identification.

It is quite likely that some of the Czech Brethren in Moravia (within the Major Party) who had been influenced by the Zwinglian writings of Zeising and his associates in the mid-twenties, joined the Habrovanite Unity.[159] Their numbers must have been small and limited to the geographical area around Habrovany. To our knowledge, there was no split on the issue of Zwinglianism among the Brethren in Moravia.[160]

3. THE RECORD OF NEGOTIATIONS

At least three separate records of the merger negotiations between the Anabaptists and the Czech Brethren in 1528 are known to have been prepared.

(1) The official Czech report of the elders of the Unity written and released at Mladá Boleslav on November 11, 1528.

(2) A letter by Vavřinec Krasonický and Jan Roh to Brother Ma-

---

Baptize all nations into the name of the Father, Son and Holy Ghost"; (3) They believe that no one can be saved unless he avoids entanglement in civil power; (4) They oppose oathtaking. The letter is preserved in Ms. Codex of Jan Kamenický (copied in 1572), fol. 31a-b (in Stuttgart) and in Ms. Codex Crupp, 1082 f. Cf. the quotation in Odložilík, 1923, 12, n. 1.

[158] After Dubčanský's imprisonment in Prague in 1537, King Ferdinand submitted a copy of the Czech *Apologia* of the Habrovanites (1536) to Bishop Faber for theological evaluation. In his *Censura super nova apud Moravos Picardorum et cujusdam Habrowansky secta et falsa religione* (printed by Döllinger, 1890, 641-661) Faber regarded the Habrovanites as "tertia Picardorum Synagoga". The other two were the Brethren in Bohemia and those in Moravia who in Faber's opinion held different views (cf. his *Summa Picardicarum rerum tum in Bohemia tum in Moravia*, printed *ibid.*, 635-641). Faber's criticism of the Habrovanite Apology is summarized by Odložilík, 1923, 312 f. and Hanák, 1928, 85 f.

[159] A view expressed by Müller, I, 451 and Hrejsa, V, 19 (no reference to sources).

[160] In a different context, Molnár, 1961d, 48 f. admits that during the era of Lukáš there existed in the Unity other theological views different from the official position publicized in the books. This applies, of course, to any ecclesiastical group at any time.

touš, the minister of the Unity at Dačice in southwest Moravia, written about the same time, or earlier.[161]

(3) A written or printed report (likely in the German language) which was issued by the negotiating Anabaptists in the fall of 1528.[162]

Of the three records only the first has been preserved [163] and contains the following review of the negotiations.

A Report of the Brethren Elders made unto certain lords upon their accusation that they [the elders] held in contempt those people, namely the Anabaptists.

Some time in the past, we [the elders of the Unity] were approached by people of distinction [164] who in their letter bore a good testimony about the Anabaptists and asked that they be received into our Unity. Yielding to their request and to the desire of the Anabaptists themselves, we agreed to hold disputations with them.

The Anabaptists ("the brethren") came to Litomyšl twice and held many colloquies with us about whatever subjects they chose, such as "faith, the ministrative means of the Scriptures,[165] all sacraments,[166] the ministers of the church and their order, and also the civil power, i.e. whether those who participate in it might be saved".

When they heard and considered our doctrines, orders and customs, they recognized them, readily and gratefully, as truly Christian and confessed that they also held such views. Thus in all things, they

---

[161] Both the official report and the letter to Brother Matouš are mentioned in *HF*, Vol. I, fol. 650: "The Brethren were accused, especially by the Moravians, that they despised the Anabaptists. They issued a letter and a report to certain lords because of such accusation. Also Brother Vavřinec Krasonický and Brother Jan Roh sent a letter about the same thing to Brother Matouš at Dačice." The wording would suggest that the official report (see footnote 163) by the elders was accompanied by a letter which was not preserved.

[162] It is mentioned in the official report of the Unity. If printed the work might have been done by the printer Kašpar Neděle "Aorg" who printed two polemical books of Jan Dubčanský against the Unity in 1527 and 1528 (cf. footnotes 145 and 149 above). Dubčanský might have arranged the printing and encouraged the release of such a report against the Unity.

[163] *AUF*, V, fol. 333b-335a. Critical edition of the Czech text by Zeman, 1958, 23-36; German translation by Müller, 1910, 189-193. It should be noted that no other sources, whether Anabaptist or of the Czech Brethren, make any allusion to the merger negotiations. Our English summary of the report is not a verbatim translation but merely a paraphrase. A few sentences which are literal translations are marked by quotation marks.

[164] "od znamenitých lidí", persons of renown, perhaps of noble origin.

[165] "služebnost slova Čtení svatého": cf. the interpretation of this terminology by Fousek, 1965, 55 ff.

[166] In the era of Lukáš, the Unity still recognized seven sacraments.

abandoned their own position,[167] accepted the teachings of the Unity and submitted themselves unto its oversight in accordance with our rules.

They departed with great friendliness and promised to inform their brethren about the talks and to lead them to the same decision. It was agreed that additional negotiations, both written and oral, would take place in order to further those things which are necessary for salvation, unanimity and unity. We were anxious for a consummation of the initial dealings and did not hesitate, therefore, to attend several more meetings which involved us in wearisome journeys on account of some elderly persons.

When a meeting (schůze) of the Unity was scheduled to be held at Boleslav, we invited the Anabaptists to come. We even sent a wagon nine miles to meet them and looked after all their needs. On the next morning, when the talks about union were reopened, we asked the following two questions: Do they believe that the Unity is of God and truly Christian? Are they confident that they can find their salvation in the Unity according to the ordered ways of God, and are they prepared to submit themselves to the rules of the Unity?

To our great surprise, the Anabaptists gave an answer which was altogether different from the initial agreement reached at Litomyšl. Not to offend them, we suggested that they should take more time to study our books. Thus they might be able better to comprehend how we follow the Scriptures in our ministrations ordered unto salvation.[168] We offered to clarify any problems they might encounter while reading our books. They were quite willing and we gave them two volumes of our Czech writings — for they said they had an interpreter — and something in Latin.[169]

They agreed to read our books and to contact us if they needed any further explanation. They also promised to keep the negotiations

---

[167] This is a contradiction of the immediately preceding statement.

[168] "kterak my se pravdou Čtení svatého v zřízeném spasení spravujeme": the phrase expresses the key concept of the soteriology of Lukáš. Cf. Fousek, 1965, 51 ff.

[169] It is impossible to identify the Czech books which the Anabaptists received. A large number of the writings of Bishop Lukáš were printed in the 1520's. Cf. the list in Müller-Bartoš, 334-350. The only known printed Latin works of the Unity at that time were the four confessional statements (1503, 1507, 1508 and 1511; cf. Chapter III footnote 206). The Brethren might have presented to them some Latin translations in manuscript since the report does not refer explicitly to Latin books. It is surprising that the Anabaptists received no German books, such as the catechism, Kinderfragen.

secret for the time being. We parted in peace and love. For their return journey, we provided again free transportation for fourteen miles.

However, they did not keep their word. For very soon after their departure, they wrote a onesided and incomplete report which did not state the reasons nor the aims of our negotiations. Without sending any communication to us, they issued (*vydali*) [170] their report and circulated it not only among their own Brethren but also among other people until it came into the hands of enemies. Finally, we received a copy, not from them but from others. As we read it, we wondered how and why they changed their mind.

Furthermore, one of those who met with us in Boleslav visited our brother in Dačice [171] and asked for a copy of our hymnary.[172] Through an interpreter [who came with him] he copied what he wanted. He refused to give any explanation why he was interested in copying the words. Afterwards, he spoke disparagingly about our hymns, called them idolatrous [173] and spoke evil of the Brethren. Another one slandered our Brethren at Ivančice, called them idolaters and hypocrites until a travelling craftsman who had known the Brethren in Boleslav and elsewhere rebuked him for his ignorant denunciations.

Rumours of other similar incidents have reached us. We also hear that they pay no attention to our books. Up to this day [November 11, 1528] we have received no direct word from them. They, not we, have broken the agreement [reached at the initial meetings at Litomyšl].

The report closes with an appeal to a lord [174] that on the basis of

170   The Czech term "vydali" is ambiguous. It refers likely to a written report rather than to a printed pamphlet (personal letter from Dr. J. Hovorka, Olomouc, Czechoslavakia). Cf. also footnote 162 above.

171   Brother Matouš, the minister at Dačice, to whom Krasonický and Roh wrote their letter about the negotiations (see footnote 161 above).

172   Most likely the Czech hymnary published in 1519 (Hrejsa Bohuš, 1931, 18 f.). The first German hymnal of the Unity was not published till 1531 (by Michael Weisse, *Gesangbuch*, 1531).

173   No doubt, the Anabaptist charge of "idolatry" referred to the teaching of the Unity concerning the presence of Christ, "sacramentaliter, spiritualiter, potentialiter et vere", in the eucharist (cf. Chapter II at footnote 68). The Hutterite chronicles praise Hubmaier for having taught the truth about the Lord's supper and having refuted "the great error in the idolatrous sacrament" (ZGL, 52: "das abgöttische Sacrament"; cf. *ibid.*, 59). Cf. also the title of Carlstadt's booklet, *Dialogus oder ein gesprechbüchlin Von dem grewlichen vnnd abgöttischen missbrauch des hochwirdigsten sacraments Jesu Christi*, printed in Basel, 1524 (Carlstadt, II, 5 ff.).

174   The singular, "your grace", implies that the report was sent to one (unnamed)

the submitted evidence he might decide who is to be blamed for the failure of negotiations. Dated at [Mladá] Boleslav, on St. Martin's day [November 11], 1528.

4. LITERARY ANALYSIS OF THE RECORD

The record of the negotiations is found in Volume Five of the official collection of sources, *Acta Unitatis Fratrum*. According to the recent research by Štěříková,[175] the copying of source materials into the fifth volume took place at Ivančice during the last years of Blahoslav's life (he died in November 1571), which means about forty years after the original document was written.

There is no reason to doubt the authenticity of the preserved text. A copy of the report sent to the anonymous Moravian nobleman in November 1528 was kept in the "bishop's archives" of the Unity at Mladá Boleslav until Blahoslav took it along with many other documents to Ivančice in 1558 and then had it copied into the fifth volume of the *AUF* about ten years later.

The report was prepared most likely by Bishop Lukáš himself.[176] One could not hope for a more reliable source than the one in our hands. One would only wish that the complementary report issued by the Anabaptists were also extant.

5. HISTORICAL ANALYSIS OF THE RECORD

The report has received considerable attention in the literature[177] but no one thus far has undertaken a proper historical analysis of the

---

member of the Moravian nobility who was likely expected to share it with others whose interest in the Anabaptists is implied in the opening sentence as well as in the title of the report.

[175] Štěříková, 1964, 99 and 103. Müller, 1913, 112 mentions that the particular folios which contain the report under discussion were written by Vavřinec Orlík who was coeditor with Blahoslav for the later volumes of the *AUF*. In her analysis, Štěříková, *ibid.*, 86 does not mention Orlík. On Orlík, a reputable historian of the Unity, cf. Krofta, 1946, 111 ff.

[176] The style of the report is similar to that in the writings of Lukáš. Cf. Müller, 1910, 189, n. 21. Kaňák, 1957, 77 confused the report with another letter and ascribed authorship to Krasonický. Cf. footnote 161 above.

[177] Gindely, I, 214 f.; Müller, 1910, 186 ff.; Müller, I, 451 f; Müller-Bartoš, 283 f.; Hrejsa, V, 22 f.; Molnár, 1952a, 111 f. and 1962c; Malínský, 1956. All of these authors limited themselves to a summary of the report in the *AUF* without analysis or interpretation.

document. The main task of such analysis is the exact identification, if possible, of the particular Anabaptist group which entered into negotiations with the Czech Brethren. The extant record does not include any names of Anabaptist emissaries, nor does it specify the congregations or groups which they represented. It offers, however, several clues which make the identification possible, or at least highly probable.

a. *Chronology of the Negotiations*

According to the report, there were two distinct phases of the negotiations. The first phase included two meetings at Litomyšl and subsequently "several more meetings" elsewhere (not specified) to which the representatives of the Unity travelled some distance (from Litomyšl to Moravia?). During the first stage, Anabaptist emissaries were prepared to subscribe to the doctrines and practices of the Unity and a merger seemed to be assured.

The second phase brought a reversal in the hopeful developments. It began with "a meeting" (*schůze*) of the Unity at Mladá Boleslav to which the Anabaptists were invited. They expressed a different attitude and from then on the negotiations were interrupted and not resumed up to the date of the written report, November 11, 1528.

To what meeting at Mladá Boleslav does the source refer? An important meeting [178] took place in Boleslav in November 1527 at which time the ailing bishop Lukáš, seated, ordained six new ministers of the Unity.[179]

---

[178]   From 1494 on, the main administrative body of the Unity was known as the central council ("úzká rada", "der Enge Rat"). It consisted of four elders or bishops (two for Bohemia, two for Moravia) and eight to twelve co-elders ("spolustarší") also called co-councillors ("spoluradní"). The leading bishop was designated as the Judge ("sudí"). The council did not meet regularly but rather according to need. It transacted most of the business. A larger body called "sněm" (later known as synod) had no clearly defined constitution. Sometimes it included all ministers and some lay representatives of the congregations. At other times, particularly during persecutions, it consisted only of the central council enlarged by additional selected ministers. During the sixteenth century, the Unity was controlled more and more by ministers. Lay representation in the central bodies was minimized in order to avoid control of the Unity by nobility. Cf. Říčan, 1957a, 61 and 82 f.; Müller, III, 393.

[179]   There are conflicting dates in the sources. *HF* (Šafařík, 1862, 201) and Todtenbuch, date 1527 whereas Jafet, 147 records the ordination for November 11, 1528. Müller, I, 452 and Hrejsa, V, 17 chose 1528 while Molnár, 1952a, 111, n. 145, decided for 1527. We accept Molnár's solution. Jafet, written after eighty years (1607), regarded the two separate meetings as one. The ordination took place in November 1527 but there was also a meeting of the central council and "of all ministers" on November 11, 1528 (*HF*, I, fol. 650; Šafařík, 1862, 202).

For 1528, two meetings are recorded: one in the second half of September,[180] and the other on November 11th.[181]

There can be little doubt that the Anabaptist representatives were invited to the meeting in September 1528. The source [182] does not stipulate whether it was a meeting of the central council or of some other specially invited group. Whoever else might have been present at the last official merger talks with the Anabaptists, one can assume that the meeting was attended by Lukáš and by the two men who had carried on the earlier phase of negotiations at Litomyšl and other places, Vavřinec Krasonický and Jan Roh.[183]

In addition to the September and November dates, the beginning of the negotiations should also be determined as accurately as possible. The report offers no clues beyond the general review of the negotiations which must have been carried on for several weeks, perhaps for several months. Two meetings at Litomyšl were followed by "not a few" meetings elsewhere. Müller and others [184] have suggested that the main motive of some Moravian barons who were responsible for the contacts was the persecution of Anabaptists in Moravia. If such were the case, one might date the beginning of the negotiations into the late spring, after the diet at Znojmo. It ordered the expulsion of Anabaptist preachers and leaders, and prohibited their meetings. It should be noted, however, that the text of the

---

[180] Jafet, 147: "And elsewhere it is noted that in the same year [1528: in spite of the mistaken dating of the ordination, the source now refers definitely to 1528; cf. the subsequent mention of the death of Lukáš] there was a meeting ("shromáždění") at Boleslav on "Wednesday of the dry days after St. Cross" ("k středě suchých dnů po sv. kříži"). The feast of Exultatio S. Crucis was on September 14, 1528, and Wednesday fell on the 16th.

[181] A meeting on November 11, 1528 is confirmed by several sources. The report under discussion was signed by the elders at Boleslav on November 11. There must have been a meeting of, at least, the central council. HF, I, 650 refers, in a not altogether clear context, to a meeting of all ministers which might have taken place on the same day, or soon afterwards (cf. Molnár, 1952a, 112). Finally, in his last will, Lukáš stated that he had been sick until November 11 (Müller, I, 453).

[182] Both Goll, I, 80 ff. and Krofta, 1946, 146-156 expressed admiration for the critical work of Jafet as a historian of the Unity. He had access to sources which have since been lost.

[183] Their names are not mentioned in the official report but their own letter to Brother Matouš (see footnote 161) confirms that they conducted the negotiations. Krasonický was pastor at Litomyšl and a close friend of Roh who had been trained under him there. No doubt Roh was invited not only as an interpreter but also as a man experienced in ecumenical relations with Luther. He was also personally acquainted with Zeising, Weisse and 'John the Monk'.

[184] Müller, 1910, 188; Molnár, 1952a, 111; Říčan, 1957a, 131 and 1957b, 92.

report makes no reference, not even by implication, to the persecution. It probably provided one of the motives.

The exact date of the beginning of the negotiations cannot be established. In a general way, one might suggest the period from May to July 1528.

b. *The Motives*

Along with the outward pressure of persecution, there was inward motivation. The report states explicitly that the Moravian lords who approached the leaders of the Czech Brethren were persuaded that the reception of the Anabaptists into the Unity would be "very beneficial" (*pokládajíc toho užitek mnohý*), presumably for both sides. The barons must have recognized basic doctrinal affinity between the two groups.[185]

Furthermore, the Anabaptists themselves desired the negotiations (*takových lidí k žádosti, i těch Bratří*). A contributing factor might have been the realization that once before, in 1480, a large group of German-speaking refugees, the Waldensians from Mark Brandenburg, had been received into the Unity.[186]

c. *The Nature of Negotiations*

It must be stressed that the 'union talks' between the Anabaptists and the Czech Brethren did not resemble the modern negotiations for church unions at which two ecclesiastical bodies enter into a type of bargaining for a common doctrinal position and a constitutional agreement. Instead of such a mutual adjustment, the talks in 1528 represented a "one-way surrender" of the particular Anabaptist group to the theology and order of the Unity. For that reason we have avoided consistently the use of the term 'union' and refer instead to 'merger' or 'joining'.[187] In principle, the reception of the particular Anabaptist group was not different from the reception of individual persons into the membership of the Unity.

[185]   Cf. also the report of Faber, 1528a according to which many compared the burning of Hubmaier to John Hus' death at the stake: "er sey wie Johannes Huss vnschüldenclich verbrennt" (reprinted by Loserth, 1893, 216).
[186]   Cf. Chapter II at footnotes 50 ff. See also Müller, 1910, 181 ff. for a discussion of the relationship of both the Unity and the Anabaptists to the medieval Waldensians.
[187]   There does not appear to exist an exact English equivalent of the German word "Anschluss" which expresses the concept well. Cf. the statement by Müller, 1910, 189: "Darum ist auch nicht von einem Vergleich die Rede, sondern nur von einem bedingungslosen Anschluss der Täufer an die Brüder."

d. *Identification of the Moravian Lords*

It is to be expected that the barons who advocated Anabaptist merger into the Unity must have had some acquaintance with the Anabaptist congregations or leaders in Moravia. A number of lords and knights fall into such a category.

In the first place, there were those to whom Hubmaier had dedicated his writings printed in Moravia: Leonhart and Hans of Liechtenstein, Jan of Pernstein, Arkleb of Boskovice, Jan Dubčanský and Burián Sobek of Kornice.[188] Of these, the last three can be excluded from our considerations. Arkleb of Boskovice died on the same day as Hubmaier. Dubčanský and Sobek were knights. The report about the negotiations refers expressly to members of the higher nobility.

In the second place, one might suspect that the initiative could have come from the same three lords who in 1527 had furthered union colloquies between the Unity and the Habrovanites: Jan of Lipé at Krumlov, Dobeš of Boskovice at Rosice and Krištof of Boskovice at Třebová.[189] The three influential lords maintained close relations with those mentioned in the previous paragraph. Dobeš of Boskovice (died 1540), married, in 1522, Bohunka of Perstein, the widow of Jindřich of Lipé and a sister of Jan of Pernstein.[190] The sister of Dobeš, Kateřina, was the wife of Leonhart of Lichtenstein. Krištof of Boskovice (died 1550) married, also in 1522, Kunigunda, daughter of Duke Karl of Münsterberg, and thus became brother-in-law of Georg, margrave of Brandenburg.[191]

In 1528, Dobeš of Boskovice, Hans of Liechtenstein, Jan of Pernstein and Bernart the Elder of Žerotín were members of a special Moravian military council which was in charge of defense against the Turks. All the lords mentioned were very active in Moravian political life and occupied the highest offices of the margraviate from time to time.

As for their religious views, some of them belonged to the Neo-Utraquist circles, with great sympathies for the Zwinglian and more

[188] Cf. our list in Chapter III at footnote 178. Biographical information on all of these is provided there, or in Chapter II (Sobek at footnotes 16 ff., and Dubčanský at footnotes 36 ff.).

[189] Cf. footnote 145 above.

[190] Šembera, 1870, 84 f. The subsequent information on the barons listed above is taken mostly from the same source. On the family of Lipé, see also Brunner, 1910, 322 ff. and 1911.

[191] One can see to what extent family relationships between nobility conditioned contacts within the camp of the 'Radical Reformation'. Georg of Brandenburg was among those to whom Hubmaier dedicated one of his writings (cf. Chapter III footnote 190).

radical views (Habrovanites), others were members or adherents of the Unity. Nearly all of them were protectors and generous supporters of the Unity.

It was hardly a mere coincidence that virtually all early Anabaptist settlements in Moravia were established on the domains of these few noblemen. To the original congregation at Mikulov and in the surrounding villages on the estate of the lords of Liechtenstein were soon added congregations at Ivančice (on the domain belonging to Jan of Lipé), perhaps also at Dačice and then at Rosice (owned by Bohunka of Pernstein and her husband Dobeš of Boskovice). It should be noted also that another relation of the lords of Boskovice, Johanka, granted, in her capacity as abbess of the Queen's nunnery in Old Brno,[192] permission to the Philippite Brethren to settle on the nunnery's estate at Hustopeč (Auspitz) in 1529 after they left Rosice. One might almost suggest that the earliest reception and protection of the Anabaptists was a "one family affair".

The only exception was Slavkov (Austerliz) on the domain of the four brothers of Kounice where the pacifistic communitarian *Stäbler* found refuge in April or May 1528, after their secession from Mikulov.[193]

The residence of Jan of Pernstein, Tovačov (Tobitschau) near Přerov (Prerau), lay outside the area of Anabaptist settlement. One should recall, of course, that Zeising found refuge there after his excommunication from the Unity in 1526. From there Johann of Zwola, as guest of Jan of Pernstein, wrote his letter in April 1528 to Dr. Johannes Hess in which he reported the decisions of the Znojmo diet concerning the Anabaptists and mentioned the burning of Hubmaier, Zeising and others.[194]

The fact that in the same localities there were also flourishing congregations of the Czech Brethren (Dačice, Ivančice, Rosice,[195] Slavkov and Tovačov) should further confirm our conclusion that the

[192] Cf. Chapter III at footnotes 200 f.
[193] Cf. footnote 70 above.
[194] Loserth, 1893, 216 f. Cf. footnotes 88 f. above. In his court testimony on May 6, 1531, Julius Lober of Zürich referred to Anabaptists on the domains of lords of "Bernstein, Lichtesteiner zu Nikelsburg vnd andere" (*TQ*, II, 238). See also Chapter III footnote 184.
[195] A congregation with a resident minister was not established at Rosice until during the second half of the century. There was probably a small group of the Czech Brethren at R. much earlier, under the protection of Bohunka of Pernstein. Her death in 1549 is recorded in the Necrologue of the Unity (Todtenbuch, 235). Cf. Hrejsa, B, 78 and Císařová, 1942, 324 f.

Moravian lords who advocated the reception of the Anabaptists into the Unity must be sought within the group which we have just described. It should be remembered that Ivančice and Dačice are mentioned in the report of the negotiations.

The precise designation will depend further on our identification of the particular Anabaptist group involved in the merger talks.

e. Identification of the Anabaptist Group(s)

To the best of our knowledge there were, in the summer of 1528, Anabaptist congregations or groups in the following localities: Mikulov and the villages nearby, Ivančice, Rosice, Slavkov and probably also Dačice and Neuwitzsch.[196] The congregations in the royal cities, Brno, Jihlava, Olomouc and Znojmo were dispersed by the fierce persecution of Ferdinand in April 1528 [197] and the fugitives probably found shelter in the four or five centers just mentioned.

The Anabaptist groups in these towns were by no means identical in character. The majority of the large congregation at Mikulov and in the surrounding villages were *Schwertler*, the followers of Hubmaier. No doubt there were also a considerable number of his opponents, *Stäbler*. With the arrest of Göschl in April 1528 and the expulsion of Spittelmaier possibly at about the same time, Hubmaier's large flock must have felt like sheep without a shepherd. Under such circumstances, Hans and Leonhart of Liechtenstein, through their contacts with the lords of Boskovice, Pernstein and Lipé, could have given consideration to merger talks with the Unity. However, two facts speak against such an hypothesis.

In the first place, the lords of Liechtenstein had no dealings with the Czech Brethren since their domains were located almost entirely in a German-speaking area of South Moravia. Furthermore, Leonhart himself was an Anabaptist and does not appear to have wavered in his position after Hubmaier's death. The sources, ingroup and outgroup, refer to him as a protector of Anabaptists, beyond 1528.[198] In 1531-1532 he corresponded with Capito and Schwenckfeld in Strasbourg about Oswald Glaidt's Sabbatarian views.[199]

In the second place, the strong emphasis which Hubmaier laid on

[196] Cf. the information on Anabaptist settlement in each place in Zeman, 1966, List A.
[197] Cf. at footnotes 86 ff. above.
[198] Cf. ZGL, 147; TQ Elsass, I, 229 and elsewhere.
[199] TQ Elsass, I, 363 and 412. Cf. CS, IV, 444 ff.

believer's baptism and his absolute rejection of infant baptism makes it highly improbable that his followers, both Anabaptist refugees and local German Evangelicals who had embraced Anabaptism under his preaching, would have consented to infant baptism as it was practised by the Unity. They would have agreed, of course, with the Czech Brethren on oathtaking, Christian participation in government and defensive war.

Hubmaier's opponents, both on the Mikulov domain and at Slavkov, must be ruled out on account of their opposite stand on the same ethical issues. Besides, the *Stäbler* who had settled at Slavkov established their colony on a communitarian basis. The issue of 'communism' was not discussed in the negotiations.

The elimination of the *Schwertler* and the *Stäbler* leaves only Ivančice and Rosice (and possibly Dačice and Neuwitzsch) for our consideration. In these two towns, the early Anabaptist congregations developed rather independently of Hubmaier and of his work at Mikulov.

In the history of Moravian Anabaptism the town of Rosice (Rossitz) is associated with the original settlement of the Gabrielite Brethren, mostly of Silesian origin, and of the Philippite Brethren who came mainly from the southwestern regions of Germany, i.e. Swabia, Hesse, Württemberg, Baden, the Palatinate, and from Alsace. The first followers appear to have arrived in Moravia with their respective leaders, Gabriel Ascherham [200] and Philip Plener or Weber, "Blauärmel".[201] The time of their settlement at Rosice has been set by some historians in 1527, by others in 1528.[202]

The dating of their arrival is of course crucial for our analysis. If the Gabrielites did not arrive at Rosice until sometime in the early or late fall of 1528, after Ferdinand's mandate for Silesia, issued on August 1, 1528, had forced Anabaptists to leave for Moravia,[203] then they could not have been the group involved in the negotiations with

---

[200] On Gabriel and the Gabrielites, see Beck, 69 ff.; Wiswedel, 1937a; Heck, 1961; Maleczyńska, 1961; the art. "Ascherham" and "Gabrielites" in *ML* (Hege and Loserth) and in *ME* (Friedmann); Williams, 1959, 225 f. and 1961, 418 f. *et passim.*

[201] On Philip and the Philippites, see Beck, 71 f.; Wiswedel, III, 146 ff.; Friedmann, 1958 and 1961a, 242-253; art. "Plener" and "Philippites" in *ML* (Neff and Loserth) and *ME* (Friedmann).

[202] Some authors give both dates in the same book, without any explanation, e.g. Williams, 1961, 412 (1528) and 418 (1527).

[203] Such is the opinion expressed by Wiswedel, 1937a, 3. Cf. also his ambiguous dating in a later work, Wiswedel, III, 223.

the Czech Brethren. The merger talks must have begun before August.

If, on the other hand, the exodus of the Gabrielites from Silesia to Moravia was not occasioned by Ferdinand's mandate but had taken place already in 1527,[204] or at least in the first half of 1528, then the Gabrielite participation in the negotiations is highly probable for the following reasons.

The theology of Ascherham was greatly influenced by Silesian spiritualism,[205] especially in the concept of baptism. In his most important book, *Unterschied göttlicher und menschlicher Weisheit*, printed in Silesia in 1544,[206] Ascherham stresses baptism of the Holy Spirit to such a degree that the external observance of water baptism becomes almost superfluous and the disputes about infant and believer's baptism irrelevant. "If someone asks me: Is infant baptism sin? I will answer: No." [207]

This statement must not be interpreted, of course, as a general approval of infant baptism. It must be understood within the frame-

[204] The recent Polish research favours the earlier date related to localized peasant uprisings that took place in Silesia in 1526-1527. Cf. Maleczyńska, 1961, 20 ff. In this connection, one should note the dates in the title of a lost (printed) booklet by Ascherham: *Was sich verloffen hat unter den Brüdern, die aus aller deutschen Nation vertrieben waren umb des Glaubens willen, die darum in derselben Zeit in das Mährerlandt kommen, zu Aufenthalt ihres Lebens von dem 1528. bis auf das 1541. Jahr.* Title in Friedmann, 1929, 172 and Wiswedel, 1937a, 9, n. 3. The work is known only from excerpts in Fischer, 1607a and Ottius, 1672.
[205] Cf. our discussion of Silesian spiritualistic influence on the German Evangelicals in South Moravia, Chapter II, beginning at footnote 172.
[206] The only extant copy is in the Nationalbibliothek in Vienna. The complete text was reprinted by Wiswedel, 1937a, 13-35 and 235-260. Brief excerpts in English translation in Friedmann's art. "Ascherham", *ME*, I, 174 ff. Cf. also Loserth, 1894, 156 ff.
[207] Wiswedel, 1937a, 240. Cf. also the following statements: "Die Taufe gibt niemand den heiligen Geist, aber durch das Gebet der Heiligen, das im heiligen Geist geschieht, bringt man den heiligen Geist dem Täufling, der getauft wird und geschieht solches entweder vor oder nach der Taufe. Daraus folgt, dass alles Taufen so ausserhalb des heiligen Geistes in der christlichen Kirche geschieht, niemand nutz ist. . . . Dieweil nun die Taufe den heiligen Geist nicht vermag zu bringen, so kann in der christlichen Kirche niemand damit gebessert oder gebösert werden. . . . Darum ist die Taufe kein Gesetz, sondern sie hat Freiheit bis auf die Ursach wie alle christliche Ordnung, denn der heilige Geist hat seine Kirche an keine elementische Creatur gebunden. . . . Um der Unordnung und mancherlei Aberglaubens willen ist es billig, die Kindertaufe zu unterlassen, dieweil auch soviel Missbrauch daraus erstanden ist. . . . Darum wäre es nicht gesündigt, aus Ursache in der christlichen Kirche die Kinder zu taufen. Dieweil aber die Taufe kein Gesetz ist, so ist es besser, sie zu unterlassen, um der vorgemeldeten Ursache willen. So stellt Paulus das Gebot des Gesetzes in eine Freiheit, sich zu beschneiden oder zu unterlassen . . ." (*ibid.*, 238 ff.; cf. Eng. tr. in *ME*, I, 175 f.).

work of Ascherham's emphasis on the primary realities of the inward Christian experience of new life in the Spirit, and also as part of his sharp criticism of the Hutterites for their tendency to stress the outward expressions of Christian life such as water baptism or the communitarian way of life. In some respects, Ascherham's minimal evaluation of water baptism represents a distinct parallel to Schwenckfeld's stress on the inward communion and to his neglect of the outward observance of the Lord's Supper. The leader of the Gabrielites probably never declared a *Stillstand* with regard to baptism as Schwenckfeld did concerning the eucharist,[208] but there can be little doubt that Ascherham's spiritualizing concept of baptism was influenced by the theology of Schwenckfeld and by the basic premises of Silesian spiritualism.

A similar emphasis can be detected in Ascherham's concept of the eucharist except that his practical conclusions are quite the opposite of Schwenckfeld's suspension of the Supper. Ascherham pleads for a more solemn observance. Basing his argument on an exposition of the *locus classicus*, John chapter six, he denounces his Anabaptist brethren, presumably the Hutterites, for treating the Lord's Supper too lightly, like any other meal. He rejects the Roman and Lutheran bodily presence of Christ in the eucharist but he also disapproves of mere symbolism. The communion involves "a mystery of Christ".

At the Lord's table, the believers who truly discern the body of Christ share, through the Holy Spirit, in the very nature of the body and blood of Christ.[209] Even though Ascherham does not employ such terms, his views resemble Calvin's concept of *vera, realis sed spiritualis* presence of Christ in the eucharist.[210] They parallel even more closely the definition of Christ's presence in the eucharist as it was expressed in the theology of Bishop Lukáš and the official pronouncements of the Unity in the 1520's, namely *sacramentaliter, spiritualiter,*

---

[208]   Cf. our summary of Schwenckfeld's views and the Silesian spiritualism in Chapter II at footnotes 172 ff.

[209]   "... wie man denn jetzt auch Leute findet, die da sagen: Ei, es ist ja nur ein Brot, wie ein ander Brot, und Wein wie anderer Wein und essen und trinken ohne Erkenntnis des Geheimnisses Christi. ... O lieber Freund, es gehört noch mehr dazu von der Gemeinsame [sic!] des Leibes und Blutes Christi unsers Herrn essen und trinken. ... Nicht den Leib im Brot, sondern das Brot im Leibe und nicht das Blut im Wein, sondern den Wein im Blut, wie Paulus sagt: Der Trank des neuen Testaments ist in meinem Blut .... Und das Trinken der Gläubigen aus dem Kelch, nämlich eine abgesonderte Gemeinschaft des Blutes Christi und werden also durch den heiligen Geist solches Verstandes Mitgenossen der Natur des Fleisches und Blutes Christi." Wiswedel, 1937a, 258 f.

[210]   So interpreted by Friedmann in *ME*, I, 176.

potentialiter et vere.[211] The mystery of the spiritual presence of Christ makes it imperative that the communion should be administered with great dignity.[212]

It is quite possible that Ascherham became familiar with the eucharistic theology of the *Unitas Fratrum* during his repeated stays in Moravia. Even though one must not forget that the views which we have summarized above were so stated in 1544, one may assume that they were typical of Ascherham's theology from the days of his first contact with Silesian spiritualism around 1526-1527. The same influence was at work among the pre-Anabaptist German Evangelicals in South Moravia and in the 'Zwinglian' group of the Unity (Zeising) when Ascherham first arrived in Moravia. The city of Litomyšl, where the initial phase of negotiations between the Anabaptists and the Czech Brethren took place in 1528, was one of the known points of contact with Silesia.[213]

The combination of these historical and theological factors furnishes the basis for our hypothesis — and it is nothing more — that the Anabaptists who negotiated with the Unity, or at least one of the several groups that might have been involved, were the Gabrielite brethren under the personal leadership of Gabriel Ascherham.[214] A group which was not insistent on an outright rejection of infant baptism and which believed in the mystery of the spiritual presence of Christ in the eucharist was more likely to subscribe to the theology of the Unity than some other Anabaptist parties in Moravia.

[211] Cf. our description of the eucharistic controversy in the Unity in 1525 ff., Chapter II, esp. at footnotes 68 ff.

[212] (Continuation of the text quoted in footnote 209): "Und darum so heiligt der Verstand, der da ist das Sakrament, das Brot und auch der Wein, welches denn gegeben ist zu einem löblichen Gedächtnis des Todes Christi. Und darum ist dieses Brot und dieser Wein heilig und soll mit hoher und grosser Würdigkeit gegessen und getrunken werden, gleichwie die Kinder Israel das Osterlamm . . .". Wiswedel, 1937a, 259. Cf. also the references of the Hutterite chronicle to Gabriel's ceremonial observance of the communion (chalice covered with cloth), ZGL, 250 (under the year 1545).

[213] Cf. Chapter II at footnotes 171 ff.

[214] Another bit of evidence may point in the same direction. The record of the colloquy between Anabaptists and Czech Brethren at Ivančice in 1559 contains a marginal note written by Jan Blahoslav in which he identified the group as Gabrielites (AUF, IX, fol. 255a; cf. Chapter V footnote 47). As we shall see, Blahoslav was mistaken in his identification, but his note betrays some acquaintance with the Gabrielites. Were there later contacts between them and the Unity? Or did Blahoslav learn about them at Goldberg, in the territory of Friedrich II of Liegnitz, during his year of studies there, 1543-1544? Ascherham's booklet which we have just reviewed appeared in Silesia in 1544.

If such were the case, what brought the sudden change of attitude which was manifested at the meeting held at Mladá Boleslav in the latter part of September 1528? There are only two possible explanations. One might suspect that the theological position of the Unity which was outlined to the Anabaptist emissaries by Krasonický and Roh at Litomyšl was somewhat different from the official statement made to them later at Boleslav. Krasonický was well acquainted with the Zwinglian and spiritualizing teachings of Zeising and his group within the Unity.[215] He and Roh might have expressed the doctrines of the Unity in terms which were more acceptable to the Silesian Anabaptists than those put to them later by the elders of the Unity. However, such conjecture cannot be substantiated from the known sources. Krasonický stood in full agreement with Bishop Lukáš and opposed Zeising's camp.

One must look, therefore, for a change of attitude among the Anabaptists from Rosice. It is known that the Gabrielite Brethren were joined, some time after their settlement at Rosice, by the Philippites. As in the case of the Gabrielites, the time of the arrival of the Philippites has not been determined accurately by previous research. Both 1527 and 1528 have been cited by different authors.[216]

Small groups of Anabaptist refugees from southwestern Germany kept arriving in Moravia during 1527 and 1528. Some settled in the Mikulov area, others at Ivančice and still others must have joined the Silesian refugees at Rosice.

Philip Plener (Weber, Blauärmel) spent at least July and August 1528 in Augsburg as leader (*Vorsteher*) of the diminishing Anabaptist group after the execution of Hans Leupold.[217] For part of the time, he stayed at the house of Leupold's widow but later complained that he could not find shelter with the brethren and had to stay with "the heathen".[218] When he could not find work as a weaver and the little group decided not to meet any more for the time being,[219] he and

---

215   Cf. Chapter II at footnotes 57 ff. Zeising and the other two Silesian refugee monks stayed in Krasonický's house at Litomyšl.
216   Wiswedel, III, 147 (1528); Friedmann, 1958, 273 ff. (1527).
217   Detailed accounts about the Anabaptists in Augsburg during the spring and summer of 1528 are preserved in the court testimonies of the imprisoned brethren; dated September 9-October 6, 1528 and published by Roth, 1901a, 14-137. Hans Leupold was beheaded on April 25, 1528. Cf. also Roth, 1901b, 248-254.
218   Roth, 1901a, 127 f. and 136.
219   Testimony of Jacob Walch on September 9: Two or three weeks ago, about twenty persons met and decided not to meet again, "... und nit weitter lernen noch tauffen, sonder ain jeder in seinem hertzen warten, was im got ereffnen wolt,

Georg Schachner left the city on August 31, 1528, supposedly for Strasbourg.[220] It is quite probable that in the court testimonies Strasbourg was indicated as Plener's destination simply because he had come from there. The Strasbourg sources from the early fall 1528 do not mention Plener at all.[221] In all likelihood he went from Augsburg to Moravia and could have arrived at Rosice during the first or second week of September.

This timing of his arrival would have given him and his followers just enough time to introduce a strong emphasis on believer's baptism [222] and a strictly commemorative interpretation of the eucharist into the Gabrielite congregation at Rosice and thus to upset the hopeful negotiations for a merger with the Czech Brethren. It would also explain the unexpected change of attitude on the part of the Anabaptist emissaries who attended the meeting with the elders of the Unity at Boleslav in the middle part of September.

Such sudden reversals of doctrinal views are known to have taken place on other occasions among Anabaptists in Moravia and elsewhere. The Hutterite chronicles report that at first, Ascherham received Plener and his group into his house and even entrusted the preaching and teaching office to him. But very soon, because of disagreements, the Philippites moved into another house and Gabriel resumed leadership for his own (Silesian) group.[223] The tensions grew worse and in 1529 the Philippites left Rosice and established a settlement at Hustopeč (Auspitz).

Before we bring our analysis to a conclusion we must examine also

---

und mit dem tauffen und lernen still steen solten, dann die zeit were verschinen, darin got den widertauff genugsam geoffenbart und bestätt hab . . ." (Roth, 1901a, 125). Nevertheless, Plener baptized several persons on the day he left Augsburg (*ibid.*, 129).

[220] *Ibid.*, 126. Cf. also the description of Plener's appearance and clothes, *ibid.*, 128 and 130.

[221] *TQ Elsass*, I, 181, n. 7. Cf. also the names of Anabaptists at the Strasbourg hearing on October 22, 1528 (including Marbeck and Reublin but no mention of Plener), *ibid.*, 184 ff.

[222] According to another court testimony in Augsburg (Matheus Unform von Brauneggen, i.e. Bruneck in Tirol, on September 2, 1528) Plener taught that believer's baptism was necessary unto salvation: "Der Philip hab im anzaigt, der tauff sei nott zu der seligkait; welher den erlangen mög und sich nit lass tauffen, der werd nit selig; welher aber sich gern liess tauffen und solhs nit kende erlangen, derselb werde selbs in seinem plut getaufft . . ." (Roth, 1901a, 130). It was views such as this against which Gabriel Ascherham reacted in his spiritualizing concept of baptism.

[223] *ZGL*, 86.

the early phase of Anabaptism at Ivančice (Eibenschitz). Our knowledge of the Anabaptist group there in 1526-1528 is based on several independent sources.

The oldest one is Hubmaier's brief mention of Johannes Sylvanus and Christian Entfelder, *Ecclesiasten zů Ewantzig*, in the dedicatory preface to his baptismal agenda.[224] Hubmaier suggested to Jan Dubčanský to confer with the two men and "with other Christian brothers" and to discuss with them whether or not Hubmaier's form of baptism was scriptural.

The reference to Sylván (also spelled Silván) has probably resulted in more historical and literary research than any other biographical reference in Hubmaier's works. The early life and career of the Slovak-Czech hymnwriter Ján Sylván (1493-1572/1573) remains obscure in spite of meticulous research by several authors.[225] Nothing is known about his life from his birth at Trnava in western Slovakia in 1493 till 1527 when Hubmaier recorded his presence at Ivančice.[226] The claim of earlier historians that Hubmaier was referring to another Johannes Silvanus, the German Socinian beheaded at Heidelberg on December 23, 1572, has been ruled out by subsequent research.[227]

In 1530 and again in 1534, one of Sylván's earliest hymns was printed in the hymnbook of the Habrovanite brethren.[228] The same hymn was later included, revised by Jan Roh, in several editions of the Czech hymnbooks of the *Unitas Fratrum*, beginning with Roh's hymnal in 1541. It was reprinted in the famous hymnals of Šamotuly (1561) and Ivančice (1564) and also in the hymnbook prepared in exile by Comenius (1659). Another of his hymns bears the remark: "composed in the year 1536, in my great hardships and persecu-

---

[224]   *HS*, 348.

[225]   The best monograph which summarizes all previous research and proposes several new solutions is Čuprová, 1958. A helpful chronological list of biographical data on Sylván and a bibliography was prepared by Bálent, 1957, 145-171. Of the other recent works, Čaplovič, 1955 and 1957 must be mentioned. Cf. also Bergsten, 1961, 427 f. and Urban, 1966, 26.

[226]   A certain "Johannes Silvanus de Merica" was matriculated at the University of Vienna for the summer semester 1516. It is not certain whether he can be identified with the later hymnwriter. Nothing is known about Sylván's education. Cf. Čuprová, 1958, 14 ff.

[227]   Čuprová, 1958, 12. The German Silvanus was a Catholic priest until 1559. Cf. Veesenmeyer, 1800, 310, note and 326 as an example of the wrong identification.

[228]   "Spomoziž mi z hoře mého", reprinted in facsimile from Sylván's own hymnbook (1571) by Bálent, 1957, 45 ff.

tions".[229] Its fourteenth stanza reveals Sylván's sympathies with the Zwinglian camp. He condemns "the Swabian *Bund*", most likely the alignment of several South German cities, formerly Zwinglian, with the Lutherans on the issue of the eucharist, in the Wittenberg *Concordia* of 1536.[230]

It is not clear why Sylván should have suffered persecution in the year 1536. If he was still in Moravia, perhaps at Ivančice, he might have been affected by the persecution of the Anabaptists. Alternately, he might have been involved in the suppressive measures against the Habrovanite Unity which were initiated by King Ferdinand at the diet of Znojmo in February 1535 [231] and finally consummated by the arrest of Dubčanský in 1537.

Sometime in the late 1530's Sylván probably left Moravia for western Slovakia.[232] But in the 1540's, he was already in Bohemia, first as a secretary to Jan Popel of Lobkovice, a Roman Catholic, at Horšův Týn and then, from about 1570 until his death in 1572-1573, at Domažlice (Taus), the birthplace of Jan Roh.

We shall not analyze the many Czech hymns and psalm paraphrases written by Sylván except to mention that one of them found its way, in a revised form, into the hymnbooks of the Unity.[233] The assumption that Sylván became a member of the Unity was refuted by Blahoslav in 1561.[234] At his death, he was either an Utraquist, or a Roman Catholic.[235]

[229] "Z hlubokosti volám k tobě", reprinted in facsimile by Bálent, 1957, 53 ff.

[230] "Zrušíť švábský punt Kristus Pán, kterýž spuntoval ďábel sám . . .". We accept the interpretation by Čuprová, 1958, 23 ff. Others have explained the allusion as a condemnation of the German domination in the Slovak cities, or of the German advisers of King Ferdinand. On the Wittenberg *Concordia*, cf. Köhler, 1953, 432-525.

[231] At the instigation of Ferdinand, the Moravian diet (February 14, 1535) ordered Dubčanský to abstain from all propagation of his teachings. Ignoring the order, Dubčanský published, in 1536, an Apology and had a copy presented to the King (Odložilík, 1923, 303 ff.).

[232] In 1540, Andreas Fischer, an Anabaptist who had visited the area around Mikulov several times, was executed in western Slovakia (Ratkoš, 1958, 56).

[233] See at footnote 228 above.

[234] Blahoslav, "De novo Cantionali bohemico" (*AUF*, IX, fol. 318-341; excerpts in Jireček, 1862): "Jan Sylvanus, secretary of Popel . . . . Musicus quidem elatus et eruditus ac plane poeticum ingenium, sed ebriosus et furiosus subinde. [Continued in Czech:] Well known to many Brethren, including myself. However, he never was a Brother, and cannot be one because of his drinking and vanity, [in Latin:] et propter furorem" (Jireček, 1862, 41). In 1561, Blahoslav was already living at Ivančice and might have heard local stories about Sylván.

[235] Čaplovič, 1955, 76 ("old Utraquist"); Čuprová, 1958, 34 ("probably Catholic"). The latter is a deduction from the fact that Sylván was employed by a Catholic lord.

It is doubtful that Sylván was, in the late 1520's, a baptized member of the Anabaptist congregation at Ivančice unless such definite association was only a passing phase in his religious development. Hubmaier referred to him and to Entfelder as *Herren,* not brothers.[236] Perhaps he hoped that a colloquy between Dubčanský and the two men might clarify their stand on baptism. More will be said on the type of Anabaptism at Ivančice further below.

Sylván's relationship to the Habrovanite Brethren is documented only by the inclusion of one of his hymns in their hymnbooks. That in itself is no proof that he joined their Unity. Nor is it possible to substantiate his allegiance to Zwinglian theology. His hymns contain no references to the eucharist, nor to the other sacraments.

Most likely, Sylván was yet another of the many restless Czech religious seekers who flocked to Moravia in the 1520's. In all probability Sylván understood the German language, and if the Anabaptists from Ivančice were involved in the negotiations with the Unity in 1528 he might have been the anonymous interpreter mentioned in the record. It is questionable that he was a minister with theological training. In the circles of the Radical Reformation with which he seems to have been in contact in Moravia, he would have been recognized as a local leader without any training or previous ordination.[237]

According to Hubmaier, Sylván's associate at Ivančice was Christian Entfelder.[238] We know nothing about his early life or education prior to his stay in Moravia, 1526-1528. Some time in 1528 or 1529,[239] he left for Strasbourg where he published two booklets in 1530 and a third one in 1533.[240] The first of these, *Von den manigfaltigen im*

[236]   *HS,* 348. Cf. also Chapter II at footnote 146.

[237]   Bergsten, 1961, 427, n. 14 interprets Hubmaier's reference to "Ecclesiasten zu E." as probably applicable only to Entfelder. Čaplovič, 1955, 81 reports that he failed to find any sources in the State Archives at Brno which would throw additional light on religious life at Ivančice around 1527 and on Sylvánus. He suggests, however, that S. was "Czech minister" while Entfelder preached to the Germans. Urban, 1966, 26 suggests that Sylván might have been linked with the Minor Party of the *Unitas Fratrum.* A friend of Kalenec, Jan Drštka, lived at Ivančice in later years (source from 1543).

[238]   *HS,* 348. On Entfelder, see Hege's art. in *ML,* I, 594 f. and *ME,* II, 226 f.; W. Köhler's art. in *RGG* (both 2nd and 3rd ed.); Veesenmeyer, 1800; Keller, 1885, 433 f. *et passim;* Jones, 1914, 39-45; Schottenloher, 1921, 85, n. 2; Čaplovič, 1955, 81; Fast, 1956, 222; Williams, 1962, 267 ff. *et passim; TQ Elsass,* I, 252.

[239]   Hege (*ML,* I, 594) refers to Entfelder's expulsion from Ivančice without any further explanation. As a minister (*Ecclesiastes*) at Ivančice, Entfelder would have been affected by the decree of the diet at Znojmo. Cf. footnote 84 above.

[240]   For titles, content and excerpts, see the art. "Entfelder" in *ML* and *ME;*

glauben Zerspaltungen (January 24, 1530) is especially important for our investigation since it contains, at the end, a message addressed "to the Brethren at Eywatschůtz".[241] Entfelder's ministry in Moravia is thus confirmed by a second contemporary source. Obviously he remained in contact with the congregation at Ivančice and might have revisited it in the early 1530's before he moved to ducal Prussia. He served as adviser to Duke Albrecht of Prussia at Königsberg from 1536 till 1546. Since only a few years earlier, on August 16, 1532, the Duke had banished three other Anabaptist leaders, Johannes Bůnderlin, Oswald Glaidt and Johannes Spittelmaier — who had taken part in the colloquy at Kętrzyn (Rastenburg) on December 29-30, 1531 — the subsequent employment of Entfelder would suggest that he must have turned away from Anabaptism.[242]

Influenced greatly by Denck, Entfelder represents a type of spiritualizing Anabaptism which drew heavily from medieval mysticism and despised "the dead letter of the Scriptures".[243] As in the case of Schwenckfeld, so for Entfelder and Bůnderlin — with whom Entfelder was associated at Strasbourg [244] — the emphasis on the inner mystical experience of spiritual realities led to a minimization or

---

Veesenmeyer, 1800, 311 ff.; Jones, 1914, 40 ff. and Williams, 1962, 269 f. The three booklets were printed first in Strasbourg and then reprinted by Philipp Ulhart in Augsburg (Schottenloher, 1921, 85, n. 2).

[241] Entfelder, 1530, fol. E 6r - 8r. A Dutch translation by Petrus Serrarius, under the title *Bedenckinge over de veelderley Scheuringen ende Dwalingen ... vervat in viif Sluyt-Reden door Christian Entfelder, weleer Dienaar des Woorts onder de Doopsgezinden tot Eywatschutz voor 128 Jaren ...* was printed as an appendix to Serrarius' book *De Vertredinge des Heyligen Stadts ...* at Amsterdam in 1659 (*ME*, II, 227).

[242] Cf. Williams, 1959, 224 and 1962, 408 f. Cf. footnote 72 above. In his decree of June 23, 1535, Albrecht refused to grant refuge in Prussia to Anabaptist exiles from Moravia (Maleczyńska, 1960, 247). Veesenmeyer, 1800, 329-334 printed Entfelder's Latin letter to Johann à Lasco written in Königsberg in March 1544.

[243] In spite of such views, the text of his second book, *Von warer Gotseligkeit*, is included in the Ms. Codex Kunstbuch (fols. 336-345) which originated in the Marbeck fellowship. Cf. Fast, 1956, 222 for explanation of the possible reasons for inclusion.

[244] Hans Bůnderlin (Johann Wunderl, 1499-1533) was born in Linz and educated at the University of Vienna. He became a personal friend of Sebastian Franck. See the art. by Neff in *ML*, I, 298 ff. and *ME*, I, 469 f.; Nicoladani, 1893; Jones, 1914, 32-39; Williams, 1962, 156 *et passim*, and Foster, 1965. In 1531 Marbeck published two brief refutations of Bůnderlin's views (Klassen, W., 1959). He spent some time with Leonhart of Liechtenstein at Nikolsburg (probably in 1527-1528) as he confessed during his imprisonment at Strasbourg, March 11-18, 1529 (*TQ Elsass*, I, 229). We do not know whether he became acquainted with Entfelder in Moravia.

total neglect of the outward ceremonies of the church, including the
sacraments. In the concluding part of his first booklet — which was
addressed to the brethren at Ivančice — Entfelder defined the church
as "a chosen, anointed, purified, sanctified group in whom God dwells,
upon whom the Holy Ghost has poured out his gifts and with whom
Christ the Lord shares his offices . . .".[245] He bewailed the divisions
in Christendom which resulted, in part, from different interpretations
of the sacraments and stated expressly that those who baptized infants and those who baptized adults "for the second or third time"
could live together in one church as they seemed to have done in the
early church.[246]

It is quite possible that through statements such as these Entfelder
was reacting to the regrettable divisions among Moravian Anabaptists
and perhaps even directly to the failure of merger negotiations with
the *Unitas Fratrum*. Since we do not know when Entfelder left
Moravia it would be pointless to suggest that he himself was personally involved in the negotiations at Litomyšl and elsewhere. However,
one may assume that the early Anabaptist congregation at Ivančice
accepted, for a while at least, Entfelder's views. Allowing, as these
spiritualizing Anabaptists did, different concepts of the sacraments
to exist side by side within one church and regarding all of them as
peripheral,[247] the brethren from Ivančice were the most likely to
favour a merger with another group such as the Unity.

But what brought the abrupt change of attitude on the part of the
negotiating Anabaptists if these can be identified with the congregation at Ivančice?[248] Another source preserved from the year 1528
explains a change in the theological outlook which must have taken
place in Ivančice during 1528.

In the late fall of 1528, Hans Sturm, an Anabaptist from Upper

---

[245] Entfelder, 1530, fol. E 7r. Eng. tr. by Jones, 1914, 41.
[246] Commenting on the rebaptism of John's disciples at Ephesus (Acts 19:1 ff.),
Entfelder wrote: "Es war auch dieselbige zeyt, zum andern oder dritten mal
tauffen, nitt so ain grosse sünd, als seider worden, nach dem das bäpstlich recht
mit dem bann, vnd das kaiserlich mit dem schwert, die ainige kindertauff haben
gezieret. Darumb bedorffts dazumal wenig disputirens, Vnd wer auch noch heüt
leicht, mit disen Ceremonien der partheyen ainigkayt zuraten, wo sich die aine nit
mehr annäm weder jr beuolhen, vnd die ander, niemants mit jr zu glauben vnd
tauffen, durch das schwert, wider die art des glaubens lieb vnd des gaists Gotes
bezwung . . .". (Entfelder, 1530, fol. D 5v; reprinted by Weesenmeyer, 1800, 317 f.)
[247] Cf. the similar views of baptism and eucharist held by Denck and Bünderlin;
summarized by Foster, 1965, 123 f.
[248] Such identification is suggested also by a reference to Ivančice in the record
of the merger talks. Cf. our text at footnote 173 above.

Austria,[249] left Moravia and made his way through Bohemia to Zwickau. He was arrested there in February 1529, subjected to repeated interrogation and eventually moved to Wittenberg on April 5. After vain attempts of several Reformers, including Luther himself, to convert Sturm, he was condemned as a "blasphemer and insurrectionist" to lifelong imprisonment. He died in the jail at Schweinitz in 1536.

When he was arrested at Zwickau, a brief tract *On the Lord's Supper and Baptism* was found in his possession. Sturm had carried it, as a precious treasure, folded under his shirt.[250] It was written by *Wetel von Ey waczitz, der von garlitz [Görlitz] bürtig ist*[251] and addressed to an anonymous brother and "to all my beloved brethren in Prague" (*Zů proge*).[252] At the end, the short undated epistle contains greetings "from all brethren of Ivančice". Sturm confessed that he had received communion at "Neuwitzsch" in Moravia.[253] Both the records of his hearings and Wetel's epistle provide a picture of the theological trends which either existed at Ivančice side by side with the spiritualizing views represented by Entfelder, or more likely, were introduced there by new refugees in 1528, perhaps after Entfelder's departure.

According to Sturm's testimony, many people bewailed the death of Hubmaier.[254] The influence of Hubmaier's teachings on baptism, eucharist, magistracy and community of goods is discernable in Sturm's statements.[255] However, Hans Hut's views on eschatology,

---

[249] Cf. Neff's art. "Sturm, Hans" in *ML*, IV, 265 and *ME*, IV. Sturm had been imprisoned at Steyer and his sister had been drowned at Freistadt. Nicoladani, 1893 and *TQ*, XI contain the records of persecution in Steyer and Freistadt in 1527-1528 but do not mention Hans Sturm. All information is based on the records of hearings held at Zwickau after Sturm's imprisonment there. Printed by Wappler, 1908a, 31 ff. and 168 ff.

[250] Cf. Wappler, 1908a, 28, n. 3. The complete text of the tract was reprinted by Wappler, *ibid.*, 183-186.

[251] In spite of continued search, we were unable to find any information about Wetel. It is doubtful that he could be identified with Bastl Wardeiner (Schlosser) who had contacts with the Anabaptists at Brno and Znojmo in 1528 (Beck, 66 f.; *ZGL*, 63 and 72) and in 1548 was elected a deacon by the Hutterites (*ZGL*, 321).

[252] "Proge" is identified as Prague by Wappler, 1908a, 29, n. 3.

[253] *Ibid.*, 28 and 169. The geographical identification of Neuwitzsch is uncertain. Cf. Zeman, 1966, 55.

[254] "Sagt, das viel leute doctor Künlein, ein rabbi der widdertauffer, beweynet haben, da er ist umbracht worden" (*ibid.*, 33 and 168). Identified as Hubmaier by Wappler.

[255] Cf. Wappler, 1908a, 34 ff. and 168 ff. "Von der weltlichen obirkeit helt er gross, wenn sie recht thut, vnd sie soll sein zur straffe den bosen vnd zu schutz

secret revelations and "the dead letter" of the Scriptures are also echoed.[256] Sturm even defended Müntzer and preferred celibacy for Christians.[257] Quite obviously, Sturm visited different Anabaptist centers in Moravia and was exposed to conflicting influences.

Wetel's tract expresses Hubmaier's theology of baptism and eucharist. Scriptural texts which were used by Hubmaier to defend believer's baptism are quoted also by Wetel. Baptism must be preceded by repentance. Like Hubmaier, Wetel distinguishes threefold baptism: of the Spirit, of water and of fire or blood.[258] The Lord's Supper is an outward sign (eusserlich zeichen) of the inward remembrance (innerlich gedechtnuss). Christ cannot be present in the sacrament since his body is at the right hand of God.

Throughout the tract, there is a strong polemical note against the Roman Catholic mass and church (bapstler, Romisch khirch), particularly in the context of the symbolic interpretation of the eucharist. One should recall that the record of the merger negotiations mentions an Anabaptist at Ivančice who accused the Czech Brethren of hypocrisy and idolatry, quite obviously because of their concept of the presence of Christ in the eucharist. It is not unthinkable that Wetel's written attacks against the Roman doctrine of the eucharist could have been occasioned by the merger talks. If one did not read carefully the Unity's own explanation of its peculiar eucharistic terminology — as the Anabaptists, according to the preserved record, did not — one could easily misinterpret the Brethren's concept of the real presence as a version of the Roman Catholic doctrine.

The clear baptismal and eucharistic theology preserved in Wetel's tract represents a parallel to the strong emphasis on believer's baptism which was introduced by Philip Plener and his followers at Rosice. In both cases, the introduction of such theology by newly arriving refugees led not only to the correction of the earlier spiritualizing trend represented by Entfelder and Ascherham in the two respective communities, but also to the change of attitude towards a merger into the Unitas Fratrum.

---

den fromen" (ibid., 38). To the question, "Ob die Oberherren können Christen sein", Sturm answered: "Ja, wo sie fürgehen vnd wo sie sein nach dem befehl des Herrn Jhesu" (ibid., 48). "Die christen sollen nicht reich sein doch mügen sie wol gütter haben, sehen aber zu, das sie sie nicht irren, vnd derhalben hab ich meine gütter verlassen ..." (ibid., 36).

256   Ibid., 38 ff.
257   Ibid., 37.
258   Ibid., 185 f. Cf. HS, 275 and 313 f.

f. *The Issues*

The only extant record of the merger negotiations does not specify all issues that were on the agenda of the several meetings. It merely reports that the talks concerned any subjects which the Anabaptists wished to discuss, "such as faith, the ministrative means of the Scriptures, all sacraments, the ministers of the church and their order, and also the civil power (magistracy) and whether those who participate in it might be saved".[259] One may interpret this brief reference as an indication that the entire scope of the Unity's theological and ethical position was included in the talks during the first amicable phase of the negotiations.

The issues which caused the sudden change of attitude are not spelled out. However, the accusations of 'idolatry' made by the Anabaptists against the Unity would suggest that the main issue, during the second phase, became the theology of the eucharist.[260] The Anabaptists with their basically Zwinglian concept of the Lord's Supper could not subscribe to, and perhaps did not even understand the teaching of the Unity according to which Christ was present in the sacrament "sacramentally, spiritually, efficaciously and truly".[261]

To what extent the question of baptism contributed to the breakdown of negotiations cannot be determined. The record does not mention baptism as such. One can only surmise that infant baptism as it was practised by the Unity side by side with adult baptism [262] could hardly have been acceptable to the stricter Anabaptist party which appears to have gained control over the congregations at Rosice and Ivančice in the early fall of 1528.

On the ethical issues, such as Christian participation in government and warfare, the two negotiating parties seem to have been in agreement.[263] The question of the community of goods obviously was not

[259] Cf. at footnote 165 above.
[260] Cf. footnote 173 above.
[261] For an analysis of the eucharistic theology in the period of Lukáš see Dobiáš, 1940; Müller, I, 486 ff. and Štrupl, 1964a, 254 ff.
[262] On Lukáš' concept of baptism, see Müller, I, 466 ff. and Štrupl, 1964a, 246 ff.
[263] In 1528, the influence of Hubmaier's endorsement of Christian magistracy — quite similar to the position of the Major Party of the Unity — seems to have been widespread among the Anabaptists in Moravia. In addition to the testimony of Hans Sturm (cf. footnote 255 above) the following statement by Hans Nadler should be noted: ". . . und auch der bruder vil unter uns, die wollen, wir solten die schwerter wer gar hinlegen; das hab ich getan, es ist doch aber kein sazung nit, es mags einer dragen aber mags lassen, darnach er stark oder schwag ist im glauben" (*TQ*, II, 136; cf. also Wiswedel, II, 44 and *ML*, III, 196). Nadler spent

included in the discussions.[264] Similarly, the radical chiliastic hopes which characterized many Anabaptist conventicles in the spring and summer of 1528 were not among the concerns of the particular group which met with the Unity.[265]

6. CONCLUSIONS

On the basis of our foregoing historical analysis we may draw the following conclusions.

The main initiative for the merger colloquies seems to have come from the Lord Jan of Lipé at Krumlov and the Lord Dobeš of Boskovice at Rosice. Both Lords were vitally interested in the German and Swiss Reformation. They were also in sympathy with the radical domestic movements. They favored closer contacts between the different religious parties in Moravia. In 1527 they co-sponsored the publication of Dubčanský's correspondence with the Unity. It is possible that other members of the Moravian nobility, such as Jan of Pernstein and Krištof of Boskovice, were also involved.

---

only two weeks at Mikulov in 1527 or 1528. The statement on magistracy was made during his trial at Erlangen on January 17, 1529. In his letter to the brethren at Ivančice (January 24, 1530), Entfelder expressed admiration for the Moravian nobility: "Befleisst euch gegen ewr öbrigkait schuldige pflicht, dann nit vil solcher herschafft hat dise welt verhanden." (Entfelder, 1530, fol. E 8r.)

[264] Without any historical and theological analysis of the record of the negotiations, Müller, I, 452 claims that "the communist organization and the fanatical rejection of infant baptism" by the Anabaptists were among the main causes of the failure. The only group which is known to have established its settlement on a communitarian basis in the summer of 1528 were the "Stäbler" in Slavkov (Austerlitz). According to our analysis, they were not involved in the merger talks. Cf. also Entfelder's reference to communitarian Anabaptists in his letter to the brethren at Ivančice: "Last ander alle ding gemain haben, allain jre brüder grüssen, jnen selbst wolthůn, wer aim andern übel thůt, gibt jnen nit vil zuschaffen, sy seind von den aussern." (Entfelder, 1530, fol. E 7v.)

[265] Cf. the chapter "Huts Lehre von der Endzeit" in Zschäbitz, 1958, 49-64. Many Anabaptists expected the return of Christ at Pentecost or in the fall of 1528 (*ibid.*, 50, n. 103). To some, Moravia was "the little land" where the brethren were to gather for the final days (Wappler, 1913, 289): "So weher auch ein lendlein, darinne ein herre, den er, auch das lendichen mit dem namen nicht anzuzeigen weiss [Liechtenstein in Moravia; cf. *ibid.*, 40 and 257], der solt sich mit sambt seinen undirthanen allenthalb anderweit hab teufen lassen. Daselbst wurden sich die prudere versamlen" (March 11, 1528). See also Stayer, 1965, 184 ff. The Codex *Kunstbuch*, fol. 242b, contains a brief prophecy of Albrecht Gleicheisen of Erfurt from the year 1372 concerning the year 1528 with no reference to Moravia (cf. Fast, 1956, 219). See also our discussion at footnotes 76 ff. above.

It is highly probable that the official report of the elders of the Unity was sent to Jan of Lipé. The incident at Dačice mentioned in the report probably occasioned the (lost) correspondence between Matouš, the minister of the Unity in Dačice, and Vavřinec Krasonický and Jan Roh. If there was an Anabaptist group resident at Dačice one might suspect that Brother Matouš could also have played some role in initiating the contacts. The Moravian leaders such as Bishop Škoda were bypassed and the Anabaptist emissaries were directed towards Litomyšl. Quite likely the minister at Litomyšl, Vavřinec Krasonický, a native of Krasonice, maintained personal contacts with the centers of the Unity in South Moravia.

The Anabaptist groups which initially expressed willingness to join the Unity and accept its teachings and orders were the 'spiritualizing' Anabaptists, either from Ivančice (influence of Christian Entfelder), or from Rosice (the early Gabrielites under Gabriel Ascherham), or more likely, from both places. In their emphasis on the inward spiritual realities, the outward observance of all ceremonies was of minimal importance. Thus they were prepared to subscribe to a concept of baptism which allowed for both adult and infant baptism, and to eucharistic theology which among other things defined the presence of Christ in the sacrament as 'spiritual'.[266]

The unexpected reversal of attitude towards a merger was brought about by the influx of new Anabaptist refugees who — under men like Philip Plener at Rosice, or Wetel at Ivančice — insisted strictly on believer's baptism and on a symbolic interpretation of the eucharist. They represented the main stream of Anabaptism.

The violent persecution of Anabaptists in Moravia in 1528 had probably little to do with the motives for the negotiations. The Moravian lords who provided the main impetus were themselves sympathetic with the spiritualizing trends among the two particular Anabaptist groups.[267] The earlier influence of Silesian spiritualism

[266] The theology of the *Unitas Fratrum*, with its strong emphasis on salvation which must be accepted by personal faith but at the same time can only be "mediated" by the ministrative acts of the church, cannot be regarded as "spiritualistic". Its concept of the presence of Christ in the eucharist was open to misunderstanding. It could be misinterpreted either as "catholicizing" (*sacramentaliter, potentialiter, vere*) or as "spiritualizing" (*spiritualiter*). The group around Zeising represented a one-sided emphasis on the latter.

[267] Williams, 1962, 412 regards Ascherham, "in the end as a spiritualist, like Entfelder and Bünderlin". Cf. footnote 271 below. See also our account of the Silesian and other spiritualizing influences in Moravia, Chapter II, beginning at footnote 172.

among the German Evangelicals in South Moravia and in the *Unitas Fratrum* (controversy with Zeising) had prepared the way for a receptive attitude toward spiritualizing Anabaptism. The eclectic trends leading to the formation of the Habrovanite Unity served a similar purpose.

It cannot be stressed enough that a positive result of the negotiations would have been of little consequence for the subsequent relationship between Anabaptism and the *Unitas Fratrum* in Moravia. If the Anabaptists from Ivančice and Rosice had merged with the *Unitas Fratrum*, their decision could not have been followed by the other 'mainstream' Anabaptist groups in Moravia. Apart from all other considerations, such as the linguistic and cultural contrasts, the doctrinal differences between the *Schwertler*, the *Stäbler* and other subsequent Anabaptist groups in Moravia [268] on the one side and the Czech Brethren on the other side, were such that a union would have been impossible unless one side had been prepared to give up, in part, its dogmatic and ethical position.

Perhaps the greatest benefit of our detailed historical analysis of the merger talks in 1528 is the evidence thus gathered for the existence of a third major type within early Moravian Anabaptism. In addition to the followers of Hubmaier (*Schwertler*) and his opponents (*Stäbler*) who can be classified as the proto-Hutterites, there existed in Moravia a significant group of spiritualizing Anabaptists. Their ideas and leadership came mainly from South Germany or Austria (Entfelder, Bűnderlin, Denck) and Silesia (Gabriel Ascherham).

However, Moravian Anabaptists also maintained relations with Saxony. The case of Hans Sturm who carried a tract from Ivančice, via Prague, to Zwickau, confirms connections with that area. Like Entfelder and Ascherham, some of the early opponents of infant baptism at Zwickau did not seem to have been greatly concerned about the outward observance of water baptism nor about a consistent practice of rebaptism.[269]

One cannot, therefore, agree with Műller that the Czech Brethren came into contact with Anabaptists only from Switzerland, South

---

[268]   Cf. the list of ten different Anabaptist groups in Moravia in Zeman, 1966, 96 ff.

[269]   Cf. the comment of Nicholas Storch in 1522 by which he showed his indifference towards rebaptism: "Ey, was liegt dan an disem artickel!!" (Husa, 1957, 93, n. 279.) On Storch's spiritualism, see Oyer, 1964, 9 ff. Cf. also Wappler, 1908b, 35 ff.

Germany and Austria.[270] In Moravia all types of Anabaptism were represented.

The center of spiritualizing Anabaptism seems to have been removed from Moravia to Strasbourg in 1528-1529.[271] It is probable, however, that a spiritualizing trend continued to exercise influence in Moravia — not only among the Gabrielite Brethren — into the 1530's and 1540's. Its existence might have contributed to the desire of Pilgram Marbeck to establish contact with Moravian Anabaptism and to counteract spiritualism there as he had done in Strasbourg and elsewhere.[272]

Interestingly enough, the only other important colloquy between the *Unitas Fratrum* and the Anabaptists again involved 'the Brethren', Czech and Anabaptist, residing at Ivančice. It did not take place until a generation later (1559). The participants on the Anabaptist side were not the spiritualizing Anabaptists but rather their opponents, the followers of Marbeck. We shall examine the record of the colloquy in the following chapter.

[270] Müller, 1910, 181.
[271] Outside of Silesia, Strasbourg was probably the main cradle of spiritualism in the Radical Reformation. "Spiritualism was clearly indigenous to Strasbourg and may well have influenced in that direction such Anabaptist refugees as Entfelder and Bünderlin" (Williams, 1962, 338). Cf. Williams' summary of the theology of Clement Ziegler (1524), *ibid.*, 245 ff. and 337 f.
[272] Cf. Bergsten, 1958b; Klassen, W., 1959 and Williams, 1962, 453 ff.

V

LATER CONTACTS

In contrast to the hopeful negotiations, for a merger in 1528, the later known contacts, personal or literary, between the Anabaptists and the Czech Brethren in Moravia were less amicable. None of the recorded colloquies was convened in order to reach an agreement. Rather, they represented unofficial enquiries by small local Anabaptist groups or individuals. The few preserved literary exchanges are even more indicative of the 'passive coexistence' which characterized the relationship between the two groups.

Apart from one or two meaningless references to the Picards in the Hutterite chronicles — which were copied from Franck's *Chronica* — the Anabaptist sources known to us do not contain a single direct mention of the *Unitas Fratrum*. The literary contacts, if they should be designated as such at all, and the records of colloquies were preserved with one exception (colloquy in 1543) in the sources of the Unity. There might have been other debates and written polemical exchanges. Most certainly, the opportunities for regular personal contacts were plentiful as our topographical studies will show.

In this brief chapter we shall not attempt to describe in detail the historical and theological background for each contact as we have done in the preceding chapters for the beginnings and origins of Anabaptism in Moravia. In most cases, the records are nearly self-explanatory and do not require a thorough-going analysis. Besides, the encounters between representatives of the two religious groups from 1529 onward are far less determinative for the basic issue of the historical and theological relationship between Anabaptism and the *Unitas Fratrum* than the initial contacts during the years 1526-1528.[1]

---

[1] See also our explanation in Chapter I at footnote 148.

1. THE PARTING ROAD

Without trying to sketch, even in the most condensed way, the historical and ideological development of Anabaptism and of the Unity during the one hundred years which extend from the deaths of Hubmaier and of Bishop Lukáš (1528) to the final expulsion of all non-Catholics from Moravia (1628), we shall point out two basic trends.[2]

In a general way, the outward history and the inner life of the Unity after the death of Bishop Lukáš may be characterized as a gradual approximation to the Magisterial Reformation, first the Lutheran and later the Calvinistic.[3] The trend affected the theological as well as the socio-ethical aspects of Czech Brethrenism.[4] Of necessity, such rapprochement also meant a growing estrangement from the Radical Reformation.[5]

Even though Molnár may be right in his thesis that the *Unitas Fratrum* never ceased to lead a dialogue between the "first" and "second" Reformation,[6] the outward and inward changes which took place in the Unity after 1528 — and in some respects already after 1495 — represented a deepening of the gulf which separated Czech Brethrenism from Anabaptism. Several bridges remained which should have facilitated understanding between the two groups. The Unity was still a free church, both in the political sense and as a gathered fellowship of believers. It also retained, to a surprising extent, its character as a disciplined community which did not hesitate to censure the misconduct of any member, whether of humble or noble origin.

Nevertheless, the gulf beneath these bridges became deeper and wider as the basic theological orientation of the Unity kept changing. In 1533, the German *Rechenschafft* of the Unity appeared in Witten-

---

[2] For the developments in the Unity, see Müller, II and III; Říčan, 1956; 1957a-b and 1961; Hrejsa, V and VI. No definitive history of Moravian Anabaptism has been written as yet. The following books and articles may be consulted: Loserth, 1894; Horsch, 1931a; Hrubý, 1935a; Friedmann's art. "Anabaptism in Moravia" in *ME*, III, 747 ff. and other articles reprinted in Friedmann, 1961a.

[3] Cf. the periodization quoted in Chapter I at note 51.

[4] See our discussion in Chapter I at notes 109 and 121 ff.

[5] We are employing this convenient terminology (Magisterial and Radical Reformation) suggested by Littell and Williams even though we cannot fully subscribe to it. Cf. Chapter I at footnote 92 ff.

[6] Cf. our summary and evaluation of Molnár's thesis in Chapter I beginning at footnote 121.

berg with Luther's preface[7] and a Latin Confession, endorsed even more fully by Luther, followed five years later.[8]

The most conspicuous change which was bound to affect the future relationship between the Unity and the Anabaptists was the abolition of rebaptism in 1534.[9] One of the stated reasons was the necessity to differentiate the position of the Unity from the teachings of the Anabaptists.[10] There can be little doubt that the decision was motivated not only by the changing theological orientation of the Czech Brethren but also by political considerations. The establishment of the 'Anabaptist kingdom' in Münster in the early spring of 1534 gave occasion to new suppressive steps against the Anabaptists in the Czech lands. In March the Bohemian diet decreed that all persons spreading Anabaptist views in Bohemia were to be punished immediately by barons, knights or by the councils of the royal cities. In extreme cases, the death penalty was to be imposed. Anabaptist refugees from other lands were to be delivered to the castle in Prague.[11] One month later (April 19), the synod of the Unity meeting at Mladá Boleslav, passed the decree abolishing rebaptism.[12]

The decision did not meet with unanimous approval among the membership at large. The preserved sources of the Unity refer only

[7] Another edition of the *Rechenschafft*, showing Zwinglian influence, was printed in Zürich in 1532. Both the Zürich and the 'corrected' Wittenberg editions were reprinted by Philipp Ulhart in Augsburg. On the history of the two editions and the theological differences, see Müller, II, 40 ff.; Štrupl, 1964a, 59 ff.; Molnár, 1952a, 130 ff.; Fast, 1959, 33, 164, 180, 188; Říčan, 1961a, 102 ff.

[8] *Confessio Fidei ac Religionis*. On its origin and significance see the references quoted in the preceding footnote (except Fast) and also Pelikan, 1946 and 1964, 125-146.

[9] Müller, II, 51 ff.; Říčan, 1961a, 104 f. The long decree by which the synod justified the abolition of rebaptism is printed in full (in Czech) by Gindely, 1865, 149-152.

[10] The decree recalls the practice of rebaptism in the days of Cyprian and the subsequent condemnation of rebaptism by Augustine. It also refers to contemporary writings of the Reformers against Anabaptists, "who in recent years revived many old heresies, Arian, Novatian and Donatist, and renewed the practice of rebaptism altogether and despised all who did not agree with them" (Gindely, 1865, 150).

[11] Czech text in Sněmy, I, 381. Similar measures against the Anabaptists were enforced also in Moravia. Cf. Hrubý, 1935a, 10 ff.

[12] See also the evaluation of the decree by Müller, II, 52 f.; Molnár, 1952a, 126 f. and Hrejsa, V, 50. The statement by Müller, II, 53 is worth noting: "Also nicht weil die Brüder sich von der Verwerflichkeit der Wiedertaufe überzeugt haben, sondern nur um Luther gefällig zu sein, haben sie wider besseres Wissen die Wiedertaufe abgeschafft." Molnár's interpretation is similar. On the concept of baptism and the theological justification of rebaptism in the theology of Lukáš, see Lukáš, 1521a-b; Müller, I, 466-486 and Molnár, 1948a, 89 ff.

to opposition in several congregations located east of Kroměříž (Kremsier) in Moravia.[13] One may assume that the disagreement with the synod's decree was more widespread.

However, such localized and short-lived protests could not reverse the general trend within the Unity towards a closer alignment, first with the Lutheran and then with the Reformed wing of the Reformation. The increasing proportion of ministers who were trained at Lutheran or Reformed universities and academies [14] accelerated the process. Repeated attempts were made to recall the Unity to the theological heritage of its own founders and early leaders, in particular to the position of Lukáš. One might even suggest that "during the time of its culminating theological creativity (1575-1612) the *Unitas Fratrum* placed itself doctrinally within the Reformed camp, but it did so by reclaiming the theological heritage of Brother Lukáš".[15]

Whatever classification one might choose to describe the successive stages in the theology of the Unity one fact cannot be questioned. Its theological development represents a shift from the left to the right if one regards Anabaptism, with Bainton, as part of the "Left Wing of the Reformation".[16]

A similar trend can be discerned in Moravian religious life in general. By the middle of the century, the two most vocal radical groups, the Habrovanites and the Minor Party of the Unity (under the leadership of Jan Kalenec) disappeared altogether. With few exceptions, the Utraquist church in Moravia yielded to the Lutheran Reformation during the second half of the century.[17] Most of the German-speaking parishes in Moravia became Lutheran as well.[18]

---

[13] The only record is preserved in *HF*, I, fols. 908-911 (summary in Šafařík, 1862, 206 f.). Three congregations (Holešov, Hulín and Záhlinice) which were under the pastoral care of Brother Valenta left the Unity until Valenta's death which followed soon after the split in 1534 or 1535. Two local barons were also involved in the opposition. Two other leaders are mentioned, Tůma "the Cutler" from Lipník and Brother Barton in Dřevohostice. All five places mentioned in the record are located east or north-east of Kroměříž and therefore outside the geographical area of Anabaptist settlements in Moravia (cf. Chapter VI). Unfortunately, the extensive correspondence between the leaders of the opposition and Jan Roh (referred to in *HF*) has not been preserved. Cf. also Müller, II, 53 f.

[14] Cf. the bibliography of lists of Czech students at foreign universities in Říčan, 1961a, 346. See also Odložilík, 1964, 13 f. (students in Geneva).

[15] Štrupl, 1964a, 480.

[16] Cf. Chapter I at footnote 91.

[17] Cf. the well-documented study, Hrubý, 1935c. Hrubý's conclusions were criticised by Hrejsa, 1938 but defended (with additional evidence) by Hrubý, 1939.

[18] Cf. Chapter II footnote 8.

The interest in the more radical streams of the Reformation — so typical of the situation in the 1520's and 1530's [19] — faded out altogether. Such a theological trend could not but increase the isolation of Anabaptist refugee congregations and colonies from the Moravian population, Czech and German.

If one seeks to describe a basic trend within Moravian Anabaptism one might call it a process of splintering. The long lists of Anabaptist sects published by several sixteenth-century authors [20] may be exaggerated. Yet our own topographical research has furnished evidence of no fewer than ten different groups in Moravia.[21] Some of these were short-lived but at least three could be classified as continuing groups which survived the vicissitudes of the 'Anabaptist century' in Moravia: the Hutterites, the Cornelians or Pilgramites (Marbeck fellowship) and the Swiss Brethren.[22] Other groups, such as the *Schwertler* (the followers of Hubmaier), the *Stäbler* (the non-resistant opponents of Hubmaier), the Austerlitz Brethren, the Philippites and the Gabrielites passed out of the picture before the middle of the century or, in the case of the Gabrielites, soon afterwards.[23]

Several factors contributed to the divisions among the Anabaptists,

[19]   See our analysis in Chapter II beginning at footnote 63.
[20]   See the comparison of four such lists with particular reference to Moravia (Varotto in 1567, Eder in 1573, Erhard in 1589 and Středovský in 1600) by DeWind, 1955a. Cf. Williams, 1962, 674 ff.
[21]   Cf. List D, Zeman, 1966, 96 ff. The list does not include "spiritualizing Anabaptists" (e.g., Entfelder's congregation at Ivančice) nor the Italian refugees many of whom showed anti-Trinitarian leanings.
[22]   An interesting Czech source, *Knížka Jana Kalence*, written by the leader of the Minor Party at Letovice on May 1, 1542, contains a series of censorious pronouncements against all religious groups in Moravia. Kalenec singled out only three Anabaptist groups by name. He praised the "Brethren from the upper lands" for their practice of believer's baptism and community of goods but objected to their spiritual pride and lack of love. They (i.e. the Hutterites) condemned all who did not practice community of goods. He rebuked the Sabbatarians for their "Jewish legalism". He criticized the Austerlitz Brethren for "holding erroneous beliefs with Athanasius" (Kalenec became an anti-Trinitarian) and tolerating harmful occupations among their brethren such as merchants, woodcarvers, painters, jewellers and innkeepers (Czech text in *AUF*, IV, fol. 221a-b; brief excerpts in Gindely, I, 508, n. 40; cf. Ch. IV, note 156). He also mentioned "all others who were baptized and differed from one another" but did not specify other groups by name.
[23]   On all these groups, see the corresponding articles in the *ML* and *ME* and our Group Analysis in Chapter VI. Referring to the recent identification of the Marbeck fellowship (the Pilgramites) as a separate group with a distinct theology, Friedmann stated: "I am sure that still other Anabaptist groups will be distinguished as research becomes more detailed and new sources are discovered" (Friedmann, 1958, 272).

particularly in Moravia. In his analysis of the schism between the Gabrielites, the Philippites and the Hutterites in 1533, Friedmann pointed out "two basic principles: the principle of liberty of conscience and the principle of charismatic authority or leadership".[24] In addition to these theological motives there were sociological and political factors involved in the process of splintering. The unusual degree of religious freedom in the margraviate minimized group cohesion and allowed for unlimited ecclesiastical pluralism.[25] More important, however, was the ethnic diversity within the Anabaptist camp.

Even though the vast majority of them were German-speaking, the refugees came from many geographical areas of Germany, Switzerland, Austria and Silesia. Their particular origin was betrayed by the dialect they spoke. In the schism of 1533, the theological differences were probably secondary to the ethnic contrasts between the (mainly) Tirolese followers of Jörg Zaunring, Simon Schützinger and Jakob Hutter (the Hutterites), the Swabian Phillipites and the Silesian Gabrielites.[26] Similar ethnic stratification played a role in the differentiation between the Pilgramites, chiefly of South German provenience, and the Swiss Brethren.[27]

From time to time, the splintering process was counteracted by genuine efforts to bring about reunion of divided groups. In some situations, such attempts succeeded. In other cases, they failed.[28]

The plurality of the Anabaptist movement in Moravia may be interpreted both as a negative and as a positive element in the rela-

---

[24] Friedmann, 1964a, 329.
[25] We have described the genesis of ecclesiastical pluralism and religious individualism in Moravia in our essay, Zeman, 1962, 3 ff. Cf. also Říčan, 1964b. One must not overemphasize religious liberty as a factor in Anabaptist schisms in Moravia. Most of them occurred during the 1530's and 1540's when Ferdinand tried to curtail the broad religious toleration and enforced two successive expulsions of Anabaptists. So far as we know there were no additional schisms during the second half of the century when the Anabaptists enjoyed the greatest freedom in Moravia.
[26] Cf. Friedmann, 1964a, 330.
[27] The role of ethnic stratification as a factor in religious pluralism can be observed today in Canada or the U.S.A. Immigrant and refugee communities, with both state church and free church backgrounds, have suffered repeated divisions which could be traced mainly to different areas of origin. In some cases, both parties involved in a split spoke the same language but represented different cultural strata.
[28] The Hutterite chronicles record several unions with the Philippites, Gabrielites and the Swiss Brethren, e.g. ZGL, 251 ff., 429 f., 258 ff. They also record Marbeck's vain efforts for unity in 1541 (ZGL, 224).

tionship between the Anabaptists and the Czech Brethren. On the one hand, the existence of several groups side by side, especially in such centers as Slavkov (Austerlitz) and Ivančice (Eibenschitz), could not but contribute to a general attitude of indifference. If one Anabaptist group was unable to reach some degree of understanding and enjoy fellowship with another Anabaptist group, how could it be expected to seek a rapprochement with the *Unitas Fratrum*? On the other hand, the lack of a centralized control rendered it possible for any local Anabaptist group to establish contact with the Czech Brethren if there were some particular reasons to warrant such interest. This in fact was the case in the few colloquies of which we learn from the preserved records.

2. THE COLLOQUIES BETWEEN THE ANABAPTISTS AND THE CZECH BRETHREN

a. *The Colloquy at Hustopeče (Auspitz) in 1543*

The only record of a debate which involved not only the Anabaptists and the 'Picards' but also the local Lutherans is a brief excerpt from local sources which was published in 1856.[29]

The brief record presents several problems of interpretation. So far as we know, the Czech Brethren did not have a congregation in the German town of Hustopeče although an unspecified source refers to their *sbor* (chapel) in the Czech suburb Böhmdorf.[30] It is most unlikely that in 1543 the *Unitas Fratrum* would have shared the parish church with the (German) Lutherans as the report of the colloquy claims.[31] Occasionally the term 'Picard' was applied, in Bohemia and

---

[29] "In eben diesem Jahr [1543] sammelten sich ohne denen Röhmisch-katholischen (welche nebst ihren Priester das Hospital-Kirchl innen hatten) dreierlei Glaubens-Genossen, als: lutherische und Pikartische (welche einander ziemlich gleich waren und die Pfarrkirchen in der Stadt im Besitz hatten), dann endlich die Wiedertauffer, welche ausserhalb der Stadt an der Strassen, wo man von hier nach Nikolsburg reiset, und der sogenannte Rayggen-Brunn befindlich, sich aufhielten; und vermeinte jede Sekt, sie hätten den wahren und rechten Glauben." The reference was printed, along with other excerpts, in a report entitled, "Abschrift der vom Herrn Bozek 1836 aus hiesigen Privilegien und sonstigen alten Schriften excerpirten Denk- und Merkwürdigkeiten der mähr. Stadt Auspitz in hist. Beziehung", in *Schriften der hist.-statist. Sektion* (ed. Chr. d'Elvert), Vol. IX (1856), 312 (published in Brno). We were unable to find anything more about the source or about the colloquy itself.

[30] Cf. Hrejsa, B, 35.

[31] In the latter part of the sixteenth century, ministers of the Unity are known to have been placed in charge of at least six Utraquist parish churches in Moravia

Moravia, not only to the Czech Brethren but also to any one who did not believe in the real presence of Christ (in the Roman Catholic sense of the term) in the eucharist. It is possible, therefore, that the source refers to two German congregations, one Lutheran and another with Zwinglian or other symbolic eucharistic theology, both of which were meeting in the parish church at Hustopeče. Nevertheless, one should not rule out altogether the *Unitas Fratrum*. The source claims that the Lutherans and the Picards were "very much alike". The Lutheran influence in the Unity reached its climax in the early 1540's and it is therefore possible that there was a small congregation of the Unity (Czech? German?) in Hustopeče in 1543 of which nothing else is known.

The identification of the Anabaptist group is also difficult. Both a Philippite and a Hutterite congregation existed in Hustopeče until the first major persecution in the year 1535. The Hutterites are known to have returned,[32] but it is extremely doubtful that they would have been involved in a colloquy with the Lutherans and the Picards. It is more probable that the Philippite Brethren reestablished their settlement at Hustopeče soon afer the persecution subsided.[33]

Whoever was involved in the debate in 1543, the participants could not reach agreement. Each side maintained that its faith was the true one.

b. *The Colloquy at Ivančice (Eibenschitz) and Znojmo (Znaim) in 1559*

In June 1558, Jan Blahoslav, recently-elected bishop of the *Unitas Fratrum*, moved to Ivančice. His arrival signalled not only a new era for the old congregation but also the removal of the main center of the Unity from Bohemia (Mladá Boleslav) to Moravia.

In the theological development of the *Unitas*, Jan Blahoslav (1523-

---

(see our introduction to List F in Chapter VI), among them one where they conducted both Czech and German services (Pohořelice). However, no such case has been known thus far from the middle of the century.

[32] Cf. the letter written by Hans Amon in the name of the congregation in Auspitz to the Brethren in Hesse in 1540, printed in *TQ Hesse*, 276 f.

[33] In his art. "Philipper" (*ML*, III, 367) Loserth claimed — perhaps on the basis of local sources — that the Philippites were able to stay at Auspitz till 1544. Friedmann, 1958, 275 f. assumes that they left A. in 1535. Cf. Zeman, 1966, 18 f. The exact localization of the Anabaptist colony "on the road to Nikolsburg, near Rayggen-Brunn" may facilitate the identification of the group if additional local or in-group sources are discovered.

1571) [34] represents the most admirable synthesis of the Czech Reformation with the beneficial influence of the German and Swiss Reformation as well as with the vision of the late Protestant humanism.

Blahoslav's parents were members of the Unity in the Moravian town of Přerov. After elementary education in the Brethren's schools, Blahoslav studied in Goldberg (Silesia, 1543), Wittenberg (1544), where he learned to know personally Luther, and especially Melanchthon, and in Königsberg (for three months in 1549). His studies in Basel (winter and spring, 1549-1550) were interrupted by sickness. In his early thirties he was sent by the Unity on four diplomatic missions to Vienna (1555-1557) where he tried in vain to present to Maximilian a petition asking for the release of Bishop Jan Augusta.[35] He became acquainted with Sebastian Pfauser, Maximilian's court preacher,[36] with the royal physician, Dr. Johann Crato of Crafftheim and with other prominent men.

Shortly after the thirty-five-year-old bishop established his residence at Ivančice, he was approached by Anabaptists living at Ivančice and Znojmo with a request for an interview or colloquy.

Since none of them spoke Czech or Latin and Blahoslav's knowledge of German was very limited, a German-speaking minister of the Unity's German congregation at Fulnek (North Moravia) was invited to meet with them and to serve as an interpreter. Blahoslav intended to be present and to lead the discussion. To his regret, he had to leave town for an extended journey on the very day on which Brother Jan Jelecký arrived from Fulnek. In Blahoslav's absence, the debate was conducted by Jelecký and by Václav Solín, minister in Třebíč.

---

[34] The most recent selected bibliography will be found in Škarka, 1958, 175 f. and Janáček, 1966, 154 f. For our present study, the following books and articles must be mentioned: Novotný, 1923 (the best symposium, including Hrejsa's analysis of Blahoslav's theology and its roots); Malínský, 1923; Urbánek, 1923; Odložilík, 1940 (the only brief essay on B. in English); Bartoš, 1964a, 92-98 and 1948a, 121-124 (Blahoslav's brief stay in Basel and contact with Sigismund Gelenius and Sebastian Castellio); a biographical sketch in Kaňák, 1957, 152-163; Škarka, 1958 (reprinted in a revised form in Hrabák, 1959, 363-379) and Janáček, 1966 (biography). On Blahoslav as historian of the Unity, see Krofta, 1946, 81-119. An anthology from Blahoslav's writings appeared in Blahoslav, 1949. The sources for Blahoslav's four diplomatic journeys to the court in Vienna, 1555-1557, and his visit to Magdeburg in 1556 were reprinted by Zelinka, 1942, 91-183. Several shorter treatises and sources related to his educational work were printed by Molnár, 1956a.

[35] On Augusta and his long imprisonment (1548-1564), see the sources reprinted in Bílek, 1942. Cf. also Odložilík, 1940 (in English).

[36] In 1558, Pfauser interceded on behalf of a Hutterite prisoner, Conrad Schuster, who was then released by Maximilian (ZGL, 396; cf. also Fast, 1959, 43, n. 201).

Solín wrote a summary (*krátká suma*) of the discussions in Ivančice (April 17) and Znojmo (April 18). It is our only source.[37]

The Anabaptists were represented by their minister (*správce*), Balcar 'the cabinet maker' (*truhlář*), and an unnamed tanner (*jirchář, Weissgerber*). Balcar admitted that his brethren approved of the teachings of the Unity, except in the following articles which they wished to have clarified: (1) the procedures followed in the reception of new members; (2) steps in church discipline according to the rule of Christ (Matthew 18:15-17); (3) the biblical basis of infant baptism as practised in the Unity; (4) Christian participation in magistracy which involves the duty to condemn evildoers to death.

The Anabaptist spokesmen expressed their general approval of the Unity's position in the first two questions only. They did not state clearly their views on Christian magistracy. The main discussion concerned infant baptism which was condemned by Balcar as "an institution of the Antichrist and of the pope".[38] Balcar claimed that the original Unity had not baptized infants at all. When questioned, he admitted that he had heard about it from "the splintered brethren" (*odtrženci*), i.e., members of the Minor Party.

Afterwards, Jelecký addressed five questions to Balcar. (1) What order do his brethren follow in choosing and appointing elders? Balcar replied that they observed no particular rules. Anyone who was moved by the Spirit unto such responsibility was granted the authority.

(2) In what way do his brethren differ from other Anabaptists and how many groups (sects) are there? Balcar stated: "We are different

---

[37] The account of the two colloquies (Ivančice and Znojmo) is preserved twice: *AUF*, IX, fols. 255a-262b and X, fols. 134b-142a. According to the latest research by Štěříková, an anonymous scribe copied the text of Vol. IX (from original documents) in 1565-1566 under the direct guidance and supervision of Blahoslav in Ivančice. The completed volume did not contain all materials that should have been included for the years 1558-1566. The next volume (X) duplicates, therefore, the years 1558-1566 which were already covered, in part, by Vol. IX, and then continues until 1569. It was written by Ondřej Štefan under the direction of Vavřinec Orlík, probably during the last two years of Blahoslav's life (1570-1571). Cf. Štěříková, 1964, 101 ff. See also our Appendix I. The preserved manuscript in *AUF*, IX is a copy made from the original record which was written by Václav Solín, a participant in the colloquies. Blahoslav read the account in Vol. IX and added one marginal note. A critical edition of the Czech text (based on Vol. IX but compared with the text in Vol. X) was published by Zeman, 1958, 39-43 and 53-57. A German translation, in part verbatim, in part abbreviated and not without a few minor mistakes, was published by Müller, 1910, 197-208.

[38] We do not reproduce the arguments since they can be followed in the Czech or German texts published by Zeman, 1958 or Müller, 1910.

from all other sects, including the Sabbatarians and the Communitarians (*společníci*, i.e., the Hutterites). The Communitarians have all been excommunicated from our brotherhood."

(3) When Balcar was asked how many Anabaptists there were, he replied: "There are many in Moravia, Bohemia, Switzerland and in the Upper Lands".[39]

(4) As for the time and place of their origin, Balcar stated: "Our group began about thirty-six years ago [1523], in the days of Zwingli".[40]

(5) Finally, Balcar was asked whether he had ever belonged to another Anabaptist group. He replied that he had always been with the same group.

On the next day, April 18, Jelecký and Solín met with an unnamed Anabaptist watchmaker in the city of Znojmo. He had been acquainted with Solín and with several members of the Unity in Ivančice for some time and had asked repeatedly for an interview. Many years earlier he had bought a printed German *Apology* [41] of the Czech Brethren. He became interested in their teachings and when he found out that they lived in Moravia he left "the Upper Lands" and settled in Znojmo. Because he was a skilled craftsman the citizens of Znojmo protected him, even against Ferdinand's orders of expulsion.[42]

The discussion at Znojmo was focused mainly on the question of baptism. Two other issues were mentioned briefly. The watchmaker claimed that the writings of the Unity contained contradictions in the concept of the eucharist. He paged through a catechism and another book "on the body and blood of the Lord" [43] but could not find any statements in support of his accusation. On the issue of Christian

---

[39]   The mountainous regions of South Germany and Austria. Cf. the interpretations of "oben" (letter of Hans Felix in 1538) listed in *ME*, IV, 444 and a similar reference to "bratří z horních zemí" by Jan Kalenec in 1542 (Urban, 1966, 21).

[40]   It should be noted that Balcar did not refer explicitly to Zürich as the place of origin of the Anabaptist movement. However, the mention of Zwingli's name and the (approximate!) dating in 1523 should likely be accepted as an indication that Balcar's group was conscious of the Zwinglian background of Anabaptism. Cf. *ZGL*, 42 ff. and Blanke in *MQR*, 31 (1957), 220.

[41]   Probably one of the several editions of the *Rechenschafft* printed in 1532 f. Cf. footnote 7 above.

[42]   Probably in 1535, or in 1547 ff.

[43]   The German catechism could have been either one of the many editions of the *Kinderfragen* (1522 ff.), or the German catechism of Johann Gyrck (1554 f). However, Gyrck's catechism did not contain any questions on the sacraments. Cf. Appendix 4 and 6. It is impossible to identify the other (German) book dealing with the eucharist.

magistracy, he did not express any of his own views but promised to consider the position of the Unity. The report on the interview in Znojmo closes with the comment: "So the second disputation ended again almost without any benefit."

Meanwhile, according to the same source, Balcar "and his brethren" held a consultation at Ivančice on Wednesday (April 19), and "perhaps for three days". After Brother Jelecký [44] left Ivančice, Balcar sent a note to Solín on which someone had copied the German, Latin and Greek text of Matthew 18:6 together with a quotation from Erasmus' *Annotationes*.[45] The quoted text had not been debated on Monday. In his written reply to Balcar, Solín expressed surprise as well as bitter resentment of "the foolish attempt" of the unlearned Anabaptists to impress the well-educated ministers of the Unity with Greek letters. "For believe me", he added, "we do not take the Word of God and the Sacred Scriptures lightly, nor do we misuse them for polemics.... If someone showed me — as we did for you — the teachings of the Scriptures so clearly that I could not refute them honestly but only reject them in sheer stubborness, I would search for the truth in a different way."

Which Anabaptist group was represented by Balcar, the anonymous tanner of Ivančice and the unnamed watchmaker in Znojmo?

The title of the Czech report on the two debates refers to the "Austerlitz Anabaptists".[46] We do not know whether the title was part of the original record written by Solín, or whether it was provided later by the editor of the particular volume of the *Acta Unitatis Fratrum*. However, the manuscript contains also a marginal note written by Blahoslav: "The Gabrielites and not the Communitarians."

Blahoslav's note was accepted without questioning by Müller and his identification of the group has been perpetuated by Wiswedel and, until recently, by Friedmann.[47]

The scholarly report on *Codex Kunstbuch* by Heinold Fast in 1956

---

[44] On Jelecký and Solín, cf. the biographical note by Müller, 1910, 197.

[45] First ed. (Basel, 1519), 60. We have not been able to identify the particular edition used by Balcar. Erasmus' biblical works were also used by Hubmaier (*HS*, 233), by the Hutterites (Friedmann, 1965b, 40 and 98) and by Kalenec (Urban, 1966, 23).

[46] "*Krátká suma rozmlouvání toho, kteréž mezi Bratřími, jenž slovou Boleslavští, a mezi těmi, jenž slovou Novokřtěnci Austrličtí, bylo ...*" (Zeman, 1958, 38).

[47] Müller, 1910, 194; Wiswedel, 1937a, 8; Friedmann's art. "Gabrielites", *ME*, II, 429. Friedmann, 1949, 31 seems to imply that the contacts involved the Hutterites. Friedmann, 1962, 352 refers to the Marbeck group.

furnished for us the initial clue for a different identification of Balcar's group. There can be no doubt that the leader of the Anabaptist congregation at Ivančice, Balcar 'the cabinet maker', is identical with "Balthasar Grasbanntner, Tischler zů Eybenschůtz" who signed, along with four other elders, a letter written to Pilgram Marbeck at Ivančice on March 19, 1553.[48] The Czech record of the colloquy in 1559 thus provides additional important evidence for the existence of the "Marbeck fellowship" (the Pilgramites) in Moravia. The original identification of Balcar's group with the Anabaptists of Austerlitz was probably based on the fact that the Pilgramite Anabaptist group in Ivančice had connections with Austerlitz where there also existed a Marbeck group.[49] The Czech Brethren had an old and large congregation there.

Nothing is known thus far about Balthasar's origin and life prior to 1553. Sometime after 1559, he must have moved to Znojmo. Local sources there report that on October 23, 1571, Balthasar Tischler, Hans Truchel, a woman and an old glazier were expelled by the city council.[50]

The unnamed tanner who accompanied Balthasar might be identical with Sebastian Neudorfer, a tanner (*Weissgerber*) from Chur (Switzerland) who was a personal friend of Leopold Scharnschlager, co-leader of the Marbeck brotherhood. According to an unconfirmed hypothesis of Traugott Schiess, Neudorfer was sent by Scharnschlager's widow as a messenger from Ilanz to Moravia in 1563.[51]

The anonymous watchmaker in Znojmo — who was acquainted with Balcar — was perhaps Hans Felix Uhrmacher, the son-in-law of Leopold Scharnschlager.[52] He first went to Moravia with his wife

[48]   *Kunstbuch*, fol. 170a: "Von uns Dienern. Ander Schůster zů Aussserlutz. Peter Fruewirt [Feuerwirt?] vmb den Stein vnd zů Boppitz [Poppitz]. Balthasar Grassbanntner Tischler zů Eybenschütz. Růp Dachennsteiner Pfannenschmid am Wald vnd zů Jemnitz vnd Bastel Schlosser zů Wien. Vnd von den elteren vnd gemainen im Lande Merhern euere Br. im Herren Christo." (Cf. Fast, 1956, 233, n. 85.) On the same folio, there are greetings from the same six congregations (named) in Moravia to which is added "Znům" [Znaim] and Wien. The letter is dated "am Sonntag Judica anno 1553" (March 19; *ME*, IV, 1062 dates it October 7). The identification of Balcar with Balthasar Tischler was suggested by Zeman, 1958, 42, n. 14 and reported in a paper read at an Anabaptist Seminar in Elkhart, Indiana, in June 1959. Subsequently, it was included by William Klassen in his art. "Balthasar Grassbanntner" and "Uhrmacher" in *ME*, IV, 1062 f. and 1131.
[49]   Cf. the signature of Ander Schůster in Austerlitz (footnote 48) and additional data on Austerlitz in Zeman, 1966, 19 ff.
[50]   See Loserth's art. "Znaim", *ME*, IV, 1034 and Dedic, 1922, 285. The expulsion from Znaim is not mentioned in the art. "Balthasar Grassbanntner" (*ME*, IV, 1062).
[51]   Schiess, 1916, 88. Cf. also Doornkaat, 1926, 332.
[52]   The identification was first proposed to us by William Klassen in 1959 (cf.

Ursula in the mid-thirties [53] and on October 29, 1538 he wrote a letter
to his parents-in-law from Austerlitz.[54] These known data are seem-
ingly contradicted by the statements made by the unnamed watchmaker in Znojmo during the colloquy in 1559. According to his words,
he settled in Znojmo immediately after his arrival in Moravia "from
the Upper Lands". Hans Felix is known to have visited his in-laws at
Ilanz, probably more than once, during the years 1546-1559. He might
have established his residence in Znojmo when he returned from one
of his trips "to the Upper Lands". Such interpretation is supported
by the known fact that the second husband of the deceased Ursula,
Stoffel Krieger, a weaver, and a daughter from the second marriage
(Esther) lived in Znojmo in 1565.[55]

Our identification of the Anabaptist congregations at Ivančice and
Znojmo in 1559 as part of the Marbeck fellowship has furnished a
new and important link for the chain of fragmentary evidence which
proves the continued existence of the Pilgramite group in Moravia
from the early 1530's until the final expulsion of all Anabaptists
in 1622.

Pilgram Marbeck himself [56] probably was in Moravia several times.
He might have visited the margraviate already in the late spring of

footnote 48) and then incorporated in his art. "Uhrmacher" in *ME*, IV, 1131. See
also the art. "Scharnschlager", *ME*, IV, 443 ff. (with extensive bibliography) and
Schiess, 1916. Cf. Hein, 1939 (letter to Moravia in 1546).
[53] Klassen (*ME*, IV, 444 and 1131) suggests 1533; Schiess, 1916, 81 refers to
"about 1535". Klassen's date is probably based on his identification of Hans Felix
with Hans of Strasbourg who defended Gabriel Ascherman against Jakob Huter
in 1533 (*ZGL*, 116). If this were correct one might wonder whether the Marbeck
group in Ivančice and Znojmo maintained friendly relations with the Gabrielites.
Cf. Blahoslav's marginal note!
[54] Printed in full by Schiess, 1916, 81 ff.
[55] Leopold Scharnschlager died at Ilanz in the spring of 1563. The widow sent a
messenger (Sebastian Neudorfer, Weissgerber?) to Moravia to request her daughter
and her second husband — Hans Felix Uhrmacher must have died before 1563 —
to come to Ilanz to live with her. Before the messenger returned, the widow had
passed away. In any case, he had not been able to find the couple in Moravia.
A second messenger dispatched to Moravia by a court (which was disposing of the
inheritance) met only the second husband and a daughter. They lived at Znojmo.
Ursula had died meanwhile. The court finally (March 1566) divided the inheritance
between the daughter from the second marriage and two sons from the first marriage. See Schiess, 1916, 88 f. (summary of the court proceedings) and Loserth,
1928b, 9 ff.
[56] See the list of bibliography on Marbeck in *TQ*, X, Nos. 1848-1873. The most
important recent works are Fast, 1956; Kiwiet, 1957a; Klassen, W., 1958, 1966a-b
and 1968; Bender, 1964 and art. "Marpeck" in *ME*, III.

1528 on his way to Strasbourg.[57] In 1533 it was reported at a trial in Speyer that Marbeck had been commissioned (ordained) as an elder by the church in Moravia.[58] On January 26, 1531, Wilhelm Reublin wrote a letter to Marbeck from Hustopeče in which he described the recent split at Slavkov.[59] From the 1530's, the daughter of Marbeck's closest associate, Scharnschlager, lived at Slavkov.[60] Marbeck might have been in Moravia on several occasions after his expulsion from Strasbourg (January 1532) but the only recorded visits are the one with Wolfgang Sailer in Slavkov in May 1540 [61] and the other in 1541 when he visited the Hutterite colony at Šakvice on an unsuccessful mission "to unite all Anabaptists".[62]

A congregation which recognized Marbeck's and Scharnschlager's leadership existed in Slavkov certainly in the 1540's and afterwards but it may be postulated for the late 1530's after the persecution in 1535.[63] Their leader in the 1540's was Cornelius Veh [64] after whom they were called, at least in Slavkov, the Cornelians.[65] His closest associate and afterwards his successor was a certain Paul, "a German who also spoke Italian".[66] The *Codex Kunstbuch* contains a number

---

[57] A letter of King Ferdinand written in Prague on July 2, 1528 and sent to Český Krumlov mentions that "Pilgram Marchpeckh" — who had been the initiator of Anabaptism in the Inn Valley — was reportedly staying with his wife on the estate of Český Krumlov. Winter, 1895, 308 and Mareš, 1907, 26. Ferdinand's letter is preserved in the Archives at Třeboň in Bohemia.

[58] *TQ*, IV, 422. Cf. Bender, 1964, 241 f., n. 40.

[59] Cornelius, II, 253 ff. and *TQ*, VII, 300 f. (Eng. tr. in *MQR*, 23 [1949], 69-75). Cf. Bender, 1964, 243 f.

[60] See footnotes 53 and 54 above.

[61] *CS*, VII, 161-167. Marbeck visited Wolfgang Sailer whom he knew from Strasbourg. He also acted as letter carrier between Sailer and Schwenckfeld (in Augsburg).

[62] *ZGL*, 224. It is quite possible that the dating in the Hutterite chronicle should be corrected to 1540, in which case there was only one visit (1540). Cf. Fast, 1956, 230 f.

[63] On October 29, 1538, Hans Felix (Uhrmacher) wrote to his father-in-law Leopold Scharnschlager: ". . . dass ich alhie zu Austerlitz . . . imerdar gewesen und mit der bruederschafft im herrnn daselbst ainig gelebt, wölche ich erkhennt hab mit uns zu gleichen glauben steundt, wie du villiecht vorhin wol vernumen und jetzo durch unnsere gesanndten zu euch noch völliger vernemen magst . . ." (Schiess, 1916, 82). Cf. footnote 54 above.

[64] See art. "Veh" in *ME*, IV, 803. Cf. *ZGL*, 224 (1541 or 1540); Fast, 1956, 231; Kiwiet, 1957, 158.

[65] The earliest mention of the Cornelians is preserved in the report of Marcantonio Varotto on his visit in Slavkov in 1567 (printed by DeWind, 1955a, 45). Local town registers report Cornelians and Pilgramites for the period 1598-1617 (see Zeman, 1966, 22).

[66] DeWind, 1955a, 45 (Varotto's report in 1567). Paul is mentioned already in

of letters which were exchanged between the 'Pilgramite' congregations in Moravia and Marbeck in the 1540's and 1550's.[67] The most
noteworthy of these is the reply sent to Marbeck in the name of five
ministers and seven congregations located in Moravia in March 1553.[68]

One might expect that after the death of Marbeck (1556) the loose
and scattered fellowship of the Pilgramite Brethren would gradually
disintegrate. One could also suspect that the contact with the *Unitas
Fratrum* which the Marbeck group at Ivančice and Znojmo initiated
in 1559 was due, in part, to a feeling of uncertainty typical of "sheep
without a shepherd". However, such was not the case. Leopold
Scharnschlager lived till 1563. His and Marbeck's writings continued
to exercise influence in Moravia. A letter written at Klein Teschau in
1579 confirms the existence of the Marbeck brotherhood in Moravia.[69]
This source has been regarded until now as the latest reference to
the Marbeck fellowship anywhere.[70]

Our topographical research has brought to light out-group sources
which demonstrate the presence of the Pilgramites and Cornelians, at
least at Slavkov, until the final expulsion of Anabaptists from Moravia.[71] The two names were obviously used interchangeably to designate the same group.[72]

Marbeck's correspondence with Moravia preserved in *Kunstbuch*, e.g., Marbeck's
letter to Moravia and Alsace in 1544: "... du meiner geliebter und geschenkter
sun nach dem glaub, Cornellj, vnd du mein geliebter B. Paul ..." (fol. 8a). Cf.
Fast, 1956, 231 ff., notes 79 and 88; Kiwiet, 1957, 158, n. 26.
[67]   Cf. the list (Nos. 1, 3, 16, 17, 24 and 37) and analysis by Fast, 1956, 214 ff.
and 230 ff. See also Kiwiet, 1957, 154 ff.
[68]   *Kunstbuch*, fol. 170a. See note 48 above. Kiwiet, 1957, 158 assumed that Marbeck was dealing with the Hutterites. Fast, 1956, 233 pointed out that only one of
the ministers whose names appear on the letter to Marbeck in 1553 is known also
as a Hutterite "Diener der Notdurft": Bastel Schlosser (Wardeiner) (*ZGL*, 63, 72,
321). In our opinion, the identification of the two men is not at all certain, particularly since Bastel's congregation was located in Vienna in 1553.
[69]   Ms. Codex III, 19, fols. 12a-13b (University Library in Olomouc). Loserth,
1928b, 11 and 1929a, 35 and 52. Cf. art. "Scharnschlager", *ME*, IV, 444 and
topographical analysis in Zeman, 1966, 79. See also Loserth, 1925b (Pilgramite
correspondence with Moravia in 1559).
[70]   Friedmann in *ME*, III, 749. Cf. also Bender, 1964, 252, n. 65, for a list of all
sources known to Bender (and William Klassen) which mention the Pilgramites
(Billgere, Bilgisch) as a separate Anabaptist group. Only Erhard, 1589 (cf. DeWind,
1955a, 49) dates from a period after 1579.
[71]   See footnote 65 above. The Pilgramite and Cornelian brethren jointly held
properties in Slavkov (records for the years 1597-1617). The Cornelian sect is
mentioned as late as 1632.
[72]   This is borne out by the fact that none of the lists of sects published by DeWind,
1955, 48 ff., includes both the Pilgramites and the Cornelians. Similarly, a letter

The relationship between the Marbeck brotherhood and the Swiss Brethren has not been defined satisfactorily up to the present. Kiwiet underscored the contrasts between the theology of the Swiss Brethren and that of Marbeck and South German Anabaptism in general.[73] Bender, Bergsten and William Klassen tend to minimize the doctrinal differences.[74]

The issue involves both historical relationships in terms of church organization and leadership, and theological concepts. If we limit our observations to the Moravian scene, it is most difficult to make a theological comparison between the two groups for the simple reason that practically nothing is known at the present time about the doctrinal position of the Swiss Brethren in Moravia, particularly during the latter part of the sixteenth and the early seventeenth centuries. One of the most striking differences between the Swiss and the Pilgramite Brethren was the wavering attitude toward Christian magistracy displayed by the Pilgramites at the colloquies in 1559 and attested elsewhere.[75] It should be recalled that the same issue loomed large in the protracted controversy between the Major and Minor Parties of the *Unitas Fratrum.*

In terms of organizational relationship, the Cornelians, the Pilgramites and the Swiss Brethren seem to have constituted, in Moravia, one basic type of Anabaptism which existed under one of the three names in different localities. The nomenclature was determined largely by the personal ties of the local leaders with Anabaptist groups and leaders in other countries.[76] Different ethnic origin (Swiss, South German) no doubt contributed to the differentiation.[77]

---

describing the sects at Mikulov in 1568, mentions only the Cornelians. Cf. Zeman, 1966, 58.

[73]   Kiwiet, 1957, 40 ff. and 154 f.

[74]   Bender, 1964, 249 ff. (Bender's last statement on the subject); Bergsten, 1958, 65 f.; Klassen, W., 1958, 229 and his art. "Scharnschlager" in *ME*, IV, 443 ff.

[75]   Out-group sources in Slavkov report that the Pilgramites took part in municipal government, paid taxes, loaned money, etc. Marbeck himself seems to have taken a mediating position between the consistent apolitism of the early Swiss Brethren and Hubmaier's endorsement of Christian magistracy. Cf. *TQ Elsass*, I, 505 f.; Bergsten, 1958, 87 ff. and 1961, 488. See also Scharnschlager's brief tract, "Ob ein Christ Obrigkeit sein mag" (*Kunstbuch*, fols. 246b-247b).

[76]   We have reached this conclusion on the basis of our topographical research. E.g., local out-group sources in Ivančice and Znojmo know only the Swiss Brethren but the Pilgramites are attested there by in-group sources. At Mikulov and Slavkov, local sources mention the Cornelians (the Pilgramites) but not the Swiss Brethren (except in Varotto's list). In some places, both groups are reported, but at different times.

[77]   See our discussion at footnote 27 above.

A more thoroughgoing historical analysis of the colloquy in 1559 would examine the wider context of contemporary events in Moravian Anabaptism and in the *Unitas Fratrum*. In particular, one might notice the attitude of Melanchthon, a personal friend of Blahoslav, towards the Anabaptists. In 1557, Melanchthon signed, with other Lutheran theologians, a treatise condemning the Anabaptists and endorsing the strictest legal measures against them.[78]

The synod of the Unity held in Žeravice in 1559 issued instructions to its members concerning Christian participation in war. War was described as "a terrible scourge of God". The Brethren should not volunteer for military service. But if they were conscripted for militia service they should "conduct themselves in all things submissively, obediently and humbly, stand up for the common good, so that they would not be reckoned as traitors or Anabaptists, and should not say: 'I do not know; let the Turk come if he must etc.'".[79]

The colloquy in 1559 might be compared with other colloquies in which the Czech Brethren were involved during the same decade.[80] Similarly one might place side by side the articles discussed at Ivančice and Znojmo and those which were the basis for negotiations between Anabaptist groups such as the Swiss Brethren and the Hutterites in 1556 and 1557.[81] But such broad analysis would take us far beyond the scope and purpose of our present study.

c. *The Colloquy in 1565*

In the year 1560 the *Unitas Fratrum* established official contacts with the Swiss Reformers.[82] In May, Peter Herbert and Jan Rokyta left

[78] *Prozess wie es soll gehalten werden mit den Wiedertäufern.* The Hutterites issued their own answer to it, *Handbüchlein wider den Prozess* .... Cf. *TQ*, I, 161-168; Wiswedel, III, 171-183; Friedmann, 1962a, 221 ff. (*ME*, II, 645 f.); Oyer, 1964, 177 f.

[79] The Czech text in Gindely, 1865, 202. Cf. Brock, 1957, 272.

[80] In particular, the record of the debate with the Lutheran theologians in Königsberg (Prussia) in 1548 (Czech text printed in full by Sliziński, 1958, 152-199; reference to Anabaptism on p. 164) and the discussions with the delegates of the Polish Unity at Lipník in 1558 (Gindely, 1865, 188-201). The former practice of rebaptism in the Unity was discussed in Poland (1556 and 1559) between the Polish branch of the Unity and the Polish Reformed church (cf. Williams, 1959, 228).

[81] *ZGL*, 357 ff. (Beck, 225 ff.) and 384.

[82] The sources for our brief résumé are printed in Gindely, 1859, 185 ff. The extended mission of Peter Herbert is described by Müller, III, 102ff.; Hrejsa, V, 275 ff.; Bartoš, 1956b, 137 ff. and Bidlo, 1900, 236 ff. The first contact with

Bohemia to visit the main centers of the Swiss Reformation. They were to clarify the doctrinal position of the Unity on which the Reformers had received conflicting and distorted reports from Poland.

On the way, the two emissaries met P. P. Vergerius in Göppingen (near Stuttgart), Duke Christoph of Würtemberg and his Chancellor, Johann Brenz. The contacts in Switzerland were made by Herbert alone. In Zürich he held discussions with Heinrich Bullinger and Pietro Martire Vermigli but also visited Lelio Sozzini unofficially. In Bern, he talked with Wolfgang Musculus and finally, in Geneva he met with Calvin several times, as well as with Beza, Viret and other ministers. On the way home, Herbert again saw Vergerius in Tübingen.

The Swiss journey was not the only important task entrusted to the young minister by the leaders of the Unity. In 1564, he translated a new Czech confession into German and accompanied two barons, members of the Unity, to Vienna where a copy was presented to Maximilian.[83] Two years later, he prepared — with two other German-speaking ministers of the Unity, Michael Tham and Johann Jelecký — a new edition of the German hymnbook and took part in a cere-monial presentation of a copy to Maximilian.[84]

Who was Peter Herbert? He was born in Fulnek and brought up in the German congregation of the Unity. He began his preparation for the ministry there as helper to the local minister, Michael Tham. In 1557 he studied in Wittenberg, five years later he was ordained minister of the Unity and in 1567 he was elected to the central council. After Jelecký's death in 1568, Herbert became pastor of the German congregation at Fulnek. He died at a young age at Ivančice on October 1, 1571, a few weeks before the premature death of Blahoslav, his close friend. With his gifts, education and dedication to the task, Herbert was regarded by his contemporaries as the second leading man of the Unity. The *Necrologue* praised him as "an exceptional, conscientious and hard-working man, extremely well educated and better known to the learned men in other countries than anyone else in the Unity".[85]

Calvin took place during Matěj Červenka's visit in Strasbourg in 1540 (see the sources printed in Gindely, 1859, 40 f. and 68 f. and Zelinka, 1942, 84 f.).

[83] Müller, II, 409 and Hrejsa, VI, 20. Herbert was also asked to prepare a Latin translation but did not find time to do so (Hrejsa, VI, 188).

[84] Müller, II, 379 ff. and Hrejsa, VI, 69 f.

[85] Todtenbuch, 255. The text also contains the following words of Blahoslav:

This was the man who, in 1565, met with an Anabaptist, Martinus Behem of Bzenec and engaged in a theological debate on the new birth, predestination, Adam's nature and Christ's, and the work of redemption. The manuscript source (*Anabaptistarum Sententia* and *Responsio P. Herberti*)[86] does not provide any information beyond the two names and a series of Latin theses. We do not know where the debate took place[87] nor by whom and for what reasons it was initiated. The record seems to consist of notes written hastily by Herbert after the colloquy. The disputation itself might have been held in the German language. We were unable to identify the particular Anabaptist group which was involved in this last recorded disputation. Perhaps Martin Behem was not attached to any congregation.

On November 29, 1565, Peter Herbert and others met with the Lutheran Count Johann Friedrich of Hardegg at his castle at Letovice to discuss "the basic agreement" between the Lutherans (*Confessio Augustana*) and the *Unitas Fratrum*. A few weeks later, the leaders of the Unity agreed, with considerable hesitation, that their members on the Count's domains should join the local Lutheran parishes under certain conditions.[88]

Herbert's manifold contacts with the Lutheran and Reformed theo-

---

O quam te memorem semper doctissime Petre?
Quo vivente mihi vivere dulce fuit,
Quis fueras praesens non vidit postera tandem
Aetas heu sentit, sentiet illa magis.
PIB [Preroviensis Joannes Blahoslav]

Similar words of appreciation were written by Esrom Rüdinger, rector of the school at Ivančice (1575-1588) in the preface to his *Psalmorum Paraphrasis*, Book Three, in 1579 (reprinted in Molnár, 1956a, 214). Rüdinger had known Herbert from his studies in Wittenberg. Cf. also Regensvolscius, 1652, 327.

[86] The Latin record is preserved in *AUF*, X, fols. 273b-275b, and is printed, for the first time, in our Appendix 7. The Latin text was probably written by Herbert himself in 1565 and then copied by Ondřej Štefan into the tenth volume of *AUF* at Ivančice some time before Herbert's death in 1571 (cf. note 37 above and Appendix 1).

[87] The designation of the Anabaptist spokesman, Martinus Behem of Bzenec, does not necessarily imply that the debate took place at Bzenec. There was a Hutterite colony at B., 1545-1547, and an earlier Gabrielite settlement. In 1556, Anabaptists were reported on the domain of B. (see Zeman, 1966, 24). The name Martin Behem does not appear in any published Anabaptist sources. The name might imply a person of Bohemian (Czech) origin, or one who came from Bohemia. It is doubtful that he can be identified with "Martinus zu Pfedersheim" mentioned in 1563 (*TQ*, IV, 161).

[88] Cf. Gindely, 1865, 217 f.; Müller, II, 394 f. and Hrejsa, VI, 42 f.

logians which we have outlined above make it obvious that there was little hope for an agreement between the Czech Brethren and the genuine members of any Anabaptist group in 1565.

3. A CZECH DEFENSE OF INFANT BAPTISM WRITTEN AGAINST THE ANABAPTISTS (1589)

One of the best illustrations of the unique position of the *Unitas Fratrum* within the sixteenth-century Reformation is the fact that the Czech Brethren, with one known exception, never directly attacked the Anabaptists. After the death of Lukáš (1528), the Unity moved closer and closer to the Lutheran, and later to the Calvinistic Reformation. The leaders of the Unity maintained personal and literary contacts with most Reformers in Germany and Switzerland. But in contrast to men like Bullinger, Luther, Melanchthon, Urbanus Rhegius, Calvin and many others, all of whom published fierce attacks against the Anabaptists,[89] the Czech Brethren never released a printed polemic against them. The fact stands out even more when one recalls the numerous polemical and apologetical writings which were issued officially in the name of the Unity against such varied camps as the Roman Catholics, the Utraquists, the Habrovanite Brethren, the Minor party of the Unity and the Zwinglian wing within the Unity led by Zeising in the 1520's.[90]

In the present context we shall not discuss the possible reasons for such peace with the Anabaptists. It might have been motivated, sometimes, by an awareness of a basic affinity with the Radical Reformation,[91] or by an unusual appreciation of religious toleration,[92] or perhaps, by sheer indifference towards the isolated communities of

---

[89]   Cf. the many titles listed in *TQ*, X, Nos. 3543 ff. See also the analysis of these writings by Horsch, 1931b-c; Fast, 1959; Oyer, 1964 and others.

[90]   Cf. our discussion of the polemics with the last three groups in Chapter II and IV.

[91]   Cf. Molnár's thesis on the dialogue between the first and second Reformation in the Unity (Chapter I at note 121).

[92]   The best example of how the Czech Brethren, even during the period of their pro-Lutheran orientation, defended the concept of a free church, is the letter of Bishop Jan Augusta to Bucer and Capito in Strasbourg, in July 1541. Augusta asked Bucer for permission to omit in the Czech translation of his book, *Von der wahren Seelsorge* (1538), the section dealing with the right of the state to coercion in matters of religion ("cogite intrare"). See Molnár, 1951, 142 (Augusta's letter) and Molnár, 1949b, 201 f. and 1950, 317 f. (Molnár's commentary).

Anabaptist refugees in Moravia. Most likely, all three motives contributed, at different times, to the 'peaceful coexistence'. No Anabaptist polemical writings against the Unity are known. Since there were no attacks, there was no need for replies.

The only polemical treatise written against the Anabaptist rejection of infant baptism and of original sin has been preserved in a manuscript codex from the year 1589. No one thus far has paid any attention to the short work entitled *A Letter Written to Lord F. of Ž. against the Anabaptists by Brother O. S. on the Subject that Children Should be Baptized.*[93]

In a brief introduction and conclusion the author recalls his recent visit with the baron at which time they briefly discussed two questions: (1) whether or not children (infants) should be baptized and (2) whether or not they are sinful (original sin). He implies that his noble friend has been inclined towards the Anabaptist rejection of infant baptism and of original sin but that "by the grace of God and with the help of faithful teachers" he has renounced the Anabaptist error. The author, likely a minister of the Unity, is writing his epistle in order to establish the baron further in the truth so that he might be better prepared to talk — as he must from time to time — with those who persevere in error.

The treatise itself is divided into three parts. The first part lists the following "Arguments of the Anabaptists that infants should not be baptized":[94]

(1) There is no expressed command in the Scriptures to baptize children.

[93] Psaní, 1589: for the full title in Czech see our Bibliography, under Bohemica, Manuscripts. The treatise has been preserved in two copies, the one in *Codex Skalský* and the other in *Codex Crupp*. The former was copied in 1589 (see footnote 99 below), the latter not until 1633 ("Tento traktát přepsán v Bisonný [?] pod Krkonoši v vyhnání léta 1633 den sv. Jiljí", *Codex Crupp*, 1073). A comparison shows that the later copy could not have been made from *Codex Skalský* but rather from a different source. There are only minor textual variations. The content and outline are identical except that in *Codex Crupp* the eighth and ninth "reasons for infant baptism" are combined and the total number of reasons is thus reduced to nine (see at footnote 95 below). *Codex Skalský* was described by Hrejsa, 1931, 10 f., note 1. According to Hrejsa, the codex was written by two scribes in Moravia during the years 1583-1596. Most of the twelve tracts included in the codex are known from other sources. Three of them are translations of German booklets printed in the 1570's. Their provenience indicates connections with Heidelberg and Zürich at that time.

[94] Psaní, 1589, fol. 47b. The refutation of the six arguments follows on fols. 48a-53a.

(2) Faith must precede baptism [Mark 16:16]. Since "faith comes by hearing" [Romans 10:17], infants cannot hear the Word of God, do not have faith and therefore ought not to be baptized.

(3) Baptism is a sign of mortification and regeneration. Since infants cannot be born again, they should not be baptized.

(4) Children cannot enter into a covenant with God. Since baptism should be a covenant, children cannot be baptized.

(5) Children are not able to confess (the articles of) faith. Therefore they cannot be baptized.

(6) The Acts of the Apostles testify that only adult persons capable of understanding, were baptized. Therefore, children should not be baptized.

The six propositions are then refuted, mostly by scriptural arguments and by two references to the writings of Augustine.

The second part contains ten "Reasons why Children should be Baptized": [95]

(1) God's promise to Abraham and to his posterity [Genesis 17:2 ff.] included a seal or sign of the promise. Such sign is given through baptism, whether of children or adults.

(2) Whoever wants to be included among the people of God must receive the sacraments which are appointed by God as a confirmation of his covenant. Since children are part of the people of God, they should be baptized.

(3) Circumcision was instituted by God as a sign of an everlasting covenant [Genesis 17:7 ff.]. Baptism replaces circumcision as the sign of the covenant [Colossians 2:11 ff.].

(4) Jesus rebuked his disciples for trying to prevent children to come to him. Theirs is the kingdom [Matthew 19:14].

(5) The command of Christ "to baptize all nations" [Matthew 28:19] implies baptism of children since they are part of every nation.

(6) Since Christ is "the Saviour of all men" [I Tim. 4:10 and Luke 2:10 f.] he is also the Saviour of children.[96]

---

[95] *Ibid.*, fols. 53a-57a. We intend to publish an English translation of the full text at some other time. We do not, therefore, include all arguments in our brief summary above. They are important for the knowledge of the Czech Brethren's hermeneutics and should be considered in a theological comparison of Anabaptism with the *Unitas*. They are not essential for our present historical analysis.

[96] The author ridicules the biblical literalism of Anabaptists and suggests that if they were to take the angels' message to the shepherds literally ("unto you is born . . ."; Luke 2:11) they would believe that Christ is the Saviour of shepherds only (fol. 54b).

(7) Since the church is the sum total of all elect and since children are known to be chosen of God even before their physical birth, they constitute part of the church and should "be sanctified and cleansed with the washing of water" [Eph. 5:26], i.e., by baptism.

(8) The example of the Israelites who were "all baptized unto Moses" [I Cor. 10:2 ff.] shows that children must not be excluded from baptism.

(9) Peter did not withhold baptism from Cornelius and his household when they received the Holy Spirit [Acts 10:47]. Children, too, can be filled with the Holy Ghost as is exemplified by John the Baptist [Luke 1:15]. Why should they not be baptized?

(10) With the exception of heretics, there has been universal agreement in the church through the centuries to baptize children.

In the third part, which is much shorter, the author takes issue with the Anabaptist claim that infants are not born in sin and quotes a number of scriptural references in support of the concept of original sin.

In addition to biblical arguments, the treatise contains many references to the writings of Augustine and also mentions Dionysius, Origen, Cyprian, Irenaeus, Ambrose, Chrysostom, Jerome, Lactantius and other patristic writers, as well as Luther, Pomeranus, Melanchthon, Calvin, Beza, Peter Martyr Vermigli, Bucer, Bullinger and other contemporary defenders of infant baptism.

The author praises Peter Dathenus, "the excellent disputer with the Anabaptists",[97] the main spokesman of the Reformed party at the Frankenthal debate (1571), and recommends to his noble friend to read the Protocoll [98] "published recently in the German language".

[97] Psaní, 1589, fol. 57a (spelled Batenus). On Peter Dathenus (1531/1532-1588) see the art. "Dathenus" in ML and ME; Yoder Jesse, 1962a, 69 ff. and 1962b, 26 f.
[98] Protocoll, 1571. Four printed editions, nearly identical, appeared. Two German editions (Sept. 4, 1571 and 1573) were printed in Heidelberg. The two Dutch editions bear the dates November 25 and December 6, 1571. TQ, IV, 174-200 contains other important sources for the Frankenthal debate, incl. the lists of participants. A commentary on the thirteen articles debated at F. is preserved in a Ms. Codex written in 1590 (Burgerbibliothek, Bern, Codex 628; cf. Bender, 1956a, 77). Two recent doctoral dissertations dealt with the Frankenthal debate: Yoder Jesse, 1962a (summarized in Joder Jesse, 1962b) and Gerhard Greulich, "Das Religionsgespräch mit den Täufern zu Frankenthal 1571" (unpublished, Heidelberg, 1953). The latter was not accessible to us. See also Güss, 1960, 73-91 (the book reviews the changing religious situation in the Palatinate from 1508-1619); Wolkan, 1903, 50-57; Wiswedel, III, 155 ff.; Hillerbrand, 1959b; and the art. "Frankenthal Disputation" in ML and ME.

The identification of the author and the addressee of the epistle presents several problems. The text was copied into the manuscript codex in the Moravian town of Kyjov (Gaya) on July 1, 1589.[99] It is not certain whether the treatise was composed at that time or merely copied from an older text.

The author uses the general name 'Anabaptists' (*novokřtěnci*, sometimes *křtěnci*) but he is referring clearly to the Hutterites. He objects to the Hutterite nurseries for children and condemns the parents for trespassing against the expressed command of Scriptures according to which parents are to bring up their children (Eph. 6:4).[100] He mentions the Hutterite production of ovens (*kamna*), knives, carriages and ornamental roofs, and accuses them of robbing local craftsmen of work, of spoiling the local markets by buying out all the grain and of bringing many people into poverty by leases of large fields and vineyards.[101] Then he describes two "recent" incidents. At Žadovice the Hutterites stole several barrels of beer from the manorial brewery because "they had nothing to drink". They also stole wood from the forest belonging to the blacksmith in Žeravice but were caught and had to return the wood with shame. "And such people", he adds, "claim that they have mortified their flesh" and are born again.[102]

A Hutterite colony existed in Žadovice (Schadowitz) from 1553 to 1622.[103] No Anabaptist settlement is recorded for Žeravice but there was an old and important congregation of the *Unitas Fratru*m there.[104] Both localities were near the royal city of Kyjov where there used to be a congregation of the Unity until 1578-1579 when the minister Jan Brotan was expelled by the emperor.[105] However, a minister must have lived in Kyjov in 1589, for on April 12 the Bishop of Olomouc wrote to the city council demanding that they prevent the growth of the Brethren and that they expel their minister according to the orders of the emperor.[106] His name is not known but it is possible

[99]   Psaní, 1589, fol. 59a: "Kyio: 1 die Julij 89".
[100]   *Ibid.*, fol. 48a.
[101]   *Ibid.*, fol. 48b. The accusations are very similar to those contained in the polemical pamphlets written against the Hutterites by Johann Eysvogel ("Ein Ander schön neues Lied . . .", 1581; reprinted by Erhard, 1589, 35-38; cf. *ME*, II, 283) and Hans Jedelshauser ("Zwelf Ursachen . . .", 1587; cf. *ME*, III, 103).
[102]   *Ibid.*, fol. 51a.
[103]   Zeman, 1966, 71.
[104]   Hrejsa, B, 100 f.
[105]   Hrejsa, *ibid.*, 55; Cvrček, 1900 and Brunner, 1911, 466 ff.
[106]   Quoted by Kameníček, III, 373 from a manuscript in Kroměříž. Presumably the letter refers to the Czech Brethren. Cf. also *TQ*, I, 682 at footnote 7 and information on Gaya in Zeman, 1966, 35 f.

that the same minister wrote or copied the text of our epistle at Kyjov on July 1, 1589. He would have been acquainted with the Hutterite colonies in the area.

The mention of Dathenus and the printed *Protocoll* (1571 or 1573) not only provides a *terminus a quo* for the dating of the treatise but also offers additional clues. The author endorsed the arguments presented by Dathenus at the Frankenthal debate[107] and was in general sympathy with the Reformed theology.

The initials of the author, O. S. might point to Ondřej Štefan, who was elected bishop of the Unity in November 1571 and became Blahoslav's successor at Ivančice from 1571. He had studied at Wittenberg with Peter Herbert. In 1573 he established contact with Heidelberg so that the following year four students from the Unity were able to attend the university there.[108] Undoubtedly they brought back a number of books, among them the *Protocoll*. The presence of so many Anabaptists in Moravia made the subject quite relevant.[109] Štefan leaned more and more towards the Reformed position. In addition to his share in the writing of the *Acta Unitatis Fratrum* he was author of several theological writings.[110] The date of his death, July 21, 1577,[111] would suggest that the original treatise against the Anabaptists — if it was written by him — must have been composed sometime during the years 1574-1577, or a little earlier. In that case,

---

[107] The analysis by Yoder Jesse, 1962b, 35 indicates that with the exception of the fifth article on the church, Dathenus made more pronouncements on the twelfth article concerning baptism than on any other article. A comparison of the Czech Psaní, 1589 with art. 4 (orig. sin) and 12 (baptism) as recorded in *Protocoll*, 1571 shows that the Czech author borrowed several arguments from the Frankenthal debate but that he followed his own outline and used additional arguments. He might also have been familiar with Riedemann's *Rechenschaft* (cf. Psaní, 1589, fols. 49b and 54b with Riedemann, 1938, 71 f.: the argument about children who are part of all nations and should be baptized; reference to II Thess. 3:10: Since children do not work they should be starved to death). Dathenus quoted from the *Rechenschaft* at the Frankenthal debate (*Protocoll*, 1571, 210 f.).

[108] Hrejsa, VI, 232, 253, 257 f.; Hrejsa, C, 99.

[109] Two of the Anabaptist spokesmen at the Frankenthal Debate, Peter Scherer and Leonhart Sumner, might have been Hutterites from Moravia. The identification of Scherer with Peter Walpot, the famous Hutterite author and bishop (from 1565-1578) and of Sumner with Leonhart Summerauer (martyred in 1585) is by no means certain. See the discussion by Wolkan, 1903, 51 ff.; Friedmann, 1961a, 280; Güss, 1960, 79 and Yoder Jesse, 1962a, 78 f. During the debate, Scherer stated openly that no one present wished to defend the Hutterite doctrine of the community of goods (*Protocoll*, 1571, 534).

[110] Krofta, 1946, 105 ff. *et passim*.

[111] *Todtenbuch*, 269.

the anonymous writer who copied the text into the preserved codex in 1589 probably made a few editorial changes such as the references to the Hutterites at Žadovice and Žeravice. In view of the distance between Ivančice (the residence of Bishop Štefan) and Kyjov it is difficult to assume that Štefan would have known of such local incidents.[112] There are other factors besides which make it impossible to ascribe the authorship to Štefan with certainty.[113]

The most obvious identification of the "Lord F. of Ž." is the well-known protector of the Hutterites and member of the Unity, Fridrich of Žerotín.[114] On his domains of Židlochovice (Gross Seelowitz, from 1569 on) and Pouzdřany (Pausram, from 1574 on) the Hutterites had established no fewer than eight households by 1589.[115] According to Fischer, the Hutterite Brethren referred to Fridrich as 'unser Fritz'.[116] A Hutterite chronicler recorded his death (May 31, 1598) with the following eulogy:

... He permitted many [Hutterites] to live on his estates, and protected them as a father does his children. Not in vain did the Brotherhood seek refuge with him in times of danger. But finally in the year 1598, he too came to the end of life when God the Almighty summoned him home from this vale of sorrows. How the Lord will requite him for all the kindness he manifested toward the Brotherhood remains in God's own hands. May he grant him the eternal heavenly kingdom.[117]

[112]   We were unable to find any other references to the two incidents reported in Psaní, 1589. Their dating (either during the 1570's or 1580's) would in turn help to identify the author or editor of Psaní. Erhard, 1589 reports many incidents, including thefts, but does not record the two cases mentioned in the Czech manuscript. The preface of his book (printed in München) is dated in Salzburg on March 28, 1589. The copying of Psaní was finished on July 1, 1589.

[113]   The title of the treatise as preserved in Codex Crupp spells out the first name of the author: "od B. Oniáše S.". Even with the kind assistance of Prof. R. Říčan in Prague we have been unable to discover in other sources a person with such a name. The added name might represent nothing more than an attempt of the late copyist (1633) to identify the author. In order to clarify the question of Štefan's authorship one should compare the literary style of the treatise with the style in Štefan's other writings.

[114]   Cf. the art. "Zerotin" by Odložilík and Friedmann in ME, IV, 1024 f. No monograph on Fridrich of Z. has been written. A number of references will be found in Chlumecky, 1862 and Hrubý, 1935a.

[115]   Hrubý, 1935a, 65. Cf. the reference of the chronicles to the beginning of the household at Přibice in 1565, "aus erlaubnus vnd guetem willen des Herren Friedrich Herren von Scherotijn vdn auff Selowitz" (ZGL, 419). The subsequent references to Fridrich deal with the period after 1589.

[116]   Fischer, 1607b, 39. In 1596, Fridrich defended the Hutterites against the imperial chamber which sought to extract from them a loan of money (Loserth, 1884, 448).

[117]   Beck, 327 f. (not in ZGL). English tr. by Horsch, 1931a, 52.

Fridrich's stand on broad religious liberty[118] and his sympathetic dealings with the Hutterite Brethren could easily have aroused suspicions that he himself would subscribe to their position, at least as far as baptism was concerned. Tensions between him and the leaders of the Unity are known to have arisen from time to time.[119] If the treatise on baptism was addressed to him it provides unique evidence of Anabaptist influence on one of the leading lay representatives of the *Unitas Fratrum* in the last quarter of the sixteenth century.

4. REFERENCES TO THE CZECH REFORMATION IN THE HUTTERITE CHRONICLES

Besides mentioning several Moravian noblemen who were Utraquists or members of the *Unitas Fratrum* and with whom the Hutterite Brethren had dealings,[120] the *Large Chronicle* contains only five brief references to the Czech Reformation. All of them were copied, in an abbreviated form and with revisions, from Sebastian Franck's *Chronica*, the chief source for all pre-Anabaptist historical narratives in the chronicle.[121] Franck himself translated most of his items about the heretical groups in Bohemia and Moravia from the *Catalogus haereticorum* (Bernardus of Luxembourg)[122] who in turn had drawn them from *Historia bohemica* by Aeneas Sylvius Piccolomini (Pope Pius II).[123]

The following table indicates the scope of knowledge about the Czech Reformation movement displayed by the *Large Chronicle*:

[118] Hrubý, 1935a, 38 f. quotes Fridrich's letter to a neighbouring baron, Christoph Teuffenbach, in 1581 in which he defended the widow of a Lutheran minister in Pohořelice (a town on his domain) who decided to join the local Hutterite colony: "Dass Gott der Herr villeicht die nachgelassne Wittib meines Pfarhers zu Poherlicz erleicht hat, dass sie sich under die Teutschen Brieder [Hutterites] geben wolt, wider solliches ich nicht sein kan. Der Glaub ist gewis ein Gab Gottes und keiner kan keinem den Glauben geben noch nemen . . .". The friendship with the Anabaptists did not prevent sharp disagreements on such issues as armsbearing (cf. Hrubý, *ibid.*, 46).
[119] Cf. Krofta, 1946, 92 f. and 110 f.; Müller, I, 611.
[120] Mainly several members of the Žerotín family, the lords of Kounice, of Boskovice and others. See the register of personal names in ZGL, 937 ff.
[121] On Franck, 1531 as a source for the Hutterite chronicles, see Beck, 9, n. 1; ZGLK, p. XLII, n. 1 (examples) and Friedmann's art. "Chronica" in ME, I, esp. 588. Cf. also Friedmann, 1931, 234 ff. for Walpot's dependence on Franck.
[122] First ed., Bernardus, 1522. Franck likely used the fourth edition published in Köln in 1529. Cf. Chapter III, footnotes 63 and 106.
[123] Aeneas Sylvius, 1475 and many subsequent editions.

Item	ZGL page	Franck, 1531 fol.	Bernardus, 1529 fol.
(1) Waldo and Waldenser (in Bohemia — Anno 1218)	39	432b-433a	L 6b-L 7
(2) 'Picardi' — a teacher 1394	40	434b	M 2a-b
the contemporary 'Picarden' or 'Gruebenhaimer'	40	483a & 403a-b	P 1b
(3) Hus	40	407b	H 6b-H 7
(4) Jeronimus of Prague	40	409b-410a	
(5) 'Johannes Bacius' [Roháč] [124]	40	412b	I 2b

In addition to these,[125] Beck has copied from three other Hutterite
codices a very general reference to the Picards or Waldensians.[126]
Neither this reference, nor the one in the Large Chronicle says any-

[124] Both ZGL, 40 and Wolkan, 30 read Bacius. Either the modern editor, or the
Hutterite copyist of the codex misread an 'R' for 'B': Both Franck and Bernardus
have Roatius: Jan Roháč of Dubé, a Taborite leader, who was among the last to
offer resistance to the armies of Sigismund at his castle Sion. He was hanged, together with fifty-two associates, in a mass execution in Prague on September 9,
1437 (Hrejsa, III, 24).

[125] In addition to the five items listed in the text above, the following articles in
Franck, 1531 represent a free, abbreviated translation of the same entries in
Bernardus, 1529: Adamite, Bohemi, Hussite, Iacobellus [Jakoubek of Stříbro],
Johannes Zischa [Žižka], Hus, Hieronymus, Iohannes alius, ein münch Prämon-
stratenser [Jan Želivský], Matthias ein Boehem [Matěj Louda z Chlumčan, Hrejsa,
II, 259], Medius [priest Martin Prostředek, Hrejsa, III, 24], Orphani, Orebitae,
Petrus de Anglia [Petr Payne], Procopius [Prokop Holý, successor of Žižka], Rokycana, Taboritae. In the following articles, Franck departed from his Catholic
source and presented a more sympathetic treatment: Jerome of Prague, Gruben-
haimer, Picardi (treated twice: fol. 434b and 483a; cf. also a reference to Luther's
criticism of their doctrine of baptism, fol. 422a) and "Der Boehem glaub, oder
Hussen orden" (Utraquists, fol. 483a). Cf. Chapter IV, footnotes 153 ff. Without
quoting the source, Franck also reprinted Velenský's arguments against Peter's
stay in Rome, on fols. 257-263. Cf. footnote 195 in Chapter III. For an analysis of
other sources used by Franck in his treatment of the Czech Reformation (also in
parts other than "Ketzerchronik"), see Bartoš, 1946b, 95 ff. Franck's personal
knowledge about the Czech Brethren as well as his surprising knowledge about
Anabaptist life in Moravia as early as 1531 must be ascribed to contacts during his
stay in Nürnberg 1528-1531 (where he married, a week after Hubmaier's death,
Ottilia Behaim, a relative of the 'godless' painters, Sebald and Barthel Behaim; cf.
footnote 204 in Ch. II) and in Strasbourg where the Chronica was printed on
Sept. 5, 1531. In 1531, Franck also met Jakob Ziegler in Strasbourg (cf. footnote
54, Ch. III). According to Peuckert, 1943, 550 the inventory of Franck's books at
the time of his death (1542) included "Ein picardisch gsangbüchlin".

[126] Beck, 11: "allain die Pickarten oder Waldenser genannt, noch gar ein klainen
schein der wahrheit gehabt". Cf. also Beck, xxvi on Cod. I. ". . . die einen gueten
Anfang der warheit gehab . . .".

thing specific about the teachings of the Czech Brethren, and this in spite of the fact that Franck's *Chronica* mentions, among other things, their concept of the Lord's Supper, opposition to oaths and even a division into two or three parties (*hauffen*) of whom "the small[est] agrees altogether with the Anabaptists".[127]

One can understand the reasons for Hubmaier's lack of knowledge about the Czech Reformation. He spent only one year in Moravia and stayed in a German-speaking town. By way of contrast, the introductory historical survey of the Hutterite Chronicle was compiled by Caspar Braitmichel, in the late 1560's or early 1570's. From 1538 onward he served the Hutterite brotherhood in Moravia and died in Slavkov in 1573.[128]

The relationship between the Hutterites and the Czech Brethren constitutes one of the most ironical, if not tragic, episodes of ecumenical history. The two groups, so much alike in their protest against the established Christendom, lived side by side in one land for several decades. Yet they ignored each other so completely that the only information which the Hutterite chronicler was able to incorporate into his manuscript was derived from a hundred-year-old book written by the arch-enemy of the Hussites, Aeneas Sylvius. Its contents were mediated by the catalogue of a Dominican inquisitor and the chronicle of a spiritualist!

5. BRIEF REFERENCES TO ANABAPTISTS IN THE SOURCES OF *UNITAS FRATRUM*

The sources of the Czech Brethren contain a number of brief references to Anabaptism and to the Anabaptists. Most of them are apologetical statements in which the Brethren disassociated themselves from Anabaptism. One should remember that similar declarations were made repeatedly with respect to the Unity's relationship with the Waldenses. The following quotations will serve as illustrations only. Additional examples could be found in the manuscript and printed sources.

The reference to Anabaptists in the decree by which the Unity abolished the practice of rebaptism in 1534 was cited earlier.[129]

---

[127] Franck, 1531, fol. 434b and 483a. Cf. Chapter IV at footnotes 154 f.
[128] See *ZGL*, xxiii, LXIX and 470 f. and Friedmann, 1965b, 105 f.
[129] Gindely, 1865, 150. Cf. footnote 10 above.

In the preface to their Czech confession printed in 1536 and to the Latin version printed in Wittenberg, with Luther's preface, in 1538, the Brethren assured the reader that they had nothing in common with the Anabaptists. Their Unity had existed for a long time before the rise of Anabaptism. Their former practice of rebaptism had been based on different theological presuppositions from the Anabaptist concept of adult baptism.[130]

In 1537, a member of the Unity in Mladá Boleslav, Jakub Poledne, publicly defended views which he had derived from the writings of Johann Denck. Poledne was excommunicated in January 1538.[131]

When Matěj Červenka, a young emissary of the Unity, visited Strasbourg at the end of May 1540, Bucer enquired, among other things, about Anabaptists in Bohemia and Moravia and whether "they were causing trouble (bouřku) in the Unity". Červenka admitted that he did not know much about them. "A few have tried but without success".[132]

At a colloquy between Lutheran theologians and representatives of the Unity at Königsberg (Prussia) in 1548, the German spokesman mentioned a rumour according to which the Brethren despised priestly offices just as the Anabaptists did. The accusation was immediately refuted by the Brethren.[133]

The decree of the synod held at Žeravice in 1559 reminded members of the Unity of their restricted participation in war. They were not to be mistaken for Anabaptists.[134]

In a letter written in 1578, the bishop of the *Unitas Fratrum* in Poland, Jiří Izrael, asked: "What came out of our negotiations with Kalenec, or with the Habrovanites, or with the Anabaptists?" He implied that the contacts had been useless.[135]

Writing at Ivančice in 1579, the former professor in Wittenberg

---

[130] "Nos ex factione Anabaptistarum non esse, nemini ignotum est ...". The Czech and the Latin text were reprinted by Sklenář, 1957b, 88 f. The Latin text had been reprinted also by Niemeyer, 1840, 780 f. Cf. also Art. XII (on baptism) in the same confessions and the analysis by Sklenář, 1957a.

[131] See Molnár, 1952a, 140 and Souček Bohuslav, 1921, 75 for further details and sources. Cf. also Appendix 2, note 4.

[132] The ambiguous statement, probably applicable chiefly to Bohemia, is part of Červenka's long report on his visit in Strasbourg. Printed by Gindely, 1859, 64 (Czech) and 39 (German translation) and Zelinka, 1942, 77 (Czech). Also in Lasicki, 211.

[133] The Czech record of the colloquy ("Examen") was reprinted by Sliziński, 1958, 164.

[134] Gindely, 1865, 202. Cf. our full quotation at note 79 above.

[135] *AUF*, XIV, fol. 311. Quoted by Hanák, 1928, 64, n. 2.

and later principal of the Brethren's school at Ivančice, Esrom Rüdinger, regretted the fact that the name 'Brethren' was being also used
and put in ill repute by the Anabaptists.[136]

On the other hand, at the insistence of Jiří Strejc, one of the
representatives of the *Unitas Fratrum* on the committee which prepared the text of *Confessio Bohemica* in 1575, a condemnation of
"Arians, Zwinglians, Calvinists, Anabaptists and all other heretics"
was omitted from the preface.[137]

Much later, the last bishop of the old Unity, Jan Amos Komenský
(Comenius, 1592-1670) made several kind remarks about the Anabaptists. In 1661, he recalled his personal acquaintance with them
during his youth in Moravia.[138] In an earlier writing, he praised their
inner order and discipline by which they surpassed all other 'unities'
(denominations).[139] He criticized, however, their "sacramentarian"
view of the Lord's Supper as a mere sign and remembrance.[140] He
saw their origin in Switzerland.[141]

A *Commentary on the Book of Acts* from the year 1595 [142] includes
a number of polemical references to the Anabaptists. The main criticism of the anonymous author is directed against their rejection of
infant baptism [143] and against the Hutterite community of goods.[144]
In a minister's manual, *Agenda*,[145] the author tries to refute the tra-
ditional Anabaptist arguments against infant baptism.[146]

---

[136] "Fratrum nomen (quod et ipsum de origine nostra testatur) retinent non tam
ipsae Ecclesiae nostrae . . . et infamant Fratrum nomen in his terris Anabaptistarum
examina." Printed in Camerarius, 160. On Rüdinger, see Molnár, 1956a, 200 ff.
[137] Hrejsa, VI, 292.
[138] "Simplices istos Fratres Moravicos a puero novi et ab Antitrinitariis Polonicis
saepius fuisse tentatos, semper autem in fide perstitisse sciebam" (*De iterato
Sociniano Irenico iterata ad Christianos admonitio* (Amsterdam, 1661), 46. Quoted
by Müller, 1910, 209). Cf. also Měšťan, 1955, 459 and Urban, 1966, 72.
[139] *Otázky některé o Jednotě bratří českých* (1632), reprinted in Komenský, 1912,
276. Cf. Müller, 1910, 209 and Friedmann, 1949, 33.
[140] *Ohlášení*, 1635, reprinted in Komenský, 1912, 322.
[141] *Otázky*, 1632, reprinted in Komenský, 1912, 267.
[142] *Výklad krátký na Skutky apoštolské*, in Ms. Codex XVII G 26 (University
Library of Prague), fols. 110-209. According to Truhlář, 1906, 121 Václav Štefan
Teplický, Utraquist dean in Kutná Hora (Kutenberg, Bohemia) might have been
the author. We are indebted to Prof. R. Říčan for excerpts from the codex.
[143] *Ibid.*, fols. 123a-b (commentary on Acts 2:39).
[144] *Ibid.*, fols. 123b-124a (Acts 2:44 ff.) and fols. 133b-134b (Acts 4:32 ff.).
[145] *Agenda zprávy a posluhování církevního na Horách Kutnách*, in the same
codex, fols. 210-237, with no date but written before 1597. The note about authorship in footnote 142 above applies also to this writing.
[146] *Ibid.*, fol. 230b. The Anabaptist arguments against infant baptism (quoted by

Both writings originated in the Czech Utraquist circles. We have included them here in order to show that toward the end of the sixteenth century there was little or no difference between the Czech Brethren and the Utraquists in their attitudes toward Anabaptism and its distinctive doctrines.

6. OTHER CONTACTS

It would be desirable to write an account of the personal and correspondence contacts between the Anabaptists in Moravia, particularly the Hutterites, and members of the Moravian nobility on whose domains they established their settlements. A number of the barons and knights were members or adherents of the Unity, especially in the families of Žerotín and Kounice. However, in many cases their religious affiliation cannot be established with certainty and it would be difficult, at the present stage of research, to differentiate between the Czech Brethren and other Protestants.[147]

It would be interesting to know how many Czech-speaking or Slovak-speaking Anabaptists are reported in the sources, and on the other hand, to list the German-speaking ministers of the Unity. But such investigations properly belong to the area of sociological comparison which we have designated as a separate project of research not included in our present study.[148]

---

the author) and the refutations are very similar to the "Arguments" and "Reasons" presented in Psaní, 1589 (see above at footnotes 94-95).

[147] Cf. an analysis for the year 1622 by Hrubý, 1922. Hrubý, 1935a includes examples of contacts with Moravian nobility. Hrubý utilized many local sources, e.g. private correspondences. Karel of Žerotín maintained contacts with the Hutterites even after their expulsion from Moravia. He corresponded with their leaders and physicians in Slovakia. Cf. Hrubý, I, 16, n. 1 (1624), 433 (1633), 511 ff. (1635). See also Hrubý, 1937; Hrejsa, C, 93; Friedmann, 1961a, 60; art. "Zerotin" in ME, IV.

[148] Cf. our "Proposed Plan of Study", Chapter I at footnote 145.

VI

OPPORTUNITIES FOR CONTACT
(HISTORICAL TOPOGRAPHY)

The preserved sources can never tell the whole story. People meet
and exchange views, learn to know one another and influence one
another and yet no written record of their contacts and conversations
is extant.

A historian who seeks to reconstruct relationships between individuals and groups cannot limit himself to a critical interpretation of
the written or printed sources. He must also use imagination in order
to envisage the manifold situations in which the heroes of history —
be they leaders or common folk — found themselves and acted out
the role of their lives. Only thus history becomes 'his story' which
he resurrects from the dusty documents and relives with the past
generations.

The written records of contacts between the Anabaptists and the
Czech Brethren in Moravia are disappointingly few. Yet the daily
contacts between the two groups must have been numerous. In order
to show the opportunities for communication we shall gather and
evaluate evidence of topographical research.

To what extent do the areas in which the Anabaptists and the
Czech Brethren are known to have settled overlap? In how many
localities in Moravia did the two groups live side by side and for
how many years or decades were they neighbours? Did the Anabaptist refugees prefer to settle in German-speaking communities?
These are some of the questions which we shall seek to answer, in
part at least, in this chapter.

Anyone who attempts to collect topographical data for a religious
group in a land from which it was eventually expelled, or in which
it was suppressed, soon discovers that he has embarked upon a life-
long task. To undertake a topographical comparison of two such

groups, and to do it without access to the archives and libraries in that particular country, may appear to be a futile exercise in fruitless labor. Nevertheless, if our present investigation of historical contacts between the Anabaptists and the Czech Brethren in Moravia is to be complete, topographical research cannot be avoided.

Fortunately, such study of the settlements of the Unity in Moravia, as well as in Bohemia and other countries, has been carried out by Hrejsa.[1] As does any work in topography, so also the exhaustive book by Hrejsa requires continuous revision and supplementation. We have taken note of several minor corrections which have been published by the author himself or by others in the intervening years.[2] However, apart from further research of local sources in Moravian archives, most of the important in-group sources as well as many out-group sources have been utilized by Hrejsa and no major changes in his list are likely to be necessary. We have accepted, therefore, his work, with only a few minor changes, as the basis for our lists of the Moravian settlements of the Czech Brethren.

The main task of our research was the gathering and critical sifting of topographical data on Moravian Anabaptism. In order to make a reliable comparison of the geographical and chronological distribution of the two groups, the Anabaptists and the Unity, a comprehensive listing of all places of Anabaptist settlement in Moravia had to be prepared to match the work done by Hrejsa for the Czech Brethren.

The results of our topographical research have been published elsewhere.[3] In the present context we shall merely reproduce the lists.

---

[1] Hrejsa, A. (Introduction and Bohemia), B. (Moravia), C. (Prussia, Poland, Latvia, Silesia, Brandenburg, Saxony, Slovakia, Moldavia and other countries). The three parts of the monumental work, each with a map showing all settlements, were published in RS, V (1935), VI (1937) and VII (1939) and then as a reprint in one volume (1939) with complete index. We have used the original edition in RS.

[2] Corrections and additions for the topography of the Unity in Moravia were published in Hrejsa, C, 110-114. Prior to Hrejsa, B, Cvrček, 1898 and 1899 published excerpts from AUF concerning several congregations of the Unity in Moravia.

[3] Zeman, 1966. The work includes a brief review of topographical research of Moravian Anabaptism.

1. TOPOGRAPHY OF MORAVIAN ANABAPTISM

List A: German-Czech Alphabetical List [4]

Explanatory Note:

One asterisk (*) in front of the name of an entry means that the sources establishing evidence of an Anabaptist settlement in that locality are of dubious value, or that their interpretation is uncertain.

Two asterisks (**) designate entries which in our judgment represent mistaken localizations of Anabaptist settlement. They are included among the numbered entries because they have been classified as Anabaptist settlements by other authors.

1. Aichhorn — Veveří
2. Alexowitz — Alexovice, Olexovice
3. Altenmarkt — Stará Břeclav
4. *Aspernitz — ?
5. Auerschitz — Uherčice
6. Auspitz — Hustopeče
7. Austerlitz — Slavkov
8. Bellowitz — Bedřichovice or Bílovice nad Svitavou
9. *Biharschowitz — Běhařovice
10. Bilowitz, Gross — Velké Bílovice
11. Birnbaum — Hrušky
12. *Birtnitz — Brtnice
13. Bisenz — Bzenec
14. Bochtitz — Bohutice
15. Bogenitz — Purkmanice
16. Bohuslawitz — Bohuslavice
17. *Bojanowitz, Unter — Dolní Bojanovice
18. Boretitz — Bořetice
19. **Borotitz — Borotice
20. *Bratelsbrunn — Prátlsbrun, now Březí
21. *Braumowitz, Brumowitz — Brumovice
22. *Braunseifen — Brunzejf
23. Brünn — Brno
24. Budkau — Budkov
25. **Budkowitz — Budkovice
26. *Budwitz (Mährisch) — Moravské Budějovice

27. Butschowitz — Bučovice
28. Damborschitz — Dambořice
29. **Dannowitz, Ober — Horní Dunajovice
30. Dannowitz, Unter — Dolní Dunajovice
31. Datschitz — Dačice
32. Deckenwitz — Dětkovice?, Tikovice?, Tavíkovice? Tvrdonice?
33. Durchlass — Tvoři(h)raz
34. Eibenschitz — Ivančice
35. Eibis — Iváň
36. Eisgrub — Lednice
37. *Eulenberg — Sovinec
38. Freiberg — Příbor
39. Frischau — Fryšava, now Břežany
40. *Gaiwitz — Kyjovice
41. Gaya — Kyjov
42. Gobschitz — Kubšice
43. Göding — Hodonín
44. Grünwies — Krumvíř, Gronvíř
45. Gurdau — Kurdějov
46. Gurwitz — Krhovice
47. *Harasy (Harasice, Harásky)
48. Herspitz — Heršpice
49. Hödnitz — Hodonice
50. **Hosterlitz — Hostěradice
51. Hrubschitz — Hrubšice
52. Iglau — Jihlava
53. Jaispitz — Jevišovice
54. Jamnitz — Jemnice

---

[4] The local names appearing in the German Anabaptist sources often consist of mutilated Czech forms whereby the refugees attempted to approximate the Czech sounds they heard. But even in communities which had German names, the Anabaptist sources display a great variety in spelling. We have adhered to the modern German forms where available. All known variations in spelling of the German names in the Anabaptist and other sources are listed in Zeman, 1966.

55. *Jawornik — Javorník
56. Jermeritz, Jarohnewitz — Jarohněvice
57. *Kamenetz — Kamenec
58. Kanitz — Dolní Kounice
59. *Klentnitz — Klentice
60. *Klobouk — Klobouky
61. Kobelitz — Kobylí
62. **Kobelnitz — Kobylnice
63. Kostel — Podivín
64. Kremsier — Kroměříž
65. Krenowitz — Křenovice
66. Krepitz — Křepice
67. Kreutz — Vsisko? Křížov?
68. Kromau, Mährisch — Mor. Krumlov (distinguish from Krumau, Böhmisch — Český Krumlov)
69. *Kukvice (German name not known)
70. Landshut — Lanžhot
71. *Langendorf — Loučka
72. *Lautschitz — Blučina
73. Lenovice (German name not known)
74. Lettonitz — Letonice
75. *Litentschitz — Litenčice
76. Lundenburg — Břeclav
77. *Malspitz — Malešovice, Malešice
78. Mayberg — Děvín
79. *Mikultschitz — Mikulčice
80. Milonitz — Milonice
81. Milotitz — Milotice
82. Mistrin — Mistřín
83. Mödritz — Modřice
84. Mohelln — Mohelno
85. **Morkowitz — Morkovice
86. *Morkuwetz, Morkuwek — Morkůvky
87. Moskowitz — Mackovice, Máčkovice
88. Muschau — Mušov
89. Mutenitz — Mutěnice
90. Napajedl — Napajedla
91. *Naschmeritz — Našiměřice
92. Nasselowitz — Násedlovice
93. Neslowitz — Nes(u)lovice
94. Neudorf — Nová Ves Ostrožská (not Moravská)
95. Neumühl — Nové Mlýny
96. Neuwitzsch — Nevojice?
97. Niemtschan — Němčany

98. *Niemtschitz, Gross — Němčice (Velké)
99. Niemtschitz, Klein (near Auspitz) — Němčičky
100. Niemtschitz, Klein (near Kanitz) — Němčičky
101. Nikolsburg — Mikulov
102. Nikoltschitz — Nikolčice
103. Nuslau — Nosislav
104. **Olkowitz, Gross — Velké Oleksovice
105. Olmütz — Olomouc
106. Pausram — Pouzdřany
107. Pawlowitz, Gross — Velké Pavlovice
108. Pergen — Perná
109. Platsch — Plaveč
110. Plumlůvky (German name not known)
111. Podax — ?
112. Pohrlitz — Pohořelice
113. Polehraditz — Polehradice, now Boleradice
114. Pollau — Polany, now Pavlov
115. *Popelin — Popelín
116. Poppitz — Pop(ov)ice
117. *Posoritz — Pozořice
118. **Pozlowic — Bohuslavice
119. *Prahlitz — Pravlov
120. Pribitz — Přibice
121. Prittlach — Příkluky, Přítluky (Mašovice)
122. Prossnitz — Prostějov
123. Pruschanek — Prušánky
124. Pulgram — Pulgarov, now Bulhary
125. Pürschitz — Prštice
126. Qualitz(en) — Chvaletín
127. Rakschitz — Rakšice
128. Rakwitz — Rakvice
129. Rampersdorf — Lanštorf, now Ladná
130. Raschowitz — Rašovice
131. *Rohatetz — Rohatec
132. Rohrbach — Hrušovany
133. Rossitz — Rosice
134. Saitz — Zaječí
135. Schabschitz — Žabčice
136. Schadowitz — Žadovice, Žádovice
137. Schakwitz — Šakvice (not Žákovice)
138. Schenkhof — Čeňkov?

139. Seelowitz, Gross — Židlochovice
140. Seelowitz, Klein — (Malé)
     Zelovice, Želovice
141. Seletitz — Želetice
142. *Sirowin — Syrovín
143. Skalitz — Skalice
144. Starnitz, Sturnitz — Starnice,
     Sturnice
145. Steinitz — Ždánice
146. Steurowitz, Gross — Starovice,
     Velké Štarvice (not Stránovice)
147. Stiegnitz — Trstěnice, Křtěnice
148. Strassnitz — Strážnice
149. *Stri(e)lek — Střílky
150. Swatoborschitz — Svatobořice
151. Swetlau — Světlov
152. Tasswitz — Tasovice
153. Teikowitz — Tavíkovice
154. Teinitz — Týnec
155. Terezín (German name not
     known)
156. Teschau, Klein — Těšánky?,
     Těšany?, Těšice?, Těšov?,
     Tetčice?
157. Tracht — Strachotín, Trachtín
158. *Trebitsch — Třebíč
159. Tscheikowitz — Čejkovice
160. Tscheitsch — Čejč

161. Tschermakowitz — Čermákovice
162. Turnitz — Tvrdonice
163. Ungarisch Ostra — Uherský
     Ostroh
164. Urbau — Vrbovec, Vrbovce
165. Urschitz — Uhřice
166. Voitelsbrunn — Sedlec
167. Watzenowitz — Vacenovice
168. **Weimisslitz — Vémyslice,
     Výmyslice
169. Weisstätten — Pasohlávky
     (Kroatendorf — Charváty)
170. Welka (or Hulka) — Velká nad
     Veličkou
171. Wessely (Wesseli an der
     March) — Veselí nad Moravou
172. *Wischau — Vyškov
173. Wischenau — Višňové
174. Wisternitz, Ober and Unter —
     Věstonice, Vistonice (Horní a
     Dolní)
175. Wolframitz — Olbramovice
176. Wolframskirchen —
     Olbramkostel
177. Wostitz — Vlasatice
178. Wratzow — Vracov
179. Z(i)erotitz — Žerotice
180. Znaim — Znojmo

List B: Czech-German Alphabetical List

Alexovice — Alexowitz
*Aspernitz — ?
Bedřichovice — see Bellowitz
*Běhařovice — Biharschowitz
Bílovice nad Svitavou — see
     Bellowitz
Bílovice Velké — Bilowitz (Gross)
*Blučina — Lautschitz
Bohuslavice — Bohuslawitz
**Bohuslavice — Pozlowic
Bohutice — Bochtitz
*Bojanovice Dolní — Bojanowitz,
     Unter
Boleradice — Polehraditz
**Borotice — Borotitz
Bořetice — Boretitz
Brno — Brünn
*Brtnice — Birtnitz
*Brumovice (Broumovice) —
     Braumowitz
*Brunzejf — Braunseifen
Břeclav — Lundenburg

Břeclav Stará — Altenmarkt
*Březí — Bratelsbrunn
Břežany — Frischau
Bučovice — Butschowitz
*Budějovice Moravské — Budwitz
     (Mährisch)
Budkov — Budkau
**Budkovice — Budkowitz
Bulhary — Pulgram
Bzenec — Bisenz
Čejč — Tscheitsch
Čejkovice — Tscheikowitz
Čeňkov? — Schenkhof
Čermákovice — Tschermakowitz
Dačice — Datschitz
Dambořice — Damborschitz
Dětkovice — see Deckenwitz
Děvín — Mayberg
Dunajovice Dolní — Dannowitz,
     Unter
**Dunajovice Horní — Dannowitz,
     Ober

Fryšava — Frischau
Harasice — Harasy
Heršpice — Herspitz
Hodonice — Hödnitz
Hodonín — Göding
**Hostěradice — Hosterlitz
Hrubšice — Hrubschitz
Hrušky — Birnbaum
Hrušovany — Rohrbach
Hustopeče — Auspitz
Charváty — see Weisstätten
Chvaletín — Qualitz(en)
Ivančice — Eibenschitz
Iváň — Eibis
Jarohněvice — Jermeritz,
   Jarohnewitz
*Javorník — Jawornik
Jemnice — Jamnitz
Jevišovice — Jaispitz
Jihlava — Iglau
Josefov — see Kukvice
*Kamenec — Kamenetz
*Kašnice — see Kamenetz
*Klentice — Klentnitz
Kobylí — Kobelitz
**Kobylnice — Kobelnitz
Kounice Dolní — Kanitz
Krhovice — Gurwitz
Kroměříž — Kremsier
Krumlov Český — Krumau,
   Böhmisch
Krumlov Moravský — Kromau,
   Mährisch
Krumvíř — Grünwies
Křenovice — Krenowitz
Křepice — Krepitz
Křížov — see Kreutz
Křtěnice — Stiegnitz
Kubšice — Gobschitz
*Kukvice
Kurdějov — Gurdau
Kyjov — Gaya
*Kyjovice — Gaiwitz
Ladná, Lanštorf — Rampersdorf
Lanžhot — Landshut
Lednice — Eisgrub
Lenovice
Letonice — Lettonitz
*Litenčice — Litentschitz
*Loučka — Langendorf
Mackovice — Moskowitz
*Malešovice — Malspitz
Mašovice — see Prittlach

*Mikulčice — Mikultschitz
Mikulov — Nikolsburg
Milonice — Milonitz
Milotice — Milotitz
Mistřín — Mistrin
Modřice — Mödritz
Mohelno — Mohelln
**Morkovice — Morkowitz
*Morkůvky — Morkuwetz
Mušov — Muschau
Mutěnice — Mutenitz
Napajedla — Napajedl
Násedlovice (Staré) — Nasselowitz
*Našiměřice — Naschmeritz
Nesklovice — see Nasselowitz
Nes(u)lovice — Neslowitz
Němčany — Niemtschan
*Němčice (Velké) — Niemtschitz,
   Gross
Němčičky (u Hustopeče) —
   Nietschitz, Klein (No. 99)
Němčičky (u Dolních Kounic) —
   Niemtschitz, Klein (No. 100)
Nevojice — see Neuwitzsch
Nikolčice — Nikoltschitz
Nosislav — Nuslau
Nová Ves — Mariahilf: see
   Lenovice
Nová Ves Moravská — Neudorf
   (No. 94/1)
Nová Ves Ostrožská — Neudorf
   (No. 94/2)
Nové Mlýny — Neumühl
Olbramovice — Wolframitz
Olbramkostel — Wolframskirchen
**Oleksovice Velké — Olkowitz,
   Gross
Olomouc — Olmütz
Pasohlávky — Weisstätten
Pavlov — Pollau
Pavlovice, Velké — Pawlowitz,
   Gross
Perná — Pergen
Plaveč — Platsch
Plumlůvky
Podax — ?
Podivín — Kostel
Pohořelice — Pohrlitz
Polany — Pollau
Polehradice — Polehraditz
*Popelín — Popelin
Popovice (Popice) — Poppitz
Pouzdřany — Pausram

*Pozořice — Posoritz
*Prátlsbrun — Bratelsbrunn
*Pravlov — Prahlitz
Prostějov — Prossnitz
Prštice — Pürschitz
Prušánky — Pruschanek
Přibice — Pribitz
Příbor — Freiberg
Příkluky (Přítluky) — Prittlach
Pulgarov — Pulgram
Purkmanice — Bogenitz
Rakšice — Rakschitz
Rakvice — Rakwitz
Rašovice — Raschowitz
*Rohatec — Rohatetz
Rosice — Rossitz
Sedlec — Voitelsbrunn
Skalice — Skalitz
Slavkov — Austerlitz
*Sovinec — Eulenberg
Starnice (Sturnice) — Starnitz
Starovice — Steurowitz, Gross
Strachotín — Tracht
(Stránovice — see Steurowitz, Gross)
Strážnice — Strassnitz
*Střílky — Strilek
Svatobořice — Swatoborschitz
Světlov — Swetlau
*Syrovín — Sirowin
Šakvice — Schakwitz
Štarvice, Velké — Steurowitz, Gross
Tasovice — Tassowitz
Tavíkovice — Teikowitz
Terezín
Těšany, Těšánky, Těšov, Těšice —
   see Teschau, Klein

Tetčice — see Teschau, Klein
Tikovice — see Deckenwitz
Trachtín — Tracht
Trstěnice — Stiegnitz
*Třebíč — Trebitsch
Tvoři(h)raz — Durchlass
Tvrdonice — Turnitz
Týnec — Teinitz
Uherčice — Auerschitz
Uherský Ostroh — Ungarisch Ostra
Uhřice — Urschitz
Vacenovice — Watzenowitz
Velká — Welka
**Vémyslice — Weimisslitz
Veselí nad Moravou — Wessely
Věstonice (Vistonice) — Wisternitz
Veveří — Aichhorn
Višňové — Wischenau
Vlasatice — Wostitz
Vracov — Wratzow
Vrbovec — Urbau
Vsisko — see Kreutz
**Výmyslice — Weimisslitz
*Vyškov — Wischau
Zaječí — Saitz
Zelovice (Malé), Želovice —
   Seelowitz, Klein
Znojmo — Znaim
Žabčice — Schabschitz
Žadovice — Schadowitz
(Žákovice — see Schakwitz)
Ždánice — Steinitz
Želetice — Seletitz
Žerotice — Z(i)erotitz
Židlochovice — Seelowitz, Gross

List C: Combined Chronological and Group Lists

Abbreviations:

A	Austerlitz Brethren	P	Philippites
C	Cornelians	S	Sabbatarians
G	Gabrielites	SR	Schwertler (followers of
H	Hutterites		Hubmaier, only 1526-1535)
M	Marbeck fellowship	ST	Stäbler (opponents of
	(Pilgramites)		Hubmaier, only 1526-ca. 1530)
O	Other groups	SWB	Swiss Brethren

? A question mark behind the letter (identifying a group): the identification of the group is not reliable.

? A question mark behind the name of a place (without any letter identifying a (group): no particular Anabaptist group is specified in the sources.

( )   A place in brackets: there was no Anabaptist settlement here; contact with the local population was occasioned only by short term work contracts (e.g. installing a clock) or by agricultural work on properties located here but owned by the colony in a neighbouring village.

*   Either the sources establishing evidence of Anabaptist settlement in a particular place, or their interpretation, is uncertain.
       Localities which have been marked with two asterisks (in list A) are omitted here.

Period I: 1526-1535 (from Anabaptist settlement in Moravia till the first expulsion)

1. Auspitz: P, H
2. Austerlitz: ST, A, H
3. (Bogenitz: ST)
4. Brünn: ST, SR
5. Butschowitz: A
6. Datschitz: ?
7. Eibenschitz: ? SR? ST?
8. Iglau: ?
9. Jamnitz: P
10. Jermeritz: G
11. *Klentnitz: SR
12. Neuwitzsch: ST
13. Nikolsburg: SR, ST, S
14. Olmütz: ?
15. Pergen: SR, ST
16. Pollau: SR, ST
17. Pulgram: P
18. Rossitz: G, P
19. Schakwitz: H
20. (Starnitz: H)
21. Steurowitz, Gr.: H
22. Tasswitz: SWB
23. Tracht: SR?
24. Urbau: SWB
25. Voitelsbrunn: SR
26. Wisternitz: SR
27. Znaim: ?

Period II: 1536-1547 (between the first and second expulsion)

1. Altenmarkt: H
2. Auspitz: H, P?
3. Austerlitz: A, C, H. M?
4. Bilowitz: H
5. Bisenz: G, H
6. Bochtitz: H
7. Bohuslawitz: H
8. Boretitz: H
9. *Budwitz: ?
10. Butschowitz: A, G, H
11. Dannowitz, Unter: H
12. Eibenschitz: H
13. Gobschitz: H
14. Göding: H
15. Gurdau: H
16. Hrubschitz: H
17. Iglau: ?
18. Jamnitz: P, SWB?
19. Kostel: H
20. Lundenburg: H
21. Milonitz: H? A? G?
22. Muschau: SWB
23. Napajedl: H
24. Nikolsburg: C? G? S? SWB?
25. Olmütz: ?
26. Pausram: P, H, SWB
27. Pawlowitz, Gr.: H
28. Pollau: SWB
29. Poppitz: H
30. Pulgram: P, H
31. Rakschitz: H
32. Rakwitz: H
33. Rampersdorf: H
34. (Rohrbach: H)
35. Saitz: H
36. Schakwitz: H
37. Seletitz: SWB
38. Tasswitz: SWB
39. Tscheikowitz: H
40. Wessely: H
41. Wratzow: G?, H
42. Znaim: H, SWB, M?

Period III: ca. 1550-1564 ('The Good Times' of Moravian Anabaptism)

1. Alexowitz: H
2. Altenmarkt: H
3. Auspitz: ?
4. Austerlitz: A, C, H, M, S, O
5. Bilowitz: H
6. Bochtitz: H
7. Boretitz: H
8. Damborschitz: H
9. Deckenwitz: H
10. Eibenschitz: A? G? H? M

11. *Gaiwitz: ?
12. Gobschitz: H
13. Herspitz: H
14. Hrubschitz: H
15. Jamnitz: M
16. Kostel: H
17. Krenowitz: H
18. Kreutz: G
19. Lundenburg: H
20. (Mayberg: ?)
21. Muschau: SWB
22. Neumühl: H
23. Niemtschan: H
24. Niemtschitz, Klein (near
    Auspitz): H
25. Niemtschitz, Klein (near
    Kanitz): H
26. Nikolsburg: C, C, H, S, O
27. Pausram: H, SWB
28. Pergen: H

29. Polehraditz: H
30. Poppitz: M, SWB?
31. Pulgram: H
32. Rampersdorf: H
33. (Rohatetz: H)
34. Schadowitz: H
35. Schakwitz: H
36. Seelowitz, Klein: H
37. Skalitz: H
38. Stiegnitz: H
39. (Strassnitz: H)
40. Tasswitz: SWB
41. Teikowitz: H
42. Tracht: H
43. Tscheikowitz: H
44. Urschitz: H
45. Voitelsbrunn: H
46. Watzenowitz: H
47. Wratzow: H
48. Znaim: G? M

Period IV: 1565-1592 ('The Golden Times' of Moravian Anabaptism)

1. Alexowitz: H
2. Altenmarkt: H
3. Auerschitz: SWB
4. Auspitz? SWB?
5. Austerlitz: C, H, M, S, SWB, O
6. Bellowitz: SWB
7. Bilowitz: H
8. Birnbaum: H
9. Bisenz: ?
10. Bochtitz: II
11. Boretitz: H
12. *Bratelsbrunn: H
13. Brünn: H, O?
14. Damborschitz: H
15. Dannowitz, Unter: H
16. Durchlass: SWB
17. Eibenschitz: SWB, H?
18. Eibis: H
19. Frischau: H
20. Gobschitz: H
21. Herspitz: H
22. Hödnitz: SWB
23. Iglau: ?
24. Jaispitz: SWB
25. Jamnitz: H, SWB
26. Kanitz: H
27. Kobelitz: H
28. Kostel: H
29. (Kremsier: H)
30. Krenowitz: H
31. Krepitz: H

32. Kreutz: H
33. Landshut: H
34. (Lenovice: H)
35. Lettonitz: H
36. Lundenburg: H
37. Milotitz: ?
38. (Mödritz: H)
39. Moskowitz: H
40. Muschau: SWB
41. *Naschmeritz?
42. Nasselowitz: H
43. Neslowitz: SWB
44. Neudorf: H
45. Neumühl: H
46. Niemtschan: H
47. *Niemtschitz, Gr.: H? SWB?
48. Niemtschitz, Klein (near
    Kanitz) H
49. Nikolsburg: C, G, H, S, O
50. Nikoltschitz: H
51. Nuslau: H
52. Pausram: H, SWB
53. Pergen: H, SWB?
54. Platsch: H
55. Pohrlitz: H
56. Polehraditz: H
57. Pollau: H
58. Poppitz: H, SWB? S?
59. *Prahlitz: SWB?
60. Pribitz: H
61. Pruschanek: H

62. Pulgram: H
63. Pürschitz: H
64. Qualitz: SWB?
65. Rampersdorf: H
66. Schadowitz: H
67. Schakwitz: H
68. Schenkhof: H
69. Seelowitz, Gr.: H
70. Seelowitz, Kl.: H
71. Skalitz: H
72. Steinitz: H
73. Stiegnitz: H
74. Strassnitz: H
75. Tasswitz: SWB
76. Teikowitz: H
77. Terezin: H
78. Teschau, Klein: M

79. Tracht: H
80. (Trebitsch: ?)
81. Tscheikowitz: H
82. Turnitz: H
83. Urschitz: H
84. Voitelsbrunn: H, SWB?
85. Watzenowitz: H
86. Welka: H
87. Wessely: H
88. (Wischau: H)
89. Wischenau: H
90. Wolframitz: H
91. Wolframskirchen: SWB
92. Wostitz: H
93. Zerotitz: SWB
94. Znaim: M, SWB

Period V: 1593-1622 (Times of War, Destruction and Final Expulsion)

1. Aichhorn (1627): H
2. Alexowitz: H
3. Altenmarkt: H
4. *Aspernitz?
5. Auerschitz: H, SWB
6. Auspitz? SWB?
7. Austerlitz: C, H, M, O
8. Bilowitz: H
9. Birnbaum: H
10. Bochtitz: H
11. Bojanowitz: H?
12. Boretitz: H
13. Budkau: H
14. Damborschitz: H
15. Dannowitz, Unter: H
16. Durchlass: SWB
17. Eibenschitz: SWB, H?
18. Eibis: H
19. (Eisgrub: H)
20. (Freiberg: H)
21. Frischau: H
22. *Gaiwitz?
23. Gaya?
24. Gobschitz: H
25. Göding: H
26. Grünwies: H
27. Gurdau: H?
28. Gurwitz: SWB
29. Herspitz: H
30. Hödnitz: SWB
31. Jaispitz: SWB
32. Jamnitz? SWB?
33. *Jawornik: H
34. Jermeritz: H

35. *Klentnitz: H or SWB
36. Kobelitz: H
37. Kostel: H
38. (Kremsier: H)
39. Krenowitz: H
40. Kreutz: H
41. *Kukvice: H
42. Landshut: H
43. *Lautschitz?
44. (Lenovice: H)
45. Lettonitz: H
46. *Litentschitz?
47. Lundenburg: H
48. *Malspitz?
49. Milotitz: H
50. Mistrin: H
51. Mohelln: H
52. Moskowitz: H
53. Mutenitz: H
54. *Naschmeritz?
55. Nasselowitz: H
56. Neslowitz: SWB
57. Neudorf: H
58. Neumühl: H
59. Niemtschan: H
60. Niemtschitz, Klein (Kanitz): H
61. Nikolsburg. H, SWB?
62. Nikoltschitz: H
63. Nuslau: H
64. Pausram: H, SWB
65. Plumluvky: H
66. Podax: H
67. Pohrlitz: H
68. Polehraditz: H

69. Poppitz: H, SWB?
70. Pribitz: H
71. (Prittlach: H)
72. (Prossnitz: H)
73. Pruschanek: H
74. Pürschitz: H
75. Rampersdorf: H
76. Raschowitz: H? M?
77. Schabschitz: H
78. Schadowitz: H
79. Schakwitz: H
80. Seelowitz, Gr.: H
81. Seelowitz, Kl.: H
82. Skalitz: H
83. Steinitz: H
84. Stiegnitz: H
85. Strassnitz: H
86. *Strilek?
87. Swatoborschitz?
88. Swetlau: H

89. Tasswitz: SWB
90. Teikowitz: H
91. Teinitz: H
92. Terezin: H
93. Tracht: H
94. Tscheikowitz: H
95. Tscheitsch: H
96. Tschermakowitz: H
97. Turnitz: H
98. Ung. Ostra: H
99. Urschitz: H
100. Watzenowitz: H
101. Weisstätten: H
102. Welka: H
103. Wessely: H
104. Wischenau: H
105. Wolframskirchen: SWB
106. Wostitz: H
107. Zerotitz: SWB
108. Znaim: SWB

Na Dating Available for the Following Places:

1. *Biharschowitz: H?
2. *Birtnitz: H?
3. *Braumowitz: H?
4. *Braunseifen: ?
5. *Eulenberg: ?
6. *Harasy: H?
7. *Kamenetz: H
8. *Klobouk: ?

9. Kromau, Mähr.: H
10. *Langendorf: ?
11. *Mikultschitz: G?
12. *Morkuwetz: H?
13. *Popelin: ?
14. *Posoritz: ?
15. *Sirowin: ?

List D: Group Lists

Explanatory Note:

( ) A place in brackets: there was no Anabaptist settlement here. Contact with the local population was occasioned only by short term work contracts (e.g. installation of a clock) or by agricultural work on properties located here but owned by the colony in a neighbouring community.

* An asterisk before the name of a place: either the sources establishing evidence of Anabaptist settlement, or their interpretation with respect to a particular group, are uncertain.

I. Austerlitz Brethren
1. Austerlitz
2. Butschowitz
3. *Eibenschitz
4. *Milonitz

II. Cornelians (cf. Pilgramites)
1. Austerlitz
2. Nikolsburg

III. Gabrielites
1. Bisenz
2. Butschowitz

3. *Eibenschitz
4. Jermeritz (Jarohnewitz)
5. Kreutz
6. *Mikultschitz
7. *Milonitz
8. Nikolsburg
9. Rossitz
10. Wratzow
11. *Znaim

IV. Hutterites
1. Aichhorn
2. Alexowitz

3. Altenmarkt
4. Auerschitz
5. Auspitz
6. Austerlitz
7. *Biharschowitz
8. Bilowitz
9. Birnbaum
10. Bisenz
11. Bochtitz
12. Bohuslawitz
13. *(Bojanowitz)
14. Boretitz
15. *Bratelsbrunn
16. *Braumowitz
17. (Brünn)
18. Budkau
19. Butschowitz
20. Damborschitz
21. Dannowitz, Unter
22. Deckenwitz
23. Eibenschitz
24. Eibis
25. (Eisgrub)
26. (Freiberg)
27. Frischau
28. Gobschitz
29. Göding
30. Grünwies
31. Gurdau
32. *Harasy
33. Herspitz
34. Hrubschitz
35. Jamnitz
36. *Jawornik
37. Jermeritz
38. *Kamenetz
39. Kanitz
40. *Klentnitz
41. *Klobouk
42. Kobelitz
43. Kostel
44. (Kremsier)
45. Krenowitz
46. Krepitz
47. Kreutz
48. Kromau, Mähr.
49. *Kukvice
50. Landshut
51. *Langendorf
52. (Lenovice)
53. Lettonitz
54. Lundenburg
55. *Milonitz

56. Milotitz
57. Mistrin
58. (Mödritz)
59. Mohelln
60. *Morkuwetz
61. Moskowitz
62. Mutenitz
63. Napajedl
64. Nasselowitz
65. Neudorf
66. Neumühl
67. Niemtschan
68. Niemtschitz, Gross
69. Niemtschitz, Kl. (Auspitz)
70. Niemtschitz, Kl. (Kanitz)
71. Nikolsburg
72. Nikoltschitz
73. Nuslau
74. Pausram
75. Pawlowitz, Gross
76. Pergen
77. Platsch
78. Plumluvky
79. Podax
80. Pohrlitz
81. Polehraditz
82. Pollau
83. Poppitz
84. Pribitz
85. (Prittlach)
86. (Prossnitz)
87. Pruschanek
88. Pulgram
89. Pürschitz
90. Rakschitz
91. Rakwitz
92. Rampersdorf
93. *Raschowitz
94. (Rohatetz)
95. (Rohrbach)
96. Saitz
97. Schabschitz
98. Schadowitz
99. Schakwitz
100. Schenkhof
101. Seelowitz, Gross
102. Seelowitz, Klein
103. Skalitz
104. (Starnitz)
105. Steinitz
106. Steurowitz, Gross
107. Stiegnitz
108. Strassnitz

109. Swetlau
110. Teikowitz
111. Teinitz
112. Terezin
113. Tracht
114. Tscheitsch
115. Tschermakowitz
116. Turnitz
117. Ung. Ostra
118. Urschitz
119. Voitelsbrunn
120. Watzenowitz
121. Weisstätten
122. Welka
123. Wessely
124. (Wischau)
125. Wischenau
126. Wolframitz
127. Wostitz
128. Wratzow

V. *Philippites*
1. Auspitz
2. Jamnitz
3. Pausram
4. Pulgram
5. Rossitz

VI. *Pilgramites*
(Marbeck Fellowship)
1. Austerlitz
2. Eibenschitz
3. Jamnitz & "am Wald"
4. Poppitz & "Um den Stein"
5. *Raschowitz
6. Teschau, Klein
7. Znaim

VII. *Sabbatarians*
1. Austerlitz
2. Nikolsburg
3. *Poppitz

VIII. *Schwertler*
(followers of Hubmaier),
up to ca. 1535
1. Brünn
2. *Eibenschitz
3. *Klentnitz
4. Nikolsburg
5. Pergen
6. Pollau
7. Tracht

8. Voitelsbrunn
9. Wisternitz

IX. *Stäbler*
(→ Austerlitz Brethren and Hutterites)
1. Austerlitz
2. (Bogenitz)
3. Brünn
4. *Eibenschitz
5. Neuwitzsch
6. Nikolsburg
7. Pergen
8. Pollau

X. *Swiss Brethren*
1. Auerschitz
2. *Auspitz
3. Austerlitz
4. Bellowitz
5. Durchlass
6. Eibenschitz
7. Gurwitz
8. Hödnitz
9. Jaispitz
10. Jamnitz
11. *Klentnitz
12. Muschau
13. Neslowitz
14. *Niemtschitz, Gr.
15. Nikolsburg
16. Pausram
17. Pergen
18. Pollau
19. *Poppitz
20. *Prahlitz
21. Qualitz
22. Seletitz
23. Tasswitz
24. Urbau
25. *Voitelsbrunn
26. *Wisternitz
27. Wolframskirchen
28. Zerotitz
29. Znaim

XI. *Other or non-specified groups*
1. Aspernitz
2. Austerlitz
3. *Birtnitz
4. Bisenz
5. *Braunseifen
6. Brünn
7. *Budwitz

8.	Datschitz	18.	*Naschmeritz
9.	*Eulenberg	19.	Nikolsburg
10.	*Gaiwitz	20.	Olmütz
11.	Gaya	21.	*Popelin
12.	Iglau	22.	*Posoritz
13.	Lautschitz	23.	*Sirowin
14.	*Litentschitz	24.	*Strilek
15.	*Malspitz	25.	Swatoborschitz
16.	(Mayberg)	26.	(Trebitsch)
17.	*Mikultschitz	27.	Znaim

List E: Settlements in German or Partially German Communities

For explanation of brackets and asterisks, see List D.

I. *Settlements in German-speaking communities:*

1.	Auspitz	15.	Nikolsburg
*2.	Bratelsbrunn	16.	Pausram
3.	Dannowitz, Unter	17.	Pergen
4.	(Eisgrub)	*18.	Prahlitz
5.	Frischau	19.	Pulgram
6.	Gobschitz	20.	Saitz
7.	Gurdau	21.	Schakwitz
8.	Gurwitz	22.	Steurowitz, Gross
*9.	Klentnitz	23.	Stiegnitz
10.	Moskowitz	24.	Tracht
11.	Muschau	25.	Voitelsbrunn
12.	Nasmeritz	26.	Wolframitz
13.	Neumühl	27.	Wostitz
14.	Niemtschitz, Klein (near Kanitz)	28.	Znaim

To these should probably be added the following communities (we were unable to verify their ethnic composition):

In North Moravia:

*29.	Braunseifen	35.	Jaispitz
*30.	Eulenberg	36.	Neslowitz
*31.	Langendorf	37.	Seletitz
	Around Znaim:	38.	Tasswitz
32.	Durchlass	39.	Urbau
*33.	Gaiwitz	40.	Zerotitz
34.	Hödnitz		(Nos. 32-40 were settlements of the Swiss Brethren)

II. *Settlements in communities with a German majority:*

1.	Auerschitz	6.	Niemtschitz, Gross
2.	Brünn	7.	Pollau
3.	Dannowitz, Ober	8.	Poppitz
4.	Iglau	9.	(Prittlach)
5.	Olmütz		

III. *Settlements in communities with a German minority:*

1.	Austerlitz	5.	Nuslau
2.	Eibenschitz	6.	Pohrlitz
*3.	Lautschitz	7.	Rakwitz
4.	Malspitz		

These lists are based on a maximum allowance for the German ethnic element in South Moravia in the 16th and early 17th century. In the case of several localities exact classification was most difficult.[5]

2. TOPOGRAPHY OF THE *UNITAS FRATRUM* IN MORAVIA

Earlier in this chapter,[6] we have discussed the topographical study of the *Unitas Fratrum* in Moravia which was published by Hrejsa in 1937. In spite of the impressive collection of source materials, Hrejsa did not attempt a clear chronological classification of the congregations and settlements such as we have done for the Anabaptist topography.

He did, however, group the localities into the following categories:

I. Independent congregations with a resident pastor.
II. Smaller or branch congregations with regular services but usually without a resident pastor.
III. Localities with only a few Czech Brethren who were under pastoral care elsewhere.

For a number of places which had been reported as congregations or settlements of Czech Brethren by other authors, Hrejsa found no supporting evidence in the sources. In our list, such places will be designated with two asterisks.

On Hrejsa's map, each place is marked in accordance with these categories.[7] Furthermore, special lists arranged by the four categories, are printed in Hrejsa's concluding analysis.[8]

We reproduce Hrejsa's list with only a few minor changes. One asterisk in front of the number designates localities where the evidence of the sources is uncertain. The local names in brackets indicate the nearest larger town or city.

Towards the end of the sixteenth century, ministers of the Unity were placed in charge of the Utraquist parish churches in the following six localities: Kynice, Měrovice, Písek, Pohořelice, Radostice and Slavíkovice. In our list, these places bear the note 'Parish Church'. German-speaking congregations and groups of German-speaking Brethren are also marked in our list.

---

[5] Cf. Zeman, 1966, 15, n. 35.
[6] See footnotes 1 and 2 above.
[7] Hrejsa, B, 24 f. Actually Hrejsa employed six different markings. They can be reduced to the four basic categories.
[8] Hrejsa, B, 102 ff. There are a few discrepancies between the lists and the map.

For the purpose of our comparative study, we have divided the list into two sections: the one for South Moravia, i.e. the geographical area where nearly all Anabaptist settlements were located, and the other for North Moravia. The dividing line is based entirely on the topographical spread of Moravian Anabaptism and is not derived from the usual geographical division of Moravia into a southern and a northern part.

List F: Unitas Fratrum in South Moravia

The area of Anabaptist settlement, south of the line connecting the cities of Jihlava (Iglau), Brno (Brünn), Kroměříž (Kremsier), Napajedla (Napajedl) and Uherský Brod (Ungarisch Brod).

1. Arklebov (Ždánice), II
2. Bílovice, Velké (Podivín), II
3. Biskupice, Biskoupky (Mor. Krumlov), III
4. Blatnice, Velká (Uher. Ostroh), III
5. Boršov (Kyjov), III
6. Brankovice (Vyškov), I
7. Brno, III
8. Broumovice, Brumovice (Hustopeč), I
9. Březník (Náměšť), III
10. Březolupy (Napajedla), II
*11. Budějovice Moravské, III
12. Budišov (Třebíč), II
13. Budkov (Mor. Budějovice), II
14. Buchlovice (Uher. Hradiště), I
15. Bzenec (Kyjov), I
16. Cetechovice (Zdounky), I
17. Dačice, I
**18. Dalešice (Mor. Krumlov)
**19. Dambořice (Kyjov)
20. Dobročkovice (Vyškov), II
21. Domčice (Znojmo), II
22. Dražov(ice) (Ždánice), II
23. Drnovice (Vyškov), I
24. Drslavice (Uher. Brod), II
25. Dubenky Horní (Dačice), III
26. Dunajovice Horní (Znojmo), I (Czech and German congregation)
27. Hartvíkovice (Náměšť), III
28. Havřice (Uher. Brod), III
29. Heršpice (Slavkov), I
30. Hodonín, I
31. Hostěhrádky (Klobouky), I
32. Hrušky (Břeclav), II

*33. Hustopeče, II (in the Czech suburb Böhmdorf?)
34. Ivančice, I (Czech and German congregation)
35. Jaroměřice (Mor. Budějovice), III
36. Javorník (Strážnice), I
**37. Jemnice (Dačice)
**38. Jeřice (Miroslav)
39. Jihlava, III
40. Kobylí (Hustopeč), I
41. Kojátky (Slavkov), III
42. Koněšín (Náměšť), III
43. Kostice (Břeclav), III
44. Kounice (Ivančice), I
45. Kožišice (Vyškov), II
46. Kralice (Náměšť), I
**47. Krasonice (Jemnice)
**48. Krokočín (Náměšť)
49. Kroměříž, III
50. Krumlov Moravský, II
51. Krumvíř (Hustopeče), III
*52. Křtěnice (Mor. Krumlov), III
53. Kunovice (Uher. Hradiště), II
54. Kyjov, I
55. Kynice (Mor. Krumlov): Parish Church
**56. Lanžhot (Břeclav)
**57. Letonice (Slavkov)
*58. Lhota Červená (Třebíč), I
59. Lideřovice (Strážnice), II
60. Lipov (Strážnice), II
61. Mikulčice (Hodonín), II
*62. Milonice (Bučovice), I
63. Miroslav (Mor. Krumlov), III
**64. Mladenovice (Jemnice)
65. Mohelno (Náměšť), I

66. Moravany (Kyjov), I
67. Morkovice (Kroměříž), II or III
68. Mutěnice (Hodonín), I
**69. Myslibořice (Mor. Krumlov)
70. Naloučany (Náměšť), III
71. Náměšť (Třebíč), I
72. Napajedla, I
73. Násedlovice (Ždánice), III
74. Nečice (Kyjov), II
75. Němeč Dolní (Uher. Hradiště), I
76. Nenkovice (Ždánice), III
77. Nivnice (Uher. Brod), I
78. Nosislav (Židlochovice), III
79. Oslavany (Ivančice), III
80. Pačlavice (Zdounky), II
81. Pavlovice Velké (Hustopeče), II
82. Petrov (Strážnice), II
83. Písek (Uher. Ostroh): Parish Church
84. Podivín (Hodonín), I
85. Pohořclice (Mikulov): Parish Church (Czech and German)
*86. Popovice (location uncertain), III
87. Přibice (Židlochovice), I or II
88. Radějov (Strážnice), II
89. Radostice (Brno), I
90. Rašovice (Slavkov), III
91. Rataje (Kroměříž), I
92. Ratiškovice (Hodonín), II
93. Rosice (Ivančice), I
94. Roštín (Zdounky), III
95. Rousinov (Slavkov), III
**96. Slatina (location uncertain)
97. Slavíkovice (Jemnice): Parish Church
98. Slavkov, I

99. Sležany, Slížany (Kroměříž), I
100. Sobůlky (Kyjov), III
101. Starč (Třebíč), III
102. Stavěšice (Ždánice), II
103. Strážnice, I
*104. Střílky (Zdounky), II
105. Šimice, Šumice (Pohořelice), III
*106. Švábenice (Vyškov), III
107. Tasov (Strážnice), II
*108. Tavíkovice (Mor. Krumlov): probably only a chaplain in the local castle
**109. Teplice Petrovská (Strážnice)
110. Troubsko (Rosice), III
111. Třebíč, I
112. Uherské Hradiště, III
113. Uherský Brod, I
114. Valč (Mor. Krumlov), I
115. Valtinov (Dačice), II
116. Vanč (Náměšť), III
117. Velká (Strážnice), I
118. Veselí (Uher. Hradiště), I
119. Věteřov (Ždánice), III
120. Vícenice (Náměšť), III
121. Vlčnov (Uher. Brod), II
122. Vrbka, Hr. (Strážnice), II
123. Výmyslice (Mor. Krumlov), III
124. Zdounky (Kroměříž), I
125. Ždánice (Kyjov), I
*126. Želetice (near Znojmo or Ždánice?), II
127. Žeravice (Kyjov), I
128. Žerotice (Znojmo), III (probably only in the local castle)
*129. Židenice (Brno), III
130. Židlochovice (Hustopeče), I

List G: Unitas Fratrum in North Moravia

1. Bezouchov (Bystřice pod Hostýnem), I
**2. Bludov (Šumperk)
3. Bojkovice (Uher. Brod), I
4. Borovnice (Jimramov), III
5. Boršice (Uher. Ostroh), II
6. Boskovice (Brno), I
7. Brumov (Valašské Klobouky), III
8. Březová (Nivnice), III

9. Bystřice nad Perštýnem, I
**10. Bystřice pod Hostýnem
11. Byteš (Bíteš) Velká (Velké Meziříčí), I
12. Crhov (Olešnice), II
13. Čekyně (Přerov), III
14. Čelechovice (Kokory), III
15. Dobromělice (Kojetín), I
16. Doubravice (Boskovice), I
**17. Doubravník (Tišňov)

18. Drahotuše (Hranice), I
19. Drnovice (Vyškov), I
20. Dřevohostice (Bystřice pod Hostýnem), I
21. Fryšták (Zlín), I
**22. Fryštát ve Slezsku
23. Fulnek: German congregation, I
24. Gerlichov-Jerlochovice (Gerlsdorf near Fulnek): German, III
25. Hodslavice (Nový Jičín), III
26. Holešov (Kroměříž), I
27. Hranice, I
28. Hrobice (Vizovice), I
29. Hulín (Kroměříž), II
30. Hustopeče (Hranice), III
31. Chropyň (Kroměříž), I
32. Chřenovice (Kojetín), III
**33. Iváň (Tovačov)
34. Ivanovice (Brno), I
35. Jaroměřice (village near Jevíčko), I
36. Jestřabí (Jastersdorf near Fulnek): German, III
**37. Jevíčko (Mor. Třebová)
38. Jičín Nový, I
**39. Jičín Starý
40. Kletné (Klötten, Klithen near Suchdol): German, III
41. Kojetín, I
42. Kokory (Přerov), II
43. Količín (Holešov), II
44. Komna (Uher. Brod), II
45. Kostelec (Prostějov), II
46. Kostelec (Holešov), II
47. Krásno (Valašské Meziříčí), I Krumpach — a suburb of Zábřeh (see Zábřeh)
48. Křetín (Kunštát), III
49. Křižanov (Vel. Meziříčí), I
50. Kujavy (Klantendorf near Fulnek): German, III
51. Kunštát (Boskovice), II
52. Kunvald (Kunewald near Nový Jičín). German, III
53. Kvasice (Napajedla), III
*54. Kvítkovice (Napajedla), I
55. Lechotice (Holešov), II
56. Letovice (Boskovice), I
57. Lipník, I
**58. Lípovec (Blánsko)
59. Liš(t)ná (Dřevohostice), I

**60. Litovel
61. Lomnice (Tišnov), I
62. Losín Velký (Gross Ullersdorf near Šumperk): German, II
63. Lukovec (Holešov), I
64. Lysice (Kunštát), III
65. Malenovice (Napajedla), I
66. Měrovice (Kojetín): Parish Church
67. Město Nové na Moravě, I
68. Meziříčí Valašské, III
**69. Meziříčí Velké
70. Meziřícko (Litovel), II
71. Místek, I
72. Mohelnice (Zábřeh): German, III
73. Moravec (Nové Město na Moravě), I
74. Mos(t)kovice (Plumlov), III
75. Myslošovice (Holešov), III
*76. Náměšť (Olomouc), III
77. Nýdek (Hranice), III
78. Olešnice (Kunštát), I
79. Olomouc, III (also a joint German congregation with the Reformed in 1620)
80. Olšovec (Hranice), II
81. Parešovice (Hranice), III
82. Paskov (Místek), I
83. Pavlovice nad Bečvou (Přerov), III
84. Petřvaldík (Nový Jičín), II
85. Petřvald Veliký (Nový Jičín), III
86. Plumlov (Prostějov), I
87. Prostějov, I
88. Prusenovice (Holešov), I
**89. Pržno (Vsetín)
90. Předmostí (Přerov), III
91. Přerov, I
*92. Račice (Vyškov), I
**93. Radostín (Velké Meziříčí)
**94. Rouštka (Vsetín)
95. Rychaltice (Místek), II
96. Řečkovice (Brno), III
97. Sebranice (Kunštát), III
98. Soběchleby (Lipník), III
99. Stachovice (Stechenwald near Fulnek): German, III
100. Stichovice (Prostějov), II
*101. Stražkov (Bystřice nad Perštýnem), III
**102. Strumeň (Bílsko ve Slezsku)

103. Střítež nad Bečvou (Valaš.
   Meziříčí), I
*104. Studénky (Zábřeh): German,
   II
105. Suchdol (Fulnek): German,
   II
106. Šternberk, I
**107. Teplice Šumperská (Losín)
**108. Tišňov (Brno)
**109. Tlumačov (Uher. Hradiště)
110. Tovačov, I
111. Trnávka (Příbor), II
112. Troub(k)y (Přerov), II
113. Vanovice (Boskovice), III
114. Věrovany (Tovačov)

*115. Vídeň (Velké Meziříčí): a
   branch of the German congregation at Ivančice?, II
*116. Vizovice (Zlín), III
117. Vlachovice (Valaš.
   Klobouky), I
118. Vrbětice (Uher. Brod), III
119. Vsetín, III
120. Zábřeh: Czech and German
   congregation, I
121. Záhliní(ce) (Kroměříž), II
122. Záhorovice (Uher. Brod), I
123. Zlín (now Gottwaldov), I
124. Životice (Seitendorf near
   Fulnek): German, III

3. RESIDENTIAL OPPORTUNITIES FOR CONTACT BETWEEN THE
ANABAPTISTS AND THE *UNITAS FRATRUM* IN MORAVIA

The preceding topographical research makes it possible to compile
a list of places in Moravia where both an Anabaptist group and
members of the Unity lived together for some time. The following
list includes concise information on the dates and types of the respective groups. For further details, the preceding lists should be
consulted.

The abbreviations used in the following list are explained in the
introduction to our lists C and F. The chronological data and other
information about the congregations of the Unity are based on
HREJSA B.

*List H: Localities with recorded Anabaptist and
Czech Brethren Settlements*

Anabaptists

Unitas Fratrum

1. *Bílovice Velké*
   H: 1545-1605, 1614-1622

   II (branch congregation of Ždánice):
   (before) 1536-1624

2. *Brno:* German majority
   ?: 1527-1528 (congregation)
   ca. 1570-ca. 1600: Individuals?
   Hutterite occupational contacts.

   III (records only of German members in 1587 and 1620 when joint
   services for the German Reformed
   and Unity were planned)

3. *Brumovice, Broumovice*
   * H: no dates

   I: second half of the century and up
   to 1624

Anabaptists	*Unitas Fratrum*
4. *Budějovice Moravské* * H: 1540 (a settlement is doubt- ful)	* III: no dates
5. *Budkov* H: 1597-1602, probably resettled before 1619	II: (before) 1563-until? (1624?)
6. *Bzenec* G: 1535-? (1545?) H: 1545-1547 (and later?) ?: 1565: disputation between Mar- tin Behem of B. (Anab.) and Peter Herbert (Unity)	I: source references only from 1594 and 1601; probably an earlier con- gregation or group
7. *Dačice* ?: 1528	I: 1507-1624
8. *Dambořice* H: 1550-1622	**: Hrejsa rejects the claim by some authors that there was a congrega- tion here
9. *Dunajovice Horní:* German majority **: a mistaken localization rejected in our List A	I: 1531-1622 Czech and German services
10. *Heršpice* H: 1561-1622 Some of the Hutterite household- ers had Slavic names. *Note:* There was no other church in the town. A great opportunity for personal contacts	I: 1565-1622
11. *Hodonín* H: 1545-1547, 1593-1622	I: (before) 1564-1624
12. *Hrušky* H: 1587 (or earlier)-1605	II: (before) 1581-1624
13. *Hustopeče:* German community P: 1529-1535 H: 1531-1535, 1536-1540 and probably also later ?: a non-Hutterite group 1536- 1618? 1543: a colloquy between "the Lutherans, Picards and Anabap- tists"	* II: a Czech congregation in the Czech suburb Böhmdorf

Anabaptists   *Unitas Fratrum*

14. *Ivančice:* German minority
Early congregation: 1526-1530
(1535?)
H: 1545-1547 (and a colony in
near Alexowitz, 1552-1622)
A? G? 1559
M: 1553-1559 (probably also earlier and later'
SWB: ?-1622
There probably was a continuing
group from the original congregation to the Marbeck fellowship and
the Swiss Brethren.

I: (before) 1498-1622; Czech and
German congregation; the main center of the Unity in Moravia from
the arrival of Jan Blahoslav at I.
(1558).
Colloquy with Balthasar Tischler in
1559.

15. *Javorník*
* Perhaps a small Hutterite settlement around 1610

I: ca. 1495-1624

16. *Jemnice*
P: before 1535
M: before and after 1553
SWB: ca. 1535-1622? (identical
with M?)
H: around 1589 (on the domain
of J.)

**: Hrejsa rejects the claim by some
authors that there were Czech Brethren in J.

17. *Jihlava:* German majority
a small group around 1528, 1536 f.
and 1592, perhaps also at other
times

III: a few members belonging to the
congregation in Třebíč

18. *Kobylí*
H: 1589-1605

I: ca. 1560-1624

19. *Kounice, Dolní*
H: ca. 1575-ca. 1590, perhaps also
later

I: (before) 1560-1624

20. *Kroměříž*
H: only work contracts, in the
Bishop's castle and mill, 1584,
1599, 1604; perhaps also a lease
of the mill in 1584

III: a few members belonging to the
congregation in Rataje (1577)

21. *Krumlov, Moravský*
H: a colony in Rakšice on the out-
skirts of K. (1545-1547), perhaps
also individual Anabaptists in town

II: a branch congregation of Ivančice (sources only ca. 1570). Jan
Blahoslav died here when on a visit
on Nov. 24, 1571.

22. *Krumvíř*
H: a meierhof, ca. 1595-1605, perhaps also later

III: members belonged to the congregation in Brumovice or Kobylí
(only source: 1581)

Anabaptists	Unitas Fratrum
23. *Křtěnice:* German village H: ca. 1560-1622	* III: end of the 16th century
24. *Kyjov* ?: ca. 1590 (isolated brethren, or a small Hutterite group?)	I: 1543-1579, later probably only II or III. On April 12, 1589, Bishop Stanislav Pavlovský of Olomouc wrote to the citizens of K. not to allow further growth of the Brethren nor to tolerate their minister in the city. On July 1, 1589 a tract against the Anabaptists was written or copied here.
25. *Lanžhot* H: 1565-1619	**: Hrejsa rejects the claim of one author that there was a congregation here.
26. *Letonice* H: 1589-1620	**: no Czech Brethren here. The sources referring to the Hutterites had been applied wrongly by some authors to the Unity.
27. *Mikulčice* *: possibly a small non-Hutterite group (no dates)	II: ca. 1585-1619 (1624)
28. *Milonice* H? A? G? second half of the century?	I: end of the century?
29. *Mohelno* H: staff for a new mill in 1614	I: ca. 1590-1625
30. *Morkovice* **: a mistaken localization rejected in our List A	II or III: 1536-1568 (and probably later)
31. *Mutěnice* H: 1593-1618, perhaps longer	I: 1503-1594 (and later?)
32. *Napajedla* H: 1545-1546	I: 1505-1620 ff.
33. *Násedlovice* H: meierhof and properties ca. 1570-1616 (1622)	III: two members of the congregation in Ždánice lived here in 1611
34. *Nosislav:* German minority H: 1583-1622	III: no dates

Anabaptists	*Unitas Fratrum*
35. *Olomouc:* German majority; executions in 1528 and 1538; probably secret Anabaptists from time to time	III: records only from 1620 when joint German services for the Reformed and the Unity were held.
36. *Pavlovice, Velké* H: 1545-1547	II: 1581-1624
37. *Podivín* H: 1536-1547, ca. 1555-1622	I: (not later than) 1533-1626
38. *Pohořelice:* German minority H: 1581-1622	The congregation at Ivančice provided Czech and German ministers (for services and pastoral work) for the local parish church in 1581. The arrangement lasted probably no more than several years (cf. "Pohrlitz", List A).
39. *Prostějov* one (former?) Hutterite is reported living at P. in 1607	I: 1494-1625
40. *Přibice* H: 1565-1622	I or II: at least in the 17th century
41. *Rašovice* H or M: only source 1597	III: only source, prior to 1572
42. *Rosice* G: 1527-1535/1536 P: 1527-1529 H: after 1537? (doubtful)	I: (after) 1550-1625 (cf. also Chapter IV note 195)
43. *Slavkov* ST: 1528 ff. A: 1531-1537? H: 1537/1538-1622 C and M: ca. 1540-1622 S and SWB: 1567	I: 1510-1623
44. *Strážnice* H: probably a colony in the latter part of the century and up to 1620	I: 1495-1628
45. *Střílky* * H? no dates	* II: no dates
46. *Tavíkovice* H: (1558?) 1567-1622	* probably only a chaplain for the local castle, prior to 1625

47. *Třebíč*
    *: No Anabaptists are reported by   I: ca. 1490-1628
    the sources, except an Italian ref-
    ugee who joined the *Unitas* but
    was suspected of Anabaptism.

48. *Velká*
    H: 1595 and "many years before",   I: ca. 1490-ca. 1624
    also perhaps in the early 17th cen-
    tury

49. *Veselí*
    H: 1545-1547 and (before) 1575-   I: ca. 1500-ca. 1624
    1621

50. *Výmyslice*
    **: a mistaken localization   * III: end of 16th century

51. *Ždánice*
    H: ca. 1550-1622   I: (before) 1540-1624

52. *Želetice:* German community?
    SWB: from the 1540's till 1622?   * II: second half of century (the
                                             localization is ambiguous; cf. List F)

53. *Žerotice:* German community?
    SWB: towards the end of the cen-   III: probably only in the local castle
    tury and until 1613 (or 1622)   (only source: 1588)

54. *Židlochovice*
    H: possibly from 1560's, certainly   I: early 16th century-1624
    in 1590's, perhaps also in the early
    17th century

4. SUMMARY AND INTERPRETATION OF TOPOGRAPHICAL LISTS

An analysis and comparison of the preceding eight lists (A to H) makes it possible to draw the following conclusions.

a. *Geographical Distribution*

For reasons which we have been unable to discover [9] the Anabaptist refugees settled in an area which we have designated as South Moravia. It can be described as a wide belt spread along the Austrian

---

[9]   Even Kuhn, II, 309-333 who studied the Hutterite settlement in Moravia within the wider geographical and economical context of the German emigrations to the east, did not suggest any explanation. A number of the earlier Anabaptist refugees entered Moravia from the north (Silesia) and yet settled in South Moravia.

border and located south of an imaginary line which connects the Moravian cities of Jihlava (Iglau), Brno (Brünn), Kroměříž (Kremsier), Napajedla (Napajedl) and Uherský Brod (Ungarisch Brod). In surface area, it represents only about one third of Moravia.

There were no real Anabaptist settlements north of the outlined imaginary boundary line. Of the seven 'northern' places included in our List A, three (Braunseifen, Eulenberg and Langendorf) are based on uncertain sources, three represent only occupational or occasional contacts (Freiberg, Prossnitz and Olmütz) and one (Aichhorn) became a hiding place after nearly all Anabaptists had left the margraviate.

As for the geographical distribution of the particular Anabaptist groups (List D) the Hutterite settlements, because of their numerical preponderance alone, were spread across the whole area. A look at a map of their colonies and settlements will suggest, however, that these were not distributed equally. The choice of settlement depended to a large extent on the attitudes exhibited and conditions set by the owners of each particular domain. Generally speaking, the Hutterite households were concentrated more in the eastern part of South Moravia. There were only a few to the north and east of Znojmo (Znaim) and with one or two exceptions (Budkau, Jamnitz) none to the west of Znojmo. By contrast, the settlements of the Swiss Brethren were found mostly in the area around Znojmo. Another area of their concentration seems to have been the oldest area of Anabaptist settlement around Mikulov (Nikolsburg). The Gabrielites, the Philippites and the Pilgramites were scattered but tended more towards the western half of South Moravia.

The congregations and groups of the *Unitas Fratrum* were divided almost equally between the southern and northern parts of Moravia (in our use of the terms).[10] This means, however, that in relation to the geographical area, the Unity was numerically stronger in the southern part. Its leading and largest congregations were in the south, especially during the second half of the sixteenth century.[11]

If one compares the number of places with recorded Anabaptist residence and the number of recorded settlements of the Unity in the

---

[10] Cf. List F: 130 places (minus 12 rejected by Hrejsa) and List G: 124 places (minus 17 rejected by Hrejsa).

[11] E.g., Dačice, Ivančice, Podivín, Slavkov, Sležany, Strážnice, Třebíč, Uh. Brod, Ždánice, Žeravice, Židlochovice. There were, of course, old and important congregations in the northern part as well, e.g. Fulnek, Hranice, Lipník, Přerov, Tovačov.

same area (South Moravia) the ratio is about 4:3 in favour of the Anabaptists.[12]

b. *Chronological Distribution*

Our "Combined Chronological and Group Lists" (List C) enable us to trace the growth of Moravian Anabaptism in five successive periods.

The periodization is not an artificial one. It is inherent in the history of Moravian Anabaptism and is derived primarily from varying degrees of religious toleration displayed by the Habsburg rulers of Moravia. The first (1535 f.) and second (1547 f.) main persecutions, the death of king Ferdinand (1564) and the beginning of the turbulent times (1593) leading to the final destruction and expulsion (1622) have set the milestones for Anabaptist history in Moravia. The periods are reflected clearly in the Hutterite chronicles and their meaningful references to 'The Good Times' (ca. 1550-1564) and 'The Golden Times' (1565-1592).

The story of the 'Anabaptist Century' in Moravia could hardly be told more vividly than in terms of the following topographical statistics.[13]

1526-1535 : 25 (2 A, 2 G, 4 H, 4 P, 9 SR, 7 ST, 2 SWB)
1536-1547 : 41 (3 A, 5 G, 32 H, 3 P, 2 M, 8 SWB)
1550-1564 : 45 (2 A, 4 G, 37 H, 5 M, 4 SWB)
1565-1592 : 88 (2 C, 1 G, 70 H, 3 M, 22 SWB)
1593-1622 : 102 (1 C, 82 H, 2 M, 17 SWB)

The Anabaptist movement in Moravia as a whole had three successive beginnings: 1526 ff., 1536 ff. and 1550 ff. In 1535 and again in 1547, the brethren were ordered to leave the country and most of their settlements were abandoned. After a short time, the persecution subsided and the households or congregations were reestablished, either in the same places, or elsewhere. In addition, there were many interruptions of residence caused by specific local conditions.

If one were to depict the growth of Moravian Anabaptism with a graph, it would not show as an uninterrupted ascending line but

[12]   Anabaptists: 164 (180 minus 7 located in the northern area and minus 9 rejected in our List A). Unity: 118 (List F; cf. footnote 10 above).

[13]   The first number is the total number of settlements for each period in our List C, reduced by the number of places which are printed in brackets (no permanent settlement). The following numbers represent the total for each Anabaptist group in the same period (see explanation of abbreviations at List C). None of these figures can be treated as exact statistics. However, they can serve as an index of growth.

instead would resemble three rising steps with alternate drops to near zero.

During the first decade (1526-1535), Anabaptism spread from Mikulov to 24 other localities with several types of congregations, about a third of them in the Hubmaier tradition (*Schwertler*).

In the second decade (1536-1547), the total number rose from near zero to about 40, i.e., an increase of slightly more than 50 per cent. The Hutterites became the largest group (32) although the combined non-communitarian groups were still strongly represented (21).

The second persecution dealt a death blow to the non-communitarian Anabaptists. With their lack of centralized organization they were not as well prepared as were the Hutterites to gather again their dispersed followers and to begin anew. In the subsequent decade and a half (1550-1564) the Hutterites succeeded in regaining their former strength and even increased it slightly (to 37) whereas the non-Hutterite groups, with the exception of the Marbeck fellowship, seem to have dwindled in size and significance (10 localities, plus 5 or 7 places with Pilgramite congregations).

The fastest growth came during the three decades of 'The Golden Times'. The total number of Anabaptist settlements increased twofold (around 90). The Hutterites doubled their strength in terms of geographical spread. But so did also the non-Hutterite groups. While the Austerlitz Brethren, the Gabrielites and the Philippites practically disappeared, the Swiss Brethren displayed a phenomenal expansion (from 4 to 22 localities). It is obvious that many of the refugees arriving in Moravia from different parts of Germany and Switzerland in the latter part of the century did not join the Hutterite colonies but rather associated themselves with the non-communitarian Anabaptist congregations.[14]

There was very little or no growth during the last period (1593-1622). As in previous times of turmoil, so now again the Hutterites were able to withstand crises. When one household was destroyed by plundering troops, the survivors were received by another colony. The number of the Hutterite settlements actually reached the peak during this period (82 localities, including small settlements in mills etc.). The other groups showed a small decrease.

[14] Cf. a similar interpretation in Kuhn, II, 317. Kuhn estimates that "several thousand" Anabaptist refugees joined the non-Hutterite groups. Still others, disappointed with the strict communitarian order, left the Hutterite colonies and settled in the German-speaking villages or towns in Moravia (cf. Kuhn, II, 316 f. and several examples from *TQ* quoted in Zeman, 1966, List A).

The final expulsion in 1622 brought, therefore, an abrupt end to a century of heroic struggle and witness. The only bitter comfort was the fact that all other non-Catholic groups in Moravia were driven out too onto the paths of fugitives and exiles which the Anabaptists had trodden, almost alone, for so many long decades.

A similar chronological analysis of the geographical growth of the Unity in Moravia is not possible at the present stage of topographical research. The chronological data are quite incomplete. One should remember of course that the gradual growth of the congregations of the Unity in Moravia suffered no general violent interruptions comparable to those which afflicted the Anabaptists. The expulsion of many Czech Brethren from Bohemia after the Smalcaldian War, in 1548, meant further strengthening of the Unity in Moravia where some refugees found new homes. Others turned to Poland and Prussia.

Many congregations of the Unity antedated the arrival of the first Anabaptists in Moravia. Others were not established until during the second half of the century. In our List H we have attempted to provide dating for congregations or groups of the Unity in localities where they shared residence with the Anabaptists.

c. Typological (Group) Analysis

For the first time in topographical studies of Moravian Anabaptism, we have paid systematic attention to the non-Hutterite groups. In spite of our limited access to local sources in Moravia the evidence which we were able to furnish for the existence and topographical spread of the non-Hutterite groups is surprising.

In contrast to the Hutterite topography which can benefit from the detailed records kept by the well-organized brotherhood, the research of non-Hutterite topography is greatly handicapped by lack of preserved sources. It is our firm persuasion that the continued existence and growth of some of the non-Hutterite groups will be demonstrated more fully as additional sources are discovered in and outside Moravia.

The list of Hutterite settlements will be augmented also as the records of ownership or leases of properties (mills, estate farms, breweries, bath houses etc.) are brought to light.[15] We were able to expand the Hutterite list from 89 entries in the *Mennonite Encyclopedia* to 128.

[15]   Zeman, 1966, 13 at footnote 37.

The following observation can be made on the basis of our List D. In terms of the total number of places with recorded Anabaptist residence,[16] the ratio between Hutterite and non-Hutterite (all other groups combined) places of settlement is 115:67, or approximately 9:5. This does not take into consideration the additional 25 places with "other or non-specified groups", most of which were likely non-Hutterite. Their inclusion would further reduce the Hutterite margin.

However, one must remember that some of the non-Hutterite groups could actually be classified as proto-Hutterites. In their views and origins they constituted the first stage of the emerging communitarian Anabaptism. This applies especially to the *Stäbler*. Of the Austerlitz Brethren, the Gabrielites and the Philippites, the majority of those who remained in, or returned to Moravia after the first two expulsions, eventually joined with the Hutterites.

One might further suggest that all groups within Moravian Anabaptism be classified under two categories: the continuing groups which remained in existence during most of the century of Anabaptist sojourn in Moravia, and the non-continuing groups which disappeared from the scene after a few decades. The latter would include the Austerlitz Brethren, the Gabrielites, Philippites, *Schwertler* (followers of Hubmaier) and *Stäbler* (the early opponents of Hubmaier). The only continuing groups were the Hutterites, Cornelians, Pilgramites (Marbeck fellowship) and the Swiss Brethren.[17] Most likely, the last three constituted, in Moravia, one basic type of Anabaptism which existed under different names depending on the personal ties of the local leaders with Anabaptist groups and leaders in Germany and Switzerland.

If one applies such simplified typological classification to our topographical List D and if one takes into consideration also the chronological data provided in List C, then the topographical ratio between the communitarian and non-communitarian groups in Moravia can be expressed with the following figures:

(1535-1547) 35 (H, P): 18 (A, G, M, SWB)
(1550-1564) 37 (H): 15 (A, G, M, SWB)
(1565-1592) 70 (H): 27 (C, M, SWB)
(1593-1622) 82 (H): 20 (C, M, SWB)

[16] In our present analysis, we exclude the places with non-residential evidence (work contracts, cultivation of land etc.) which are printed in brackets in our List D.
[17] The Sabbatarians might also be included. However, they seem to have survived only in two or three isolated settlements with little or no relationship to Moravian religious life, especially in the second half of the century.

One can see readily, that in the four successive periods [18] the ratio changed gradually from 2:1 to 4:1. In our opinion, the latter figure (4:1) represents a realistic appraisal of the respective strength of the Hutterite and non-Hutterite Anabaptism in South Moravia during the last quarter of the sixteenth century. Further research will increase the total number of settlements for both Anabaptist camps in Moravia. We doubt, however, that it will modify, to any considerable extent, the ratio between the two.

No typological analysis is needed for the *Unitas Fratrum*. The Minor Party which became extinct by the middle of the century seems to have had only one congregation in Moravia, namely Letovice near Boskovice (north of Brno).[19] The Habrovanite Brethren who disappeared from the scene at about the same time were concentrated on the small domain of knight Jan Dubčanský of Habrovany.[20] The topographical locus of both groups lay on the border line of the area of Anabaptist settlement even though Dubčanský maintained regular contacts with the centers of radicalism in South Moravia. Our Lists F and G include only the topography of the official Unity (Major Party).

d. *Ethnic Analysis*

One of the decisive factors in the contacts between the Anabaptists and the Czech Brethren was the difference in ethnic origin and language.

The *Unitas Fratrum* was an indigenous Czech movement. Its small German-speaking branch consisted almost exclusively of the descendants of the Waldensian refugees from Mark Brandenburg who established two main settlements. One was located in and around Lanškroun (Landskron) on the Bohemian-Moravian border, east of the city of Litomyšl (Leitomischl). The other was in and around Fulnek in north-eastern Moravia.[21]

---

[18]   In this particular analysis, we have omitted the first period (1526-1535) because in terms of Anabaptist typology, it constituted a preliminary, "unsettled" stage of Moravian Anabaptism.

[19]   Hrejsa, B, 56 and Brock, 1957, 249 ff.

[20]   Dubčanský owned only three villages (Habrovany, Lulč and Nemojany) north of Slavkov (Austerlitz), near Vyškov (Wischau). They were on the border line of the area occupied by Anabaptists. The founding meeting of the Unity of Habrovanite Brethren (1528) took place in the small village Routka, near the town of Letovice, the center of the Minor Party and residence of Jan Kalenec. Cf. Odložilík, 1923, 16 and 45 and Hrejsa, V, 18.

[21]   Cf. Chapter II at footnotes 50 ff.

For almost a century and a half, the German Brethren lived isolated in their two large congregations with a number of small branch congregations in the immediate area of Fulnek. In addition, German services were held in a few places around Zábřeh in northwest Moravia.[22] In South Moravia there were only three places where ministers of the Unity conducted German services: Horní Dunajovice (near Znojmo), Ivančice and Pohořelice. In the first two cases, the local congregation of the Unity was bilingual. At Pohořelice (Pohrlitz), Czech- and German-speaking ministers from Ivančice merely provided preaching and pastoral services in the local parish church (at the request of the town council) and for a limited period of time only.[23] Joint German services with the Reformed Germans were arranged, for a very short time during the revolution in 1620, at Brno and Olomouc.

As for the ethnic composition of the communities in which the Czech Brethren lived in South Moravia, all these towns and villages (List F) were Czech except in the following cases. A few members of the Unity are reported in the German villages Stiegnitz (Křtěnice) and Seletitz (Želetice) but the evidence is doubtful in both places. In Zerotitz (Žerotice)[24] the 'congregation' seems to have consisted only of a Czech group in the local castle. In the German town of Auspitz (Hustopeče) uncertain sources refer to a small congregation in the Czech suburb Böhmdorf. One is, therefore, inclined to dismiss all four cases until better topographical evidence can be furnished.

Regular contacts of the Czech Brethren with the local German population can be registered only for the following three localities which had German minorities in the sixteenth century: Ivančice (Eibenschitz), Nosislav (Nuslau) and Slavkov (Austerlitz). To these might be added Pohořelice (Pohrlitz) where the ministers of the Unity served both the Czech and the German population in the local parish church.

The ethnic composition of the communities where Anabaptist settlements were found is indicated in our List E. Of the total 170 places,[25] 28 were certainly German and 12 more were probably Ger-

---

[22] All such places are designated as 'German' in our List G. Cf. also the summary by Hrejsa, B, 103.

[23] Cf. details in Zeman, 1966, 63 f.

[24] The ethnic composition of Seletitz and Zerotitz is not certain. Cf. our List E, section I.

[25] The total of 180 in List A, minus 9 places which were proved to be wrong localizations, and without Mayberg which was a mountain area without a com-

man.[26] Nine others had a German majority and seven showed a German minority. In other words, only about one fifth of the Anabaptist settlements in South Moravia were located in purely German environment. An additional one tenth was found in communities with ethnically mixed population. The vast majority (approximately 70 per cent) was surrounded by Czech population.

The proportions would vary somewhat from one Anabaptist group to another. Without quoting additional figures,[27] we may summarize our findings as follows. The percentage for Hutterite settlements in Czech environment was higher than for any other Anabaptist group in Moravia. By way of contrast, all but five of the congregations of the Swiss Brethren were found in German or mixed communities. The reasons are obvious. The Hutterite colonies and smaller households represented economically self-sustaining units. Social isolation from the local population was a preference, not a handicap for their way of life. It did not matter too much whether the population of the area was Czech-speaking or German-speaking.

The Swiss Brethren and the Pilgramites desired, on the contrary, normal contacts with the population. As craftsmen, they depended on the people of the town or village for their living.[28] It was to be expected, therefore, that the non-communitarian Anabaptists would purposely seek out German, or at least partially German communities. In contrast to the apolitical Swiss Brethren, the Cornelians and Pilgramites even participated in local government.[29]

The differentiation between the communitarian and non-communitarian Anabaptists in their respective attitudes to the ethnic environment in Moravia is of great significance for their contacts with the local population, Czech and German. On the one hand, the involve-

---

munity. In fact, the total might be reduced further by the number of Anabaptist settlements which were limited to a mill or a meierhof. However, most of these were located near a particular town or village, the ethnic character of which is classified in our List E.

[26] In the case of the latter, we were unable to find reliable information about their ethnic composition in the 16th century. Of the 12, three were located in the northern part of Moravia.

[27] These can be obtained easily by comparing the data appearing in our Lists D and E.

[28] Cf. the case of the Pilgramite watchmaker in Znaim whom the residents defended and retained against Ferdinand's orders of expulsion. See *ME*, IV, 1131 (Uhrmacher, Hans) and our analysis of the Znaim colloquy (1559) in Chapter V at footnote 52.

[29] Cf. local sources on Austerlitz in Zeman, 1966, 22 and Bergsten, 1961, 488 (at footnote 30).

ment of the non-communitarian Anabaptists in the everyday life of the German towns and villages provided a regular opportunity for missionary impact on the native German population in South Moravia. The best known case is of course the work and witness of Hubmaier in Nikolsburg and in the surrounding villages where hundreds of the local Germans, including their clerical leaders, responded to the Anabaptist preaching and joined the refugee congregation. On a much smaller scale, the story must have been repeated in other German localities in later days. By contrast, the Hutterite chronicles do not record many cases of local Germans who joined their brotherhood.

The concentration of the non-communitarian Anabaptists in the German-speaking communities considerably reduced the missionary impact of Anabaptism on the Czech population in Moravia. If the vast majority of the Anabaptists with whom the Czech-speaking Moravians came into contact were the Hutterites one can understand why there were so few converts to Anabaptism from among the Czech population. For a conversion to Hutterite Anabaptism involved a double reorientation of life. It included not only a doctrinal change but also the most radical social and economic revolution. While the social security which a Hutterite colony could offer would have appealed to a destitute refugee from Germany or Switzerland, it would be far less inviting to a native peasant, let alone a burgher.

The ethnic stratification of the localities in which Anabaptist settlements, both Hutterite and non-Hutterite, were found, must be regarded, therefore, as of great consequence for the relationship of Anabaptists to the native population of Moravia, both Czech and German.

e. *Topographical Contacts between Anabaptists and Czech Brethren*

For the sake of completeness, the list of localities with recorded Anabaptist and Czech Brethren settlements (List H) includes 54 places. A careful examination of each entry leads, however, to a considerable reduction of the list.

Seven places of 'joint residence' must be ruled out for the simple reason that the listing of either the Anabaptist or the Unity settlement has been rejected as a mistaken localization.[30] In the case of the three

---

[30]   Nos. 8, 9, 16, 25, 30 and 50 (List H).

royal cities which were predominantly German (Brno, Jihlava and Olomouc) the presence of the few isolated Czech Brethren from time to time can hardly be interpreted as a sufficient basis for residential contacts. The Anabaptist settlement in these cities was also very sporadic. Similar reservations must be expressed about three towns with respect to the Anabaptists (Kroměříž, Prostějov and Třebíč) and likewise, about the town Žerotice with respect to the Czech Brethren.

Since the known periods of settlement do not coincide for the two groups in eight other places, these must be dropped from the list.[31] No dating is available for one or both settlements in five places.[32] This makes evidence of contact doubtful. Localization remains ambiguous in one case.[33] An examination of the presently known sources in support of three other settlements (one Anabaptist and two of the Unity)[34] should probably result in their elimination from the list.

Such critical sifting leaves a list of the following 23 places: Bílovice, Velké (H),[35] Budkov (H), Dačice (?), Heršpice (H), Hodonín (H), Hrušky (H), Hustopeče (P, H & ?), Ivančice (H, A? G?, M, SWB), Kobylí (H), Kounice, Dolní (H), Kyjov (H?), Mohelno (H), Napajedla (H), Násedlovice (H), Podivín (H), Pohořelice (H), Přibice (H), Slavkov (ST, A, H, C, M, S, SWB), Strážnice (H), Velká (H), Veselí (H), Ždánice (H) and Židlochovice (H).

It will be seen at first glance that with the exception of the two well-known centers with multiple group settlement, Ivančice (Eibenschitz) and Slavkov (Austerlitz), the contact of the Czech Brethren with the Anabaptists was narrowed down to the contact with the Hutterites. This fact is related to the ethnic composition of the localities. As we have pointed out earlier, the majority of the Hutterite colonies and practically all congregations of the Unity (in South Moravia) were found in Czech communities. The only exception in the list above is Hustopeče where the Czech Brethren were settled (reportedly) in a Czech suburb of the German town. Three of the 23 localities had German minorities: Ivančice, Pohořelice and Slavkov.

One might be inclined to interpret our topographical evidence of contacts between the Anabaptists and the Czech Brethren as negligible. Such a conclusion, however, would be unfounded. The pre-

[31] Nos. 6, 21, 22, 31, 36, 41, 42 and 46 (List H).
[32] Nos. 3, 4, 27, 34 and 45 (List H).
[33] No. 52 (Czech Brethren).
[34] Nos. 15, 23 and 28.
[35] The capital letters in brackets designate the particular Anabaptist group. See the explanation at List C.

dominance of residential contacts with the Hutterites may explain a great deal of the 'ecumenical failure'. At the same time, one must recognize that several leading congregations of the Unity and several well-established Hutterite colonies were involved in these contacts.

As for the non-communitarian Anabaptists, one might wish that there had been more numerous points of residential contact between them and the Czech Brethren. Nevertheless, one must admit that the two towns of Ivančice and Slavkov offered opportunities for contact unparalleled anywhere else in Moravia and perhaps in the entire continent at that time. A number of groups lived here side by side. Exchange of views took place. It was no coincidence that the town of Ivančice, with a bilingual congregation, serving as the seat of the bishops of the Unity in the second half of the century, set the stage for the colloquy with the Pilgramites in 1559 and that it probably had played an important role in the early negotiations for a merger in 1528.

The total number of localities on our reduced list (23) represents the minimum of documented topographical contacts. A maximum list would be about double that number. If one were to accept a median number of thirty-five as a reasonable estimate of the number of communities in which topographical contact actually took place — even though it may not be documented sufficiently by the sources known at the present time — one might draw the following con- clusions.

Approximately one out of every four congregations (and smaller local groups) of the *Unitas Fratrum* in the area designated by us as South Moravia was located in a community where there was also, for a shorter or longer period of time, an Anabaptist settlement, in most cases a Hutterite colony. Likewise, one out of every four Hutterite settlements (regular colonies and smaller households) was in residen- tial contact with the Czech Brethren. Opportunities for contacts be- tween the Unity and the non-Hutterite Anabaptists seem to have been limited to two localities, Ivančice and Slavkov.

In our opinion, the number of these residential opportunities was sufficient to allow for a reasonable mutual acquaintance and personal relationships between the Anabaptists and the *Unitas Fratrum*. The fiasco of an ecumenical rapprochement was not caused by lack of opportunities for contact.

VII

CONCLUSIONS

In the preceding chapters we have described and analyzed all historical (personal and literary) [1] contacts — known to us at the present time — between the Anabaptists and the Czech Brethren in Moravia during the one century of Anabaptist sojourn in the margraviate (1526-1628).

It would be premature to try to define the historical and theological relationship between the two ecclesiastical movements on the basis of such a limited study. The greater part of the research which must include theological, sociological and typological analyses and comparisons of the two groups [2] remains to be undertaken in subsequent studies. When all these aspects have been examined and the results of such exact scholarship have been collated, then and only then will it be possible to solve the complex problem of the relationship between Anabaptism and Czech Brethrenism and of their respective relatedness to medieval theology and piety on the one hand, and to the sixteenth-century Reformation on the other hand. [3]

Nevertheless, the following partial answers can be given on the basis of our present study.

(1) There was no genetic influence on the rise of normative Anabaptism [4] in Moravia, either by the different parties of the Czech Reformation (the Utraquists, the Major and Minor Party of the *Unitas Fratrum*) or by the German Evangelicals in South Moravia, whether by incoming refugees or by persons of native origin. The emergence

---

[1] With the exception of hymnology; cf. Chapter I at footnote 155.
[2] See our "Proposed Plan of Studies", Chapter I.
[3] Cf. the three basic questions stated in Chapter I, Section "Proposed Plan of Studies", under (4).
[4] For our discussion of "normative Anapabtism" see Chapter I at footnote 100 and Chapter II at footnotes 154 ff.

of Anabaptism in Moravia is connected with the arrival of Balthasar Hubmaier and of other Anabaptist refugees in the early summer of 1526 (Chapter II). Our findings should not be interpreted, of course, as the final answer to the problem of the genetic influence of the *Unitas Fratrum* upon the rise of Anabaptism. There were other geographical areas of contact besides Moravia.

(2) Hubmaier's relationship to the Czech Reformation in general, and to the *Unitas Fratrum* in particular, can be characterized as one of ignorance and indifference. Through painstaking exploration of all known opportunities for literary knowledge about the Czech Reformation and by a careful analysis of evidence of such knowledge in the preserved writings of Hubmaier (Chapter III) we were led to conclude that Hubmaier knew practically nothing about the Czech Reformation prior to his arrival in Moravia and that he did very little to become acquainted with the Czech religious parties, and especially with the Czech Brethren, during his one-year stay in Moravia. He lived, isolated, in the German town of Mikulov (Nikolsburg) and remained oriented towards the Swiss and German Reformation. The meagre information about the Moravian religious scene as it is reflected in his works, seems to have been channelled mainly by Oswald Glaidt, Martin Göschl and Johann Zeising. There is a slight possibility that Hubmaier was acquainted with the German catechism (*Kinderfragen*) of the Unity (see Appendix 5).

(3) After Hubmaier's death, the known contacts between the two religious groups were limited to four colloquies (1528, 1543, 1559, 1565). All but one of these are recorded in the sources of the Unity. The Anabaptist sources make no mention of them and generally maintain a surprising silence about the *Unitas Fratrum*.

In contrast to the subsequent colloquies, the first contacts between the two groups were of an official nature and aimed at a merger. The reasons for the failure of these initial negotiations (1528) were explained in Chapter IV. It should be noted that all disputations under our study differed from similar debates in other countries such as Switzerland and Germany in one important respect. There were no magisterial arbiters present at any colloquy because there was no state church involved. The spokesmen met as representatives of two free churches.

They did not meet, however, in order to seek a better knowledge of the divine truth. During the merger negotiations in 1528 the Anabaptists were expected to make an unconditional surrender to the doctrinal position of the Unity. At the later colloquies, the well-educated ministers of the Unity did not regard the simple Anabaptist believers as equal partners in a common search for a better understanding of the Gospel. They were prepared to instruct them but not to learn from them, or with them. In that respect, the representatives of the Unity — including such leading men as Lukáš, Krasonický, Roh, Blahoslav and Herbert — did not conceive their role too differently from the Zwinglian spokesmen at the colloquies in Zürich, or the Reformed 'disputators' at the Frankenthal debate (1571). The initiative towards the merger negotiations and the colloquies came in each case [5] from the Anabaptists and not from the Czech Brethren who are known to have sought contact with so many groups, from the Waldensians and the Eastern Church to the Reformers of the sixteenth century.

(4) In contrast to the numerous friendly or polemical literary and epistolary exchanges between the *Unitas Fratrum* and other domestic and foreign Reformation groups or leaders (the Utraquists, the Minor Party, the Habrovanite Brethren, Luther, Bucer, Calvin etc.) only one unofficial and indirect polemical writing of the Czech Brethren against the Anabaptist concept of baptism has been preserved (from the year 1589, see Chapter V). We do not know of a single written Anabaptist treatise dealing with the *Unitas Fratrum*.

Their relationship in Moravia seems to have been characterized by strange ambiguity. They did not attack each other but neither did they seek fellowship with one another. Both sides probably recognized basic kinship between the two free church movements but at the same time they were aware of important theological differences.

(5) The historical relationship between the Anabaptists and the Czech Brethren in Moravia may be fittingly described by the modern expression 'peaceful coexistence'. The records of the colloquies and the one polemical treatise would suggest that the main issues of disagreement were (a) baptism, (b) the eucharist, (c) anthropology (original sin, free will) and (d) the ethical issues of magistracy, oathtaking and armsbearing.

It is actually misleading to compile such lists of articles since in each recorded contact the Czech Brethren dealt with representatives of a different Anabaptist group: with the spiritualizing followers of Christian Entfelder and (probably also) of Gabriel Ascherham in 1528,

---

[5]   Except in the disputation in 1565 about which no historical data is known.

with the Philippites in 1543, with the Pilgramites in 1559, with an unidentified group in 1565 and with the Hutterites in the treatise of 1589.

The particular Anabaptist groups disagreed among themselves on many doctrinal issues. Nor can one identify the theology of Brother Lukáš (in 1528) with the views of his pro-Lutheran successors (in 1543), or with the theology of Jan Blahoslav (in 1559) and Peter Herbert (in 1565), or with the pro-Calvinistic orientation in the Unity towards the end of the century.

One thing is certain. The outright rejection of the Zwinglian theology, particularly of its concept of the eucharist, by the *Unitas Fratrum* under the leadership of Bishop Lukáš in the 1520's — just prior to the appearance of Anabaptists in Moravia — could not but have far-reaching consequences for the future relationship to Anabaptism. With few exceptions, the Anabaptist eucharistic theology was and remained Zwinglian.

(6) Our topographical research (Chapter VI) has furnished evidence of sufficient residential opportunities for regular personal contacts, especially between the Hutterites and the Czech Brethren. The minimal communications and the fiasco of an ecumenical rapprochement was not due to a lack of opportunities for contact.

(7) As a useful by-product of our investigation, we were able to redraw the general picture of Moravian Anabaptism. For the early period (1526-1535) we have documented the existence of a third major type of Anabaptism in Moravia. In addition to the followers of Hubmaier (the *Schwertler*) and to his opponents (the *Stäbler* who might be designated also as the proto-Hutterites) there was a large group of 'spiritualizing' Anabaptists with main centers at Ivančice (Christian Entfelder) and Rosice (Gabriel Ascherham).

For the second half of the century and up to the final expulsion of Anabaptists from Moravia in 1622, we have gathered and analyzed (Chapters V and VI) convincing evidence that Moravian Anabaptism remained pluralistic from the beginning until the end. The Hutterite brotherhood represented its most numerous sector. But in addition to it, there were other 'continuing groups' (up to 1622), such as the Cornelians, the Pilgramites and the Swiss Brethren, all three of whom probably represented one common type of Anabaptism which existed, in Moravia at least, under different names in different localities and at different times.

It is our sincere hope that in the years to come an increasing number of studies will be devoted to the relationship of the Anabaptists to the Czech Brethren and, vice versa, of the *Unitas Fratrum* to the Radical Reformation. Our present historical investigation represents but an initial step towards the solution of the complex issue.

APPENDIX 1

ACTA UNITATIS FRATRUM

	Volume and Initials on Cover	Period of Time Covered	Notes on Editors and Scribes. Dates and Places of Copying
	I	1461-1485	Jáchym Prostibořský, first part only. Second part was copied at Ivančice, 1558-1571, with marginal notes by Blahoslav.
Collection B	II, IBP III, IBP IV, IBP V, IBP VI, IBP	1463-1546 The majority of the documents dates from the period preceding 1510. They are not arranged in chronological order.	Collection B consisting of older documents was started by Blahoslav at Mladá Boleslav after 1553, brought to Ivančice in 1558. Editing and copying was done by Blahoslav, later by Vavřinec Orlík, mostly during the 1560's. All volumes were finished and checked by Blahoslav prior to his death in 1571. The volumes were completed in the following order: III, IV, II, VI and V.
Collection A	VII, IBP VIII IX, IBP X, ASP, 1574	1547-1549 1549-1557 1558-1566 (not in strict chronological order) 1557-1569	Collection A of contemporary documents was started by Jan Černý in Boleslav around 1551 and developed by Blahoslav who himself copied Vols. VII and VIII. Vols. IX and X contain many duplicate materials. Vol. X was written by Ondřej Štefan who was guided first by Blahoslav, then by Vavřinec Orlík. Most materials were copied at Ivančice. (See also Vols. XII and XIII.)
	XI, W.O., 1582	1468-1522 1547-1559	An independent volume edited by Vavřinec Orlík (died 1589) and written by several scribes.

	Volume and Initials on Cover	Period of Time Covered	Notes on Editors and Scribes. Dates and Places of Copying
Collection A	XII, 1589	1570-1579	Entries till 1574 by Ondřej Štefan (d. 1577), subsequent entries by Jan Eneáš (d. 1594) at Ivančice.
	XIII, 1589	1580-1589	Jan Eneáš, assisted by Jan Kapito (d. 1589) at Ivančice.

The present numbering of the thirteen volumes of *AUF* comes from the hand of Johannes Plitt, librarian at Herrnhut, who was responsible for the purchase and transfer of the codices to Herrnhut in 1840. A literary and historical analysis [1] by a number of scholars has led to the identification of the following four [2] separate collections:

Collection A represents the original collection of contemporary documents which was started by Jan Černý in Mladá Boleslav around 1551, developed fully by Jan Blahoslav and continued by Ondřej Štefan and Jan Eneáš. It covers the years 1547-1589 in volumes VII-X and XII-XIII. The initials on the leatherbound volumes mean Iohannes Blahoslav Preroviensis and Adreas Stephanus Prosniciensis.

Collection B was also initiated by Jan Černý and Jan Blahoslav in in order to preserve documents from the first three generations of the Unity (1463-1546). All volumes (II-VI) bear Blahoslav's initials.

Collection C consists of Volume XI for which materials (1468-1522 and 1547-1559) were compiled independently by Vavřinec Orlík.

Collection D consists also of one volume only (I) which was prepared independently of the Blahoslav series but was added to his collection during his life-time and contains his marginal notes.

Two other volumes are often referred to as part of the *AUF* collection. Volume XIV [3] contains a copy of a Diary in which Ondřej Štefan and Daniel Jindřich Švarc described the important diet of 1575 (nego-

[1] Our table and description of the *AUF* is based on the published results of research in Müller, 1913, 63-80; Müller, I, 578 ff.; Bidlo, 1923 and (Bidlo's introduction in) Akty, I, 8 ff.; Krofta, 1946, 85 ff.; Štěříková, 1964 and Hobza, 1967. See also Chapter I, beginning at footnote 156.

[2] The classification A, B, C, D was suggested by Bidlo in Akty, I, 12 ff. Cf. also Müller, 1913, 71 ff.

[3] When the *AUF* codices were found in the archives of the Reformed Church in Leszno (Lissa) in the 1830's (cf. Müller, 1913, 78 f.), thirteen volumes were acquired by the Archives (then called Library) of the Brüderunität in Herrnhut, Saxony. Volume XIV had been purchased earlier by the National Museum in Prague (sign. II D 8, old 2 G 10). Müller, I, 282 designated it originally as Vol. XIIa or *AUF*. M (Museum). For contents of Vol. XIV, see Hobza, 1967, 238 ff.

tiations concerning the *Confessio Bohemica*).[4] It also includes a number of documents covering the period from 1576 to 1584 and edited by Jan Eneáš (died in 1594).

Volume "P"[5] bears the initials I (an) K (álef) 1579. It represents an independent collection of documents, in particular the correspondence with Luther, Melanchthon, Bucer and others from the years 1530-1546. Most likely, the volume was edited by Kálef, bishop of the Bohemian Unity, at Mladá Boleslav, from 1571 till 1588.

---

[4]   Krofta, 1946, 107 f. and 138 f.
[5]   The "fifteenth" volume was preserved independently in the University Library in Prague (sign. XVII C 3), Müller classified it first as Vol. VIa and later as "P" (Prague). Although it had its origin in the same official circles of the Unity, it obviously never formed an integral part of the large collections. Contents and critical analysis by Souček Bohuslav, 1921.

OSWALD GLAIDT'S *HANDLUNG* (1526)
(A Comparison of the Different Editions)

1. REVIEW OF BIBLIOGRAPHICAL DATA BY OTHER AUTHORS

Weller listed three different editions:

No. 3806, n.d., n.p., 4°: printed by Simprecht Sorg in Nikolsburg, 1526, and edited by Hubmaier. Copy in Vienna.

No. 3807, n.d., n.p., 8°: printed by Chr. Froschauer in Zürich, 1526. Copies in Zürich, Freiburg i. B. and Vienna.

Supplement, No. 387: n.d., n.p., 8°: a different edition, no designation of printer. Copy in Nűrnberg.

Rudolphi, 1869, 17, No. 133 listed only a Zürich ed. by Chr. Froschauer, edited by Hubmaier.

Sachsse, 1914, 102 f. rejected the mistaken claim of several older authors (Dudík, Tschackert, Weller) that Hubmaier composed the booklet, or at least arranged its printing either in Zürich or in Nikolsburg. He also questioned the printing of one edition by Chr. Froschauer in Zürich. Sachsse seems to have examined only one copy (Freiburg i. B.).

Bergsten, 1961, 403 and in *HS*, 59 defended the printing by Froschauer and suggested that the manuscript of Glaidt's *Handlung* could have arrived in Zürich some time in April just prior to Hubmaier's departure from the city. He ruled out, however, the possibility of Hubmaier's personal arrangements for the printing in the office of Froschauer, the printer of Zwingli's works.

Friedmann, 1965b, 63 and 133 listed "the only extant copy" of the booklet, preserved in the Austrian National Library in Vienna, without any identification of printer, or reference to the different editions. He appears to have drawn his information from *TQ*, X, 125, No. 2749).

2. LIST OF KNOWN COPIES

We have examined the originals, or photocopies, of the following three editions:

A. *Handlung yetz den. xiiii. tag/ Marcy dis. xxvi. iars./So zů Osterlytz inn Merhern durch erforderte versam/ lung viler Pfarrer vnd priesterschafften auch / etlicher des Adels vñ anderer in Christ / licher lieb vñ ainikayt beschehē. Vñ / in Syben Artickel beschlossen / mit sambt der selbenn Artickel Erklärũg. / Non quod . . . fide statis. I. Cor. I.*

[n.d., n.p., 4°; copy in Vienna, Nationalbibliothek, sign. 43.K.112].

B. *Handlung yetz den/ xiiij. tag Marcij diß. xxvj. Jars, So/ zu Osterlytz inn Merhern durch erfor-/derte versamlung, viler pfarrer vñ prie-/sterschafften, ouch etlicher des Adels vñ/ anderer in Christlicher lieb vnd einig-/ keit beschehen. Vnnd in siben/Artickel beschlossen mit sāpt/ der selbenn Artickel / Erkla°rung./ Non quod . . . fide statis. I. Cor. I.*

[n.d., n.p., 8°]; copy in Vienna, sign. *43.X.102 and two copies in Zürich (sign. 5.290 and III B 135) with slight variations on fol. a v only. Another copy (reported by Weller) in Freiburg i. B., Universitätsbibliothek (sign. N. 3359) is missing and was probably destroyed during the war].

C. *Handlung ietz den xiiij / tag Marcij diß xxvj. Jars, So zu/Osterlitz ĩn Merhern durch erforder/te versamlung viler pfarhern vnd / priesterschafften, auch etlicher des / Adels, vnnd anderer ĩn christ-/licher lieb vnd eynigkeyt be/schehen, vnd ĩn siben / artickel beschlossen /mit sampt der/selben Arti-/ckel/Erklerung. /2. Corin.1./ Nit das wir herren seien . . . ihr steht ĩm glauben.*

[n.d., n.p., 8°; copy in Nürnberg, Stadtbibliothek, sign. 5 an Theol. 480.8°].

3. THE PRINTERS

None of the three editions indicate the year or place of printing, or the name of the printer. With the kind assistance of Dr. J. Benzing, Universitätsbibliothek, Mainz, we were able to identify the printers as follows.

Edition A was printed by Simprecht Sorg Froschauer probably at Nikolsburg (Mikulov) in July or August 1526. It was set in the same type as the first ed. of Hubmaier's *Der Vralten vnnd gar neuen Leerern Vrteil* (*HS*, 227 ff.). Its preface was dated by Hubmaier on July 21, 1526 and presumably, the book was printed soon afterwards.

Since Sorg is known to have used his type also elsewhere (in Zürich, and later at Liegnitz) there is a slight possibility that he could have printed Glaidt's report somewhere else prior to his coming to Moravia. In our opinion, such possibility should be ruled out.

Edition B was printed unmistakenly in Switzerland (Swiss spelling) but not by Christopher Froschauer as has been assumed but by the other printer in Zürich in the 1520's, Hans Hager. Leemann, 1931 did not list Glaidt's *Handlung*. According to a personal letter from Dr. J. Benzing, the identification of Hager can be regarded as absolutely certain. On Hager, cf. Benzing, 1963, 490.

Edition C was produced by Peter Schöffer Jr. in Worms who printed a number of Anabaptist books, including four works by Hans Denck (1527-1528) and the translation of the Prophets by Denck und Hätzer (first ed., April 13, 1527; cf. *DS*, 1, 8 and 32). On Schöffer, cf. Benzing, 1963, 478.

4. A TABLE OF MAJOR TEXTUAL VARIANTS

The following examples of major textual variants between the three editions can be listed:

	Edition A Nikolsburg	Edition B Zürich	Edition C Worms
(a) *Scripture text on title page (II. Cor. 1:24):*	in Latin "I. Cor. I."	in Latin "I. Cor. I."	in German "2. Corin. 1"
(b) *Marginal Scripture references:*	all	all but one	omitted altogether
(c) *End of historical introduction:*	"zů Nycolspurg am 29. Marcy dises anzaigten 26. Jars."	"zů Nycolspurg am 29. Marcij jm 26. Jar."	"zu Nicolspurg am xxix Marcij im xxvi jare."
(d) *Title of articles:*	"Nun volgen die artickel verteuscht"	"Nun volgen die artickel"	"Nun volgen die artickel"
(e) *Explanation of the fourth article:* [1]	"Dises Sacrament aber, das die kriechē nennē das ist dancksagung ..."	"dises Sacrament aber, dz die kilchen nennet, das ist danksagung ..."	"diss Sacramēt aber, das die Kirche nennet, ist dancksagung ..."

[1] Edition A left an empty space for the Greek word *eucharistia* for which Simprecht Sorg in Nikolsburg did not have the Greek letters. The printers of Edition B and C did not insert the Greek word but "amended" the text reading "Kirche" in place of 'kriechen", i.e. the Greeks.

	Edition A Nikolsburg	Edition B Zürich	Edition C Worms
(f) *Explanation of the fifth article:*	"priester weyhen, praytling, ayer ..."	"priester wyhen, fladen, eyer ..."	"priester weihen, fladen, eyer ..."
(g) *Explanation of the sixth article:*	"wie eine yedes ... wohlbehertzigenn kan"	"wie ein yedes ... ermessen kan"	"wie eun iedes ... ermessen kan"
(h) *The end of the text:*	"Jesus est Cristus. Actū 2."	omitted	omitted

5. CHRONOLOGICAL SEQUENCE AND MUTUAL DEPENDENCE OF THE THREE EDITIONS

On the basis of the preceding table we can draw the following conclusions.

Edition C followed Edition B as it shows the same omissions (plus the total omission of marginal Scripture references) and amendments in text. Edition B could not follow Edition C since it includes marginal Scripture references (left out in C).

Edition B followed Edition A (omissions listed under b, d, and h; amendment listed under e). Edition A could not follow Edition B for the same reasons.

Without such careful textual comparison, these conclusions could not be made. For in terms of mere chronology, both B and C could have been printed before A. Glaidt signed his preface at Nikolsburg on March 29, 1526. Simprecht Sorg did not print the first work of Hubmaier in Moravia till the end of July 1526. There was, therefore, ample time for the other two editions to precede the Nikolsburg edition.

However, our textual comparison established the sequence of the three editions. There is only one other possible solution. Glaidt, or someone else, could have sent a second copy of the manuscript to Zürich [2] where the book could have been printed independently of

---

[2]   By coincidence, a Silesian messenger from Schwenckfeld and Krautwald visited Oecolampad in Basel and Zwingli in Zürich in the first part of April 1526. If he had travelled through Moravia, he could have brought Glaidt's manuscript with him. Glaidt's preface is dated March 29. The Silesian messenger was in Basel on, or before April 9 (Z, VIII, 559; cf. Chapter II note 166). However plausible the conjecture might appear, it must be rejected on the basis of our textual analysis of the three editions.

the Nikolsburg edition. However, the textual amendment listed in our table (under e) makes such a hypothesis highly improbable, if not entirely impossible. The printer in Zürich had Greek letters and would not have found it necessary to amend the original text of the manuscript. In our opinion, this particular amendment proves unmistakenly that he was following the printed edition A.

One might recall also that Simprecht Sorg maintained contacts with Zürich after he had settled in Moravia, and later in Silesia. Hubmaier's works printed by him at Nikolsburg were known in Switzerland promptly (cf. Bergsten, 1961, 417).

6. CONCLUSION

Our examination of the five known copies of Glaidt's *Handlung* has not only led to a reliable identification of the printers but also clarified, for the first time, the chronological sequence and mutual dependence of the three editions.

There can be no doubt that Simprecht Sorg printed the first edition soon after his settlement at Nikolsburg. In the absence of other sources, one may only suggest that the printing took place in July or August 1526. Glaidt's book might have been the first book printed by Sorg in Moravia.

The second (Hager in Zürich) and third (Peter Schöffer Jr. in Worms) editions followed some time later in 1526, or perhaps not until in 1527. A more precise dating is not possible at the present time.

These conclusions have important bearing on our discussion of the motives which led to Hubmaier's decision to go to Moravia.[3]

Our findings also furnish an additional proof of the widespread contacts between Moravia and the centers of the German and Swiss Reformation. The connection with the printer of Denck's writings in Worms is particularly worth noting.[4]

---

[3] Cf. Chapter III, at footnotes 133 ff.
[4] In 1537, a member of the *Unitas Fratrum* in Mladá Boleslav, Jakub Poledne, followed and publicly defended the teachings of Denck. He was excommunicated in January 1538. Cf. Molnár, 1952a, 140; Souček Bohuslav, 1921, 75 and Chapter V, note 131.

APPENDIX 3

THE POLEMICAL WORKS OF JOHANN FABER AGAINST THE ANABAPTISTS AND AGAINST THE CZECH BRETHREN

A detailed literary and theological analysis and comparison of Faber's polemical works against the Czech Brethren (Picards) and those against the Anabaptists, espccially Hubmaier, in Moravia, would go far beyond the scope of our present inquiry.[1]

We are reprinting a list of topics covered by Faber in his several writings in order to show, side by side, the theological *loci* of the two groups as seen by their common Catholic opponent. One must remember, however, that even in these works, the real targets of Faber's polemics were not the Czech Picards, nor the Anabaptists in Moravia, but Zwingli and Luther.[2]

1. COMPARISON OF THE THEOLOGICAL *LOCI* OF THE CZECH BRETHREN AND OF HUBMAIER

Articles discussed with Hubmaier (Faber, 1528e)[3]

1. De sana expositione intelligentiaque scripturae sacrae.
2. De Baptismo parvulorum.
3. De non scriptis ecclesiae traditionibus.
4. De baptizandis infantibus.

[1] A thoroughgoing examination of Faber's works and their relationship to the source materials of the Czech Brethren and of Hubmaier is sorely needed. What Peschke, 1964 did with the polemical works of Jakob Ziegler and Dungersheim of Ochsenfurt should be undertaken for the writings of Faber. A short descriptive paper on Faber, 1528a, 1528c and 1528e, yet without a full historical and theological analysis, was prepared by Eisenblätter, 1964 and 1965.

[2] Cf. Faber's own statements quoted in Chapter III, footnotes 149 f.

[3] We have used the text reprinted in Faber, 1537a, fols. Mij^v - b vj^v. The list appears on fol. N j^v. These articles should be compared with Hubmaier's "Rechenschaft", *HS*, 460 ff. Cf. footnote 51 in Chapter IV.

5. De veritate corporis et sanguinis Christi in venerabili Sacramento altaris.
6. De Sacrificio Missae.
7. De sanctorum intercessionibus pro nobis ad Deum.
8. De purgatorio animarum.
9. De imaginibus Christi et sanctorum.
10. De fide et operibus.
11. De satisfactione pro peccatis.
12. De libertate Christiana.
13. De absoluta necessitate.
14. De libero arbitrio.
15. De genitrice dei Maria et filio eius vere Deo.
16. De perpetua virginitate Mariae.
17. De assumptione Mariae gaudioque sanctorum in coelo.
18. De extremi die iudicii.
19. De agenda poenitentia pro peccatis.
20. De auriculari confessione peccatorum.
21. De clavibus Petri.
22. De operibus satisfactoriis.
23. De ieiuniss ab ecclesia institutis.
24. De excommunicationibus.
25. De ecclesia, quid sit.
26. De Zvinglii tyrannide varioque sacrilegio.
27. De inconstantia doctrinae Zvinglianae.
28. De inconstantia Lutheri.
29. De concensu et concordia Conciliorum et Doctorum in fide.
30. Conclusio, ut perstemus in Ecclesia, quia in fide nunquam errat.

Articles of the Picards (Faber 1528 f.)[4]

1. De Symbolo Apostolorum.
2. De Nicaeno Concilio.
3. De Symbolo Athanasii.
4. De Ecclesia Christi.
5. De Septem Sacramentis.
6. De Baptismo parvulorum.

---

[4] We have used the text reprinted in Faber, 1537a, fols. g vj^v - i j^v. In the much briefer German version, Faber, 1526b, fols. a j - a iij^v, the articles of the Picards (only 28 of them) follow the same order, except that (a) an article on church councils (concilia) is inserted after art. 19, (b) art. 20-27 are numbered as 21-28, (c) the last three articles are missing. Cf. footnotes 140-145 in Chapter III.

7. De gratia sacramentorum.
8. De S. Dionysio Areopagita.
9. De Confirmationis sacramento.
10. De ritu confirmandi.
11. De Forma Baptizandi.
12. De officio Sacredotali.
13. De Confectione Eucharistiae.
14. De Communicatione Eucharistiae.
15. De digna sumptione Eucharistiae.
16. De sacerdotum ordinatione.
17. De Poenitentia.
18. De extrema Unctione infirmorum.
19. De sanctorum Communione.
20. De libero arbitrio.
21. De obedientia erga superiores.
22. De libro Apocalypsis.
23. De potestate consecrandi.
24. De virginitate Mariae perpetua.
25. De Presbyteris.
26. De S. Petro.
27. De dissonantia doctrinae.
28. De sanctis in coelo.
29. De bello contra Turcas.
30. De seditionibus.

2. THE CONTENT OF FABER'S SERMONS AGAINST THE ANABAPTISTS AT THE DIET IN ZNOJMO, APRIL 1528

(Faber, 1528b-c) [5]

Common Theme: Defense of infant baptism against the arguments of the Anabaptists.

Common Text: I John 4:1a.

Each of the first five sermons consists of three parts.

Part I: Faber's defense of infant baptism:
    Sermon 1: general arguments.

[5] The sermons were preached and originally published in German (Faber, 1528b). A Latin translation, dedicated to Bishop Thurzo of Olomouc (Prague, April 24, 1528) followed in three editions (Faber, 1528c). We have used the Latin text reprinted in Faber, 1537a, fols. i iiij^v - m j.

Sermon 2: arguments from the Old Testament.

Sermon 3: arguments from the New Testament.

Sermons 4 and 5: arguments from the tradition and theology of
the church.

Part II: Refutation of Anabaptist hermeneutics used in support of
their rejection of infant baptism (e.g. their objections to fides
infantium).

Part III: Rejection of specific Anabaptist heresies:

Sermon 1: Chiliasm (predictions of the end of the world at
Pentecost 1528).

Sermon 2: Denial of the divinity of Christ.

Sermon 3: Sleep of the soul.

Sermon 4: The ultimate salvation of demons.

Sermon 5: Attitude to government, and the divisions among
Anabaptists.

In his fifth sermon, Faber included a long quotation from Urbanus
Rhegius' *Wider den neuen Taufforden* (Augsburg, September 6,
1527).

The last, sixth sermon, "Sermo paraeneticus ad orthodoxos indubitatae
veteris fidei Christifideles", contains exhortations to the orthodox
(Catholic) believers and a final condemnation of the Anabaptists for
their hypocrisy. They regard themselves as the only pure (catharos)
believers and hold all others in contempt.

LIST OF EDITIONS OF THE FIRST GERMAN CATECHISM
OF THE UNITY (1522-1530)

The following editions of the German catechism are described by Zezschwitz, 1863, 252-269; Müller, 1887, 4 f. and Cohrs, I, 11 ff. *et passim*. We have arranged them into four groups.

A. *Editions with the Original Text* (contain Question 61 which prohibits adoration of Christ in the eucharist, according to the teaching of the Unity):
All of these bear the title (with variations in spelling):
Ain schöne Frag vnd Antwurt den Jungen Kindern, zu vnderweysen . . .
1. 1522, 4°, n.p. [probably Augsburg, Hans Schönperger]. The title of this ed. includes the phrase *Aus Doct. Mar. Lut. Leer.* Müller, No. 2; Zezschwitz, 260.
2. 1522, 4°, n.p. [reprint of the previous ed., probably by the same printer]. No reference to Luther in the title. Müller, No. 3; Zezschwitz, 261.
3. 1523, 4°, n.p. [another reprint from the same shop]. Müller, No. 4; Zezschwitz, 262.
4. 1524, 4°, n.p. [printed perhaps by Grünenberg in Wittenberg]. Müller, No. 5; Zezschwitz, 263 f.
5. 1523, n.p. [Strasbourg?]. Listed by Cohrs, I, 11.
6. 1523, 4°, n.p. [Basel?]. Listed in the Catalogue of the British Museum in London.

B. *Editions with a Revised Text*: changes in Q. 60 (adoration of images) and 61 (adoration of Christ in the eucharist).
All of these bear the title (with variations in spelling):
Ein christliche vnterweysung der klaynen Kinder im Glauben, durch ein weysz einer Frag . . .

1. 1522, 8°, n.p. [probably Nürnberg, Fr. Peypus]. Omits Q. 61. Müller, No. 1; Zezschwitz, 252. This copy was the basis for the text published by Zezschwitz.
2. 1522, 8°, Erfurt, Michel. Listed by Cohrs, I, 11 ff. This ed. rewords Q. 61 to allow adoration of sacrament and besides adds "Lutheran propaganda" at the end (reprinted by Cohrs, I, 14).
3. N.d., 8°, Strasbourg. Q. 60 and 61 omitted. Listed by Cohrs, I, 12.
4. 1523, 8°, n.p. [Strasbourg]. Listed in the Catalogue of the British Museum, perhaps identical with the previous edition.

C. A *Later Edition*: It claims to be a reprint of the original edition and identifies the "Waldensian Brethren" in the title.
Catechismus. Ein Christliche vnderweisung vnd Vorschrifft den Jungen im Glauben, Wie vor Neun Jarn vonn den Valdenser brudernn, Rechnung yres Glaubens dadurch zegebenn, vszgangen. Dem ersten Original (so hieuor etzlich mal, durch andere geenderet) nachgetruckt.
N.d., n.p. [perhaps Zürich, Chr. Froschauer, 1530]. Müller, No. 5; Zezschwitz, 255 f. and 269. This text was reprinted first by Ehwalt, 1756 and served also as the basis of Müller's crit. ed. It contains Q. 61 although its title corresponds to the title of Group B (with revised text).

D. *Editions with Adapted Text*:
1. The Magdeburg Version (Low German) 1524
   a) *Eynn buchleyn wie man die Kinder lerenn schall yhn dem rechtenn Gelo^euen dorch eyne wysse eyner Frage vnd Antwort.*
   Magdeburg, Hans Knap Jr., 1524. Q. 61-76 left out. Zezschwitz, 265; Müller, 148 f.; Cohrs, I, 103 ff. Full text reprinted in Müller, 151-158.
   b) *Eyne schone vnnd ser nutte Christlike vnderwysunge allen Christgelouigen mynschen. . . .*
   Rostock, (Feb.) 1525. Listed by Cohrs, I, 103-108 with a list of text variants.
2. The Wittenberg Version (Low German) 1525
   a) *Eyne schone nye vorklarynghe, des kynder bo^eckelyns. . . .*
   Wittenberg, Hans Barth, 1525. Full text reprinted in Müller, 163-188.

b) Reprint of the same ed. and by the same printer on Feb. 10, 1526. Listed by Cohrs, I, 146 ff. with a list of text variants.

3. The St. Gallen Catechism 1527

a) *Ain Christliche vnderwisung der Jugend jm Glouben.* ... Zürich, Chr. Froschower, 1527. Zezschwitz, 267 f.; Müller, 191-208 (with full text); Cohrs, II, 203 ff.

b) Reprint by Froschauer in 1528. Cohrs, II, 205.

c) Reprint by Froschauer in 1530. Cohrs, II, 205.

We did not have access to the old prints. Many identifications of the printers (esp. in Group A and B) were made by Zezschwitz more than a century ago, with uncertain conclusions in several cases. The bibliographical data would merit further research.

THE OLDEST GERMAN CATECHISM OF THE CZECH BRETHREN (1522) AND THE CATECHISM OF HUBMAIER (1526) [1]

1. COMPARISON OF OUTLINES

The Catechism of the Czech Brethren

Introduction
Man was created to know and to love God (Questions 1-2).

A. *Salvation*
   a. Depends on faith, love and hope (3-5).
   b. Faith — the first ground of salvation (6-8).
   c. Faith "objectively": THE APOSTLES' CREED (9-10).

B. *Living and dead faith*
   a. The twofold faith (11).
   b. The dead faith (credere deum, de deo, deo) (12).[2]
   c. The living faith (credere in deum)
      in God the Father, Son and Holy Spirit (13):
      (1) *God the Father*:
         (a) faith, love and obedience (14-15).

---

[1] For our comparison, we use the crit. ed. of the German text (*Kinderfragen*) in Müller, 1887, 9-28. In the crit. ed. of the original Czech text in Molnár, 1948a, 120-133, the numbering of questions differs by minus one from Q. 29 on. (The Czech Q. 28 combines the German Q. 28 and 29.) The editors of the crit. ed. of Hubmaier's catechism (*Leertafel*, 1526) failed to provide the useful numbering of questions (*HS*, 311-326). For the purpose of our study, we have numbered them 1 to 99.
[2] Question 12 shows variant readings in the different ed. of the catechism. In Latin equivalents, the Czech printed version (1523) would read "Credere dominum deum, domino deo, sed non in dominum deum". The German 'Nürnberg' ed. (1522) would read: "credere dominum deum esse, domino deo et de domino deo, sed non in . . .". Other variants in Müller, 1887, 12, note.

(b) THE TEN COMMANDMENTS (16-17).

(c) Love as fulfilment of commandments (18-22).

(2) *God the Son:*

    (a) Christ — the foundation of love (23-26).

    (b) THE SIX COMMANDMENTS OF CHRIST (Mt. 5:22-48) (27).

    (c) The highest command of Christ:
        to believe in him (28-29).

    (d) The promises of Christ:
        THE EIGHT BEATITUDES (Mt. 5:3-12) (30-31).

    (e) Eternal life, present and future (32-33).

(3) *God the Holy Spirit:*

    (a) Faith, love and hope — gifts of the Spirit (34).

    (b) Faith in the Holy Spirit (35).

    (c) The triune God (36-40).

C. *Genuine and false religion (worship)*

  a. Genuine religion (worship):

    (1) Worship with heart, mouth and works (41-44).

    (2) Worship in prayer.
        THE LORD'S PRAYER (45-46).

    (3) Worship of creatures forbidden (47-48).

  b. False religion: fourfold ("threefold" in text)[3] (49).

    (1) *Idolatry* — what it is (50).

      (a) veneration of Mary (51-53).

      (b) veneration of saints (54-59).

      (c) veneration of images (60).

      (d) adoration of Christ in the eucharist (61-62).

    (2) *False piety* (63).

      (a) true piety (64-65).

      (b) outward forms (66).

    (3) *False hope.*

      (a) false hope (67 and 71).

      (b) true hope (68-70).

    (4) *Mortal desires* (73).
        THE SEVEN MORTAL SINS (74).

Conclusion

How to avoid false religion and how to practice true religion in the fellowship of the faithful (74-76).

---

[3] Müller, 1887, 103 explains how the term "threefold" from the Czech manuscript version was retained in the later versions in spite of a fourfold division.

The Catechism of Hubmaier

"The First Part" (so marked in the text)

Introduction
   What is your name? (Question 1-3).
   What are you? (4).

A. *Knowledge of God*
   a. Almighty (5-6).
   b. Allknowing (7).
   c. Allmerciful (John 3:16) (8).

B. *Salvation*
   a. Sin and knowledge of sin (9-10).
   b. THE TEN COMMANDMENTS (11-12).
   c. Repentance (13-14).
   d. Prayer (15-16).
      THE LORD'S PRAYER (17).
   e. God's promises and the gospel (18-22).
   f. Faith (23).
      (1) Living and dead faith (24-26).
      (2) Fruit of the Spirit and of the flesh (27-28).
      (3) THE APOSTLES' CREED (29-30).

C. *Baptism*
   a. Only after preceding faith (31).
   b. Threefold baptism (32-33).
      (1) of spirit (34).
      (2) of water (35).
      (3) of blood (36).
      (4) their institution by Christ (37).
   c. Infant baptism (38-40).
   d. Baptismal pledge (41).
   e. Baptism in the Apostles' and Nicene Creeds (42).

D. *Church*
   a. What it is (43).
   b. Twofold: universal and local (44).
   c. Built on public profession of faith (45).
   d. Church discipline (46-50).
   e. Excommunication (51-54).

"The Second Part" (so marked in the text)

E. *The Lord's Supper*
   a. Its meaning (52-56).
   b. Adoration of Christ (57).
   c. The mass (58).

F. *Worship and religious observances*
   a. Confession of sins (59-60).
   b. Fasting (61).
   c. Blessing of food (meals at table) (62-66).
   d. Sabbath (67).
   e. Veneration of Mary and the saints (68-70).
   f. Veneration of images (71).
   g. The greatest worship:
      to believe the word of God (72-75).
   h. Love as sum and substance of all preaching (76-77).
   i. Singing in the church (78).

G. *Man's nature and eternal redemption*
   a. Good works (79-80).
   b. Free will (81).
   c. Rewards (82-84).
   d. God's call ("ziehung") to man:
      outward (preaching) and inward (illumination) (85-88).
   e. The good and evil works (Mt. 25:31-46 (89-93).
   f. The last day (94).
   g. Eternal life through suffering and cross (95-96).
   h. THE BEATITUDES (97).
   i. Hell (98).

Conclusion
   "The peace of God be with us all" (99).

2. BRIEF ANALYSIS OF OUTLINES

The modern editors of the German catechism of the Unity have complained about the lack of systematic outline. The attempt of Zezschwitz (1863, 61-86) to arrange the questions according to the trichotomy "faith-love-hope" was corrected by Müller (1887, 95-104) who pointed out that the catechism is structured according to several dichotomies and trichotomies which overlap, or are not even carried

out. His analysis served as the basis for the outline suggested by
Cohrs (I, 15-16). It is similar to ours which we have prepared on the
basis of the text itself, independently of Müller and Cohrs.

Even a cursory glance at the outline shows that the catechism is
developed according to a dual dialectic, namely the tension between
the living and the dead faith on the one hand, and between genuine
and false religion on the other. The dual contrast represents the two
aspects of the vital concern which characterized the Unity from its
inception to the last days of Brother Lukáš: the anxiety about the full
assurance of personal salvation (*nouze spasení*) and the quest for the
living church. These two leitmotifs of the Brethren's theology, the
one soteriological (in the sense of a personal experience), the other
ecclesiological, constitute the two main parts of the catechism.

By the same token, one cannot overlook what appears to be the
fragmentary nature of this oldest catechism of the Brethren. Baptism
is not even mentioned,[4] the eucharist is treated only in connection
with false adorations as an example of idolatry. There is no explicit
teaching on the church and its ministry. However, this seeming lack
can be understood readily from the fact that the German catechism
represents no more than the first part of the complete Czech catechism, *Spis tento otázek trojiech* which was printed on November 5,
1523.

The first part, *Otázky dětinské* [Questions for Children], was
meant for children who had been baptized in the Unity and who
were growing up under the spiritual care of their parents, godparents
and pastors, or for such adults who became interested in the Unity
and began to learn its teachings (*počínající*, the beginners). The expressed goal of this initial instruction, whether of the children or of
the adult inquirers, was that they might "experience the second birth
in faith". Only after such spiritual rebirth were the children, at a
minimum age of twelve, or the adult inquirers, permitted to learn the
second part of the catechism in preparation for the confirmation (or
believer's baptism and confirmation in the case of adults). At that
time, they studied in detail the meaning of baptism and the other
sacraments, as well as aspects of Christian living. After confirmation
and reception into the Unity, the members were expected to learn the

---

[4] The editors of the St. Gallen Catechism (1527) added a section on baptism at
the end (Müller, 1887, 207). Cf. also their frustrating attempt to divide the
Brethren's catechism into seven parts. The titles supplied by them reveal a complete minundersanding of the dual dichotomy referred to above.

final part of the catechism. Thus the tripartite catechism corresponded
to the concept of the threefold membership.[5] Only the first part was
translated into German. For the purposes of our comparative studies,
we limit ourselves to it.

In their later catechisms, Czech and German, the Brethren abandoned this original theological and pedagogical pattern. They followed the "classical" order established by Luther in 1529: Exposition
of (1) the Decalogue, (2) the Apostolicum, (3) the Lord's Prayer, (4)
the sacraments of baptism and of the Lord's supper.[6]

It should be noted that both the elementary catechism of the Unity
and Hubmaier's catechism contain the three basic elements of catechism, although they order them in a different sequence and do not
provide an exposition, sentence by sentence.[7]

The outline of Hubmaier's catechism [8] shows originality and re-
flects the purpose for which it was written at the request of Martin
Göschl at Mikulov in the fall of 1526, viz., to provide a textbook for
instructing baptismal candidates.[9] Although in his preface Hubmaier
envisaged a wider use of the booklet for regular catechetic instruction of children who were growing up in the Anabaptist congregations, the difficult language employed in some paragraphs as well as
lengthy answers to many questions made the catechism hardly suitable for children.[10]

[5]   The different goals of catechetical instruction at the three levels of membership
are stated clearly in the prefaces of Lukáš to the three parts of his Catechism (1523),
reprinted in Molnár, 1956a, 66-69. Cf. extracts in German tr. in Müller, 1887, 98
et passim. On the Catechism, see also Müller, I, 296 ff. and 481 ff.
[6]   Cf. Bednář, 1939, 113 and Katechismus, 1615. On the catechisms of the Reformation era, see the art. "Katechismus" by L. Fendt in EK, II, col. 561-566, by
H. W. Surkau in RGG, 3rd ed., III, col. 1179-1186, and "Katechismen u. Kate-
chismusunterricht" by Ferd. Cohrs in RE, 3rd ed., vol. 10, 135-164.
[7]   Hubmaier wrote a brief exposition of the Apostolicum (HS, 216-220, composed
during his imprisonment in Zürich, 1526) and of the Lord's prayer (HS, 221-223,
dating probably from the same place and time).
[8]   No one, thus far, has attempted an analysis of Hubmaier's catechism. Sachsse,
1914, 40-43 merely reviews the sequence of questions. The exhaustive work of
Cohrs, I-V does not even mention Hubmaier. Hubmaier's use of the term Ein
Catechismus oder Leertafel (HS, 172 and 307) may well justify the claim of
chronological priority over Andreas Althammer's Catechismus (Nürnberg, 1528)
which is usually regarded as the first book bearing that title.
[9]   HS, 172 and 307.
[10]   See HS, 307 (the last sentence) about catechetic instruction of children. As an
example of a lengthy answer, see Q. 81 on the nature of man and freedom of will
(almost two pages: HS, 321-323). With the exception of the Hutterite catechisms,
Hubmaier's Leertafel seems to have been the only Anabaptist catechism during
the 16th century (Neff in ML, II, 469 f. and ME, I, 529).

In comparison with the catechism of the Czech Brethren, Hub-maier's *Leertafel* lacks a clear theological outline. He himself divides it into a first and a second part but the distinction between the two is difficult to guess unless the first part was meant to be a preparation for the act of water baptism and the second part followed as a cate-chetical initiation into church membership. Theologically speaking, the section on the sacraments (baptism and the Lord's supper) is dissected by the section on the church (D.) which in turn becomes divorced from the paragraph dealing with the practical aspects of the church's life (F.). The last section (G.) reads like a postscript. The questions dealing with anthropology and soteriology (79-93), as well as the brief treatment of eschatology (94-96, 98) might have been included in the section on salvation (B.).

However, the outline as it stands reveals the main concerns of Hubmaier's theology more than any other of his preserved writings. In fact, it is his only work in which he attempted to summarize, in an elementary form, the entire scope of Christian faith and life. All of his other works deal with specific issues.[11]

3. THE QUESTION OF DEPENDENCE

Since Hubmaier wrote his catechism at the expressed request of Martin Göschl, a native Moravian German who might have been acquainted with the catechism of the Czech Brethren, the comparison of the two becomes more than an exercise in historical theology. Does Hubmaier's *Leertafel* (1526) show any direct dependence upon the *Kinderfragen* (1522-1524)?

The outlines of the two catechisms indicate no similarity compa-rable to that of the Magdeburg, Wittenberg or St. Gallen Catechisms which incorporated an adapted text of the *Kinderfragen*. Hubmaier developed his outline independently.

On the other hand, a careful textual comparison has brought to light a number of parallelisms in thought and expression.

[11]   The short treatise, *Eine Summe eines ganzen christlichen Lebens* (*HS*, 108-115) deals only with baptism and the Lord's supper. The only work comparable in scope with the catechism is Hubmaier's *Rechenschaft* (*HS*, 460-491) in which he sum-marized his teachings in 27 articles. It was composed for King Ferdinand during Hubmaier's final imprisonment. The account is characterized not only by a strong polemical note against the teachings of Hans Hut but also by Hubmaier's effort to minimize his deviations from the position of the Roman church. It was not printed until by Sachsse, 1914. A comparison of the *Rechenschaft* with the *Leertafel* would provide additional insights into Hubmaier's theological development.

Kinderfragen	*Leertafel*
Q. 1 "Was bistu? Ein vernunfftige schöpfung Gottes, vnd ein tödliche."	Q. 4 "Was bistu? Ein leybliche vernunnfftige Creatur ... erschaffen."
11 "Welcher vnderscheyd ist dises glaubens? Diser, das ein glaub ist lebendig, der ander todt."	24 "Wie vilerlay seind Glau- ben? Zwairlai. Namlich ein todter vnd ein lebendiger."

(It should be noted that the definition of the living and dead
faith differs considerably in the two catechisms.)

61	57

Rejection of adoration of Christ in the eucharist, using the same
argument about Christ seated at the right hand of God until
the day of his second coming.

53	68

A similar statement concerning the Virgin Mary and her per-
petual virginity.

57	69

Obedience ("gehorsam") of Mary and the saints, with the same
reference to Mary's command: "Alles was euch saget mein sůn
das thůt" (John 2:5).

60	71

Prohibition of veneration of images.

63	96

The use of the same phrase, "erdichte geistlichkeit", albeit in a
different context.

In our opinion, none of these parallels in thought and expression are
of such nature as to warrant the conclusion that Hubmaier was
familiar with the German catechism of the Unity. In view of Hubmaier's contacts with Göschl and Zeising (Čížek) one cannot rule out
such a possibility. However, the few textual similarities — which
might be explained by a common rejection of Roman Catholic
teachings and practices — cannot be regarded as sufficient evidence
of literary dependence.[12]

[12]   Cf. Chapter III, footnote 212.

THE LATER GERMAN CATECHISMS
OF THE CZECH BRETHREN AND THE CATECHISMS
OF THE HUTTERITES

1. THE PRINTED EDITIONS OF THE CATECHISMS OF THE UNITY [1]

A. Earlier Versions, Not Preserved (in Czech)

a. 1531, 16°, 16 fols. Mentioned in *HF*, fol. 867 and 913. Cf. Müller, 1887, 211 f.; Müller, II, 5, n. 13 and Říčan, 1957a, 134.
b. 1564, 16°, *Katechismus menší* [The Smaller Catechism]. Title page preserved in a writing of the Jesuit Václav Šturm, 1584. Cf. Müller, 1887, 214 f., n. 1 and Daňková, 1951, 103.

B. The Czech Large Catechism [2]

a. 1581?, 12°, without the title page. *Müller*, No. 3; *Bednář*.
b. [1590?], 16°, printed in Kralice without the title page. *Daňková*, No. 48, dates 1594-1601. Molnár, 1956a, 232 suggests 1590.
c. 1604, 12° (Kralice), *Daňková*, No. 49; *Müller*, No. 4.
d. [1608/1609], 12° (Kralice), *Müller*, No. 5; *Daňková*, No. 50 (dates 1594-1609); *Bednář*.

---

[1] No comprehensive study on the catechisms of the Unity in the period which followed the death of Lukáš (1528) is available. We have used the following accounts in preparing our list: Müller, 1887, 214 f. (The Large Catechism) and 294 f. (The Small Catechism, *Summa*); *Katechismus*, 1615, VII ff. (introduction by J. K. Smetana); Bednář, 1939, 110 f.; Daňková, 1951, 102 ff. and Molnár, 1965a, 231 f. We did not have access to any of the old prints which are deposited in Czechoslovakia. The list, which is likely not complete, was compiled simply to facilitate a chronological orientation in our comparison of the catechisms of the Unity with the catechisms of the Hutterites. We include both the Czech and the German versions.

[2] The numbering by Müller refers to his list in Müller, 1887, 214 f.; the numbering by Daňková to her list in Daňková, 1951, 102 ff.

e. 1615, 12° (Kralice), *Daňková*, No. 51. Modern ed. *Katechismus*, 1615, by J. K. Smetana.

f. 1633, 12° (Lešno) (Lissa in Polen), *Müller*, No. 6; *Bednář*.

g. 1661 (Amsterdam, published by Comenius), *Bednář*.

C. The Czech Small Catechism, "Summa" [3]

a. [1590?], 16° (Kralice), Printed together with the Catechism listed under B b. *Daňková*, No. 52.

b. 1600, 12° (Prague) (Daniel Adam of Veleslavín), *Müller*, No. 1. Reprinted in full by Molnár, 1956a, 232-237.

c. [before 1601], 12° (Kralice), *Daňková*, No. 52a.

d. [1608/1609], 12° (Kralice), *Müller*, No. 2. *Daňková*, No. 50.

e. 1615, 12° (Kralice), *Daňková*, No. 51.

f. 1633, 12° (Lešno), *Müller*, No. 5.

g. 1661 (Amsterdam), *Bednář*.

D. Edition in Four Languages

"*Summa Catechismi, In usum scholarum orthodoxarum unitatis fratrum in Bohemia et Moravia, Graece, Latine, Bohemice et Germanice*" (Bremen, Thomas Villerianus, 1615). Reprinted in full by Müller, 1887, 296-315.

E. German Catechisms of The Unity [4]

a. 1554, 8° (n.p.), The Catechism of Johann Gyrck (Jirek): "*Catechismus der Rechtgleubigen Behemischen Brüder, Welche der*

---

[3] The numbering by Müller refers to his list in Müller, 1887, 294 f. In most cases, the Czech *Summa* was published in conjunction with the Large Catechism.

[4] The textual relationship between the Czech and German catechisms (after 1528) requires further study. Müller, 1887, 213 and 293, and Říčan, 1957a, 202 claim that Jirek (Gyrck) translated, in 1554, his catechism from a Czech text. Neither of them explains which Czech catechism he translated (cf. the phrase "verdeutscht" in the title). Apart from the very short catechism of 1531 (16 fols., not preserved) no edition of the Czech catechism is known from the period 1529-1554. One should compare Gyrck's Catechism of 1554 with the text of the tripartite Czech catechism of Lukáš, *Spis tento otázek trojiech*, of 1523. Bednář, 1939, 112 assumes that the Czech large catechisms of the end of the 16th and the beginning of the 17th centuries were translations or adaptations of the German text of 1554, at least in their exposition of the Decalogue and the Apostolicum. No one has defined the textual relationship between the German (Large) Catechism of 1609 and 1618, as well as the German *Summa* of 1619, and the Czech versions of the same period. Since only the German catechisms could have exercised influence on the Hutterite catechisms, we shall not include a textual comparison of the Czech and German catechisms of the Unity in our present study.

*Antichrist mit seinem Gotlosen anhang verfolget, vnd auss Teuffe-
lischem eingeben, Hass, Neid, vnd vnwarheit, für Verfürer, Pic-
carden, vnd Waldenser, etc. schilt vnd lestert* ... *Verdeutscht
Durch Johannem Gyrck, Strelnensem, Pfarherrn zu Neidenburgk,
in Preussen.* 1554. Reprinted in full in Müller, 1887, 227-292. With
a dedicatory preface to Duke Albrecht of Prussia, *Müller*, No. 1
(list in Müller, 1887, 214 f.).

b. 1555, 8° (n.p.), An identical reprint of the 1554 ed. *Müller*, No. 2.

c. 1560, 4°, Königsberg (Prussia), Johann Daubman. The second part
   of Gyrck's catechism dealing only with the sacraments (which
   were not included in the Catechism of 1554): *Das ander theil des
   Heyligen Catechismi, Das ist: Lehre und Bericht von der Heyligen
   Tauff, Beicht, Vergebung (oder Aufflösung) der Sünden, vnd dem
   Abentmal des Herren* ... *Gezogen aus gemeiner Lehr der Rechtgleubigen Behemischen Brüder, Für die Jungen Christen. Durch
   Johannem Gyrck von Strelen.* Since the title does not refer to a
   translation, Müller, 1887, 224 concludes that this catechism was
   Gyrck's own work. It comprizes only 65 questions (baptism, 1-7;
   absolution of sins in the church, 8-10; confession, 11-29; Lord's
   Supper, 30-37; salvation through faith alone, 38-65) on 39 folios
   of print. Reprinted by Ehwalt, 1756, 291-352.

d. 1609. German Large Catechism, Listed by Molnár, 1956a, 232
   (with no particulars).

e. 1618. German Large Catechism, Listed by *Molnár, ibid.*

f. 1619, 12° (Kralice), *Summa der Christlichen Lehre. Aus dem
   Behemischen verdeutscht.* Müller, 1887, 295 (No. 4); *Daňková*,
   No. 53. The text is identical with the German text printed in the
   four language ed. of the *Summa* (Bremen, 1615; see item D a-
   bove).

2. THE CATECHISMS OF THE HUTTERITES

There are at least three main versions of the Hutterite catechism
from the 16th and 17th centuries, all preserved only in manuscripts.

a. *Kinderlehre*, 1568, probably written by Peter Walpot. Preserved
   in Ms. Codex 365 in Olomouc (written after 1568) and in Beck's
   Collection, Brno, No. 54. Brief excerpts in *TQ*, III, 257 f.

b. *Kinderbericht für die erwachsene Jugend in und ausser den
   Schulen,* 1620. Preserved in Ms. Codex A b 12 in Budapest (written
   ca. 1640) and in Beck's collection No. 63, fols. 1-21. Complete text

(based on Beck's copy) was published, in modern German, by Wiswedel, 1940b, 44-60.

c. *Kinderbericht vom Tauff und Abendmahl*, 1662. Preserved only in Beck's collection, No.62.[5]

3. OUTLINE OF THE GERMAN CATECHISM OF THE UNITY (GYRCK 1554)[6]

Introduction

Q. 1. What are you? ("ein vernünfftige Creatur Gottes").
2. For what purpose did God create you?
3. Why did you become mortal?
4. How can you be saved and enter eternal life?
5. Of what faith are you?
6. Are you a true Christian?
7. What is a Christian?
8. How were the Christians called in the beginning?
9. What should a Christian know?
10-14. The church through its ministry "mediates" the knowledge of God.
15. The Word of God as the foremost "ministrative thing".
16. What do you learn from the Word of God?
17-20. The full text of the Ten Commandments, the Apostles' Creed and the Lord's Prayer.

A. *The Ten Commandments*

a. The story of the exodus (Questions 21-25).
b. The summary of the law (love of God and neighbour) (26).
c. The uses of the law (27-28).
d. Exposition of the Ten Commandments (29-58).
e. Obedience and disobedience to the commandments (59-67).

---

[5] Our list is based on Friedmann, 1965b, 155 who includes other catechisms besides. The three listed above were studied by Wiswedel (in Beck's copies only) but no critical comparison of the three is included in his article, Wiswedel, 1940b, 42 f. Nor does he explain why he decided to publish the text of the later version. Friedmann, 1965b uses the titles *Kinderlehre* and *Kinderbericht* interchangeably (cf. pp. 50, 60, 130, 134, 155).
[6] Text reprinted in Müller, 1887, 227-292.

B. *The Apostles' Creed*

a. The living and the dead faith (68-72).
b. Exposition of the twelve articles of faith (73-119).

C. *Prayer*

a. What is prayer? (120-121).
b. Exposition of the Lord's Prayer (122-145).

D. *New Testament Doctrines Concerning the Status and Vocation ("Stand und Beruff") of a Christian*

The greatest commandment of the New Testament:
a. Concerning God:
   (1) Love and obedience of Christ (146-151).
   (2) Obedience of Christ's ministers (152-159)
      (concept of the ministry as apostolic office).
b. Concerning fellow men:
   (1) In general (160-164).
   (2) By status and vocation:
      (a) authorities ("Obrigkeit") (165-167).
      (b) married people (168-169).
      (c) parents and their children (170-171).
      (d) heads and members of household (172-173).
      (e) the Christian congregation (174-177).
      (f) the cross and patience (178-181).
      (g) fasting and almsgiving (182-185).
      (h) celibacy (186-187).

NOTE. The later (large) catechisms of the Unity follow a very similar outline in the Introduction and Parts A to C. However, Part D is replaced by a section on the "ministrative things" which include: (1) The ministry of the Word of God, (2) the power of the keys (church discipline) and (3) the sacraments (only baptism and the Lord's supper). Cf. Katechismus, 1615, questions 172-202. The Appendix (*ibid.,* 113 f.) includes the "Six Commandments of the New Law" and the Beatitudes. It should also be noted that Gyrck's catechism of 1554 contains no questions on the sacraments. These were presented in a separate booklet, "The Second Part of the Catechism", printed six years later (cf. the list above).

4. OUTLINE OF THE HUTTERITE CATECHISM (1620)[7]

Introduction

a. „God and his creation" (Questions 1-4).
    (1) What is God?
    (2) How can God be known?
    (3) For what purpose did God create the world?
    (4) What was the original will of God?
b. "The first disobedience" (Adam and Eve) (5).
c. "The first penalty for sin" (6-11).

A. The Ten Commandments

a. "The Exodus from Egypt" (12-13).
b. "The Ten Commandments" (full text and exposition (14-25).
c. The summary of the Commandments and how to keep them (26-27).

B. The Apostles' Creed

a. "Faith" (28-29).
b. The Apostolicum (text) (30).
c. Exposition of articles on God as Creator and Father (31-35).
d. "Jesus Christ" (incl. virgin birth) (36-52).
e. "The Holy Spirit" (53-54).
f. "The Christian Church" (incl. forgiveness of sins, resurrection and eternal life) (55-60).

C. The Lord's Prayer

a. Prayer (61-62).
b. Text and exposition of the Lord's Prayer (incl. the doxology) (63-75).

D. The Sacraments

a. "Baptism" (76-77).
b. "The Supper" (78-82).

[7] Text reprinted by Wiswedel, 1940b, 44-60. We have numbered the questions 1-82. The themes in quotation marks are part of the text of the catechism as published by Wiswedel.

5. FOUR QUESTIONS ABOUT LITERARY DEPENDENCE

In our attempts to discover traces of historical contacts and literary
influence of the Czech Brethren upon the Anabaptists, or vice versa,
we have compared in detail the texts of four German catechisms: the
Kinderfragen (1522), Hubmaier's *Leertafel* (1526),[8] Gyrck's catechism
(1544) and the Hutterite catechism (1620).[9] We have explored four
possible channels of literary influence.

(1) Did Gyrck in his catechism (1554) draw from the *Kinderfragen?* Müller, 1887, 216 ff., found only one slight similarity between
the two: the differentiation between the living and the dead faith.
However, the definition of the two kinds of faith is quite different in
the two versions. Our comparison produced a negative answer.

(2) Did Gyrck know Hubmaier's *Leertafel?* The only parallel we
were able to discover was the differentiation between the living and
the dead faith. There is no similarity in the understanding of the
terms in the two respective catechisms.

(3) Did Hubmaier's *Leertafel* influence the author of the Hutterite
catechism? We were unable to find evidence of such influence, either
in the outline, or in the phrasing and treatment of individual questions.[10]

(4) Did the author of the Hutterite catechism know Gyrck's catechism? This is perhaps the most intriguing aspect of our comparative
studies. The two catechisms show great similarity in the outline of

[8] One should keep in mind that the *Kinderfragen* and the *Leertafel* differ from
the later catechisms in that they do not include a detailed exposition of the Decalogue, the Apostolicum or the Lord's Prayer. According to Müller, 1887, xii, Ludwig
Keller suspected influences of the *Kinderfragen* in "a modern catechism of the
Mennonites" (*Taufgesinnte*). Müller was unable to identify such a catechism.
Wiswedel, 1940b, 41 misunderstood Müller and applied Keller's statement to the
Hutterite *Kinderbericht*. In vain did he search for parallels between the *Kinderfragen* and the Hutterite *Kinderbericht*. Cf. also Keller, 1885, 297, n. 2.
[9] It is highly desirable that some one compare the text of Gyrck's catechism (1554)
with the text of the oldest version of the Hutterite catechism (1568) preserved in a
16th century Ms. Codex in Olomouc. On Gyrck's Silesian background and his career
in the Unity, see Matusik, 1960, 218 ff.
[10] According to Friedmann, 1965b, 134 Beck claimed that the Hutterite catechism
(which one?) was dependent, in part, upon Hubmaier's *Leertafel*. Similarly, Wiswedel, 1940b, 42 stated that one could discern the influence of Hubmaier's theology in the Hutterite catechism, particularly in the section dealing with the church,
baptism, communion and church discipline. Nevertheless, our analysis has shown
that there are no traces of a direct literary dependence upon Hubmaier's *Leertafel*
nor evidence of a specific theological influence beyond a general agreement on the
basic principles of Anabaptism such as believer's baptism, regenerate membership
and church discipline.

the first three parts (the Decalogue, the Apostolicum and the Lord's Prayer). One might suspect that both authors followed the pattern of the Lutheran catechisms. However, in contrast to these, both Gyrck's and the Hutterite catechisms omit the section on sacraments.

Gyrck left it out altogether (replacing it with an unusual Section D) and later published a supplementary catechism (1560) which dealt with the sacraments exclusively. The Hutterite catechism includes a section on baptism and the Lord's supper but it is surprisingly short and unsatisfactory, especially the two questions on baptism. (Cf. the prominent place Hubmaier assigned to baptism and the Lord's supper in his *Leertafel*). Like Gyrck, the Hutterites later produced a supplementary brief catechism on the sacraments. Was it a mere coincidence, or were they influenced by the catechism of the Unity?

A detailed textual comparison of the two catechisms produced no traces of influence.

COLLOQUY BETWEEN THE ANABAPTISTS AND THE CZECH BRETHREN IN 1565 [1]

Again in the same year [1565] the Anabaptists held a disputation with the Brethren about the new birth. Martinus Behem of Bzenec was disputator, Brother Peter Herbert was Respondens.[2]

ANABAPTISTARUM SENTENTIA

Prior Adam per lapsum amisit imaginem Dei.

Posterior restituit omnem gloriam toti humano generi. Per suam incarnationem, sanitatem et mortem sustulit peccatum, omnemque maledictionem, reconciliauit nos Deo, et regenerauit nos in spem uiuam. 1. Pet. 1.

Hinc sumus omnes in Christo noua creatura et nisi tamen excidant per proprium peccatum, omnes saluantur.

Nam promissio et redemptio extenditur ad omnes sine exceptionem. Genes. [3] In semine tuo benedicentur omnes gentes. Rom. 5. Vt per unum hominem introiuit peccatum et mors, sic etiam iustitia et uita.

Vetera praeteriere, omnia sunt noua. 1. Corint. 15. In Christo omnes uiuificamur. Eph. 2. Cum Christo mortui sumus resurreximus. Si autem tandem exciderint proprio peccato, tum denuo eos regenerari oportet, et huc tendunt illae admonitiones de ueteri homine exuendo, mortificando. Eph. 4.

---

[1] The text is preserved in AUF, X, fols. 273b-275b. See Chapter V footnote 86.
[2] The title is in Czech, the record itself in Latin except for two marginal notes in Czech which we shall quote in the footnotes. In our transcription of the Latin text, we write in full all abbreviations. Only a few changes in punctuation have been made.
[3] Czech marginal note: "Genesis. God did not take pleasure in all [people]."

Nisi haec sententia constaret, non esset plena redemptio, Christi meritum esset inefficax, nos essemus ad huc in maledictione, fides nostra fieret inanis.

Sunt haec plane figmenta phantastici hominis.[4]

RESPONSIO P. HERBERTI

[274a]

Omnia per Christum, quae in coelo et in terra sunt, restaurata esse, affirmat D[ivinus] Paulus. Col. 1.

Omnes thesauros sapientiae et scientiae in Christo absconditos esse predicat. Col. 2.

Hos thesauros exuperantos et imperuestigabiles diuitias Christi appellat. Eph. 3.

Hanc plenitudinem reuerenter commendat. Joh. Cap. 1.

Nos quoque libenter fatemur, quod in predicanda divinae gratiae amplitudine nobis nunquam satisfacere possumus. Si inexhaustum dei gratiae fontem eiusque consilij mysterium respicimus, tum sumus nos electi, dilecti et saluati ante conditum mundum et ad dextram cum Christo antequam nascimur. Eph. 1 et 2.

Vel omnino aliquid sumus.

Quae in Christo capite apparent ad membra certe pertinent propter arcanam unitatem.

Sed si mentem in nos conuertimus quaeritur de applicatione et participatione huius gratiae, quo modo nobis patefiat, in nos conferatur, a nobis recipiatur, in nobis operetur. In summa quo modo saluemur.

Deus quidem fiduciam nostram ad se erigit, sed habens nostrae infirmationis rationem, nostra captui sese accommodat. Proinde ad Ecclesiam nos remittit cui proferit Spiritum sanctum. Media constituit, quibus nobiscum agat suaque beneficia nobis communiret Spiritu sancto. Ex Christi merito accipit, quos Ecclesiae impertit, ministerio praedestinauit ministros. Ideo enim ascendit Dominus, ut daret dona hominibus ad colligendam et aedificandam Ecclesiam. Eph. 4. 2. Cor. 5.

In ministerio primas partes obtinet Verbum quo salutis mysterium reuelatur, unde fides oritur. Rom. 10.   [274b]

Fides autem est illud unicum medium, quo oblata beneficia ap-

---

[4] Czech note: "Are we all born of Christ as of Adam?"

prehenduntur. Haec itaque requiritur et ueluti conditionis loco poni-
tur ab ipso domino. Joannes 3.

Exemplum huius processus describit Johannes Euangelista cap. 1.
qui, cum de uita, luce et plenitudine gratiae disseruisset, dedit Dominus, inquit, illis potestatem filios Dei fieri, qui credebant in
nomine eius et ex Deo nati erant.

Hunc modum etiam Paulus declarat. Eph. 1. 2. 3. Hac igitur ratione
salutem acquisitam in Christo per fidem possidemus, perfectionem
eius in spe expectamus, et sumus noua creatura et transformamur
quotidie in eandem imaginem. 2. Cor. 3.

Qui uero hunc Dei ordinem inuertunt, temeritatis vitium effugere
non possunt.

IAM OBIECTA ARGUMENTA DISCUTIEMUS DE INCARNATIONE

Cum filius Dei assumpsit humanitatem nostram, magno honore totum
genus humanum affecit.

Verum haec coniunctio non est salutaris nisi ijs, qui uicissim illi,
tanquam uerae oleae, inserantur, ut fiat utrinque, plena communi-
catio. Haec uisitio aliter fieri nequit nisi per fidem. Infantibus piorum
peculiari ratione communicatur, habent enim in foedere [5] ius adop-
tionis, quo in Christi communionem cooptantur. Actorum 26. S. Paulus
Christum ita loquentem inducit. Mittam te inter gentes, ut accipiant
remissionem peccatorum et sortem inter sanctos per fidem quae est
in me. Corde creditur ad iustitiam. Rom. 10.   [275a]

COMPARATIO ADAE CUM CHRISTO. ROM. 5

1. Cor. 15.

Si unius delicto mors regnauit, multo magis uita regnabit per gratiae
exuberantiam.[6]

Differentia inter Christum et Adamum.

(1) Non per solam imputationem peccato Adae damnamur, ac si
alieni peccati poena exigeretur a nobis, sed ideo poenam sustinemus
quia et culpa sumus rei, dicit enim apostolus qua omnes peccauimus,
istud peccare est corruptos et uitiatos esse. At Christi iustitia nobis

---

[5] Ms. reads "infaedre".
[6] Marginal note: Caluin.

imputatur, non qua intra nos sit, sed quod Christum ipsum possidemus.

(2) Quod non ad omnes homines peruenit Christi beneficium, quemadmodum uniuersum genus suum damnatione Adam inuoluit. Nam cum maledictio per naturam deriuasit, non est mirum, si totam massam complectatur. At ut in participationem gloriae Christi ueniamus, in eum inseri nos per fidem oportet.

Comunem omnium gratiam facit, non quod ad omnes extendatur re ipsa. Nam et si Christus passus est pro peccatis totius mundi, atque omnibus indifferenter Dei benignitate offertur, non tamen omnes apprehendunt.

Non tantum ab originali peccato, ceu corruptione ab Adamo contracta liberamur per Christum, sed ex multis delictis inquit apostolus. Rom. 5. Vetera praeteruerunt, omnia fiunt noua creatura.

De uniuersali promissione an cum conditione quadam offeratur:

[275b]

Extra foedus Deus non agit, nec illud praestitit promissum. Hinc formulae conditionales. Quisquis inuocaverit nomen Domini, saluus erit. Is qui credit non confundetur.

Haec conditio in ipsa electione iacet. Act. 13. Crediderunt quotquot erant praeordinati ad uitam aeternam. 1. Thes. 4. Paulus fidem fructum electionis asserit reprobi aliquam umbram percipiunt.

BIBLIOGRAPHY *

A. Anabaptistica

1. PRIMARY SOURCES

a. *Manuscripts*

Kunstbuch: *Codex 464* (Burgerbibliothek) (cf. Fast, 1956b).
Codex III, 19 (University Library, Olomouc, Czechoslovakia).

b. *Printed Sources*
(See also List of Abbreviations for Sources)

Alker, Hugo,
    1955 "Eine Täuferhandschrift des 16. Jhts. aus der Universitätsbibliothek in Wien", *ARG*, 46, 228-243.
Amerbach, Bonifacius,
    1943 *Die Amerbachkorrespondenz*, ed. Alfred Hartmann, II. Band (Basel).
Annales,
    1571 *Annales Gentis Silesiae* ... a Ioachimo Cureo Freistadiensi (Wittenberg).
Beck, Josef (ed.),
    1883 *Die Geschichtsbücher der Wiedertäufer in Oesterreich-Ungarn* (Wien).
Bergsten, Torsten (ed.) (see also under Anabaptistica, Secondary),
    1958a "Two Letters by Pilgram Marpeck", *MQR*, 32, 192-210.
Bernardus de Lutzemburgo,
    1522 *Catalogus haereticorum*, editio prima (Köln).
    1529 *Catalogus haereticorum*, editio quarta (Köln).
Böhmer, Heinrich (ed.),
    1933 *Urkunden zur Geschichte des Bauernkrieges und der Wiedertäufer* (Berlin).
Brandt, Otto (ed.),
    1933 *Thomas Muentzer. Sein Leben und seine Schriften* (Jena).

* Our classification of bibliography made it necessary to list different works of the same author in several sections of the bibliography. Many items classified as "Secondary Works" contain also source materials. Some primary sources are listed under the name of the editor rather than of the author.

Bullinger, Heinrich,
> 1526 *Verglichung der uralten vnd vnser zyten ka^etzeryen. Zů warnen die einfaltigen Christen, durch Octauiū Florentem beschriben*, n.d., n.p. [Zürich, 1526].
> 1838 *Reformationsgeschichte*, ed. J. J. Hottinger and H. H. Vögeli, Vol. I (Frauenfeld).
> 1904 *Heinrich Bullingers Diarium*, ed. Emil Egli (Basel).

Carlstadt, A. Bodenstein von,
> I-II *Karlstadts Schriften aus den Jahren 1523-1525*, ed. E. Hertzsch, Vols. I and II (Halle [Saale], 1956 and 1957).

Dialogus,
> 1527 *Dyalogus von Frembden glauben. Von Glauben der Kirchen. Von Tauff der Kinnder*, n.p.

Erasmus,
> 1519 *Farrago noua epistolarum* (Basel).
> 1521 *Epistolae ad diuersos* (Basel).
> E, 1-12 *Opvs epistolarvm Des. Erasmi Roterodami*, ed. P. S. Allen and H. W. Garrod (Oxford).

Ehrenpreis, Andreas,
> 1652 *Ein Sendbrief* (reprinted in Wilson, Alberta, Canada, 1953).

Entfelder, Christian,
> 1530 *Von den manigfaltigen im glauben zerspultungen* [Augsburg, Philip Ulhart].

Erhard, Christoph,
> 1589 *Gru^endliche kurtz verfaste Historia* (München).

Faber, Johann,
> 1524 *Malleus in haeresim Lutheranam* ... (Köln) (reprinted in Corpus Catholicorum 23/24, Münster i. W., 1941 and 1952).
> 1526a *Moscouitarum iuxta mare glaciale religio* ... (Basel).
> 1526b *Christenliche beweisung ... über sechs Artickel ... Vlrich Zwinglins* ... (Tübingen).
> 1528a *Ursach warumb ... Balthasar Hubmayr zu Wienn ... verbrennet sey*, n.p. [Wien].
> 1528b *Ettliche Sermon von Doctor Johan Fabri gepredigt wider die gotlossen Widertauffer zu Znaym auf dem Lanndtag der Marggraffschafft Merhern jm Monat April* (Wien).
> 1528c *Sermones ... adversus ... Anabaptistas habiti, apud Morauos, in Conventu Znoimensi, Mense Aprili* (Wien).
> 1528d *Etliche Sermonn von dem hochwirdigen Sacrament warens leib vnd Plut Christi, geprediget zu Prag ... auf die Osterliche zeyt* (Wien).
> 1528e *Adversvs Doctorem Balthasarvm Pacimontanvm ... orthodoxae fidei catholica defensio* (Leipzig).
> 1528f *Wie sich Johannis Huhs, der Pickarder vnd Joannis von Wessalia, Leren vnd buecher mit Martino Luther vergleichen* (Leipzig).
> 1529a *Sermones ... Habiti Prague apud Bohemos, de sacrosancto Eucharistiae sacramento* (Freiburg i. B.).
> 1529b *Christenliche ableynung des erschröckenlichen yrrsal, so Caspar Schwenckfelder in der Schlesy wyder die warheyt des hochwirdigenn Sacraments ... auffzurichten understandenn hat* (Wien).
> 1537a *Opvscvla quaedam* ... (Leipzig).
> 1537b *Censura super nova apud Moravos Picardorum et cuiusdam Habrowansky secta* ... (Wien).
> 1537c *Confvtatio Gravissimi Erroris* ... (Leipzig).

Fast, Heinold (ed.) (see also under Anabaptistica, Secondary),
    1962b *Der linke Flügel der Reformation* (Bremen).
Fischer, Christoph Andreas,
    1603 *Von der Wiedertauffer Verfluchten vrsprung* ... (Bruck a.d. Thaya).
    1604 *Antwort auff die Widerlegung so Clauss Breuᵉtel, ... hat gethan ...* (Bruck a.d. Thaya).
    1607a *Der Hutterischen Widertauffer Taubenkobel* ... (Ingolstadt).
    1607b *Vier und funfftzig Erhebliche Ursachen Warumb die Widertauffer nicht sein im Land zu leyden* (Ingolstadt).
Franck, Sebastian,
    1531 *Chronica, Zeytbůch vnd geschichtbibel* ... (Strasbourg).
Friedmann, Robert (ed.) (see also under Anabaptistica, Secondary),
    1945 "Reason and Obedience", *MQR*, 19, 27-40.
    1955b "Claus Felbinger's Confession of 1560", *MQR*, 29, 141-161 and 30, 78.
    1957a "A Notable Hutterite Document Concerning True Surrender and Christian Community of Goods", *MQR*, 31, 22-62.
    1960 "An Epistle Concerning Communal Life ...", *MQR*, 34, 249-274.
    1961b "A Newly Discovered Source on the Transmigration of the Hutterites to Transylvania, 1621-1623", *MQR*, 35, 309-314.
    1964a "Jakob Hutter's Epistle concerning the Schism in Moravia in 1533", *MQR*, 38, 329-343.
Gastius, Johannes,
    1544 *De Anabaptismi exordio, erroribvs, historijs abominandis* ... (Basel).
Gerlach, Stephan,
    1674 *Stephan Gerlach ... Tage-Buch* (Frankfurt a. M.).
Glaidt, Oswald,
    1526 *Handlung yetz den xiiii tag Marcij diss XXVI Jars, So zů Osterlytz inn hern* ... (see Appendix 2).
    1527 *Enntschuldigung Osbaldi Glaidt von Chamb, Etwan zu Leybm in Oesterreich, yetz predicannt zu Nicolspurg in Merhern* (Nikolsburg).
Hillerbrand, Hans J. (ed.) (see also under Anabaptistica, Secondary),
    1958a "An Early Anabaptist Treatise on the Christian and the State", *MQR*, 32, 28-47.
    1960a "Ein täuferisches Missionszeugnis aus dem 16. Jahrhundert", *ZKG*, 71, 324-327.
    1961 "A Sixteenth-Century Anabaptist Evangelistic Testimony", *MQR*, 35, 314-317.
    1964a "Thomas Muentzer's Last Tract against Martin Luther", *MQR*, 38, 20-36.
Jenny, Beatrix (ed.),
    1951 *Das Schleitheimer Täuferbekenntnis 1527* (Thayngen).
Kameníček, František (ed.) (see also under Bohemica, Secondary),
    1894 *Prameny ke vpádům Bočkajovců na Moravu* ... (Prague).
    1899 "Zpěvník novokřtěnců", *ČMM*, 23, 74-75.
Kessler, Johannes,
    1902 *Sabbata*, ed. Emil Egli and Rudolf Schoch (St. Gallen).
Loserth, Johann (ed.) (see also under Anabaptistica, Secondary),
    1914 "Zwei Miszellen aus der Wiedertäuferzeit in Mähren", *ZDVGMS*, 18, 168-170.
    1919a "Zur kirchlichen Bewegung in Mähren im Jahre 1528", *ZDVGMS*, 23, 176.
    1919b "Zwei Briefe des Kardinals Dietrichstein zur Ausweisung der Wiedertäufer aus Mähren", *ZDVGMS*, 23, 173-175.

1925c "Aus dem Liederschatz der Mährischen Wiedertäufer", ZDVGMS, 27, 46-51.
1929a Quellen und Forschungen zur Geschichte der oberdeutschen Taufgesinnten im 16. Jahrhundert. Pilgram Marbecks Antwort auf Kaspar Schwenckfelds Beurteilung des Buches der Bundesbezeugung von 1542 (Wien and Leipzig).

Lumpkin, William L. (ed.),
1959 Baptist Confessions of Faith (Philadelphia).

Mais, A. (ed.),
1964 "Das Hausbuch von Neumühl 1558-1610, das älteste Grundbuch der huterischen Brüder", JGPÖ, 80, 66-88.

Menčík, Ferdinand (ed.),
1896 "Ueber ein Wiedertäufergesangbuch", VKČSN, No. XI, 1-15.
1911 "Ein Schreiben über die Wiedertäufer" [1607], ZDVGMS, 15, 364-372.

Meshovius, Arnoldus,
1617 Historiae Anabaptisticae Libri Septem (Köln).

Oecolampad, Johannes,
1927 Briefe und Akten zum Leben Oekolampads, ed. Ernst Staehelin, Vol. I (Leipzig).
1934 Vol. II (Leipzig).

Ottius, Johannes Henricus,
1672 Annales Anabaptistici (Basel).

Protocoll,
1571 Protocoll. Das ist Alle handlung des gesprechs zu Frankenthal ... (Heidelberg).

Riedemann, Peter,
1545 Rechenschafft vnserer Religion Leer vnd Glaubens, n.p., n.d. [ca. 1545].
1938 Rechenschafft ... (reprint, Cotswold-Bruderhof, England).
1950 Account of Our Religion, Doctrine and Faith (English translation by Kathleen E. Hasenberg, London).

Schreiber, Heinrich (ed.),
1863 Der deutsche Bauernkrieg. Gleichzeitige Urkunden, Vol. I, Jahr 1524 (Freiburg i. B.).

Schwenckfeld, Caspar,
1524 Ermanung Des missbrauchs etlicher fürnempsten Artickel des Euangelij ..., n.p. [Zürich].
1528 Ein anwysunge das die opinion der leyplichen gegenwertigheyt ... gericht ist (Zürich).

Simler, Josias,
1575 Narratio de ortv, vita et obitv reverendi viri, D. Henrici Bvllingeri (Zürich).

Spittelmaier, Joannes,
1524 Entschuldigung Ioannis Spitelmayer prediger zu Nicolspurg ..., n.d., n.p. [Wien].

Stumpf, Johannes,
1952 Johannes Stumpfs Schweizer- und Reformationschronik, Vol. I (Basel).

Szczucki, Lech and J. Tazbir (ed.),
1958 "Korespondencja anabaptystów morawskich z arianami polskimi", ORP, 3, 197-215.

Vadian,
I-VII Die Vadianische Briefsammlung, ed. Emil Arbenz and Hermann Wartmann, Vols. I-VII (St. Gallen, 1888-1913).

Williams, George Hunston (ed.) (see also under Anabaptistica, Secondary),
    1957   *Spiritual and Anabaptist Writers* (= *Library of Christian Classics,*
        Vol. XXV) (Philadelphia).

Wiswedel, W. (ed.) (see also under Anabaptistica, Secondary),
    1937a "Gabriel Ascherham und die nach ihm benannte Bewegung", *ARG,*
        34, 1-35 and 235-262.

Wolkan, Rudolf (ed.) (see also under Anabaptistica, Secondary and Bohemica,
        Secondary),
    1923   *Geschicht-Buch der Hutterischen Brüder* (Wien).

Wolny, Gregor (ed.),
    1850   "Die Wiedertäufer in Mähren", *Archiv für Kunde österreichischer
        Geschichts-Quellen,* 5 (Wien), 67-138.

Wotschke, Theodor (ed.),
    1908   *Der Briefwechsel der Schweizer mit den Polen* (Leipzig).
    1929   "Urkunden zur Reformationsgeschichte Böhmens und Mährens", *Jahr-
        buch der Vereines für die Geschichte der Deutschen in Böhmen,* II.

Zieglschmid, A. J. F. (ed.),
    1941   "Unpublished 16th century letters of the Hutterian Brethren", *MQR,*
        15, 5-25 and 118-140.

Zwingli Hauptschriften,
    1 ff.   *Zwingli Hauptschriften,* ed. Fritz Blanke, Oskar Farner, Rudolf Pfister
        (Zürich, 1940 ff.).
    Note. The new critical edition *Thomas Müntzer: Schriften und Briefe* (ed.
        Günther Franz, Gütersloh, 1966) was not accessible to us before the
        completion of the manuscript.

2. SECONDARY WORKS

Altrichter, A.,
    1910   "Materialien zur Geschichte Iglaus in der Cerronischen Sammlung
        des mährischen Landesarchivs", *ZDVGMS,* 14, 147-153.
    1928   "Zur Geschichte der Wiedertäufer in Iglau", *ZDVGMS,* 30, 157-159.

Armour, Rollin Stely,
    1966   *Anabaptist Baptism: A Representative Study* (Scottdale, Pa.).

Auer, Alfons,
    1954   *Die vollkommene Frömmigkeit des Christen, nach dem Enchiridion
        des Erasmus von Rotterdam* (Düsseldorf).

Bahlow, Hans,
    1928   *Die Anfänge des Buchdrucks zu Liegnitz* (Liegnitz).

Bainton, Roland H.,
    1940   *Bernardino Ochino* (Firenze).
    1941   "The Left Wing of the Reformation", *The Journal of Religion,* 21,
        124-134. Reprinted in *Studies on the Reformation (Collected Papers
        in Church History,* II) (Boston, 1963), 119-129.

Barge, H.,
    I-II   *Andreas Bodenstein von Karlstadt,* 2 vols. (Leipzig, 1905).
    1935   "Die gedruckten Schriften des evangelischen Predigers Jakob Strauss",
        ARG, 32, 100-121 and 248-252.
    1937   *Jakob Strauss. Ein Kämpfer für das Evangelium in Tirol, Thüringen
        und Süddeutschland* (Leipzig).

Baring, Georg,
1959 "Hans Denck und Thomas Müntzer in Nürnberg 1524", *ARG*, 50, 145-181.
Baum, Johann Wilhelm,
1860 *Capito und Butzer. Strassburgs Reformatoren* (Elberfeld).
Bauman, Clarence,
1968 *Gewaltlosigkeit im Täufertum* (Leiden).
Baur, August,
I-II *Zwinglis Theologie. Ihr Werden und ihr System.* Vol. I (1885), Vol. II (1889) (Halle).
Bender, H. S.,
1949 "Anabaptist Manuscripts in the Archives at Brno", *MQR*, 23, 105-107.
1950 *Conrad Grebel* (Goshen, Indiana).
1952 "Die Zwickauer Propheten, Thomas Müntzer und die Täufer", *TZ*, 8, 262-278.
1956a "New Discoveries of Important Sixteenth-Century Anabaptist Codices", *MQR*, 30, 72-77.
1964 "Pilgram Marpeck, Anabaptist Theologian and Civil Engineer", *MQR*, 38, 231-265.
Benzing, Josef,
1952 *Buchdruckerlexikon des 16. Jahrhunderts* (Frankfurt a.M.).
1963 *Die Buchdrucker des 16. und 17. Jahrhunderts im deutschen Sprachgebiet* (Wiesbaden).
Bergfried, Ulrich,
1938 *Verantwortung als theologisches Problem im Täufertum des 16. Jahrhunderts* (Wuppertal-Elberfeld).
Bergmann, Cornelius,
1916 *Die Täuferbewegung im Kanton Zürich bis 1660* (Leipzig).
Bergmann, J.,
1848 "Die Wiedertäufer zu Au im innern Bregenzerwalde und ihre Auswanderung nach Mähren i. J. 1585", *Sitzungsberichte der kais. Akademie der Wissenschaften*, I (Wien), 106-116.
Bergsten, Torsten (see also under Anabaptistica, Primary),
1958b *Pilgram Marbeck und seine Auseinandersetzung mit Caspar Schwenckfeld* (Uppsala).
1959 "Der heutige Stand der Hubmaier-Forschung". *Bericht über den Kongress der Europäischen Baptisten*, ed. Jakob Meister (Kassel), 177-186.
1961 *Balthasar Hubmaier. Seine Stellung zu Reformation und Täufertum 1521-1528* (Kassel).
Bernhofer-Pippert, Elsa,
1967 *Täuferische Denkweisen und Lebensformen* ... (Münster).
Bílý, Dr.,
1859 "O novokřtěncích v osadách moravských", *Moravské noviny* (Brno).
Bischof, Hermann,
1857 *Sebastian Franck und deutsche Geschichtsschreibung* (Tübingen).
Blanke, Fritz,
1940a "Das Reich der Wiedertäufer zu Münster 1534/35", *ARG*, 37, 13-37.
1940b "Beobachtungen zum ältesten Täuferbekenntnis", *ARG*, 37, 242-249.
1942 *Der junge Bullinger 1504-1531* (Zürich).
1952 "Zollikon 1925. Die Entstehung der ältesten Täufergemeinde", *TZ*, 8, 241-262.
1953 "The First Anabaptist Congregation: Zollikon 1525", *MQR*, 27, 17-33.

1955 *Brüder in Christo* (Zürich).
1957 "Anabaptism and the Reformation", *The Recovery of the Anabaptist Vision* (Herschberger, 1957) (Scottdale, Pa.), 55-68.
1960 *Aus der Welt der Reformation* (Zürich).
1961 *Brothers in Christ*, tr. Joseph Nordenhaug (Scottdale, Pa.).

Bonorand, Conradin,
1963 "Stand und Probleme der Vadian-Forschung", *Zwingliana*, 11, 586-606.
1965 "Aus Vadians Freundes- und Schülerkreis in Wien", *Vadian-Studien*, 8, and reprint (St. Gallen).

Bouvier, André,
1940 Henri Bullinger (Neuchâtel-Zürich).

Brändly, Willy,
1950 "Peter Kolin von Zug", *Zwingliana*, 9, 150-171.

Burckhardt, Paul,
1898 *Die Basler Täufer* (Basel).

Cantimori, Delio,
1949 *Italienische Haeretiker der Spätrenaissance*, Deutsch von Werner Kaegi (Basel).

Čapek, Norbert F.,
1903 *Úryvky z dějin kaceřovaných křesťanů* (Brno).

Černohorský, Karel,
1931 "Počátky habánských fajansí", *Sborník k 60. naroz. E. W. Brauna* (Opava, 1930, and reprint, Opava, 1931), 103-143.

Cerroni, Jan P.,
I "Ursprung und Geschichte der böhmischen und mährischen Brüder, dann der Wiedertäufer in Mähren", n.d. [19th century], Ms. No. 471, Brno, State Archives.
II "Über die Wiedertäufer in Mähren", n.d. [19th century], Ms. Cerroni Collection, No. I: 131, Brno, State Archives.

Chmaj, Ludwik,
1957 *Bracia polscy* (Warszawa).
1958 "Komeński a bracia polscy", *ORP*, 3, 133-156.
1959 *Studia nad Arianizmem*, ed. L. Chmaj (Warszawa).

Clasen, Claus-Peter,
1963a "The Sociology of Swabian Anabaptism", *CH*, 32, 150-180.
1963b "Medieval Heresies in the Reformation", *CH*, 32, 392-414.
1965a "Nuernberg in the History of Anabaptism", *MQR*, 39, 25-39.
1965b "The Anabaptists in Bavaria", *MQR*, 39, 243-261.
1965c *Die Wiedertäufer im Herzogtum Württemberg und in benachbarten Herrschaften* (Stuttgart).

Comba, Emilio,
1897 *I nostri Protestanti*, Vol. 2 (Firenze).

Cornelius, Carl Adolf,
1860 *Geschichte des Münsterischen Aufruhrs* ..., Vol. 2 (Leipzig).

Corda, Sergio,
1962 "Giulio Gherlandi: ...", *Il Messaggero Evangelico*, 79 (Roma), 374-380.

Correll, Ernst H.,
1925 *Das Schweizerische Täufermennonitentum* (Tübingen).

Čulen, Ladislav,
1945 "Habáni na Západnom Slovensku", *Historický Sborník*, III, 68-161.

Dedic, Paul,
1922 "Die kirchlichen und religiösen Verhältnisse in Mähren im Reforma-

tions-jahrhundert". Unpublished dissertation (handwritten copy in private possession) (Wien).

1931/36 "Die Geschichte des Protestantismus in Olmütz", *JGPÖ*, 52 (1931), 148 ff.; 53 (1932), 110 ff.; 54 (1933), 118 ff.; 55 (1934), 69 ff.; 56 (1935), 120 ff.; 57 (1936), 121 ff.

1938 "Forschungen zur Geschichte des oesterreichischen Protestantismus", *ARG*, 35, 277-281.

1939a "The Social Background of the Austrian Anabaptists", *MQR*, 13, 4-20.

1939b "Zur Frage der kirchlichen Organisation des Luthertums in Mähren im Reformationsjahrhundert", *JGPÖ*, 60, 7-48.

DeWind, Henry A.,
1954 "Italian Hutterite Martyrs", *MQR*, 28, 163-185.

1955a "A Sixteenth-century description of religious sects in Austerlitz, Moravia", *MQR*, 29, 44-53.

1955b "Anabaptists in Thessalonica?", *MQR*, 29, 70-73.

Doornkaat, Koolman J. ten,
1926 "Leopold Scharnschlager und die verborgene Täufergemeinde in Graubünden", *Zwingliana*, 4, 329-337.

Durnbaugh, Donald F.,
1968 "Theories of Free Church Origins", *MQR*, 42, 83-95.

Dušek, Konstantin (pseudonym for Josef Hovorka),
1962 "Ondřej Ehrenpreis", *KJ*, 47, No. 42.

1963a "Moravští křtěnci — habáni — před 400 lety", *KJ*, 48, No. 4.

1963b "Vlastní charakteristika huterských bratří", *KJ*, 48, No. 11.

1963c "Bratří roku 1463 o Valdenských", *KJ*, 48, No. 40-41.

1964 "Valdenská myšlenka roku 1464 na Horách Rychnovských", *KJ*, 49, No. 41.

Eberlein, Hellmut
1952 *Schlesische Kirchengeschichte*, 3rd ed. (Goslar).

Ecke, Karl,
1952 *Das Rätsel der Taufe* (Güterslohe).

Egli, Emil,
1900a "Christoph Froschauer und der Meister H.V.", *Zwingliana*, I, 146-150.

1901a "Biblianders Leben und Schriften", *Analecta Reformatoria*, Vol. II (Zürich).

1901b "Briefpost im 16. Jahrhundert", *Zwingliana*, I, 229-235.

1904 "Bullingers Beziehungen zu Zwingli", *Zwingliana*, I, 439-443.

Eisenblätter, Winfried,
1964 "Der Kampf Johann Fabris von Leutkirch gegen Balthasar Hubmaier und die Mährischen Täufer in den Jahren 1527/78" (seminar paper, Zürich).

1965 "Die katholische Auseinandersetzung mit dem Täufertum", *MGB*, 22, 47-52.

Estep, William R.,
1963 *The Anabaptist Story* (Nashville, Tenn.).

Evans, Austin Patterson,
1924 *An Episode in the Struggle for Religious Freedom* (New York).

Fast, Heinold (see also under Anabaptistica, Primary),
1955 "Neues zum Leben Wilhelm Reublin's", *TZ*, 11, 420-425.

1956a "The Dependence of the First Anabaptists on Luther, Erasmus and Zwingli", *MQR*, 30, 104-119.

1956b "Pilgram Marbeck u. das oberdeutsche Täufertum", *ARG*, 47, 212-242.
1959 *Heinrich Bullinger und die Täufer* (Weierhof).
1960 "Die Sonderstellung der Täufer in St. Gallen und Appenzell", *Zwingliana*, 11, 223-240.
1962a "Hans Krüsis Büchlein über Glauben und Taufe", *Zwingliana*, 11, 456-475.

Fischer, Hans,
1956 *Jakob Huter* (Newton, Kansas).

Foster, Claude R., Jr.,
1965 "Hans Denck and Johannes Buenderlin: A Comparative Study", *MQR*, 39, 115-124.

Friedmann, Robert (see also under Anabaptistica, Primary),
1929 "Die Briefe österreichischen Täufer", *ARG*, 26, 30-80 and 161-187.
1931 "Eine dogmatische Hauptschrift der hutterischen Täufergemeinschaften in Mähren", *ARG*, 28, 80-111 and 207-240, and continued in
1932 *ARG*, 29, 1-17.
1942 "The Schleitheim Confession (1527) and Other Doctrinal Writings of the Swiss Brethren in a Hitherto Unknown Edition", *MQR*, 16, 82-98.
1947 "John Horsch and Ludwig Keller", *MQR*, 21, 160-174.
1948 "The Encounter of Anabaptists and Mennonites with Anti-Trinitarianism", *MQR*, 12, 139-162.
1949 *Mennonite Piety through the Centuries* (Goshen, Ind.).
1950 "Anabaptism and Protestantism", *MQR*, 26, 12-25.
1952 "Of Hutterite Books", *Mennonite Life*, 81-82.
1954 "A Critical Discussion of Meihuizen's study of 'Spiritual Trends'", *MQR*, 28, 148-154.
1955a "Christian Sectarians in Thessalonica and their Relationships to the Anabaptists", *MQR*, 29, 54-69.
1955c "The Christian Communism of the Hutterian Brethren", *ARG*, 46, 196-209.
1956 "A Hutterite Book of Medieval Origin", *MQR*, 30, 65-71.
1957b "Thomas Muentzer's Relation to Anabaptism", *MQR*, 31, 75-87.
1958 "The Philippite Brethren: A Chapter in Anabaptist History", *MQR*, 32, 272-297.
1959 "The Doctrine of Original Sin as Held by the Anabaptists of the Sixteenth Century", *MQR*, 33, 206-214.
1961a *Hutterite Studies*, ed. H. S. Bender (Goshen, Ind.).
1962 "Old Evangelical Brotherhoods: Theory and Fact", *MQR*, 36, 349-354.
1964b "Das täuferische Glaubensgut. Versuch einer Deutung", *ARG*, 55, 145-161.
1965a "Anabaptist Research in Progress", *MQR*, 39, 68-72.
1965b *Die Schriften der hutterischen Täufergemeinschaften* (Wien).
1966a "Hutterite Worship and Preaching", *MQR*, 40, 5-26.
1966b "Ecumenical Dialogue between Anabaptists and Catholics", *MQR*, 40, 260-265.
1966c "Die Nikolsburger Artikel", *JGPÖ*, 82, 15-29.
1967a "The Essence of Anabaptist Faith", *MQR*, 41, 5-24.
1967b "The Nicolsburg Articles", *CH*, 36, 391-409.
1968 "Newly Discovered Hutterite Manuscripts", *MQR*, 42, 73-74.

Friesen, Abraham,
1965 "Thomas Müntzer in Marxist Thought", *CH*, 34, 306-327.

Fuchs, Gerhard,
1954 "Karlstads radikal-reformatorisches Wirken und seine Stellung zwi-

schen Müntzer und Luther", *Wissenschaftliche Zeitschrift der Martin-Luther-Universität*, III (Halle-Wittenberg), 523-551.

Geiser, Samuel,
1931 *Die Taufgesinnten-Gemeinden* (ed.) (Karlsruhe).
1951 "An Ancient Anabaptist Witness for Nonresistance", *MQR*, 25, 66-69 and 72.

Gelder, H. A. Enno van,
1961 *The Two Reformations in the Sixteenth Century* (The Hague).

Goeters, J. F. Gerhard,
1957 *Ludwig Hätzer* (Gütersloh).

Gratz, Delbert,
1953 *Bernese Anabaptists and Their American Descendants* (Scottdale).

Gritsch, Eric W.,
1967 *Reformer Without a Church* (Philadelphia).

Groling, Moriz,
1908 *Die Klosterdruckerei im Prämonstratenserstifte Bruck a. d. Thaya (Mähren) 1595-1608* (Wien).

Gross, Leonard,
1968 "Newly Discovered Codices of the Hutterites", *MQR*, 42, 149-155.

Güss, Ernst Friedrich,
1960 *Die Kurpfälzische Regierung und das Täufertum bis zum Dreissig-jährigen Krieg* (Stuttgart).

Hall, Thor,
1961 "Possibilities of Erasmian Influence on Denck and Hubmaier in their Views on the Freedom of the Will", *MQR*, 35, 149-170.

Heck, Roman,
1961 "Reformacja a problem walki klasowej chłopów śląskich w XVI wieku", *ORP*, VI, 29-48.

Hein, Gerhard,
1939 "Leupold Scharnschlager", *MGB*, 4, 6-12.

Helbing, Leo,
1933 *Dr. Johann Fabri und die Schweizerische Reformation* (Einsiedeln).
1941 *Dr. Johann Fabri. Generalvikar von Konstanz und Bischof von Wien* (Münster i.W.).

Herschberger, Guy F. (ed.),
1957 *The Recovery of the Anabaptist Vision* (Scottdale).

Heuschel, A.,
1901 *Dr. Johannes Hess, der Breslauer Reformator* (Halle).

Hillerbrand, Hans Joachim (see also under Anabaptistica, Primary),
1958b "The Anabaptist View of the State", *MQR*, 32, 83-110.
1959a "Die gegenwärtige Täuferforschung — Fortschritt oder Dilemma?", *Lebendiger Geist* (H. J. Schoeps Festschrift, ed. Hellmut Diwald) (Leiden-Köln), 48-65.
1959b "Remarkable Interdependencies between Certain Anabaptist Doctrinal Writings", *MQR*, 33, 73-76.
1959c "Ein Täuferbekenntnis aus dem 16. Jahrhundert", *ARG*, 50, 40-45.
1960b "Anabaptism and the Reformation: Another Look", *CH*, 29, 404-423.
1962a "The Origin of Sixteenth-Century Anabaptism: Another Look", *ARG*, 53, 152-180.
1962b *Die Politische Ethik des oberdeutschen Täufertums* (Leiden).
1966 "Andreas Bodenstein of Carlstadt, Prodigal Reformer", *CH*, 35, 379-398.

Hirsch, Carolus Christianus,
I-IV   *Millenarius* (Nürnberg), 1746-1749.
Hochhuth, Karl Wilhelm Hermann,
1858   "Mittheilungen aus der protestantischen Secten-Geschichte in der hessischen Kirche", *Zeitschrift für die historische Theologie*, 28, 538-644.
1859   *Ibid.*, 29, 167-209.
1860   *Ibid.*, 30, 258-284.
Holl, Karl,
1923   "Luther und die Schwärmer", *Gesammelte Aufsätze zur Kirchengeschichte*, Vol. I, 2nd ed. (Tübingen), 420-467.
1957   "Habanerhöfe in Südmähren", *Südmährisches Jahrbuch*, 92-94.
Horsch, John,
1931a   *The Hutterian Brethren* (Goshen, Ind.).
1934a   "An Inquiry into the Truth of Accusations of Fanaticism and Crime against the Early Swiss Brethren", *MQR*, 8, 18-31 and 73-89.
1934b   "The Character of the Evangelical Anabaptists as reported by Contemporary Reformation Writers", *MQR*, 8, 123-135.
Horst, Irvin B.,
1964   "Report of the Täuferakten-Kommission", *MQR*, 38, 368-370.
Hošek, František Xaver,
1867   *Balthasar Hubmaier a počátkové novokřestěnstva na Moravě* (Brno).
1891   "Life of Balthasar Hubmeyer, the founder of 'New Christianity' in Moravia", *Texas Baptist Hist. and Biographical Magazine*, tr. W. W. Everts, 118-148, 226-256, 321-329, 502-559.
1892   *Ibid.*, 19-32, 127-155, 189-268, 313-328, 375-386, 435-445, 497-511.
Hovorka, Josef,
        See Dušek, Konstantin.
Hrubý, František (see also under Bohemica, Primary and Secondary),
1929a   "Nové příspěvky k dějinám moravských novokřtěnců", *Českou minulostí* (Prague), 213-229.
1929b   "Konec knihtiskárny v Louce", *ČMM*, 53, 508-511.
1935a   "Die Wiedertäufer in Mähren", reprint of articles in *ARG* (Leipzig), 30 (1933), 1-36 and 170-211; 31 (1934), 61-102; 32 (1935), 1-40.
1935b   "Ulrich Zwingli a novokřtěnci", *Tvůrcové dějin III* (Prague), 61-68.
1937   "Karel st. z Žerotína a moravští novokřtěnci", *ČČH*, 47, 68-72.
Hűbel, Ignaz,
1927   "Beziehungen Mährens zu den deutschen Universitäten im 16. Jahrhundert", *ZDVGMS*, 29, 157-198 and Beilage.
Humbel, Frida,
1912   *Ulrich Zwingli und seine Reformation im Spiegel der gleichzeitigen schweizerischen volkstümlichen Literatur* (Leipzig).
Husa, Václav,
1956a   "O původu novokřtěnství", *Zápisky katedry čs. dějin a arch. studia*, 1 (Prague), 26-28.
1956b   "K dějinám lidových hnutí na Moravě kolem roku 1525", *Zápisky*, 1, 29-31.
1957   *Tomáš Müntzer a Čechy* (Prague).
1958   "Počátky anabaptismu a Müntzerův pobyt v Čechách", *ČSČH*, 6, 501-506.
Jones, Rufus M.,
1914   *Spiritual Reformers in the 16th and 17th Centuries* (Beacon Hill-Boston).

Kasparek, Max Udo,
1956 "Zur Tracht der Wiedertäufer in Mähren und der Slowakei", *Südostdeutsche Heimatblätter*, 5, 91-95.
1957 "Habanerhöfe in Südmähren", *Südmährisches Jahrbuch*, 92-94.
Kaufman, Maynard,
1957 "Anabaptism as an Existentialist Philosophy of Religion", *Mennonite Life*, 12, 139-143, and
1958 13, 35-38.
Kautsky, Karl,
I-II *Vorläufer des neueren Sozialismus*, 2 vols., 2nd ed. (Stuttgart, 1909).
Keller, Ludwig,
1882 *Ein Apostel der Wiedertäufer* (Leipzig).
1885 *Die Reformation und die älteren Reformparteien* (Leipzig).
1887 *Zur Geschichte der altevangelischen Gemeinden* (Berlin).
1894 *Die böhmischen Brüder und ihre Vorläufer* (Leipzig).
Kiwiet, Jan J.,
1957a *Pilgram Marbeck* (Kassel).
1957b "The Life of Hans Denck", *MQR*, 31, 227-259.
1958 "The Theology of Hans Denck", *MQR*, 32, 3-27.
Klaassen, Walter,
1961 "Some Anabaptist Views on the Doctrine of the Holy Spirit", *MQR*, 35, 130-139.
1962 "Anabaptism and the Reformation", *The Canadian Journal of Theology*, 8, 34-42.
1963a "Spiritualization in the Reformation", *MQR*, 67-77.
1963b "The Anabaptist View of the Christian Life", *The Canadian Journal of Theology*, 9, 103-111.
1966a "Speaking in Simplicity": Balthasar Hubmaier", *MQR*, 40, 139-147.
1966b "The Bern Debate of 1538: Christ the Center of Scripture", *MQR*, 40, 148-156.
Klassen, Peter James,
1963 "Mutual Aid Among the Anabaptists: Doctrine and Practice", *MQR*, 37, 78-95.
1964 *The Economics of Anabaptism* (The Hague).
Klassen H, Herbert C.,
1958 "Ambrosius Spittelmayr: His Life and Teachings", *MQR*, 32, 251-271.
1959 "The Life and Teachings of Hans Hut", *MQR*, 33, 171-205 and 267-304.
Klassen W, William,
1958 "Pilgram Marpeck in recent research", *MQR*, 32, 211-229.
1959 "Pilgram Marpeck's Two Books of 1531", *MQR*, 33, 18-30.
1966a "Anabaptist Hermeneutics: The Letter and the Spirit", *MQR*, 40, 83-96.
1966b "The Relationship of the Old and New Covenants in Pilgram Marpeck's Theology", *MQR*, 40, 97-111.
Köhler, Walther,
1968 *Covenant and Community* (Grand Rapids).
1900 *Luther und die Kirchengeschichte nach seinen Schriften* . . . (Erlangen).
1906 "Die Post von Hessen nach der Schweiz zur Zeit Zwinglis und Bullingers", *Zwingliana*, II, 172-180.
1921 *Huldrych Zwinglis Bibliothek* (Zürich).
1924 *Zwingli und Luther*, Vol. 1 (Leipzig).

1940 "Das Täufertum in der neueren kirchenhistorischen Forschung", *ARG*,
37, 93-107, and
1941 *ARG*, 38, 349-364,
1943 *ARG*, 40, 246-270,
1948 *ARG*, 41, 164-186.
1951a *Dogmengeschichte* ..., Vol. 1 (Zürich), and
1951b Vol. 2 (Zürich).
1953 *Zwingli und Luther*, Vol. 2 (Gütersloh).

Kolde, Theodor,
1888 "Beiträge zur Reformationsgeschichte: 3. Zum Prozess des Johann
Denck und der drei gottlosen Maler von Nürnberg", *Kirchengeschicht-
liche Studien. Hermann Reuter zum 70. Geburtstag gewidmet* (Leipzig), 228-250.
1902 "Hans Denck und die gottlosen Maler von Nürnberg", *Beiträge zur
bayerischen Kirchengeschichte*, VIII (Erlangen), 1-31 and 49-71.

Konrad, Paul,
1917 *Die Einführung der Reformation in Breslau und Schlesien* (Breslau).

Kot, Stanislas,
1957 *Socinianism in Poland* (Beacon Hill-Boston).

Krafft, Carl,
1870 *Aufzeichnungen des schweizerischen Reformators Heinrich Bullinger
über sein Studium* ... (Elberfeld).

Krajewski, Ekkehard,
1954 *The So-Called Petition of Protest and Defence to the Zürich Council
1524/1525*. Unpublished B.D. thesis, Baptist Seminary, Rüschlikon.
1957 *Leben und Sterben des Zürcher Täuferführers Felix Mantz* (Kassel).
1962 "The Theology of Felix Manz", *MQR*, 36, 76-87.

Kraus, František,
1937 *Nové príspevky k dejinám habánov na Slovensku* (Bratislava).

Kreider, Robert,
1952 "Anabaptism and Humanism: ...", *MQR*, 26, 123-141.
1953 "Vocations of Swiss and South German Anabaptists", *Mennonite Life*,
8, 38-42.

Kretz, František,
1922 "Zpěvníky novokřtěnců", *Časopis vlast. spolku musejního*, 33 (Olomouc), 57-67.

Krisztinkovich, Maria H.,
1965 "Anabaptist book confiscations in Hungary during the eighteenth
century", *MQR*, 39, 125-146.

Krodel, Gottfried,
1956 "Nürnberger Humanisten am Anfang des Abendmahlsstreites", *ZBKG*,
25, 40-50.

Kűhn, Johannes,
1923 *Toleranz und Offenbarung* (Leipzig).

Kuhn, Walter,
I-III *Geschichte der deutschen Ostsiedlung in der Neuzeit*. Vol. I (1955);
Vols. II and III (1957) (Köln-Graz).

Landsfeld, Herman,
1962 "The Discovery of Hutterite Books", *Mennonite Life*, 17, 140-144.
1964 "Thirty Years of Excavation", *Mennonite Life*, 19, 167-173.

Laurense, Leo,
1964 "The Catholicity of the Anabaptists", *MQR*, 38, 266-279.
Leemann-van Elck, Paul,
1931 "Bibliographie der Drucke Hans Hagers 1524-1527", *Der Schweizer Sammler*, 5, 147-153 and 165-170.
1934 *Die Zürcher Druckgeschichte* (Bern).
1940 *Die Offizin Froschauer* (Zürich/Leipzig).
Lepp, Friedrich,
1908 *Schlagwörter des Reformationszeitalters* (Leipzig).
Lindsay, Thomas,
I-II *A History of the Reformation*. Vol. I (1907) and II (1908) (Edinburgh).
Littell, Franklin Hamlin,
1950 "The Anabaptist Doctrine of the Restitution of the True Church", *MQR*, 26, 33-52.
1955 "Spiritualizers, Anabaptists and the Church", *MQR*, 29, 34-44.
1957 *The Free Church* (Beacon Hill-Boston),
1958 *The Anabaptist View of the Church*, 2nd ed. revised (Boston).
1961 *A Tribute to Menno Simons* (Scottdale, Pa.).
1962a "What Butzer debated with the Anabaptists at Marburg ...", *MQR*, 36, 256-276.
1962b *Reformation Studies*, ed. by Littell (Richmond, Va.).
1963 "The Radical Reformation", *The Layman in Christian History*, ed. Stephen Ch. Neill and Hans-Ruedi Weber (Philadelphia), 261-275.
Loetscher, Frederick William,
1906 "Schwenckfeld's Participation in the Eucharistic Controversy of the Sixteenth Century", *Princeton Theological Review*, 4, 352-386 and 454-500.
Loserth, Johann (see also under Anabaptistica, Primary),
1884 "Zur Geschichte der Wiedertäufer in Mähren", *Zeitschrift für Allgemeine Geschichte, Kultur-, Literatur- und Kunstgeschichte*, 1, 438-457.
1891 "Die Stadt Waldshut und die vorderösterreichische Regierung in den Jahren 1523-1526", *Archiv für österreichische Geschichte*, 77 (Wien), 1-149.
1892 "Deutschböhmische Wiedertäufer", *Mittheilungen des Vereines für Geschichte der Deutschen in Böhmen*, 30, 404-422.
1893 *Dr. Balthasar Hubmaier und die Anfänge der Wiedertaufe in Mähren* (Brünn).
1894 "Der Communismus der mährischen Wiedertäufer ...", *Archiv für österreichische Geschichte*, 81, 135-322.
1897 "Bilder aus der Reformationszeit in Mähren", *ZDVGMS*, 1, 65-73.
1899 "Die Wiedertaufe in Niederösterreich von ihren Anfängen bis zum Tode Balthasar Hubmaiers 1525-1528", *Blätter des Vereines für Landeskunde von Niederösterreich*, 43 (Wien), 417-435.
1917 "Zum Abzug der Wiedertäufer aus Mähren", *ZDVGMS*, 21, 411-415.
1922 "Die letzten Züge der Wiedertäufer nach Mähren", *ZDVGMS*, 24, 85-94.
1925a "Studien zu Pilgram Marbeck", in Neff 1925, 134-177.
1925b "Über die Beziehungen der mährischen Wiedertäufer zu ihren Glaubensgenossen in Augsburg und in Graubünden", *ZDVGMS*, 27, Heft 3-4, 48-50.
1928a "Recent Research in the History of the Tyrol-Moravian Anabaptists", *MQR*, 2, 5-15.

1928b "Zwei Tiroler, Pilgram Marbeck und Leutpold Scharnschlager", *ZDVGMS*, 30, 1-12.

Macek, Josef,
1958a "Petr Pässler v tyrolské a salcburské selské válce", *ČSČH*, 6, 3-32.
1958b (ed.), *Mezinárodní ohlas husitství* (Prague).
1958c "Müntzer a Čechy", *ČSČH*, 6, 346-351.
1959 "Zu den Anfängen des Tiroler Bauernkrieges", *Historica*, I (Prague), 135-195.
1960a "Das revolutionäre Programm des deutschen Bauernkriegs von 1526", *Historica*, II (Prague), 111-144.
1960b *Tyrolská selská válka a Michal Gaismair* (Prague).
1960c "Středoněmečtí novokřtěnci", *ČSČH*, 8, 185-188.

Machát, František,
1897 "Společenské řády novokřtěnců na Moravě", *ČČH*, 3, 349-358.

Macoskey, Robert Arthur,
1956 "The Life and Thought of Balthasar Hubmaier". Unpublished dissertation, Edinburgh.

Maier, Paul L.,
1959 *Caspar Schwenckfeld on the Person and Work of Christ* (Assen, The Netherlands).

Maleczyńska, Ewa,
1956 *Z dziejów postępowej ideologii na Śląsku v XIV-XVI wieku* (Warszawa.)
1959 "Ulrik Stadler na tle losów anabaptystów w pierwszej połowie XVI wieku", *Przegląd Historyczny*, 50, 473-485.
1960 "Frederyk II legnicki wobec lewego nurtu reformacji na Śląsku", *Studia z dziejów polskich i czechosłowackich*, I (ed. Ewa i Karol Maleczyński) (Wrocław), 225-248.
1961 "Gabrielowcy śląscy", *ORP*, 6, 17-28.

Mareš, J.,
1907 "Novokřtěnci", *ČČH*, 13, 24-36.

Matusik, Leokadia,
1959 "Michael Weisse", *Sobótka*, 14, 457-486.
1960 "Śląskie kontakty późnohusyckie i brackie do r. 1548", *Studia*, I (see under Maleczyńska, 1960), 183-224.

Mau, Wilhelm,
1912 *Balthasar Hubmaier* (Berlin and Leipzig).

Mayer, Anton,
1883 *Wiens Buchdrucker-Geschichte 1482-1882*. Vol. 1 (Wien).

Mecenseffy, Grete,
1956a *Geschichte des Protestantismus in Österreich* (Graz-Köln).
1956b "Die Herkunft des oberösterreichischen Täufertums", *ARG*, 47, 252-259.
1956c "Das Verständnis der Taufe bei den süddeutschen Täufern", *Antwort* (K. Barth zum 70. Geburtstag) (Zollikon-Zürich), 642-646.

Meyer, Chr.,
1874 "Zur Geschichte der Wiedertäufer in Oberschwaben", *ZHVSN*, 1, 207-253.

Moser, Andres,
1958 "Die Anfänge der Freundschaft zwischen Zwingli und Ökolampad", *Zwingliana*, 10, 614-620.

Müller, Konrad,
1955 "Markgraf Georg von Brandenburg-Ansbach-Jägerndorf", *Jahrbuch für Schlesische Kirche und Kirchengeschichte*, N.F., 34 (Düsseldorf), 7-31.

Muller, Lydia,
1927 *Der Kommunismus der mährischen Wiedertäufer* (Leipzig).
Näf, Werner,
1944 *Vadian und seine Stadt St. Gallen*. Vol. I (St. Gallen).
1957 Vol. II (St. Gallen).
Neff, Christian (ed.),
1925 *Gedenkschrift zum 400 jährigen Jubiläum der Mennoniten oder Tauf-gesinnten* (Ludwigshafen a.R.).
Neubaur, L.,
1912 "Mährische Brüder in Elbing", *ZKG*, 33, 447-455.
Neumann, Gerhard J.,
1957 "Nach und von Mähren", *ARG*, 48, 75-90.
Neuser, Wilhelm,
1913 *Hans Hut* (Berlin).
Newman, A. H.,
1926 "Balthasar Hubmaier and the Moravian Anabaptists", *The Goshen College Record*, 27, 4-22.
Nicoladani, Alexander,
1893 *Johannes Bünderlin von Linz* . . . (Berlin).
Novak, Michael,
1965 "The Free Churches and the Roman Church: The Conception of the Church in Anabaptism and Roman Catholicism", *Journal of Ecumenical Studies*, 2, 426-447.
Novotný, Jaroslav,
1959 "Novokřtěnci na jižní Moravě v 16. a 17. století", *Vlastivědný věstník moravský*, 14 (Brno), 86-92.
Orchard, G. H.,
1855 *A Concise History of Foreign Baptists*, 12th ed. (Nashville, Tenn).
Oyer, John S.,
1964 *Lutheran Reformers Against Anabaptists* (The Hague).
Payne, Ernest A.,
1949 *The Anabaptists of the Sixteenth Century* . . . (London).
Peachey Paul,
1954a *Die soziale Herkunft der Schweizer Täufer* . . . (Kalsruhe).
1954b "Social Background and Social Philosophy of the Swiss Anabaptists", *MQR*, 28, 102-127.
Pestalozzi, Carl,
1858 *Heinrich Bullinger* (Elberfeld)).
Peter, Rodolphe,
1954 "Le maraîcher Clément Ziegler, l'homme et son œuvre", *RHPR*, 34, 255-282.
Peters, Victor,
1965 *All Things Common. The Hutterian Way of Life* (Minneapolis).
Peuckert, Will-Erich,
1943 *Sebastian Franck* (München).
Philoon, Thurman E.,
1962 "Hans Greiffenberger and the Reformation in Nuernberg", *MQR*, 36, 61-75.
Ratkoš, Petr,
1954 "Banícke povstanie 1525-1526 a reformačná ideológia na Slovensku", *ČSČH*, 2, 400-414.

1958 "Die Anfänge des Wiedertäufertums in der Slowakei", *Aus 500 Jahren deutsch-tschechoslowakischer Geschichte*, ed. Karl Obermann and Josef Polišenský (Berlin), 41-59.
1963 *Povstanie baníkov na Slovensku 1525-1526* (Bratislava).
Redekop, Calvin,
1962 "The Sect Cycle in Perspective", *MQR*, 36, 155-161.
1965 "The Sect from a New Perspective", *MQR*, 39, 204-217.
Rich, Arthur,
1949 *Die Anfänge der Theologie Huldrych Zwinglis* (Zürich).
Riedl, Franz H.,
1953 "Von Tirol über Mähren in die Welt", *Tiroler Heimat*, 17 (Innsbruck-Wien), 143-147.
Ritschl, Albrecht,
I-III *Geschichte des Pietismus*, Vol. I (1880), II (1884) and III (1886) (Bonn).
Robinson, Robert,
1792 *Ecclesiastical Researches* (Cambridge).
Rogge, Joachim,
1957 *Der Beitrag des Predigers Jakob Strauss zur früheren Reformationsgeschichte* (Berlin).
Roth, Friedrich,
1885 *Die Einführung der Reformation in Nürnberg* (Würzburg).
1901a "Zur Geschichte der Wiedertäufer in Oberschwaben. III. Der Höhepunkt der wiedertäuferischen Bewegung in Augsburg und ihr Niedergang im Jahre 1528", *ZHVSN*, 28, 1-154.
1901b *Augsburgs Reformationsgeschichte 1517-1530*, 2nd rev. ed., Vol. I (München).
Rudolphi, E. C.,
1869 *Die Buchdrucker-Familie Froschauer in Zürich* ... (Zürich).
Rupp, Gordon,
1959 "Andrew Karlstadt and Reformation Puritanism", *Journal of Theological Studies*, 10 (London), 308-325.
1961 "Thomas Müntzer, Hans Huth and 'the Gospel of All Creatures'", *Bulletin of the John Rylands Library*, 43 (Manchester), 492-519.
Sachsse, Carl,
1914 *D. Balthasar Hubmaier als Theologe* (Berlin), 1914. [*Note*. Sachsse's book *D. Balthasar Hubmaiers Anschauungen von der Kirche, den Sakramenten und der Obrigkeit* (Bonn, 1913) is reprinted in Sachsse, 1914, 185-220.]
1963 "Die politische und soziale Einstellung der Täufer in der Reformationszeit", *ZKG*, 74, 282-315.
Schäufele, Wolfgang,
1962 "The Missionary Vision and Activity of the Anabaptist Laity", *MQR*, 36, 99-115.
1966 *Das missionarische Bewusstsein und Wirken der Täufer* (= *Beiträge zur Geschichte und Lehre der Reformierten Kirche*, Bd. XXI) (Neukirchen-Vluyn).
Schenner, Ferdinand,
1908 "Zur Geschichte der Reformation in Znaim", *ZDVGMS*, 12, 310-337.
1910 *Ibid.*, 14, 337-381.
1911 "Beiträge zur Geschichte der Reformation in Iglau", *ZDVGMS*, 15, 222-255.
1912 *Ibid.*, 16, 84-102 and 374-406.
1913 *Ibid.*, 17, 114-159.

Schiess, Traugott,
1916 "Aus dem Leben eines Ilanzer Schulmeisters", *Bündnerisches Monatsblatt* (Chur), 73-89.
Schlesinger, Ludwig,
1866 "Wiedertäufer in Böhmen und Mähren", *Mittheilungen des Vereines für Geschichte der Deutschen in Böhmen,* 4, 149-151.
Schottenloher, Karl (see also under Bohemica, Secondary),
1908 "Johann Fabri in Rom nach einem Berichte Jakob Zieglers", *ARG,* 5, 31-47.
1921 *Philip Ulhart. Ein Augsburger Winkeldrucker* ... (München and Freising).
Schram, Wilhelm,
1899 "Der Abt von Kloster-Bruck Freitag von Cziepiroh (1573-1585)", *ZDVGMS,* 3, 312-324.
Schraepler, Horst W.,
1957 *Die rechtliche Behandlung der Täufer* (Tübingen).
Schultz, Selina Gerhard
1946 *Caspar Schwenckfeld von Ossig* ... (Norristown, Pa.).
Schulze, R. Wilhelm,
1957 "Neuere Forschungen über Balthasar Hubmaier von Waldshut", *Alemannisches Jahrbuch* (Lahr/Schwarzwald), 224-272.
Schwab, Paul J.,
1962 "Augsburg and the Early Anabaptists", *Reformation Studies,* ed. F. H. Littell (Richmond, Va.), 212-228.
Schweizer, J.,
n.d. *Reformierte Abendmahlsgestaltung in der Schau Zwinglis* (Basel).
Seeberg, Erich,
1929 "Der Gegensatz zwischen Zwingli, Schwenckfeld und Luther", *Reinhold Seeberg Festschrift,* I (Leipzig), 43-80.
Seewald, Gerd,
1953 "Balthasar Hubmaier and Civil Government", typescript (1953) deposited at the Baptist Seminary in Rüschlikon-Zürich.
Smirin, M. M.,
1952 *Die Volksreformation des Thomas Münzer und der grosse Bauernkrieg* (Berlin) (Russian orig., 1947).
Sommer, J. L.,
1953 "Hutterite medicine and physicians in Moravia ...", *MQR,* 27, 111-127.
Staedtke, Joachim,
1954 "Heinrich Bullingers Bemühungen um eine Reformation im Kanton Zug", *Zwingliana,* X, 24-47.
1955 "Anfänge des Täufertums in Bern", *TZ,* 11, 75-78.
1960 "Voraussetzungen der Schweizer Abendmahlslehre", *TZ,* 16, 19-32.
1962 *Die Theologie des jungen Bullinger* (Zürich).
Staehelin, Ernst
1939 *Das theologische Lebenswerk Johannes Oekolampad* (Leipzig).
Staub, Ignatius,
1911 *Dr. Johann Fabri, Generalvikar von Konstanz* ... (Einsiedeln).
Stauffer, Ethelbert,
1933 "Märtyrertheologie und Täuferbewegung", *ZKG,* 52, 545-598.
1945 "The Anabaptist Theology of Martyrdom", tr. by Robert Friedmann, *MQR,* 19, 179-214.

Stayer, James M.,
    1965   "Hans Hut's Doctrine of the Sword . . .", *MQR*, 39, 181-191.
Steiner, Eduard,
    1957   "Die mährischen Wiedertäufer", *Mährisch-Schlesische Heimat* (Stein-
    heim/Main), 88-96.
Strauss, Gerald,
    1966   *Nuremberg in the Sixteenth Century* (New York).
Teufel, Eberhard,
    1941   "Täufertum und Quäkertum im Lichte der neueren Forschung", *Theo-
    logische Rundschau*, N.F., 13, 21-57, 103-127, 183-197.
    1942   *Ibid.*, 14, 27-52, 124-154.
    1943   *Ibid.*, 15, 56-80.
    1948   *Ibid.*, 17, 161-181.
    1952   *Ibid.*, 20, 361-370.
Theobald, Leonhard,
    1936   *Die Reformationsgeschichte der Reichsstadt Regensburg*, Vol. I (Mün-
    chen).
    1941   "Balthasar Hubmaier", *ZBKG*, 16, 153-165.
Tobolka, Zd. V.,
    1929   "Knihtiskař Simprecht Sorg-Froschauer", *ČMM*, 53, 501-508.
Troeltsch, Ernst,
    1912   *Die Soziallehren der christlichen Kirchen und Gruppen* (Tübingen).
Tschackert, Paul,
    1891   *Paul Speratus von Rötlen, evangelischer Bischof von Pomesanien in
    Marienwerder* (Halle).
    1894   *Herzog Albrecht von Preussen* (Halle).
Urban, Wacław,
    1966   *Studia z dziejów antytrynitaryzmu na ziemiach czeskich i słowackich
    w XVI-XVII wieku* (Kraków).
Urner, Hans,
    1948   "Die Taufe bei Caspar Schwenckfeld", *Theologische Literaturzeitung*,
    73, 329-342.
Vaňáček, Michael,
    1967   *Bohutice* (Brno).
Vasella, Oskar,
    1956   "Zur Biographie des Prädikanten Erasmus Schmid", *ZSKG*, 50, 353-366.
Vedder, Henry C.,
    1905   *Balthasar Hübmaier, the leader of the Anabaptists* (New York and
    London).
Veesenmeyer, Georg,
    1800   "Etwas von Christian Entfelder", *Neues Theologisches Journal*, 15,
    4. Stück (Nürnberg), 309-334.
    1826   "Ueber Balthasar Hubmoer . . .", *Kirchenhistorisches Archiv* (Halle),
    226-248.
Verduin, Leonard,
    1964   *The Reformers and Their Stepchildren* (Grand Rapids, Michigan).
Vischer, Lukas,
    1955   *Die Auslegungsgeschichte von I. Kor. 6, 1-11* (Tübingen).
Volf, Josef,
    1934   "K literatuře o novokřtěncích", *ČČM*, 107.
Wackernagel, Rudolf,
    1924   *Geschichte der Stadt Basel*, Vol. III (Basel).

Wappler, Paul,
1908a *Inquisition und Ketzerprozesse in Zwickau zur Reformationszeit* (Leipzig).
1908b "Thomas Münzer in Zwickau und die 'Zwickauer Propheten' ", *Wissenschaftliche Beilage zu dem Jahresberichte des Realgymnasiums . . . in Zwickau* (Zwickau, 1908) (cf. rev. ed., Gütersloh, 1966).
1910 *Die Stellung Kursachsens und des Landgrafen von Hessen zur Täuferbewegung* (Münster i. W.).
1913 *Die Täuferbewegung in Thüringen von 1526 bis 1584* (Jena).
Weiss, Ruth,
1959 "Die Herkunft der osthessischen Täufer", *ARG*, 50, 1-16 and 182-199.
1961 "Herkunft und Sozialanschauung der Täufergemeinde im westlichen Hessen", *ARG*, 52, 162-187.
Weller,
Repertorium typographicum. Die deutsche Literatur im ersten Viertel des 16. Jahrhunderts (Nördlingen, 1864).
Wenger, John C.,
1961 *Even Unto Death* (Richmond, Va.).
1963 *Die dritte Reformation*, tr. by R. Grossmann (Kassel).
Westin, Gunnar,
1958 *The Free Church Through the Ages*, tr. by V. A. Olson (Nashville, Tenn.).
Widmoser, Eduard,
1951 "Die Wiedertäufer in Tirol", *Tiroler Heimat*, 15 (Innsbruck-Wien), 45-89.
1952 "Das Tiroler Täufertum, 2. Teil", *Tiroler Heimat*, 16, 103-128.
Wiedemann, Hans,
1965 "The Story of the Anabaptists at Passau", *MQR*, 39, 91-103.
Williams, George Huntson (see also under Anabaptistica, Primary),
1958 "Studies in the Radical Reformation . . ." *CH*, 27, 46-69 and 124-160.
1959 "Anabaptism and Spiritualism in the Kingdom of Poland and the Grand Duchy of Lithuania . . .", *Studia nad Arianizmem* (= Chmaj 1959) (Warsaw), 215-262.
1962 *The Radical Reformation* (Philadelphia).
Wiswedel, Wilhelm (see also under Anabaptistica, Primary),
I-III *Bilder und Führergestalten aus dem Täufertum*. Vol. I (1928), II (1930) and III (1952) (Kassel).
1937b "Oswald Glait von Jamnitz", *ZKG*, 56, 550-564.
1938 "Die Nikolsburger Artikel", *ZBKG*, 13, 34-46.
1939 *B. Hubmaier, der Vorkämpfer für Glaubens- und Gewissensfreiheit* (Kassel).
1940a "Dr. Balthasar Hubmaier", *ZBKG*, 15, 129-159.
1940b "Das Schulwesen der Huterischen Brüder in Mähren", *ARG*, 37, 38-60.
1943 "Die alten Täufergemeinden und ihr missionarisches Wirken", *ARG*, 40, 183-200 and *ARG*, 41, 115-132.
Wolf, Adam,
1878 *Geschichtliche Bilder aus Oesterreich*, Vol. I (Wien).
Wolkan, Rudolf (see also under Anabaptistica, Primary and Bohemica, Secondary),
1903 *Die Lieder der Wiedertäufer* (Berlin) (reprint, 1965).
1918 *Die Hutterer* (Wien).
Yoder, John H.,
1957 "The Prophetic Dissent of the Anabaptists", *The Recovery of the Anabaptist Vision* (= Herschberger, 1957), 93-104.

1958 "The Turning Point in the Zwinglian Reformation", *MQR*, 32, 128-140.
1959 "Balthasar Hubmaier and the Beginnings of Swiss Anabaptism", *MQR*, 33, 5-17.
1962 *Täufertum und Reformation in der Schweiz, I: Gespräche zwischen Täufern und Reformatoren 1523-1538* (Weierhof-Karlsruhe).
Yoder, Jesse,
1962a "A Critical Study of the Debate Between the Reformed and the Ana-baptists, held at Frankenthal, Germany in 1571". Unpublished disser-tation, Northwestern University, Evanston, Ill.
1962b "The Frankenthal Debate with the Anabaptists . . .", *MQR*, 36, 14-35 and 116-146.
Zeman, J. K. (see also under Bohemica, Primary and Secondary),
1966 *Historical Topography of Moravian Anabaptism*, Reprint (1-99) from *MQR*, 40, 266-278 and 41, 40-78 and 116-160.
Zschäbitz, Gerhard,
1958 *Zur mitteldeutschen Wiedertäuferbewegung nach dem grossen Bauern-krieg* (Berlin).
Zumpe, Hans,
1960 "Die Hutterischen Brüder", *Zeitschrift für Religions- und Geistes-geschichte*, 12 (Köln), 323-345.

B. Bohemica

I. PRIMARY SOURCES

1. *Manuscripts*

Acta Unitatis Fratrum (AUF) (Central State Archives, Prague) (microfilm),
AUF, IV "Psaní od Jana Habrovanského B. Lukášovi", February 9, 1527 (fol. 191a).
"Odpověď na list Jana Habrovanského", February 20, 1527 (fols. 191b-193a).
"Poznamenání hádky, neb společného rozmlouvání, kteréž spolu měli pan Jan Habrovanský s svými Bratřími, a Bratří někteří Veliké strany . . . v Kyjově", February 28, 1535 (fols. 199a-214a).
"Knížka Jana Kalence", May 1, 1542 (fols. 215a-228a).
"Psaní Kalencovo proti Janu Augustovi a jeho při, kterouž vydal proti kněžím kališným", ca. 1543 (fols. 231a-240a).
AUF, V "Zpráva Bratří starších pánům některým učiněná, na obžalování jich, že by pohrdali těmi lidmi, totiž Novokřtěnci", November 11, 1528 (fols. 333b-335a).
"Psaní Bratra Lukášovo z příčiny Michala Weysa a Čížka", 1526 (fols. 349b-350b).
AUF, IX "Krátká suma rozmlouvání toho, kteréž mezi Bratřími, jenž slovou Boleslavští, a mezi těmi, jenž slovou Novokřtěnci Austrličtí, bylo L.P. 1559 v Evančicích" (fols. 255a-262b).
AUF, X "Rozmlouvání Novokřtěnců s Bratřími o novém rodu 1565" (fols. 273b-275b), see Appendix 7.

Historia Fratrum (HF), Ms. Codex XVII F 51, University Library, Prague, Microfilm of several short portions. Cf. also Šafařík, 1862.

Codex of Jan Kamenický (copied in 1572), Stuttgart, Württembergische Landesbibliothek.

Psaní,
    1589   "Psaní Panu F. z Ž. učiněné od B. O. S. proti novokřtěncům o tom, že
           dítky mají křtěny býti", preserved in two copies:
           (a) *Codex Skalský*, Ms. Codex I K 5746, Comenius Faculty Library,
                Prague, fols. 47a-59a (photocopy).
           (b) *Codex Crupp*, Ms. Codex XXVI A 8, University Library, Prague,
                formerly in Stadtbibliothek, Zittau (Žitava, sign. B 194b), 1049-
                1073 (microfilm).
Codex XVII G 26, University Library, Prague,
    1595   "Výklad krátký na Skutky apoštolské", fols. 110-209 (copied excerpts).
           "Agenda zprávy a posluhování církevního na Horách Kutnách" by
           Václav Štefan Teplický (no date, before 1597), fols. 210-237 (copied
           excerpts).

2. Printed Sources

Aeneas Sylvius, Piccolomini,
    1475   *Historia bohemica* (Roma).
    1523   *Commentariorum Aeneae Sylvii Piccolominei Senensis De Concilio
           Basileae celebrato libri duo, olim quidem scripti, nunc vero primum
           impressi* ... [ed. Jacobus Sobius] (n.d., n.p.) [Basel, Cratander].
Akty,
    I-II   *Akty Jednoty bratrské*, ed. Jaroslav Bidlo, Vol. I (1915), Vol. II (1923)
           (Brno).
Búlent, Boris (ed.),
    1957   *Piesne Jána Sylvána*, facsimile ed. 1571 (Martin).
Bartholomäus von Sct. Aegidius,
    1859   *Chronik von Prag im Reformationszeitalter*: Chronica de seditione et
           tumultu Pragensi 1524-1531, ed. C. Höfler (Prague), Latin tr. of
           Bartoš Písař.
Bartoš Písař,
    1907   *Kronika pražská Bartoše Písaře*, ed. Josef V. Šimák, *FRB*, VI (Prague).
Bílek, Jakub,
    1942   *Jan Augusta v letech samoty*, ed. Fr. Bednář (Prague).
Blahoslav, Jan,
    1949   *Jan Blahoslav. Pochodně zažžená*, ed. Pavel Váša (Prague).
Bohemia Pia,
    1608   *Bohemia pia, hoc est historia brevis, pietatem ac vitam Bohemiae* ...
           ostendens, Georgius Bartholdus Pontanus à Braitenberg (Frankfurt).
Borový, Klement (ed.),
    1868   *Jednání a dopisy konsistoře katolické i utrakvistické*, Vol I (Prague),
    1869   Vol. II (Prague).
Brandl, Vincenc, ed. (see also under Bohemica, Secondary),
    1870   *Spisy Karla Staršího z Žerotína*, Oddělení II: *Listové psaní jazykem
           českým*. Vol. 1 (1870).
    1871   Vol. 2 (1871) (Brno).

Brown, Edward (ed.),
    1690   *Fasciculus Rerum Expetendarum et Fugiendarum* (London).
Camerarius, Joachim,
    1606   *Historica narratio de Fratrum orthodoxorum ecclesiis in Bohemia,
            Moravia et Polonia* (Heidelberg).
Capito, Wolfgang,
    1524   *Antwurt D. Wolffgang Fab. Capitons auff Brůder Conradts ... ver-
            manung* (Strassburg).
Döllinger, Ignaz von (ed.),
    1890   *Beiträge zur Sektengeschichte des Mittelalters*, II. Teil: *Dokumente
            vornehmlich zur Geschichte der Valdesier und Katharer* (München).
Dubravius, J.,
    1575   *Historia Boiemica* (Basel).
Dungersheim, Hieronymus von Ochsenfurt,
    1514a   *Confutatio apologetici cuiusdam sacrae scripturae falso inscripti ...*
            (Leipzig).
    1514b   *Reprobatio orationis excusatoriae Picardorum ...* (Leipzig).
Freherus, Marquardus,
    1602   *Rerum bohemicarum antiqui Scriptores ...* (Hanover).
Frinta, A. (ed.),
    1928   "Vyznání víry paní Johanky Krajířky z Krajku (1513)", *RS*, 2, 90-93.
Gengenbach, Pamphilus,
    1523   *Von drien Christen*, Anonymous, n.d., n.p. [Basel].
Gesengbuchlen,
    1531   *Ein New Geseng buchlen*, ed. Michael Weisse. Jungbunzlau. (Facsimile
            ed., Kassel, 1931 and 1957.)
Gindely, Anton (ed.) (see also under Bohemica, Secondary),
    1859   *Quellen zur Geschichte der Böhmischen Brüder* (Wien).
    1865   *Dekrety Jednoty Bratrské* (Prague).
Goedeke, Karl (ed.),
    1856   *Pamphilus Gengenbach* (Hannover).
Goll, Jaroslav (ed.) (see also under Bohemica, Secondary),
    I-II   *Quellen und Untersuchungen zur Geschichte der Böhmischen Brüder*
            (Prague, 1878 and 1882).
    1895   "Některé prameny k náboženským dějinám", *VKČSN*, 1-12.
Gratius, Orthvinus,
    1535   *Fasciculus Rerum Expetendarum et Fugiendarum ...* (Köln).
Hagecius (Hájek), Václav of Libočany,
    1697   *Böhmische Chronik* (Nürnberg).
Historie (J. A. Komenský *et alii*),
    1902   *Historie o těžkých protivenstvích církve české*, ed. L. B. Kašpar (later
            ed. by F. M. Bartoš in 1922 and M. Kaňák in 1952) (Prague) (1st ed.
            1655).
Hrubý, František (ed.) (see also under Anabaptistica, Secondary, and Bohemica,
            Secondary),
    I-II   *Moravské korespondence a akta z let 1620-1636*. Vol. I (1934), Vol. II
            (1937) (Brno).
Hus, Jan,
    1520a   *De Causa Bohemica. Paulus Constantius*, n.p., n.d. [Hagenau].
    1520b   *Liber Egregivs de vnitate ecclesiae, cuius autor periit in concilio Con-
            stantiensi*, n.p., n.d. [Mainz].
    1963   *Sermo de pace. Řeč o míru*, ed. F. M. Dobiáš and Am. Molnár (Prague).

1965   *O církvi* [De ecclesia], tr. F. M. Dobiáš and Am. Molnár (Prague).
Institoris (Heinrich Krämer),
1501a   *Clippeum adversus Waldensium seu Pickardorum heresim* ... (Olomouc).
1501b   *Opus perutile Sermonum* ... *adversus Waldenses haereticos.*
Jafet, Jan,
1861   "Meč Goliášův", ed. J. Jireček, *ČČM*, 35, 139-158.
Kästner, Alexander (ed.),
1902   *Die Kinderfragen: der erste deutsche Katechismus (Neudrucke pädagogischer Schriften,* 17) (Leipzig).
Katechismus,
1615   *Katechismus bratrský*, ed. Jan K. Smetana (Vilémov, 1934).
Koecher, Joh. Christoph,
1741   *Die drey Letzte und Vornehmste Glaubens-Bekenntnisse der Böhmischen Brüder* (Frankfurt and Leipzig).
Komenský, Jan Amos,
1912   *Veškeré spisy Jana Amose Komenského,* ed. J. Th. Müller and Jan V. Novák, Vol. XVII (Brno).
1938   *Anděl míru,* tr. by Jos. Hendrich (Prague).
Lasicki, Jan (Lasitius),
1869   *Obraz Jednoty českobratrské,* ed. L. B. Kašpar (Prague) (orig. ed. 1649).
Lukáš, Pražský,
1521a   *Spis dosti činící otázce protivníkuov Jednoty Bratrské, proč křest* ... *v ní se opěluje,* 1st ed. (February 21, 1521), Bělá pod Bezdězem.
1521b   2nd ed., Litomyšl (photocopies).
Lydius, Balthasar,
1616   *Waldensia, id est Conservatio verae Ecclesiae.* Vol. 1 (Rotterdam).
1617   Vol. 2 (Dordrecht).
Molnár, Amedeo (ed.) (see also under Bohemica, Secondary),
1947   *Bratří a král* (Železný Brod).
1950a   "Kšaft Mikuláše Roha z r. 1536", *ThEv,* 3, 368-369.
1951   "La correspondence entre les Frères Tchèques et Bucer 1540-1542", *RHPR,* 102-156.
1956a   *Českobratrská výchova před Komenským* (Prague).
Moryson, Fynes,
1617   *An Itinerary written by Fynes Moryson* ... (London).
Müller, Joseph Th. (ed.) (see also under Bohemica, Secondary),
1887   *Die Deutschen Katechismen der Böhmischen Brüder* (= *Monumenta Germaniae Paedagogica,* IV) (Berlin).
1910   "Die Berührungen der alten und neuen Brüderunität mit den Täufern", *ZBG,* 4, 180-234.
Niemeyer, H. A. (ed.),
1840   *Collectio Confessionum in Ecclesiis reformatis publicatarum* (Leipzig).
Palmov, Ivan (ed.),
1904   *Cheshskie bratya v svoikh konfessiyakh* ..., Vol. I, Part 2 (Prague).
Peschke, Erhard (ed.) (see also under Bohemica, Secondary),
1940   *Die Theologie der Böhmischen Brüder in ihrer Frühzeit,* Band I: *Das Abendmahl,* Teil 2: *Texte* (Stuttgart).
Regensvolscius, Adrianus,
1652   *Systema historico-chronologicum Ecclesiarum Slavonicarum* (Utrecht).
Reychart, Peter,
1523   *Ain Christenlich gesprech Büchlin vonn zwayen weybern Mit namen*

Margretha Böhemin vnnd Anna Kollerin . . ., n.p. [Augsburg, Heinrich Steiner].

Říčan, Rudolf (ed.) (see also under Bohemica, Secondary),
1951a *Čtyři vyznání* (Prague).

Šafařík, Pavel Josef (ed.),
1862 "Br. Jana Blahoslava Historie Bratří českých u výtahu", *ČČM*, 36, 99-124 and 201-212.

Schweinitz, Edmund de (ed.),
1869 "The Catechism of the Bohemian Brethren", *Transactions of the Moravian Historical Society*, 3, 90-106.

Sklenář, Jaromír (ed.) (see also under Bohemica, Secondary),
1957b "Předmluva k Bratrskému vyznání 1536-1538", *TPKR*, 73-92.
1960 "Der Artikel einer Konfession der Böhmischen Brüder von der Obrigkeit", *CV*, 3, 263-269.

Sliziński, Jerzy (ed.),
1958 *Rękopisy Braci Czeskich* (Wrocław).

Sněmy,
I *Sněmy české od léta 1526 po naši dobu*, Vol. I: 1526-1545, ed. Fr. Dvorský and A. Gindely (Prague, 1877).

Todtenbuch,
1863 *Todtenbuch der Geistlichkeit der böhmischen Brüder*, ed. by Joseph Fiedler (Wien).

Treger, Conrad,
1524 *Vermanung bruder Conradts Treger . . . an ein lobliche gemeyne Eydgenossenschafft vor der Böhemschen Ketzerey . . .* (Strassburg).

Vávra, Ivan (ed.),
1957 "Rejstra sboru evančického", *TPKR*, 144-146.

Vavřinec, z Březové,
1940 *Kronika husitská*, ed. Ant. Dolanský (Prague).

Zelinka, Timoteus Č. (ed.),
1942 *Cesty Českých bratří Matěje Červenky a Jana Blahoslava* (Prague).

Zeman, J. K. (ed.) (see also under Anabaptistica, Secondary, and Bohemica, Secondary),
1958 "Rozhovory Českých bratří s novokřtěnci", *Pravda a Slavná Naděje*, 39, 4-5, 23-26, 38-43 and 53-58 (Chicago, Ill.).

Ziegler, Jacob,
1512 *Contra haeresim valdensium libri quinque* (Leipzig).

2. SECONDARY WORKS

Allen, P. S.,
1914 *The Age of Erasmus* (Oxford).
1934 *Erasmus. Lectures and Wayfaring Sketches* (Oxford).

Bartoš, František M.,
1925 "Zapadlé dílko bratrské vědy", *VKČSN*, 1-28.
1929 "Lutherovo vystoupení a Jednota bratrská", *RS*, 3, 3-17.
1931 *Husitství a cizina* (Prague).
1932 "Husitika a bohemika několika knihoven německých a švýcarských", reprint from *VKČSN*, 1931 (Prague).
1934 "Das Auftreten Luthers und die Unität der böhmischen Brüder", *ARG*, 31, 103-120.
1939 *Hledání podstaty křesťanství v české reformaci* (Prague).
1946a *Bojovníci a mučedníci* (Prague).

1946b "Dva osamělí bojovníci světové reformace" (Sebastian Franck and J. Acontius), *Náboženská revue církve československé*, 17, 91-103.
1948a *Knihy a zápasy* (Prague).
1948b *O podstatu křesťanství a dědictví Jednoty bratrské* (Prague).
1949a *Světci a kacíři* (Prague).
1951a "Budovcova obrana Jednoty bratrské a svobody svědomí z r. 1604", *ThEv*, 4, 88-101.
1954a "Památce křesťanského humanisty Z. Gelenia", *KR*, 21, 297-303.
1954b "Nový bratrský historik", *Sborník historický*, II, 103-112.
1956a "Erasmus a česká reformace", *TPKR*, 7-12 and 34-41.
1956b "Jednota a reformátoři", *Jednota bratrská 1457-1957* (Prague), 109-146.
1958a "Erasmus und die böhmische Reformation", *CV*, 1, 116-123 and 246-257.
1959a *Ze zápasů české reformace* (Prague).
1959b "Wenceslas Budovec's Defense of the Brethren and of Freedom of Conscience", tr. and adapted by Howard Kaminsky, *CH*, 28, 229-239.
1959c "První Jednota bratrská a Devotio moderna", *TPKR*, 38-42.
1959d "Ekumenismus Václava Budovce z Budova", *O svrchovanost víry* (Sborník k 70. výročí narození J. L. Hromádky, ed. J. B. Souček) (Prague), 44-59.
1965 *Husitská revoluce*, I (Prague).
1966 *Husitská revoluce*, II (Prague).

Bednář, František,
1939 "Obsahová stránka katechismů bratrských", *Zásady Jednoty českých bratří* (Prague), 110-141.
1952 "Zwei Versuche der alten Brüderunität um einen Aufbau der praktischen Theologie im 16. Jahrhundert", *TZ*, 8, 357-385.
1954 "The Ecumenical Idea in the Czech Reformation", *The Ecumenical Review*, 6, 160-168.
1955 "Die erste Abendmahlsagende der böhmischen Brüderunität", *TZ*, 11, 344-360.

Bidlo, Jaroslav,
1900 *Jednota bratrská v prvním vyhnanství*, Vol. 1 (Prague).
1906 "O konfessi bratrské z r. 1573", *Sborník prací historických k 60. narozeninám J. Golla*, Vol. 1 (Prague), 246-278.
1918 "Vzajemný poměr české a polské větve Jednoty bratrské v době od r. 1587 do 1609", *ČMM*, 41/42 (1917/1918), 108-188.
1923 "Bratr Jan Blahoslav jako archivář a knihovník Jednoty bratrské", *Sborník Blahoslavův* (Přerov), 34-37.

Bittner, Konrad,
1954 "Erasmus, Luther und die böhmischen Brüder", *Rastloses Schaffen* (Festschrift Fr. Lammert) (Stuttgart), 107-129.

Bohatcová, Mirjam,
1962 "Počátky publikační činnosti Jednoty bratrské", *Acta Comeniana*, 21 (Prague), 44-60.

Brandl, Vincenc (see also under Bohemica, Primary),
1882 "Jan Dubčanský a bratří Lulečtí", *ČMM*, 14, 74-125.

Brock, Peter,
1957 *The Political and Social Doctrines of the Unity of Czech Brethren in the 15th and 16th Centuries* (The Hague).

Brož, Luděk,
1958a "Nové hodnocení theologie Jednoty bratrské", *KR*, 104-106.

1958b "A New Evaluation of the Theology of the Unitas Fratrum", *CV*, 1, 124-126.

Brunner, Heinrich,
1910 "Die Herren von Lipa", *ZDVGMS*, 14, 309-336.
1911 *Ibid.*, 15. 466-486.

Čapek, Jan B.,
1951 *Duch a odkaz československé reformace* (Prague).
1956 "Vývoj a význam Jednoty na poli kulturním", *Jednota bratlrská 1457-1957*, ed. F. M. Bartoš and J. L. Hromádka (Prague), 191-238.

Čaplovič, Ján,
1955 "Literárne začiatky Jána Silvána", *Slovenská literatúra*, II (Bratislava), 73-84.
1957 "Dve vydania Silvánových piesní", *Slovenská literatúra*, IV (Bratislava), 202-213.

Chaloupecký, Václav,
1925 "Pře kněžská z r. 1562", *VKČSN*, 1-207.

Chlumecky, P. Ritter von,
1862 *Carl von Zierotin und seine Zeit*, Vol. 1 (Brünn).
1879 Vol. 2: Sources (Brünn).

Čihula, J.,
1897 "Poměr Bratří českých k Martinovi Lutherovi", *VKČSN*, 1-70.

Císařová Kolářová, Anna,
1942 *Žena v Jednotě bratrské* (Prague).

Clement, David,
1759 *Bibliothèque curieuse historique et critique, ou Catalogue raisonné de livres difficiles à trouver ...*, Tom. 8 (Leipzig).

Cohrs, Ferdinand,
I-V *Die Evangelischen Katechismusversuche vor Luthers Enchiridion* (= *Monumenta Germaniae Paedagogica*) (Berlin, 1900-1907).

Čuprová, Ludmila,
1958 "Poznámky k životu a dílu Jána Silvána", *Litteraria*, I (Bratislava), 5-68.

Cvrček, Josef,
1898 "Paměti o sborech bratrských na Moravě ze stol. XVI.", *ČMM*, 22, 45-51, 150-155, 248-255 and 344-350.
1899 *Ibid.*, 23, 120-127, 261-268 and 353-360.
1900 "Z posledních dnů sboru bratrského v Kyjově", *ČMM*, 24, 39-50.

Daňková, Mirjam,
1951 *Bratrské tisky ivančické a kralické (1564-1619)* (Prague).

Dobiáš, František M.,
1940 *Učení Jednoty bratrské o večeři Páně* (Prague).
1941 *Víra a vyznání Českých bratří* (Prague).
1950 "Vyznání J. A. Komenského", *ThEv*, 3, 175-187.
1952a "Dědička husitské revoluce", *KR*, 141-146.
1952b "Theologický profil Bratra Lukáše", *KR*, 264-271.
1953a "Vznik a osudy Lukášových Zpráv kněžských", *KR*, 12-18.
1953b "Hodnocení Lukášových Zpráv kněžských", *KR*, 84-90.
1957 "Předpoklady ekumenismu v theologii rané Jednoty", *TPKR*, 136-144.
1960a "Ecumenical Motifs in the Theology of the Unity of Bohemian Brethren", *The Ecumenical Review*, 12, 455-470.
1960b "Die ökumenische Weite in der Theologie der Böhmischen Brüder",

Unitas Fratrum, ed. F. M. Dobiáš and J. B. Jeschke (Berlin), 40-55.
1961 "Aspects of Social Ethics in the Works of J. A. Comenius", *CV*, 4, 72-82.

Dudík, B.,
1874 "Dějiny knihtiskařství na Moravě od vzniku jeho až do roku 1621", *ČMM*, 7, 103-138.

Ďurovič, Ján P.,
1956 "Jednota na Slovensku", *Jednota bratrská 1457-1957*, ed. F. M. Bartoš and J. L. Hromádka (Prague), 239-263.

Dvořák, Rudolf,
1900 *Dějiny Moravy*, Kniha II: *1306-1526* (Brno).
1901 *Dějiny Moravy*, Kniha III: *1526-1648* (Brno).

Ehwalt, Joh. Gottfried,
1756 *Die alte und neue Lehre der Böhmischen und Mährischen Brüder* (Danzig).

D'Elvert, Christian,
1854 *Geschichte des Bücher- und Steindruckes, des Buchhandels, der Bücher-Censur und der periodischen Literatur . . .* (Brünn).

Enequist, L.,
1884 *Die Beziehungen der Böhmischen Brüder zu den Reformatoren* (Basel).

Fornaçon, Siegfried,
1954 "Michael Weisse", *Jahrbuch für Schlesische Kirche und Kirchengeschichte*, N.F., 33 (Düsseldorf), 35-44.

Fousek, Marianka S.,
1961 "The Perfectionism of the Early Unitas Fratrum", *CH*, 30, 396-413.
1964 "The Ethos of the Unitas Fratrum", Private Ms. of a paper read in New York, 1964.
1965 "The Second-Generation Soteriology of the Unitas Fratrum", *ZKG*, 76, 41-63.

Gindely, Anton (see also under Bohemica, Primary),
I-II *Geschichte der böhmischen Brüder*. Vol. I (1857) and II (1858) (Prague).
1854a "Über die dogmatischen Ansichten der böhmisch-mährischen Brüder nebst einigen Notizen zur Geschichte ihrer Entstehung", *Sitzungsberichte der kais. Akademie der Wissenschaften*, 13 (Wien), 349-413.
1854b "Über die Verhandlungen am Landtage zu Prag im J. 1575 . . .", *Ibid.*, 413-429.

Goll, Jaroslav (see also under Bomemica, Primary),
1916 *Chelčický a Jednota v XV. století* (Prague).

Gonnet, Giovanni,
1952 "Beziehungen der Waldenser zu den oberdeutschen Reformatoren vor Calvin", *ZKG*, 64, 308-311.

Hájek, Viktor,
1934 *Kázeň v Jednotě bratrské* (Brno).
1959 "Učení Petra Chelčického o užívání násilí a o válce", *O svrchovanost víry* (Sborník k 70. výročí narození J. L. Hromádky, ed. J. B. Souček) (Prague), 36-43.

Hanák, Jan,
1928 "Bratří a starší z Hory lilecké", *ČMM*, 52, 39-124 and 277-348.
1929 *Ibid.*, 53, 1-44.

Havelka, Emanuel,
1938 *Husitské katechismy* (Prague).

1955   "Byl B. Lukáš autorem 'Otázek dětinských' ", *TPKR*, 70-74.
Hejnic, Josef,
1957   "Humanistická zpráva o Matěji Poustevníkovi", *LF*, 5, 64-67.
Herben, Jan,
1926a *Husitství a bratrství* (Prague).
1926b *Huss and his Followers* (London).
Heubach, Joachim,
1952   "Die christliche Unterweisung bei Johann Amos Comenius". Unpublished dissertation, Göttingen (microfilm).
Heymann, Frederick G.,
1955   *John Žižka and the Hussite Revolution* (Princeton).
1959   "John Rokycana — Church Reformer between Hus and Luther", *CH*, 28, 240-280.
1961   "The Hussite-Utraquist Church in the Fifteenth and Sixteenth Centuries", *ARG*, 52, 1-16.
1965   *George of Bohemia: King of Heretics* (Princeton).
Hobza, Radek,
1967   "Akta Jednoty bratrské", in Kaňák, 1967, 152-249.
Hrabák, Josef (ed.),
1959   *Dějiny české literatury*, Vol. I (Prague).
Hrejsa, Ferdinand,
   A   "Sborové Jednoty bratrské" [Topography of congregations in Bohemia], *RS*, 5 (1935), 17-79.
   B   *RS*, 6 (Moravia) (1937), 10-111.
   C   *RS*, 7 (Poland and other countries), (1939), 10-114. Also a reprint.
   I-VI *Dějiny křesťanství v Československu*, Vols. I to VI (Prague, 1947-1950).
1912   *Česká konfese* (Prague).
1915   "K českým dějinám náboženským za prvních let Ferdinanda I", *ČČH*, 21, 161-216.
1918   "Beneš Optát", *ČMM*, 41/42, (1917/1918), 284-297.
1923   "Náboženské stanovisko B. Jana Blahoslava", *Sborník Blahoslavův* [= Novotný, 1923], 50-120.
1931   "Jednota bratrská a podobojí koncem 16. století ve světle nových zpráv", *Ročenka Husovy fakulty pražské* (Prague), 9-27.
1938   "Luterství, kalvinismus a podobojí na Moravě před Bílou horou", *ČČH*, 44, 296-326, 474-485 and German summary on pp. 681-683.
1939   "Náboženský svéráz Jednoty bratrské", *Zásady Jednoty českých bratří* (Prague), 7-109.
Hrejsa Bohuš,
1931   "Kancionály v Jednotě bratrské", *RS*, 4, 11-47.
Hromádka, Josef L.,
1937   "Ferdinand Hrejsa a Masaryk", *RS*, 6, 151-154.
1938   "The Heritage of the Bohemian Reformation", *At the Crossroads of Europe* (Prague), 103-131.
1939   "Smysl bratrské reformace", *Zásady Jednoty českých bratří* (Prague), 142-163.
1954   *Smysl bratrské reformace*, 2nd ed. (Prague).
1956   "Odkaz Jednoty dnešku", *Jednota bratrská 1457-1957*, ed. F. M. Bartoš and J. L. Hromádka (Prague), 265-290.
Hrubý, František (see also under Anabaptistica, Secondary and Bohemica, Primary),
1922   "Moravská šlechta r. 1619, její jmění a náboženské vyznání", *ČMM*, 46, 107-169.

1931 "Švýcarský svědek Bílé hory", ČČH, 37, 42-78.
1935c "Luterství a kalvinismus na Moravě před Bílou horou", reprint of articles in ČČH, 40 (1934), 265-309 and 41 (1935) (Prague), 1-40 and 237-268.
1938 "The Habsburgs and Czechs at the Period of the Reformation and Counter-Reformation", At the Crossroads of Europe, ed. K. Čapek (Prague), 133-174.
1939 "Luterství a novoutrakvismus v českých zemích v 16. a 17. století", ČČH, 45, 31-44.

Janáček, Josef,
1966 Jan Blahoslav (Prague).

Janoušek, Em.,
1923 "Konfese Jednoty bratrské od oddělení 'Malé stránky' k prvním jejím stykům s Lutherem", ČMM, 47, 15-52.

Jersák, Artur,
1965 "Německý objevitel Komenského (Památce Ludwiga Kellera)", TPKR, 108-110.

Jeschke, J. B.,
1958 "Pastýřská péče v Jednotě bratrské", KR, 146-151 and 187-190.
1959 "Návrat k prvotní církvi", O svrchovanost víry (Prague), 75-85.
1960a "Der Hirtendienst in der alten Brüderunität", Unitas Fratrum, ed. F. M. Dobiáš and J. B. Jeschke (Berlin), 7-39.
1960b "Návrat k eschatologii přes lidovou církev", KR, 27, 45-47.

Jireček, J.,
1862 "Kancionál bratrský", ČČM, 36, 24-51 and 95.

Kameníček, František (see also under Anabaptistica, Primary),
I-III Zemské sněmy a sjezdy moravské 1526-1628, Vols. I (1900), II (1902) and III (1905) (Brno).
1895 "Vpády Bočkajovců na Moravu ...", reprint from ČČM.

Kaňák, Miloslav,
1957 Význačné postavy Jednoty bratrské a jejich dílo (Prague).
1967 Československá církev a Jednota bratrská (ed.) (Prague).

Kišš, Igor,
1965 "Luther und Hus", CV, 8, 239-250.

Kleinschnitzová, Flora,
1931 "Seltene Bohemica des XVI. Jahrhunderts in schwedischen Bibliotheken", Nordisk Tidskrift för Bok- och Biblioteksväsen, 18, 1-32.

Kopřiva, Hjalmar,
1959 "Styk olomouckého biskupa Stanislava Thurza z Bethélfalvy s humanistou Beatem Rhenanem", Věstník musea v Kroměříži (Kroměříž), 78-80.

Kratochvíl, Augustin,
1906 Ivančice (Ivančice).

Kraus, Arnošt,
I-III Husitství v literatuře, zejména německé. Vols. I (1917), II (1918) and III (1924) (Prague).

Kroess, Alois,
I-II Geschichte der böhmischen Provinz der Gesellschaft Jesu. Vol. I (1910) and II (1927) (Wien).

Krofta, Kamil,
1931 Doktor Václav Mitmánek panu tatíkovi milému (Prague).
1936 Listy z náboženských dějin českých (Prague).
1942 "Zprávy o bratrských cestách do ciziny" in Zelinka, 1942, 7-54.

1946   *O bratrském dějepisectví* (Prague).

Lehmann, Emil,
1922   *Michael Weisse* (Landskron).

Lendi, Karl,
1926   *Der Dichter Pamphilus Gengenbach* (Bern).

Ličman, Alois,
1912   "Náboženské poměry ve Slavkově od počátku XVI. století do proti-reformace", *ČMM*, 36, 379-380.

Lochman, Jan M.,
1963   *Die Not der Vesöhnung* (= *Evangelische Zeitstimmen*, Nr. 14) (Hamburg).

Malin, William Gunn,
1881   *Catalogue of Books Relating to, or Illustrating the History of the Unitas Fratrum* (Philadelphia).

Malínský, František,
1923   *Život Jana Blahoslava* (Přerov).
1948a "Z dějin bratrské Litomyšle", *Památník k 25. výročí Českobratrského Evangelického sboru v Litomyšli* (Litomyšl), 3-17.
1948b *Vývoj náboženských poměrů v střední a severní Moravě* (Přerov-Olomouc).
1956   "Jednota a novokřtěnci", *KJ*, 41, No. 6.

Marek, Jaroslav,
1965   *Společenská struktura moravských královských měst v 15. a 16. století* (Prague).

Mesnard, Pierre,
1952   *L'essor de la philosophie politique au XVIe siècle*, 2nd ed. (Paris).

Měšťan, Antonín,
1955   "Komenský a polští ariáni", *Slavia*, 24 (Prague), 456-460.

Mikulova-Thulstrup, Marie,
1962   "Nye Kirkehistoriske studier i Praha", *Saertryk of Dansk teologisk tidsskrift* (Copenhagen), 65-81.

Molnár, Amedeo (see also under Bohemica, Primary),
1945   *Strážná samota Petra Chelčického* (Železný Brod) (cf. Molnár, 1964 f.).
1948a *Bratr Lukáš, bohoslovec Jednoty* (Prague).
1948b "Lukáš Pražský před svým vstupem do Jednoty bratrské", *ThEv*, 1, 21-32.
1949a "Luc de Prague et les Vaudois d'Italie", *Bolletino della Società di Studi Valdesi*, No. 90 (Torre Pelice).
1949b "Svět v bratrské theologii", *KR*, 16, 195-205.
1950b "Bratří a Bucerův spis O opravdové péči o duše", *ThEv*, 3, 168-175 and 311-318.
1952a *Boleslavští bratří* (Prague).
1952b "Valdenští a reformace", *TPKR*, 78-86.
1952c "Valdenský přítel Komenského", *TPKR*, 127-132.
1954a "Les Vaudois et la Réforme", *Bolletino della Società di Studi Valdesi*, No. 96 (Torre Pelice).
1955a "K Otázkám dětinským Bratra Lukáše", *TPKR*, 115-116.
1956b "Marcello Squarcialupi mezi Bratřími", *TPKR*, 106-111.
1956c "Marcello Squarcialupi et l'Unité des Frères Tchèques", *Bolletino della Società di Studi Valdesi*, No. 100 (Torre Pelice).
1956d "Eschatologická naděje české reformace", *Od reformace k zítřku* (Prague), 11-101.

1956e "Počínající, pokračující a dokonalí", *Jednota bratrská 1457-1957*, ed. F. M. Bartoš and J. L. Hromádka (Prague), 147-169.

1957a "Příspěvky k dějinám ekumenického působení Jednoty bratrské",*TPKR*, 24-30.

1957b "Německý překlad Husova spisu O církvi", *TPKR*, 108-109.

1957c "Cesta bratrské theologie", *KR*, 18-24.

1957d "O bratrské theologii", in *Říčan*, 1957a, 407-442.

1957e "K františkánským motivům v Jednotě bratrské", *TPKR*, 49-50.

1957f "Mírové smýšlení v české reformaci", *KR*, 53-59.

1957g "Sociální theologie Jednoty bratrské", *KR*, 213-218.

1958a "Les Vaudois et la Réforme tchèque", *Bolletino della Società di Studi Valdesi*, No. 103 (Torre Pelice).

1958b "Müntzer a Čechy", *KR*, 25, 93-95.

1958c "Thomas Müntzer und Böhmen", *CV*, 1, 242-245.

1959a "Lukáš Pražský a Martin Luther v zápase o Kristovu církev", *KR*, 184-190.

1959b "Tři studie k dějinám bratrského myšlení", *KR*, 272-276.

1960a "Etudes et conversion de Luc de Prague", *CV*, 3, 255-262.

1961a "Les premières années de Luc de Prague au sein de l'Unité", *CV*, 4, 83-89.

1961b "Luc de Prague à Constantinople", *CV*, 4, 192-201.

1961c "Luc de Prague devant la crise de l'Unité des années 1490", *CV*, 4, 316-324.

1961d "Mikoláš Konáč a Jednota bratrská", *TPKR*, 43-53.

1961e "Die Theologie der Brüder", in *Říčan*, 1961a, 283-321.

1962a "Voyage d'Italie", *CV*, 5, 28-34.

1962b "Luc de Prague édifiant la communauté", *CV*, 5, 189-200.

1962c "Rozhovory s novokřtěnci", *KJ*, 47, No. 2.

1962d "Mezi dvojí reformací", *KR*, 37-38.

1962e "Poselství reformace ve vývoji společnosti", *KJ*, 47, No. 35.

1962f "Bratrský odkaz v theologii J. B. Součka", *KR*, 121-123.

1963a "Autour du mandat royal", *CV*, 6, 39-46.

1963b "Pasteur dans la tourmenté", *CV*, 6, 276-286.

1963c "Hnutí svobodného ducha a husitství", *KR*, 37-39.

1963d "L'évolution de la théologie hussite", *RHPR*, 133-171.

1964a "Luther neboli zápas o církev", *KR*, 183-186.

1964b "Zum Gespräch zwischen Luther und den Böhmischen Brüdern", . . . *und fragten nach Jesus* (Festschrift für Ernst Barnikol zum 70. Geburtstag) (Berlin), 177-185.

1964c "Der ökumenische Gedanke im tschechischen Protestantismus", *CV*, 7, 7-15.

1964d "Les Vaudois en Bohême avant la Révolution hussite", *Bolletino della Società di Studi Valdesi*, No. 116 (Torre Pelice).

1964e "Elementi ecclesiologici della prima Riforma", *Protestantesimo*, 19 (1964) (Rome), 65-77.

1964f *Wonderful Solitude of Peter Chelčický*. Tr. by Andrew P. Slabey, Bethlehem, Pennsylvania. (Cf. Molnár, 1945.)

1965a *Bibliographie de la Réforme 1450-1648*, Fasc. 5, "Tchécoslovaquie" (Leiden), 67-100.

1965b "Hus mezi první a druhou reformací", *KR*, 32 (1965), 149-152, 179-183 and 203-205.

1965c "Theologie husitského kalicha", *TPKR* (1965), 1-9.

Molnar, Enrico C. S.,
1953 "Anglo-Czech Reformation Contacts". Unpublished Th.D. thesis, The Iliff School of Theology, Denver, Colorado.
Műller, Joseph Th. (see also under Bohemica, Primary),
I-III Geschichte der böhmischen Brüder, Vol. I (1922), II (1931) and III (1931) (Herrnhut).
1896 "Die Gemeinde-Verfassung der böhmischen Brüder in ihren Grundzügen", Monatshefte der Comenius-Gesellschaft, 5, 140-163.
1913 "Geschichte und Inhalt der Acta Unitatis Fratrum", ZBG, 7, 66-113 and 216-231.
1915 Ibid., 9, 26-79.
1920 "Die böhmische Brüderunität und Zwingli", Zwingliana, III, 514-524.
Műller-Bartoš,
Dějiny Jednoty bratrské (Prague) [= Műller, I, translated by F. M. Bartoš, with important revisions].
Novotný, Václav and Rudolf Urbánek (ed.),
1923 Blahoslavův sborník (Přerov).
Nyikos, Lajos,
1937 "Erasmus und der böhmisch-ungarische Königshof", Zwingliana, VI, 346-374.
Odložilík, Otakar,
1923 "Jednota bratří Habrovanských", ČČH, 39, 1-70 and 201-364.
1925 "Der Widerhall der Lehre Zwinglis in Mähren", Zwingliana, IV, 257-276.
1939 "Bohemian Protestants and the Calvinist Churches", CH, 8, 342-355.
1940 "Two Reformation Leaders of the Unitas Fratrum", CH, 9, 253-263.
1964 Jednota bratrská a reformovaní francouzského jazyka (Philadelphia).
1965a "Die Wittenberger Philippisten und die Brüderunität", Ost und West in der Geschichte des Denkens und der kulturellen Beziehungen (Festschrift für Eduard Winter zum 70. Geburtstag) (Berlin), 106-118.
1965b The Hussite King (New Brunswick, New Jersey).
Pelikan, Jaroslav (Jr.),
1946 "Luther and the Confessio Bohemica of 1535". Unpublished Ph.D. thesis, University of Chicago.
1948 "Luther's Attitude toward John Hus", Concordia Theological Monthly, 19, 747-763.
1949 "Luther's Negotiations with the Hussites", Concordia Theological Monthly, 20, 496-517.
1964 Obedient Rebels (New York and Evanston).
Peschke, Erhard (see also under Bohemica, Primary),
1935 Die Theologie der Böhmischen Brüder in ihrer Frühzeit, Vol. I: Das Abendmahl, Part 1, Untersuchungen (Stuttgart).
1955 "Peter Chelčický's Lehre von der Kirche und der weltlichen Macht", Wissenschaftliche Zeitschrift der Universität Rostock, 5 (Sonderheft, Festschrift E. Schlesinger), 263-274.
1956 "Der Kirchenbegriff des Bruder Lukas von Prag", Wiss. Zts. d. Univ. Rostock, 5, Heft 2, 273-288.
1957 "Der Gegensatz zwischen der Kleinen und der Grossen Partei der Brüderunität", Wiss. Zts. d. Univ. Rostock, 6, Heft 1, 141-154.
1958a "Bruder Gregors Lehre von der Kirche", Wiss. Zts. d. Univ. Rostock, 7, Heft 1, 1-10.
1958b "Die religiös-sozialen Ideen des Bruders Thomas Přeloučský", Wiss. Zts. d. Univ. Rostock, 7, Heft 2, 283-292.

1958c *Bauleute der Unität* (Hamburg).
1964   *Die Böhmischen Brüder im Urteil ihrer Zeit. Zieglers, Dungersheims und Luthers Kritik an der Brüderunität* (Stuttgart).
Raillard, Rudolf,
1936   *Pamphilus Gengenbach und die Reformation* (Heidelberg).
Rezek, Antonín,
1882   "Biskup vídeňský Jan Faber a čeští utrakvisté", *Zprávy o zasedání k.c. společnosti nauk v Praze* (Prague), 398-404.
Říčan, Rudolf (see also under Bohemica, Primary),
1939   *České náboženské tradice* (Prague).
1943   *Setkání české reformace s reformací světovou* (Prague) (mimeographed).
1951b "Členství v Jednotě bratrské", *KR*, 142-148.
1956   "Dějiny Jednoty v přehledu", *Jednota bratrská 1457-1957*, ed. F. M. Bartoš and J. L. Hromádka (Prague), 11-107.
1957a *Dějiny Jednoty bratrské* (Prague).
1957b *Das Reich Gottes in den böhmischen Ländern. Geschichte des tschechischen Protestantismus* (Stuttgart).
1959a "K otázce ekumenismu, svobody svědomí a náboženské tolerance v české reformaci", *TPKR*, 81-89.
1959b "Některé životní řády Jednoty bratrské", *TPKR*, 97-106.
1961a *Die Böhmischen Brüder, ihr Ursprung und ihre Geschichte*, tr. by B. Popelář (Berlin).
1962   "Jiří z Poděbrad a kompaktáta", *TPKR*, 118-127.
1964a "Karel Starší ze Žerotína", *KR*, 259-262.
1964b "Zur Frage des Okumenismus, der Gewissensfreiheit und der religiösen Duldung in der tschechischen Reformation", *CV*, 7, 265-284.
1965a "Georg von Poděbrad u. die Kompaktaten", *CV*, 8, 43-52 and 161-172.
1967   "Tschechische Übersetzungen von Luthers Schriften bis zum Schmalkaldischen Kriege", *Vierhundertfünfzig Jahre lutherischer Reformation* (Berlin), 282-301.
Ritter, Gerhard,
1927   "Studien zur Spätscholastik, III", *Sitzungsberichte der Heidelberger Akademie der Wissenschaften* (Phil.-hist. Klasse), Jg. 1926/27, 5. Abh. (Heidelberg).
Šašková, G.,
1925   "Jednota bratrská a konsistoř podobojí ...", *VKČSN*, 1-86.
Schottenloher, Karl (see also under Anabaptistica, Secondary),
1910   *Jakob Ziegler aus Landau an d. Isar* (Münster i. W.).
Schweinitz, Edmund de,
1901   *The History of the Church Known as the Unitas Fratrum*, 2nd rev. ed. (Bethlehem, Pa.).
Seibt, Ferdinand,
1962   "Die Hussitenzeit als Kulturepoche", *Historische Zeitschrift*, 195 (München), 21-62.
Šembera, Alois Vojtěch,
1870   *Páni z Boskovic* ... (Wien).
Sita, Karel,
1951   "Život a dílo Amanda Polana z Polansdorfu". Unpublished dissertation, Hus Faculty, Prague (copy in Universitätsbibliothek, Basel).
1954   "Studenti z českých zemí na basilejské universitě v době reformace", *TPKR*, 14-19.
Škarka, Antonín,
1958   "Jan Blahoslav", *Česká literatura*, 6 (Prague), 150-175. Also abbrevi-

ated and revised in Hrabák (1959), 363-379.
Sklenář, Jaromír (see also under Bohemica, Primary),
 1957a "Bratrská konfese o křtu", *TPKR*, 8-17.
Smolík, Josef,
 1948 "Sociální působení Jednoty bratrské", *ThEv*, 1, 87-98.
 1956 "Sociální působení Jednoty", *Jednota bratrská 1457-1957*, ed. F. M. Bartoš and J. L. Hromádka (Prague), 171-190.
Souček, J. B.,
 1933 "Theologie výkladů kralické Šestidílky", *VKČSN*, 1-140 and reprint.
 1956 "Hlavní motivy bratrské theologie ve světle novějšího biblického bádání", *Od reformace k zítřku* (Prague), 103-118.
Souček, Bohuslav,
 1921 "Rukopis pražské universitní knihovny XVII. C. 3", *RS*, 1, 45-80.
Štěříková, Edita,
 1964 "Blahoslavova Akta Jednoty bratrské", *TPKR*, 81-88 and 97-105.
Štrupl, Miloš,
 1964a "Confessional Theology of the Unitas Fratrum". Unpublished Ph.D. dissertation, Vanderbilt University, Nashville, Tenn.
 1964b "Confessional Theology of the Unitas Fratrum", *CH*, 33, 279-293.
Tapié, Victor-L.,
 1931 "Une église tchèque au Moyen-Age. L'Unité des Frères", *Revue des sciences réligieuses*, 11 (Strasbourg), 224-265.
 1934 *Une église tchèque au XVe siècle: l'Unité des Frères* (Paris).
Thomson, S. Harrison,
 1953a *Czechoslovakia in European History*, 2nd ed. (Princeton).
 1953b "Luther and Bohemia", *ARG*, 44, 160-181.
Tobolka, Zdeněk and František Horák,
 I-II *Knihopis československých tisků od doby nejstarší až do konce XVIII. století* (1936 ff.) (published in parts) (Prague).
 1930 *Dějiny československého tisku v době nejstarší* (Prague) (text in German).
Trtík, Zdeněk,
 1967 "Moderní prvky v theologii Lukáše Pražského", in Kaňák 1967, 68-81.
Truhlář, Josef,
 1894 *Humanismus a humanisté v Čechách* ... (Prague).
 1906 *Katalog českých rukopisů c.k. veřejné a universitní knihovny pražské* (Prague).
Urbánek, Rudolf,
 1923 *Jednota bratrská a vyšší vzdělání až do doby Blahoslavovy* (Brno).
 1930 *České dějiny*, Vol. III, Part 3: *Věk poděbradský* (Prague).
Válka, Josef,
 1959 "Jednota bratrská a společnost", *Kralice*, ed. Vlasta Fialová (Kralice), 129-142.
Volf, Josef,
 1928 *Geschichte des Buchdrucks in Böhmen und Mähren bis 1848* (Weimar).
Vonka, R. J.,
 1936 *Tiskařské dílo Jednoty bratrské* (Prague).
Winter, Zikmund,
 1895 *Život církevní v Čechách*, Vol. I.
 1896 Vol. II (Prague).
Wolkan, Rudolf (see also under Anabaptistica, Primary and Secondary),
 1891 *Das deutsche Kirchenlied der Böhmischen Brüder im 16. Jahrhundert* (Prague).

Wotke, Karl,
    1898   "Augustinus Olomucensis", *ZDVGMS*, 2, 47-71.
    1899   "Der Olmützer Bischof Stanislaus Thurzó von Béthlenfalva und dessen Humanistenkreis", *ZDVGMS*, 3, 337-388.
Zeman, Jarold Knox (see also under Anabaptistica, Secondary and Bohemica, Primary),
    1957   "Religious Liberty in Sixteenth-Century Moravia", seminar paper, Baptist Seminary, Rüschlikon-Zürich.
    1962   *Kolébka náboženské svobody na Moravě* (Chicago-Toronto).
Zezschwitz, Gerhard von,
    1863   *Die Katechismen der Waldenser und Böhmischen Brüder...* (Erlangen).
    1878   Article "Brüder, böhmische", *RE*, 2nd ed., II (Leipzig), 648-677.
Zíbrt, Čeněk and Josef Volf,
    I-V   *Bibliografie české historie*, Vols. I-V (1900-1912) (Prague).

ADDENDA

Two publications reached us in the final stage of printing. They could not be included in the text of our book but should be mentioned here.

Durnbaugh, Donald F.,
    The Believers' Church: The History and Character of Radical Protestantism (New York, 1968).
Heymann, Frederick G.,
    "The Impact of Martin Luther upon Bohemia", *Central European History*, 1 (1968), 107-130.

INDEX

Names of persons and places as well as book titles which appear in the main text are indexed exhaustively. Footnote references are included only when they supplement the discussion in the main text and are not already listed under the same page number. Entries for names in the Appendices (pp. 315-349) and all entries in the topical index are selective. There are no general entries for the following names: Anabaptists, Bohemia, Calixtines, Czech Brethren, Czech Reformation, Evangelicals, Germany, German Reformation, Left-Wing Reformation, Magisterial Reformation, Major Party (*Unitas Fratrum*), Moravia, Protestants, Radical Reformation, Reformation, Roman Catholics, South Germany, Swiss Reformation, *Täufer, Unitas Fratrum*, Utraquists, *Wiedertäufer*. Persons and places in the Scriptures and names appearing in the topographical lists on pp. 277-299 and 308 have also been excluded. As a rule, members of nobility are listed under their places of origin or cognomens, except for the German princes who are indexed under their personal names. On the spelling of personal and local names, see pp. 57-58. Abbreviations: A — Anabaptist, UF — *Unitas Fratrum* (usually the Major Party).

INDEX OF PERSONS, PLACES AND TITLES

INDEX OF TOPICS

MAP OF SOUTH MORAVIA

* Places with recorded major contacts between the Anabaptists and the Czech Brethren.

○ Other villages, towns and cities important for historical topography of Moravian Anabaptism and Unitas Fratrum. (Names of *royal cities* are italicized)

ST. MARY'S COLLEGE OF MARYLAND
ST. MARY'S CITY, MARYLAND